P9-DVR-530

Municipal Management Series

The Practice of State and Regional Planning

Editors

Published in cooperation
with the International City
Management Association

Frank S. So
American Planning
Association

By the
American
Planning
Association

Irving Hand
Pennsylvania State
University

Bruce D. McDowell
U.S. Advisory Commission on
Intergovernmental Relations

Municipal Management Series

The Practice of State and Regional Planning

Developing the Municipal Organization

Effective Communication: Getting the Message Across

The Effective Local Government Manager

Effective Supervisory Practices

The Essential Community: Local Government in the Year 2000

Housing and Local Government

Local Government Police Management

Management of Local Planning

Management Policies in Local Government Finance

Managing Fire Services

Managing Human Services

Managing the Modern City

Managing Municipal Leisure Services

The Practice of Local Government Planning

Small Cities and Counties: A Guide to Managing Services

Urban Public Works Adminstration

Library of Congress Cataloging in Publication Data

Main entry under title:
The Practice of state and regional planning.

   (Municipal management series)
   Bibliography: p.
   1. Regional planning—United States.   2. State
governments—United States—Planning.   I. So, Frank S.
II. Hand, Irving.   III. McDowell, Bruce D.   IV. International
City Management Association.   V. American Planning
Association.   VI. Series.
HT392.P7 1985   361.6'0973   84-72732
ISBN 0-918286-38-7
ISBN 0-918286-42-5 (soft)

Printed in the United States of America.

1 2 3 4 5 91 90 89 88 87 86

Foreword

For more than forty years, the International City Management Association has had a productive relationship with the planning profession. The collaboration has produced five editions of the basic text on planning in local government, the most prominent text in the ICMA Green Book series and the most widely read in the planning profession.

These were five editions of one book in concept, and yet they were also five different books. Different editors, different writers, and changes in approach and viewpoint distinguish each edition. Content has also changed markedly with a half century of development in planning technique and changes in the agenda of public decisions that planning addresses.

The agenda has also expanded. The editors decided that it cannot all be squeezed into one fat book. That is why the fifth edition was really edition number four-and-one-half. This book is the second half of the fifth edition.

The first half is *The Practice of Local Government Planning*. This volume covers state and regional planning. The relations among local, state, and federal government have continued to change. There are shifts in the distribution of decision-making, in program responsibilities, and in funding. States have become more systematically active in planning and programming and in pursuing development policies. Regional coordinating mechanisms

have been through two decades of intensive development, experimentation, and service to their areas. "New federalism" is no longer a label for a single set of changes. Each year brings its installment of changes in the relations among governments.

What is abiding is the necessity of conducting local government planning in the context of planning for wider geographic areas, for larger political units. Localities must influence, and are influenced by, the planning decisions around them. We have long ago learned that water and air, whether clean or dirty, respect no political boundaries; that public funds at every level come from local pockets; and that a local economy cannot be sealed off from the world.

Local planners and managers will, therefore, be as interested in the quality of state and regional planning, and in the demographic and economic data produced, as are those officials who have the direct responsibility for that planning.

We thank the International City Management Association for continuing this long and fruitful collaboration. William H. Hansell, Jr., the Executive Director of ICMA, is putting his own full-spirited stamp on the production of this edition, initiated under his predecessor, Mark Keane.

The Practice of State and Regional Planning is a collective endeavor, and we wish to thank many organizations and individuals who have given so much time and effort to this book.

Our thanks go, first, to the editors of the book: Frank S. So, Deputy Executive Director, American Planning Association; Irving Hand, Director of the Institute of State and Regional Affairs, and Chairman of the Graduate Degree Program in Urban and Regional Planning, at the Pennsylvania State University Capitol Campus; and Bruce D. McDowell, Senior Analyst, U.S. Advisory Commission on Intergovernmental Relations, in Washington, D.C.

We are also grateful to the chapter authors for their fine efforts and for their willingness to work with the editors. We want to acknowledge the work of the Merriam Center Library, and especially Sue Lannin, in helping with documentation and the bibliography.

Many persons helped in planning the content of this book and in reviewing chapter drafts in various stages of preparation. These persons are listed alphabetically with their affiliations at the time of their involvement: David S. Arnold, Senior Editor, International City Management Association; Richard S. Bolan, Professor and Chairman, Community Organization–Social Work, Graduate School of Social Work, Boston College; Paul Brace, Government Technical Representative, U.S. Department of Housing and Urban Development; Clifford W. Graves, Chief Administrative Officer, County of San Diego; David K. Hartley, Planning Consultant; Gerard Hoetmer, Staff Member, International City Management Association; Steve Hudson, Staff Member, International City Management Association; Sherman Landau, Staff Member, International City Management Association; Dean Macris, Planning Director, City of San Francisco; Frank Moreno, Planning Consultant; Stuart S. Nagel, Policy Studies Organization, University of Illinois at Urbana–Champaign; David Pampu, Denver Regional Council of Governments; Amy Paul, Staff Member, International City Management Association; David Pomerantz, Staff Member, International City Management Association; Walter A. Scheiber, Executive Director, Metropolitan Washington Council of Governments; Burt Sparer, Governmental Planning Associate, Carl Vinson Institute of Government, University of Georgia; Larry Susskind, Chairman, Department of Urban Studies and Planning, Massachusetts Institute of Technology; Revan A.F. Tranter, Executive Director, Association of Bay Area Governments; John W. Vining, Jr., Executive Director, Miami Valley Regional Planning Commission; H.F. Wise, Planning Consultant; Robert Wise, Office of the Governor, State of Arizona; and Warren T. Zitzmann, Community Planning Specialist, Soil Conservation Service, U.S. Department of Agriculture.

The Practice of State and Regional Planning is a visually oriented book with well over 100 sidebars and figures. Herbert Slobin and Frank S. So developed the ideas for most of the illustrations and sidebars, and Mr. Slobin prepared the figures in final form. David S. Arnold assisted in illustration and sidebar planning and wrote the captions.

Our thanks also go to the diligent work of our copy editors who had to work with a complex manuscript: Walter G. Glascoff, III and Judy Lola.

This book is part of ICMA's Municipal Management Series. The series is the responsibility of Barbara H. Moore, Senior Editor, ICMA. Other ICMA staff members who worked on this book were David S. Arnold, who assisted with manuscript review and development of illustrations; Rebecca Geanaros and Karen Peacock, who helped prepare some of the figures; and Christine Ulrich, who conducted most of the line cut and photo research and assisted in the final checking of manuscript, figures, and sidebars.

Israel Stollman
Executive Director
American Planning Association

Washington, D.C.

**American
Planning
Association**

The American Planning Association
and its professional institute, the
American Institute of Certified Planners, are organized to advance the art
and science of planning and to foster
the activity of planning—physical, economic, and social—at the local,
regional, state, and national levels. The
objective of the Association is to
encourage planning that will contribute
to public well-being by developing communities and environments that meet
the needs of people and of society more
effectively.

Contents

Figures

Tables

Introduction

This book is a companion volume to *The Practice of Local Government Planning*. It deals with planning at the state and regional levels of government. Planning is newer at these levels than at the local level. It responds to different needs and fills different roles.

City planning is a time-honored and well-established field of study and professional practice. Planners are an accepted part of most city administrations—and of the administrations of most other urban localities as well, such as urban counties, towns, and townships. Even some rural localities accept planners into their professional ranks. Local planning is largely supported now by local taxes, although there have been times in the past when there was substantial federal aid for local planning.

Much has been written about local planning.[1] The standard textbook in that field has been published since 1941 and now is in its fifth edition under the title of *The Practice of Local Government Planning*.[2] The literature of local planning deals extensively with topics concerning which local governments have direct responsibility, authority to act decisively, and a great deal of experience. Such topics include—most traditionally—land use zoning, regulation of the land subdivision process, urban renewal, public housing, and the provision of local parks and public works. The preparation of local comprehensive plans and capital improvements programs, in which public actions supporting orderly physical development of the local community are mapped out and budgeted, is explored in detail as the accepted means toward effective exercise of recognized local government powers. Many local governments have expanded the scope of their planning to meet the needs of their citizens for jobs, income, and a variety of social services through programs they administer themselves.

Planning at the state and regional levels is different. Its role is neither well defined nor well accepted. Its literature is sparse. Until the publication of this book, there was no standard textbook in the field. In addition, such planning usually relied quite heavily for its existence upon financial support and role definitions supplied by the federal government—leading some observers to suggest that planning by states and regions is artificial and not naturally sustainable in its own right.

This book seeks to fill the gap in the literature of state and regional planning. The editors hope that this book will become the standard textbook in its field, a useful companion to *The Practice of Local Government Planning*. *The Practice of State and Regional Planning* is designed to demonstrate that legitimate and constructive roles for planning have been developed at the state and regional levels of government. State and regional planning is not just local master planning on a grander scale. It has its own characteristics, features, topical interests, and processes.

Regional planning, in particular, is different in that it seldom is related directly to the exercise of governmental authority on a region-wide basis. Most regional planning organizations—whether of the large multistate variety encompassing the multiple local governments in a single metropolitan area or any other contiguous community of social contacts in the daily working and living environment—are intergovernmental mechanisms. They respond to region-wide problems in a single integrated area, but they usually report back to a variety of governments rather than to just one. Most regional planning organizations must persuade many independent governments to act in concert if regional objectives are to be attained.

At the state level, planning has been practiced for many years—often very professionally—in a variety of different functional fields like transportation, parks, natural resource conservation, and public health. But planning across these functional lines and in newer areas of concern is much newer, less well developed or established, and often less successful. Many states have developed strong central management systems only in the last two decades.[3] Such systems encompass (1) governors with four-year (rather than two-year) terms who are able to succeed themselves, (2) a strong executive budget process, (3) a reorganized executive branch with a small number of departments headed by gubernatorial appointees, (4) a central management staff for the governor (including some sort of planning or policy development and policy coordination office), and (5) annual sessions and full-time staffing of the legislature. The governors' recently developed roles in budgeting, central management, and cabinet government provide, for the first time, a sound managerial environment for broad coordinative or "comprehensive" policy planning.

Over the past two decades, central planning staffs have been established in all states, and about 2,000 regional planning organizations of various types—large and small, general purpose and special—have been established, virtually blanketing the whole nation. At the substate level alone—metropolitan and nonmetropolitan interjurisdictional communities of everyday activity—the 1977 Census of Governments found 1,932 regional planning organizations, spending more than $1.3 billion, employing more than 148,000 workers, and involving more than 43,000 citizens on their governing bodies.[4] These employees and policy makers, plus persons with whom they deal in the performance of their duties, and others who will join them or replace them in the future, represent a sizeable audience for a book such as this. *The Practice of State and Regional Planning* is aimed at that audience.

Scope of this book

This book examines state and regional planning in four parts. First, it looks at the planning process and how it has been established at each level. Next, it describes the main analytical techniques used in state and regional planning. Then, it describes comprehensive policy plans. Finally, it explores the content of major types of state and regional plans for specific government sectors. This sequence is explained more fully below.

Part one: The planning context and process   This part has eight chapters. The first two are concerned, respectively, with (1) the general theoretical underpinnings of planning processes and (2) the ways in which planning has developed at the various levels of government in the U.S. Chapter 1 is especially important for the reader having no previous formal training in planning, because it begins with basic definitions and explores various alternative approaches that planners may use in differing circumstances. But Chapter 1 may be of interest to more advanced readers as well, since it also summarizes the reasons why planning appears in different forms at the various levels of government and highlights a special concern that will run throughout the book with respect to the role of "central" or coordinative planning units. These are such units as an office of state planning serving a governor or a general purpose council of governments or a regional planning commission serving a whole metropolitan area or non-metropolitan region. Such units have broad responsibilities that cut across many different policy fields and allow them to take a more or less comprehensive view of policy interrelationships. Even if a state or regional plan is addressed to a particular function of government, the point stressed in this book is that it should be coordinated as well as possible with other related plans.

The point of Chapter 2 is that the style of planning being used must fit in with the political customs and practices of government where it is being practiced—and planning styles must change as governments change from time to time at each level. This chapter seeks to give the reader a feeling for the developmental process by which state and regional planning has become part of the American scene.

The next three chapters describe the state planning process as it is manifested today by specific types of organizational units, work programs, implementation methods, and management processes. This material includes current assessments of the legal basis and financing of state planning as well as an exploration of current issues concerning the future role of state planning.

The final three chapters in Part One provide a similar analysis of today's regional planning process—its organization, legal basis, financing, work programs, implementation methods, management processes, and future roles.

Part two: Analysis and information   This part has four chapters. The first two chapters emphasize techniques for analyzing state and regional planning data, first through a process known as policy analysis, and then through a technique known as impact analysis. Both are rather broad forms of analysis that subsume numerous more specialized methods of detailed analytical examination of policy proposals, relying largely on quantitative techniques. Policy analysts and other specialists in quantitative and scientific analysis often will be involved in these studies. Planners should be aware of the roles of such specialists and be ready to work with them effectively.

Chapter 11, "Basic Studies for State and Regional Planning," deals with the various types of data needed for state and regional planning, where and how to collect them on a regular basis, and the forms in which they should be maintained if they are to be most timely and useful.

Finally, Chapter 12 describes citizen participation at the state and regional levels, emphasizing its values as a source of both new information and analytical insights.

Part three: Development policies and strategies   The three chapters of this part—urban development, rural development, and economic development—discuss what might be termed general plans. They have broad goals and rely upon coordinative strategies for focusing a variety of special function plans and policies toward common purposes. Only a general purpose planning organization—such as an office of state planning or a regional planning council—would have the broad scope needed to devise and promote such plans.

Part four: Major types of state and regional plans   The last nine types of plans presented here—Chapters 16 through 24—are more specialized than those discussed in Part Three. In some cases they may be prepared by a general purpose planning organization (especially at the substate regional level in regions with a well-integrated planning structure), but in other cases they are much more likely to be prepared by specialized planning agencies (especially at the state level) concerned only with the particular function of government under consideration. These chapters cover planning for housing, transportation, energy, environmental protection, solid waste management, health, social services and education, law enforcement and criminal justice, and hazard mitigation and emergency preparedness. Other types of plans might have been included as well: parks and recreation, the arts and humanities, and natural resources. But it is unlikely that a book such as this could hope to be complete for long. The sampling offered here is enough to give most readers a sound introduction to the variety of planning activities likely to be found at the state and regional levels during the 1980s.

In studying each of these last nine chapters, the reader is urged to remember that, despite the use of the word "comprehensive"—as in "comprehensive transportation plan" or "comprehensive housing plan" for a particular state or region— and despite assurances that "all relevant physical, social, and economic factors have been taken into account," the plans described in these chapters are likely to be special purpose ones, advocating the most favorable outcomes for the particular function served by the plan. This is only natural, and there is value to such advocacy. Still, the possibility of conflict among these special-purpose plans, or the chance that opportunities might be lost for mutual reinforcement among diverse policies, should be sought out for the greater good. That is the assigned task of the central planning unit (the general-purpose state planning agency or regional planning council), and it is the purpose of preparing "general plans" or strategies for broad policy areas (as represented by the types or plans described in Chapters 13 through 15).

Recent currents

By 1982, the first year of Ronald Reagan's presidency had become history, and the second year was taking shape. This beginning already showed signs of great change in how planning had been established and funded at the state and regional levels.[5] Federal budget cuts for fiscal year 1982 were particularly severe for federal aid to states and regions (as well as to local governments).

One result was termination of the Section 701 comprehensive planning grants from the Department of Housing and Urban Development to state and regional planning organizations. The same was true for rural planning assistance from the Department of Agriculture. These cuts eliminated many required plans for housing, land use, broad development strategies, and federal aid project coordination (under Office of Management and Budget Circular No. A-95). In addition, the Administration rescinded OMB Circular A-95 and replaced it with processes specified by state and local officials, the effects of which are still uncertain.[6]

Many other federal aid cuts also made state and regional planning organizations seek new sources of funding at a time when cuts were the order of the day at all levels—a dismal process, to say the least. Energy grants were terminated. Water quality planning funds were suspended. Planning funds for economic development and coastal zone management were cut back, with proposals that both programs be eliminated in the future. The solid waste management program went dormant. Regional health systems planning agencies were set to phase out. The Law Enforcement Assistance Administration went out of existence on April 15, 1982. The federal government terminated its participation in the eleven Title V multistate economic development commissions and the six Title II river basin commissions in the fall of 1981. The Appalachian Regional Commission's program was cut and scheduled for elimination. The urban transportation planning regulations of the U.S. Department of Transportation were revised in 1983 and made less strict in accordance with President Reagan's major regulatory relief effort. Social services planning requirements, formerly specified by the federal government, were left up to the states.

The states, however, gained some new power from some federal aid cuts. Despite the fewer dollars, 77 former federal grant programs were merged into nine new block grants for which the states gained freedom to specify whatever type of planning they chose. For the most part, the states also became free to determine the nature of participation in these programs by local governments and regional organizations.

It is too early to tell, as final copy is prepared for this book, how all these federal budget changes and regulatory relief actions will affect state and regional planning organizations in the long run. There may be still further withdrawal of federal participation in the topics covered by this book, or Congress may reverse some of the actions taken in that direction. At any rate, state and regional planning organizations have begun to cope with present realities. Cutback management techniques are being invoked for staff reductions; new priorities for work programs; fees for publications, data, and services; and streamlined procedures or automation of certain tasks to increase the productivity of remaining staff. Even with such measures, it was estimated that 10 percent of all substate regional councils would go out of business during 1982, and as many as 50 percent might experience very substantial budget cuts—perhaps amounting to losses of as much as 60 percent of the dollars that had been available in 1981.[7] Although the number of councils actually lost was much smaller than predicted, very substantial budget cuts did materialize for most councils. Clearly, the 1980s started out as a difficult decade for planning at the state and regional levels.

Continuing needs for state and regional planning

The brief histories of state and regional planning contained in Chapter 2 show that federal funding and requirements have been of tremendous importance to the development of planning at the state and regional levels. They also show, however, that state planning survived—after a fashion—a total cut-off of federal funding in the 1940s, and that two-thirds of all metropolitan areas had at least begun their regional planning activities by 1960—before the federal government began requiring them to do so. This gives reason to believe that the generally recognized need for planning at these levels is strong enough to ensure its survival in most states and regions. In fact, during the first Reagan administration, when funds were being cut, Illinois and Minnesota established new state planing offices. The past two decades of federal assistance and federal requirements for such planning have enhanced the quality of work and demonstrated achievable benefits sufficient to whet the public's appetite, and that of policy officials, for continued professional planning advice. Enhanced state powers under the new block grants also may push the states toward greater planning efforts.

Thus, the years just ahead may be lean in terms of federal funds, but we will not see the demise of state and regional planning. These years will be a time for reappraisal, for sharpening the cost-effectiveness of planning efforts, and for making sure that planning studies and proposals have maximum relevance to the needs of the policy makers who will have to put up scarce dollars to keep the planning function alive during hard times. Some public officials mistakenly believe that in hard budgeting times planning is a luxury. We believe it is a necessity.

1   George C. Bestor and Holway R. Jones, *City Planning Bibliography*, 3rd ed. (New York: American Society of Civil Engineers, 1982).

2   Frank So, Israel Stollman, Frank Beal, and David S. Arnold, eds., *The Practice of Local Government Planning* (Washington, DC: The International City Management Association, 1979).

3   Advisory Commission on Intergovernmental Rela-

tions, *State and Local Roles in the Federal System*, Chapter 3 (Washington, DC: U.S. Government Printing Office, 1982).

4   U.S. Bureau of the Census, *Regional Organizations*, Vol. 6, No. 6 of the 1977 Census of Governments (Washington, DC: U.S. Government Printing Office, August 1978).

5   Bruce D. McDowell, "The Federal Role in Regional

Planning: Past and Present," in Gill C. Lim, ed. *Regional Planning: Evolution, Crisis, Prospects* (Totowa, NJ: Allenheld, Osmun Publishers, 1982).

6 Bruce D. McDowell, "A-95: Disappering or Just Shrinking?," *Planning*, Janaury 1982; and Advisory Commission on Intergovernmental Relations, *Intergovernmental Consultation: Considerations for State and Local Officials in the Transition from OMB Circular A-95 to Executive Order 12372*, an Information Bulletin (Washington, DC: ACIR, November 1982). See also The Council of State Planning Agencies, *The Promise of Partnership: A Status Report on Implementation of the President's Intergovernmental Consultation Initiative, Executive Order 12372* (Washington, DC: CSPA, February 1984).

7 National Association of Regional Councils, *Director's News*, Vol. 2, No. 5, April 24, 1981, p. 8.

8 Bruce D. McDowell, "Regions under Reagan," *Planning*, August 1984, pp. 25–29.

Part one:
The planning context and process

1 Approaches to planning

Planning is a normal and pervasive part of human existence. Individuals do it in their personal and professional lives. Businesses do it. Governments do it.

But sometimes planning is more complex than other times. Sometimes it is more controversial. Sometimes it is more successful or more effective.

These differences occur because of the diverse policy issues, situations, and actors involved in the particular planning exercise. Yet throughout this diversity run some common threads.

The purposes of this chapter are to (1) examine the fundamental definition of planning and the classical statement of the governmental planning process, (2) explore the factors leading to increasing diversity in the practice of public planning, (3) describe the relevance of such planning theory to planning practices at the various levels of government, and (4) set the tone for the rest of part I.

A basic definition of planning

Planning involves visualizing a better future and going after it. Another way to say this is that "A plan is a predetermined course of action."[1]

A plan must have three characteristics. First, it must involve the future. Second, it must involve action. Third, there is an element of personal or organizational identification or causation. That is, the future course of action will be taken by the planner or someone designated by or for him within the organization. Futurity, action, and personal or organizational causation are necessary elements in every plan.[2]

In order to enhance the quality of their plans, most organizations, public and private, and many individuals with significant personal assets engage professional assistance. For individuals, the professional may be an estate planner or an investment advisor. For organizations, the advisors may be policy planners, technical planners, program evaluators, systems analysts, statisticians, actuaries, or other professionals. The idea is to learn more about current problems and future prospects before deciding on a course of action toward the future. By this means, the decision becomes more rational, more objective and fully informed; it relies less on intuition and more on facts (as best as they can be determined).

It is important to note that professional planners are not the only advisors consulted in many decision making situations. Planners may or may not be among those involved. They have no monopoly in analyzing steps toward the future, but they do have special training and a kit of analytical tools that can be helpful. Planners are challenged constantly to show how their talents will benefit the decision makers whom they advise.

The classical planning process and its critics

One of the best and clearest modern statements of classical planning theory was written in 1956 by Martin Meyerson.[3] It incorporates scientific method, decision theory, and simple logic, and it even incorporates some new features of information theory. Meyerson argued that the long range plans typically prepared by planners in the past could not be effective unless translated into short range plans to guide immediate actions. He called these short range plans "the middle range bridge for comprehensive planning," meaning to stress their role in linking long range policy guides to everyday decision making.

In developing these necessary short range plans Meyerson outlined the following five functions for planning agencies:

1. Central intelligence function (analysis of relationships and values).
2. Pulse-taking function (periodic alert to danger signs).
3. Policy clarification function (regular revision of development objectives).
4. Detailed development plan function (specific projects furthering the long range plan).
5. Feedback review function (analyze consequences of past as guide to future).

Meyerson was not satisfied with letting long range plans sit on the shelf unused. He wanted them to be more timely, more pointed in their advice to decision makers, and more firmly based on current data and relevant factual analysis. Such planning, he reasoned, was not likely to be ignored.

The classical planning process is, above all, a rational one. It begins by recognizing a problem and logically moves ahead in sequence to analyze it and solve it through appropriate decision making. The steps in this process, including the continuous information flows and feedback for policy recycling proposed by Meyerson to relieve the "one-shot" finality implied by many plans, may be enumerated as follows:[4]

1. Problem identification (awareness of need).
2. Goal setting (statement of objectives and establishment of a work program to prepare appropriate plans).
3. Data collection and analysis.
4. Refinement of goals.
5. Development of alternative plans and/or policies (designed to achieve goals).
6. Evaluation of alternatives (determine probable effects, both good and bad, and the ease or difficulty of implementation).
7. Adoption of preferred plans and/or policies.
8. Implementation of plans and/or policies.
9. Monitoring and evaluation of results (alerts to progress toward goals and/ or danger signs calling for course correction).
10. Feedback (recycle the planning process as necessary to meet emerging circumstances).

Despite Meyerson's updating of the traditional planning process, a number of theorists continue to criticize it for being too rigid in the face of the ultra pluralistic and fluid American governmental scene.[5] Such critics point out the large number of decision points, both public and private, which operate simultaneously to create "resultants" rather than orchestrated public policies, and they despair of the possibility that any grand designs or even moderately comprehensive plans have a fighting chance of being implemented. Incremental decision making, at most, is what might be expected despite the best efforts of professional planners, according to this view. Some alternatively advocate contingency planning to prepare for any eventuality, and others suggest advocacy planning to arm all who have a stake in governmental decisions with professional planning assistance to help them promote their own views about the public policies under consideration. Still others believe that the pluralism of American government calls for formal intergovernmental negotiation of plans, with professional mediators being used to bring the main actors together in constructive dialogue. Citizen participation techniques are at the center of still other proposals for "transactive" planning in which governments and their citizens would work together, in a mutual learning experience designed to develop consensus plans that would meet citizen needs most effectively.

Apart from these reactions of planning theorists to the pluralistic fragmentation of government decision making, there is a pragmatic political reaction. The central question of politics—"Who gets what, when, and where?"—leads many public officials to favor keeping their options open as long as possible. They quite naturally want to stave off the designations of winners and losers—which occur as a result of their decisions—until after the next election (and the next, and the next). Planners, by urging "predetermined courses of action," tend to move in the direction of closing off many options and committing elected officials to specific policies. In so doing, they often may create tensions between themselves and the policy makers.

The issue, as Perloff puts it, is whether to develop firm plans which specify detailed futures (end state plans) and work unflinchingly toward their implementation, or whether to develop plans which indicate general principles and directions for policy making but stop short of detailing specific futures (open options plans).[6] He cites examples where each approach would be well advised, and urges, therefore, that the best of both approaches be used.

The conclusion must be, therefore, that planning is not a simple process in American government. Its decision making environment makes it a complex political process in which success often is ensured not only (and perhaps not even primarily) by the quality of the technical analysis performed. This is not to say that technical analysis is unimportant, for this is the planner's primary stock-in-trade; it is only a recognition that analysis is not sufficient by itself to meet the needs of public policy makers.

The planner has a responsibility to go beyond the analyses assigned, to see that they produce relevant products that policy makers can use. An examination of the various dimensions of the planning process, as they may be perceived in the public policy making process, may help the planner in that second task.

Seven dimensions of the planning process

Any planning process has at least seven "dimensions." These are types of characteristics that may be exhibited differently from one process to another. The particular combination of these characteristics found in any one planning process distinguishes it from others.

The seven dimensions examined here are: organizational location (or clientele), purpose, openness, time horizon, scope, specificity, and flexibility. Each will be described and analyzed briefly below, using Figure 1-1 as a point of departure.

Organizational location (or clientele)

The planner's affiliation—whom he or she works for—brings with it a whole set of ground rules concerning acceptable topics for planning, planning responsibilities, access to the powers of implementation, and relationships with other organizations and individuals who may be planning and/or acting in the same arena. Not all of these ground rules may be immediately apparent to the new planner, but as the planning process proceeds they will help to set him or her on a sound course. Topics chosen should be of significance to the organization, within the capability of the planning staff to analyze, and within the bounds of

Dimensions	Difficulties	Benefits
Organizational location (or clientele)	Defines interests, responsibilities, and authority for planning May be too limited to meet real needs	 May be adequate or ample
Purpose: to institute change	May arouse "the fear of change" May upset status quo and vested interests	May achieve a better future
Openness	May "tip your hand" to opponents of change May be expensive and time consuming	May provide important insights for problem solving and meeting needs May win support for needed change
Time horizon	May be too distant to: (a) interest decision-makers (b) be sure of relevant circumstances	May help to overcome long lead times in meeting needs May help to recognize future implications of present actions
Scope	If too broad, it may paralyze action	If broad enough, will help to make the most of interrelations, interdependencies, and mutually reinforcing benefits among diverse policies, programs, and projects
Specificity	Too much closes off options Not enough fails to guide decisions and actions	Right amount helps policymaker to act wisely
Flexibility	Not enough produces rigidity, irrelevance Too much fails to guide decisions and actions	Right amount helps policymaker to act wisely

Figure 1–1   Difficulties and benefits associated with
the seven dimensions of a planning process.

likely organizational policy making activity. Such criteria will help to ensure that planning will make a constructive contribution and produce results.

This necessity for good alignment applies not only to the topics chosen for planning but also to the types of policies recommended and the implementation measures proposed. That which is within the legitimate jurisdiction of the organization (or the client) obviously is safer territory than that which is under the control of others. Yet, there are many occasions when planning agencies are far removed from organizations that make the final decisions, and there is no choice but to try to influence them across that distance—unless the gap can be narrowed or closed by reorganization.

As Figure 1-1 shows, the affiliation of the planning process may serve well to promote the plan, or it may act as a significant limitation on the ability to match planning to real needs which may reach beyond the organization's (or the client's) jurisdiction. In such cases, intergovernmental cooperation or some other form of persuasion should be considered.

Intergovernmental cooperation is particularly needed in the United States because of its three-level, three-branch system of government. Seldom can the executive branch of government act without the legislative branch (except at the local level where these two branches are often combined). Increasingly, the judicial branch also has a say. And many spheres of public policy also have intertwined roles for the federal, state, and local levels—often through the operation of grant programs with planning requirements. Even within a single branch of government at a single level, public policy responsibilities have been divided so that related policies may be decided upon by various executive agencies and/or legislative committees. Centrally placed planning organizations may be charged with identifying the cross-over relationships, but more than likely, the individual agencies and committees will be allowed to make their own final decisions.

While most planners still work in the executive branch of government (or for a combined executive/legislative unit at the local level), it is becoming more common to find planners in legislative units. Planning certainly should be considered an integral part of the whole policy making and implementation process, not just part of "management." Planning can serve virtually any client, inside government or outside, within the "establishment" or without. But the planner's role will shift with his affiliation—from central coordinator, to agency advocate, to private interest advocate, to something else.

Purpose of planning

No matter what the topic of a plan, its purpose will be to affect the future in a positive way. "Positive," of course, will be defined by the responsibile policy makers and may be viewed variously by different segments of the community. But specifics aside, a plan generally calls for some sort of *change*—such as *community growth* to accommodate expected population expansion, *increased aid to the poor* to ensure at least a minimal standard of living for all and an opportunity to escape poverty, *fuller use of domestic energy sources* to limit the nation's dependence on foreign nations, *control of rapidly rising medical costs* to keep services affordable, and *new regulations and aid programs* to protect established communities from deterioration and to preserve historical sites.

Whatever the specific policy change may be, it is likely to be scary or threatening. Someone almost certainly will view it as a threat to the status quo or to a vested interest. Sometimes a proposal for change is perceived even more generally as a threat because it gets linked with the infamous "fear of the unknown." For example, while a proposal to merge small local governments into a larger metropolitan government usually promises better services, a more highly professional staff, and more efficient operations, fears about the possibility of higher taxes and more remote administrators frequently have convinced voters to say no.[8] Unless it is very clear that a plan will make the future better in a nonthreatening way, the fear of change and the inertia of the public are likely to prevent its adoption. Thus, the planner should identify any emerging fears early and seek to accommodate them in the plan.

Planning for change may be approached in at least three different ways, depending upon the situation and the relationships among the principal actors. One approach is to be cooperative—to work it out amicably among the affected parties. Another may be to fight it out, with the most powerful faction winning and others losing. A third way, when there is little if any policy difference among the parties, is simply to get on with preparation of the plan in a routine way, doing what must be done to reach agreed upon objectives.

The *cooperative approach* works when relationships among the principal actors are good and their basic interests are not threatened. In this case, those involved usually are willing to explore objectively and openly a wide range of alternative solutions to the problems they have identified, letting the chips fall where they may and then negotiating satisfactory compromises which accommodate all major interests. The idea is to communicate widely throughout the planning process and carefully build consensus.

The *competitive approach* may be necessary if major actors mistrust or dislike each other, or if all or some of their vital interests are threatened by certain proposals which might be adopted. In this case, efforts may be made to limit the scope of proposals which will be considered and to develop favored proposals rather fully before exposing them to public view. Strategic planning by a chief executive (in competition with the legislature) may have this character, as might the advocacy planning by various special interests. The issues may be highly charged political ones, overflowing with controversy and ultimately ending at the ballot box or in the courts. Policy makers caught between warring factions in this type of planning process may be delighted with a plan that will keep options open rather than force hard decisions earlier than necessary.

The *routine approach* is possible after hard decisions have been made or consensus reached on basic policies. Planning at this stage, although it may cause some friction with those most directly affected, usually can be accomplished without raising major policy issues. It becomes simply a matter of working out the details through accepted planning practice. Technical, managerial, or administrative plans, rather than policy plans, usually fall in this category.

The planner needs to be sensitive enough to each situation to know which approach is appropriate.

Openness

American government is unusually open compared to government in many other countries, and most planning processes in the United States follow this pattern. In fact, planning processes often take the lead. With respect to local planning, one observer has noted that

no other local government activity generates more citizen participation than does planning. The planning agency is responsible for holding more public hearings, conducting more attitude and opinion surveys, arranging more neighborhood meetings, and appointing more citizen advisory committees—in addition to giving official duties to unpaid citizens on planning commissions and boards and publicizing the alternative decisions being considered.

Planners are concerned with the quality of participation and the substantive degree of understanding with which it is accepted. Genuine participation has to begin before ideas are crystallized—long before a hearing is held on unchangable proposals with contracts about to be let. It must proceed without the condescension of technician-knows-best, the selective packaging of facts that will sell best, or glib replies to problems that may trip up the project.[9]

Although few aspects of government match the openness of local planning, regional planning at the substate level comes close. State planning is less open, but compared to much else in state government, it rates high. The *cooperative approach* to planning, of course, is more conducive to openness than the *competitive approach*. The *routine approach* is likely to be open more on an as needed rather than blanket basis.

The planning process which starts off as an open process is less likely to generate disrupting surprises later on. Secretive planning processes often are forced to become more open when a leak of confidential information occurs. As the process opens up, it may take the form of confrontation in the latter stages of plan preparation that can prevent adoption of the plan.

Openness, at its best, can provide important insights for solving problems, for meeting needs, and for attracting support for plans. At worst, it can be expensive, time consuming, and inappropriately revealing of delicate strategies or negotiations.

Time horizon

Every plan has a time dimension. Some are long range; some short; some are middle-range; some so incremental as to be virtually *ad hoc*. Others encompass more than one time horizon. The unique contribution of professional planners is their help in considering the lengthened horizons needed to anticipate and prepare to meet future needs and to avoid future consequences of unwise current decisions. Yet the danger that planners face lies in looking so far into the future that the link with the present is broken. Uncertainties may occur about the circumstances that will apply in far-off future times; long range proposals may be irrelevant to current policy makers. A combination of long and short horizons helps to guard against this danger.

Perloff recently urged planners to be much more time conscious.[10] He focused not just on the future which planners project, forecast, and visualize, but also on a more precise knowledge of what the inherited past predetermines for the future as well as how present understandings, data, and decision processes limit what can be done about the future. Inadequate present attention to the nation's aging public works and housing stock, for example, has led one pair of observers to predict that future needs for replacement or rehabilitation are in danger of growing so great that they cannot be met, leaving the United States in ruins.[11]

Planners should use the various aspects of time needed to make their plans most relevant to policy makers.

Scope

This dimension of planning refers to how broad or narrow a plan is. Plans may cover whole policy areas very broadly or seek to interrelate various different policies. Such plans often are labeled "comprehensive." An example would be a growth management plan which might seek simultaneously to regulate private development, provide public facilities and services, and keep local taxes reasonable.

Other plans may be limited to a more restricted policy field, and may be labeled "functional." This nomenclature refers to the fact that such plans address only a single function of government—such as transportation, health services, or parks. They do not pretend to supply policy for other functions, though they may be based upon assumptions about what is likely to occur in other fields.

Finally, there are project plans. These deal only with a particular highway segment, health service, or park, rather than with whole systems of such facilities or services.

All three types of plans are needed, but too often the need for project plans is more obvious than that for functional system plans, and the need for both of these is more obvious than the need for multifunctional comprehensive plans. In addition, it is easier to prepare project and functional plans, and it is more likely that they will be implemented in the form originally conceived. This greater ease and success results from the fact that usually there are fewer actors involved in plans of lesser scope. But the more limited scope carries with it the danger that unforeseen factors may make the project or functional system obsolete or inappropriate.

Planners promote comprehensiveness more than most other professionals, and supporting this emphasis is one of their important roles. It needs to be recognized, however, that comprehensiveness must be kept within workable limits. While it is true, in the abstract, that almost everything is related to everything else, the time and resources, and the powers available to government to affect the future, limit the number of relationships which can be dealt with profitably. Selecting the key relationships to be studied and addressed by public policies is an important part of the planning process. Failure to be selective enough, can bog down the preparation of plans with endless studies which prevent action. This often is referred to as "paralysis by analysis," a common disease of planning processes.

Specificity and flexibility

These final two interrelated dimensions concern the amount of detail within a plan and the degree to which details are specified as requirements to be followed. Plans may be quite specific, very general, or somewhere in between. As specifications within the plan become more detailed, flexibility to meet diverse or changing conditions becomes more limited; options are closed off. The alternative is to adopt performance standards which may be interpreted creatively so as to attain desired results whenever implementing actions occurs. Obviously, the flexible approach is most appropriate for plans of broad scope, and less appropriate for the more detailed system plans. Project plans, by definition, must be specific since they are the action manifestations of more general plans. Their specifics cover not only what is to be done, but when, by whom, by what means, and how the project is to be financed. General plans which never generate or guide specific projects are plans which are not being implemented.

Creative use of planning processes

Plural processes

There is no single planning process in the pluralistic United States which will satisfy everyone or answer all questions—not even at a single level of government. It is most accurate to think of individuals planning "to beat the system," local governments planning to compete with neighboring jurisdictions and obtain aid from other levels of government, regions planning to coordinate local actions, executives planning to get new legislation, legislatures planning to modify the plans of executives, private businesses planning to increase their profits—and much, much more. All deserve professional planning assistance if they want it and are willing to pay for it. The idea that planning is something special—perhaps a fourth branch of government—or that a single planning commission can pull together all factors, representing all views fairly, is outmoded. Pluralism in decision making breeds plural planning efforts.

Situational processes

A corollary of plural planning is that no particular type of planning is the right kind. In other words, appropriate planning is situational:

1. There is no single best organizational location, affiliation, or client for planning.
2. It is impossible to say whether planning should be cooperative, competitive, or routine.
3. There is no general standard about how open the planning process should be.
4. It is no better to make all plans long range rather than short range.
5. Comprehensive plans are not necessarily better than functional or project plans—or vice versa.
6. Flexible plans are not always better than specific ones.

   The planner's job is to fashion an appropriate planning process in the existing situation using the options described above for these seven dimensions.

Rational processes

Whatever the process looks like in terms of dimensional options, it should consider using most, if not all, of the steps in the classical planning process. The critics of that process are commenting more on the dimensional options than on the technical problem-solving steps in the classical formulation. Rational problem solving is the set of techniques that the planner brings to the situational process in which planning is done. Infusing as much quantitative analysis, explicit goal setting, and related policy making as possible into the situation is the planner's function.

   As the critics point out, a great deal is not always possible in this regard. The planner certainly should not expect that quantitative analysis and logical rationales will drive the planning process toward clear or easy choices, or that the technical work called for can always be completed. Poor data, lack of time or money, inadequate knowledge and expertise, political impatience or hostility all may cause short-cutting of the standard problem-solving sequence. But the process then may have the opportunity to recycle and improve upon the "first-round" results. Political situations and other circumstances may change from time to time, allowing various approaches. The planning process itself hopefully will serve an educational function which will gradually enhance the opportunity for rational analysis to make a contribution.

Involvement in the processes

If planning is to be more than a technical process pursued for the edification of professional planners, it needs the involvement of policy makers at each step. Also, depending upon how open the process is, within the guidelines established by its organizational or other affiliations, most planning could benefit from citizen participation at each step. Figure 1-2 depicts the types of inputs that might be most useful at each step. These are described briefly below.

   As public policy problems are recognized and as issues are defined, citizens should be given an opportunity to react to them or advocate their own perceptions of needs. Policy makers have the responsibility of listening to both the planners and citizens, as well as adding their own thoughts to this process. The best grasp of what needs attention probably results from rather broad consultations.

   The initial goal setting step involves the selection of problems or issues to be dealt with, authorizing a work program to address them, and establishing first-cut policy guidelines for what is to be achieved. Obviously, this step takes formal

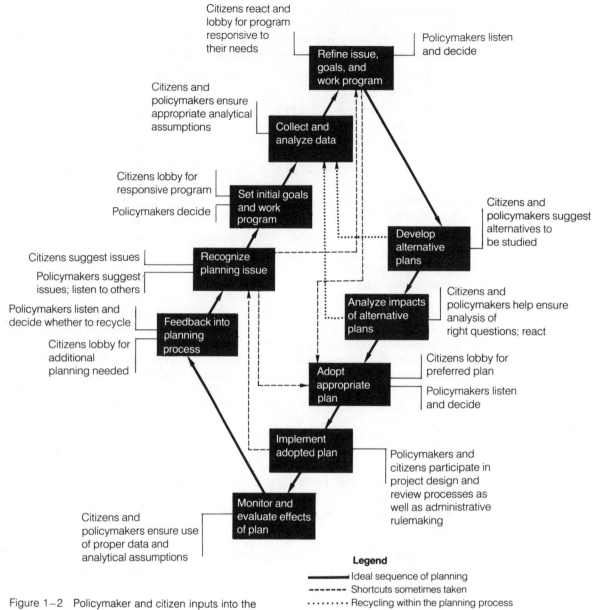

Figure 1–2   Policymaker and citizen inputs into the
classical planning process.

action by policy makers, but advice from both planners and citizens can be helpful. Citizen advice might be expected to center on the results desired from the process, while planners may concentrate more upon the administrative and technical practicalities involved in producing the plan. These two different viewpoints can work together to enrich the planning process.

Collecting and analyzing data, too often thought of as a purely technical step, also can benefit from policy maker and citizen inputs. A plan or policy often is only as good as the data and analysis upon which it is based. The wrong types of data and analytical assumptions can produce inappropriate results. Thus, it is a good cross-check to consult those for whom the plan is being prepared at this crucial step. To paraphrase a famous statement about war, planning is too important to be left to the planners. Complaints about the data and analytical methods used, when made after the work has been completed, can be much more disruptive and damaging to the planning process than if they are made early enough for constructive response.

Redefining issues and resetting goals on the basis of fuller knowledge is a step much like the first two in the planning process. Similar inputs should be sought.

The steps of developing and analyzing alternative policies or plans come back to the question of meeting people's needs. Those people should be consulted so that their insights can be incorporated in the design phase. They will view proposals from "the receiving end"; things often look different from there. Alternatives not thought of by the planners very well might come out of this consultation in addition to diverse views of policy impacts upon citizens.

Citizen inputs on alternatives design and evaluation, along with the contributions of professional planners, can enrich the thinking of policy makers when they face the task of adopting policies and plans.

The implementation stage is not just a routine administrative step. Policies can go astray here as easily as at other stages. Citizen participation and continued policy maker involvement can help to keep plans on track.

The monitoring and evaluation step returns to data collection and analytical methods. The comments on involvement made about the third step apply equally here.

Finally, a decision to use feedback from the monitoring and evaluation step to restart the planning cycle is a responsibility of the policy makers. Planners and citizens both should be consulted about the need for this before the decision is made.

A good example of how planners, policy makers, and citizens can interact throughout a planning cycle at the regional level has been written for the Minneapolis–St. Paul metropolitan area.[12] At the state level, preparation of the Massachusetts Urban Policy provides an interesting illustration.[13]

Balancing processes with products

Planning processes sometimes go on endlessly without much tangible result. Much recent planning theory seems to encourage this by its emphasis upon the increasing complexities of society, difficulties in forecasting the future, and the fluidity of plural policy making. While it is true that much of the planner's work may result in policy advice to decision makers concerning short range issues, often given behind the scenes, total emphasis upon this aspect of planning foregoes the benefits of the longer range thinking and fuller analysis that planners are trained to provide. Only the more formal planning process with publications, advisory committees, extended public debate, and adopted policies can provide the kind of two-way communications and consensus building needed to realize the full benefits of the planning process. A planning process that does not produce plans can be only partly successful.

Planning at various levels of government

As noted in the Introduction to this book, neither state nor regional planning is just local planning writ large. Planning at each level of government has its own subject matter, techniques, and products—matched to the differences in governmental responsibilities and practices at each level.

This book is largely devoted to describing the nature of state and regional planning processes. In doing so, it shows some of the differences between these two levels and among the various states and regions.

At this point, however, it is useful to present a brief overview of some of these differences as well as to sketch some of the local and national planning concerns which frame state and regional efforts. This is done below by examining successively the differentiated policy concerns to be addressed by the planning process, styles of planning, and planning situations as they vary among the levels.

Differentiated policy concerns

Figure 1-3 shows, in a very generalized way, how a number of governmental responsibilities—which create planning concerns—have been divided up among the various levels of government in the United States. Four major policy areas are covered—environmental development and protection, economic development, human resources, and governmental structures and processes. Every level of government—local, substate regional, state, multistate regional, and national—has certain responsibilities in each of these four fields that involve established planning processes.

With respect to *environmental development and protection*, the local governments typically plan and exercise land use controls, provide basic public works, and collect the trash. Substate regions plan and help to provide areawide commuter transportation, airports, water supply, sewage treatment, air quality improvements, solid waste disposal, and overall interjurisdictional equity in the sequencing of growth and change. The states plan, provide, maintain, and patrol state highways, provide aid to local transit systems, set environmental protection standards and help local governments to enforce them (including those for solid waste disposal), and establish growth policies for areas of critical state concern. Multistate regions plan for, and in a few cases administer, certain aspects of river basin management. The national government prepares a Presidential urban policy report every other year, helps to plan and finance national systems of highways and airports, aids local transit and sewage treatment works, sets various environmental protection standards which the states must meet, and controls many aspects of hazardous wastes movement and disposal. Obviously, there are many interrelationships among the environmental planning concerns of the various levels of government.

Human resources responsibilities also exhibit many intergovernmental planning relationships. In criminal justice, for example, the federal, state, and local levels each have police, courts, and corrections responsibilities—with certain degrees of concurrent jurisdiction. Increasingly, these elements of the criminal justice system are being planned in relation to one another. Substate regional organizations provide areawide planning studies aimed at interjurisdictional coordination and joint operations in such activities as crime labs, mutual aid, hot pursuit, communications, and training. State criminal justice planning may have concerns similar to areawide ones—especially for areas not planned by areawide units—but also is responsible for upgrading statewide court and corrections systems. Unique federal government responsibilities lie in the direction of criminal justice research, statistics, and record keeping. Federal grants for state and regional planning and criminal justice operations below the national level have been discontinued.

In welfare, local governments administer most programs, while the state and federal levels each establish standards and help with financing. Related social services exhibit much the same pattern, except that some of the more specialized services, such as those for the aging and handicapped and those for vocational education, are planned and provided by substate regional organizations in some areas as a means of capturing economies of scale. Some states also provide such services directly in the "balance of state" not served by local or areawide providers. Some multistate regional commissions stimulate the improvement of various social services.

Hospitals are provided separately by the local, state, and federal governments—as well as privately. The state and federal hospitals serve special types of patients (such as the mentally ill, the military, and veterans). Local and private hospitals handle most patients, while the states set standards for the operation of hospitals and nursing homes. Local governments also operate public health clinics.

Health care cost containment is a major issue involving each level of government. Avoiding duplication of health facilities is one key. State and substate regional planning organizations have been enlisted in this battle by both state and federal laws.

Special roles in the health care field include areawide emergency medical services designed to bring quick on-the-spot treatment to accident victims and swift transport to specialized trauma treatment facilities. Another specialized role is the unique health research effort by the federal government.

In the housing field, local housing authorities plan and provide public housing units for low income residents and also distribute federal rent supplement payments for other eligible persons. Substate regional organizations plan and help to allocate federal housing assistance equitably among localities within the area. Many states provide mortgage assistance over and above that available from the federal government. The federal government, of course, provides various forms of mortgage assistance, public housing grants, and rent supplements.

Jobs programs include training, placement, unemployment compensation, and planning for these programs. Much of the training is provided by local governments and private contractors. The states are largely responsible for job placement and unemployment compensation through a network of locally placed state offices. The federal government provides much of the financing (including incentives for state unemployment taxes). Areawide manpower planning is encouraged, though not required, by the federal government. Statewide manpower planning is required. The objectives of manpower planning are to analyze market area data and to coordinate job training and placement activities for whole areas.

In the field of *economic development*, planning has been very largely concentrated at the state and regional levels where potentials for business are analyzed and promoted. There has been substantial federal aid for such planning at the substate, state, and multistate levels. Local governments, of course, compete with each other to attract businesses which will increase jobs and the local tax base. Crucial to the success of all these activities is a healthy national economy, a responsibility of the federal government. Another crucial federal role relates to the interrelationships among environmental protection, energy, and import policies.

Finally, with respect to *governmental structures and processes*, the states hold the key constitutional position. They are responsible for their own structures and processes, as well as for those of local and regional bodies. Nevertheless, many local governments have been given home rule powers limited only by certain general laws of the state legislature and referendum actions of the local electorate. A few states have established permanent local government boundary commissions at the state and/or local levels—local meaning county-wide or metropolitan-wide. Other states have authorized, from time to time, temporary government study commissions at the state or metropolitan levels. The topics studied and recommended for action include home rule charters, consolidation, annexation, and intergovernmental cooperation. The plans developed by these boundary and study commissions seek to establish improved relationships between the public service needs to be met and the boundaries and powers of those governmental bodies expected to respond.

States also have the basic responsibility for establishing planning at the state, regional, and local levels. While most states have enabled such planning for many years, most did not promote it energetically. The federal government, on the other hand, has been taking major initiatives to this direction for over two

Broad areas of public policy	Local	Substate[1] regional	State	Multistate	National
Environmental development and protection	Land use compatibility	Commuter transportation	State highways	Appalachian highway system	National highway system
	Protection of property values		Transit aid		Transit aid
					National railway system
	Building safety and occupancy conditions				
	Land platting (local roads)				
	Airport owner	Airport system plan	State airport plan		National airport system
		Airport owner	Airport owner		Air safety Airport aid
	Growth timing	Growth equity	Critical areas, growth policy		National urban policy
	Local utilities and facilities	Water supply, sewage treatment	Environmental protection standards and enforcement (air and water)	River basin management	Environmental protection standards and aid
		Air quality planning and emergency plan			
	Trash collection	Solid waste disposal	Solid waste disposal standards		Solid waste aid
					Hazardous waste
Economic development		Analyze potentials of the area	Analyze state's potentials		Economic development aid for planning and promotion
			Prepare investment strategies	Prepare investment strategies	Manage the economy • Monetary policy • Fiscal policy • Social safety net
	Create a favorable business climate		Create a favorable business climate		
	Provide incentives for business development	Fairly allocate new business investment in the area	Promote new business	Natural resource allocation issues	Energy/ environment interface
		Metropolitan tax sharing			

Figure 1–3   Common planning concerns at various levels of government by policy areas.

Broad areas of public policy	Local	Substate[1] regional	State	Multistate	National
Human resources	Police patrol	Police crime labs, mutual aid, hot pursuit, communications, training	Highway patrol Crime labs Police training		FBI Crime research, statistics, and records
Criminal justice	Local courts Local jails		State courts Corrections		Federal courts Federal prisons
Welfare	Administration		Welfare standards and finance		Welfare standards and finance
Social services	Basic social services administration	Special services Aging Handicapped Vocational education	"Balance of state" services for the aging	Stimulation of critically needed social services	Social services aid
Health	Hospitals Health clinics	Health care cost control planning Emergency medical services	Hospitals Hospitals and nursing home standards	Stimulation of critically needed health services Health research	Hospitals Financial aid for health planning and services
Housing	Public housing authority Housing aid to individuals in private housing	Areawide fair share allocation of federal housing aid Realtor affirmative action training	Mortgage assistance Mortgage revenue bonds Affirmative action legislation		Mortgage assistance Public housing assistance Civil rights legislation
Jobs	Job training	Labor market data and job placement coordination	Job training Job placement Unemployment compensation	Stimulation of new jobs	Employment and training aid Emergency unemployment compensation
Governmental structures and processes	Home rule charters Consolidations	Boundary studies Control of areawide districtions Local planning assistance Model for local governments Joint purchasing Plan and coordinate federal aid	Establish local and regional government structures, functions, and finances Control local financial emergencies Plan and coordinate federal aid	Promote state and substate regional planning capabilities Plan and coordinate federal aid	Provide planning aid

Figure 1—3   (continued).

[1] This level encompasses both infrastructure and interstate metropolitan areas as well as single and multicounty non-metropolitan areas encompassing common communities of interest and being organized for areawide planning.

decades and also has enlisted the states and regions in promoting planning at other levels.

It should be apparent from this brief overview of how the many current responsibilities of government are divided among the various levels that planners need to be sensitive to the role of their own level when they pursue their trade. It is important also to recognize and plan for the intergovernmental relationships that exist in the policy fields being addressed.

As indicated in this brief review, local governments have the broadest set of public service action responsibilities matched by a commensurate set of planning processes. In contrast, most regional organizations, excepting certain single-purpose authorities, have significant planning responsibilities and very little implementation authority. States are more like local governments in having parallel responsibilities and authority for planning and action programs. The states, however, being sovereign, have fewer legal restrictions on their finances and governmental authority. While local governments must look to the states, as well as the federal government and local voters, to open new paths of planning, finance, and authority to them, the states need look only to their own constitutions and voters in most cases, or to the federal government. States have the basic responsibility for empowering local governments and regions to cope with the problems faced at those levels. Inadequate state planning and action in this regard, however, led the federal government in recent decades to provide increasing amounts of aid directly to local governments and regions, as well as to the states themselves. Such federal aid, instituted in a broad array of program fields, almost always has required planning, and frequently has funded that planning as well.

Thus, by one means or another, each level of government now is deeply involved in the planning process. Generally, it is the classical planning process that has been specified in state law, local charter, federal law, or federal aid regulations. Increasingly, emphasis has been placed upon the need for a solid connection between planning and implementation. State and local governments have been moving in this direction by incorporating their planning agencies into their top policy and budgeting offices, thereby "operationalizing" the planning process. At the same time, most regional planning remains outside any operational government body. To the extent that a regional plan is simply an aggregation of local plans, it may be linked fairly closely to implementation activities. To the extent that it seeks to resolve area-wide controversies upon which local governments cannot agree, it may be left with little access to the needed implementation powers. The main exception has been in a very limited number of federal aid programs—especially urban transportation and sewage treatment facilities—where federal approval of project funding has been largely dependent upon consistency with a regional plan.

The largely advisory role of most regional plans makes it more difficult for regional planning organizations to "deliver" results. Their planning reports, developed using the classical process, satisfy federal planning requirements but often have little other effect. State planning, on the other hand, is becoming less classical, more submerged in top policy circles, less oriented toward producing separate planning documents, and—perhaps—more effective in influencing state policies.

Differentiated styles of planning

Styles of planning relate very directly to organizational positions of the planning unit. Independent planning commissions, for example, are outside the direct flow of power. Therefore, their success depends upon persuasion, and their capability to be persuasive usually is enhanced by consensus building among concerned constituencies. Thus, an open process with major emphasis upon citizen and policy maker participation serves well.

In sharp contrast is the chief executive strategic policy planning process which may operate on a very intimate basis until a finished proposal is ready for public exposure. Participation in this process typically is limited to a close knit group of top advisors plus, perhaps, an appointed advisory group used to generate ideas for consideration by the policy group and chief executive. As the executive unveils his plan, he or she begins the process of selling it.

Legislative committees considering plans are likely to do so in public, under the requirements of "open meetings" or "sunshine" laws requiring most of their deliberations to be open to the public. This process tends to keep options open until the final committee mark-up session makes choices. As the proposal or plan takes shape, public testimony usually is taken from a wide variety of interested parties.

Such considerations lead to differing styles of planning at the various levels of government. At the local level, where policy making often is vested in a council which combines executive and legislative functions, the planning process usually follows the open legislative style. An advisory planning commission may be used to enrich citizen opportunities to consider a variety of options before debate by the local governing body. In some larger localities, elected chief executives are independent of the council, splitting the planning process into a two-stage "propose and dispose" affair. The executive typically proposes a plan, based upon a limited participation decision making process, and the council uses a more open process to examine the proposal and make some disposition of it.

State planning, located predominantly in or close to the governor's office, or in a number of executive agencies, is likely to be relatively nonparticipatory except in a few functional fields like transportation where recent political controversies and federal regulations have opened the process. Legislative involvement in state planning, now limited in most cases to approval of budgets needed to carry out planned projects, would tend to open up the process if it were used more freely.

Regional planning is more like its local counterpart with respect to openness. Most regional organizations have only a single policy making body, combining both executive and legislative functions. Unless the organization is dominated by staff—usually an unhealthy sign—its planning process is likely to be relatively open. A major incentive for regional planning to be open is its need to build consensus as its primary means of influencing implementation.

Planning requirements imposed by state law or federal aid programs may affect planning styles considerably. Such requirements often specify matters of style like the make-up and roles of advisory committees, the frequency of public hearings, the use of other citizen participation techniques, the array of alternatives to be considered, and the factors to be analyzed.

Other matters of style, like the time horizons and degree of flexibility, are likely to be determined both by the level of government and subject matter of the plan. Higher levels of government, working through other levels to achieve their ends, often can be more general. Those responsible for final action must be specific. Planning agencies not responsible for administering governmental facilities or services can concentrate more of their attention on long range considerations, but if they cannot ultimately translate long range goals into steps recommended for immediate action, they may be wasting their time and effort.

For all these reasons, and more, planning may look very different from one level of government to another and from one branch of government to another. The success or failure of any particular planning process should be judged on the basis of its location and role in the governmental system.

Figure 1–4   The complexity of planning is suggested in this aerial photo of Tulsa, Oklahoma, taken in the early 1950s. In the foreground is the fringe development of subdivisions and industry jostling the parkland and undeveloped land. In the background is the more densely developed portion of the city and the city center. Planning and financing roads, sewer and water lines, and other parts of the infrastructure are part of the development of both areas but on decisively different scales.

Diversity of situations among states and regions

The situations of states and regions differ dramatically from one to another. Some are rich; some are poor. Some are populous; some are sparsely settled. Some are highly urban; some are rural. Some have large land areas; some are small. Some have fragile environments; some seem indestructible. Some are highly subject to earthquakes, tornados, or floods; others are relatively free of such risks. Some have progressive political climates; some have conservative ones. Some have long histories of good planning; some have had shorter or less satisfactory planning experiences. Some are used to having clean and open government; some suffer back-room corruption.

Such differences inevitably show up in the subject matter and styles of planning processes. Any situation which reaches crisis proportions may cause a dramatic reaction. For example, fragile environments facing pressures for rapid development—like those in the states of Florida, Vermont, and Hawaii, and regions along coast lines—have brought forth some of the most effective environmental protection and land use management laws. Highly urbanized states like California, Massachusetts, and Michigan have been leaders in producing statewide urban policies. States with unusually large numbers of counties—like Georgia and Texas—or with very small local governments—like Vermont—have been leaders in promoting the use of substate regional planning organizations. The metropolitan consolidation of governments in Jacksonville, Florida was a response to the need for reforming local corruption and ineffectiveness. California's strongest-in-the-nation air quality laws were a response to high concentrations of urban activity in areas subject to weather conditions that often trap dirty air for long periods of time.

The list of situational differences is endless. While there are many commonalities from place to place, there also is great diversity. It is best for the planner to assume that each state or region (or other planning jurisdiction being considered) is unique, and to figure on adjusting the planning process and planning products to the situation at hand.

Focus on generalist planning organizations

Throughout Part I of this book, the emphasis is upon the central planning agency of the state and the general purpose regional planning organization. These are the units with overarching responsibilities cutting across any policy fields which may need to be interrelated or coordinated. It is important that such planning units have access to the chief elected officials of the level of government for which general plans and policies are being developed. At the state level, this means the governor and legislature. At the multistate level, it means governors, legislators, members of Congress, and the President. At the substate regional level, it means mayors, county executives, and local council or governing board members as well as the governor and legislators. In short, the clientele for general plans consists of generalists. This is the hardest clientele to serve; general purpose plans are the most difficult type to prepare; the benefits of such planning often are the most difficult to identify in tangible ways because they become so fully intertwined with political processes; therefore, central planning often becomes the most difficult type to justify and fund adequately. Yet, without some form of central, general purpose, or comprehensive planning portfolio assigned, the most important policy makers in government are left unaided by rational analysis, and many opportunities for better government are left to chance.

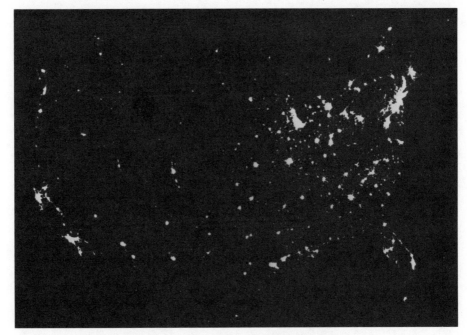

Figure 1–5 This satellite photo, taken in 1981 at night at Vandenberg Air Force Base in California, shows the major cities in the United States by light images. These concentrations of population dramatize how much of the nation's activites are concentrated in a small number of areas.

A strong state planning agency at the center of each state's decision making, and strong general purpose regional planning organizations throughout the nation, are important resources for improving government. The chapters that follow are offered for the purpose of helping to develop those resources to their fullest.

1   Preston P. LeBreton and Dale A. Henning, *Planning Theory* (Englewood Cliffs, NJ: Prentice-Hall, 1961), p. 7.

2   *Ibid.*

3   Martin Meyerson, "Building the Middle Range Bridge for Comprehensive Planning," *Journal of the American Institute of Planners* 22 (Spring 1956): pp. 58–64.

4   LeBreton and Henning, p. 14.

5   Summaries of these objections may be found in Richard S. Bolan, "Emerging Views of Planning," *Journal of the American Institute of Planners* 33 (July 1967): pp. 233–245; Dennis A. Rondinelli, *Urban and Regional Development Planning: Policy and Administration* (Ithaca, NY: Cornell University Press, 1975): chap. 2; and David E. Wilson, *The National Planning Idea in U.S. Public Policy: Five Alternative Approaches* (Boulder, CO: Westview Press, 1980): chap. 6.

6   Harvey S. Perloff, *Planning the Post-Industrial City* (Chicago: Planners Press, 1980).

7   For a slightly different list which, nevertheless, influenced my thinking greatly, see LeBreton and Henning, chap. 2.

8   Advisory Commission on Intergovernmental Relations, *Factors Affecting the Voter Reactions to Governmental Reorganization in Metropolitan Areas*, Report M-15 (Washington, DC: U.S. Government Printing Office, May 1962).

9   Israel Stollman, "The Values of the City Planner," in *The Practice of Local Government Planning*, ed. Frank S. So, *et al.* (Washington, DC: International City Management Association), p. 13.

10 Perloff, *Planning the Post-Industrial City*.

11 Pat Choate and Susan Walter, *America in Ruins* (Washington, DC: Council of State Planning Agencies, 1981).

12 Ed Knutson, *Regional Politics in the Twin Cities: A Report on the Politics and Planning of Urban Growth Policy* (St. Paul, MN: Metropolitan Council of the Twin Cities Area, September 1976); Peggy A. Reichert, *Growth Management in the Twin Cities Metropolitan Area: A Report for Planners on the Development Framework Planning Process* (St. Paul, MN: Metropolitan Council of the Twin Cities Area, September 1976). *Executive Summary* of both was published at the same time.

13 The Massachusetts Office of Planning, *City and Town Centers: A Program for Growth*, The Massachusetts Growth Policy Report (Boston: September 1977).

The evolution of American planning

Planning in America did not emerge full blown. As a matter of fact, it was very limited in the early years. Understanding planning today in the United States, and especially particular types of planning—like state and regional planning—is facilitated by a review of the history and philosophical development of planning in the particular governmental context and social environment of the nation.

Planning is practiced by individuals, businesses, private organizations, and governments. Thus, planning adapts to many different situations.

The way in which planning is practiced varies a great deal from one organization to another, from one level of government to another, and from one unit of government to another. Where there is a consensus on the goals of the organization or government, planning is likely to be used rather routinely to improve the effectiveness of reaching these goals. On the other hand, where there is no such consensus on goals, or where the consensus is weak, planning efforts often may be opposed; planning may also be dragged into controversies about whether planning is good and thereby weakened in its ability to function constructively. This is not surprising, since planning usually is viewed, and properly so, as a means of enhancing goal attainment. But planning also can be viewed as a means of goal definition.

In its public policy roles, planning sometimes is a major way of initiating new public policies, and at other times it becomes a vital part of the management process in carrying out public policies. This equates public planning with the exercise of governmental power.

The nature of public planning organizations and processes flows very directly from the evolution of public policy issues arising from a variety of technological and social changes as well as from the improving capacity of planners to collect and analyze relevant data. When the public policy goals are agreed to—as in a war effort, beating a deep depression, putting a man on the moon, or building a subway system—the planners are given great support, enthusiastic encouragement, and significant roles. But when the goals are contested, or if some of the likely means of achieving these goals are controversial, the planners are told to go slowly, to turn their efforts to other pursuits, or even in some cases to go out of business. Some of these less universally favored goals might be those which have the effect of redistributing wealth, changing the character of neighborhoods, raising taxes substantially, or having a significant adverse impact on surrounding properties or people.

The history of planning in the United States shows, nevertheless, that planning gradually has been accepted into ever widening circles of governmental jurisdictions and public policy fields, including many which are controversial. It also reveals changes in public attitudes toward the use of governmental power and toward the role of planning in the exercise of such power. This chapter summarizes the major historical, philosophical, and attitudinal developments in America which have brought planning into its present place in the governmental system—including planning at the state and regional levels.

Although state and regional planning both are quite prevalent now, such was not the case as recently as two decades ago. Both of these types of planning have roots which go back much earlier, of course, but in their present form they are relatively new innovations, probably subject to a great deal of further evolution in the decades ahead.

As background for the more direct treatment of state and regional planning in subsequent chapters, this chapter surveys the governmental context of planning in the United States, reviews the historical development of planning at each level of government in the nation, and traces the major philosophical transformations which have taken place in the planning field from colonial times to the present. The governmental context is examined in terms of both the unique philosophies of American government and the particular powers of government through which planning becomes effective. The historical development is traced with particular emphasis upon state and regional planning. And the philosophical evolution is surveyed with emphasis upon recent social, environmental, intergovernmental, and management concepts which have come forward very largely in the last 20 years—the formative years of most present state and regional planning organizations.

Each section of this chapter has special relevance to planning at the state and regional levels. The governmental context shows how limited and fragmented United States governments are in dealing with many of the planning issues at the state and regional levels. The early historical eras of public planning in the United States show how urban planning issues developed, outgrew city boundaries, and became issues for regions and states—as well as for the nation. The philosophical transformations, all maturing during the formative years of most present state and regional planning organizations, have shaped these units and have become their operating guides.

Basic elements of government in the United States: A special context for planning

Governments in the United States—whether federal, state, or local—are democracies, operating under an interlocked system of laws established in accordance with the federal Constitution and fifty state constitutions. These fundamental legal documents have been amended and reinterpreted in very substantial ways as the nation has matured, and they set very specific limits on the exercise of public powers which vary from state to state. Nevertheless, certain basic philosophies of government and types of governmental powers permeate the nation.

General legal and political principles

Government in the United States is limited in its scope and powers, divided into three basic levels (federal, state, and local), and open to the influence of the people. Each of these features is deeply embedded in the legal and political principles of the nation as explained below.

Limited government   When the United States was established, protection of personal freedoms and assurance of self rule were of paramount concern. So was the use of private enterprise, emphasizing free markets with their incentives for private initiative. The Declaration of Independence and the Revolutionary War were aimed at protecting the rights of individuals against governmental interference and establishing the principle of representation in government by the people of the colonies. Government was to be limited by the consent of the people, while private enterprise was to be relied upon to the greatest extent possible in developing the new nation. Government was to serve the people and private enterprise in limited ways, as necessary, rather than the people being expected to serve the needs of the government as too often occurred in the past.

To help ensure that government in the United States would not become too powerful, the Constitution of the United States and those of the individual states established checks and balances which separated the legislative, executive, and judicial functions of government. Soon thereafter, the Bill of Rights established the rights of individuals which government cannot violate. Thus, the nation began with the thought that individuals and private enterprises should be of first importance, while government should be the servant. The exact meaning of this attitude changes from time to time, but it is generally given a large share of the credit for the nation's success, and it remains a strongly held and very influential basis for government and politics in present-day America.

Federalism   Another major feature of American government is its federal system under which the functions and responsibilities of government are divided among the national, state, and local levels. In the constitutional sense, the states are the sovereign units. In the federal constitution, the states delegated certain enumerated powers (such as interstate commerce, national defense, and foreign affairs) to the federal government, while retaining most other powers themselves. The federal Constitution makes no mention of local governments, so the states retain full authority for creating and structuring the lower levels of government. A fairly strict separation of powers, along these constitutional lines, remained in effect very largely until the 1930s when the crisis of the Great Depression demanded federal action of much broader dimensions.

Through liberal interpretation of the interstate commerce, general welfare, and federal spending powers in the Constitution, the federal government now is allowed to participate in almost any function of government which the political process will authorize.[1] In most domestic functions, however, the prevailing constitutional interpretations and political preferences still prohibit direct federal action. Therefore, the bulk of the federal government's domestic activities— except for the administration of federal lands, the post office, and the regulation of interstate commerce—are accomplished through intergovernmental programs in which federal grants and other forms of aid are used to secure the cooperation of the state and local governments. Thus, the separation of governmental levels in the federal system and the very great recent expansion of the federal government's domestic activities have combined to make intergovernmental relations a principal mechanism for the pursuit of public policies and public programs in the United States today.

Pluralism and access to government   In a pure democracy, everyone has an equal voice in government. This ideal, of course, is never achieved. The closest we come in the United States is probably the New England town meeting form of government in small communities. Even in that part of the country, however, the larger towns have a modified "representative" town meeting form of government, and representation characterizes the rest of the governments in the United States. Generally speaking, representatives are elected to serve in the governing of our national, state, and local governments. Elected officials then appoint others to help in carrying out the functions of government.

This is far from the whole story, however. The Bill of Rights protects every citizen's right to assemble with other citizens and to petition the government for "redress of grievances." When Alexis de Tocqueville made his famous reconnaissance of the United States in the early 1830s, he was profoundly struck by the great degree to which Americans seemed to be organizing into groups for anything and everything.[2] The well-to-do always have had good access to their elected representatives, and great influence on government. But over the years, representations by all types of interest groups have become more numerous and diverse. Today there are even groups known as "citizen lobbies" which have no particular interest other than opening up the governmental system further so that anyone and everyone will have the opportunity, if he or she desires to use it, to help influence governmental decisions in the legislative, executive, regulatory, and judicial branches. Thus, the United States has not only representative democracy, but also representational democracy. Special attention is being given to allowing minorities and the disadvantaged to be heard, and citizen participation practices are being developed to new heights of effectiveness. Despite all of the difficulties involved, the commonly held belief is that everyone with the desire should be allowed to put in his or her two cents worth. Voting alone is not enough to sustain democracy in America.[3]

Comparison with other nations   On a scale of nations ranging from tyranny to pure democracy, the United States places well toward the pole of democracy. Its government is more limited than most; its federal system relies more on local government; its individual citizens enjoy greater freedoms; its private economy plays a greater role in the nation's affairs; and access to the government is among the easiest.

With so little centralization, so much separation of powers, and so much pluralism, government in the United States appears haphazard in comparison with many other nations—and less planned. Its planning is less rigid, less deterministic, and perhaps even less effective by some measures.[4] At the same time, this nation's planning is safer, more democratic, and less threatening to individual rights. It is also less pervasive, because of the more limited role of government here. The role of planning in the United States follows the role of government and is geared in large part to public opinion.

Basic governmental powers

The basic governmental powers exercised in the United States are taxing and spending, regulation, and eminent domain.[5] Planning recommendations are geared to the exercise of these powers. Therefore, planners need to be familiar with each of these powers and with their combinations.

Taxing and spending   There are many different types of taxes. The major ones in the United States are on property, incomes, and sales. Other taxes are collected on such things as imports coming into the country, licensing businesses to operate, and the purchase of particular goods or services such as amusements, gasoline, and tires.

The various levels of government rely upon different sets of taxes, and this changes from time to time. In its early history, the federal government relied primarily on taxes from imports, but its main source now is the income tax. State governments used to rely primarily on the property tax, but in recent years they have come to rely much more heavily on sales and income taxes. Local governments always have relied, and still do rely, most heavily upon the property tax, and most states have legally limited the taxing authority of their localities.

The basic purpose of taxes, of course, is to raise revenues adequate to satisfy the demands for governmental spending. Traditionally, most governmental spending has been done by local governments and financed from the property tax. However, with the two world wars, the federal government moved heavily into the income tax field and developed it as such a powerful source of funds that it has become the dominant public revenue producer in the nation. The high wartime revenue levels of the 1940s were retained very largely after the war, allowing a major expansion of federal domestic spending in the post-war years. States then joined in with smaller versions of the federal income tax, plus sales taxes, which they used to match the federal government's domestic spending increases and to supplement limited local government revenues as the public sector expanded.

Governmental revenues now quite frequently are raised by one level of government and then transferred to another level where they are spent. Most of the federal government's transfers to the state and local governments are in the form of conditional grants, supporting national purposes, while state aid to local governments most frequently takes the form of the relatively unconditional return to localities of state taxes collected in those jurisdictions (revenue sharing).

Public spending in the United States traditionally was largely devoted to education and public works, including transportation, utilities, and public buildings. Health and welfare expenditures, though very large now, only recently achieved this status. Tax programs have grown over the years in response to demands for expanding public spending programs. Today, about 30 percent of the gross national product is in the public sector, and public spending has become the primary means of effectuating public policy.

Before leaving the subject of taxation, it is important to note that taxes have effects other than simply raising revenues. This is unavoidable, so it should be thought through before any new tax proposals are adopted. In very general terms, it can be said that transactions which are heavily taxed will be discouraged, while transactions which escape taxation or have relatively low taxes will be encouraged. Thus, tax policies may be used to help implement plans as well as to raise revenues for the spending program.

Regulation   Regulation is sometimes called "the police power." Either of these terms simply refers to the authority of government to regulate the activities of society for protecting the general public's health and safety and for promoting the general welfare of the citizens of the local community, the state, or the nation. So long as such regulations do not fall disproportionately or unfairly upon particular individuals, no compensation is required. Thus, the only spending involved is for enforcement of the regulations—usually a rather modest amount.

All levels of government use regulation. At the local level, zoning, subdivision regulations, right-of-way reservations, building and occupancy codes, and the like have taken their place alongside the capital improvements program and the operating budget as mainstays of plan implementation efforts. State regulations commonly apply to such things as highway safety, hospital and nursing home operations, and natural resource protection, conservation, and extraction. Federal regulations, traditionally restricted largely to banking, money supply, and interstate commerce, now have branched out into many additional fields such as environmental protection, drinking water safety, drug abuse, working conditions, consumer protection, and various aspects of civil rights.

Eminent domain   The power of eminent domain is the power of government to buy property from an owner at a fair price whether or not the owner wishes to sell. Specific procedures are set by state law which provide that the courts monitor this transaction to ensure fairness. Federal legislation enacted in 1970 requires that most displacements of people and businesses resulting from involuntary property acquisitions involving federal funds shall be accompanied with fair and equitable relocation assistance.[6] This type of aid is also beginning to be provided in cases of state and local displacements.

A clear public purpose must be established before the eminent domain power may be used, but the definition has broadened since the 1940s to include many facets of urban renewal as well as the more traditional public works necessities.

Combinations of powers These three basic governmental powers can be used alternatively, or in combination, to implement a particular public policy in more than one way. For example, tax deductions or credits (sometimes called "tax expenditures") can be used in place of or as a supplement to the government's spending power. A tax deduction or credit for political contributions, coupled with campaign financing by matching grants from the governments, is such a case. Most tax deductions, however, simply substitute a tax policy which subsidizes certain transactions for what otherwise would have to be a governmental grant program. The tax provision may require very little administration by the government, but it may be quite costly (in terms of foregone revenues) because it provides benefits to a broad range of taxpayers including those who might otherwise do exactly the same thing even without the tax subsidy.

With respect to regulations, certain regulations might well be perfectly within the purposes of protecting the public health, safety, and general welfare, but they may at the same time unfairly impact certain individuals. In such cases, compensation might well be offered in much the same fashion as if eminent domain were being exercised. Such cases are called "compensable regulation." An example might be the preservation of open space by zoning for very low density land uses while at the same time acquiring partial development rights through the exercise of eminent domain. Alternatively, either full or partial property tax exemption might be used as compensation for a promise not to develop.

The possible combinations and alternatives are almost unlimited. New ones are being devised constantly.[7] Creative planners need to be aware of these varied possibilities for implementing their proposals.

Due process in exercising these powers The Constitution provides that the exercise of all these powers must be accomplished under due process of law. Otherwise, the use of these powers may be challenged in court and overturned as being unconstitutional. Increasingly, the definition of due process is expanding beyond narrow legal concepts which require only that a few rules and regulations be followed. The broader concept ensures open and sensitive consideration of all relevant viewpoints and careful balancing of competing interests before public policy decisions are made. The planning process plays a very major part in the identification of issues and the weighing of alternatives in the light of a broad spectrum of citizen input into the governmental decision-making process.

Due process and faithfulness to the state and local constitutions, as well as to the laws and regulations enacted thereunder, is judged by the courts. There is a large and growing body of judicial opinion on planning issues. As was the case with judicial reinterpretation of the Constitution in the 1930s, the courts update their opinions when times change and new issues develop. The expansion of planning into new fields of public policy and program has been followed by the development of new branches of case law. In fields where legislation is vague and policies are uncertain, court decisions often can be as important as laws and regulations in establishing key principles for public planning and action. Some recent examples in which the courts have had a major impact on planning include environmental protection, housing availability, growth management, citizen participation, and grant law.

Specific legal frameworks

For a large number of reasons it is very difficult to generalize about the legal framework under which any particular program must operate at any particular time and location in the United States. The nation's federal system of government, under which each of the 50 states has a separate constitution, is one of the foremost reasons. Another is the expansion of home rule authority for local governments during most of this century, enabling many localities to have their own separate charters of incorporation. Still a third factor is the relatively weak coordination among different parts of the federal government, which allows substantial differences in policies and procedures from one federal program to another—including the intergovernmental programs which affect the ways in which states, regions, and localities operate.

These differences translate directly into differences of powers, structures, tax sources, tax limitations, and intergovernmental arrangements among the various states, local governments, and regional organizations in the nation. Thus, the generalizations made here about basic governmental powers and the general legal and political principles of American government show up in very diverse forms, depending upon the particular unit of government being examined. This means that a planner must become familiar with the specific legal framework and political dynamics of the governmental organization with which he or she is serving or dealing.

Major eras of American planning

There have been five major eras of planning in the United States: (1) the early years from colonial times to the Civil War, (2) the latter part of the nineteenth century following the Civil War, (3) the early twentieth century, (4) the Great Depression and the war years following it, and (5) the post-war years to the present. Brief highlights of each of these periods are sketched below.[8]

Colonial times to the Civil War

Many colonial towns were preplanned in Europe before the settlers set off for the new world. Others were laid out on the site primarily by surveyors. Grid patterns were common, though some plans included more elaborate features such as public gathering places and ceremonial avenues and vistas. Fortifications often were featured in frontier areas. Land uses were not specialized except for a few public buildings, and most urban areas remained quite small until well into the nineteenth century. Making land available and safe for development was the primary thrust of most planning.

The late nineteenth century

By the time the Civil War ended, the Industrial Revolution was well along, and the rapid urbanization which accompanied it had made some cities quite large and crowded. Densely built, overcrowded, and unhealthy tenements were creating disease, fire hazards, and very poor living conditions for many people. Several major studies of slums were prepared. The national government and some states became concerned. Settlement houses began springing up to provide improved living conditions for immigrants. Regulation of boarding and lodging houses started. Large cities such as New York and San Francisco began to regulate tenement houses to provide a certain amount of light and air, plumbing, and relief from overcrowding. Social workers, architects, and engineers led these efforts.

Reactions against urban squalor also spurred the "city beautiful" movement in which parks, civic buildings, and monumental features were added to cities in an effort to make them more livable. This phase of planning often was the work of landscape architects.

The early twentieth century and
modern municipal planning

The theory of new town development, sometimes referred to as garden cities and advocating many of the features of what is known today as good suburban development, was published just before the turn of the century (1898). Within a decade, the first city planning commissions had been formed (beginning with Hartford, Connecticut in 1907); Wisconsin had enacted the first planning enabling act for cities (1909); Los Angeles had passed the first real land-use zoning ordinance (1909); and Daniel Burnham had presented the first modern city plan in Chicago (1909). Between 1910 and 1930 zoning spread to many cities and was upheld by the Supreme Court (1926); Cincinnati adopted the first official comprehensive plan as a guide for its zoning (1925); the first American new town was developed at Radburn, New Jersey (1928); and the Standard City Planning Enabling Act was prepared and made available by the U.S. Department of Commerce (1928). Thus, modern municipal planning and the concept of municipal master plans had been established. The national government and a number of states had become involved in urban planning issues. Lawyers led much of this work.

Rapid urbanization during this period, and the introduction of the automobile, focused attention on upgrading city utilities and streets, providing public transit systems, and accommodating suburban expansion. Many planners in this era came from the professions of civil engineering and architecture. The first professional planning school in the United States was established in Harvard in 1929, although this university had offered landscape architecture degrees with a city planning emphasis since 1923 and 33 other American universities and colleges had been offering individual courses in city planning for some time.

The early twentieth century also began the development of planning theories reaching beyond the municipal level. Through professional organizations which formed early in the century (National Conference on City Planning, 1909, and American City Planning Institute, 1917), planners began to discuss their frustrations with trying to plan for urban needs within the framework of individual city boundaries. The need for planning whole urban areas became obvious to them even before the first world war, as suburbs expanded beyond the central city boundaries. Experience in planning for war housing heightened the awareness that surburban areas were ill prepared to accommodate growth. The state role in urban planning and metropolitan affairs also was discussed as a necessary framework for planning at other levels.

During the 1920s, several metropolitan planning organizations were established in major urban areas including New York, Los Angeles, Chicago, Pittsburgh, Milwaukee, Toledo (Ohio), and Washington, D.C. Some were private organizations, while others were county-wide planning commissions or multi-county public bodies. Other areas experimenting with such organizations included Minneapolis–St. Paul, Philadelphia, and San Francisco.

A climate for national planning also began to develop in the late 1920s. In 1927, the Federated Societies on Planning and Parks established a Joint Committee on Bases of Sound Land Policy which examined a variety of national issues dealing with land and water resources and the need for national planning to address these issues as well as the urbanization of the nation. Then in 1929, Herbert Hoover appointed the President's Research Committee on Social Trends which covered much of the same subject matter but brought it into official governmental dialogue. As a result, "National planning of some sort, supported by state planning or river basin planning and more effective local planning, loomed as an imperative need the more the country drifted toward economic disintegration."[9]   (*text continued on page 41*)

Landscape, cityscape, and planning, a portfolio From the earliest settlements in the United States to the present day, planning has been the concept and means for altering the land, water, and mineral resources of the United States. Drawing on John R. Stilgoe's *Common Landscape of America, 1580 to 1845*, landscape means "shaped land, land modified for permanent human occupation, for dwelling, agriculture, manufacturing, government, worship, and for pleasure." The key word is "modified." When landscape is wholly dominated by "structure and chiseled space," it becomes cityscape. (Stilgoe, p. 3)

One of the themes in Stilgoe's book is the historic attachment to neighborhood and home. For three centuries,

Americans have striven to attain and secure neighborhood and home within the exigencies of livelihood, education, religion, and government. The love of landscape, however, and the need for cityscape create a historic tension that has permeated planning. Many people still attempt to attain and secure neighborhood and home within a landscape that is "space shaped for agriculture and gently punctuated by artifice [mills, stables, small shops, and the like] and roads." (Stilgoe, p. 25) As the nation has moved from small, isolated settlements to the urbanization, technology, and communication of the 1980s, an ideal for many has been pulled along: "Most Americans hoped to live in landscape, in communities they understood and liked." (Stilgoe, p. 208)

(continued on page 33)

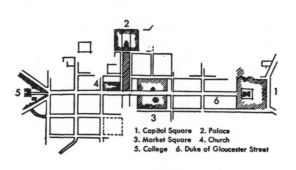

1. Capitol Square   2. Palace
3. Market Square   4. Church
5. College   6. Duke of Gloucester Street

This portfolio shows the ways in which planning, even though it was seldom called that for more than two centuries, and land, water, and resources shaped the face of the United States.

Fort Caroline on the St. John's River in Florida (1671) shows a fortified settlement with the essentials of water supply and river access. The formal plan for Williamsburg, Virginia, demonstrates the importance assigned to government, education, and com-

merce. One of the first land surveyors was George Washington, shown here in the Dismal Swamp. His work preceded the Ordinance of 1785, a national law, which established a grid system for most of the country of six-mile-square townships to be laid out by land surveys with alignments by longitude and latitude. The next line cut is identified by the Library of Congress as the "embryo town of Columbus on the Chatahoochie (Georgia, 1828)."

(continued on page 35)

The country was transformed—economically, socially, and physically—in the nineteenth century by water and rail. From the 1850s on, however, rail was the radical force in changing the landscape.

The railroad was the backbone of Aberdeen, Dakota Territory (1883). The line cut also shows the grid layout for the streets with Main Street as the axis. The grid system was widely used in cities and towns in the West. "Main Street . . . objectified the openness of an armature; villagers lived in daily contact with one another but depended for their livelihood on farm families beyond the 'ends' of the main-street axis, where the street became a road." (Stilgoe, p. 262)

Coal and the railroad came together in Johnstown, Pennsylvania (1888), and coal from the Pennsylvania mine fields literally fueled the Industrial Revolution from the 1870s to the 1930s. With the Industrial Age came the demand for cheap labor. Shown here are immigrants about to debark in New York in 1907.

Economic forces and technological developments reshaped the life of the nation from the 1870s on. By the late 19th and early 20th centuries, the United States was rapidly becoming urban, but it was an urbanization that depended on mineral resources, transportation corridors, mechanized agriculture, and a far-flung network of cities and towns linked by railroads.

The debarking immigrants shown on a preceding page quickly made their own neighborhoods as shown in the picture of a New York market on the East Side (1900). The expansion of the cities was symbolized by the skyscraper—two early examples are shown.

In the 20th century, industry, commerce, and trade in the cities and towns were linked much more closely with open areas by communication and transportation. Telephone (1910 photo) and radio (1926 photo) for the first time brought rapid, low-cost communication to millions of people. And the automobile made large-scale suburban development possible; the photo of an early highway is undated but probably was taken in the early 1920s.

All of these elements came together in an unprecedented way in the 1920s to produce the first large-scale suburban housing developments. Shown below is a photo, taken in 1965, of housing built in Queens, New York, in the 1920s—single-family homes, tightly packed, but providing even families of modest means with a home of their own.

Four photos dramatize the 1930s: unemployment (25 percent of the work force was unemployed during much of that time), mortgage foreclosures, and national work relief provided through the WPA (Works Progress Administration). Offsetting the bleak side of the 1930s was the nation's first major effort at regional resource development, the Tennessee Valley Authority. Shown here is a transmission tower and a portion of the Norris Dam.

The WPA and the TVA were highly visible parts of national planning efforts (never labeled as such) that also included the National Resources Planning Board, the Farm Resettlement Administration, new towns, and other programs that changed the lives of millions of people.

World War II brought an almost total conversion of the economy to the war effort. The photo, taken in 1943, shows production at the Ford Willow Run bomber plant. Never before had planning been done so quickly, on such a large scale, and so successfully.

(continued on page 39)

With the end of the war, urban redevelopment began to change the landscape adjacent to cities and towns, and the housing boom, mostly a suburban phenomenon, began its 30-year surge. The next photo shows a residential development of the 1950s in Woodbridge, New Jersey. Note that the lots are larger than those in the Queens development of the 1920s shown on a preceding page. Note also the Garden State Parkway, one of the early expressways that brought housing and the automobile together in the exurbs.

The baby carriages and the land cleared for building in Waldwick, New Jersey, symbolize the population explosion which started in the mid-1940s, peaked from the mid-1950s to the early 1960s, and faded away in the 1970s.

Consumer expectations rose with the prosperity of the 1950s and 1960s. The dream of the detached, single-family house became the dream of the country house. The photo shows a development in Bergen Country, New Jersey, in the early 1970s with large-lot

(one-acre) zoning. Again we turn to Stilgoe: "More than any other constituent of the pre-1845 landscape, the detached house surrounded by land kept in equilibrium remains the spatial epitome of the 'good life.' " (Stilgoe, p. 342)

Not everyone shared in the postwar prosperity, however. Many cities, large and small, could not stop the decline of their business districts. Trade moved with housing to the fringe areas, even in places with populations under 50,000. Boarded up store fronts appeared in every part of the country as highly visible evidence of urban decay.

Many social, economic, and technological trends can be projected for the next decade or so, but the one that may be the most influential is information. In just 28 years—from the invention of the transistor in 1947 to the development of the microcomputer in 1975—the information age came into being. The computer with feedback and control has many applications. Shown above is a subway train (Washington, D.C.'s METRO) that is controlled by computer.

The information world of 1984 is symbolized by the photo of an integrated work station with a microcomputer, keyboard, and screen for data and graphics. The location can be urban, suburban, or rural; the information can be drawn from anywhere in the country.

Source: See Illustration credits.

The Depression and war years: Experimentation with planning at all levels of government

Shortly after President Roosevelt was inaugurated in 1933, the National Planning Board was established in the newly created Public Works Administration.[10] This Board took on a number of very broad national planning tasks, went through several name changes, and eventually was elevated into the Executive Office of the President as the National Resources Planning Board (NRPB). During its 20 years of existence, this board established a network of 13 regional offices and several interagency advisory committees. It undertook a variety of social and economic studies as well as physical planning studies on a nation-wide basis, and it also stimulated regional, state, and local planning all across the nation. Several of NRPB's regional offices prepared significant multistate planning studies for their regions.[11]

By providing manpower to the states for state planning upon the condition that states would establish permanent state planning offices, the board succeeded in establishing state planning in almost every state. At the regional level, the Tennessee Valley Authority was established as an independent federal corporation about the same time that the National Planning Board was established, and the President later proposed similar authorities for various other river basins. However, these were turned down by Congress, and the National Planning Board proceeded to establish less formal river basin committees in several parts of the nation. The National Planning Board also supplied 10,000 engineers, architects, draftsmen, statisticians, and stenographers to 200 local planning agencies at the city and county levels who contributed to state-wide data collection efforts for planning purposes. In addition, the Board supported a seven-county interstate metropolitan planning effort in the St. Louis area as a model for other metropolitan efforts throughout the nation; the Board also urged Congress to authorize interstate compacts for metropolitan planning in the nation's 22 interstate metropolitan areas.

The Board's Urbanism Committee presented a major report in 1937 in which it recommended permanent national planning with continued support of state, multistate regional, city, and metropolitan efforts throughout the nation. Both the Tennessee Valley Authority and the Pacific Northwest Regional Planning Commission, which had been encouraged by the National Planning Board, stimulated many local planning commissions.

The development of regional planning theories and organizations in the early twentieth century, and the experiments with national, state, and regional planning in the 1930s emphasized the need to consider social and economic factors along with physical planning concerns.

With the advent of World War II, President Roosevelt recalled the difficulties of economic adjustment following the first world war and directed the National Resources Planning Board to begin planning for the post-war recovery. In doing so, the Board enlisted the aid of the state planning boards. However, by 1943, NRPB had become controversial, disliked by Congress, unessential to the war effort, and peripheral to the President's immediate needs. Congress let its appropriation lapse, and NRPB went out of business. This withdrew national support from the state planning boards, many of which went out of existence or changed their form. Some became post-war planning boards, while others became industrial development units. Frequently, state planning was downgraded to the status of a subordinate unit in some other organization.

The post-war years to 1981

In the years since World War II, planning has continued to grow and mature at all the levels of government except the national level.

Local planning matures and spreads   Local planning now is virtually universal among the nation's urban areas and has even spread out into a significant number of rural counties. This planning includes land-use controls in most cases, but vast rural areas still do not have local planning. About 75 percent of the nation's land area remains without land-use controls (as of 1975). Urban areas commonly have urban renewal powers. Housing for low and moderate income families also has become a local function in most urban areas and many rural ones as well. Federal aid for urban renewal and housing programs, along with their associated planning requirements, have been important factors in the spread and maturation of the nation's local planning programs.

Regional planning is established nation-wide   Regional planning also has spread and matured.[12] By 1980, it was more widespread than local planning at both the multistate and substate levels. Multistate regional action commissions for economic development purposes affected all states except Hawaii and Alaska, though some states were not completely encompassed in these regions. Multistate river basin planning commissions and committees, including the Tennessee Valley Authority, also covered approximately the same territory. At the substate level, metropolitan and nonmetropolitan regional councils, together with other federally encouraged regional organizations, covered 99 percent of all the nation's counties. Again, federal aid programs were responsible for much of this spread, though state legislation and some other forms of state support also helped this movement along.

State planning is reestablished   Federal aid to the states in the 1950s, 1960s, and 1970s brought about a major resurgence of state planning. As a result of these federal funds and associated planning requirements, most states now have land use and housing plans, water and air quality plans, solid waste plans, economic development plans, and plans in a number of social services and educational fields (though many of these latter plans are not really plans in the traditional sense of the term, but just funding allocation devices). These states also have transportation plans at least for highways and frequently for airports and other modes as well. Many states began developing railroad revitalization plans in the 1970s as federal aid became available for this purpose.

Most of these state plans are the responsibility of individual departments and agencies within state government. State planning offices more and more have become overall management coordination units in the office of the governor, frequently attached to or very closely interrelated with the budget office.[13] The concept of a comprehensive plan, such as might be found in a local government or regional planning agency at the substate level, has no real counterpart today in most states. Instead, the states tend to focus upon political strategy statements (such as a governor's urban policy) and annual or long-term investment strategies (akin to local government capital budgets and capital improvement programs, but broader and more flexible in concept).

National planning remains disjointed and largely unaccepted[14]   The demise of the National Resources Planning Board in 1943 did not stop planning in the federal government, but it did scatter it widely. Perhaps the most visible portion of the Board's duties which was reinstituted was planning for the post-war economy. The Full Employment Act of 1946 was enacted for the purpose of absorbing all of the returning soldiers into the economy and getting domestic production started again to avoid severe unemployment and economic depression. The act established the federal government's responsibility to help ensure full employment in the economy and set up two new institutions to pursue this policy. One was the Council of Economic Advisors in the Executive Office of the President, and the other was the Joint Economic Committee in Congress. These two institutions remain important to the present day, and the President's annual economic report is an important planning document for the nation.

Also in the economic sphere, price stabilization units have survived many reorganizations and temporary periods of suspension, and the six-year public works program which the National Resources Planning Board had developed continued to be maintained in the Office of Management and Budget. Of course, the federal government's budget is also a major planning device. It has moved over the years slowly toward the more useful program budgeting format and three- to five-year projections. Nongovernmental organizations like the National Urban Coalition and the Brookings Institution offered alternative budgets throughout the 1970s, and in the latter part of that decade the Congress established its own overall budget process to help it compete successfully with the executive branch in this most important national planning dialogue.

The post-war years have seen at least two official instances of national goals studies. The first, *Goals for Americans*, established by President Eisenhower in the latter part of the 1950s, covered the whole range of domestic and foreign policy programs of the nation.[15] The second, *A National Agenda for the Eighties*, was established by President Carter in 1979 with a similarly broad mandate.[16]

Water plans and a national water policy have been under development by interagency committees of the federal government (and more recently by federal-state river basin commissions) at least since the 1930s. This planning was formalized in 1965 by the establishment of the U.S. Water Resources Council (WRC) and by the funding of associated state and multistate water planning organizations. The second national water resources assessment was published in 1980, but WRC and the multistate commissions were abolished in 1981, leaving water policy to the Office of Water Policy in the Department of Interior rather than to an interagency body.

Land policy studies by the national government also have a long history. There have been numerous national studies of federally owned lands and lands for agriculture and forestry, with national policies and legislation evolving from them. During the 1970s, the federal government enacted the Coastal Zone Management Program to enlist the aid of the states and their localities in planning for the preservation and appropriate development of the lands along the nation's shorelines. When such plans are developed for these areas and approved by the national government, federal agencies are directed to pursue their own activities in accordance with them. An even broader national land-use bill was considered quite seriously in the Congress, but it was narrowly defeated at mid-decade. This legislation would have applied the coastal zone management planning concept nation-wide, but as of 1982 it had not been re-introduced.

Transportation also has received considerable planning attention by the federal government since federal aid for it began in 1916. In 1956, a new interstate system of freeways was authorized, and by 1980 well over 90 percent of it had been planned and built. Several special study commissions have been established and have submitted their reports since the second world war, and periodic urban transportation needs studies were a routine cooperative endeavor of the states and the U.S. Department of Transportation during the 1970s. A national airports plan is produced annually, and a number of federal studies of the nation's railroads during the 1970s resulted in major new federal responsibilities for revitalizing and helping to operate the system.

Poverty, discrimination, and inadequate housing were addressed in the latter 1960s by the establishment of several national study commissions. Partly as a result, interagency efforts to establish a system of "social indicators" similar to those in the economic field have been undertaken. Such indicators have been published at least twice, and a related study commission on population policy reported in the early 1970s.

The National Environmental Policy Act of 1969 established the Council on

Environmental Quality in the Executive Office of the President with oversight and coordinating responsibilities somewhat analogous to those of the Council of Economic Advisors. Its annual reports over the first 10 years monitored the progress toward cleaning up the environment and reaching legislatively determined standards for clean air, clean water, quiet communities, safe disposal of wastes, and other national goals.

The 1970 Housing Act established a national growth policy process in which the President issues a biennial report on this subject (beginning with 1972). HUD has taken the lead in preparing this report, with various degrees of support from other federal agencies over the years. Out of this process has developed presidential urban policy. Though there has been a good deal of criticism charging these reports with being inadequate, recent editions have been much more policy-oriented than earlier ones. A counterpart rural development policy (including policy for small communities) has developed under the leadership of the Department of Agriculture and emerged in 1980 as presidential policy.

Presidential energy policy has also begun to develop in recent years, under the leadership of the new Department of Energy. Long-range implications of strategic material supplies and shortages were studied by two national study commissions in the 1970s. However, President Reagan has proposed dismantling the Department of Energy.

President Nixon began to formalize the domestic policy staffing of the White House by establishing a coordinated domestic council under his chief domestic policy advisor, parallel to the National Security Council which had been attempting to deal with foreign affairs and defense matters in a coordinated fashion for a number of years. This basic structure was continued under President Ford, and was only slightly modified under Presidents Carter and Reagan. Although, the original design called for both long-range and short-range units within this staffing arrangment, the short-range needs of the presidency pushed out the longer range function almost from the beginning. On the other hand, policy inputs to the White House by the various domestic departments and agencies have been enhanced over the years. As the Carter administration matured, an interagency coordinating committee was established with various subcommittees and task forces functioning under the secretary of the cabinet for the purpose of bringing White House and departmental policy development efforts closer together. The Reagan White House operates several subject specific "cabinet councils" with similar roles. White House conferences also have been used rather freely for many years to bring advice on major policy issues from diverse sectors of the national community directly to the President.

This brief recitation shows that there is a substantial amount of planning going on within the federal government, even if there is no specifically identified national planning office. Much of this planning provides the policy framework for and genesis of federal aid programs which guide state, regional, and even local planning and policy implementation activities. Yet, in most people's minds, the United States does not have national planning and, indeed, there seems to be very little political support at the moment for institutionalizing it in any formal sense. In fact, several serious proposals in the 1970s to do so met very substantial opposition and were shunted aside.

Intergovernmental planning coordination begins   Instead of directly reinstitutionalizing national planning, the federal government has sought to substitute planning at the lower levels of government which can be used to coordinate the diverse federal programs and activities. Since the bulk of the federal government's domestic programs are pursued through federal aid programs, these programs have been used to require a great deal of planning at the state, regional, and local levels of government. At the same time, these federal aid programs have paid for a great deal of this planning.

In 1966, metropolitan planning agencies were tapped by national legislation for the purpose of reviewing and commenting upon a wide variety of physical development projects in those areas to be funded with federal grants. These reviews were to reflect the relationships of those projects to coordinated, comprehensive metropolitan plans developed by the review agencies, and comments were to be supplied to the grant-making federal agencies before they made their final decisions about funding projects. Then, as a result of additional legislation in 1968, this type of federal aid review and comment was broadened to include all parts of the nation (metropolitan and nonmetropolitan), and a much wider range of federal aid programs (going well beyond just physical development), and reviews by state planning agencies as well as area-wide ones. In 1981, well over 200 federal aid programs were being reviewed this way by a nation-wide network of approximately 550 area-wide (metropolitan and nonmetropolitan regions) and 50 state "clearinghouse" review agencies.

By the end of the 1970s, the federal government was inviting these state and area-wide clearinghouses to incorporate into their reviews comments about the relationship of proposed projects to the President's urban policy and environmental impacts. Also as the decade closed, the federal government was providing a procedure for local officials in one part of an urban area to call for an impact assessment of development projects proposed in another part of the area, to determine whether such developments would be in accord with the President's urban policy. These federal requirements have called for many planning and program coordination issues to be addressed below the national level and, it is hoped, resolved there. Mechanisms for resolving them at the national level are lodged almost exclusively within individual federal departments or agencies, and there is little likelihood that a generalist policy view (or comprehensive planning approach) will prevail there. Nevertheless, the Reagan Administration is deemphasizing the national interest in such coordination.

Planning innovations cumulate

The changing emphasis on different aspects of planning traced through these major eras of American history represents the growth of the planning function into ever-widening circles of public policy. For the most part, the new concerns of one era are simply added to the established concerns of prior eras. The earliest concerns of making property available and accessible for use remain as vital today as they were in colonial times. Likewise, public utilities and facilities remain major components of modern plans even though social policies and program elements have joined them. Local planning continues to mature and retain its vitality, even though new planning processes have been established at the state and regional levels. National efforts in the planning field add vitality (and at least some, though perhaps disjointed, policy guidance) to planning at the other levels, and vice versa. Thus, the planning network grows throughout the nation in an additive fashion. It is an evolutionary process rather than one of displacement.

Philosophical transformations in planning

Several major streams of thought in the planning community and related governmental sectors have helped to transform planning in America from a relatively simple activity to a highly complex, multifaceted enterprise. Six of these transformations stand out for treatment here: (1) the shift from nearly exclusive concern with the protection of private rights to broader concerns which also include positive public purposes and comprehensive plans; (2) the shift from independent planning outside the mainstream of government to planning within government; (3) the shift from almost exclusive concentration on physical de-

U.S. and world events	Year	State and regional planning events
President Garfield assassinated	1881	
Brooklyn Bridge completed	1883	First regional park system in Twin Cities
	1889	First regional sewer agency in Boston
Spanish American War	1898	
	1908	First state planning agency in Massachusetts
Sixteenth Amendment on income tax	1913	First regional planning commission in Philadelphia
World War I begins	1914	
Prohibition begins	1919	
League of Nations meets	1920	
	1923	Formation of New York and Chicago regional planning associations
Teapot Dome Scandal	1924	
	1928	Standard City Planning Act suggests regional planning commission or association of governments
Stock market crashes and Great Depression begins	1929	
Roosevelt elected president	1932	
	1933	National Planning Board and TVA established
	1938	Every state except Delaware has a state planning agency
U.S. enters World War II	1941	
	1944	Federal aid for urban roads
	1946	Employment Act of 1946
Korean War begins	1950	
Eisenhower elected president	1952	
	1954	First federal funds for metropolitan planning
Martin Luther King, Jr. leads bus boycott in Montgomery, Alabama	1955	

Figure 2–1   State and regional planning in its historical context.

U.S. and world events	Year	State and regional planning events
	1956	Federal act creates interstate highway system
Sputnik I launched by U.S.S.R.	**1957**	Formation of Advisory Commission on Intergovernmental Relations
	1961	Hawaii adopts state zoning
John Glenn orbits the earth	**1962**	River basin commissions established
Washington, D.C. civil rights rally	**1963**	Clean Air Act
Supreme Court decision on one man, one vote	**1964**	Urban Mass Transit Act of 1964
Medicare begins	**1965**	HUD and Appalachian Regional Commission established
	1966	DOT is established
Nixon elected president	**1968**	OMB issues A-95 requiring state and regional review of federal grants
U.S. lands man on the moon	**1969**	National Environmental Policy Act creates NEPA and CEQ and requires environmental impact statements
U.S. Supreme Court rules school busing legal	**1971**	
	1972	Federal Water Pollution Control Act
Nixon resigns as president	**1974**	Economic Development Administration created
U.S. withdraws from Viet Nam	**1975**	American Law Institute Model Land Development Code
Carter elected president	**1976**	
	1977	U.S. Department of Energy created
California adopts Proposition 13 to cut property taxes	**1978**	
Reagan elected president	**1980**	
	1981	701 planning assistance stops
	1982	Regional Economic Development Commission abolished, LEAA disbanded, Water Resources Council abolished
	1983	Federal Regional Councils abolished

Figure 2–1   (continued)

velopment to an equal emphasis upon people's physical and social needs; (4) the shift from plans of individual jurisdictions standing alone to an intergovernmental system of interrelated planning processes encompassing state-wide purposes; (5) the shift toward intergovernmentalization of practically everything in American government; and (6) the shift in management philosophies from authorative, "seat-of-the-pants" thinking to participatory and systematic thinking backed up by increasingly capable information systems and analytical processes. Additional transformations are still to be expected.

From private rights to public purposes

Planning in the United States, from colonial times until near the end of the nineteenth century, very largely was concentrated on the protection of private rights. The subdividing of land into plots for private ownership which could be recorded in the public records was one important focus. Then, as urban areas became larger and more crowded, nuisance abatement became a more prominent concern. Along with this came a concern for public health and safety. The tenement house laws and early attempts at zoning were based on the concept that individuals had a right to at least a minimum amount of space, light, and sanitary conditions, and that particularly noxious land uses should be segregated from others to protect as many individuals as possible from being subjected to such conditions. Even as zoning developed further in the early twentieth century, it was used very largely as a means of protecting the value of real estate by keeping objectionable uses away from the cleaner and more serene parts of the city.

With the World's Columbian Exposition of 1893 and Burnham's plan for Chicago, the concept of comprehensive urban planning began to develop. By the time the Standard City Planning Enabling Act was issued in 1928, Cincinnati had already adopted a comprehensive plan, and zoning had been redefined as one tool, to be used along with several others, for helping to achieve an interrelated set of positive public purposes in urban development reaching far beyond the protection of private rights. Zoning, at least in theory, was to be used to implement a comprehensive plan which carefully allocated land uses in a pattern which had been balanced with transportation, utility, and public facility capacities, so that the urban system as a whole would function smoothly. The comprehensive plan also was to guide the local government's priorities in funding its capital improvements and its use of subdivision regulations to help ensure adequate rights-of-way and other lands for public purposes. Thus, the comprehensive plan became the means for infusing public purposes into the planning process and pursuing them along with the more traditional goals of protecting private rights.

From independent planning to planning within government

As planning was established initially—for local governments in the first half of the twentieth century, in a handful of metropolitan regions beginning in the 1920s, and at the state level beginning in the 1930s—the independent planning commission composed of civic-minded private citizens was the typical organizational form used. The idea was to reach outside the halls of government, and above politics, to set in motion a more competent and objective process for looking to the future and preserving "the public interest." The commission, quite typically, would have control over its own staff, authority to adopt its own plans, and the power to make at least some portion of its plans become effective (for city planning only) unless overridden by an extraordinary majority of the city governing body. Regional and state planning commissions generally had less authority, but essentially the same form of organization as the cities.

As time went on, however, government became more professionalized and less subject to the political spoils system. As this occurred, it became apparent that the tensions between independent planning commissions and the state and local governments they served frequently became counterproductive. The governing officials became increasingly irritated with the "watchdogs" looking over their shoulders and began moving to integrate the planning operations into the mainstream of government.

At the local level, where the council-manager system of government was becoming quite popular by the 1950s, the planning staff usually was shifted under the control of the city manager, and the commission was retained as an advisory body, while the local governing body became responsible for adopting plans and taking related implementation actions. At the state level, the planning staffs typically moved toward the governor's office or other closely linked offices like budget or general administration, while the commission became advisory. At the regional level, where there usually is no regional government to relate to, the regional planning commissions increasingly have become councils of governments, with elected local officials from city and county governing bodies replacing the civic-minded private citizen appointees. Thus, the organization of planning in the United States has shifted quite fully from its independent "watchdog" role to a position more directly relating to the mainstream of political policy making.

The social revolution in planning

While "enlightened" planning for physical development long had taken into account the social and economic factors in the community, it was largely restricted to the use of physical improvements to meet the needs of people. As urban renewal broadened its scope in the 1950s through citizen involvement, relocation assistance, and self-help counseling, it became apparent that much more than physical solutions were needed to address the problems of the urban poor and disadvantaged. The civil rights decisions of the Supreme Court, and the implementing acts of Congress in the 1960s redefined "equal opportunities" as something more than "decent, safe, and sanitary housing." By the mid-1960s, the federal government's "war on poverty" and its model cities program brought planning at full tilt into the process of providing social services as well as physical improvements. While the model cities program stayed within the confines of city government, the anti-poverty program and such related programs as manpower planning and special services for the aging frequently involved area-wide and regional planning as well. Even the states were involved in these latter three programs.

Taking their cues from the urban renewal program, these newer social action efforts relied heavily upon citizen participation processes. In fact, the antipoverty programs experimented with nongovernmental governing bodies made up largely of poor people and operating largely as "counter governments," while the model cities legislation called for separately elected model cities commissions made up of people from the neighborhoods in which improvements were to be concentrated, and the law called for city governments to share their powers with these boards.

Since these federally aided programs all required planning, their anti-establishment features spawned a special type of planning generally referred to as advocacy planning. This type of planning provides assistance directly to, and on behalf of, the clients of the program. Advocacy plans represent the clients in their dealings with government on planning matters, much as a lawyer would represent his clients in legal proceedings. The 1970s saw some pulling back from the more radical anti-establishment forms of advocacy in the planning of social programs, but the magnitude of social programs has continued to increase rapidly, and techniques of social impact analysis have improved substantially.

The quiet revolution in land-use control

Hesitatingly, in the 1960s and 1970s, state governments began to take on major roles in land-use control.[17] Up until that time, the states had left the control of land uses almost exclusively to local governments. The states had done this by providing enabling legislation for local planning and zoning. Under this locally initiated system, however, only about 25 percent of the nation's land area had come under local land-use controls, leaving major development decisions in places outside these areas to be made with little or no public policy guidance. In addition, local land-use controls were being used in some areas to exclude sites for low-income housing, power plants, solid waste disposal, and other essential uses affecting the larger community beyond the borders of individual cities or counties. These occurrences attracted state interest, and legislation began to emerge.

Hawaii began the revolution in intergovernmental land-use controls by adopting state-wide zoning in 1961. Because of unusual climatic conditions and the scarcity of land for producing the state's vital agricultural exports, the state established four broad zoning categories covering conservation and agricultural needs as well as urban development. Within the urban zone, local government supplied more finely detailed land-use controls, while state regulations applied to the other three zones.

Massachusetts inserted itself into the wetlands protection business in the mid-1960s and stepped into the fray on exclusionary zoning by local governments in the housing field in 1969. Wisconsin undertook shoreline protection ventures in 1966. Maine took on a state role in industrial site location in 1970, the same year that Vermont established state controls over land development in localities not providing local controls. By the mid-1970s, every state had some type of land-use controls, though most relied only on permits for certain individual types of development such as surface mining, power plants, or wetlands.[18] Nevertheless, eight states had much broader state-wide land-use control programs, while a total of 26 states had either state-wide land-use planning and control or similar controls applying only in the coastal zones or only to areas of critical state concern. After a number of years of drafting and redrafting, the American Law Institute published *A Model Land Development Code* in 1975, providing for state designation of critical areas in which the state has an interest and is prepared to intervene if local development controls do not adequately reflect the state interest.

Florida and Oregon are probably the best examples of integrated state-local land-use control systems. Florida requires all of its local governments (cities and counties) to prepare plans for local land-use control and to implement them. If the local governments fail to prepare plans, the state has the power to substitute its own plans. The Florida law also defines "developments of regional impact" and provides for the review of such developments by the regional planning organizations serving the state-designated substate district system. Appeals from the decision of the regional bodies are decided by the state government.

In Oregon, the State Land Use Commission establishes standards for local planning throughout the state and must approve local plans before they become effective. Deficient local plans are sent back for revision before they may be approved.

Much of the state activity in land-use control was spurred in the early 1970s by the introduction of national land-use planning legislation in Congress which would have relied extensively upon the development of effective state land-use plans to govern both direct federal activities and federal aid programs. This federal legislation would have funded the preparation of these state plans, much as the coastal zone management program has done in the coastal areas. While the national legislation did not pass and has not been revived since the mid-1970s, it left a substantial legacy of state activity in the land-use control field.

This quiet revolution in land-use control has had the effect of broadening the concept of land to one which recognizes its value as a scarce resource with many different types of community values as well as its value as a commodity in the economic marketplace. It has also established a firm place for the states in land-use control systems, but at the same time, it has recognized the continuing role of local governments and regional planning bodies. Finally, it has helped to strengthen the linkage between planning and the exercise of land-use controls and has highlighted the need to develop new forms of land-use regulation to meet broader environmental and community objectives within the constitutional limitation that such regulation shall not amount to a "taking" of property without payment of "just compensation." A truly intergovernmental system of interrelated state, regional, and local land-use plans would appear the firmest base upon which to exercise resolute but sensitive control over the development and use of land as it is not defined more broadly in terms of the new environmental and social goals of the the 1960s and 1970s.

The intergovernmental revolution

The United States is governed by approximately 80,000 governments. Most of these are municipal, county, township, special district, and school district governments.[19] The typical metropolitan area contains about 100 of these local governments.

As pointed out previously in this chapter, federal and state financial assistance programs have become increasingly vital to most local governments. It has been estimated that about 60,000 of them receive such aid.[20] On the average, counties receive 44 percent of their revenues from intergovernmental aids, while municipalities receive 39 percent. The aid system has become this important for two reasons: (1) the insufficiency of local funds under limited tax systems for meeting local needs, and (2) the overlapping of program objectives among the three levels of government. While direct regulation by the federal government—growing from its roles in interstate commerce, the monetary system, and the protection of civil rights—has become increasingly important over the years and has been transmitted intergovernmentally in a number of cases by allowing the states to regulate in lieu of the federal government so long as federal standards are complied with, the intergovernmental grant system has achieved a much wider scope. In 1981, the federal government funded 534 different grant programs for which state and local governments were eligible.[21] Some of these programs provided funds directly to the states, some directly to both states and local governments, some to local governments alone, and some to the states to be passed through at least in part to local governments. A recent survey of these programs indicated that about 160 require state, regional, or local planning, or planning at more than one level, as a condition for receiving these funds, and about 40 of these programs were specifically designed to support planning activities. Most of the 40 planning assistance programs were for planning in individual functional program areas, though a few were for broad coordinative planning designed to integrate the objectives of a broad array of aided programs. Most federal aid programs, whether narrowly focused on an individual program or more broadly based, carry with them a broad array of national policy objectives in addition to the objectives of the individual program being funded.[22] These collateral national policy objectives are in such fields as nondiscrimination, environmental protection, relocation assistance for displaced residents and businesses, the promotion of merit systems in aided governments, and wage protection for third party contractors.

Through its regulatory and grant systems, the federal government has succeeded in recent years in intergovernmentalizing practically every function of government and in bringing state governments into a much greater range of intergovernmental activities with their localities than had previously been their practice. Thus, whatever program is being planned, and whatever level of government is doing the planning, the planner should be alert to identifying the roles, either present or potential, for the other levels of government.

Federal aids and federal regulations are not coordinated at the federal level. The expectation is that they will be coordinated by the states, the local governments, or the regional planning organizations. A number of studies made in the 1960s and 1970s have shown that this is a very difficult task, if not an impossible one, given the existing complexities and outright incompatibilities among existing federal aid programs. Yet, little action had been taken by the federal government to simplify or consolidate its grant system prior to 1981.

Nevertheless, three halting steps were taken in this direction by the federal government during the 1960s and 1970s. First, the federal aid review and comment system, mentioned earlier, was established to allow area-wide and state planning organizations to comment upon direct federal and federally aided action proposals; second, standard administrative procedures for federal aid programs were issued (though quite incompletely complied with by federal agencies); and third, stepped-up federal agency consultation with affected state and local governments and others was started in the federal rulemaking process. These salutory steps improve the potential for achieving satisfactory results from the federal grant system, but they still leave the 500 separate programs intact, with all the paperwork and potential conflict which that entails.

Planning is thrown into this breach—bringing to bear the logic of the planning process, the persuasiveness of its data collection and analysis, the evaluation of alternatives, and the reasoned choices among feasible options. Intergovernmental planning and intergovernmental review and comment processes through the A-95 process have been relied upon to enhance creative communications among the various levels of government to the point where accommodations will be reached so that projects will proceed only after reasoned consideration of all views—national, state, regional, and local. This very heavy load placed upon the planning process provides an opportunity to show that planning can be useful. Whether or not one believes that this is the best way to bring some order out of the nation's highly fragmented intergovernmental system, it is the only way currently provided.

The management revolution

Since World War II, and partly as a result of it, management philosophies and practices have undergone massive changes in two directions. First, theories of management have swung dramatically away from authoritative, top-down decision making toward a much more broadly based participatory form in which decisions are arrived at with much greater sharing of information among all those involved—including workers, middle management, and top management. This helps to ensure that important information is not overlooked, and it also paves the way for higher morale and better implementation of decisions once made.

The other direction is toward a much greater reliance on "scientific" management. The information explosion, based largely on computer technology and associated increases in the development of analytical techniques, has put a much wider range of information at the disposal of managers than ever before. Growing partly out of the operations research experiences in World War II, and also from the mental disciplines demanded by computers, new ways of thinking in terms of large systems were thrust upon the management scene. Such "systems thinking" is quite analogous to the rational planning model with which most professionally trained planners are highly coversant. This scientific management movement has spurred a number of planning related public policy efforts in government. Perhaps the most notable was the Planning, Programming, Budgeting System (PPBS) used successfully for many years for budgeting the federal government's Defense Department, and for a few years applied more generally throughout the government. While PPBS proved to be overly ambitious as the overall budgeting system for the federal government, it emphasized the need to link planning directly and strongly to specific program options and budgets, and it spawned program evaluation and policy analysis units throughout the government. The two successor budgeting systems—management by objectives, and zero-based budgeting—each continued some of the same features.

These two new directions in management—participatory decision making and systems thinking—provide a very favorable environment within which to practice planning. Planning processes—with their emphases on goals development, measurement of social conditions, testing of public reactions to alternative proposals, and use of public hearing processes—are well versed in participatory methods of policy development. At the same time, the heavy reliance by the planning process upon problem definition, data collection, and analysis of data within a systematic framework of problem solving puts it well within the orbit of program evaluation and policy analysis activities. Many large business corporations have come to rely quite heavily upon strategic planning offices to serve their top management groups in a much more central way than is typical within government at the present time.[23] But this business practice is being looked at more frequently by governors and the federal government to see what might be transferred into the public sector.[24]

The coming revolutions

The rate of change in society seems to be continuing and accelerating its rapid increase. Pluralism also appears to be broadening, and international interdependence is having increasing day-to-day effects as energy imports and trade balances shift markedly in rapid sequence. These kinds of forces imply that society will become increasingly participatory and that governments will become increasingly intertwined in intergovernmental relationships.

The major centralizing tendencies of past decades—whereby population moved increasingly toward major metropolitan areas—now appear to be weakening or reversing as population has begun moving outward toward nonmetropolitan America. Thus, planning may be called upon to cope with more dispersed patterns of population growth, and perhaps slower overall rates of growth as well, in future decades.

It is difficult to tell precisely what the future holds, but looking at the past strongly suggests that changes will abound, and the planning process will be called upon to adjust to additional "revolutions" in the future.

Summaries of state and regional planning history

The key points in the history of state and regional planning efforts have been covered in the preceding chronological and philosophical reviews. It has been seen that many of the same forces affecting planning at the local and national levels also had important influences at the state and regional levels. Nevertheless, it is useful to bring these points together now in their jurisdictional frameworks—

first viewing the whole stream of planning evolution at the state level, and then at the regional levels. This provides a picture of the current status of planning at the two levels of planning central to this book and gives an understanding of how it got that way.

The evolution of state planning[25]

As already pointed out, the need for state planning was recognized in the 1920s. A few states—including New York, Illinois, Wisconsin, Michigan, Virginia, Pennsylvania, California, Texas, New Jersey, Massachusetts, and North Carolina—undertook statewide planning projects of one sort or another between 1925 and 1932. However, these certainly were not what could be called comprehensive state planning programs.

Then, between 1933, when the national planning program began, and 1938, when the national effort reached its peak, all states except Delaware established state planning boards and embarked upon ambitious programs of their own. Forty-two of the states did this by legislation. In 1937, 82 percent of state planning personnel and 78 percent of their budgets were supplied by the federal government.

As the national planning program ran into trouble, however, it reduced its support of state planning and turned its attention to wartime and post-war concerns. By the time the National Resources Planning Board was eliminated by Congress in 1943, many of the state planning boards also were gone, and the remaining state planning functions had been dispersed to other agencies with much less ambitious and more narrowly conceived missions.

State planning had been initiated by popular movements supporting the conservation of natural resources, improvement of public management (often based upon the growing literature of corporate and business administration), and the need to support the burgeoning field of city planning. But state planning had been structured under independent boards of private citizens outside the mainstream of state politics and administrative management; its programs had been opportunistic and not well thought out; many of its social and economic concerns grew out of the depression and became politically controversial; and the improving economy plus mounting concerns about the war effort triggered a reaction against the new state programs.

Despite the withdrawal of federal support, state planning remained healthy in the southeastern states through the Southern Association of State Planning which drew its leadership largely from Harold Miller, the long-time director of the Tennessee state planning office, and from the Tennessee Valley Authority. Local planning assistance was born out of this effort, and major utility companies were enlisted in promoting planning.

It was not until 1954 that federal support for comprehensive state planning and central planning offices returned. And it was 1969 by the time that a state planning agency was needed to respond to the federal government's invitation to the states to review the growing array of direct federal and federally aided projects proposed within their borders, and to provide comments prior to approval of funding by the responsible federal agencies.

Meanwhile, the states began to reorganize their diverse, and often chaotic, administrative structures—emphasizing modern management techniques centered on the governor and a limited number of integrated departments of state government under the control of the governor. Between 1965 and 1975, 20 states enacted rather complete reorganizations along these lines, and 20 others took partial steps in this direction. Public administration theory specified planning as an important ingredient of the managerial task facing the newly empowered governors, and the governors increasingly brought planning units into their own

Table 2–1   Organizational
location of state
planning agencies, 1976.

Location	No. of states
Separate planning department	4
Governor's office	28
Department of administration	8
Economic development department	5
Community affairs department	3
Other location	2
Total	**50**

Source: Council of State Governments, *State Growth Management* (Washington, D.C. Government Printing Office, 1976), pp. 37–38.

offices or into the closely allied departments of administration where budget controls were lodged. By 1976, the Council of State Governments found that all states had some sort of overall coordinative state planning efforts. These were lodged in the governor's office in 28 states and in the department of administration in another eight states (see Table 2-1). Thus, the preferred administrative pattern prevailed in 72 percent of the states.

The rapid increase in federal aid to state governments since the mid-1960s brought some 80 programs with requirements for state plans, and the federal aid review and comment process provided by U.S. Office of Management and Budget Circular A-95 gave the governor some leverage over these plans—which were lodged in his functional departments—if he could command his state's central planning mechanism. Some federal planning assistance was used to support state reorganization studies in the 1965–1975 period, and some was used (and still is) to run the states' federal aid review and comment processes. These uses of federal aid funds have helped to strengthen the governors' overall management capabilities by strengthening state planning. Once again, the states were back in the planning business, and this time the planning offices are in the political and managerial mainstream.

Finally, there is the intergovernmental dimension of state planning. The quiet revolution in land-use controls, previously mentioned, is only one way in which the states have asserted themselves in planning processes below the state level. As partners in the federal aid system, and as increasingly significant providers of aid themselves, the states increasingly are applying for federal aid funds on behalf of local governments and regional organizations, passing such funds on to these bodies, adding state funds to the federal programs, helping to establish substate and multistate regional organizations, participating in many regional activities, and relying upon local governments and regional organizations to carry out state policies and programs. Thus, state planning not only addresses the coordination of multitudinous functional planning efforts within state government, but also seeks to form a partnership with regional and local government planning processes as well.

The role of the legislature, beyond enacting and funding the state planning process, is not well developed. It has been suggested that state planning should be a research arm of the legislatures as well as an important service to the governor, and that the legislatures should play a more forceful role in establishing state planning policies, but little has come of such suggestions thus far.

The evolution of regional planning

Regional organizations are a frequently created response to boundary limitations which arise when public problems spill beyond the jurisdiction of a single government capable of acting alone to address the problem. Very often, such problems are recognized long before a regional organization is established, and the earliest organizations to respond generally are unofficial. Gradually, as the problem becomes better defined, and as the stake in common intergovernmental solutions becomes clearer to affected governments, the informal organizations are transformed into, or supplemented by the creation of, official public bodies.

As noted earlier in this chapter, metropolitan planning got its start in the 1920s. Its theory grew out of suburbanization demands and the difficulties encountered in providing war housing during World War I. The first metropolitan planning organizations sprang up in the 1920s, and a few others appeared in the period up through the 1950s. Then, in the 1950s, federal aid for comprehensive planning and metropolitan transportation planning became available to support metropolitan planning, but most planning of this type remained largely locally initiated. By 1960, approximately two-thirds of the nation's then existing 212 metropolitan areas were engaged in some type of area-wide planning. The typical form of organization during this whole period was the independent appointed city-county or metropolitan area planning commission, composed of "blue ribbon" private citizens, although some were ad hoc transportation study committees made up largely of state and local transportation agency representatives.

Larger scale multistate regional planning also got an early start, dating back to creation of the Tennessee Valley Authority in 1933 and some river basin committees in other areas beginning in that same era.

The turning point for regional planning, however, did not arrive until the 1960s. Early in that decade the federal aid programs for highways, mass transit, and open space began requiring metropolitan planning as a condition for obtaining federal action grants in those fields. Then came 1965, a landmark year for both metropolitan and multistate regionalism.

In 1965, four pieces of legislation were enacted which dramatically changed the governmental structure of the United States by helping to establish a nation-wide system of substate regions between local government and the states, and by helping to establish multistate regions between the states and the federal government. Actually, these new regions, of whichever type, are not really governments at all, but intergovernmental mechanisms designed to fill the gaps between the existing levels, facilitate the work of the federal, state, and local governments, and guide the use of implementation powers held by these traditional levels without creating that "fourth level of government" which has been so often railed against in discussions of regionalism.

The Housing and Urban Development Act of 1965 made area-wide organizations of local elected officials (commonly referred to as councils of governments) eligible for planning funds. The Public Works and Economic Development Act of 1965 provided funding for multicounty economic development districts and authorized the establishment of federal-multistate economic development commissions. The Appalachian Regional Development Act of the same year established the multistate Appalachian Regional Commission, which has pursued much of its work through multicounty local development districts. Finally, the Water Resources Planning Act of 1965 authorized the establishment of federal-multistate river basin commissions. While these are not the only important pieces of federal legislation in the regionalism movement, they triggered what became virtually full coverage of the nation within 15 years by both substate and multistate regional planning organizations.

Substate regionalism In the five years following passage of the Housing and Urban Development Act of 1965, area-wide planning organizations developed in the remaining metropolitan areas, and local elected officials became much more prominently involved in these planning endeavors. During the 1970s, regional planning at the substate level (usually multicounty) spread throughout small town and rural America as well. By 1977, 99 percent of the nation's counties were encompassed within some sort of regional planning district.

There are two basic types of substate regional planning organizations now: (1) multipurpose regional councils which usually are composed primarily or wholly of local elected officials, and (2) special purpose regional organizations responsible for administering such single federal aid programs as the war against poverty, health systems planning, special services for the aging, or criminal justice planning. Nationally, the 1977 Census of Governments counted twice as many of the special purpose regional bodies as there are multipurpose ones, and these special units are composed mostly of program clientele and other private citizens.[26] This creates a fragmentation of regional planning responsibilities which is worse in some states and some regions than in others.

It is the combination of these two types of substate regions that encompasses 99 percent of all the nation's counties, but the multipurpose ones cover nearly as much territory by themselves. This represents a major increase in coverage since 1972 when only about one-half of the nation was covered.

Table 2-2 shows the year of establishment of the multipurpose substate regional councils in the forms in which they existed in 1979. While this table significantly understates the earlier growth of metropolitan planning, because of the changing forms of organization (creating more recent establishment dates), and because the number of metropolitan areas continues to grow, it clearly documents the metropolitan surge in the 1966–1970 period, followed by the big growth on nonmetropolitan organizations in the 1970s.

The 1977 Census of Governments provides, for the first time, an official count of substate regional organizations.[27] It identified a total of 1932 such organizations, of which 675 were general purpose organizations, while 1257 were special purpose. As shown in Table 2-3, these organizations spent almost $1.3 billion, employed nearly 148,000 people, and involved over 43,000 people on their governing bodies. Thus, substate regionalism has become a governmental sector of substantial proportions affecting virtually the whole nation.

Substate district *systems* have been established state-wide in 43 states by executive order, legislation, or a combination of the two, and Maryland has achieved the same end less formally through supportive policies and financial aid from

Table 2–2   Number of substate regional councils established in metropolitan and nonmetropolitan areas, selected years.

Established before	Total		Metropolitan		Nonmetropolitan	
	Number	Percent	Number	Percent	Number	Percent
1956	7	1	5	2	2	1
1961	36	5	25	9	11	3
1966	119	18	71	24	48	13
1971	423	64	222	76	201	55
1978	659	100	292	100	367	100

Source: National Association of Regional Councils, *1979 Regional Council Directory* (Washington, D.C.: October 1978); presentation in J. Norman Read, *Regional Councils in Metropolitan and Nonmetropolitan Areas: Some Characteristics*, ESCS Staff Report (Washington, D.C.: U.S. Department of Agriculture, September 1980).

Table 2–3 Measures of regional organization activity, 1977[1]

Measure	Regional Organizations		
	Total	General purpose	Special purpose
No. of regional organizations reporting	1,569	607	962
Total expenditures (in millions)	$1,278.2	$373.7	$904.5
No. of employees	147,852	21,611	126,241
No. of governing board members	43,111	16,673	26,438

Source: U.S. Bureau of the Census, *Regional Organizations*,
Vol. 6, No. 6, 1977 Census of Governments (Washington,
D.C.: Government Printing Office, 1978).

[1] The universe canvassed was 1,932 regional organizations
of which 675 were general purpose and 1,257 were special
purpose.

its state planning department. These systems, established mostly after 1967, are attempts by the states, with federal encouragement, to bring about some commonality of boundaries and organizations for various types of regional planning as well as for the field operations of state agencies.

Individual regional councils within these state-wide systems—which may be called by various names such as council of governments, regional council, regional planning council, regional planning and development commission, or area planning and development commission—usually are formed voluntarily by the action of local governments taking advantage of general state laws authorizing interlocal cooperation or specific state enabling acts for regional planning commissions or councils of governments. In fewer instances, regional councils are nonprofit corporations or have been established as public agencies directly by state law. While approximately 40 regional councils serve areas which cross state lines, only three have been established by interstate compacts.

The responsibilities and powers of regional councils are usually rather limited. In only rare cases do regional councils have their members directly elected or have their own taxing authority. Their responsibilities are mainly for planning and giving advice. Their powers are largely limited to reviewing and commenting upon action proposals by the various levels of government operating within the region, and in many cases these reviews are limited to projects supported at least in part by federal government funds.

As of 1977, regional councils received 76 percent of their funds from the federal government, most of which they had to match with funds from other sources. Their other funds came from the states (10 percent), from local governments (12 percent), and from other sources (2 percent). Metropolitan councils generally receive somewhat more from their local governments and less from the states than do nonmetropolitan councils.

The pattern of primary reliance on federal funding held steady from the 1960s until 1981. This dependence was even greater for the special purpose regional organizations which received 92 percent of their funds from the federal government, 4 percent from the states, 2 percent from local governments, and 2 percent from other sources. In fiscal year 1982, the Reagan Administration began a sudden withdrawal of most federal funds for both general purpose and special regions.

The nation-wide network of substate regional councils, which developed over the past two decades, proved itself useful in many ways (as will be seen in following chapters) and developed a strong cadre of regional planners. This network is buttressed by a major national interest group in Washington known as the National Association of Regional Councils.

Nevertheless, most regional councils remain voluntarily structured; they have uncertain finances, depending too heavily, perhaps, upon a complex array of federal grants; they often find it difficult to grapple effectively with major political controversies; they exist side by side with several other single-purpose regional organizations in their own regions; and they often are controversial themselves because they cannot perform up to expectations and because proposals to strengthen them raise questions about the propriety of their new roles in relation to the established state and local governments. Obviously, then, substate regionalism has not yet evolved fully.

Multistate regionalism   At the multistate level, the picture is very similar to that at the substate level. All states except Hawaii and Alaska are members of one or more multistate regional economic development commissions, though eight states are not completely encompassed. Multistate river basin commissions also affect all states except Hawaii and Alaska, and the omitted portions of the few states not completely covered is even smaller than for the economic development commissions.

Both of these types of multistate regions were joint federal/state endeavors until the federal government withdrew from them in 1981. The commissions were composed of both federal and state officials—state governors and a presidentially appointed federal cochairman in the economic development case, and representatives of about 10 federal departments and agencies plus five to ten state representatives in the river basin case.

A third type of multistate regional organization is the federal regional council (FRC) of which there now are 10—one for each of the standard federal regions. The FRCs are not joint federal/state bodies, but they do focus largely upon intergovernmental coordination issues, including administration of the federal aid system.

These three nation-wide sets of large multistate regions developed over a period of many years. Their forerunners were the federal interagency river basin committees which began meeting in the 1930s. They gradually took in state representatives, and then in 1965 were given the legislative means (Title II) to convert to official Federal/State River Basin Commissions, establishing an equal voice on both sides of the table. The 1965 federal legislation also established the U.S. Water Resources Council to coordinate the work of regional commissions and grants to support not only the commissions but also state water resources planning offices and noncommission types of river basin planning organizations (where agreement could not be reached to establish formal Title II commissions).

Adding together the Title II River Basin Commissions, the three unconverted interagency river basin committees (all having state representatives), the three interstate compact commissions (for the Delaware, Susquehanna, and Potomac Rivers), the Tennessee Valley Authority, and the Mississippi River Commission, nearly the whole nation was covered by 1980. The only exceptions were Alaska, Hawaii, the Hudson River in New York, the coastal portion of New Jersey, the Chesapeake Bay, and the Rio Grande and Texas Gulf basins in Texas and New Mexico. The Water Resources Council was actively encouraging the organization of comprehensive regional water resources management plans in these remaining areas, and a Congressional hearing was held in August 1980 concerning the fragmented condition of current research and planning in the Chesapeake Bay.

Except for the interstate compact bodies for the Delaware and Susquehanna Rivers, which have some implementation authority, these river basin organizations were limited to preparing plans and giving advice.

Suddenly, in 1981, the federal government abolished the Title II river basin commissions.

The Tennessee Valley Authority is a combined river basin and economic development region organized as a federal government corporation. While it has been quite successful in developing the river and related resources for the betterment of the region, and has involved the people and governments of the region in its activities, its corporate form of organization has been rejected for transfer elsewhere. The regional economic benefits of TVA, however, were obvious, and made other regions envious. A number of unofficial regional associations of state officials, some state-supported research organizations—like the Southern Growth Policies Board and the Federation of Rocky Mountain States—and regional Congressional caucuses have formed from time to time to promote the special interests of particular parts of the nation.

TVA's success helped to establish a philosophical basis conducive to passage of the 1965 legislation authorizing the Appalachian Regional Commission and the Title V Regional Economic Development Commissions. The governors of the Appalachian states had firmly requested a commission for their area to help deal with the aftermath of serious floods in the early 1960s and the depressed economic conditions highlighted in the Kennedy presidential primaries. Therefore, it was established outright by federal law, while the Title V commissions were simply authorized to be established by the President upon request of the states involved. Boundaries were not set ahead of time for the Title V commissions, but a carefully balanced federal/state sharing of decision making roles and costs was established. By 1979, every state except Alaska and Hawaii had been given membership in one or more of the 11 official Title V regional commissions (or Appalachia) at its own request. Alaska for several years had a special relationship with the federal government through the Joint Federal/State Land Use Planning Commission for Alaska and applied for Title V status as well. Hawaii also applied for Title V status. Various other applications have involved portions of the states never formally encompassed within the Title V system (largely in California and Texas).

The Appalachian Regional Commission (ARC) has been well funded and regarded as quite successful by most evaluators, but the Title V commissions have been poorly funded and much less highly regarded. In fact, the final three established (in 1979) never were funded or activated. ARC and five of the Title V commissions have helped to fund substate regional councils and looked to them to help plan and improve the larger region of which they are a part. But, in 1981, the federal government withdrew its participation from the Title V commissions and began phasing out ARC. At least five of the Title V commissions, however, have become nonprofit corporations intending to maintain some form of regional activity.

The third type of multistate region—in addition to river basins and large economic development areas—consisted of the 10 standard federal administrative regions and the Federal Regional Councils (FRCs) serving them. While the FRCs were not federal/state commissions like the others, their principal role is to facilitate the smooth operation of the federal aid system through federal interagency coordination and consultation with state and local governments and regional organizations. These 10 regions cover all 50 states plus Puerto Rico and the Virgin Islands.

The Councils are committees of the chief regional administrators of the major grant-making federal departments and agencies plus a few other federal units. Once informal committees, these Councils were established officially in 1969 by Executive Order, were expanded and strengthened more than once, but were reduced in size and scope in 1981, and then abolished in February 1983. They never were independently staffed, funded, or chaired, and most FRCs received fairly low marks from most evaluators. In 1979, in an effort to improve this situation, the federal cochairmen of the Title V commissions were given memberships on the FRCs with eligibility to be appointed to the FRC chairmanships. In the case of New England, where the Title V and FRC boundaries coincided, this option was exercised, bringing a full-time regional generalist and regional planning staff on board in support of FRC activities. Of course, this experiment ended in 1981 when federal participation in Title V commissions ended.

All of these multistate regional organizations—except the FRCs and TVA—were intergovernmental mechanisms rather than governments in their own right. Their stock-in-trade has been intergovernmental communication and cooperation. Even the two multistate organizations that are exceptions to this "rule" generally act as though it applies to them as well. Multistate regionalism seemed to have been accepted throughout the land as a necessity up until 1981, but was given very few powers beyond planning and persuasion. Regional organizations traditionally have been looked upon quite gingerly, almost as "necessary evils," not to be trusted with governmental authority, and certainly not to be viewed as panaceas.

Federal action and federal funding created multistate regionalism with overlapping regional boundaries and multiple regional organizations serving the same areas. Perhaps this was inevitable, but such intergovernmental coordination mechanisms created an additional need for coordination among themselves. Now that most federal support for multistate regionalism has been withdrawn, the future is uncertain. Some of the river basin and economic development bodies have become non-profit corporations, but their operations have shrunk and they are limping along at best.

Conclusion

State and regional planning programs and organizations now seem to be firmly established in the United States despite the recent withdrawal of federal support. State planning seeks to influence directly the exercise of basic taxing and spending, regulatory, and eminent domain powers of state government, while regional planning seeks indirectly to influence the exercise of these same powers by all levels of government (federal, state, and local) as they act within the various substate and multistate regions. Planning at both of these levels—state and regional—is limited by the basic American governmental predispositions favoring the protection of personal freedoms, reliance on private enterprise, restricted governmental roles, separation of powers, federalism, and pluralism.

At the regional level, there is the additional limitation that, except for a few special districts and authorities, there is no regional government to which the planning process can relate directly. Regional organizations still are too new for the electorate to be comfortable with, and the federal government recently seems to have lost much of its commitment to them. So regional planning is faced with the most complex of intergovernmental problems, and given few if any governmental powers to apply. It works mostly in an advisory capacity, relying largely upon its powers of persuasion to move a broad array of governmental units—none of which is directly responsible for the total geographic region addressed by the region's planning process—toward common goals.

1   Advisory Commission on Intergovernmental Relations (ACIR), *The Condition of Contemporary Federalism: Conflicting Theories and Collapsing Constraints*, Chap. 2: "Breakdown of Constitutional Constraints," Vol. 2, *The Federal Role in the Federal System* (Washington, DC: U.S. Government Printing Office, 1981).

2   Alexis de Tocqueville, *Democracy in America*, ed. Richard D. Heffner (New York: A Mentor Book, New American Library, 1956).

3   ACIR, *Citizen Participation in the American Federal System* (Washington, DC: U.S. Government Printing Office, 1980).

4   James L. Sundquist, *Dispersing Population: What America Can Learn from Europe* (Washington, DC: Brookings Institution, 1975).

5   Institute for Training in Municipal Administration, *Local Planning Administration*, 2nd ed. (Chicago: International City Managers' Association, 1948), pp. 22–23.

6   *Uniform Relocation Assistance and Real Property Acquisition Policies Act of 1970*, P.L. 91-646, 84 STAT. 1894.

7   Donald Hagman and Dean Misczynski, *Windfalls for Wipeouts: Land Value Capture and Compensation* (Chicago: American Planning Association, 1978).

8   For further information about these eras, see Laurence Conway Gerkens, "Historical Development of American City Planning," in Frank So *et al.*, editors, *The Practice of Local Government Planning* (Washington, DC: International City Management Association, 1979), pp. 21–57; and Mel Scott, *American City Planning Since 1890* (Berkeley: University of California Press, 1969), pp. 265–266.

9   Scott, *American City Planning Since 1890*, p. 278.

10 Marion Clawson, *New Deal Planning: The National Resources Planning Board*, Published for Resources for the Future. (Baltimore: Johns Hopkins University Press, 1981).

11 Ibid.pp. 11, 169–170, 248.

12 ACIR, *Multistate Regionalism* (Washington, DC: U.S. Government Printing Office, 1972); ACIR, *Regional Decision Making: New Strategies for Substate Districts* (Washington, DC: U.S. Government Printing Office, 1973); ACIR, *Regionalism Revisited: Recent Area-wide and Local Responses* (Washington, DC: U.S. Government Printing Office, 1977); ACIR, *State and Local Roles in the Federal System* (Washington, DC: U.S. Government Printing Office, 1982), Chap. 5: "Area-wide Organizations."

13 Lynn Muchmore, *Concepts of State Planning*, State Planning Series 2 (Washington, DC: Council of State Planning Agencies, 1977).

14 For further information about national planning, see Otis L. Graham, Jr., *Toward a Planned Society: From Roosevelt to Nixon* (New York: Oxford University Press, 1976); and David E. Wilson, *The National Planning Idea in U.S. Public Policy: Five Alternative Approaches* (Boulder, CO: Westview Press, 1980).

15 President's Commission on National Goals, *Goals for Americans* (Englewood Cliffs, NJ: Prentice Hall, 1960).

16 The President's Commission for a National Agenda for the Eighties, *A National Agenda for the Eighties*, Report of the Commission (Washington, DC: U.S. Government Printing Office, 1980).

17 Fred Bosselman and David Callies, *The Quiet Revolution in Land Use Control*, prepared for the Council on Environmental Quality (Washington, DC: U.S. Government Printing Office, 1972).

18 Council of State Governments, Task Force on Natural Resources and Land Use Information and Technology, *Land: State Alternatives for Planning and Management* (Lexington, Kentucky: 1975), pp. 10–11.

19 U.S. Bureau of the Census, *Governmental Organization*, Vol. 1, No. 1, *1977 Census of Governments* (Washington, DC: U.S. Government Printing Office, July 1978).

20 ACIR, *A Crisis of Confidence and Competence*, Vol. 1, *The Federal Role in the Federal System* (Washington, DC: U.S. Government Printing Office, 1980), p. 64.

21 ACIR, *A Catalog of Federal Grant-In-Aid Programs to State and Local Governments: Grants Funded in FY 1981* (Washington, DC: U.S. Government Printing Office, February 1982).

22 ACIR *Categorical Grants: Their Role and Design* (Washington, DC: U.S. Government Printing Office, 1978), Chap. 7.

23 George A. Steiner, *Strategic Planning* (New York: Free Press, 1979).

24 Susan M. Walter, editor, *Proceedings of the White House Conference on Strategic Planning* (Washington, DC: Council of State Planning Agencies, 1980).

25 Harold F. Wise, *History of State Planning: An Interpretive Commentary*, State Planning Series 1 (Washington, DC: Council of State Planning Agencies, 1977).

26 For further information see ACIR, *State and Local Roles in the Federal System*, Chap. 5 (Washington, DC: U.S. Government Printing Office, 1982).

27 U.S. Bureau of the Census, *Regional Organizations*, Vol. 6, No. 6, *1977 Census of Governments*, (Washington, DC: U.S. Government Printing Office, August 1978).

3 State planning today

This consideration of state planning should help to clarify and identify the purpose and direction of state planning. What is being done, why is it being done, and what is expected to be achieved as a result are important criteria to test the purpose and direction of planning in the particular state.

The changes in the function and practice of state planning over the past 50 years may leave some observers wondering where it is headed. Over the course of this period it has certainly been affected by such national initiatives as the New Deal, the Great Society and, most currently, New Federalism. These initiatives have interacted with other factors such as the new breed of pro-active Governors, the dynamics of state decision making, and the rise in the influence of the states through ad hoc multistate coalitions to produce contemporary state planning. Through the process of observing its evolution, one can begin to better understand the forces that have shaped state planning and perhaps to more clearly identify the role and function of the planning process in state government.

This chapter provides a perspective for state planning, accordingly. By this examination of where we have been and where we are, perhaps state planning in the decade of the 1980s can build on that experience rather than repeat the errors of the past.

Introduction

Recognition of state planning

After several decades of evolution, the art and science of state planning is now an integral part of state government. Virtually every state has recognized the essential role that planning can play in the management of state affairs—in addressing key state issues, in the formulation of state policies and strategies, and in the provision of reliable, dependable, and continuous information that is critical to the effective management of the state.

Location of state planning agency

Planning seems to have found its niche in state government, overcoming years of concern about the location of this function in both the wide-ranging array and the hierarchy of state affairs. Most planning offices today are lodged within the office of the Governor. Others may be found in departments of administration, economic development, or community affairs. A few are state departments in their own right. While the organizational location may vary, nearly every state relies on the state planning agency for advice and assistance on a variety of major issues, policy needs, and policy and management initiatives. In short, state planning has established a certain credibility among its constituents—the elected officials, line agencies, and the general public—a level of confidence which, in most states, has generally paralleled the development of the policy/issue-oriented process of state planning that exists today.

Practice of state planning

The practice of state planning has changed radically over time, reflecting the dynamics of the environment within which it operates. In many states, current emphasis is on policy formulation and coordination and issue-oriented planning rather than the more generalized comprehensive planning of an earlier era. Planning offices throughout the country are involved in staffing strategic planning, development policy, energy and natural resource policy, management improvement, and other high priority issues confronting states. A number of states have undertaken long-range strategic planning programs to attempt to gain some perspective of the longer term and to establish mutually consistent short- and long-range objectives against which current policy decisions can be measured. With the expected redefinition of government responsibilities in the 1980s, state government will face new challenges, and state planning can be instrumental in determining how those challenges will be met.

To some observers, contemporary state planning is a management tool to be used in the communication of policy to state agencies and substate units of government and in the allocation of resources.[1] Planning offices in many states have become the policy arm of the administration and are used to identify and provide substance to new initiatives, to guide the day-to-day decisions of state government as well as to formulate strategic plans that provide longer range direction.[2] In reaching this stage, planning has survived numerous challenges as to its legitimate role in the functioning of state government. In the past, it has been criticized as being an ill-conceived art, centering on superficial issues and activities without coming to grips with problems of the real world. But the evolution of state planning has been linked with the development of the states. It has been influenced by the same forces that have shaped state government. And just as the states are evolving into more sophisticated mechanisms for dealing with contemporary issues and problems, state planning generally has been structured into the state policy making and management system.

In both acknowledging and taking on this issues-oriented policy role, state planning in many states has undergone additional fine tuning during the last 10 years. Planning has been positioned to serve in the dual capacity of providing a quick response on short-term issues while developing longer range functional and/or strategic plans to help ensure consistency of policy actions. This is in contrast to what has been seen as an elusive search for the state comprehensive plan, a concept borrowed from local government and local planning practice apparently much too literally in its expected application. Time and experience, and the determination of what works best in state government, may yield a profile of state planning that tempers comprehensiveness with a definition of functional responsibilities and strategies and their interrelationships, and how desired results best might be achieved.

State planning, as we know it today, emerged out of a desperate need for states to come to grips with highly complex issues and equally complicated solution alternatives that, in part, were being addressed at the federal level beginning with the Great Society programs in 1965. While we will look closely at the impact of federal programs on state planning later in this chapter, this relationship is illustrative of the external forces that have shaped both state government and the state planning function. Consequently, to understand contemporary state planning, we must look to its past, its evolution and maturation, and its relationship with the private and public sectors. This, indeed, should help to gain an appreciation of the dynamics involved and alert one to the volatility of the redefinition of responsibilities in the 1980s, a redefinition which, with planning, can mean policy on the basis of understanding, program on the basis of knowledge, project on the basis of fact, and action to achieve desired results.

State planning history: a brief review

During the 1930s a state planning fever swept the nation. National and state planning programs were launched from the White House and from the state houses. Planners from all over the nation gathered annually in cities like Detroit and Cincinnati to consider and discuss the new-found concepts of national and state planning. Many of the President's advisors attended along with Governors and members of Congress. And their discussions invariably recounted the wasteful exploitation of natural resources, which was both possible and profitable throughout much of the history of the country, and the need for a public response to finally come to grips with this problem.

State planning roots

In an address to the American Society of Planning Officials in 1936, George Peery highlighted events that prompted the initiation of state planning programs. From his vantage point as Governor of Virginia, Peery saw the private sector planning for and developing the nation's resources in the absence of any meaningful effort by the states to promote and protect the public good. Prior to the Civil War there was little need for state or national planning. Private enterprise was small-scale and did not operate in conflict with the interests of the public at large.[3]

But following the war, larger enterprises were launched, and intensive planning on their behalf extended their power and control over large areas of industry. Often, these efforts by the private sector did not consider the public interest. For example, railroads, which were flourishing under government subsidies of land and money, were insensitive to individual rights and practices which were contrary to business ethics and morality. In the process of building the nation's railroads, the resources of one area were destroyed for the benefit of other areas. From Peery's perspective, during this early period in the development of the nation, "Planning for such private enterprise outstripped for the time planning for the public good; and it became necessary to plan for the common good to meet this condition."[4]

It was not only the private side, however, but also the public sector that contributed to the depletion of the nation's resources. During the nineteenth century, states invested heavily in the construction of public works projects—canals, railroads, and highways that would encourage new economic growth and development.[5] Competition among the states for economic superiority flourished as every effort was made to develop the frontier.

States were virtually on their own in building new projects. Neither the federal or local governments nor the private sector were inclined to participate in public works development. As a result, public investment in the canal system built between 1815 and 1860 totaled nearly 70 percent. During the same period, public investment in railroads totaled between 25 and 30 percent. At least two-thirds of all public investment was provided by state governments, exceeding the local share by a two-to-one ratio and the federal share by 40-to-one.

State efforts during this era concentrated mainly on resource utilization—building projects—rather than on allocating resources efficiently based on market demand. The result by the mid-1800s was a serious case of overdevelopment, a default in state bonds, and a corresponding decline of state initiatives and development.[6]

Most American cities of the nineteenth century were dominated by the same commercial-expansionist ideology which produced material growth but also social displacement and great environmental degradation. In his article on planners and the American city, University of North Dakota Professor John L. Hancock

described the cities of the 1800s as being "dominated by profit minded oligar-
chies following 'settle and sell, settle and boom-bust' practices in pursuing growth
at whatever social costs."[7] It was the "manner" of settlement and the values
associated with it that were profoundly disruptive, according to Hancock.

In evaluating the cities which flourished during this era, Hancock reported
that most subordinated all values to economic development objectives. In contrast, cities such as Savannah, Georgia, in which social and environmental considerations were rigidly maintained, did not share in the economic prosperity of
the period. Consequently, most cities pursued a growth-at-any-cost philosophy,
rejecting any attempt to consider noneconomic factors in the physical patterning
of development. The common grid approach for street layout was used almost
exclusively because it was most accommodating to laissez-faire development. By
1900, 200 American cities looked almost exactly alike: streets positioned in grid
fashion, small lots featuring 20–40 percent substandard housing, tenements near
the city centers, few open spaces, high speed grade-level movement on main
streets, the best locations reserved for commercial and industrial uses, few public
controls, and unchecked peripheral growth.[8]

The conservation and resource ethic

It was against this backdrop of haphazard growth and physical disorder, economic
exploitation, and political corruption that the mood of the country changed. The
early 1900s saw the emergence of the progessive era (1906–1916) and the call
for social reform.[9] From a social and technical perspective, society was moving
forward at a pace faster than anyone could calculate. New technology was being
advanced, and cities were about to assume a major role in twentieth century
America. It was an appropriate time to take stock in America, to assess its
accomplishments, its problems, and its opportunities. For many this meant the
first real chance to stop the wanton depletion of the nation's resources. These
sentiments were not universally shared, of course, for the spirit of free enterprise
development was a basic tenet of the American system. But support for resources
conservation was backed by the highest office in the country, by President
Theodore Roosevelt. The President, along with many of the state Governors,
would set in motion the conservation ethic that was to be a factor in national
and state affairs until the outbreak of World War II. Resources conservation
would also become the principal focus of state planning which, in 1909, was still
waiting in the wings.

As the reform movement gathered momentum during the early 1900s, focusing
initially on business and political corruption, public affairs, and conservation
issues, President Roosevelt convened the nation's Governors at the White House
in 1908. The topic of the meeting, which was attended by 33 of the nation's
Governors, was to create mechanisms within each state to deal with conservation
and forestry issues. Assisted by Governor Gifford Pinchot of Pennsylvania,
Roosevelt urged the Governors to establish state planning offices to focus on
natural resources management.

About half of those represented at the White House conference responded
affirmatively to the President's request, and within a few years the first state
conservation plans began to appear. In 1915, Massachusetts produced a general
outline of a state conservation plan and in the early 1920s the Iowa State Conservation Commission initiated studies that culminated in a "Twenty-Five Year
Conservation Plan," published in 1925.[10]

Most of these early state planning efforts concentrated on the use of land,
physical development, and resource conservation. Gradually, the focus of state
planning began to broaden with the recognition of the close relationship between

economic development and planning. The Illinois State Chamber of Commerce sponsored a study on the need for a comprehensive approach to planning for the development of the state. In 1925, the work of the New York State Planning Commission produced a state plan that included a housing component along with the traditional land use and conservation elements.[11] (See Chapter 12, "Report of the New York State Commission of Housing and Regional Planning," in *Planning the Fourth Migration.*)

Other states attempted to merge economic development and resources planning into a state organizational framework to promote the development of commerce and industry. This broadened concept of planning was generated, in part, by state Governors who were amassing more power within their respective states and more control over state affairs. New state planning agencies were established in states like Virginia and North Carolina which created state departments of conservation and development in the mid-1920s. A few years later, 15 states had established similar agencies which combined the state planning function with economic promotion and development activities.[12] The relationship between state planning and economic development was a marriage that would for the most part continue into the present, although there would be periods of separation followed by reconciliation, after which the relationship would change.

By the end of the 1920s state planning was emerging into a field that was considerably broader than originally conceived by Teddy Roosevelt in 1908. City planners of that period were casting hopeful glances at what appeared to be a promising newcomer on the scene. The public's seeming indifference to city planning efforts and the questioned success of the city planning movement suggested to some that perhaps the broader, more comprehensive overview of state planning could provide valuable assistance to the urban planners.

At the 1932 conference on city planning, Jacob Crane described the reorganization of cities as an essential element of the whole planning movement that would not be replaced but rather, aided, by state planning. Crane believed that state planning could help make local planning work by establishing a larger conception of the physical environment and of the city's place in that greater area; by providing new methods of studying and forecasting and even guiding population distribution and concentration; by determining the most desirable use of major land areas and the effect of that use upon all elements of local planning; by establishing a handhold on the puzzle of industrial location in relation to urban development; and by dealing with the area-wide problems of water sources, power supply, and transport, and with their influence on city building. "All told," Crane suggested, "state planning promises to become a new and sounder background for city and regional planning."[13]

A principal accomplishment of state planning during this period was its contribution to the realization that public and private endeavors could be guided toward the achievement of a specific objective, and that hit-or-miss, uncoordinated development efforts belonged to a bygone era.

The Depression and recovery

It has been suggested that "in great emergencies more intensive planning becomes imperative."[14] Emergency conditions of worldwide significance prevailed at the beginning of the 1930s. American prosperity had broken in 1929, and in the Great Depression years that followed unemployment reached 13–15 million, one-fourth of the labor force in 1933. Hunger and destitution spread. Franklin D. Roosevelt defeated Herbert Hoover in the 1932 Presidential race and launched his domestic New Deal policies in 1933. The Administration of Public Works appointed a National Planning Board (NPB) which Roosevelt converted to a

Presidential board in 1934, after incorporating the functions of the Committee on Natural Land Problems. The functions of the new NPB were:

To advise and assist the administrator in the preparation of the "Comprehensive Program of Public Works" required by the Recovery Act through:

1. The preparation, development and maintenance of comprehensive and coordinated plans for regional areas in cooperation with national, regional and state and local agencies based upon—

2. Surveys and research concerning:
   (a) The distribution and trends of population, land uses, industry, housing and natural resources; and
   (b) The social and economic habits, trends and values involved in development projects and plans; and through

3. The analysis of projects for coordination in location and sequence in order to prevent duplication of wasteful overlaps and to obtain the maximum amount of cooperation and correlation of the effort among the departments, bureaus and agencies of the federal, state and local governments.[15]

Roosevelt's NPB consisted of three members, including the President's uncle, Frederick Delano. One of their earliest initiatives was to provide incentives to the states to encourage the formation of permanent state planning boards and a professional staff. The NPB wanted the states to undertake specific studies of land use and public works programs and to coordinate these efforts with regional or interstate planning organizations that might be established.

The states responded to the NPB's proposal by establishing 30 state planning boards within three months of the NPB's request. By 1936, most of these early planning boards were established by executive order of the Governor. But by 1938, with 47 state planning boards in place, 42 had been given permanent statutory status by the state legislatures—perhaps an indication of the value potential associated with the idea of state planning.[16]

The missions of the state planning boards in the 1930s   The meaning of the state planning boards which have recently sprung into life is the expression of a desire to . . . (1) Take a comprehensive view of the resources and planning problems of the several states: (2) To relate the work of the local planners, already under way in many cities and in a number of counties, to the work of the state as a whole; (3) To relate the work of the states to each other by better cooperation and coordination, as in the case of water users; (4) To relate the work of the state planning agencies to that of the national government; and (5) Finally, to relate the work of the several public planning agencies to that of private and semipublic agencies within the state, as in the development of transportation and power.

Source: National Resources Board, *State Planning, Review of Activities and Progress* (Washington, D.C.: National Resources Board, 1935), pp. *iv–v*.

By executive order of the President, the functions of the NPB were merged with the National Resources Board which would serve in an advisory capacity to the National Resources Committee. The Committee was composed of six Cabinet Secretaries and the three members of the National Resources Board.

The first report of the National Resources Board was published in 1934. It brought together information on land use, water use, minerals, and related public works in relation to each other and to national planning. It was the most comprehensive report since Theodore Roosevelt's Commission on Country Life published its findings in 1909; it contained detailed recommendations that many believed would provide the basis for a comprehensive long-range national policy for the conservation and development of the nation's resources.[17]

The report was essentially a plan for planning. Charles Merriam, one of the original members of the Board, described the Board's intent in developing its report:

There are three outstanding considerations in looking at plans for planning:

1. The necessity and value of coordinating our national and local policies instead of allowing them to drift apart or pull against each other, with disastrous effect;

2. The value of looking forward in national life, of considering in advance rather than afterward, of preventive measures as well as remedial;

3. The value of basing plans upon the most authentic collection and analysis of the facts.[18]

It was generally concluded that the work of the National Resources Board was fact-finding as opposed to planning; to "estimate the situation" rather than to prescribe the remedies; and to submit its findings and whatever recommendations it might develop to the President and to the Congress.

Coordination and decentralization were basic tenets of the Board's philosophy, and it attempted to reflect these principles in its reporting and its actions. In addition to providing financial assistance to states that established planning boards, a planning network was created to maintain contact between the states and the National Resources Board. Technical consultants were made available to the states to provide advice and assistance in developing and carrying out their plans.

As a result of the National Resources Board's efforts, the states were engaged in a variety of state planning programs by 1937. The Board had established special committees on water, power, land, minerals, industrial resources, and public works and had staffed the committees with experts drawn from federal agencies, universities, and the private sector. The intent of the Board was to formulate national plans and policies by bringing together the individual planning work in each of the states. For example, in the planning for nonfederal public works, the first movement toward a coordinated national plan began in 1935 when the state planning boards prepared for the Public Works Administration a comprehensive inventory of public works in their respective states. The magnitude of this effort was significant. The inventory involved more than 130,000 public works projects reported by over 20,000 units or agencies and exceeded $20 billion in estimated cost.[19] Efforts of this type were notable in that they

---

The state planning movement in the 1930s There have been many explanations for the rapid growth of the state planning movement. Presumably, many governors and leaders of legislative groups saw in the establishment of a planning agency a logical and useful service to their states. The fact that this new agency would cost the state very little because of the help available from the National Planning Board or the National Resources Board and from the Relief Organization, certainly did not deter them. In some states there was doubtless also the feeling that compliance with the suggestions from the administration in Washington might help the position of the state in seeking public works allotments or other help in the war against depression. Whatever the reasons might have been in the early days of the movement, there was extraordinary unanimity of support from all kinds of sources without regard to political party or economic group.

Source: Charles W. Eliot, 2nd, assisted by Harold A. Merrill, *Guide to the Files of the National Resources Planning Board and the Predecessor Agencies, Ten Years of National Planning, 1933– 1943* (December 31, 1943), p. 95.

brought to the attention of substate officials the advantages of planning for public works and other projects and a recognition of the importance of regional and city planning as part of the national-state planning network.

In extolling the virtues of advance planning, Harold Ickes, Chairman of the National Resources Board and Secretary of the Public Works Administration commented:

I hope State Planning Boards, backed by legislative and popular approval, will develop continuous six-to-ten year programs, annually revised, and that larger goals of attainment can be visualized and reached. . . . Their effectiveness will depend on the character of their personnel, the wisdom and vision of their plans, the scope and accuracy of their research and, more particularly, on the firm support of the public.

If public works are to be timed to aid in counteracting industrial fluctuations, one of the essentials is a long-range program, constantly kept up-to-date, such as State Planning Boards are now attempting. To embark on public works expansion without such advance planning is to increase the danger of including ill-advised projects. . . .

I believe that the catch-as-catch-can method which ignores the necessity of national planning is a thing of the past. It is wasteful, futile and unscientific method which deserves oblivion.

In the National Resources Committee, which is an integral part of the present Administration, we have a body that is gradually evolving a national plan which I am sure will fit into an adequate social vision of the future.

I am convinced that long after the necessity of stimulating industry and creating new buying power has been removed, national planning will continue as a permanent government policy.[20]

As history has been written, Ickes was wrong in his assessment about the permanency of national planning as part of government. While the President's Committee on Administrative Management recommended the establishment of a National Resources Planning Board in 1939, its Congressional expression was not forthcoming, and a desired statutory basis was not achieved. As a result, the hoped-for permanency was short-lived. The activity of the state planning boards would also peak by 1939 as rising international tensions and war in Europe focused attention on world affairs.

As America prepared for World War II, federal interest in the planning agenda as heretofore developed declined. State planning activities, largely dependent on federal funds, contracted significantly between 1939 and 1941 as federal nondefense funds were reduced to a trickle. More than a dozen state planning boards either folded entirely or were buried in line departments and assigned new functions. With support for planning declining, Congress broke under pressure from the Corps of Engineers and repealed the National Resources Planning Board legislation in 1943. But by that time little was left of the planning network created by the NRB as state after state had dismantled its planning apparatus.

The loss of federal funding and the outbreak of the war were not the only problems contributing to the demise of state planning. There were operating agencies at both the federal and state level who had rather substantial constituencies and who saw other than functional planning as an encroachment.[21] They worked to ensure the protection of their turf. There was also a lack of interest among many Governors in the work of their state planning boards.[22] Only about a half dozen Governors really used their planning boards in a meaningful way, and planning at the state level did not have a strong constituency of its own. As structured by the NRB and NRPB, state planning did not belong to either the Governor or the legislature and, as a result, has no political base.[23] Finally, there was no clear and widely understood purpose for state planning. There was no definition as to what constituted the function of state planning for there was no previous experience or planning doctrine on which to draw.[24] State planning was involved in a variety of social and economic projects which did not fit into the established governmental framework of the period.[25]

During their peak years of 1935–1938, state planning board activities were indeed varied and far-ranging. There were, however, certain characteristics common to many of these efforts such as the emphasis attached to rural and resource related problems. This focus very likely stemmed from state planning's conservation lineage and earlier efforts to deal with natural resources issues. As the concept of comprehensive planning for orderly growth and development emerged during the 1930s, the scope of state planning broadened to encompass transportation, recreation, land use, and water use—but, too often, only within a rural context. When the state planning boards attempted to carve out their niche in the already crowded field of public affairs, they apparently preferred not to impinge on the territory of city planners. As a result, those city planners who had looked to the broader reach of state planning for support and assistance for their urban efforts received little help.

With the repeal of the National Resources Planning Board's legislation, the states became the highest level of government possessing planning agencies. A few states, such as Pennsylvania, Maryland, Connecticut, and Tennessee, maintained the planning functions that were similar to those established and carried

---

Early findings and recommendations in state planning In a report to the governor and the National Resources Board in 1934, the Pennsylvania State Planning Board set forth its findings as follows:

Population.
Pennsylvania's population shows a tendency to stabilize by 1960.

Land and its utilization.
The State lacks a longtime program of forest development.
The State needs information on flood control.
Many streams and other bodies of water necessary to human life are badly polluted.

Working and living conditions.
In the last 15 years relatively few dwellings have been constructed within the price range of a majority of the people.

Industry, trade, and transportation.
Marked changes in industries and in their location are having serious effects on the workers dependent on them.
Pennsylvania's transportation system, covering railways, highways, airways, waterways and pipelines, is not adequately coordinated.

Social activities.
More than 5600 taxing bodies exist in this State and many of them have outlived their usefulness and should be combined.
The present system of relying mainly on taxation of real property makes the carrying on of services by local units of government exceedingly difficult.

The board then presciently set forth its recommendations for basic state policies:

Recommendations.
Research with a view to maintaining the relative importance of Pennsylvania's mineral industries.
A long time program of forest redevelopment.
Collection of information on flood control.
Rigid enforcement of laws for control of stream pollution.
Legislation to govern the use and development of streams, with a view to better allocation of water, and reduce the number of separate local units of government in order to increase the quality and reduce the cost of public services rendered.

out during the 1930s. But these states were the exception. More than 60 percent of 46 state planning boards active in 1938 either had disappeared completely or were transformed into other agencies by 1946.[26]

Those state planning agencies that were still active during the first half of the 1940s were engaged in military and other war-related planning and research, or in postwar planning projects such as employment for returning military personnel, housing, and conversion of wartime industrial facilities. As the war began to wind down, many state efforts were directed to postwar reconstruction and development programs. Responsibility for these programs was usually vested with state economic development agencies or special commissions established for this purpose. State planning agencies, which in more and more states were becoming lodged in economic development agencies, participated in these programs by conducting local postwar planning seminars, administering grants to local units of government for blueprinting postwar construction, or providing technical assistance to local governments in the development of their long-term capital improvements programs.[27]

The comprehensive plan idea was not part of the planning function as perceived by the states throughout the 1940s and early 1950s. State planning activities turned, with increasing emphasis, to assisting local governments with capital construction projects which were being financed with federal assistance. Economic and industrial development programs were launched in many smaller communities as part of the reconstruction effort and as a way of promoting community development and providing jobs and job opportunities in a postwar economy.

State planning agencies were providing local planning commissions with substantive assistance with their industrial promotion programs, and although this generated criticism that in several states the planning function was being underutilized, state planning was existing in a transitory mode and, as such, was making a contribution to achieving state and local objectives of that period.

The 1950s and 1960s: "We can do it all"

By the mid-1950s there was a renewed interest at the federal level in comprehensive planning. Congress enacted the Housing Act of 1954 which included under Title VII, Section 701, a program that initially provided federal assistance to smaller communities and metropolitan and regional planning agencies for comprehensive planning activities. Grants flowed to the states to be passed through to the substate level for comprehensive planning. The federal government required that local urban renewal projects must conform to a local comprehensive plan. In many states, the job of administering the 701 program fell to the state planning agency which tended to reinforce its preoccupation with local communities and away from issues of statewide scope and concern.

The 1954 Housing Law was amended by Congress many times during the next two decades. In 1959, responding to expressions from the Council of State Governments and the American Institute of Planners, among others, Congress modified the Housing Act to extend support for comprehensive planning programs to the state level. The amendment provided for two-thirds federal funding for state comprehensive planning. The states were required to provide the one-third match.

With the 1959 amendment, the federal government rekindled the fires of state planning. But the response from the states was considerably less enthusiastic than in 1933 when the National Resources Board first offered to support state planning. Several states in the East responded quickly but most states failed to qualify or were reluctant to provide the matching funds.[28] In time, however, nearly all states would receive federal support for one or more state planning activities. The 1959 Housing amendment marked the rebirth of federal assistance for state planning that would continue for more than two decades.

Acknowledging this rekindling of effort and activity with respect to state planning, the American Institute of Planners directed its attention to an examination of State Planning: Its Function and Organization.

In a 1959 report of the AIP Committee on State Planning, it was noted:

To be effective state planning must meet the organizational as well as functional needs of present-day state government. This report does not lay down hard and fast rules as to how state planning should be organized. It does suggest principles of organization for state planning based on the general concept that the chief executive has the responsibility for formulating long-range policies and for directing programs to carry them out. Moreover, in many states the chief executive is becoming more and more the focal point for legislative leadership. The planning staff should be in a position to help him in preparing policy and program recommendations for administrative and legislative considerations.

Within these general concepts, the following principles of organization for state planning are suggested:

1. State planning must be an integral part of the administrative structure of state government.

2. The staff concerned with over-all state planning should be advisory to the chief executive. The staff should act at his direction in its relationships with the legislature and with individual state departments.

3. The director of planning must be acceptable to the chief executive and should be a person qualified by training and experience in state and regional planning. The trained technical staff should be within the career service.

4. An advisory commission may or may not be needed. If such a commission is created it should be advisory to the director of planning who takes full administrative responsibility for recommendations.

Any organization for state planning should be based on the concept that the continuity of the planning function can be assured only by the technical competence of the staff. An independent board is no assurance of the continuity or even performance of the planning function.[29]

A Survey of State Planning Agencies, 1960, conducted by the AIP Committee of State Planning, reported on the status, organization, and activities of state planning agencies and provided an appropriate reference point in examining the application of those principles; see the bibliography.

If the 1950s can be characterized as a period of physical development and expansion throughout the country, the 1960s were the age of social reform.

As the 1960s dawned, very few people perceived the problems that we as a nation would face throughout this tumultuous decade. The country was on a racial collision course: it would soon feel the effects of generations of resource waste and consumption; there would be serious mistakes made in foreign affairs that would nearly drain the vitality of America; and there would be the riots in the Watts section of Los Angeles, campus riots, and other urban confrontations.[30]

The new domestic programs that would emerge in this period, which would have an effect on state planning, began to take shape after 1963. They would be programs that would be based in part on a concept of structural change in the relative power and income of groups and would be the first such attempt at restructuring since the early days of the New Deal. They would begin with President John F. Kennedy and would continue and intensify after his death under the leadership of Lyndon Johnson. And they would incorporate Western European planning concepts, particularly the French experience, of combining decentralized decision making with national goals.[31]

Social policy under President Johnson consisted primarily of more money and more government for social problems. There was no direct effort to embrace the national planning idea of the early New Deal era which attempted to incorporate longer range, planned social interventions by restructuring government. But there was under Johnson a feeling that the market forces alone would not produce more equality, that there was a need for a more comprehensive social policy and some structural change to affect the distribution of power and money, and for more information on social problems and better methods for using it. The tragic death of President Kennedy seemed to open the door for President Johnson to move pending fiscal legislation and antipoverty and civil rights bills which would take social policy several steps closer to the New Deal concept of national planning, although there would be many miles left to cover.[32]

In the wake of new federal programs initiated during the 1960s, the number of active state planning programs increased from 13 to 39. Much of their activity was in response to the Great Society programs emanating from the Johnson Administration. Federal aid between 1959 and 1969 increased from $6 billion to $20 billion. By 1967, there were about 162 major federal programs, of which nearly one-third provided aid directly to the states.[33] There were new or expanded federal programs for open space, outdoor recreation, water and sewer, highways and mass transit, economic development, resource conservation, health, and crime. Most of these programs required states to prepare individual state functional plans as a precondition to the receipt of federal funds. In one state, Georgia, the planning office estimated that the state was responsible for the preparation of some 80 programmatic state plans that would generate about $300,000,000 of federal assistance under the Great Society programs of 1965.[34]

There was virtually no coordination of planning and programming at the federal level during this period, and the situation within the states was just as loose. The federal program deluge had caught most states off guard, and throughout most of the 1960s states were in the position of attempting to react to federal planning and programmatic requirements rather than to assess where all this activity would lead them. There was little intergovernmental exchange between the states and their substate entities which had their own program pipelines and problems with Washington. Special interest groups emerged around many of the federal programs and continued to keep the heat on Congress and the national administration to ensure that their favorites were well treated.

In some instances, the state planning agency was tapped by the Governor to prepare one or more of the federal functional plans, but usually these assignments fell to line agencies. The new planning requirements generally increased the level of planning capability within the states, and the planning function became considerably more visible in line agency operations. The sheer number of functional plans stimulated consideration for some type of state overview or coordination among the various planning responses. To be effective, this coordination would require that states have identified their longer range goals and objectives in a comprehensive manner and have established a framework within which functional planning could take place. Unfortunately, in most states this was not the case and, the functional plans continued to be produced in relative isolation and without consideration of any longer term impacts or objectives. While it might be assumed that the development of some type of overall framework plan into which the functional plans could fit was a logical extension of the state planning function, this rarely happened. Most Governors, while recognizing the need for planning, did not understannd it and did not see the need for centralized state framework plans.

There were, of course, exceptions such as in Hawaii, California, and New York. These states had recognized the need to anticipate change even before the onslaught of federal programs, and to consider structural changes in government to deal with the future.

The first was Hawaii, which in 1958 enacted strong legislation linking state planning with the Governor's Office. This relationship established the pattern that most states would attempt to emulate, with varying degrees of success, throughout the 1960s. In 1961, Hawaii published a general plan for the state from which a state land policy emerged and which set the stage for the adoption of state level zoning of conservation and watershed areas, agriculture and urban areas. California and New York followed with the preparation of state development plans which, although they did not meet with the same success as the Hawaii effort, had a profound effect on shaping the developing of state planning in the 1960s.[35]

The 1960s and 1970s: Reappraisal

The Hawaii, New York, and California experiences by and large still reflected state planning's hesitation to deal with the problems of metropolitan areas and depressed rural areas. Many of the federal programs that were coming on line in the 1960s were inspired by Watts and urban confrontations, directed to these kinds of issues, and were designed to bypass the states and provide support and assistance directly to the affected areas. Programs such as HUD 701 Local and Areawide Planning Assistance, Economic Development Planning Assistance, Comprehensive Health Planning, and Community Action were examples of direct federal-local initiatives. Recognizing the impact of the federal-local relationship, states began to become increasingly involved in intergovernmental efforts and become willing partners in such programs as model cities and economic planning and development programs. The states' efforts to crack the direct federal-local relationship were designed to maintain the integrity of state programs and budgets which were being distorted by federal funds flowing into the state but which were not being funneled through the state budget process.[36]

State efforts in this area were considerably enhanced with the passage of the Intergovernmental Cooperation Act of 1968. Implemented through OMB Circular A-95, this legislation enabled the Governor to establish state clearinghouses through which all federally assisted planning and development activities must pass for review. A-95 provided the states with the first real mechanism for getting a handle on federal activity within the state and the opportunity to affect that activity. Substate agencies were provided with the same opportunity to coordinate local initiatives with state efforts through the A-95 clearinghouses.

States were also beginning to experiment with the Planning Programming Budgeting System (PPBS) as a mechanism to set long-term state objectives and priorities. PPBS was primarily the result of substantial improvements in state budgeting techniques coupled with a strong desire on the part of the states to better direct the deluge of federal programs through improved planning. The new system caused controversies to arise in some states over responsibility for the planning component of the PPBS. Functional line agencies, the state planning office, and the budget office, who initiated the system, each claimed they were in the best position to set the state's longer range objectives. In many states this argument was never resolved, and PPBS has gradually faded out of vogue. But the system brought the state budgeting and planning functions closer together, and in many states permanently linked planning and budgeting, if not structurally, at least for the purpose of setting longer range state objectives. Many planning agencies today direct part of their work to establishing the program policy guidelines around which state budgets are developed. This is true particularly in those states where the planning function is part of the Governor's office.

For much of the 1960s and 1970s there was an evolution in thought about the location of state planning within state government and its technical mission. In 1962, for example, the Subcommittee on State Planning of the Governor's Conference offered recommendations dealing with: providing state planning services, elements of state-wide planning, and the characteristics of a state planning office.

In providing state planning services there should be a central planning unit, and planning units in major operating agencies. Assuming necessary authority and financial support, the functions should include fact gathering and analysis, overall development policy, implementation programs, capital improvements programming, and assistance to operating agencies.

It was felt that effective state-wide planning must include a state-wide development plan, provide a coordinating mechanism for all state programs, and provide information for agencies throughout state government.

The state planning office was perceived as a staff service to the Governor, which engaged in legislative participation, worked closely with operating agencies, had relationships with local planning agencies, encouraged regional planning, participated in interstate activities, and was the lead agency in relation to federal programs.

In the latter part of the 1960s, only a handful of state planning agencies had a significant relationship to the Governor's office. Many critics of state planning during that period, while agreeing that planning had shown impressive vitality in bounding back during the decade, claimed that it was still not institutionalized and would not be until it was a staff function within the Governor's office. Most executive decisions, they charged, still were not being made in relation to long-range state goals. And what was passing for state planning was really nothing more than an accumulation of budget decisions on proposed projects.

Former Governor Terry Sanford of North Carolina wrote that: "Few Governors concern themselves with planning, for planning simply to help the next Governor seems irrelevant to the everyday tasks that pile up in a busy Governor's Office."[37]

To Sanford, state planning was a process, not a plan. It was a process for bringing about changes necessary to reach desired goals. And as a process it must be comprehensive and it must be at the Governor's right hand. For Sanford, the Governor was the only person sufficiently powerful to effectuate change, to bring agencies together, to determine priorities, and to resolve conflicts. There are, of course, those who did not share this view of planning and who saw a broader relationship between planning and the executive and legislative branches as well as with substate regional planning organizations.

Regardless of one's point of view, the situation at the close of the 1960s saw more state planning agencies established than ever before, a general recognition of the key role of the Governor in regard to state planning, general agreement on what the focus of state planning should be and how it should be concentrated, but very few state planning agencies measuring up to these expectations.

The nation's Governors, in a 1968 Report of the Committee on State Planning, National Governor's Conference, suggested several components be included in the activities of a central state planning agency:

1. Goal setting and issue formulation.
2. Problem solving research.
3. Coordination of effort.
4. Organizational planning.
5. Education.

In summary, that report noted:

The state planning agency should serve as the key advisor to the governor, the legislature, and the state executive agencies in organizing and coordinating the functions and applying them in the state. In some cases the planning agency may carry out several of these functions, but at no time should the broad overview be lost in administrative morass.

There should be no protective efforts of 'empire building' notions here—. The job at hand is to see that these functions are performed somewhere and have an impact throughout state government.

The charge of the state planning agency is clear—make sure the state planning process is operating and affecting the activities of state government. This can be done by all parts of state government working together, not just by a group of isolated planners.

There is one further key ingredient. If the planning process is to gain broad acceptance throughout state government, planners must be issue-oriented. They must operate within the political framework of government. Those planners who would desire to be 'professional' in the tradition of the early reformers, avoiding politics, political controversy and issues, will find themselves working outside the context of modern government.

The genesis of planning and the primary motivation of political action is one and the same—the desire to shape the patterns of society for the greatest benefits to all. This means controlling the forces affecting us, channeling the changes sweeping us forward, reordering the institutions burdening us, and predicting the challenges yet facing us. By its very nature, government, a political institution, deals in issues, problems, and controversy. If planning is to serve government, and that is its only rationale, it must operate within this context.

If the state planner would adopt an issue-orientation and curb his emphasis on the master or comprehensive planning document, he will discover himself to be a planner, not an information scientist. The information scientist is a spectator who produces a status report or a statistical analysis; the planner is a participant who produces real-world decisions or prepares for a contingency. There is far too much mere reporting and commenting on the state of affairs. Planning today needs men who advocate causes and press for solutions.[38]

Throughout the 1970s state planning was in for more changes. First, it was substantially impacted by the wave of state government reorganization that swept the country. In state after state, government agencies were being consolidated by function and the number of line agencies and points of responsibility were being reduced. Similarly, the number of independent boards and commissions were being reduced with the resulting, more direct, functional control of the Governor and legislature.

Much of the reorganization was in response to the vast array of new federal grant programs and the need for the states to improve their administrative ability to deal with these programs. Governors and members of the legislature also were becoming more involved in personally dealing with major issues, and reorganization was imperative if effective management was to be applied to these issues. Most reorganization plans regarded the Governor's office as the focal point of administrative arrangement.

Some of the reorganization impetus may be traced to the federal level as President Richard Nixon openly considered and then discarded the concept of national planning, preferring instead his (Nixon's) New Federalism policy of turning more responsibility back to the state and local governments.

Congress in the early 1970s involved itself with the consideration of national legislation dealing with land use and development, under which states would engage in comprehensive land-use planning in accordance with state policies and involving a state-regional-local interaction.

The primary federal land-use measure, the Land Use Policy and Planning Assistance Act, passed the Senate in 1973. A companion bill in the House failed to win approval, however, and Congress, in 1974, amended the Housing and Urban Development Act to require the preparation of state land use and housing elements by recipients of HUD 701 comprehensive planning assistance.

Although operating under a much lower funding level than was proposed in the defeated land use legislation, the new HUD 701 program had a major impact on states receiving 701 planning assistance for state, areawide, and local planning. For the first time, the 701 program contained performance requirements, in the form of acceptable housing and land-use plans, which all 701 recipients had to meet in order to continue their program eligibility.[39]

Table 3–1　State populations, 1980, and rate of growth, 1970–1980.

		% Growth rate	Population			% Growth rate	Population
1.	Nevada	63.5	799,200	26.	Mississippi	13.7	2,520,638
2.	Arizona	53.1	2,717,900	27.	Montana	13.3	786,690
3.	Florida	43.4	9,740,000	28.	Maine	13.2	1,124,660
4.	Wyoming	41.6	470,816	29.	Alabama	12.9	3,890,061
5.	Utah	37.9	1,461,037	30.	West Virginia	11.8	1,949,644
6.	Alaska	32.4	400,481	31.	Delaware	8.6	595,225
7.	Idaho	32.4	943,935	32.	Maryland	7.5	4,216,446
8.	Colorado	30.7	2,888,834	33.	Minnesota	7.1	4,077,148
9.	New Mexico	27.8	1,299,968	34.	Wisconsin	6.5	4,705,335
10.	Texas	27.1	14,228,383	35.	Indiana	5.7	5,490,179
11.	Oregon	25.9	2,632,663	36.	Nebraska	5.7	1,570,006
12.	Hawaii	25.3	965,000	37.	North Dakota	5.6	652,695
13.	New Hampshire	24.8	920,610	38.	Kansas	5.1	2,363,208
				39.	Missouri	5.1	4,917,444
14.	Washington	21.0	4,130,163	40.	Michigan	4.2	9,258,344
15.	So. Carolina	20.4	3,119,208	41.	South Dakota	3.6	690,178
16.	Georgia	19.1	5,464,265	42.	Iowa	3.1	2,913,387
17.	Arkansas	18.8	2,265,513	43.	Illinois	2.8	11,418,461
18.	California	18.5	23,668,562	44.	New Jersey	2.7	7,364,158
19.	Oklahoma	18.2	3,025,266	45.	Connecticut	2.5	3,107,576
20.	Tennessee	16.9	4,509,750	46.	Ohio	1.3	10,797,419
21.	No. Carolina	15.5	5,874,429	47.	Massachusetts	.8	5,737,037
22.	Louisiana	15.3	4,203,972	48.	Pennsylvania	.6	11,866,728
23.	Vermont	15.0	511,456	49.	Rhode Island	– .3	947,154
24.	Virginia	14.9	5,346,279	50.	New York	– 3.8	17,557,288
25.	Kentucky	13.7	3,661,433	51.	D.C.	– 15.7	637,651
	U.S. Total	**11.4**	**226,504,825**				

Source: U.S. Bureau of the Census, 1980 Census of Population, Series II-B Projections, 1979.

Since land-use planning in most states was the responsibility of substate units of government, state land-use planning under the new HUD 701 program was geared to providing growth and development guidance rather than the more traditional form of the mapped land-use plan. HUD responded to this approach by shaping the 701 program regulations to fit the growth and development strategy mode.[40]

A number of states, notably Vermont, Rhode Island, Oregon, and Florida, produced significant programs during this period with much of the work provided either by the state planning agency or a specific organization charged with the land-use function.[41]

Emphasis on land-use planning, even when future federal funding was at stake, was not viewed as adequate justification for maintaining a strong and vital state planning function in many states during the mid-1970s, especially in the wake of widespread government reorganization. Land-use issues were often arguable and highly personalized with a resulting political volatility. By and large, planning was not enjoying more than limited acceptance as a useful function of state government. As new functional agencies were established, the planning capability in line departments was being enhanced. State planning agencies still seemed to lack a specific mission and often attended to activities such as land-use planning or growth and development strategies which did not fit neatly into line agency functions and yet touched a number of those responsibilities. Very often state planning staffs were considerably smaller than those in line agency planning offices, a direct result of inadequate funding and mission. These factors contributed to the dismantling of important state planning agencies in mid-decade in states such as New York, California, Oregon, and Kentucky. Planning was said to be suffering from some serious image problems. Some believed these problems were due in part to a failure of planning to become results-oriented; to the extensive lead time required to produce a product; to competition between line agency planning and the central planning function; to the lack of public or special interest support for planning; to the too close relationship between planning and the Governor; to the overreliance on federal funding; to the generally poor public relations performance carried out by planners.[42]

In a 1976 report of the Council of State Governments there was the realization that with declining government revenue that state government and state planning had to do more with less. Governors needed a process to assist them in defining goals, coordinating policies and plans, and keeping track of the programs that proliferated at the local level. The fundamental purpose of a state planning process was to provide the Governor with a planning capacity. However, it was realized that producing truly comprehensive state plans had proved to be an impractical job for most states. In determining an overall state policy framework the key elements might be land use, economic planning, and capital improvements programming. Interestingly, it was felt that the budget, if it were prepared in a program format, was at least a short-term comprehensive plan. Moreover, it was felt that the division of planning functions may vary widely among the states with divided responsibilities among various types of units such as a planning office, a community affairs agency, the budget office, and line agencies.[43]

In spite of these problems and the fact that in many states the state planning function tended to be underfunded, a sense of mission for state planning began to emerge during the latter part of the 1970s. Several factors were responsible for the shift including the energy crisis and the economic recession in 1973; a new breed of Governor who tended to be out front on the issues and problems facing the states; the Governor's need for quality staff work to provide issue analysis and support data; a need for a state policy framework on which executive and legislative decisions could be based and which could be used to coordinate line agency activities; an increasing competence among state planners in using new data techniques, particularly for policy simulation; the need for a closer relationship between state planning in a policy sense and the budget function to identify state policy objectives and priorities in a period of increasing costs and diminished resources; and the increasing importance of multistate and substate regionalism as a mechanism to facilitate the coordination and implementation of state objectives.

In concluding this discussion on the essential ingredients for state planning, let us summarize the views of one observer of the state planning scene:

1. Gubernatorial leadership—the leadership and participation of the governor is essential; that personal interest is the key to effectiveness.
2. State development policy—policy guidelnes are the output of planning and the preparation of a comprehensive development policy should be a mandated responsibility of a state planning office.
3. State legislature—must be actively involved; its absence has been an Achilles heel for state planning.
4. Implementation—must receive explicit attention and priority as part of the planning process; too little implementing has been a primary shortcoming of state planning.

5.   Regional planning network—the geography of virtually every state indicated the need and usefulness of a sub-state regional structure particularly in the implementation of state planning.

Can state planning make a difference?

The situation near the end of the 1970s may be summed up generally as follows:

1.   Several important states had dismantled the state planning function, although some, like New York, were in the process of reconsidering this action.
2.   A number of state planning offices were engaged in functional planning for health, crime, recreation, housing, etc., while others were focused primarily on land-use plans. The land-use plan was more than a physical plan for development and included other selective social and economic issues such as housing, transportation, natural resources conservation, social service facilities, and industrial development.
3.   The most significant new trend emerging in state planning was the policy and planning relationship in which the planning office was becoming a more direct staff function in the Governor's office. Longer term strategic plans were being developed in hot issue areas like economic development and energy. The planners were engaged in providing the Governor with a wide range of policy advice backed up with hard data. Increasingly, these governors were relying on the planning staff to flesh out policy positions, to develop a policy framework, and to coordinate the activities of line agencies to ensure consistency with state policy. Governors using the planning agency in this fashion generally viewed their role as chief executive officer of the state as well as a political leader. Under this concept, issue and policy analysis and the strategic planning process were part of the Governor's day-to-day decision-making process.

These two models, functional and policy, generally reflect the status of the state planning function moving into the 1980s. Increasingly, emphasis is shifting to the policy model with a special focus on economic development and alternative futures planning. The significance attached to economic development as an issue among the states may be generally attributed to multistate regional competition for new industry and jobs that has emerged in a transitory economy. This shift is not universal, however, and many planning offices are engaged in various functional planning activities which are usually written under federal sponsorship for the purpose of coordinating program development and investment. It is the responsibility of the state to ensure compatibility among these plans and state policy objectives.

   The New Federalism of the Reagan administration may bring yet another dimension to state government and state planning. With actions taken concerning budget and taxes in its first "200 days," that administration has triggered a review of state and local government responsibilities not experienced since the New Deal. This reassessment and the use of funding resources diminished at least for a time will place greater urgency on the quality of state decision making. If, indeed, the art and science of state planning is now an integral part of state government, then state planning will be central to those deliberations and actions.

Experiences in state planning

A preface to these selected state planning vignettes may be found in the panel discussion "New Directions for State Planning," which took place at the National Conference of the American Planning Association in Baltimore, Maryland, in

1979. The Secretary of the Maryland Department of State Planning observed "a definite movement away from the Comprehensive Master Plan approach . . . in this world of uncertainty where change is the only thing that is guaranteed." She foresaw, as well, "a continuation of the well-documented movement away from the traditional physical planning orientation of state planning agencies toward a policy/management planning process." She offered one practicable admonition that "the State Planning Agency must realize the Governor is its primary client and that it cannot serve equally that client and others—no matter who they may be. To put it more directly, the State Planning Agency cannot run about advocating programs and policies which are contrary to the position and policies of the Governor. . . . The State Planning Agency . . . unable or unwilling to provide accountable and responsive services to the Governor— particularly in policy sensitive areas—may well find itself in the untenable position of being a non-entity at best and a pariah at worst." She noted that while state planning has received its greatest stimulus from the federal funding sources "the fact remains that it is often fiscally unsound and unwise for a state to build programs around promised federal funding . . . especially . . . when programs are started in response to or at the insistent urging of the federal government to further . . . national objectives which may give little consideration to the realities at the state and sub-state levels." She concluded that "State Planning Agencies [must make] a stronger, more concerted approach to securing increased state funding support—[promoting] the planning process and [selling the] case to the Governors, the state legislatures and the citizenry; and [this can be done] only . . . by high performance which is competent, visible and results oriented."[45]

With the foregoing in mind, consider the following experience and judgments as a relatively current expression concerning state planning and its application.

Kansas

In October, 1980, the Kansas Chapter newsletter of the American Planning Association reported that the state's Division of Planning and Research (P&R) had been abolished by the state legislature.

The newsletter offered two key factors that may have prompted the legislature's action:

1. P&R was not immune to the problems of state planning agency role definition which have surfaced in most states. There appeared to be little understanding or interest on the part of the newly elected Governor as to how P&R could be most effectively used.
2. There appeared to be a similar lack of understanding of the role of P&R by the state legislature which may have viewed the agency as being too closely tied to the Governor.

While the newsletter attempted to pinpoint blame for the actions against the state planning agency, the experience in Kansas was not unlike similar situations in other states in which the state planning function was dismantled during the 1970s. One important difference, however, was the fact that the Kansas state planning agency had only been in existence since the mid-1970s. For that period of time it functioned within the Governor's office. The dismantling of this agency after only a few years of operation may be the manifestation of the risk that such agencies encounter when closely aligned with the Governor's office and faced with political changes.

In abolishing the state planning function, the Kansas legislature allocated the agency's responsibilities between the Department of Economic Development and the Division of the Budget, indicating that the legislature perceived value to P&R activities, but preferred a new organizational arrangement.

A survey of the status of state planning nationwide undertaken in connection with the preparation of this chapter brought a response from the Director of the Budget in Kansas that there was a small cadre of planning and policy analysts in his office to conduct some of the research oriented functions often found in state planning mission statements.

At the annual meeting of the American Planning Association in Cincinnati, Ohio in October, 1980, the State Planning Division sponsored a program session: "The Many Faces of State Planning."

In the papers that were presented and the discussions which followed, principles were presented which were not novel or new. But, they bear emphasis particularly in light of the Kansas experience.

Florida

Howard Pardue, in his paper,[46] observed that his review of the state planning experience in Florida made several objectives for the 1980s clear:

1. Create not only the image but the actuality of success.
2. Serve the management needs of state government at all levels of responsibility and authority.
3. Fully integrate planning into the functioning management systems of state government including, but not limited to, the budget.
4. Gain legislative acceptance of the system.

In profiling state planning in Florida, Pardue noted that, riding sequential waves of governmental reorganization and environmental concern, it emerged from ashes of obscurity in 1967 and was significantly strengthened in 1969 and 1972. In 1967, the state legislature identified the Governor as the chief planning officer, established the Office of State Planning and Programming, and required the preparation of a long-range plan and an annual development program. By 1971, a less than successful program budget "plan" had been prepared and state planning had evolved into an ill-fated planning-programming-budgetary system (PPBS) effort. In 1972, the state legislature broke new ground for state planning by establishing a state and regional role in local land and water management decision making, reaffirming the mandate to develop a state comprehensive policy plan, creating a new state planning agency with status equal to the budgetary agency, and establishing new planning-oriented, state-level programs for water resource management and state lands acquisition.

By 1978 and the election of a new Governor, there had been a half-dozen years of experience with these new resource management programs, and a state comprehensive plan with several hundred policy directives had been formulated and adopted. The gubernatorial election that year appeared to signal two distinct possibilities for state planning in Florida: one candidate held a keen interest in planning and a reputation for long-range thinking; the other expressed little inclination toward planning responsibilities. The planning oriented candidate won.

Two years later, a major reorganization of state planning agencies and functions has come about; gubernatorially appointed task forces have readdressed urban, economic, and natural resource planning and management issues; and new policy initiative from the Governor's office are overshadowing the previously adopted State Comprehensive Plan.

State planning in Florida has become an executive planning and policy-making system. It is a process aimed at bringing goals, policies, priorities, and needed background information and analysis to bear on decisions. Its purpose is to obtain good, comprehensively based decision making. It aims at "charting a course," defining and anticipating the future, and taking actions accordingly. It provides an alternative to crisis-oriented problem solving.

State planning includes distinct activities such as needs assessment, goal-objectives-policy-priority development, evaluation of alternatives, resource allocation, and other forms of decision-making implementation and evaluation. At times, the planning and policy making occurs as part of a formalized approach such as the biennial planning-budgeting-management system (PBMS) or the development of the Governor's Policies and Priorities materials and statement. It also occurs on a more informal basis when issues are raised and resolved at the gubernatorial level. In either case, the planning-policy making process is considered more important than specific planning products.

Today, in Florida, state planning is decentralized throughout state agencies with the focal point for integration, coordination, and control being the Governor and his Office of Planning and Budgeting. Other key elements within the system include the strategic use of task forces, state agency heads, and agency planning activities and responsibilities.

State government in Florida has made a major shift in its concept, definition, organization, and expectations of state planning. It now is designed and intended to focus state planning on the management needs of the Governor.

The change is a continuation of the maturing of a state planning function which generated much awareness in 1967. Since that time, state planning has emerged as a legitimate and sometimes forceful instrument in influencing governmental decision making.

The future of state planning is dependent on the commitment and ability of the Governor to incorporate what it does into governmental management processes and in decision making.

Looking forward, state planning in Florida must successfully confront many challenges, including:

1. Continuing the conceptualization and design of specific components of the state planning system.
2. "Field testing" and refining those parts of the system that have been designed.
3. Pinpointing responsibility for and assigning staffing to the various components of state planning.
4. Maintaining the intended and legitimate function of planning and policy management in budgeting and daily decision making.
5. Establishing the linked policy and implementation mechanisms required for any state planning that may be found useful and worth sustaining, including comprehensive plan and background studies; agency operational and program plans; a management information system; review processes; performance measurement methodologies; rule making and legislative programs; and conflict resolution mechanisms.
6. Gaining acceptance and use of state planning functions and services by state agencies.
7. Meeting these challenges with the prospects of limited resources and staffing.
8. Be responsive to the Governor and yet be capable of surviving the transition from one administration to another.

Pennsylvania

It is a widely shared view in Pennsylvania that a strong planning and policy analysis function in the Governor's office enables state government to work more effectively and efficiently, permits policies to be formulated with greater opportunity for consistency among the state departments and agencies whose responsibilities and activities are involved, and permits a fuller consideration of the options available at the time decisions are made.[47] It represents a recognition that planning isolated from and not directly tied to decision makers cannot be expected to be viewed with enthusiasm for implementation and action.

The Thornburgh administration, which took office in 1979, has brought about a reorganization of state planning in accordance with the following general principles:

1. State planning must be linked to and be a key aspect of the policy development function of the Governor in order for planning to be effective.
2. The products of state planning must be implementable within a relatively short period.
3. State planning should not carry out functional planning programs that could be accomplished by line agencies.
4. State planning should not be a creature of federal funding that would focus its activities on federal, rather than state, objectives.
5. The purpose of state planning is to serve the Governor and not interest groups or organizations that have embraced planning.

As a result, the Governor's Office of Policy and Planning is now deeply involved in:

1. Providing substantive, in-depth policy research and analysis directly to the Governor and key cabinet officials; and, in some cases, such as welfare reform, working with the state legislature.
2. Assisting in the preparation of the Governor's legislative agenda and program; developing new legislation, executive orders, and regulations.
3. Developing new state initiatives—policies and programs—in such areas as economic development, community conservation, and human services.
4. Assisting in the preparation of annual state agency budget guidelines (called Program Policy Guidelines), that identify specific areas in which state agencies must direct their resources and efforts.
5. Providing staff support to the Governor for his involvement as Chairman of the Economic and Community Development Committee of the National Governor's Association and in the Coalition of Northeast Governors.
6. Developing a longer range strategic plan to address economic development and community conservation issues which are a critical concern in Pennsylvania.
7. Seeking out and receiving special federal grant assistance to meet identified state needs, such as a National Science Foundation three-year grant to rebuild the scientific and technical policy advisory capacity of the Commonwealth which was demonstrated to be inadequate by such events as the Three Mile Island nuclear plant accident.
8. Reviewing state agency functional plans to assure their consistency with the policies and overall direction of the Administration.

As viewed in Pennsylvania, one of the primary objectives of planning must be to improve the quality of day-to-day decision making. Among the products of planning should be a consistent set of short-term policy decisions which, over time, result in the achievement of longer range objectives.

To help ensure that the day-to-day policy decisions of state government are internally consistent and consistent with longer term objectives, a two-year "Choices for Pennsylvania" program was initiated in 1979. As a strategic planning program to address critical state issues of economic development and community conservation, "Choices for Pennsylvania" is geared to gaining a greater control over the Commonwealth's future by understanding the forces that will shape it; by setting some policy objectives against which short-term policy decisions can be measured; and by developing specific action alternatives that will help answer the question "What can we do, and how?"

The effort has involved examining Pennsylvania's place in the Northeast-Midwest region; undertaking major citizen participation activities using public meetings, television media, and a citizen survey to elicit citizen views about the state's future and how to get there.

The Pennsylvania State Planning Board, established in 1933 and used variously or not at all by different governors over the years, has been particularly involved in the "Choices" program and the articulation of long term goals for the Commonwealth. With a membership of 24 (five cabinet officers, four state legislators, and 15 citizen members) a representation is provided that is sensitive to a composite of interests and views that will have a bearing on whatever actions may be taken to implement "Choices" recommendations when these are offered.

It is important to note that interim products have been drawn from "Choices" activities including new initiatives in a complete restructuring of the state's efforts to stimulate business and industrial expansion including: major emphasis on small business; legislative changes in the Pennsylvania Industrial Development Program (PIDA), one of the oldest and most successful in the nation; a "one-stop shop" for business and industry information and services; and the establishment of an Economic Development Committee of the Cabinet to target opportunities and actions necessary to accomplishment.

The planning structure and process currently found in Pennsylvania relates directly to the Governor's concept of his role as the chief executive officer of the state as well as the leader of state government. In this position, the Governor insists on the demands a vigorous policy formulation and planning process that values the in-house research, analytical, and planning capability that a vigorous state planning office should offer.

Illinois

In reporting on the work of the Task Force on the Future of Illinois, a commission of 17 members (nine citizens appointed by the Governor and eight members of the state legislature) established by the Illinois General Assembly and instructed to ". . . evaluate and articulate state goals and objectives regarding the future of Illinois and to recommend an agenda of implementing actions," its Executive Director summarized the recommendations under consideration for their final report:

1. In the Governor's Office—to create an official to be designated as the Director of Strategic Planning; to work with Governor on state strategic planning, to review and coordinate state plans and federal funding with long-range implications in mind, and to serve as the Governor's Office link to the regional planning agencies in the state.
2. In the Bureau of the Budget—to support the long-range economic and population forecasting process, to enforce the state clearinghouse process, and to strengthen the projections and fiscal relationships with the annual budgeting and agency review process.
3. In State Departments—to identify a staff link with the Governor's Office of Strategic Planning, and to strengthen the internal management and planning process looking toward longer-range objectives.
4. In the State Legislature—to minimize the use of legislative commissions, such as the Task Force, and rather concentrate resources on strengthening the legislative committee process assisting on legislative oversight as well as foresight efforts.

5. For the Citizens of the State—to provide a way to see a "balance sheet" or score card on how the state is doing in reaching its goals and to establish a State of the State Reporting Council.[48]

Minnesota

The Deputy Director of the Minnesota State Planning Agency judged that new directions for state planning was not the issue; rather new directions for state government was the more overriding concern. As state government became increasingly large, complex, and with a growing role and range of responsibilities, the next decade, it was observed, would be a difficult period for state government, a period of "limits" with the federal role diminishing in state affairs, with local governments constrained in dealing with facility and service demands and with funding support reflecting a decline in light of reduced federal grants and expected tax reform.

He suggested a distinction between state planning and state planning agencies, noting that state government plans and that state planning may or may not help in that endeavor. He outlined several key considerations for state planners in that regard, including:

1. The department heads are the "true" planners in state government—how can they be assisted in making better decisions.
2. Planning as problem solving—how can problem solving skills be improved.
3. Focus on those skills that would help make better decisions.
4. Emphasize priority setting and making choices and recognize the futility of excessive detail.
5. Manage knowledge as an integral part of managing the planning process.[49]

State planning in the 1980s: a prognosis

In view of the foregoing considerations, some observations can be made about state planning and where it is headed in the decade on the 1980s.

A recent survey, with responses from more than half the state planning agencies throughout the country, reveals that several are on the leading edge of state policy development and are actively involved in helping to assure that line agencies are engaged in implementing state policy through plans, programs, and requisite activities.[50] In those states, there appears to be a strong relationship between the Governor and the state planning staff; see Figure 3-1. The administration appears to rely on the planning agency for a rigorous evaluation of policy options and for policy recommendations. In almost every instance the Governor is providing strong leadership in the management of state affairs and has sent signals throughout the administration that the planning staff is a principal "mover and shaker" in the administration. This recognition of the planning agency has enhanced its prestige within the administration, helped to neutralize the opposition to the state planning agencies' involvement in line agency affairs, and generally has made the mission of the state planning agency easier.

It should be noted, however, that a great deal of the success of the state planning agency depends on the leadership of the Governor and the Governor's desire for the kind of services that the agency can provide. There will be some Governors who will have very little interest in the research and planning capabilities of the agency. There will be others who will not know how to use those capabilities. Generally, those Governors who will use the state planning function for policy research and development, new initiatives, and the like will be the type who see their role not only as the chief political leader of the state but also as its chief executive officer and chairman of the board.

Clearly, there is some danger that the planning agency could become so closely

State	Agency location	Relationships with state legislature	Relationship with state agencies	Relationship with private sector	Use advisory boards
Arizona	Governor's office	Regular	Clearinghouse; policy committees	Private sector advisory board	Several advisory
Colorado	Office of state planning and budgeting (independent by statute)	Joint budget committee	On implementing governor's agenda	On major economic planning efforts	Ad hoc
Connecticut	Governor's office	Regular and frequent	Coordination; plan review	Periodic and varied	Ad hoc on selective issues
Florida	Governor's office	Indirect; prepares executive budget, policy guides, legislative package	Plan review	Through advisory councils	Functional advisory boards; housing, economic, hospital costs
Hawaii	Department of Planning and Economic Development	Hearings and informational workshops	Coordination; plan review	State plan advisory council representation	Functional plan advisory committee
Indiana	Governor's office	Minimal	Prepares state agency functional plans under contract	Minimal except housing	Statutory advisory committee
Iowa	Governor's office	On selective programs	Coordination; plan review	—	Ad hoc advisory and regulatory
Kansas	Abolished (functions transferred to Department of Administration and Department of Economic Development)	Regular and frequent	Instructs and supervises agency financial and operations planning	Minimal	No
Kentucky	Department of Finance	Regular; systematic exchange of information	Monitors program and financial activities	Consideration of private sector impact in budget policies	Several advisory
Maine	Governor's office	Frequent. Works with legislative committee on issues of mutual concern	On specific projects	On economic development projects	Land and Water Resources Council; Rural Development Committee
Michigan	Department of Commerce; Office of Community Development	Informal (information support); develops legislative proposals; reviews selected legislation	Participates in interdepartmental task forces on comprehensive policy development; assists agencies in policy research	Ad hoc task forces, especially economic development	Ad hoc advisory

Figure 3–1 Organizational relationships of state planning agencies with executive, legislative, and other agencies.

State	Agency location	Relationships with state legislature	Relationship with state agencies	Relationship with private sector	Use advisory boards
Mississippi	Governor's office	Informal (information requests)	Coordination; plan review; grant request review	Minimal	Ad hoc Governor's Planning Council
Nebraska	Policy Research Office (independent by statute)	Full-time legislative analysis function	Coordination	Limited	No
New Mexico	Department of Finance and Administration	Provides information and reports per requests	Plan coordination and review	Through state planning conference	No
New York	Governor's office	Prepare legislation; coordinate with legislative committees	Monitors activities; prepares new initiatives	Frequent ad hoc	Several advisory on selected topics
North Dakota	Lieutenant governor's office, Office of Federal Aid Coordination, Division of Planning	Works with interim committees	Reviews state agency plans	Ad hoc on specific issues	Advisory committee on block grant guidelines anticipated
Oklahoma	Department of Economic and Community Affairs	Formal through state legislative council	Through A-95	On project basis	Standing boards and committees
Pennsylvania	Governor's office	Administrative relationship— Office of Policy and Planning, Office of Legislative Council, Office of Legislative Relations	Prepares governor's program policy guidelines; reviews agency plans and budget	Through public participation program on long-range strategic planning policies; participation on private sector councils	State planning board (statutory)
Rhode Island	Department of Administration	Informal; prepares components of governor's legislative program	Formal and informal mechanisms in place	Participation on various public interest and private sector committees	Three standing committees; others ad hoc
South Dakota	Governor's office	Prepares governor's legislative package	Reviews state agency plans	Ad hoc	State planning commission; various cabinet subgroups
Tennessee	Governor's office	Informal (information requests)	Reviews capital and operating budgets; assists in planning preparation	Informal; information and reports	Ad hoc advisory or technical
Vermont	Governor's office	Selected formal linkages	Formal mechanism for state agencies to prepare and update five-year management policies	Through governor's council of economic advisors	Governor's council of economic advisors; ad hoc advisory committees

Figure 3–1   (continued).

State	Agency location	Relationships with state legislature	Relationship with state agencies	Relationship with private sector	Use advisory boards
Virginia	Department of Planning and Budgeting	Prepares fiscal and policy analysis of legislation	Reviews agency budgets and plans	Indirect; information and reports	Not directly
Washington	Governor's office	Regular	Coordination; plan review, analysis of agency legislation	—	Several advisory committees and issue task forces
Wisconsin	Department of Administration	Provides technical analysis on budget and policy issues, analysis of bills and programs under legislative review	Analysis of agency budget and policy issues; undertakes joint studies and reviews agency activities	—	—
Wyoming	Governor's office	Provides legislative liaison	Coordination; plan review	Participation on private sector committees	Eight advisory committees

Figure 3–1 (continued).

aligned with the Governor that a backlash of resentment could be forthcoming from the legislature or other sources, and efforts could be made to strip the Governor of the agency's resources. Survey results have indicated that most planning agencies have established either formal or informal relationships with the legislature and private sector. The success of these relationships depends in large measure on the effectiveness of the planning director, the Governor, and other key administration officials in managing executive/legislative and private sector relationships. The key to this success is a sharing of executive initiatives and new policies and programs with the legislature, and providing mechanisms for private sector participation in the consideration of issues and policy options in order to avoid the sometimes disastrous consequences of "surprise."

While the executive/legislative relationship is indeed an important element in the successful management of the state planning function, the most critical relationship is that which exists between the Governor and the planning agency. For the state planning agency to be effective, policy guidance must be the product of planning. Without a strong relationship between the Governor and the planning agency, there can be a great deal of planning but no product. This is especially important in states where the legislature has not mandated the preparation of an overall development policy. Most new policy initiatives must then come from the executive branch.

While many state legislatures would probably define their role as the chief policy arm of the state, in reality very few have mandated the preparation of a comprehensive state development policy. Consequently, much state policy is developed ad hoc or on the basis of the Governor's legislative agenda. This is sometimes supplemented or expanded by executive policy initiatives in the form of strategic plans prepared by the state planning agency. These policy plans are geared to coping with specific issues, often identified by the Governor as a priority concern of the administration. The issues may be primarily of state concern, such as the emphasis on environmental matters in Vermont in the 1970s. They may be of multistate regional significance, such as economic development in the Midwest and Northeast in the late 1970s and currently. Or they may be issues that affect virtually every state, such as coping with the transition from federal categorical grants to block grants and the New Federalism of the Reagan administration. Emphasis on strategic policy planning to deal with these kinds of issues that require a quick turnaround and accurate assessment and response is perhaps the major factor contributing to the resurgence of state planning in many states today.

Strategic planning is a new dimension for many state planning agencies and one that has been borrowed from the corporate sector for application in public affairs. It is particularly attractive to Governors who view themselves as the chief executive officers of their states and who engage in the day-to-day battle of issue identification and analysis, policy evaluation, and implementation. From a process perspective, strategic planning is relatively short-term (that is, needs to be done quickly), when contrasted with state planning of an earlier era. It is also more narrowly focused. But the scope of strategic planning is long-range, with considerable attention directed toward clarifying and assessing external factors that may influence the planning. There may be a number of strategic policy plans undertaken by an administration to address a variety of issues, and the issues are often highly diversified reflecting that they can be generated externally, for example, through changes in federal policies, programs, and funding, as well as from within the state.

When state planning agencies throughout the country were asked to identify the major issues in their states for the 1980s, those who were engaged in carrying out policy analysis and strategic planning for the Governor cited the state response to changes in federal programs and funding levels (block grants), economic development and jobs, water supply, hazardous waste management, and tax policy as areas of principal concern. These were followed by related issues such as the provision of government services in the face of revenue constraints, energy issues, and fiscal impact of growth on local governments.

Many of these issues are not new. But the method being used by many states to deal with them is. The strategic or policy plan appears to be one of the most promising techniques in the state planner's arsenal to address these areas of special concern.

In states utilizing this process for policy decisions, a system of policy planning has evolved that generally incorporates a rigorous issue evaluation, including projection of consequences over a long term; an identification of the impacts of the issue under consideration; the assessment of the external environment and its implications; the formulation of objectives and options for dealing with the issue; the identification of advantages and disadvantages associated with each option; and a recommendation and rationale or strategy for a preferred course of action. Very often, the policy is reviewed throughout its preparation process with the Governor and his chief aides. The Governor may elect to release publicly the policy plan when announcing his policy decision or initiative, in an effort to show that his position was reached after a very careful consideration of the issue and options. This technique can be helpful in developing an image of the Governor as an individual who does not take the public decision-making process lightly. The policy paper or strategic plan also places the Governor far ahead of any opposition who must cope with a well-developed background piece on the Governor's decision.

Is policy planning the direction state planning agencies will be pursuing during the 1980s? For many states the answer is yes. It will, of course, depend on the Governor, whether or not his style and method of operation are consistent with or adaptable to this approach, and whether the planning agency is capable of providing timely and effective responses to the Governor's needs.

The state planning agency of the 1980s will still have a variety of functions on its agenda which it must pursue regardless of any policy planning efforts it may undertake. This will include maintaining close and effective contact with the state legislature and with substate regional planning and development organizations. Those states with mandates from the legislature or engaged in assisting line agencies with functional plans will continue to carry out important responsibilities.

But as state/federal relationships change, and every indication now is that they are changing, and, as new issues emerge and some older ones intensify, it is incumbent on the state planning agency to anticipate, evaluate, and prepare for change.

Conclusion

It has been noted that, in many instances, state planning is a variety of endeavors lacking strong interrelationships and continuity that distinguish a systematic process from activity.

Many states are seeking to achieve a systematic process. They are finding out that it is not enough for the elements of a state planning process to exist; they are determining that these elements must be organized to achieve a policy formulating capacity, its effective expression and application, and the resulting management of change.

A useful state planning program and process will be a composite of many units of government. Where it exists, state planning is the organized and continuous interaction of goal definition, issue identification and analysis, policy development, program design, resource allocation, project application, monitoring, and evaluation. Among those states with an articulated program and process, there is a delineation of responsibilities among the Governor's executive staff, the budget office, the state planning office, the line agencies, regional organizations, and local government. They know what to expect from each other and how they must interact to fulfill their respective responsibilities in achieving desired results.

In this perhaps idealized situation, the state planning office is responsible for making the system perform with sustained effectiveness. The state planning office director reports directly to the Governor. The state planning office and the budget office have worked out the basis for collaboration, respecting their particular mission and not seeing one become the victim of the other.

A strong bond of state-local partnership is gained by the state encouragement and support of multipurpose regional planning organizations, statutory legitimization, participation in funding, and providing the opportunity for regional involvement in state decision making.

The state legislature considers planning a significant responsibility and an important legislative activity. Its organizational units are accordingly assisted in dealing with planning matters by the central and line agency planning offices.

The decade of the 1980s has opened with an economic and political climate that augers an era of financial restraint, a condition that demands rigorous consideration in public program selection and management. New priorities will demand a careful reexamination of goals and purposes, if not a first coherent expression of goals and purposes. The ability to anticipate and prepare responses to future possible events and the ability to evaluate future consequences of current policies, programs, and efforts as a basis for action call for a capability in state government yet to be uniformly achieved. The challenge to state planning in the 1980s, the measure of its usefulness, will be its contribution to helping bring about that achievement.

1   Harold F. Wise, *History of State Planning—An Interpretive Commentary*, The State Planning Series 1 (Washington, DC: Council of State Planning Agencies, 1977).

2   Ibid.

3   George C. Peery, "State Planning," *Planning for City, State, Region, and Nation*, Proceedings of the Joint Conference on Planning, Chicago, IL, 1936, p. 158.

4   Ibid.

5   U.S. Department of Housing and Urban Development, "Historic Background of State Planning," State Planning Intergovernmental Policy Coordination, Washington, DC, 1967, p. 132.

6   Ibid.
7   John L. Hancock, "Planners in the Changing American City, 1900–1940," *Journal of the American Institute of Planners*, 33 (September 1967): p. 292.
8   Ibid.
9   Ibid., p. 293.
10 Jacob L. Crane, "Whither State Planning," Planning Problems of Town, City, and City, and Region, Pittsburgh, 1932, pp. 142–150.
11 Alan W. Steiss, *A Framework for Planning in State Government* (Chicago: Council of State Planning Agencies, 1968), p. 17.
12 Ibid., p. 16.
13 Crane, "Whither State Planning," p. 143.
14 Peery, "State Planning," p. 159.
15 Ibid., pp. 159–160.
16 Steiss, *A Framework for Planning in State Government*, p. 18.
17 Maury Maverick, "A Permanent National Resources Board," *Planning for City, State, Region, and Nation*, Proceedings of the Joint Conference on Planning, American Society of Planning Officials, Chicago, IL, 1936, pp. 153–154.
18 Charles E. Merriam, "National Planning in Practice," *Planning for the Future of American Cities*, Proceedings of the Joint Conference on City, Regional, State, and National Planning, American Society of Planning Officials, Chicago, IL, 1935, p. 181.
19 Fred Schnepfe, "Planning for Public Works," *Planning for City, State, Region, and Nation*, Proceedings of the Joint Conference on Planning, American Society of Planning Officials, Chicago, IL, 1936, p. 135.
20 Ibid., p. 138.
21 Steiss, *A Framework for Planning in State Government*, p. 22.
22 Ibid.
23 Wise, "History of State Planning," pp. 12–13.
24 Ibid.
25 Ibid., p. 13.
26 *State Planning: Intergovernmental Policy Coordination*, U.S. Department of Housing and Urban Development, Washington, DC, 1976, p. 136.
27 "How States are Preparing for the Post-War Period," *Planning*, 1944: pp. 118–181.
28 *State Planning: Intergovernmental Policy Coordination*, p. 137.
29 "State Planning: Its Function and Organization," Report of the Committee on State Planning, American Institute of Planners. *Journal of the AIP*, 21, November 1959.
30 Otis L. Graham, Jr., *Toward a Planned Society* (New York: Oxford University Press, 1976), p. 127.
31 Ibid., p. 136.
32 Ibid., pp. 149–151.
33 U.S. Department of Housing and Urban Devel-

opment, *State Planning Intergovernmental Policy Coordination*, p. 137.
34 Harold F. Wise, "History of State Planning," p. 18.
35 Ibid., pp. 14–15.
36 Ibid., p. 18.
37 Terry Sanford, *Storm Over the States* (New York: McGraw-Hill, 1967), pp. 193–194.
38 *Relevance, Reliance, and Realism*, 1968 Report of the Committee on State Planning, The National Governor's Conference, pp. 15–16.
39 Wise, "History of State Planning," p. 27.
40 Ibid.
41 Ibid., pp. 28–29.
42 Norman F. Kron, Jr., "Planectomy—The Surgical Removal of State Planning Agencies," *State Planning Issues*, (Summer 1977): p. 000. See also the book review by Irving Hand on *The States and Urban Strategies: A Comparative Analysis and Ten Case Study Reports*, in *Journal of the American Planning Association* 48 (April 1982) 260–261.
43 *State Planning: New Roles in our Times* (summary report) (Lexington, Kentucky: Council of State Governments, 1976).
44 See statement of Richard T. Anderson, President, American Planning Association, and Vice-President—Administration, Regional Plan Association, NYC; "Why Small Communities Need State Planning," the Francis Pitkin Memorial Lecture, 1980, Annual Conference of the Pennsylvania Planning Association, State College, PA, September 29, 1980.
45 "New Directions in State Planning," a statement by Constance J. Lieder, Secretary, Maryland Department of State Planning, presented by Clarence J. Harris, Executive Assistant; at the annual national conference of the American Planning Association, Baltimore, MD, October 17, 1979.
46 "The Status of State Planning in Florida"—a paper presented at the 1980 Conference of the American Planning Association by Howard W. Pardue, Jr., AICP, Chicago, 1980.
47 "The Many Faces of State Planning: Pennsylvania"—a statement by Robert G. Benko presented at the APA National Planning Conference, Cincinnati, OH; October 28, 1980.
48 Based on the statement "Illinois: the State of the Future," comments on the Task Force on the Future of Illinois prepared by Franklyn H. Moreno, AICP, Executive Director, and presented at the 1979 Baltimore conference of the American Planning Association.
49 Remarks by A. Edward Hunter, Deputy Director, Minnesota State Planning Agency, at program session "New Directions for State Planning," 1979 APA Conference, Baltimore, MD.
50 A survey of state planning agencies throughout the country was conducted by the authors especially for this publication.

Techniques for implementing state plans

Introduction and perspective

The implementing tools of state planning theoretically include all the constitutional powers of state government. These powers include (1) taxing and spending, (2) regulation, and (3) eminent domain. All authority under these powers can be used to achieve the desired future results which are embodied in the products of the planning process. The role of the planner thus would be to show precisely how these powers can be used to these ends and to illustrate that this is the way in which planning is made relevant to governing.

While one could find examples of the use of each of these fundamental powers of state governments in the planning process, they have not been the dominant focus of state planning implementation. Two major themes have dominated state planning implementation over the past two decades. They are (1) orientation to the executive authority of the governors, and (2) policy formulation in intergovernmental relations, especially the implementation of federal grants-in-aid. Since 1961, these two themes have been closely interrelated.

The governors, meeting in Hawaii in 1961, "discovered" state planning. Hawaii had begun to develop a state plan in 1959 largely modeled after local planning and presented the published document to the assembled governors. Governor Rockefeller of New York immediately moved to develop a plan for his state, and the National Governors' Conference created a subcommittee on state planning with the following purposes:

1. To devise in collaboration with the United States executive office, the Congress and the various federal agencies, procedures and policies looking toward the objectives of a more comprehensive approach to joint federal-state planning and to closer federal-state coordination in the development of plans and programs affecting such vital policy areas as use of the public lands, transportation, water resources, open space for recreation and metropolitan expansion.

2. To develop a policy statement with regard to comprehensive physical planning on a statewide basis, including consideration of the factors making such planning a pressing necessity at this time, the measures necessary to carry out effective state planning and the status of present state planning activities, together with such significant current examples as may support the committee's position.[1]

The subcommittee report issued in 1962 as "State Planning: A Policy Statement" left no doubt as to the governors' perspective. The report stated:

The subcommittee recommends that the agency responsible for planning services be located where it will be most effective in the overall policy development of state government as a staff service to the chief executive.[2]

Since the creation of the 701 program in 1954, that program had been focused on local planning, essentially on the comprehensive physical planning model. The 701 program was revised to include state planning grants in 1979. The 1966 program guidelines left no doubt as to the orientation of state planning to executive authority:

State comprehensive planning is most effectively employed as an element of the executive function of State government. The Governor, therefore, is the official primarily responsible for its conduct and execution. The State comprehensive planning program should be conceived as a continuing process to provide central policy formulation for the inter-related social, economic, and physical aspects of State development, to give direction to the various governmental programs involved, and to effect coordination of departmental or functional agency activities and programs.[3]

As more and more federal grant-in-aid programs were developed during the 1960s, two requirements became standard. The first was that the governors be given the authority to assign the program within their state administrative structure. The second was that there would be a program planning requirement which rationalized program expenditures within a larger planning framework. These two factors strengthened executive authority and provided the components for implementing state planning strategies. In 1969, the Council of State Governments (CSG) published the report *State Planning and Federal Grants*. It reflected and reinforced the twin themes of state planning implementation when it stated:

The degree of gubernatorial response and commitment to comprehensive planning is evidence that governors fully recognize the implications of the comprehensive planning program and the singular opportunity it represents for unifying and leading the multiple programs and diverse energies of the state government. The governors realize that such planning provides a unique opportunity to effect dramatic improvements in governmental coordination and intergovernmental cooperation. The states have responded with the institutional capabilities and policy priorities essential for success. If state planning is to avoid yet another false start, the federal government must give equal priority and commitment to the opportunity which comprehensive state planning represents for both the challenge and resolution of difficult intergovernmental responsibilities. If coordination is to be achieved, there must be some federal-state sharing of purposes and higher objectives; some sharing of both resources and authority.[4]

In addition to increased administrative authority granted to governors in federal-aid programs, executive authority was enhanced during the 1960s through a variety of state reorganizations. Invariably, the results of state reorganization was increased executive authority through appointments, span of control, and administrative consolidation. Often the stimulus to state planning was the need to respond to a rapidly changing federal system with structural changes occurring at all levels simultaneously. Effective implementation centered on rationalizing administrative systems and intergovernmental relations.

Governors rarely chose as their state planner a person trained in the traditional local comprehensive planning mode. Only a few states adopted a state planning approach resembling local planning at a larger scale. State planners were most often politically sensitive economists, public administrators, lawyers, and the like. The traditional implementation tools of taxing and spending (capital program), regulation (zoning), and eminent domain (public works) were not the central grist for state planning. While physical planning had some relevance in the late 1960s and early 1970s as related to initiatives in land use and environmental programs, physical planning was secondary to the tools of administration, budgeting, intergovernmental negotiation, and policy development.

The first meeting of state planners as a group was held informally at a conference of the American Society of Planning Officials (ASPO) in Toronto in 1964. For a time, the American Institute of Planners (AIP) provided some secretariat support to the group. However, the state planning directors, acting on their own, held a meeting in Lexington, Kentucky, in 1967 to establish the Council of State Planning Agencies (CSPA). The meeting, by invitation only,

Figure 4–1   State planning implementation is dominated
by the executive authority of the governors.

established ground rules for the future. CSPA would move to be affiliated with the Council of State Governments, to be closely associated with the Governors' Conference which received secretariat services from CSG, and to achieve parity with the National Association of State Budget Officers. This was accomplished at the Governors' Conference annual meeting in 1968 at Cincinnati. CSPA also decided that it would not relate to any professional association such as ASPO or AIP, but would be instead an organization of the chief state planner in each state as designated by that state's governor. Community affairs agencies were typically dominated by personnel with local planning backgrounds and were excluded explicitly from the ranks of CSPA unless designated by the governor. The result of these actions was to reinforce the concept of state planning as an activity of the executive function.

The Carnegie-funded Institute on State Programming for the 1970s centered on the potentials of state planning as an executive tool. The Institute was headed by Jack Campbell, former Governor of New Mexico, and advised by some of the most activist governors of the 1960s. In 1967, the staff of the Institute collectively visited all 50 states, interviewing governors, department heads, legislators, and a variety of other state government officials. Francis H. Parker, a staff member, reflected the dominant view:

Finally we see the possibilities for a small staff working directly with the Governor, performing the largely innovative function of looking at major policy areas from his point of view, with an eye to changes and proposals which he, as chief executive, can advocate and then implement within the organization over which he tenuously presides. His real power is the power to innovate, to call attention to, and to legitimize new areas of concern, and to the extent that he is interested in doing so he should have planning capability to investigate the complexities of major problem areas. His planning staff would essentially cut across the program orientation of the different functional planning groups, and would seek to focus the impact of all program areas on certain sub populations of the state, either social or geographic. His planning staff would probably be the smallest and the least permanent of any of the elements of our system.[5]

The 1970s continued the basic themes in state planning. Executive authority continued to increase through both reorganization and federal program guidelines. The federal system continued to strain under both expanded programmatic funding pressures for response at both the state and local levels. This called for creative and innovative solutions which could be provided by loosely structured, responsive state planning staffs serving the governors. The tools and techniques for implementing state planning were tied integrally with those available to the offices of the governors. From time to time, lip service was given to the role of legislatures in state planning, but while some serious attempts were made to institutionalize the process in Florida, Hawaii, Minnesota, and Vermont, legislative-executive integrated state planning has never been achieved in any state.

A wide range of subthemes have been used to implement a state planning system and the goals of the planning process. Administration of local planning assistance and coordination of state-local relations has been a persistent function of state planning agencies in many states. Basic demographic and economic data used by all state agencies have often been considered an important technique for coordination. Combining state planning with budgeting in a single agency has been used as a technique for more effective implementation. Often, this was combined with the latest budgeting approach with planning taking the lead in directing program budgeting (PPBS), zero-based budgeting, or similar techniques of the time. Futures, growth policy, and land-use planning have been combined with the above techniques as a means for effective state planning implementation. Geographic approaches have been easily understood as a means of planning implementation, and substate and multistate regional approaches have been largely directed by state planning agencies as a tool of implementation. This is less the result of theory than the fact that these jurisdictions are within the province of the governor and federal program requirements.

Most of these tools have fallen under the rubric of policy planning implementation or, stated another way, techniques for implementing executive authority. As we begin the 1980s, the current phrase is "strategic planning." Strategic planning was first used in the private sector and is considered more acceptable than policy planning due to a shifting public rhetoric. In effect, however, it is the same. Techniques for implementing state plans are synonymous with the techniques of governors to fulfill their responsibilities. From time to time, state planning solutions are ratified by legislatures and become the tools of state government as a whole.

Consequently, the techniques for implementing state plans and the planning process are largely synonymous with administrative and executive leadership techniques in state government. At the state level, this makes planning more closely aligned with the rapidly changing field of public administration than it does with local physical planning. Implementing powers are less the province of constitutional authority than they are of the political and leadership prerogatives of the governors. While governors vary widely in their styles of leadership and their interest in change, the tools available to them are largely identifiable. These are the techniques which comprise the core of implementing opportunity for state planning.

Finally, while the state planning function has become institutionalized within the executive branch of the states over the past two decades, its purposes and objectives have shifted over time with changing political climates. Implementing techniques have shifted accordingly. Writing in 1976, Leonard Wilson, a long-time state planning participant and keen observer, set the contemporary stage:

The current economic situation and political climate portend an era of imposed financial restraint that will force States to be rigorous in program selection and management. The need to set priorities will require a careful reconsideration of goals and purposes. To be efficient and effective, States will have to improve their planning and coordination processes. In particular, the ability to anticipate and prepare responses to future possible events, and the ability to evaluate future consequences of current events, programs, and policies, will have to be developed to a much higher degree of sophistication than is now common in the states.[6]

Executive leadership

Newly elected Montana Gov. Ted Schwinden (D) in January called for reductions in executive spending and employment and major executive branch reorganization, including establishment of a Department of Commerce. He urged repeal of the income tax surcharge for Montanans earning less than $20,000 and a uniform motor vehicle licensing system. The governor also proposed a comprehensive water development program.

State Government News
April, 1981

The offices of the governors provide the most visible platform from which to define and articulate issues and initiate solutions. The governors represent a majority of the electorate and are endowed with authority to direct most of the actions of state government. Consequently, an effective governor is listened to as an authoritative observer of trends and issues, he is watched by an articulate press, and he is expected to initiate change by the legislatures. The cumulative power of this executive leadership is considerable.

Gubernatorial messages

The governor has several formal responsibilities to interpret the status and needs of state government to the legislature. Typically, governors routinely present a "State of the State" and a "Budget" message at the opening of a legislative session. These constitute an interpretation of the condition of state government from the executive branch to the legislative branch of the government and are attended as formal occasions of state. The skill with which the governor can perform this duty frequently determines the shape and substance of subsequent legislative debate and deliberation.

Preparation of formal messages to the legislatures often involves the entire executive branch leadership. Current and future issues must be identified, program needs must be evaluated, revenues and expenditures for all programs must be considered, and priorities must be determined. Since much of the message will be translated into a legislative program, views of the legislators, citizen interests, and possible opponents must be evaluated. Consequently, the governor must motivate the entire executive branch to define, shape, and articulate the needs of the state. His role in this enterprise is much more than a passive spokesman.

Once the material has been gathered and the choices made clear, it is the governor and his immediate staff who must make the final decisions. The governor himself must imprint his own values on the final product since he publicly commits himself to a course of action with political consequences for his and the state's future. His style of conciliation or conflict, challenge or support, vision or response, are all imprinted on the interpretation and program he presents. He will seek to sound like and be a leader.

As your Governor, I intend to offer active leadership for the next four years. I will devote all my efforts and energies to the Governor's Office. As the top elected officer in the State, I feel it is my duty to work closely with you to achieve the goals of the people of Texas.

State of the State Address
Governor William P. Clements, Jr.
January 23, 1979

He will seek to establish the ground rules for action programs in coming years.

The state of our State is good. The budget I have recommended is balanced. It proposes that we increase spending next year by only 2 percent from all funds, well within our nation's anti-inflation guidelines, and 7.3 percent in the general funds, below the rate of inflation.

Even with the addition of the increases I recommended in road fund resources . . ., vital to the economic and social life of the State, spending will be within presidential guidelines. Clearly, we in Illinois are *practicing* what the nation *preaches*—fiscal conservativism, balanced budgets, economic growth and containment of the cost and size of government. I pledge to you my co-operation to extend those goals in the next year. I ask your help in achieving them.

> State of the State/Budget Message
> Governor James R. Thompson
> March 7, 1979

Most state of the state and budget messages take on a standard form. The state of the state is a formal speech and reflects the constraints of that format. They include an interpretation of trends, recommend an action program, and most often reflect contemporary attitudes toward politics and government. From time to time, however, there are departures from tradition. One of the most innovative departures was Governor Daniel J. Evans's 1976 "Report to the Stockholders of the State of Washington." It is instructive both as an example of form and as a reflection by a three-term governor on the problems of communicating the special issues of state government leadership. He began:

Why don't you run government more like a business? In the past 11 years I have heard that question more than any other. Of course, people never specify whether we should run government like Boeing or Weyerhaeuser, or like Penn Central or Lockheed. The following report will enable you—the stockholders of Washington State government—to decide just how well your state government performs.

First, let's examine the organizational structure of state government. More than 25 department heads report to the Governor, not but choice by by statute. Few corporations, even of major size, have that many who report directly to a chief executive officer . . .

Next, let's compare the budget of the State of Washington with that of a major corporation. We deal with 245 appropriated funds and more than 120 additional non-appropriated funds ranking in size from the state general fund of $4 billion to some with as little as $13.95.

The options of the chief executive officer or the board of directors (the legislature) of a governmental corporation are not quite as unlimited as they are for most businesses. When sales (revenues) go down, the state can't always cut the product line to fit. In fact, when sales go down it is not because the state can't sell its product. Rather, government often is confronted with the unhappy prospect of revenues decreasing during a period of economic downturn while at the same time products, the services of state government, are under immense pressure. The pressure comes in the form of increased demand for public assistance unemployment compensation, and for education . . .[6]

The press

Exposure in the press provides another forum for the governor in articulating issues and shaping approaches to solutions. The press conference, while treated differently by individual governors, is a standard means for communicating to the public and shaping the dimensions of state government problems. In 1974, the National Governors' Conference prepared a handbook for new governors entitled "The Critical Hundred Days." It warned:

You must realize that your relationship with the press changes the minute you become Governor-elect. You are no longer a candidate in quest of office; you are now the person who will be running the state administration. The press will be looking for clues as to your goals and programs and your stand on various issues. Consequently, you must prepare for press conferences, especially those early in your tenure—they are very critical to your image as governor.

Some Governors try to maintain a schedule of periodic press conferences regardless of whether particular announcements need to be made. Others hold press conferences only when they feel the need to make a statement on some issue.[7]

Policy development and management

The governor, as the executive branch leader, must articulate within his administration an approach to policy development and management. Most emerging problems are highly interdependent and do not yield to narrowly focused programs or traditional units of management. Energy, economic development, and community affairs are examples of problem areas which require coordinated strategies among agencies and levels of government.

The academic community has sought to teach programs in "the policy sciences." However, it is generally agreed that "policy development" includes the full range of analytical techniques and strategies for innovation which have been developed by the management professions, including business, public administration, and planning. Policy development is less a science than the application of management techniques by executive leadership.

Within the executive branch, only the Governor wields sufficient authority to command the attention of major department heads, to create a common agenda, to overlay programmatic thinking with emphasis on strategy. Thus policy development is identified by Governors, and sometimes by the legislature, as a responsibility of the central planning office.[8]

Executive orders are the formal mandates from the governor to direct administrative agencies of the state on common agenda or strategy. They are used primarily to announce a policy or to implement a program. How extensively a governor uses executive orders varies among states depending on tradition, the political situation, relationship between the governor and the legislature, and the governor's personal management style. As state executives have become stronger and more management conscious, use of executive orders has increased.

While executive orders do not carry the force of legislative action, they do have force to guide administrative action. Often they are used in areas where jurisdiction is unclear and multiple agencies must act in a coordinated manner. An example of this was the creation by executive order in most states of standard planning regions or districts for substate planning. The substate regions were designated by the governors as a framework for regional planning, technical assistance to local government, coordination of federal grants-in-aid, and regional clearinghouses. Consequently, these executive orders affected not only state actions, but those of federal and local governments.

State planning as staff assistance to the governor

No governor can fulfill the responsibility of spokesman for state government without substantial staff assistance. State of the state and budget messages require complex policy development and administrative decision. All of these require staff attuned to the governor's needs, priorities, and strategies.

At least 37 state planning agencies are located in the governor's office. Three out of four state planning directors are directly responsible to the governor. The role of staff assistant depends in large measure upon the personal relationship of the assistant to the governor and on the governor's confidence on him or her. Consequently, formal planning systems and techniques are secondary in state planning's influence on executive leadership and the governor's role as spokes-person for state government.

Lynn Muchmore, a former planning director in two states and presently the budget director of a third, developed a checklist for state planning agencies relating to effective staff assistance to the governor.[9] The checklist is a test of the activities of state planning agencies in their linkage with the power of executive leadership. In effect, it is a measure of potential influence for implementing state plans.

State planning personnel are regular participants in gubernatorial staff meetings.
The Governor frequently refers pending policy decisions to the state planning agency for in-depth analysis of alternatives and for recommendation.
The state planning director is expected to initiate new or innovative policies that, in his judgement, will serve the public interest, and is assured that his proposals will receive serious consideration by the Governor.
The state planning agency is often called upon to furnish draft material or information for use in gubernatorial speeches.
The planning director or his subordinates frequently discuss gubernatorial priorities and objectives with line-agency managers.
State planning personnel often represent the Governor in meetings with state agencies, local governments, or federal officials.
State planning personnel frequently promote, explain or defend gubernatorial policy before the public, the press or legislative committees.
The state planning agency consciously assumes an "early warning" responsibility in order to advise the Governor of potential developments that may require gubernatorial action.
The planning director or his subordinates frequently act as third parties to resolve conflicts among state agencies, between state government and citizens, or between the federal government and the state agencies before they require gubernatorial attention.
In the event of "crises" requiring gubernatorial response, the state planning agency is expected to supply information, short-term analysis and alternative solutions.

Executive appointment[10]

One of the first and most important jobs of the newly elected Governor is the selection of the staff that will make or break his administration.

The Critical Hundred Days: A Hand-
book for New Governors

The appointment power of the governors is considered to be one of his most significant opportunities for directing state government programs and policies. This power was weak or nonexistent for nineteenth-century governors, but successive reorganizations of state governments in this century have increasingly rationalized the structure of state agencies and centralized appointment authority in the hands of the governor. Nevertheless, the governors make fewer than one-half of all appointments, and all but one-third of those must be confirmed by some other board or institution.

A seeming contradiction of this has been the growth of the civil service which has eliminated much lower-level patronage. The civil service has encouraged the professinalization of career administrators. Most contemporary governors have supported this trend since it does not interfere with top-level appointments and reduces the pressures for petty nepotism.

Governors differ greatly in their approach to appointments and the power they wish to exercise personally. The *Handbook for New Governors* spells out the basic strategic choices:

At one extreme are those who in many circumstances would just as soon avoid power and the responsibility that goes with it. Such individuals tend to favor administrative arrangements such as independent boards and commissions to handle various hot subjects and are not afraid to have subordinates with their own political base and a long-standing reputation in office. Such cabinet officers provide the Governor with less effective control over the activities of the department but with corresponding shifts in public and legislative accountability from the Governor to the cabinet officer. The Governor cannot, of course, avoid some ultimate responsibility for the department, but can dilute that responsibility substantially. On the other hand, a Governor seeking to maximize his power and influence in a department will make sure that cabinet officers are "fireable," which generally suggests avoiding appointing people who could not be fired without offending a major special interest group or faction of the Governor's political party.[11]

Thad Beyle, the foremost academic authority on governors and former research director of the National Governors' Association, conducted interviews with 15 former governors on their views in seeking appointees. While the governors differed slightly in emphasis, a strong set of criteria emerged as follows:

1. Management and administrative skills.
2. Experience, expertise, and competence in the field of their charge.
3. Basic commitment to the administration and its policy direction.

Beyle continued, "In addition, the governors looked for a variety of other qualities, of which two groups stand out. One was intelligence, common sense, and good judgment. Exxon wanted people who 'could think,' Holshouser sought 'common sense,' Lee recruited 'bright' staffers, and Wollman looked for persons with 'just plain intelligence.' The other set of qualities was sensitivity to people, compassion, and a sense of fairness especially in the human services areas. Askew made 'empathy to people and constituencies' a standard, and Dukakis watched for 'sensitivity to people and constituencies.' All in all, the governors looked for administratively skilled persons with intelligence, flexibility, understanding of human needs and foibles, and the willingness to follow the governor's overall policy direction."

To the extent that the incoming governor may have a plan, the appointment power can be a technique for implementation. The appointees establish a context within which state planning must be exercised. However, rarely does a governor have a plan beyond his own special objectives. The state planner, as an appointee himself, is part of the governor's team and, in most cases, is in a position to work effectively with the special set of individuals who will be responsible for the shaping of policy and its implementation.

Executive reorganization

State governments vary widely in their basic organization. While the trend over the past two decades has been toward consolidation of functions into eight to fifteen cabinet agencies, many states retain highly fragmented structures. Consolidation has been in progress since 1965 when Michigan inaugurated the modern wave of state reorganizations, but much state government remains compartmentalized. Constitutional problems in many states prevent full reorganization without constitutional revision, with the result that hybrid structures are common. In these states, control of some agencies is in the hands of elected constitutional officers other than the governor, commonly the attorney general, but also, variously, the secretary of state, the commissioner of education, the commissioner of agriculture, and others. Policy control of some agencies remains in the hands of boards and commissions which in many instances are dominated by appointees of predecessor governors.[12]

Twenty-two states have undergone major reorganization since 1965, while most other states have reorganized one or more departments. Reorganization has been a response to pressures on the states to rationalize functional responsibilities, to create clearer lines of authority, and to increase accountability.

Reorganization has generally strengthened the governor's authority and responsibility, but not universally. Governors have increased their control over human services and development agencies. They have also gained increased control over the administrative services component of state government. Control over police and safety functions has been reduced, as has power over regulatory agencies. Governors have increased control over managerial functions, generally, through reorganization.[13]

Reorganization has been a tool to strengthen executive management. In general, states have moved toward creation of cabinet type administrative departments headed by a cabinet secretary directly appointed by the governor and responsible to the governor. The cabinet style, or super-agency form, has been designed to combine in one department all related programs and agencies and to reduce or eliminate the number of multiheaded boards and commissions with administrative responsibilities.

New Mexico's reorganization in 1977 is typical of the general pattern. The governor formed an executive cabinet by executive order. Then, the New Mexico legislature formally adopted the changes which combined 117 agencies, 176 boards, commissions, and committees, and 102 other governmental entities into 12 cabinet level departments.[14]

Individual agencies or groups of related agencies have also been combined or reorganized in many states. Twenty-six states have created comprehensive human services agencies combining programs such as public assistance and social services, health, mental health, mental retardation, corrections, vocational rehabilitation, employment security, and manpower training. Thirty-seven states have created departments of transportation. The purpose of these combinations is to strengthen administrative coordination in program implementation and to achieve organizational efficiencies. One result has been to enhance the governor's role in policy analysis, planning, and implementation.[15]

Planning agencies within the organization of states vary according to purpose, emphasis, and tradition. Considerable shifts in organizational location have occurred over the past 10 years depending upon the governor's needs and use of the planning function. Robert Wise, staff director of the Council of State Planning Agencies, points out that there are three basic forms of state planning organization. They are: (1) state planning, community affairs, and budget in separate agencies; (2) state planning and community affairs together and budget separate; and (3) budget and planning in the same agency and community affairs apart. Most states use some modification of one of these forms.

Where there is a clear organizational distinction between the three functions, state planning is usually in the governor's office, budget in a department of finance, and most community affairs activities in a separate agency. Where state planning and community affairs are combined, state planning is either a separate department or in the governor's office. Community affairs then becomes a division of the state planning office. The association of planning with budgeting usually occurs within a department of administration, office of planning and budget, or office of policy and management. In 1975, seven states were organized with planning and budgeting related structurally. By 1978, 19 states had moved to this approach, although with many variations on the general theme.[16]

A less formal organizational technique, task force, is often used to focus attention on special problems overlapping existing structures. Task forces are most often created to bring together government officials, citizens, and private sector experts to recommend solutions to planning issues. Task forces are also used to implement recommended solutions. Management task forces have recently been utilized by a number of states to promote efficient and effective government administration and management. Occasionally, task forces become permanently institutionalized as ongoing state programs, such as the case with the productivity commission in North Carolina and the Hawaii Institute for Management and Analysis in Government.[17]

Legislation and the legislature

Legislative reform and strengthened staff support have gone hand in hand with executive reform via reorganization and increased appointment power. Both branches have increased their powers and management capacities generally and necessarily.

While state planning is most closely associated with the executive branch, it can also serve as a valuable aid to the legislature. State legislatures deal with an enormous range of complex issues, usually on a limited time schedule and with little staff assistance. State planning can assist in (1) providing information and problem analysis; (2) presentations at public hearings; (3) staff reports for task forces and special commissions; (4) drafting and reviewing proposed legislation; (5) program review and evaluation; and (6) identifying potential long-range consequences of proposed actions.[18]

The state planning agency in Minnesota has enjoyed a close working relationship with its legislature and is frequently turned to for special studies. The Minnesota Legislature joined with the state planning agency and the Commission on Minnesota's Future in sponsoring a unique three-day legislative symposium, Minnesota Horizons. The seminar provided the opportunity for the legislators to participate in an extensive review of the significant issues confronting the state and how these issues could be addressed. Members of the Commission, citizen experts, and members of the state planning staff briefed the legislature on the status of the state—people, economy, and natural and man-made environments—and examined important trends and developments that could be expected to influence the future of the state.[19] The entire proceedings were made available to the state on public television.

The Florida Legislature provided a major planning initiative when it created the state land-use program following the consequences of drought. Within a few years, the Speaker of the House of Representatives took the lead in consideration and passage of a concurrent resolution on growth policy for the state and in convincing the legislature to make growth policy its priority issue and evaluate other programs in light of this policy. The legislators issued policy statements on issues ranging from "quality of life" to "local responsibility" to "sound economy."[20] The legislative directives on growth policy served as a guide for legislative and state and local action.

Hawaii instituted state planning with statehood in 1959. Consequently, Hawaii has not had to overcome former traditions in establishing a planning program as an integral part of state management. This, coupled with the constraints of an island environment, has provided the setting for a sophisticated planning process. The legislature has provided strong support for planning and has involved itself in significant planning decisions. After extensive deliberation and debate, the legislature adopted the Hawaii State Plan in 1978. In his introduction to the Plan, Governor Ariyoshi wrote:

The passage of The Hawaii State Plan . . . [was a] significant [event] in Hawaii's history. Hawaii by these actions became the first State in the Nation to enact a comprehensive State plan setting forth goals, objectives, and policies to guide it into the future. I consider this new law . . . second in importance only to our State Constitution.[21]

Under Vermont's land-use program, its legislature was to adopt a plan and implementation policies. However, its legislature could not agree on its provisions and failed to act positively on the plan. Few other attempts have been made at the state level to have comprehensive plans adopted by the legislative body as is done routinely by local governments.

As federal grants became more pervasive in the late 1960s and 1970s, legislatures moved to reduce the governor's sole discretion in their use. They expanded their review of federal program use and increasingly required that federal funds be appropriated in the legislative budget process. Specialized legislative staffs were expanded to enhance the capacities of legislatures for research and policy analysis, expanded review of federal funds coming into the states, enlarged budget review of administrative regulations, and expanded use of sunset legislation.

As budgets have become more complex, intergovernmental transfers more important, and political pressures for fiscal restraint more powerful, legislatures have moved toward computerized fiscal information systems in such states as Colorado, Florida, Michigan, and Washington. These systems provide an enhanced legislative ability to track the budget through the decision process, provide better identification of policy choices for legislators, and establish more effective review of expenditures after legislative budget decisions have been made. Fiscal information systems also allow more legislators to participate with greater knowledge in fiscal policy decisions, thus diluting the long-held concentration of power in budget and appropriations committees.

Budget and taxes

Logically, everything ought to come first.

Jean-Jacques Rousseau

States operate under annual or biennial budgets which are important and powerful policy instruments. The budgeting process itself is a significant tool for defining and evaluation alternatives. A budget helps develop and implement policy by:

Stating and defending the governor's programs and policy

Providing an operating framework for determining productivity

Measuring programs with costs

Providing for accountability.

The relationship of planning to budgeting has been a major concern to the states for at least the past 15 years. Most states have attempted to more closely link planning and budgeting staffs and, in many cases, have joined them in the same management or administrative agency.

Planning and budget formats

A series of budgetary reforms swept the states during the past 15 years challenging the traditional line item budget which utilizes categories such as salaries, supplies, and travel as budget items. The first of these reforms was program and performance budgets; then planning, programming, and budget systems (PPBS); and most recently zero-based budgeting (ZBB). No reform has fulfilled the expectations of its proponents, but all have contributed to an increased emphasis within the budgetary process on program analysis, long-term planning, and the application of a policy approach to budget decisions.

Program budgeting is a format for evaluating state expenditures in terms of programmatic objectives. The process usually begins with the governor issuing general policy guidelines containing broad goals and objectives. Agencies then prepare program plans that outline, usually under a multiyear perspective, the missions of each program or subprogram unit within their jurisdiciton, describe the activities or the agency as they reflect a commitment to the mission, and relate the resource needs of the agency to levels of expected performance.

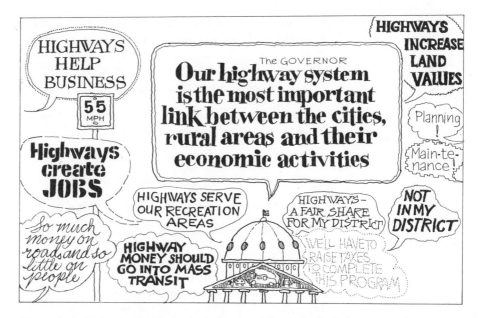

Figure 4–2 State planning is dominated by executive authority, but responses to gubernatorial decisions reflect local diversity.

Program plans and agency requests are then reviewed by the central budget staff, and the governor's budget document is prepared to reflect estimated revenues and the governor's priorities.[22]

PPBS was the major budgetary reform format of the 1960s. It shares some similarities with program budgeting. It is a process which emphasized output of government expenditures. The process includes collection and analysis of data pertaining to the operations and activities of each state agency in categories which represent the agency's purposes and identification and comparison of alternative objectives and alternative methods to pursue those objectives. The process is intended to formulate the information needed to facilitate budget decisions.

Zero-based budgeting was the innovative budgetary technique of the 1970s. It employs techniques developed in the private sector by Texas Instruments. These include "decision packages" and "priority ranking." Because ZBB tends to be time-consuming and assumes more flexibility than exists in the public sector, many states have modified ZBB to reflect political and administrative realities. ZBB was first introduced at the state level by Governor Jimmy Carter of Georgia and has been tried by approximately a dozen states.[23] The theory of zero-based budgeting is that every program, every budgetary item, must be fully justified each year. It attempts to replace the attitude of "incrementalism" which accepts continuation of a given level of program expenditures and concerns itself with proposed new expenditures. Under the incremental approach, almost all agency budgets grow and programs are rarely, if ever, eliminated for budgetary reasons.

After a period of relative high growth in revenues and expenditures, states are facing major cuts in revenue. In a time of budgetary constraints, the budgetary planning and decision making process looms increasingly important. Planning for slow growth or reduction in government services through the budget process will continue for some time to be an important function of the state planning process.

All three of the above formats are designed to link more closely planning with budgeting. Whatever the budget format, states are utilizing the following techniques to implement planning goals through the budget process:

Assist in developing annual or biennial program plans for each line agency.

Evaluate program plans in relation to the governor's policies.

Utilize program plans to justify budget requests, negotiative changes when conflicts arise, and evaluate agency programs.

Provide technical assistance to line agencies.

Identify potential future long-range problems and issues.

Prepare estimates of future resources or revenues.[24]

Legislatures vary considerably to the extent that they examine and modify the executive budget. Legislative fiscal offices have been strengthened in recent years, and sophisticated computer systems have been installed for budget tracking. California's legislature has its own budget staff and legislative planning program which exercises considerable independence in budget review. In most states, however, the final approved budget closely reflects the policy and direction of the governor.

Capital programs

Planning the location, scale, and timing of major state capital projects is a significant state activity. Traditionally, capital improvement planning has been carried out by programmatic agencies. Some states have undertaken long-range capital investment planning for both fiscal management and growth management purposes. Comprehensive capital investment planning can be a means to reduce duplication, overlap, and conflict among programs. It can help determine effective utilization of state financial resources to compare the state's needs for such disparate facilities as college dormitories, state office buildings, park facilities, prisons, highways, or assistance to local capital projects. Capital investment planning is often viewed as a way to guide state growth patterns and minimize adverse environmental and social impacts of state development.

Preparation of five-year capital improvement programs and an annual capital budget are major responsibilities of the Maryland and Hawaii state planning agencies. The five-year plan classifies projects by need, recommends a time sequence for construction, and estimates the cost of each project and its potential impact on operations and maintenance. Current projects are evaluated in depth and, if recommended, are scheduled in the annual capital budget. The planning agencies are actively involved in preparation and distribution of detailed instructions and project submittal forms, application of space criteria, departmental hearings, and evaluation of program and facility need in coordination with other state agencies and institutions.[25]

Those states with capital investment programs often experience conflict between planning and budget officers which must be dealt with, because, as one participant has noted:

an effective capital investment planning program requires a smooth working relationship between the budget office and the planning office. In particular, it requires a mutual understanding as to the separate responsibilities of the two organizations, an appreciation of the two perspectives that each will contribute and a settled procedure for resolving inevitable disputes.[26]

The governor pays attention to planning Together, in partnership, this government will work with labor and industry to plan rationally and creatively, to look beyond the political moment to the projects that will mean to New York's future what Roebling's bridge across the East River and Governor Clinton's canal meant to the whole state.

This idea of partnership is particularly important. It is simply no longer practical to pretend that our work can be neatly divided into public and private sectors, that the one can ignore the other, cooperating only when we are faced with the collapse of our bridges or the bankruptcy of agencies and industries, that we can afford to have government by itself, business with itself, labor of itself.

Because this partnership is a prerequisite to any lasting succes, I will create a State Council of Economic and Fiscal Priorities composed of leaders from business, leaders from labor, leaders from local government and leaders from our universities, to help the state define a long-range, coherent economic strategy.

The council will be asked immediately to prepare a five-year capital plan, covering all capital financing and construction, in which the state and all of its authorities will engage. The Assembly initiated and the Comptroller and the Senate have already reviewed this concept.

Together, then, I think that for the first time in our history we will be able to put in place a clear and distinct capital budget that will replace what we have now, which is nothing more than a jumble of plans and financing.

Source: Excerpted from an address by Governor Mario Cuomo to the New York State Assembly on January 5, 1983.

Conflict resolution

Conflict resolution and various techniques of negotiation have become standard tools for both planning and budget agencies seeking to implement executive policy among state agencies. Conflict resolution is a technique for obtaining agency conformance with policy and/or redefining state policy. Even when goals, policies, and priorities have been properly coordinated among the governor's office and agency heads, case-by-case conflicts will occur within and among agencies. Conflicts within agencies routinely are handled by department heads. In other situations in which conflicts arise to the gubernatorial level, the approach taken is to have meetings, decision papers, etc., with the governor and/or key staff members to resolve issues, to create greater sensitivity among department heads to each agency's needs and purposes, and to "lock in" the new or refined policy.[27]

Program evaluation

Evelution of program performance is an increasingly important component of the planning and budget process. Program operations are being periodically reviewed to see if they are fiscally sound and consistent with program objectives. The evolving concept of evaluation is identified by various names. In some states it is called executive evaluation, while in others it is known as program review, performance auditing, effectiveness auditing, and legislative oversight. Despite the different labels and approaches, the objective is clearly to determine the effectiveness and impact of state programs. This type of evaluation appears to differ from past efforts in that (1) it focuses on programs, not organizational units; (2) it emphasizes not only resource application, but also efficiency and program achievement; and (3) it is based on more intensive data collection and analysis.[28]

Management objectives and impact indicators are thus playing an increasingly important role in program evaluation. Evaluation is being closely linked to planning, and such states as Wisconsin, Washington, and South Dakota have added an evaluation phase to their program budget process.

Legislatures are also expanding their use of program evaluation and performance audits. The Massachusetts Legislature created the Joint Committee on Post Audit and Oversight which reviews reports of the state auditor and legislative auditor and presents its findings and recommendations to the legislature. The Connecticut Program Review Committee established procedures for monthly meetings, for selecting review topics, for developing liaison with target agencies, for developing issues, and for making preliminary investigations. A number of states have adopted "sunset" laws for comprehensive agency reviews on a periodic basis.[29]

State plans

Functional plans and program planning

A wide variety of functional or program plan documents is prepared by states each year. These plans vary in scope and content. Additionally, the utility and effectiveness of these plans varies considerably from state to state and from program area to program area. Many state functional plans, such as health, criminal justice, or water and sewer, are developed in response to federal mandates or as a precondition to receiving federal aid. A number of states, however, do have their own program planning programs which reflect internally perceived needs. These states attempt to use program planning to help facilitate state policy formulation and implementation by raising issues, identifying problems, and evaluating alternative strategies of action.

States differ in how they define the relationship between functional planning and overall policy planning and coordination. A few states such as Maine and Florida prepare comprehensive plans which serve as an overall framework for coordinating all state planning activities. Similarly, such states as Hawaii, Oregon, and Vermont use growth management planning as an overall structure to which other more specific economic and social planning relates. In other states, for example, Kentucky, economic development planning is the overall planning framework for specific functional planning efforts. In states such as Maryland, Minnesota, and Utah, which view state planning primarily as part of an executive management system, an emphasis is placed on the administrative capacity to coordinate individual planning programs.[30]

The comprehensive plan

State comprehensive plans represent an attempt to apply the principles of local comprehensive planning at the state level. The magnitude and dynamics of state activities make it extremely difficult to attain truly comprehensive plans. Comprehensive plans have been criticized for taking too long to prepare, for being too difficult to relate to current decision making, and for being too soon out of date. Yet several states undertake preparation of a comprehensive plan. Maine, for example, has a statutory requirement for a state comprehensive plan.

The basic goal of a state comprehensive plan is to formulate a document that defines state policies and provides guidelines for functional planning, program coordination, and resource allocation. The goal of total comprehensiveness that encompasses all the major facets of state government has proven illusive to most states, but comprehensive planning remains as a testament to the desirability of an articulated overall policy framework.[31]

Land use plans

States which have pioneered in state land-use planning have done so in reaction to the threat or actuality of major adverse environmental and economic impacts from rapid growth, growth that local government was unable or unwilling to regulate. Potential or immediate disaster has usually provided the catalyst for the coalescence of interests including farmers, environmentalists, resource and tourist-based activities, and outdoor sportsmen who have pushed for managed development of resources and land.

In the absence of a unifying "crisis," state land-use planning has tended to produce strong political antagonism. Opponents arguing that state land-use planning infringes on local values and property rights have kept many states from undertaking an explicit land-use planning program. Almost every state government activity from program implementation to business regulation to taxation affects the use of land within a state.[32]

Since 1977 recipients of 701 Housing and Urban Development planning funding have been required to include a land-use element including (1) criteria and procedures necessary for guiding major growth decisions and (2) general plans with respect to the pattern and intensity of land use for residential, commercial, and other activities.[33]

Vermont, Florida, Oregon, and Hawaii have developed the most comprehensive state land-use programs involving state agencies, local government, and citizen participation. In other states, critical issues such as wetlands protection, flood plain, or coastal zone management have been the focus of more specialized land-use planning. Almost all states have increased their planning activity related to land use.

The issues of growth policy and management have become a major area of concern in several states. Hawaii's Growth Policies Plan represents one of the most extensive state efforts at growth management. In addition to the basic general plan, there are functional plans, such as open space, recreation, housing, etc., and continuing land-use and economic planning. The growth policies plan includes a detailed analysis of alternatives, a recommended strategy, and implementation actions.[34]

Economic plans

States are becoming increasingly sophisticated in analysis of their economies. Input-output analyses, simulation models, and econometric forecasting are regularly applied techniques. The impact of policy changes and other external factors on market forces is being carefully scrutinized to aid policy makers and administrators in both the public and private sectors. Most states have consolidated a number of programs affecting economic development into a major state cabinet department. Additionally, the U.S. Economic Development Administration's (EDA) 302 program of federal grants to state planning agencies has been supporting expanded economic resource planning.

Economic planning is not new to states, but it has changed emphasis in recent years. All but two states began economic planning programs during the 1930s with the financial assistance and encouragement of the National Resources Planning Board. After the disruption caused by World War II, those states which continued these programs turned mainly to industrial promotion. Tax incentives, locational assistance, and other inducements were offered as states competed for manufacturing and industrial firms. What resource management was done was primarily by the federal government.

The 1970s saw a shift in the issues of economic planning. The concerns of the environmental movement, the energy crisis, depleting natural resources, and awareness of the costs incurred with unplanned or inappropriate economic development have led to new approaches to economic planning which include resource development, environmental protection, and community development. While sharing similar concerns, states vary in their particular approach to economic planning. At least four different broad approaches have been noted: public investment, alternative futures, strategic issues, and, most recently, natural resource management.[35]

Pennsylvania and Massachusetts have demonstrated two variations of public investment planning. The objective of the Pennsylvania program is to determine potential sources of funding for future investment by (1) making projections of future growth potentials, population, income, and social service requirements; (2) matching these with desired expectations; (3) analyzing past investment expenditures; and (4) examining the investment expenditure required to reconcile the difference between the probable and desired future trends. In order to revitalize central cities, Massachusetts has focused on developing a state locational policy which coordinates taxation, regulation, and capital investments.

South Dakota and Hawaii are examples of the alternative futures approach which entails the examination of goals and objectives through the use of alternative future scenarios. Scenarios are developed reflecting different rates of economic growth. Then the impact of each of these scenarios is evaluated usually with extensive involvement of state officials and the public. Finally a program, plan, or strategy is developed to encourage the desired pattern of growth. South Dakota's futures program evaluated three industrial development and two farming scenarios. A series of issues were identified which reflected the possible effects of different 20-year policy projections. Hawaii, after studying four alternative future scenarios varying from continuation of present growth to accelerated growth, designed a program

to encourage selective growth through attempting to moderate and change the past trends and location of growth in order to create a rational development program for achieving economic progress while preserving the unique environmental character of the islands.[36]

The strategic approach aims at identifying those few critical activities which are likely to have a broad impact on the economic condition of the state. The approach involves

the creation of a rather detailed and intricate process design divided into three subprocesses: (1) collecting and organizing existing data and identifying information; (2) reorganizing the accumulated information in order to identify those elements that will principally guide state growth and development; and (3) examining the management structure necessary to carry out the objectives laid out in the strategy design.[37]

Maryland is utilizing a variant of the strategic issues approach to develop an economic development plan through the use of a goals-by-subject-area matrix and an objectives-by-governmental-functions matrix. Major attention has been devoted to issue identification, development, resolution, and implementation in order to promote a set of government activities to encourage economic development.[38]

States are exploring a number of ways to maximize economic activity while using wisely the state's natural resources and integrating overall development objectives with quality of life concerns of the citizens. States such as Hawaii have a comprehensive approach to resource management including active programs in forestry, foodcrops, aquaculture, livestock, and feed grains. Some states, however, have more specialized resource planning such as gasohol in Nebraska, wood energy in Georgia, coal conversion technologies in Kentucky, coal desulfurization in West Virginia, and fishing in Alaska. Because of the state's role in community development, environmental protection, and economic development, it is likely that the role in resource management will continue to expand during the 1980s.

Federal functional planning

Almost all federal grant-in-aid programs require planning as a condition to receiving financial aid. Approximately 80 programs mandate state plans, including employment and training, health, aging, air and water pollution control, and solid waste management. Some planning requirements are for fairly specific categories such as nutrition; others are for rather broad categories such as transportation. The federal requirements have been introduced to provide a means to achieve overall goals and objectives, to provide a measure of federal control, and to relate state and local needs to broad national purposes.

Federal planning requirements have encouraged planning in areas where systematic planning would not likely occur. The federal government has helped to finance and promote the role of state planning in administering programs. Yet there have been problems that have accompanied the growing number of functional plans prepared in response to federal mandates. Federal planning requirements have been haphazardly imposed with little uniformity of format or purpose. Functional planning may absorb large amounts of staff time producing analysis and plans that are not utilized in program implementation. The relationship of the functional planners to the central state planning staff has also caused problems of effective coordination. If functional planning is located in separate agencies, the process often fragments, producing single purpose plans which may be in conflict with other state programs or goals. Locating functional planning in the central agency, however, tends to isolate the planning from line operations, and the plans may not be very useful to program administrators. In an attempt to avoid both these pitfalls, most functional plan preparation is done within the agency or department responsible for program implementation with the state planning office serving to review, coordinate, and provide technical assistance.[39]

Permits, licenses, and other regulations

Administrative rules, regulations, ordinances, and procedures are the means by which many state agencies execute legislative and executive mandates. Regulations add specificity to general principles and policy. They help determine when and in what manner laws are implemented. Utility regulation, insurance, consumer protection, agriculture, business, labor, and occupational licensing are areas of state government where administrative regulation is widely utilized to promote public welfare and other specific policy objectives.

Only in recent years has state planning begun to use the broad regulatory powers of state government, focusing upon land use and environmental controls. State planning took the lead in establishing facility siting procedures now used in more than half the states. These most often pertain to the location of major energy processing and generating plants which use contemporary technology. Their intent is to ameliorate broad-scale impacts on resources and related development. Vermont, Florida, and other states review certain land-use decisions affecting regional development or critical natural areas of concern. Procedures vary from state to state, but they generally establish a process by which a proposed development is evaluated, affected parties are involved, examination of alternative locations is considered, and conditions under which the development may proceed.

The federal government has enticed the states into use of regulatory powers which are not otherwise available to implement national goals, especially in the area of environmental quality. Federal grants-in-aid are often contingent on states acting to impose certain regulations or administrative processes. The middle ground between state and federal regulation is often the threat of federal preemption of state regulatory systems if the states do not perform in a prescribed manner. Surface mining regulations are a current example of this in determining "state primacy."

Media campaigns

Media campaigns are very little used as a technique in state planning. Since most state planning directors are the appointees of the governor, they are dependent on the governor's strategic use of the media. However, several approaches to public education and media use on state planning issues have been used.

Task forces and special commissions are often staffed by state planning agencies. The reports of progress and recommendations of such bodies make good news and provide an opportunity for in-depth coverage of special problems.

Newspaper supplements of state plans have been used in Vermont and a few other states. These can provide statewide information to all citizens on overall policy.

The Washington Alternatives program was an extensive effort to secure citizen input to choices for the future. More than 200 citizens participated in extensive weekend retreats, and polling was used to determine citizen interests. Public television was used to provide background for neighborhood home meetings to consider issues. Finally, the report was used to establish the format for the governor's state of the state message to the legislature.

Intergovernmental relations and technical assistance

Contemporary intergovernmental relations bear little resemblance to the comparatively simple Cooperative Federalism of a generation ago. Dysfunctional Federalism is a better label for today's federal-state-local relations.[40]

As noted above, there has been a close linkage between the growth of state planning and the growth of federal grant-in-aid programs. The chapter on intergovernmental relations explores the history and current trends in this area. However, the federal budget has been radically cut, especially in domestic assistance programs to state and local governments. What these cuts portend for the future of intergovernmental relations and state planning is not yet clear, especially since they come at a time of major institutional changes in the intergovernmental system.

Planning with a community focus

Departments of Economic Development in the 1950s typically created divisions of community affairs to administer local 701 programs for small communities. These divisions were staffed by local planners who provided a variety of "hands-on" assistance to encourage and support local planning efforts. They were the precursors of the contemporary planning and public administration "circuit riders" of today's regional planning districts or state departments of community affairs.

As community affairs activities became more popular in the 1960s, many states created separate departments of community affairs and included newly emerging functions of state planning. In the late 1960s, some of the leading state planning directors closely related to their governors moved to separate themselves from identification with community affairs in order to move more directly into the workings of state governments. Organizationally, however, there are many combinations of community affairs and state planning. Currently, there is a rediscovery of economic development and some return to the organizational form of the 1950s.

Whatever the organizational form, the function of state-local relations is performed in each state for two fundamental objectives:

1. To provide a variety of assistance services directly or through a regional structure, especially to smaller, less well staffed communities;
2. To provide a mechanism for implementing state policies affecting local governments, especially as they relate to growth and development.

Perceptions of the function of state-local relations vary because of the frequent contradiction between the objectives of the two levels of government. Frequently, local officials look to the community affairs agency as an "ombudsman" for local government within the precinct of state government. However, community affairs agencies are often line agencies with little special clout with either their peers or cabinet secretaries. Implementation of state programs at the local level assumes a variety of forms through functional line agencies, and the chief executive is as likely to look at the human services agency for implementing policy as to the community affairs agency.

Joseph Marinich, former executive director of the Council of State Community Affairs Agencies, posed the dilemma in his overview report of 1978:

There is a major question as to whether DCAs in the future will be able to play a strong role in bringing about changes in policies and programs affecting local government form and functions. A review of the experiences of DCAs indicates that the services which DCAs bring into supportive relationships with local governments are essential to the development of the DCAs' credibility as spokespersons and advocates for local concerns. This credibility is threatened when DCAs become strong advocates for changing local practices and local government structures.[41]

Local assistance activities

State planning agencies and departments of community affairs (DCAs) have developed a broad range of local assistance programs despite the frequently shifting ground upon which they must operate. Many of these activities have been strongly encouraged by federal programs and policies, especially those of the U.S. Department of Housing and Urban Development. For example, substate regionalization and its attendant planning assistance activities resulted directly from program actions of HUD and EDA. Nevertheless, by 1978, state appropriations to DCAs had grown to $326,000,000.

State planning and community affairs agencies have greatly accelerated their activities intended to assist local government upgrade quality of service and most effectively coordinate state and local service delivery. In addition to providing technical assistance in planning, these agencies are often heavily involved in administration of both federal and state grant-in-aid programs. Most programs are variations of the state community affairs agency model demonstrated by Paul Ylvasaker in New Jersey during the mid-1960s. It provided a state counterpart to the then recently created HUD. A recent listing of the range of assistance activities includes:

1. Encouraging intergovernmental cooperation.
2. Coordinating certain state services and assistance programs.

3. Assisting localities in obtaining state and federal aid.
4. Economic development planning.
5. Economic development programs such as industrial, tourism, and trade development; economic adjustment; and growth impact assistance.
6. Local planning assistance, both technical and financial.
7. Regional planning coordination.
8. Research, policy analysis, and how-to-do-it manuals.
9. Human services programs such as day care, aging, and community action agency programs.
10. Housing, including planning, research, technical assistance, finance, management, and regulation.
11. Disaster preparedness, e.g., emergency housing.
12. Personnel training and development.
13. Financial management and general management technical assistance.
14. Local government regulation, including audits, bond issuance, and uniform relocation.
15. Home rule and charter-revision technical assistance.
16. Information clearinghouse.
17. Legal advisory services, including model ordinances.[42]

Intergovernmental coordination

Typically, the governor's chief state planner also carries the title of intergovernmental coordinator. This function covers many responsibilities, but basically requires his monitoring of state-local and state-federal relations. The state-federal role usually necessitates continuing contact with federal agencies on behalf of the governor and representation and negotiation of state interests. The continuing dialogue resulting from these contacts provides the opportunity to package federal programs to the state's and the governor's best interests for implementing strategic objectives.

Conclusion

One of the major themes of this chapter is that state planning takes many forms depending largely on the special issues of the individual states, the leadership style of the governors, and the evolution of executive management functions related to planning. State planning has been one of the most dynamic activities of state government in a period of rapid change in the states since 1965. While state planning is largely institutionalized in most states, it is likely to face significant changes in the 1980s as the dimensions of the intergovernmental system shift and as new issues command the attention of state policy makers.

Some dimensions of change can be foreseen. Among these are:

1. While growth of state planning has paralleled growth in intergovernmental funding for nearly 20 years, constrained federal and state resources will cause new emphasis in the state planning process. Governors have become more interested in fiscal restraint than in program development. Consequently, state planning will shift to concerns of productivity, administrative efficiency, and internal accountability.
2. While social programs, urban development, and environmental regulation have been the program focus of state planning, it is now shifting to economic and resource development. Economic development, out of vogue for many years, has now become the measure of executive performance due to national attention on inflation, productivity, and federal budget reduction. Natural resources have assumed an economic importance for the first time since the 1930s due to the attention on

energy and related scarcities and will result in new state program activities in timber, fisheries, agriculture, energy, and other resource opportunities.

3. While state planning has received considerable attention as a new function of state government in the past, its implementing techniques will be increasingly integrated as routine practices throughout state government. Its unique character will be diminished, and its contribution will be less on establishing position than in achieving output objectives tied to executive leadership.

Finally, state planning is likely to continue in the mode forecast by Francis Parker more than 10 years ago:

We see the possibilities for a small staff working directly with the Governor, performing the largely innovative function of looking at major policy areas from his point of view, with an eye to changes and proposals which he, as chief executive, can advocate and then implement within the organization over which he tenuously presides.[43]

1 The Governors' Conference, *Proceedings of the Governors' Conference 1961* (Chicago: The Governors' Conference, 1961), p. 150.

2 The Council of State Governments, *State Planning: A Policy Statement* (Chicago: Council of State Governments, 1962), p. 22.

3 US Department of Housing and Urban Development, *Urban Planning Program Guide: State Comprehensive Planning* (Washington, DC: Department of Housing and Urban Development, 1966), Chap. 5.

4 The Council of State Governments, *State Planning and Federal Grants* (Chicago: Public Administration Service, 1969), p. 72.

5 Francis H. Parker, "Strategy and Effectivenss of Planning in State Government" (unpublished dissertation) (University of North Carolina: Chapel Hill, 1970), p. 226.

6 The Council of State Governments, *A Summary for Governors State Planning New Roles in Hard Times* (Lexington, KY: Council of State Governments, 1976), p. 16.

7 National Governors' Conference, *The Critical Hundred Days–A Handbook for New Governors* (Washington, DC: National Governors' Association, 1974), p. 10.2.

8 Lynn Muchmore, *Evaluation of State Planning* (Washington, DC: The Council of State Planning Agencies, 1977), p. 6 (State Planning Series 3).

9 Ibid., pp. 3–4.

10 See Thad L. Beyle and Robert Dalton, "Appointment Power: Does It Belong to the Governor?" *State Government* 54 (1981), pp. 2–12.

11 *The Critical Hundred Days*, pp. 3.2–3.3.

12 The Council of State Governments, *State Planning: Intergovernmental Policy Coordination* (Lexington, KY: Council of State Governments, 1976), p. 58.

13 Beyle and Dalton, "Appointment Power," pp. 4–6.

14 Judith Nicholson, "State Administrative Organization Activities 1976–1977," *The Book of the States 1978–1979* (Lexington, KY: Council of State Governments 1978), p. 105.

15 Ibid., pp. 108–110.

16 Robert N. Wise, "State Planning," *The Book of the States 1980–1981* (Lexington, KY: Council of State Governments, 1980), pp. 234–236.

17 Nicholson, "State Administrative Organization Activities," p. 114.

18 Muchmore, *Evaluation of State Planning*, pp. 10–11.

19 The Council of State Governments, *State Planning: Intergovernmental Policy Coordination*, pp. 34–35.

20 Ibid., p. 35.

21 1978 Annual Report, Department of Planning and Economic Development, State of Hawaii, 1978, p. 1.

22 The Council of State Governments, *State Planning: Intergovernmental Policy Coordination*, pp. 43–50.

23 Muchmore, *Evaluation of State Planning*, pp. 6–7.

24 Ibid., p. 7.

25 The Council of State Governments, *State Planning: Intergovernmental Policy Coordination*, pp. 50–53.

26 Muchmore, *Evaluation of State Planning*, p. 8.

27 Howard W. Pardue, Jr., unpublished paper, "The Status of State Planning in Florida," delivered at the 1980 Conference of the American Planning Association, October 1980, p. 17.

28 The Council of State Governments, *State Planning: Intergovernmental Policy Coordination*, p. 53.

29 Ibid., pp. 54–55.

30 Ibid., see chap. II.

31 Ibid., pp. 24–26.

32 Ibid., pp. 17–18.

33 Ibid., p. 21.

34 Ibid., pp. 19–22.

35 Robert N. Wise, "State Planning," *The Book of the States* (Lexington, KY: Council of State Governments, 1978), pp. 486–487.

36 The Council of State Governments, *State Planning Intergovernmental Policy Coordination*, p. 23.

37 Ibid., p. 23.

38 Ibid., p. 24.

39 Muchmore, *Evaluation of State Planning*, p. 5.

40 David B. Walker, "Dysfunctional Federalism–The Congress and Intergovernmental Relations," *State Government* 54 (1981), p. 53.

41 Joseph S. Marinich and Frank A. Kirk, "Community Affairs," *The Book of the States 1978–1979* (Lexington, KY: The Council of State Governments, 1978), p. 599.

42 Ibid., p. 595.

43 Francis H. Parker, "Strategy and Effectiveness," p. 226.

5 State planning administration

In Chapter 3, we reviewed the maturing of state planning and the various organizational arrangements undertaken by the states to carry out a state planning function. Initially, the responsibility for state planning in general was frequently assigned to a special state planning board or commission. Later, it was often housed in a line agency, usually a department of commerce or community development. The particular organizational relationship typically reflected the mission of state planning at a specific point in time.

Today, an increasing number of state planning agencies are part of the Governor's office or the executive offices of the Governor. This, too, appears to reflect the current view that the state planning agency is a central resource to assist the incumbent administration in making policy and management decisions as well as in formulating new initiatives.

Chapter 3 concluded with a prognosis for state planning in the 1980s which suggested that state planning agencies will increasingly be used in helping to formulate incumbent administration policy decisions. Under this scenario, most functional planning would be carried out in the state departments and agencies, while the policy context for functional planning will be established by the central state planning agency in the Governor's office. State planning agencies would increasingly make use of the short-term, highly focused strategic planning process developed and used in the private sector. Emphasis would be on establishing a state policy framework, on issue analysis, and on the formulation of options or action alternatives which would form the basis for decisions by the Governor.

The extent to which the state planning agency will be involved in policy formulation will depend entirely on the Governor and his closest aides. During the last 10 years, we have seen the introduction of a new breed of Governors who see their roles as not only political leader of the state but also its chief executive officer. This added dimension, which places the Governor in the lead administrative position within the state, may have been born of necessity as state government has grown more complex and more in need of strong leadership as well as the Governor's personal management of state affairs. To accomplish this task, the Governor must have adequate staff support capable of dealing on a timely basis with virtually any issue that may cross the Governor's desk. With the state planning agency frequently lodged in the executive office in many states, it is not surprising to find these agencies transformed into resource and policy staff for the Governor. Within this context, the state planning agency can apply planning principles to a variety of issues via a strategic planning approach that will help ensure that the day-to-day decisions within state government are in the long-term best interests of the state.

The focus of this chapter is to provide an overview of the activities, organization, and structure of a state planning agency serving as principal research and policy planning staff of the Governor. Since each state and every Governor is different, it should be clear from the outset that this is not intended to be prescriptive. Nevertheless, as state planning agencies become more involved in the policy planning process, there are a few dos and don'ts which seem to stand out as common factors to be considered in organizing and implementing the state planning function. Thus, what is presented here is derived in part from a consensus among states involved in policy planning and in part from the authors' judgment as to what appears to be the appropriate role and function of the planning agency in this process. Only time and experience will confirm or deny these findings.

Dimensions of practice in state planning

This volume provides a basis for understanding what state planning is and where it stands at the advent of the 1980s. The reader is made aware of the sweep of issues and activities that will have a bearing on the direction of state planning in the 1980s.

A checklist for state planning

As one seeks to apply this discussion to a particular state in order to assess the current status of its state planning efforts as a context for plotting its future, the following outline may be useful:

1. State planning organizations
    a. State planning office (central or comprehensive):
        (1) What is its legal basis: state law, executive directive, press release?
        (2) Where is it in the state's governmental structure: Governor's office, Office of Administration, other state department, separate agency?
        (3) Is there a state planning board or advisory group; how do they interrelate?
        (4) What does the state planning office do?
        (5) How is it organized to do it?
        (6) What is its budget: state appropriation, federal funds?
        (7) How does it relate to Governor, Governor's staff; state legislature and legislative leadership; other state agencies; regional structure and capacity within the state; interact with federal government, local government, private sector, public?
    b. State planning offices (departmental or functional):
        (1) How is planning provided for in the various agencies or functions of state government; in the respective state agency?
        (2) What is the legal basis for its respective existence: statute, Secretary's directive?
        (3) Where is the planning responsibility—the planning office—in the structure and organization of the particular state agency: policy unit in Office of the Secretary, Deputy Secretary of Planning, Bureau of Planning?
        (4) Is there an advisory committee; how do they interact?
        (5) What does the planning office do?
        (6) How is it organized to do it?
        (7) What is its budget: state appropriation, federal funds?
        (8) How does it relate to head of agency and other units within agency; to other parts of state government (executive, legislative, departmental); to regional structure of state, etc.
    c. Reorganization of state government:
        (1) Recent and current efforts.
        (2) How was work of State Planning Office(s), central and departmental, related to these activities?

       (3) How is state planning responsibility being reflected in resulting structure and decision-making processes?

2. Formulating and applying state policies and plans
   a. Who prepared them—who gets involved in the process, why and how?
   b. Who gives them status—what kinds of status do state policies and plans customarily have; how do they get status or some measure of official recognition such as executive or legislative endorsement?
   c. How are they applied—what actions are taken; what difference do they make with respect to actions taken? With respect to results of particular efforts?

3. Content of state planning, and state policies and plans
   a. Physical development
   b. Environmental protection
   c. Social and economic well-being

4. Implementing state policies and plans
   a. State executive, legislative, and administrative actions, with particular reference to:
      (1) Gubernatorial—State of the State reports, legislative programs, budget message, executive directives, etc.
      (2) Legislative—statutes, resolutions, committee reports.
      (3) Budgets and taxes—includes operating budgets; capital budget and program; funding formulae, tax, revenue, and grant policies and programs; debt structure, use of official funds.
      (4) Actions of state agencies.
      (5) Permits and licenses—consistent with state regulations and applicable criteria, whether responsibility of state agency or delegated to regional or local body.
   b. Local executive, legislative, and administrative actions; as above, and including:
      (1) Local plans.
      (2) Local financial actions.
      (3) Local codes and ordinances.
   c. Substate, regional linkages and actions:
      (1) Regional policies and plans.
      (2) Regional processes for implementation and action.
   d. Federal linkages and actions:
      (1) Federal policies and programs.
      (2) Federal processes for implementing activities.

5. Issues in state planning
   a. Who are the "clients" and how can they best be served:
      (1) Governor.
      (2) Legislature.
      (3) State agencies.
   b. How should state planning relate to:
      (1) Federal policies and programs, their formulation and application?
      (2) Multistate regional organizations and activities?
      (3) Substate regional structure and capacities?
      (4) Local government?
      (5) Private sector?
      (6) Public?
   c. How can citizen participation work in state planning?
   d. Is there a role for a state planning board?
   e. What is a "comprehensive" plan within the context of state planning?
   f. State planning and the political process—can planning survive?

A factual determination will not only provide a useful status report on what exists under the rubric of state planning but also bring together pertinent insights and judgments about its relative quality and effectiveness, a consideration of no small moment in determining the climate within which a desired state planning responsibility must function (at least initially).

The authors' 1981 survey of the states, previously referred to in Chapter 3, brought forward a listing of Major Issues for the 1980s and a further enumeration of Planning and/or Policy Research Activities (see Figure 5-1) which indicate an agenda in the states that, if responded to, could include a planning capacity drawing from each of those organizational entities.

One would expect to find in a state Department of Transportation a planning capacity concerned with the transportation programs, facilities, and services within that state, participating in the process which gives those considerations more precise identification, definition, location, and impact.

A similar configuration would not be unusual or without value in relating to a variety of responsibilities which, at this time, are judged to be the issues for the 1980s: jobs and economic development; housing; resource development and environmental protection; land use, growth management, and patterns of development; law enforcement and public safety; and human services.

As the states move into the 1980s, particularly with the renewed attention being directed to state government in the Reagan administration's New Federalism and the ensuing debate, executive leadership moves center stage. And, as the process which can usefully undergird the substance of that leadership, planning should move center stage as well. The discussion which follows deals with what is involved and how that might be done.

Planning of state policy

What is it that distinguishes "policy planning" from other kinds of planning?

The term "policy" has never been used with a great deal of precision in government. It has tended to be a catchword for the official government position on issues of concern. In fact, however, a check with the dictionary finds "policy" specifically defined as: "1) prudence or wisdom in the management of affairs," and "2) a definite course or method of action selected from among alternatives and in light of given conditions to guide and determine present and future decisions."

For a long period of time the definition of planning was subjected to a fair amount of debate, particularly among those in the profession who attempted to define planning to reflect what it was they were doing. As noted in Chapter 3, the function, organization, and administration of state planning changed over time, which, as could be expected, influenced how planners tended to define planning.

Nearly 20 years ago, Paul Davidoff and Thomas Reiner developed what they called a "choice theory of planning" which they defined as "a process for determining appropriate future action through a sequence of choices."[1] This definition appears to have withstood the test of time as well as some substantive changes in the practice of state planning and seems to be particularly well suited to state policy planning in the 1980s.

The idea of providing decision makers with some choices in the form of policy options from which they can pick and choose the most appropriate course of action is both appropriate and constraining. It is appropriate because it makes explicit what public policy specialists, economists, and the like always talk about and that is the necessity to make choices. Every decision maker—legislator, Governor, President, or businessman—has to make choices.

However, it is artificial and perhaps misleading to suggest that every decision

State	Major issues for the 1980s	Planning and/or policy research activities
Arizona	Growth Transportation Effects of federal budget cuts	Planning and policy research activities facing curtailment due to federal program budget cuts

California	Early 1980s:
	  Finance
	  Housing
	Late 1980s:
	  Assimilating Pacific immigration
	  Water distribution throughout the western states
	  Economic competitiveness
		Preparation of policy for the Governor

Colorado	Provision of government services vs. revenue constraints Block grants	Policy coordination Program evaluation Federal budget impact on state (block grants)
Connecticut	Housing Infrastructure deterioration Limited public funds Competitive position of Northeast Job opportunities and training Transportation Waste and hazardous materials management Human services Criminal justice Education cost Economic development vs. environmental protection	Physical resources and human services Policy analysis of issues related to national priorities
Florida	Law enforcement/public safety Transportation Economic development Education Fiscal impact of growth on local governments Senior citizens Water and coastal management	Growth management Budgeting/financial planning management Mining regulations Water management Financing Housing Education Federal budget impact on state (block grant)

Hawaii	Safety and protection from crime
	Housing
	Education
	Jobs
	Energy self-sufficiency
	Population growth
	Land use and water allocation
		Special analysis of issues of statewide concern
		  Resort condominums
		  Sugar industry
		  Land use planning and management
		  Functional plan

Indiana	State expenditures and revenue Financing local government services	Federal budget impact on state (block grants) Government reorganization
Iowa	Inadequate revenue Taxation Employee morale and productivity	CDBG administration Other block grant administration
Kansas	Highway financing Revision of property tax Health and hospital financing Water supply Water quantity	Medicaid cost containment Scope and placement of state energy activities Highway funding alternatives Reconstruction of juvenile justice system Federal funding reductions
Kentucky	Limited revenue growth Increasing demand for additional state services	Policy analysis related to preparation and execution of state budget

Figure 5-1   State planning for the 1980s.

State	Major issues for the 1980s	Planning and/or policy research activities
Maine	Provision of government services vs. revenue constraints Energy issues and policy Natural resource management Economic development Public finance Energy Effects of industrial shifts	Intergovernmental relations Public finance Resource management
Michigan	Economic development Community development Matching growth trends to available resources	Overall policy analysis function including: Community development Surplus land disposition Infrastructure placement Development initiatives
Mississippi	Economic development Education Government services vs. revenue constraints	HUD 701 FmHA 111 ARC EDA Block grants
Nebraska	Water Redefinition of federal, state, local roles	Analysis of federal actions and state options
New Mexico	Federal funding cutbacks Block grants "MX" missile development	Administer eight federal functional programs Will undertake comprehensive planning program and administration of federal CDBG program
New York	Financing infrastructure maintenance and development Ensuring access to education and training Providing for private new business development Coordinating education/training activities with economic development Control of environmental pollutants and toxic waste disposal	Economic development policy research and analysis
North Dakota	Economic development Water Energy	Overall policy analysis function Program administration of block grants
Oklahoma	Water and water management Oil and gas development impact Reform and modernization of local governments	Community economic development program administration Public works development Manpower planning Data center
Pennsylvania	Economic and community development Water Matching available resources to needs	Overall policy analysis function including: Income maintenance programs Economic development and community conservation Crime Development policy Federal budget impact on state (block grants)
Rhode Island	Resource allocation Waste management Economic development Water Housing	Preparation of State Guide Plan Overall policy analysis function Data management Governmental management and coordination

Figure 5–1   (continued).

State	Major issues for the 1980s	Planning and/or policy research activities
South Dakota	Water Government efficiency	Overall policy analysis and research
Tennessee	State and local tax policy Environmental regulations Substate districting Technical assistance to local governments Block grants and revenue sharing	Taxation Revenue production Cash management Economic concerns Capital budgeting Government organization State–local relationships Social services CDBG Environment Resource conservation
Vermont	State response to federal–state relations Resource allocation Policy management State/local relations Provision of government services vs. revenue constraints New job opportunities Environmental quality	Federal budget impact on states (block grants) Federal–state relationships State response to federal regulatory reform
Virginia	Maintenance and expansion Governmental service vs. revenue limitations Government employee relations Energy policy and issues Transportation needs vs. revenue constraints Correctional programs	Policy research on social, economic and physical issues Federal budget impact on states (block grants)
Washington	Impact of energy costs Impact of revenue constraints on state–local government services Prison facilities construction and location Impact of higher interest rates on economy Water resources Boldt II impacts	Impact assessment of federal budget cuts Executive policy research, analysis and coordination Legislative coordination Federal coordination assistance
Wisconsin	Attraction and redevelopment of economic activity Ground water and hazardous waste management Maintenance of capital assets Level of support University support Reduction in governmental regulations and mandates Adjusting state–local fiscal policies and priorities to new federalism	Special policy analysis of issues having broad fiscal implications
Wyoming	Multiplying effects of energy growth and the impact of energy growth Renewable and nonrenewable resources	Preparation of comprehensive state plan Coordination of state agency policy activities

Figure 5–1   (continued).

maker has a set of real options or choices, each of which is equally attractive. In fact, most decision makers act in highly controversial environments. The appropriate approach is not to think of unencumbered options from which decision makers pick and choose ambiguously. Nor is the task to construct three more options which are not in any way realistically attuned to environment. The task of state policy planning is to identify what's going on in the environment and to develop certain analytical approaches or the capacity to identify substantive factors which can be applied to specific policy decisions as the need arises.[2]

To Davidoff and Reiner, "determining" means "finding out"; "appropriate" implies establishing a basis for making "judgments" concerning preferred conditions and suggests the need to set objectives; and "action" embodies specifics which are the eventual end products of planning. "Choices" in the process of planning are made at three levels: first, in establishing the objective; second, in identifying a set of realistic alternatives and selection of the desired alternative; and third, in guiding actions toward achievement of the objective. Each level requires the exercise of judgments in making the choices. For Davidoff and Reiner, the judgment basis of decision making is the crux of planning. If policy is wisdom in the management of affairs, and wisdom implies good sense or judgment, then planning is the basis of making informed judgments about policy.

On this basis, state policy planning, or more precisely, "planning of public policy," can be defined as: a process for establishing a course of action, selected from among alternatives and in light of given conditions, to guide and determine present and future state government decisions.

This definition provides a reasonably clear identification of the major elements involved in the planning of state policy. First, it is a process rather than an ad hoc approach to establishing policy. It implies that issues having policy implications are placed into this process in which they will be subjected to various analyses and evaluated or judged in relation to established criteria or objectives. Second, the process will include an examination of the issue environment, i.e., an examination and evaluation of existing and future external factors or conditions that will affect the issue and must be taken into account when formulating action alternatives. And third, action alternatives or options will be considered, including an identification of their current and long-term consequences in relation

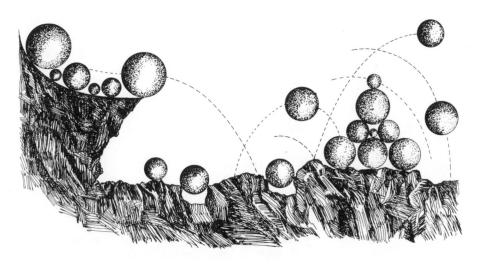

Figure 5–2 Planning is not an ad hoc process.

to the environment, from which the decision maker can choose a specific course of action that will become state policy.

Organizing for state policy planning and execution

From an operating perspective, in order for policy planning to be effectively carried out at the state level, several basic principles concerning the function and organization of the state planning agency should be considered:

1. The state planning function must be linked to and be a key aspect of the policy development process of the Governor.
2. The principal purpose of state planning should be to assist the Governor. The state planning agency should not be the advocate for interest groups or organizations that have embraced planning.
3. The state planning agency should not carry out functional planning programs that could be accomplished by line agencies.
4. The products of state policy planning should be implementable within a relatively short time period.
5. The state planning agency should be funded primarily from state revenues rather than from federal sources.

Under the policy planning model the state planning agency would be part of a policy management team in the Governor's office, responsible for coordinating the development and implementation of policy on an administration-wide basis. Ideally, this policy management team would have three components: policy and planning, legislative counsel, and legislative relations. Each would be a separate office such as the Office of Policy and Planning, Office of Legislative Counsel, and Office of Legislative Relations. All administration policy, legislative initiatives, and planning and research would be accomplished within this small, tightly knit organization, under the overall direction and supervision of one of the Governor's principal aides. Each component of each office would have a director and staff, whose function and responsibilities can be summarized as follows:

Policy and planning

1. Issues and policy research and analysis, state policy planning, and interagency planning and policy coordination.
2. Working with executive branch agencies, legislators, and legislative staff in developing policies and programs as appropriate.
3. Monitoring and reporting progress and status of all the Governor's policy and legislative positions and initiatives; in so doing, working closely with the state budget director.
4. Providing staff assistance to the Governor for his participation in the National Governor's Association, multistate regional organizations and endeavors, and other intergovernmental efforts.

Legislative counsel

1. Reviewing all legislation developed in the executive branch.
2. Reviewing all testimony before presentation to the legislature by representatives of the executive branch.
3. Preparing legislative analysis of all proposed or introduced legislation and reviewing agency positions to assure compliance with administration goals.
4. Directing and coordinating line legislative analysis and proposed positions.

5. Coordinating the development of the Governor's position on all legislation.
6. Coordinating the Governor's position on a bill following passage by the state legislature.

Legislative relations

1. Communicating daily with legislative leadership and rank and file as representatives of the Governor.
2. Resolving problems and responding to requests of individual legislators.
3. Planning and execution of legislative events for rank and file.
4. Communicating the Governor's legislative and policy priorities to the legislature with support of the policy planning and legislative counsel teams.
5. Coordinating communications to interested business, labor, citizen, and other groups regarding legislative and policy priorities.
6. Coordinating all legislative liaison activities in executive agencies.

From this organizational arrangement, it is clear that most policies and implementation actions would initiate within the state policy and planning office, developed for the legislative process by the legislative counsel staff, and managed in the legislature by the legislative relations group. This division of labor must be carefully managed to ensure that the activities underway and made within each group are compatible across the board and that taken together they support the overall objectives of the administration.

The relationship of the state planning agency to the state legislature has appropriately been the subject of considerable debate over the years. Many have correctly argued that without a strong relationship to the state legislature the planning agency cannot expect implementation of its recommendations. Others have suggested that budget cuts and sometimes outright abolition of the state planning function is an indication that the legislature may not be well informed about the function and activity of state planning, a circumstance not foreign to lack of understanding and support.

There is merit to these arguments as evidenced in the latter part of the 1970s when several state planning agencies were abolished. The demise of state planning agencies in a number of states can be traced to ineffective legislative relations, due in part to the fact that many were only nominally associated with the Governor's office or executive branch, received little support or recognition from the administration, and were forced to compete on their own for state funding. The difficulty in competing for scarce state dollars more than likely influenced many state planning agencies to seek federal funds to augment meager appropriations from the state legislatures.

The policy planning model presented here seeks to overcome this problem by incorporating the state planning function in the overall policy management team in the Governor's office. In reality, the state planning office may have no more contact with the legislature under this arrangement than it did previously. In fact, as noted above, both the Office of Legislative Counsel and the Office of Legislative Relations by definition of function would be the appropriate representatives of the administration to interact on a regular basis with the legislature. However, under the policy planning model, these offices would bring to this interaction the product of state planning agencies' work in the form of policy analysis, legislative initiatives, and the like. As appropriate, the state planning staff may be directed to work with legislators or their staff on specific assignments; it is to be noted that this would not be expected to occur on their own initiative or without the concurrence of the directors of the policy management team.

There are a number of advantages to this approach. First, it preserves the central policy management function of the Governor's office. Second, it maintains the functional specialization of each component of the policy management team. For example, the policy and planning staff is hired because its expertise is in issues research or public policy development and not in legislative relations. Similarly, it is the job of the Director of Legislative Relations to fully understand the legislative leadership and their needs and to be able to coordinate administration initiatives accordingly. No one would expect the Director of Legislative Relations independently to have developed the administration's position on welfare reform, but rather to be responsible to convey and coordinate it with the legislature. Finally, within this organizational framework the state planning agency is perceived to be a critical component of the administration's policy staff. As legislators and others come to realize that policy measures under consideration have been developed by the policy and planning staff, when tough policy issues are being discussed, the Governor's policy and planning staff will be expected to be available in that consideration.

It should not be assumed that a solid relationship with the legislative leadership will assure smooth sailing of administration policy initiatives through a General Assembly. The reality of the situation is that most lawmakers are not only influenced by what they perceive to be the needs and wants of their constituents; they are also influenced by major corporations, business, and other power brokers operating within the state, who have vested interests in what is happening at the state house.

Clearly, it is in the best interest of the administration to fully comprehend the impact of any new policy initiative on the affected parties prior to taking any steps toward implementation. This is a responsibility that can fall to the state planning staff as part of its assessment of the issue environment and the consequences of an action alternative or option being developed for consideration.

While there may be selected issues, the discussion of which may be constrained with respect to all parties of interest, they are not expected to constitute the majority of an administration's new initiatives.

Careful attention should be given to the need for establishing these relationships and how they are carried out. The objective here is multifaceted and includes not only learning first-hand about the issue environment and getting expert analysis on the impact of the options under consideration; the objective also is to have the affected party support the policy initiative or at least agree to its substance and direction.

To ensure policy coordination and issues management within the Governor's office, it is vital that a close working relationship exist between the policy management team and other key administration staff. This would include the Governor's administrative assistant who is responsible for scheduling the Governor's time and appearances. Strategic management of the Governor's schedule can be of significant value in furthering the achievement of policy objectives among groups important to the legislative process and among the legislature itself.

The Governor's communications staff, the press secretary and the speech writers, also should be part of the policy management loop. It is important that the Governor's public posture on policy issues and new initiatives be a product of the research and analysis coordinated by the state planning agency. A special working relationship should exist between the policy and planning staff and communications staff to coordinate all major public positions in order to ensure that a voiced public posture can sustain a rigorous review by the media and the public.

By linking the state planning process to the overall policy management function of state government, a number of benefits can be achieved. First, the state planning agency becomes a significant administration resource. The agency adds a research and analysis dimension to the Governor who is intent on providing strong leadership in the administration of state affairs. Second, the state planning agency can be considerably more effective under this organizational arrangement in which its efforts are focused on specific research and analytical tasks. Problems that plagued state planning agencies under other organizational structures, such as its relationships to the legislature and the public at large, are virtually non-existent in this arrangement. Under the policy management model there is a clear division of the responsibilities with the planning agency primarily responsible for providing policy research and analysis and working closely with other members of the management team to achieve administration policy objectives.

The policy planning agency

The role of management

Management staff in the state planning agency would be characterized by policy specialists who possess desired experience and knowledge in dealing with substantive issues of state concern. A strategic component of this qualification should be an understanding of the planning process and its application. This is particularly true of the director, who is responsible for providing detailed policy advice and recommendations to the Governor and who must structure a state planning organization that is capable of responding to the demands of the administration for policy and issue analysis on a quick-turnaround basis.

The particular responsibilities of the state planning agency may require a chain of command that purposefully preserves the anonymity of the planning director. For many reasons it is not prudent to have the Governor's policy staff a highly visible part of the administration. One obvious reason is that it reduces efficiency. Another is that the director's role is to provide policy advice, not to make policy. Furthermore, planning directors are not public relations persons, and one of the criticisms frequently leveled at state planning agencies in the past is that they simply are not well equipped to carry out this activity if, indeed, it is desired.

The idea of anonymity for the planning director is not meant to imply that he be confined to his office. In fact, the administration often may tap the director as the "point-person" on specific issues. This can and should be a frequent assignment when working on policy issues within the administration that will involve Cabinet heads and other officials. It has clear value in that it facilitates centralized management, and it keeps the line agency heads focused on administration issues and initiatives.

One of the most important relationships the state planning director will have is with the budget director. Virtually every administration issue or initiative will be placed before one of these two individuals. To facilitate communication, the state planning director should be a regular participant in budget office staff meetings. This should further understanding between these two key agencies and facilitate the implementation of cooperative initiatives such as issuing annual program and budget guidelines to line agencies that set forth the Governor's priorities and initiatives for the upcoming budget year.

As part of the "front office," the planning director will be involved in the Governor's scheduling meetings, in cabinet meetings, and in private discussion between the Governor and his top advisors. These relationships will facilitate the work of the planning agency by making the planning director aware of the range of demands placed on the chief executive. This type of intelligence will permit the formulation of policy recommendations by the planning agency which take into account the realities associated with a specific issue.

In addition to his role within the administration, the planning director will often be called upon to carry out specific assignments external to state govern-

The creative manager   In the various discussions of Theory X, Theory Y, and Theory Z, we often overlook the creativity of management. Managers in the eighties and nineties will face requirements far different from their predecessors' as they balance conventional managerial wisdom with the demands of a complex society. The following excerpts show six of the most important functions of the manager as a creative person:

1. *The Manager as Manager.* This is the traditional role, the subject of all basic texts. In fulfilling it, the manager becomes the person "in charge," the one who in the face of uncertainties or indecision, decides—or helps to decide—and then, see to it that the decision is carried out. In this role, the manager is expected to be fair, firm, insightful, and, above all, prudent.

2. *The Manager as Negotiator.* A managerial function that has increased in geometric proportions during recent years is that of negotiating with others the many vexatious issues and problems which involve a variety of people, offices, and organizations. At higher levels, the majority of the executive's time is spent in external relationships. There are matters to be worked out with governing bodies, with other organizations which share an interest in the problem, with clients, with suppliers, with associations (supporters as well as opponents), with unions, with the media, and even with the courts.

3. *The Manager as Leader.* Effective managers are more than managers. They are also leaders. The two roles, however, are by no means the same. The manager is the expert in the processes of administration. The leader, on the other hand, is someone chosen by those who follow his or her example because, for whatever reasons, they approve it. We identify leaders by their followership, by the fact that others *voluntarily* accept their influence.

4. *The Manager as Developer.* As the requirements of the organization become more complex and more demanding, the need for a work force able to cope with them increases also. The marketplace cannot be expected to supply more than the raw talent, if that, which is required to meet these needs. It is, accordingly, part of the manager's job to see to it that people are recruited and trained to do what is needed not only for the present but for the future as well.

5. *The Manager as Innovator.* Managers themselves do not . . . need to be the primary source of organizational innovation. What is suggested here is that innovation per se be seen as the important contributor it is to productivity, and that the manager become one of the major catalysts in producing it.

Most of us will produce few patentable products, but much is possible if we use another term, innovation, which recognizes new uses for existing equipment, new methods for making existing goods, the value of novelty, renovation, deviation, modernization, and adaptation.

6. *The Manager as Human Being.* In a world which is increasingly emphasizing the importance—and rights—of the individual, the manager needs to be seen as someone who feels for others, who shares their hopes and expectations, who understands—or at least tries to understand—their problems.

Source: David S. Brown, *Managing the Large Organization: Issues, Ideas, Precepts, Innovations* (Mt. Airy, Md.: Lomond Publications, 1982), pp. 219–24.

ment. The director may staff the Governor's participation on committees of the National Governors Association and on multistate regional organizations. The planning director may also be selected to work closely with special groups outside the state in order to convey administration policy and relay outside reactions to the administration. These external relationships must be carefully selected and defined since the principal role of the planning director is to provide the Governor with information on issues and with policy options. Any external activities that unnecessarily infringe on this primary function may blur and ultimately diminish the value of the policy planning process.

The role of staff

The state planning staff will be faced with developing the administration position on a wide variety of public issues. In a number of instances, a considerable amount of time will be required for analysis, the development of a position, and the formulation of new initiatives or actions necessary to successfully resolve the issue. There will be other issues of less complexity that can be handled by the staff on a quick-turnaround basis. It is important that the administration develop a consistent position on both long- and short-range issues.

The planning staff should be organized to respond to the needs of the Governor for policy research and advice. This suggests that the staff be organized into two units. First, a policy analysis unit comprised of personnel who, in addition to a knowledge of planning and its application, have a capability in selected subject areas of particular emphasis so important in meeting the short-term, day-to-day demand for issue research and analysis. The second unit, a strategic planning staff, would focus on resolving longer term issues that may be more complex in that they require a broader response and new initiatives to be put forth by the administration.

The strategic planning issues are generally selected by the administration as areas of principal concern of the Governor. They may have been campaign issues or issues carefully selected as part of the Governor's legislative or budget program. Generally, the administration itself comes to be identified with these issues, and they become key components of the Governor's record. Unlike the day-to-day policy issues which are often thrust upon the administration and which force it to be reactive, albeit creative, the strategic issues are targeted by the administration and become a focal point of its efforts. Indeed, the treatment of this activity may be the avenue through which the administration asserts its leadership in dealing with state affairs, giving voice to overall as well as specific policy direction and substance and expression to proactive initiatives.

Strategic planning issues are usually more global than the short-term policy variety. For example, the administration may be concerned with the overall economic climate in the state, the availability of jobs and job opportunities, the state's ability to compete with other states in attracting new firms, and the relationship between the state's economy and the economic well-being of its communities. Economic development may have been a campaign issue or the Governor may have singled out this problem as one of his primary concerns.

The state planning agency will face a major test in considering this type of issue, its current and longer term consequences, the capability of the state to affect the level of economic development, and the options available to deal with its many considerations. These kinds of issues will require a substantial staff commitment, a high level of expertise in the particular issue area, and the use of sophisticated techniques to fully address those concerns. It is clearly the type of assignment to be carried out by a strategic planning staff. The product of those efforts will be one the administration will want to put forward as its response to a campaign pledge or other commitment to resolve.

Figure 5–3 It's up to the planner to
provide direction in implementing executive
policies.

The short-term issues can usually be handled in less time and with less formality by the policy analysis staff. Often, this effort will be geared to developing the administration position on various legislative proposals, formulating alternate proposals, working with state agencies in functional areas to develop specific policies, programs, and legislative measures to be put forth by the administration. For the most part, these efforts are of the quick-turnaround variety, although they may sometimes take several months to complete. Since the policy analysis staff is small, assignments should be handled by individual policy specialists rather than the entire unit.

Within every administration, there will be crises that require an administration response. The policy planning staff can play a special role in these situations with the administration tapping a policy specialist from the agency to carry out the administration's staffing requirement, coordinating line agency involvement in the crisis situation, and providing a communications link between the administration and outside parties.

Advisory boards and commissions

A number of states have established planning advisory committees or have maintained state planning boards to assist in the state planning function. These advisory bodies can play an important role in the state policy planning process in those states where they are providing technical and policy advice to a state planning staff in the Governor's office.

The use of advisory committees, commissions, or boards is particularly relevant in the strategic planning activity which requires the involvement of representatives of interest groups in helping to formulate long-term policy objectives and providing selected technical assistance. For example, the strategic planning assignment may require an assessment of the current and long-term environment which involves identifying factors that must be taken into consideration in formulating the administration's strategies. While the strategic planning staff may have highly sophisticated technical models for understanding the external environment, the task of forecasting remains terribly complex and cannot be regarded solely as a mechanical, numbers-crunching endeavor. Often informed judgment, such as can be provided by a planning board or advisory committee, can prove to be more reliable than the most sophisticated projection. Most strategic planning processes will use more than one method of forecasting the future. Clearly, a consensus provided by such a panel on the state of the economy five years hence can be of significant value to the strategic planning process and important to any economic projection that is offered.

Financing state planning

Since its inception in the 1930s, state planning has substantially relied on federal agencies for financial assistance to support its work programs. When federal financial support waned in the late 1930s, state planning in a number of states ceased to exist. Throughout the last two decades, state planning agencies have typically relied on federal agencies such as HUD and EDA to support planning programs. These sources are diminishing, if not vanishing, under the Reagan administration, forcing state planning agencies to become considerably more creative in securing federal financial support.

The demise of many of the broad-based federal assistance programs that supported state planning in the past should not be of serious concern to the viability of the state policy planning model. Relying on federal funding programs for financial assistance is not consistent with the concept and function of state policy planning. To accept significant federal funding means that the state planning agency must fulfill specific federal program requirements. Under this arrangement, the planning agencies would not, for example, have the flexibility to provide the Governor with a policy position on welfare reform if the federal program requirements call for the agency to produce a state land use plan as a more immediate priority.

The state policy planning agency, to effectively fulfill its role and responsibility of providing policy assistance to the administration, must be fully funded from state revenues. No one would suggest that the state budget office seek federal funds as the principal support to maintain that function. It is similarly incongruous in fulfilling the responsibility of state policy planning for that agency to rely on substantial federal financial assistance.

Other considerations

Functional planning   This policy planning model anticipates that a functional planning capability of some competence will be established and available in various of the state's departments (i.e., transportation, environmental resources, education, health, welfare, commerce, community development, etc.). It is on that basis that the role of the policy planning agency can be projected as *not* including federal functional planning but rather setting the policy context within which the functional planning will take place and in relating to those agencies as particular issues assignments might require or the strategic planning agenda makes appropriate. There must be an understanding within the administration, however, that a planning frame of reference is provided by the policy planning office both in substantive as well as operational terms. Just as that office should not be managerially or bureaucratically viewed as cutting off a Cabinet Secretary from access to the Governor, that department should be sensitive to the state planning structure and its role as a participant in that structure.

Regional planning   Substate regional planning should be taken into acccount in the functioning of state planning. This network of agencies and activities can be important to the substance of the work undertaken by the policy planning unit in state government. An understanding of how the planning process might best be applied in a particular state must include a consideration of the status of substate planning, the mutual interests to be addressed, how this relates to the administration's agenda, and an explicit policy expression dealing with regional planning and its interaction with state government. Within that context, regional planning and what it produces has the potential for important contribution and participation in the activities of the policy planning agency.

Conclusion

Planning in state government continues to evolve in definition, purpose, application, accomplishment, and continuity of effort.

It has been pointed out that state governments in the United States are not monolithic enterprises where everyone single-mindedly seeks to advance the policies of the chief executive. Legislators have their own constituencies and their own basis of authority. Executive officials all have different operating responsibilities, different clientele groups, and different perspectives on public issues, which lead them to support a Governor's policies with varying degrees of enthusiasm. When Governors announce the development of a particular strategy, they often are not able to eliminate the other responsibilities of state officials or resolve the competing policy preferences of the state's citizens. Implicit in such a statement, however, is an expression of that Governor's willingness to struggle to overcome competing priorities.

A recent analysis of the states and urban strategies brought forward this observation:

Whether one's expectations are modest or more expansive, those who advocate and formulate comprehensive strategies do so on the assumption that the judicious application of state powers in the regulatory area, in land use and environmental protection, and through the timing and staging of public investments, can shape and influence private market decisions and yield positive, long-term results. The state efforts reported upon in this comparative analysis would seem to justify those beliefs.[3]

Planning is politics, and action to implement planning often requires political action. Given those qualities, planning can be institutionalized in the organization and operation of state government, building on the richness that can be gained from the experience of one administration to another, only by a continued demonstration of its usefulness, a usefulness viewed not only in technical, analytical terms but also in terms of results accomplished in the management of public affairs.

1   Paul Davidoff and Thomas Reiner, "A Choice Theory of Planning," *Journal of the American Institute of Planners* 28 (May 1962): 102–115.

2   Arnold R. Weber, Provost, Carnegie-Mellon University; speech before the Benjamin Franklin Symposium, the Pennsylvania General Assembly, Harrisburg, PA, 3–4 January 1979.

3   Charles R. Warren, *The States and Urban Strategies: A Comparative Analysis*; report prepared by the National Academy of Public Administration for the U.S. Department of Housing and Urban Development, September 1980.

6 Regional planning today

As noted in Chapter 2, regional planning organizations have been established virtually nationwide at both the substate (county and multicounty) and multistate levels. This has happened very largely since 1965.

This chapter describes the regional planning processes currently being pursued by organizations of this type in terms of the various different needs to which they are responding, their existing organizational structures and financial arrangements, their work programs and the products they produce, their limited powers to implement regional plans and policies, the theories which guide them, and the issues now being faced in efforts to strengthen regional planning processes.

Diverse needs for regional planning

Metropolitan areas (large and small), rural regions of one or more counties in size, large multistate regions of the nation, and major river basins all have different needs for regional planning. These are examined briefly below.

Metropolitan areas

The average metropolitan area contains approximately 100 units of local government—counties, cities, towns or townships (in nearly half the states), school districts, and various other special purpose districts. While approximately 100 of the nearly 300 metropolitan areas defined by the U.S. Census in 1980 are encompassed by only one county, the other 200 spread across two or more counties. Some of the larger metropolitan areas have half a dozen or more counties. Adding to the complexity of this local government fragmentation is the fact that approximately 40 metropolitan areas cross state lines. Most of these involve local governments in only two states, but several spill over into three. When this happens, there usually are two or three different sets of rules (established by state law) governing the structures, functions, and finances of the local governments in the area, and governing their ability to establish regional organizations and pursue mutual objectives through formal interlocal cooperation agreements and contracts.

This fragmentation of local government in metropolitan areas is very different from the wide-ranging activities of the area's citizens. People frequently live in one locality and work in another; they may do much of their shopping in still another and attend cultural events elsewhere. They need easy transportation throughout the area; they depend daily upon the same sources of water; the quality of the air they breathe is affected by the automobiles, industries, housing, and other facilities throughout the area; burglary rings and drug dealers operate without regard for local boundaries; and parking tickets issued in one locality may be difficult to enforce against someone living in another.

Often, central city and suburban governments experience very different pressures even though they are in the same area. The central cities may be much older, experiencing population decline, finding that increasingly larger proportions of their populations are older, poorer, or more disadvantaged than the average for the area, and experiencing financial difficulties arising from a declining tax base combined with increasing needs for public services. Thus, for the same tax effort, suburban jurisdictions may be able to provide better schools and other essential services. Such inequities frequently may be quite apparent.

While state and federal governments can and do get involved in helping to solve some of these interjurisdictional problems, an area-wide metropolitan planning organization can more easily involve the local governments and citizens of the region in addressing such needs.

Regions of rural and small urban communities

For many years, population moved away from the farms and small communities of rural America to the big cities and metropolitan areas. In the past decade, however, nonmetropolitan counties have begun to grow faster than metropolitan areas in many cases. These trends have brought mixed problems to rural regions. The evident needs may be a combination of shoring-up a shaky agricultural economy with nonagricultural industry and business, responding to sudden new pressures for urban development which may be large relative to existing population and activity, guarding against potential damages to natural resources and environmental quality, and providing urban types of services never before contemplated but now being demanded by new residents.

These needs are especially difficult to meet in rural and small urban areas. Although more than two-thirds of the nation's local governments are outside of metropolitan areas, most of them serve very small populations, and few of them are professionally staffed and administered. Rural areas also typically have more than their share of poor housing, unemployed and poor residents, and inadequate medical and social services. Thus, greater needs for public service are combined with less capable local governments. At the same time, it is more difficult and more expensive to provide urban types of services and basic functions of government in highly dispersed rural areas and small communities. This disparity between needs and capabilities can reach crisis proportions very quickly when a large new recreation development, retirement community, or energy development suddenly appears. Even a modest development by metropolitan standards may appear huge and completely overwhelming in the rural governmental environment.

Regional planning organizatiions in rural and small community areas often can help to supply the professional government capacity otherwise lacking there. Promoting and responding to economic development in an orderly fashion, and providing the public services being demanded, with limited governmental resources, are the challenges to be met.

Multistate economic regions

When the Tennessee Valley Authority was established in 1933, the region drained by the Tennessee River was one of the poorest and most backward in the nation. The hydroelectric potential of the Tennessee River was seen as the means of bringing new prosperity to this suffering region and putting the Valley to work for the benefit of the whole nation.

When the Appalachian Regional Commission was established in 1965, the mountain range running from the old South all the way up into New York State was an economic backwater of dwindling coal mining and inaccessible old communities housing a declining and increasingly poor populace.

The New England states—similar to parts of the Mid-Atlantic and Midwest regions—now are suffering economic decline related to their age, costliness of

Many types of regions *Webster's Collegiate* has nine definitions of the term "region," but none match the terms below which are used in this book.

Substate regions. These typically encompass the one or more counties included in a metropolitan area or a non-metropolitan community organized for planning, administrative, or service delivery purposes. Some include counties from more than one state and may be called interstate regions. In states without counties, groups of towns or townships are used to define boundaries. Often, state government plays a part in defining the boundaries and functions of these regions and the boundaries are fixed as part of a statewide set of substate regions. Usually a substate region is served by a general purpose or multipurpose regional planning council composed largely of representatives of participating local governments.

Metropolitan areas. These encompass one or more counties (or county-type areas in states without counties) which include at least one urbanized area of 50,000 population or more plus socially and economically related urban and rural territory. Each such area is officially defined by the U.S. Bureau of the Census using a complex set of criteria. Many metropolitan areas have the same boundaries as substate regions, but some small metropolitan areas merely serve as an urban center of a larger substate region, and some substate regions encompass more than one metropolitan area.

Special purpose substate regions. These regions usually are formed for purposes of a single federal aid program that is required or encouraged to be administered on a regional basis. The boundaries may coincide with those of metropolitan areas or substate regions, or multiples of such areas or regions. These special regions also may have boundaries of their own. The process of establishing boundaries for these regions is separate from those for establishing metropolitan area or substate region boundaries, and it may be guided by unique federal guidelines for the individual federal aid programs.

Multistate economic regions. The boundaries of two of these—the Tennessee Valley Authority and the Appalachian Regional Commission—are established specifically and explicitly by federal law. Others—the Title V commissions—have boundaries requested by one or more states and agreed to by the federal government. Usually, such regions cover all or a large portion of several states. These boundaries have no necessary relationship to multistate statistical analysis regions established by the U.S. Census Bureau or the U.S. Bureau of Economic Analysis. They also have no necessary relationship to the Standard Federal Regions used for internal administrative purposes by the U.S. government. Only in New England and the Pacific Northwest is there boundary coincidence among these different geographic systems.

Multistate river basins. These are large watersheds for major rivers or complex coastal drainage areas. Their boundaries are largely the result of the topographic features of land. Political considerations enter only to subdivide massive river systems or coastal areas into smaller, more manageable segments. These regions bear no necessary relationship to any others. Only in New England and the Pacific Northwest is there boundary coincidence with other types of regions.

Standard federal regions. This is a specific set of ten multistate regions established by presidential executive order for the purpose of conforming the boundaries and regional office locations for the administrative regions of many federal departments and agencies. These boundaries have no necessary relationships to those of other multistate regions. All of these boundaries follow state lines, unlike many boundaries of other multistate regions. Only in is there boundary coincidence with New England and the Pacific Northwest other types of regions.

their governments, migration of their industries to the south and west, increasing welfare burdens, an unfavorable energy position (as consumers rather than producers), and increasing foreign competition for many of their traditional industries.

Western regions in the United States have been awakened since 1973 to their great potentials as energy resources (such as coal and oil shale) for the nation, but realize that full development of these resources could endanger their water reserves and cattle industries, not to mention the quality of their environment.

These are the major forces in the nation that are too big for individual communities and states to counteract through their own individual efforts. Natural resources potentials and conflicts; poverty, backwardness, and inaccessibility requiring an infusion of outside capital; and declining economies resulting from a complex of industry trends and historically derived competitive factors—all of these and more pull states together to pursue common purposes through multistate regional organizations. Often, national action is required by the federal government—and it has been forthcoming in varying degrees as noted in Chapter 2—but the regional organizations provide the opportunity for maximum state participation in these larger issues.

Multistate river basins

Rivers are a major source of water for many different and often competing uses—so long as the quality of the water is protected. Rivers also are often major transportation routes, energy sources, recreational assets, habitats of endangered species, and sources of natural disasters in the form of floods. Maximizing the various different types of benefits available from a river, while minimizing its dangers, requires overall management of the whole river basin (including related land resources) as a single system. Yet, major rivers are much larger than any single state in the nation, and no single government—whether federal, state, or local—has complete governmental jurisdiction over all the interrelated activities necessary for effective management of the river. Therefore, joint action is required. River basin commissions or committees plan these activities on a basinwide (regional) basis, so that actions by all the governments affecting the basin may be consistent with each other.

The Mississippi is a major resource
The Mississippi . . . is in all ways remarkable. Considering the Missouri its main branch, it is the longest river in the world—four thousand three hundred miles. . . . It discharges three times as much water as the St. Lawrence, twenty-five times as much as the Rhine, and three hundred and thirty-eight times as much as the Thames. No other river has so vast a drainage-basin: it draws its water supply from twenty-eight States and Territories; from Delaware, on the Atlantic seaboard, and from all the country between that and Idaho on the Pacific slope—a spread of forty-five degrees of longi-

tude. The Mississippi receives and carries to the Gulf water from fifty-four subordinate rivers that are navigable by steamboats, and from some hundreds that are navigable by flats and keels. The area of its drainage-basin is as great as the combined areas of England, Wales, Scotland, Ireland, France, Spain, Portugal, Germany, Austria, Italy, and Turkey; and almost all this wide region is fertile; the Mississippi valley, proper, is exceptionally so.

Source: Mark Twain, *Life on the Mississippi* (New York: Oxford University Press, 1962), p. 1.

Other regions

The types of regions enumerated above are the major ones created to achieve broad public purposes through separate, at least partially independent, regional organizations incorporating representation from a variety of participating governments. Other types of regions are established from time to time for a wide variety of special purposes. For example, individual departments of state government frequently establish a regional office structure to deal with a manageable number of areas within the state for their own program purposes. Likewise, the federal government has established a standard regional office structure for most of its departments and agencies which deal with state and local governments, and certain other federal departments and agencies have their own regional office structures. While the regions of state departments frequently are used for regional planning purposes as well as for administrative purposes, federal regional offices generally are used for administrative purposes only.

A number of individual single-purpose federal aid programs require or allow a substate regional approach. Criteria are established for delineating regions for these specialized program purposes and for designating regional organizations to plan program activities (and in some cases—such as special services to the aging, landfills, and carpool matching—to administer them as well). Sometimes the organizations aided are multipurpose regional councils in the metropolitan and the rural and small urban community regions mentioned above, but other times they are separately established, single-purpose organizations concerned with only an individual federal aid program. The single-purpose bodies constitute a distinct class of regional organizations.

The other major type of region frequently established in the United States is the special district. These are areas in which special taxes and/or services apply. Usually a separate governmental organization is established to meet the area's special need. Sometimes these organizations are simply administrative conveniences serving individual local government jurisdictions, or portions of such jurisdictions, but other times they serve intergovernmental regions spanning two or more local jurisdictions and providing planning as well as administration of a particular function such as transportation, water supply and pollution control, soil conservation, mosquito control, parks and recreation, fire protection, housing and urban renewal, hospitals, or flood control. Special districts usually have boundaries drawn for very specific functional and administrative purposes; they seldom conform to the boundaries of the whole metropolitan area or multipurpose rural region.

Structure and financing of regional organizations

There are two basic types of regional organizations—those which are governments themselves (holding taxing and administrative powers so that they can perform assigned governmental functions and deliver services), and those which are participatory intergovernmental planning and coordinating bodies which rely upon others, completely or in large part, for the financing and provision of public services. Of course, there are a few organizations which have certain traits of both types, and are difficult to classify either way. Examples are:

1. The Metropolitan Council of the Twin Cities, with members appointed by the governor, some independent financing, some policy-making authority over certain areawide special districts and local planning processes, but very largely serving the same planning and coordinating roles common to most of the participatory, intergovernmental regional organizations.
2. The Metropolitan Service District of Portland, Oregon, with a governing

body consisting of directly elected metropolitan representatives and certain limited service delivery responsibilities, but without an assured tax base, and with its overall planning and coordinating role remaining very similar to the advisory status it held under the predecessor council of governments before it was merged into the service district.

3. Interstate compact organizations for regional planning in such areas as Philadelphia, New York, and Lake Tahoe, where the existence and form of the organization are mandated by parallel state laws enacted by the participating states, but where the functions of the organization are primarily to prepare plans and give advice to other units of government.

4. Interstate compacts for river basin commissions for the Delaware and Sesquehanna Rivers which firmly establish the organizations and certain limited policy making and administrative powers, but which in practice rely almost exclusively on their planning and advisory functions.

Regional offices of state or federal departments and agencies likewise do not fit this two-part typology. While they may hire regional planners and produce regional plans, they are not independent regional organizations. Their organizational structure and financing are integral parts of the state or federal organization which they serve.

Actual regional governments, though proposed quite often by political scientists ever since the 1930s, are still not very common even though there are more of them than there are hybrids such as those mentioned above. Most regional organizations in the United States today are intergovernmental participation bodies.

The paragraphs which follow describe these regional governments and intergovernmental participation bodies and examine the external support provided to buttress the commonly used but fragile intergovernmental organizations.

Regional governments

There are three types of regional government in the United States today— consolidated local governments resulting from the merger of cities and counties, area-wide special districts usually serving only a single function (or a very few functions), and the Tennessee Valley Authority (TVA) which is a semi-independent federal corporation. Each of these is examined below.

Consolidated local governments   There have been 16 city-county mergers since World War II. These are many more consolidations than occurred in the whole previous history of the nation, but one (Carson City/Ormsby County, NV) has since been overthrown by the courts, and even this number is miniscule compared to the more than 300 metropolitan areas now in existence. Most consolidation proposals are turned down by the voters, and even those which do succeed seldom encompass the whole urban area except where the areas are quite small. Then, unless additional mergers take place, the consolidated government later becomes just the core jurisdiction in a larger metropolitan area which again spans a number of localities. Nevertheless, for a time following the consolidation local planning for the new government may, for all practical purposes, amount to area-wide planning for an urban region. It can be seen from the table that consolidation has not been accomplished in any of the largest metropolitan areas (all being in areas with populations significantly under one million), nor in interstate areas where there would be definite legal barriers.

Planners working on area-wide plans for the whole city-county during the period while the consolidation still covers all or nearly all of the urban area may find themselves addressing many of the substantive regional issues mentioned in this book, but the legal, financial, and governmental organization frameworks within which they will be working would more closely resemble those within which the local planner normally works.[1]

Area-wide special districts   Of the nation's approximately 26,000 independent special districts, roughly 1,000 are metropolitan area-wide in jurisdiction. Of course, many more than that serve two or more local jurisdictions, even though they fail to encompass the whole region.

Most of these districts serve only a single function, and they are governed by boards of appointed members. The appointments may be made by city or county governing bodies, mayors, or governors. In some cases they are elected. The special district board then appoints an administrator who hires and manages the necessary staff to perform the district's function. This works much like a council-manager form of government at the city or county level. The planning staff of such a district typically would report to the administrator.

The legal basis for a special district generally is either a special act of the state legislature, a general enabling act allowing local governments to establish such a special district, or an interlocal agreement established by local governments in accordance with a general state law authorizing interlocal cooperation. Some special districts have their own taxing authority, but others do not. Those which do not usually have authority to issue revenue bonds which they pay off from the proceeds of their operations (such as water bills or bus fares). Both types of special districts often receive grants from other levels of government.

The functions of TVA and ARC   Two of the most successful multistate regional organizations are the Tennessee Valley Authority and the Appalachian Regional Commission. Their functions are broad, especially in conservation and resource development.

Tennessee Valley Authority. Power production, including hydroelectric, coal, and nuclear generation plants; power distribution; navigation; flood control; recreation; improvement of agriculture and forestry; promotion of local planning; and planning for all of these functions.

Appalachian Regional Commission. The major functions of ARC are funding a special Appalachian highway system; health; child development; construction of vocational and technical schools; housing; community development; and water and sewer facilities.

Other ARC functions are mining restoration; funding the administrative and planning expenses of local development districts; research; and technical assistance, including support for state planning.

TVA[2]   The Tennessee Valley Authority is a semi-independent federal corporation established to develop the Tennessee River for power production, navigation, flood control, and recreational purposes, and to promote improved agriculture and forestry throughout the valley. Its power production activities subsequently developed well beyond the hydroelectric capability of the river itself, relying upon both coal and nuclear generation plants. The Authority's independence derives from the nine-year overlapping terms of its three board members, its right to retain earnings from its sale of electric power so long as they are needed to meet operating and construction costs, and by its exclusive power to develop the river—displacing the U.S. Army Corps of Engineers. On the other hand, much of the Authority's work does depend on annual appropriations from the Congress, and its power distribution as well as agricultural and forestry programs depend importantly upon the cooperation of local governments, cooperatives, state extension services, and the like. Congressional appropriations, however, have been made in lump sum, so the autonomy of the Authority's board has been maintained.

Originally, the three board members divided the administrative duties of the organization among themselves. This changed in the later part of the 1930s when administrative responsibilities were transferred to a general manager. Nevertheless, the four main programs of the Authority have operated relatively independently—river development, power production, agriculture, and forestry. The river development and power programs have been more centrally planned for the region as a whole than the agriculture and forestry programs.

Proposals to duplicate this corporate style of federal enterprise in other river valleys were rejected in the later 1930s and 1940s and seem unlikely to be revived. TVA remains a unique regional development organization in the American experience.

Intergovernmental participation bodies

The small number of consolidated local governments and the uniqueness of TVA are signs of the nation's political rejection of the idea that a "fourth level of government" is needed, as well as the idea that the third level (local government) should be thoroughly reformed in terms of its boundaries. The widespread use of special districts has been limited rather strictly to individual functions and geographic areas where they provide an administrative and/or financial advantage without displacing other functions and powers of existing localities.

This decision in favor of retaining existing local governments and supplementing them only piecemeal by the pragmatic use of boundary-bridging special districts leaves many area-wide issues unaddressed. To bridge this gap, several different types of intergovernmental mechanisms have been devised. These regional bodies are public purpose organizations which stop short of being governments in their own right. They prepare studies and plans, and they provide a forum for discussion of regional issues by the various governments and nongovernmental interests affected, but their role in implementing plans is largely limited to giving advice to others who possess the governmental powers which would need to be exercised.

The four main types of these intergovernmental participation bodies are substate regional councils, special purpose substate regional organizations, multistate regional economic development commissions, and multistate river basin commissions and committees. All of these organizations have basically the same form—a relatively large governing body composed wholly or primarily of representatives of participating governments, with a professional staff headed by an executive director. Descriptions of these four types of regional organizations follow.

Substate regional councils   Substate regional councils, of course, trace their roots back to metropolitan planning commissions. The traditional metropolitan planning commissions established up through the mid-1960s drew their memberships mainly from citizen appointees. Usually these members were outstanding community leaders, and the commissions were considered to be composed of the elite. They often were known as "blue ribbon" organizations. Their membership, however, set them apart from local government decision making. Metropolitan councils of governments, as differentiated from planning commissions, were rather rare in 1965 when federal funding for regional planning was broadened to include support for regional planning bodies of the council of governments form. Since that year, however, the council of governments type of organization rapidly became the most common one in metropolitan areas and later spread to nonmetropolitan areas as well.

According to a 1977 survey, 26.4 percent of metropolitan regional councils had memberships totally composed of local elected officials, about 90 percent had at least a majority of such members, and only 1.6 percent had none.[3] This compares with 16.8 percent of nonmetropolitan councils consisting entirely of local elected officials, about 80 percent with at least a majority elected, and nearly 5 percent without this type of representation. This pattern is fairly consistent throughout the United States, although the northeastern states tend to have somewhat fewer regional councils with a majority of elected officials than do states in other parts of the nation.

The average size of the regional council governing body is 33. In contrast to the participation of local elected officials on almost every regional council, about half of the councils had members who were appointed local officials, and about one-third had private citizen members. Only 15 percent or less had (in descending order) elected officials of special districts, state legislators, representatives from the executive branch of state government, appointed officials from special districts, or other types of members.[4]

Most substate regional councils are established voluntarily by the action of participating local governments in accordance with state enabling legislation (63.4 percent) or state legislation authorizing the joint exercise of local powers (14.3 percent). A little over 7 percent of them are established formally as private nonprofit corporations.[5] Responsibilities usually mentioned for these organizations in the enabling legislation include the preparation of comprehensive regional plans which set public policy goals and priorities, the preparation and/or coordination of functional plans in relation to overall coordinative policies, and the provision of technical assistance to local governments. Less frequently mentioned are the responsibilities to provide a forum for local government policy coordination and plan implementation, as well as for the development of recommendations regarding the distribution of state and federal aid within the region.[6]

While most of these state laws mention at least some of these responsibilities, fewer than half of the states actually provide even minimal powers to help the councils carry out their responsibilities. The most frequently authorized power is for "the adoption" of plans and programs, but in only five states does this adoption carry with it a requirement for other units of government to act consistently with such adopted plans and programs. The power to review and comment upon projects that might affect the regional plan also is quite common, but fewer than half the states extend this power to projects being pursued without federal funds, and only a handful of states supplement it with additional powers related to the allocation of state and federal funds within the region, budget control of special districts, or certificates of need for certain types of projects. About 20 percent of the states authorize regional councils to perform regional services—such as landfills, public transit, water supply, and sewage treatment— under certain specified conditions.

It can be seen from this brief review of responsibilities and powers that the responsibilities are considerably broader and more commonly specified in state legislation than the powers to back them up.

Special purpose regional organizations The more than 1200 single-purpose substate regional organizations in the United States are established primarily to administer four specific federal aid programs—community action (anti-poverty programs), special services for the aging, health systems planning, and criminal justice planning. Eighty percent of these organizations are organized as nonprofit corporations, and 62 percent of their governing board members are private citizens representing the target groups being served or the providers of services.[7]

Another federal aid program—comprehensive employment and training

(CETA)—also encourages regional planning, but of a less formal nature. Large local governments with populations of 100,000 or more are eligible to receive this type of aid directly from the federal government, but smaller ones must join together to aggregate at least this much population among them, and there is 10 percent extra money as an incentive for such joint action. Of the 400 or so recipients of CETA funds, approximately 130 are joint action consortia. Nevertheless, the intergovernmental committees administering them were not independent enough or separately staffed apart from member local governments sufficiently to be counted in the 1977 Census of Governments as independent regional organizations. Many of the consortia are not fully area wide in relation to their labor markets, and their planning appears to be centered for the most part in participating local governments rather than in a separate regional staff.

Certain other federal aid programs also have fostered regional planning outside the substate regional councils. For example, the metropolitan planning organizations required by the U.S. Department of Transportation for urban transportation planning purposes now are about equally divided between regional councils and separate single purpose regional planning organizations—down from 75 percent regional councils in the mid-1970s. The water quality planning required by Section 208 of the Federal Water Pollution Control Act has been carried out by regional councils in about 125 areas, but by separate single purpose planning bodies in 11 other areas; although the federal funding for this purpose has lapsed, the requirement remains (with restoration a live option in Congress), and there is no reason to believe that the established pattern of regional responsibilities will change significantly. Likewise, solid waste and air quality planning usually have been carried out by regional councils, but sometimes by other special purpose bodies. The Department of Agriculture's resource conservation and development committees always have been separate bodies representing the various soil conservation districts and other cooperating organizations in their areas, but they have not been separately staffed or funded. Finally, the community mental health center program has operated with an organization tailored directly to the specific center or constellation of interrelated centers being administered;[8] it now is encompased within a broad block grant subject to whatever administrative patterns the individual states may establish.

Multistate economic development commissions[9] The Appalachian Regional Commission (ARC)—now being phased out—and the Title V Regional Development Commissions (abandoned by the Federal government in 1981) were established by the Federal Public Works and Economic Development Act of 1965. The act designated members consisting of the governors of the states involved (one chosen annually as chairman of the commission and state co-chairman) and a presidentially appointed federal co-chairman. The Commission then was charged with appointing an executive director to hire and administer a professional staff. In the case of the Appalachian Regional Commission, there is also a states' representative who is a full-time staff member representing the states' interests within the organization as a physical counterpart to the full-time federal co-chairman. All three staffs of the Appalachian Regional Commission—including the executive director's nonpartisan staff and the more partisan staffs of the states' representative and federal co-chairman—are located together in Washington. However, for the Title V Commissions, the executive directors and general staffs were located within the respective regions, while the federal co-chairmen and their special staffs all were located in Washington, D.C. within the U.S. Department of Commerce.

The regional development commissions were charged with developing goals, policies, plans, and programs for the economic and social improvement of their multistate jurisdictions, and with coordinating the use of federal funds consistent with the regional planning process. Congress appropriates funds to them for administration, planning, research, and demonstrations, as well as for supplementing many of the action programs funded by regular federal aid programs. In the case of Appalachia, this additional federal funding is quite substantial in several fields—especially for highways—and has had a major impact within the region. Funding for the Title V Commissions was much less significant, providing the governors with an opportunity to pursue a number of special projects, but making relatively little overall impact in those regions.

ARC has systematically used its planning funds to help support state and substate regional planning programs which feed into the multistate planning program and support it on a sound basis. Only five of the eleven Title V Commissions attempted to use their planning funds this way, and the effort was much more sporadic than in Appalachia, due to the scarcity of funds. Criticisms of the Title V planning processes often are heard to the effect that the commissions did little more than compile the federal aid funding proposals of the states. In Appalachia, there has been a much greater balance of planning inputs from all levels and more evidence of overall regional goals and priorities.

Multistate river basin commissions and committees Federal interagency committees for coordinating the development of rivers have been active in individual river basins throughout much of the country beginning in the 1930s. Gradually, state representatives were invited to participate. These committees had no separate staffs, but relied upon the work of the various participating federal agencies.

In 1965, the Federal Water Resources Planning Act established the opportunity for states to consent to the establishment of joint federal-state river basin commissions which would have official state representation appointed by the states to balance federal agency representation, and a full-time presidentially appointed chairman with a staff to perform planning and coordinating functions. While these commission staffs were small (averaging about one dozen) and therefore had to rely substantially on the work of other federal agencies, they had begun to make some difference in the traditionally construction-oriented planning for the several basins in which commissions have been established.[10]

These commissions covered approximately 40 percent of the nation by 1981 when the federal government disbanded them. Where they did not exist, most of the nation's remaining territory was covered by the old style interagency coordinating committees. The few remaining river basins are subject to individual planning efforts of the states and separate federal agencies.

Portions of the nation that were not incorporated into formal river basin commissions were eligible for this form of organization upon the consent of at least half of the states involved in any particular basin. Prior to its demise in 1981, the Federal Water Resources Council promoted the formation of additional river basin commissions among the states, and the President established them by executive order when agreement was reached among the states. The federal government financed the operations of the commissions and provided water resources planning funds to the states to help them participate effectively. However, federal funding levels were quite modest.

State and federal support for intergovernmental participation bodies

Most of the initiative and funding for regional organizations has come from the federal government. For substate regions, federal support began with one program of grants for metropolitan planning in the 1950s, grew to 24 programs for both metropolitan and nonmetropolitan regions by 1972, and offered 39 different forms of support by 1979.[11] As noted in Chapter 2, these federal programs supplied approximately 76 percent of all the funds for substate regional councils by 1977, and 92 percent for all of the special purpose substate regional organizations. With the matching funds required by many of these federal grant programs, nearly the total budgets of most substate organizations were devoted to federal program purposes and administered in accordance with federal rules and regulations.

States merely consented to the formation of these organizations within their boundaries until the latter part of the 1960s when a number of states began to take advantage of the potential for positive state action in directing this movement in a more coordinated fashion which could meet state objectives as well as federal and local ones. As states began to reorganize their own structures to establish the governors as overall managers and coordinators of state programs during this period, and as they began to take new interest in the state role in land-use controls, many of the programs taking root at the substate regional level came into focus in state government. Also, the states received federal aid in many of these same program areas. Yet, the regional offices of state departments and agencies usually were established with highly divergent service area boundaries from one department to another, seldom coinciding with one another or with the boundaries of substate regional councils or special purpose regional organizations. The federal government called upon the states to help establish common boundaries for all the different area-wide federal aid programs, and some of the states took this opportunity also to rationalize the administrative boundaries for their own departments and agencies. The idea was to reinforce the various planning and coordination efforts at the regional level and tap that expertise for use in state planning, budgeting, and program coordination efforts. To accomplish this purpose, most states established statewide substate districting systems. These statewide systems were established by legislation in 19 states by 1980 and by executive order in an additional 24 states. Maryland established a comparable statewide system by action of its state planning department, bringing the total number of states joining this effort to 44.[12]

By the end of the 1970s, over half the states were providing general financial support to their regional councils. Although this support is much below the level traditionally supplied by the federal government, it grew modestly during the 1970s. Nevertheless, 60 percent of these funds were still being provided by only six states—Texas, Kentucky, Georgia, Virginia, Michigan, and Minnesota.[13]

Both the National Association of Regional Councils (NARC) and the Advisory Commission on Intergovernmental Relations have recommended that each state should create a statewide system of multipurpose regional councils, direct that all of the area-wide federal programs be carried out through them, provide the councils with a broad set of responsibilities and powers adequate to meet emerging area-wide needs, supply a substantial amount of general support funds unfettered by specific program requirements, and establish direct links between regional planning and policy making, on the one hand, and the states' own planning and budgeting processes, on the other. A 1978 survey by NARC showed that most states had taken some action along these lines, but that the degree of support varies widely from one state to another.[14] On the rough scale used, only about half the states scored better than 50 percent, and the best state scored only 80 percent. Thus, most states could do more to support their regional councils.

Work programs of regional organizations

As should be readily apparent by now, the work programs of regional organizations result from a combination of local desires and needs, federal aid priorities and requirements, and state legislated purposes. The multistate river basin commissions, of course, devote most of their attention to river development, the allocation of water, and the protection of water quality. Special purpose substate regional organizations are confined to the purposes of the individual federal aid programs which they serve. The multistate economic development commissions have somewhat more varied programs, but differ substantially from each other depending upon the needs of their regions.

1. In Appalachia, over half of the budget goes for the special Appalachian highway system, while other major amounts are spent for health and child development programs, construction of vocational schools, and the supplementation of a variety of other federal grant programs operating within the region. Increasingly, in recent years, supplementation of federal grants for housing, community development, water and sewer facilities, and other forms of infrastructure have become important. Minor amounts go for mining restoration, administrative expenses of local development districts, research, and technical assistance.
2. The Ozarks Commission has devoted its attention to (in descending order) job development, human resources, transportation, and community development.
3. The Pacific Northwest Commission gave first priority to natural resources, followed by agriculture and forestry, human resources, and regional economic analysis.
4. Old West also put natural resources first, followed by agriculture and forestry, regional economic analysis, and energy management.
5. Four Corners stressed industrial development, and then human resources, transportation, and natural resources.
6. Upper Great Lakes also stressed industrial development and human resources, with energy, transportation, and tourism next in order.
7. New England concentrated first on transportation, then on energy and the development of commercial and industrial opportunities.
8. Coastal Plains began with human resources concerns, followed by marine resources, industrial development, agriculture, and forestry.[15]

Among the most complex work programs are those of the multipurpose substate regional councils. The remaining discussion here, concerning the work programs of regional organizations, focuses upon these regional councils.

Programs pursued by substate regional councils

Regional councils were involved in a wide variety of planning and coordinating programs by the late 1970s. The federal government provided grants for most of these programs. The programs spanned the fields of community and economic development, transportation, environmental protection, natural resources, energy, health and social services, public safety, fire protection, surplus property disposition, and the arts. Other activities in which the regional councils were involved included: noise control, tourism, regional library cooperation, mental health, alcoholism/drug abuse, nutrition, and child development/day care.[16] Comprehensive planning (with federal grants from the U.S. Department of Housing and Urban Development) and the review of federally pursued or federally assisted projects (under authority of U.S. Office of Management and Budget Circular A-95) were the only two programs almost universally undertaken.

Services to local governments and to the citizens of the region are also provided by regional councils, but aside from grantsmanship and professional planning services to the local governments, relatively few regional councils are involved.

Figure 6-1 shows the relative importance of the different programs in regional council budgets, and how they differ between metropolitan and nonmetropolitan

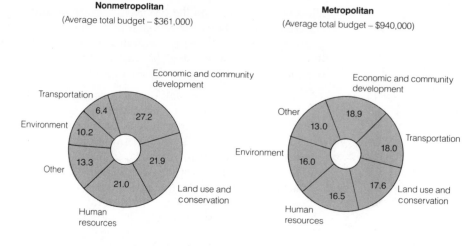

Figure 6–1   Expenditures of general regional organizations, by function, 1977 (unweighted averages).

areas. In metropolitan areas, typically, there is a fairly even balance among the five main program areas—economic and community development, transportation, land use and conservation, human resources, and environment. Nonmetropolitan regional councils devote much less of their effort to transportation and environment, with correspondingly more to the other three areas. Economic and community development stands out largest in the nonmetropolitan budgets.

Regional council work programs have changed substantially over the decade of the 1970s. Social services, special programs for the elderly, and energy concerns each have come to occupy a much more prominent position in the work of more councils, while fewer councils now deal with airports, recreation and open space, water quality, solid waste, health systems, and manpower.[17] Housing probably also became much more important for a larger number of regional councils, although available data are somewhat unclear about this.

Federal influences

As noted earlier, most of the programs which regional councils pursue have federal grants available. Regional councils were the officially designated agents for carrying out federal responsibilities under a number of those programs.

Figure 6-2 lists all 39 federal aid programs available for the support of regional councils as of 1979. While this list has grown over the years, the growth has been in single-function programs and in programs that do not apply to all regions in the nation. While planning assistance remained steady overall—through 1980—at about 1 percent of the growing amount of federal aid, the share allocated to comprehensive planning dropped from 38 percent to 20 percent in recent years. At the same time, functional planning rose from 47 percent to 54 percent, and project planning nearly doubled from 15 percent to 26 percent.[18]

With multipurpose planning funds drying up—including discontinuance of HUD's Section 701 program and Agriculture's rural development program in fiscal year 1982—and with applicability of many programs limited to only certain parts of the nation, regional councils increasingly are having to piece together the major portions of their budgets from a wide variety of diverse federal grant programs and other sources. By the late 1970s, the average regional council had managed to become designated as the official agent for carrying out four federal programs—with councils in the mideast, southeast, southwest, and Appalachia doing somewhat better than this, while those in other states averaged fewer.[19] Most councils also had managed to become involved one way or another in some additional federal aid programs for which an official designation was not required. By fiscal year 1982, however, most of these federal programs had been terminated or were being phased out (see Figure 6-2).

As area-wide federal aid programs increased in number, moved more predominantly toward single-purpose functional planning, shifted priorities, and remained the dominant part of regional council budgets in the 1970s, funding the regional council work program became increasingly complex. Grantsmanship became a major staff function, as the staff always sought to have an additional new source of grant funds available to take the place of one no longer forthcoming, or of another which was reduced in amount. Frequently this meant dropping an established program from the council's activities, and adding a new one to reflect the new source of funds. In the grantsmanship competition, some of the federal funds went to special purpose regional planning organizations, rather than to the general regional council.

These characterisitics of the federal grant system made it difficult to maintain a stable work program for a regional council, with a sound balance of functional planning efforts tied together by an overall coordinated public policy framework. Creativity in writing grant applications so that they would meet the needs of the regional council and its participating local governments as well as federal program objectives was essential.

Regional councils, with their very heavy reliance upon federal funding, were in the forefront of federal aid recipients taking advantage of the Joint Funding Simplication Act. This act allowed funds from several different grant programs to be combined into a single application and work program supervised by a single federal agency under an interagency agreement. While joint funding agreements were difficult to arrange among federal agencies, they did simplify paperwork and allow the integration of federal aid objectives by regional councils. However, the decline in federal aid for regional councils has contributed to the dormancy of the joint funding process.

State purposes

Although most states still require very little of regional councils, some have begun to expect them to act on behalf of state government. One example is the state of Florida. Under 1980 legislation, Florida has expanded its expectations of help from regional councils and restructured them to include appointment of one-third of the members of council governing bodies by the governor. Roles to be played by the councils on behalf of the state now include (1) assisting in the preparation of the state comprehensive plan, (2) coordinating with regional water management districts and the substate districts of the state department of environmental regulation, (3) reviewing local plans mandated by the state to be prepared by the counties and cities, and (4) reviewing developments of regional impact, electric power plant siting plans, and coastal zone management plans.[20] Although taking shape slowly, the trend appears to be in the direction of growing state expectations for help from the substate regional councils. According to a recent survey, nine states have policy and planning information exchanges between certain state agencies and the regional councils, while 10 states provide for inputs from the regional councils to state priority setting and budget processes.[21]

Products of the planning program

The products of the regional council's planning program generally fall into three categories—planning reports, intergovernmental agreements, and project reviews.

Figure 6–2 Availability of federal programs supporting substate regional activities, 1977–79, and FY 1982.

Name of program	Availability of program, 1977–79		FY 1982
	Throughout the nation	Limited number of substate regions	
Rural Development			
1. Sec. III Planning*		rural areas only	terminated
2. Rental Housing		rural areas only	reduced funds
3. Energy Impacted Area Development		inland areas with major energy-related employment growth only	terminated
4. Resource Conservation and Development		rural areas only	reduced funds
Community and Economic Development			
5. Economic development*		regions with local depressed areas	reduced funds (may be phasing out)
6. Sec. 8 Housing	X		areawide features dropped
7. Sec. 701 Planning*	X		terminated
8. Community Development Block Grants	X		areawide features dropped
9. Historic Preservation	X		reduced funds
10. Appalachian Planning*		Appalachian states only	reduced funds (phasing out)
11. Coastal Plains Planning		Coastal Plains states only	terminated
12. Four Corners Planning		Four Corners states only	terminated
13. Upper Great Lakes Planning		Upper Great Lakes states only	terminated
14. Old West Planning		Old West states only	terminated
15. Pacific Northwest Planning		Pacific Northwest states only	terminated
Environmental Protection			
16. Coastal Zone Management		regions along the nation's coast only	reduced funds (phasing out)
17. Coastal Energy Impact		certain impacted regions along the nation's coast only	reduced funds (phasing out)
18. Air Pollution Control		large urban areas mostly	being revised
19. Quiet Communities	X		phased out
20. Water Pollution Control	X		being revised
21. Solid Waste Planning	X		terminated

Transportation

#	Program		
22.	Airport Planning	urban or metropolitan regions only	terminated
23.	Urban Highway Planning	urban or metropolitan regions only	being revised
24.	Mass Transportation	X	being revised

Health and Social Services

#	Program		
25.	Alcohol Abuse Control	X	**
26.	Drug Abuse Control	X	**
27.	Emergency Medical Services	X	**
28.	Health Systems Planning	X	reduced funds (phasing out)
29.	Community Mental Health Centers	X	**
30.	Special Programs for the Aging	X	continuing
31.	Title XX Social Services	X	blocked, no areawide requirements
32.	Comprehensive Employment & Train.	X	reduced funds
33.	Highway Safety	X	being revised
34.	Community Action (Anti-Poverty)	X	blocked, no areawide requirements after FY 1982

Protective Services

#	Program		
35.	Law Enforcement	X	terminated
36.	Juvenile Justice & Delinquency Prevention		reduced funds

General Purposes

#	Program		
37.	Project Notification and Review Process (A-95)*	X	being revised
38.	Intergovernmental Personnel Grants	X	terminated
39.	Excess Property Transfer	X	reoriented to states

Total Number of Programs	**23** (59%)	**16** (41%)

* Support comprehensive planning
** In block grants—no areawide requirements

Source: Compiled by ACIR staff, based upon: Reid, Sam, Kestner, and Godsey, *Federal Programs Supporting Multi-county Substate Regional Activities: An Analysis.* ESCS Staff Report (Washington, DC: U.S. Department of Agriculture, May 1980); Reid, J. Norman, and Stam, Jerome M., "Funding Cuts Hit Substate Regions," *Public Administration Times,* January 15, 1982, p. 3.

Regional planning reports   These reports may take several forms and fulfill several different purposes. Some will simply provide information about the region—perhaps findings of fact, data, or directories. Up-to-date maps and computer tapes may even be included in this information dissemination type of reporting. The purpose is to inform the governments, citizens, and businesses of the region about the status of the region. Some regional councils organize this information systematically once each year into a state of the region report. Some councils also make their information available through a staffed information center where the public can get help in finding what they need.

Other reports may set forth plans, policies, and priorities for public action. These types of reports frequently are published first as draft reports for the purpose of eliciting discussion of important public policy issues and drawing out comments from various segments of the community which can be used in revising the draft before final action is taken on it. When issues are particularly complex or controversial, second and third drafts (or even more) may be issued before a final plan or policy is decided upon. Action by the regional council usually is only an advisory recommendation to other units of government but may carry greater authority than this in certain cases.

Special sections in these policy reports, or perhaps separate, more detailed follow-up reports, may be devoted to the programming of plan implementation projects or actions, and the identification of needed legislation. Such documents detail the actions to be taken, those responsible for taking action, the amount of money involved, and the schedule for accomplishing the objective.

Intergovernmental agreements   Building consensus is one of the most important roles of regional councils. Publishing, discussing, revising, and adopting reports is one way to do this. However, regional planning reports seldom commit governments or others to take particular actions. Formal agreements achieve this commitment.

Regional councils may develop memoranda of understanding among local governments and regional bodies in their area concerning procedures for planning processes, for the exchange of information, and for coordinating interrelated programs. Signatories to such memoranda agree to follow these procedures.

Another type of agreement is the negotiated investment strategy in which the signatory parties (which may include state and federal agencies, local governments, and regional bodies) agree to spend their funds in particular ways at particular times consistent with an overall regional plan and program. Agreement on such strategies may be developed through the use of professional mediators. By this means, it is hoped that all or most federal and state aid funds and direct expenditures by the federal and state governments in the region will contribute positively to the implementation of the overall regional plan and program.

Project reviews   When a specific public action is proposed to be taken in the region, which would have regional significance, it should be referred to affected governmental units and other interests for their comments, and the regional council should prepare official comments for submission to the proposing unit and to any grant-making unit or other authority whose approval would be required before the proposal could move ahead. Most federal actions and federal aid projects in recent years have been subject to this process, and several states require that nonfederal projects also must be.

Difficulties in implementing regional plans

Most regional councils issue reports for the purpose of communication, education, and consensus building. They develop agreements about what should be done in the region and work toward voluntary commitments to those agreements by important actors. They review proposed projects and issue advisory comments concerning them. In a few cases, adopted regional plans can have the effect of vetoing projects that would be inconsistent with them, but this is the exception rather than the rule. Regional councils that perform services may have some additional influence in their regions, but the number of councils with this kind of authority is rather limited.

Some of the special purpose substate regional organizations actually provide services in accordance with the plans for the particular functions that they serve. Even when they do not provide service themselves, as in the case of health systems planning agencies, they may still be able to veto actions that would be inconsistent with their plans. Multistate economic development commissions can exercise some positive influence on the implementation of their plans by the allocation of their own special funds for projects which they favor. But the river basin commissions have no such leverage. They are more in the advisory planning category, along with most substate regional councils.

Overall, then, regional planning organizations have very few implementation powers themselves. They are generally in the position of trying to persuade other actors to follow regional plans voluntarily. The various means of doing this are explained in Chapter 7.

In general, though, it can be said at this point that regional organizations as they are presently constituted need to develop stronger linkages with the state and local governments, special districts, and federal agencies which possess the powers needed to realize the goals and objectives of regional plans. For the most part, regional powers do not exist and cannot be applied directly. The traditional units of government still retain the needed powers and must be persuaded to use them in the best interests of the region.

Regional planning theories

The theoretical basis for all this regional planning activity rests upon the reasons that regions are organized, the nature of the regional needs to be met, some principles which seem to guide planning within regions, and the directions in which regional planning is evolving. These elements of planning theory are treated next.

Reasons for organizing regions

Regions are geographical areas with problems of public policy or administration for which no existing unit of government is organized. Organizing such a region provides a governmental body that will focus on the region's needs, study them, and try to meet them or move others to do so. In many regional organizations, planning is the principal activity; often it is the only activity authorized. Regional planning plays the key role of informing regional decision makers about the issues they face, if there are any such decision makers, or if not, it informs decision makers at other levels of government whose policies and projects affect regional affairs.

The region (an area big enough to encompass whole problems) should have a clear organizing concept which sets the theme for planning. A metropolitan area and a river basin are good examples. The former is a continuously urbanized community cut by numerous local jurisdictional boundaries but struggling to function as a single entity for many purposes. The second is a large interdependent land and water resource—also cut by many local jurisdictional boundaries as well as state lines—whose long-term preservation and productivity depends heavily upon its management as a single system. The stronger the organizing concept, the clearer will be the purposes of the region—and the benefits to be planned for.

The regional plan attempts to visualize a better future for its geographical area and recommend steps to achieve it. This involves the "ordering of activities and facilities in space and time."[22] The realism of the regional plan depends upon (1) the degree to which the regional problems, needs, and organizing concept are politically recognized as legitimate subjects of public policy at the regional level, and (2) the degree to which the regional organization itself is authorized to implement its own plans or is likely to be able to convince other units of government to take the steps recommended in the plan on behalf of the region.

Organizing the region is an effort to provide the political visibility, accessibility, responsibility, and accountability necessary to deal with regional problems as public policy issues. Proper representation in the regional planning organization helps to ensure that decisions with interjurisdictional consequences will be made jointly by those jurisdictions affected. This, in itself, is a goal to be valued highly.

The nature of regional needs

Regions may be organized either to deal more effectively with "the outside world" or to provide a forum within which to work out internal issues—or to do both. Examples of the first are to enhance the region's competitive position among other regions (perhaps in the market place for economic growth) and to generate greater "clout" in dealing with the state and federal governments (as in seeking financial aid or other benefits). Internal issues generally have to do with enhancing effectiveness, efficiency, economy, opportunity, equity, and livability within the region. In its dealings with the "outside," the regional organization becomes an advocate, while its role in internal issues is that of reconciler and balancer of multiple interests.

It is important to note that regional purposes and plans should deal with issues that local plans cannot.[23] Not only will this avoid a direct challenge to established local prerogatives, but it also will help local governments to achieve goals that would be out of reach otherwise. Such a focus would be expected to enhance the acceptance of regional planning.

Most regional organizations are highly intergovernmental. As such, they focus their planning heavily upon efforts to coordinate the activities of constituent (local or state) governments and to allocate resources among them. The regional offices of state and federal agencies, however, focus their efforts on administering policies already established above and/or on furnishing information and planning

TAXING BODY	CURRENT RATE	CURRENT AMOUNT	CHANGE FROM PRIOR YEAR	TAXING BODY	CURRENT RATE	CURRENT AMOUNT	CHANGE FROM PRIOR YEAR
CORPORATE	.080	31.95-	.38	COUNTY HIGHWAY	.068	27.16+	.56
COUNTY BRIDGE FUND	.003	1.20-	.03	FED AID MATCH FUND	.021	8.39-	.21
DET YOUTH HOME	.017	6.79+	1.06	I M RET FUND	.066	26.36-	.24
VETERANS ASSIST	.009	3.60+	1.55	CIVIL DEFENSE	.001	.40-	.40
DEPT OF MAPS	.005	2.00+	.36	HEALTH DEPT	.088	35.14+	3.22
COUNTY AUDIT TAX	.002	.80-	.02	PUB BLDG COMM RENT	.042	16.77-	.83
HISTORICAL MUSEUM	.002	.80-	.02	ELECTION EXPENSE	.030	11.98+	.11
SUPV OF ASSMTS	.011	4.40-	.51	EXT & COLL TAXES	.000	.00+	.00
PROP REC CARDS	.005	2.00+	2.00	NURSING HOME	.025	9.99-	.24
FOREST PRESERVE	.151	60.30+	.14	TOWNSHIP	.068	27.16+	.15
MOSQ ABATE	.009	3.60-	4.10	PK DIST	.662	264.34-	.01
NORTH SHORE SAN	.561	224.01-	34.61	CITY	1.387	553.83-	20.28
COLL LK CO 53	.220	87.85-	.54	SCHOOL DIST NO 10	2.484	991.87+	37.20
HIGH SCHOOL NO 11	2.240	894.33+	20.27				

PERMANENT INDEX NUMBER	TAX CODE	ACRES	(OVER)	TOTALS →		
26-204-01	8005			8.257	3297.02+	5.00

Figure 6-3 What is regional? What is local? Here is an example of extreme localism—a tax bill from Highland Park, Illinois, showing twenty-seven allocations for the property tax. The overlapping governments, special districts, and special programs make regionalism a containment operation.

proposals to higher level decision making. As noted earlier in this chapter, some states also expect their substate regional councils to furnish such inputs to the state. In addition, the federal government has flirted with a similar "bottom-up" idea for its budget making.[24] Of course, state and federal planning requirements also help to determine the issues with which regional planning will deal. Thus regional planning must look outward as well as inward.

Some principles guiding regional planning

If ordering activities and facilities in space and time is the core of regional planning, as Perloff has emphasized, then allocating resources to a region and within the region is the prime concern. At least three basic principles lie behind regional allocation decisions:

1. Regionwide systems should be effective and efficient regardless of how local boundaries or state lines intervene.
2. The region should take advantage of available economies of scale.
3. Opportunities and burdens should be distributed equitably throughout the region (or among regions).

Examples of the system principle occur in the fields of transportation, utilities, and the environment. Highways should fit together to give easy access throughout the region. Utilities should serve developed areas without being either seriously overloaded or underutilized. Shared water supplies, in particular, should keep pace with the needs for both economic and domestic use and be alloated equitably throughout the region with adequate interconnections to help avoid spot shortages, while sewage treatment capacity adequate to safeguard the region's shared waterways is essential. Ecological systems also should be kept intact.

Examples of the economies of scale principle are numerous. Health planning focuses heavily upon sharing of expensive facilities and avoiding excess facilities which would raise health care costs for everyone. Other expensive facilities also might be shared among jurisdictions; these could include zoos, sports arenas, convention centers, vocational high schools, community colleges, regional parks, museums, jails, and airports.

The equity principle would guide planning toward such goals as equal opportunity housing, meeting the needs of the area-wide job market, and sharing the metropolitan tax base. Usually this type of regional planning is the most difficult because its goals are newer and less firmly established in public attitudes. Political controversy frequently swirls around these issues.

Planning to meet all these regional goals is a complex task. Many of the goals, or at least the means of attaining them, are interrelated. While much planning focuses on just one type of regional system, or an individual economy of scale, or a single type of equity, the comprehensive regional planning organization should attempt to illuminate and accommodate at least the most critical interrelationships. Many such relationships come together in growth management plans wherein local governments set out to schedule the types and speed of development to match their own interests and fiscal capacity. If these local plans fail to accommodate fair shares of regional growth, to accept essential regional facilities, and to provide equal opportunities in the housing and job markets, regional planning can demonstrate the burdens placed on neighboring jurisdictions. Regional plans should establish specific targets for local governments to meet and seek to back these up with a counterbalancing allocation of state or federal grants that would assist neighboring localities overburdened by the inadequate performance of those that fail to meet their targets.[25] Regional planning targets also may be enforced by the courts if localities use exclusionary zoning to avoid their regional responsibilities.

Directions of evolving regional planning theory

Until the mid-1960s much regional planning was largely based upon intuitive concepts of ideal metropolitan growth patterns.[26] Physical planning was almost the exclusive concern, and metropolitan plans looked much like local master plans; they were largely focused on multicolored maps showing land-use patterns, major transportation routes, large open spaces, and certain other major facilities. But metropolitan planning organizations had little say in these matters, and the plans had little value other than for educational purposes.[27] The goals in such plans far outstripped the public's ability to implement them.

At about this time, some planning theorists began calling for a broader scope of analysis, covering program activities as well as facilities, but narrowing goals to less ambitious ones that were more nearly manageable within the given governmental setting. They urged that intuitive planning methods be replaced with quantitative ones as new computer, aerial photography, and satellite sensing technologies made large-scale data gathering and analysis more feasible. A good deal of progress was made along these lines in the 1970s, but little has changed with respect to the political authority of regional planning organizations to put improved plans into use.

Politically, there are three basic modes of operation for a regional planning organization: (1) to provide information and analytical studies, (2) to give politically significant planning advice to policymakers, and (3) to allocate regional resources itself. Of course, it takes differing sets of authorized powers for the regional planning organization to operate in each mode. Unfortunately, the greater the political controversy attached to each mode, the more unlikely it is that the necessary powers will be granted.

Figure 6-5 carries this analysis one step further by showing the typical mode of operation and most important skills needed for effectively pursuing the type of planning associated with the major types of regional planning organizations.

	Mode of operation		
	Information provider	Planning advisor	Allocator of resources
Authorized powers:			
Staff/study	●		
Policy adoption	●		
Mandatory referral	●	●	
Governing authority	●	●	●
Controversial nature of the mode:			
Low	●		
Medium		●	
High			●

Figure 6–4   Modes of operation of regional planning organizations by powers and controversiality.

	Major types of regional organizations			
	Blue ribbon regional planning commission	Council of governments	Authoritative regional council	Regional special district
Mode of operation:				
Information provider	●			
Planning advisor		●		
Allocator of resources			●	●
Prime skill needed:				
Research and analytical	●			
Negotiating		●		
Managerial			●	●

Figure 6–5   Modes of operation and prime skills needed by major types of regional planning organizations.

The old-style citizen planning commissions often provide high quality planning reports which, too often, sit on the shelf unused. The now more commonly encountered councils of governments, while often producing sound analytical reports as well, are in a better position to emphasize their advice to elected officials and sometimes can advance significant intergovernmental planning negotiations on selected high priority issues. The few authoritative regional councils (like those in Minneapolis–St. Paul and Portland, Oregon), as well as the somewhat more numerous regional special districts, can actually allocate certain types of regional resources themselves; consequently they need to emphasize responsible managerial skills, including sound management and financial planning.

In actuality, regional planning organizations follow no neat patterns of operation. They do the best they can under the diverse circumstances in which they find themselves. A recent classification of areawide regional councils (Figure 6-6) shows their wide variations in styles of operation—ranging from those that barely function to those that authoritatively govern. Most are somewhere in between, leaving a great deal of room for improving the organizational position of the regional planning process.

Current issues in strengthening regional planning processes

Current issues facing regional organizations are only new wrinkles in the age-old governmental debates about area and power.[28] Among the issues are drawing appropriate boundaries, assigning proper functions and powers, and figuring out how to organize, fund, plan, and proceed to perform assigned responsibilities effectively, fairly, and compassionately. These decisions are intermeshed, and their dimensions are both technical and political. Agreeing that some problem or need is regional in scope may not lead to agreement that there should be a strong regional organization capable of solving the problem or meeting the need.

Name	Description
In name only	Barely functions
Tourist board	Promotes development of the region with an "advertising" approach
Stalemate	Unsuccessfully attempts to resolve major interjurisdictional policy issues
Regional broker	Provides the policy forum within which major interjurisdictional issues are resolved
Local entrepreneur	Constantly invents and pursues new ways to serve the region's local governments and area-wide interests
National emphasis	Pursues policy objectives of various federal aid programs
State extension	Carries out state policies autonomously within the region
State agent	Acts within the region on behalf of state government
Regional provider	Provides agreed-upon regional public services
Regionweal	Authoritatively governs areawide policies and programs

Figure 6–6 Functional types of regional councils.

In the paragraphs which follow, defining what is regional and examining the role that a regional organization should play will be addressed separately.

Defining regional functions[29]

Some public problems or needs are simply bigger than others. They may be so costly, for example, that they require a larger tax base than the individual local governments in the area can tap separately, but combining their tax bases may provide adequate resources.

Some problems simply cannot be stopped by local political boundaries. For example, air pollution generated in one locality frequently is blown by the wind into another. Likewise, water pollution from upstream communities flows through downstream ones. Increased taxes or tougher regulations in one locality may push economic or other activities into neighboring communities.

Examples such as these can be multiplied many times over. The point is that the geographic extent of a problem or need, however, it may be defined by principles of economics, social impact, or environmental effects, is the first step in determining whether the governmental response should be regional or local. If the problem falls completely within the borders of a local government, that problem reasonably may be considered to be a local one. If, however, this problem should spread across the boundaries of two or more local governments, then a regional solution is something to be considered. If a regional approach will lead to greater effectiveness and efficiency, reduced costs, more fairly distributed costs and benefits, and more compassion, the case for a regional approach is strengthened. Each of these advantages helps to make the case, and the more of them that can be documented, the stronger the case becomes.

Nevertheless, the regional exercise of governmental powers is perceived as more dangerous than the local exercise of the same powers. Regional organizations often are equated with "super-governments" because the exercise of their powers affects so many more people than the powers of an individual locality. A regional decision tends to homogenize the levels of service across the whole area, diminishing the amount of choice arising when some communities provide fewer services and lower tax rates. So the tendency is for voters to avoid defeat proposals that would give major powers to regional organizations unless the benefits are very clear and would substantially outweigh other disadvantages.

The extent to which a regional approach would disturb the status quo in other governmental activities within the region may also help to determine whether it is acceptable. If the proposal would diminish the present powers of local governments or other regional organizations, or work to the political disadvantage of officials currently in power, or lead to higher taxes (or even just the fear of higher taxes), then the political defeat of the proposal is likely.[30]

Ways of making a regional proposal more acceptable include limiting the regional functions quite strictly, making regional organizations clearly accountable to the political process by the use of elected officials (either directly elected for a regional job, or elected to local government and representing the local view at the regional level), heavy use of citizen participation, and procedures by which the regional organization shares its functions with the local governments or other limited purpose regional bodies in the area (in a planning, coordinating, consensus-building, "balance of powers" mode of operating). Major governmental functions may be broken down into a number of separate activities, some of which might remain local while others become regional. Even these activities might sometimes remain shared rather than clearly divided into independent local and area-wide responsibilities.

Ultimately, decisions about which functions and activities remain local and which become regional are made politically. This occurs in at least five different ways. The most basic way is for the assignments to be made specifically in the state constitution or state laws. Frequently, though, state laws may provide that such decisions may be made by local referenda—usually requiring separate majorities of the voters in each local jurisdiction affected. Most states also have general legislation allowing their local governments to cooperate with one another by entering into interlocal agreements or contracts for the joint provision of services or the provision of services to one locality by another. A large number of functions have been transferred from one government to another or are being performed either jointly or by contract in accordance with interlocal agreements.[31]

The remaining two means of political decision making for the assignment of functions among local jurisdictions and regional bodies are federal aid programs and court decisions. While not specifically provided for in state constitutions and laws, these means have had major effects. As pointed out earlier in this chapter, federal aid provides the major funding for many types of regional organizations, and the purposes of the federal grants become the functions of the regional organizations; the decision making roles of the regional organizations as specified in the grant programs and associated regulations become the "powers" of these bodies.

Two types of court decisions in recent years also have required a regional approach. One type holds that local communities cannot exclude certain types of development within their borders unless that is consistent with a formal regional planning process in which all of the region's needs are accommodated.[32] The other upholds federal laws requiring that federal aid be used in such a way as to avoid discrimination among particular segments of the population and enlist the positive actions of central cities and suburbs alike in addressing urban problems.[33] Therefore, federally required regional planning prerequisite to the approval of action grants must satisfactorily address these issues.

The assignment of functions and activities to local and area-wide units varies a good deal from one place to another and continues to evolve from time to time. As products of the political process, these decisions tend to evolve gradually in a continuing manner and are unlikely ever to be made "once and for all." In recent years, there has been more or less equal emphasis upon revitalizing local government while broadening and strengthening regional organizations.[34] It is not a question of one or the other, but the proper balance between them. Many experts believe that this is not simply a matter of coexistence, but that strong local governments and strong regional organizations can be of mutual benefit to each other. The National Association of Regional Councils has a motto, "Regionalism is local power," by which it means to point out that joint action can be more effective than separate action in many circumstances, and that such action taken on a regional basis can enhance the decision-making role of local leaders, as compared with state and federal officials, in those areas where regionalism is strong.

Figure 6-7 shows how local and area-wide activities may supplement, complement, and strengthen each other. Of course, these are just a few examples designed to illustrate more or less typical situations in moderate sized regions. In regions with very small populations, many of the local activities in this table might become area-wide, while in big regions large local governments might perform a number of the area-wide activities themselves. Nevertheless, the regional phenomenon is universal. No matter what the size of local governments, there are public problems and needs which spill across their boundaries into adjoining areas, creating the need for regional approaches and regional plans.

Improving the performance of regional organizations

Studies of regional organizations all conclude that such bodies almost always lack the power to implement their plans, usually coexist with other regional units in their area, are hampered by inconsistent federal policies concerning different types of regional activities, rely almost exclusively upon federal project notification and review processes as their source of power, and receive too little support from state government. Largely because of these difficulties, regional organizations generally are judged to have disappointing performance records. This raises the question whether such difficulties can and should be overcome.

Provide governmental authority for regional organizations? As already noted, most regional organizations are planning and coordinating units rather than regional governments. Their coordinating ability comes from their knowledge, advisory activities, and persuasive capabilities, rather than from authority or governmental power. This is true for both substate and multistate regional organizations.

With voluntary membership being the present norm, major controversies cannot be pushed too far without endangering the very structure of the organization. If consensus does not develop, often the planning issue is abandoned or simply sent back for further study. State legislation or interstate compact authority, which would establish definite boundaries, a stable membership, and independent revenue raising authority, would allow regional organizations to tackle tougher issues, decide them by majority vote, and move ahead to implement them without fear that the organization would dissolve.

It is a big jump from the present intergovernmental mechanisms of substate regional councils, multistate economic development commissions, and river basin commissions to the establishment of regional governments for these areas. The dilemma in crossing this gap is that policies designed to enhance support for voluntarily established planning advisory bodies are very different than those designed to create new governments. The intergovernmental mechanisms concentrate on providing noncontroversial services, developing consensus, and "going along to get along." Establishing a regional government means tackling major

Functions	Typically local activities	Typically areawide activities
Police	Patrol Routine investigation Traffic control	Crime laboratory Special investigation Training Communications Hot pursuit and backup agreements
Fire	Fire prevention Fire fighting	Training Communications Backup agreements Special investigations

Transportation	Local streets,
	  sidewalks, alleys:
	  repairs, cleaning
	  snow removal,
	  lighting, trees
		Expressways
		Major arteries
		Mass transit
		Taxi regulation
		Ports
		Airports
		Terminals

Refuse	Collection	Disposal/recycling
Environmental protection	Sanitation Noise control	Air pollution control River quality

Water and sewer	Local mains
	Retail distribution/
	  billing
		Water sources and treatment
		Trunk lines/wholesale
		  distribution

Parks and recreation	Small parks and tot lots Recreation centers Playgrounds Swimming pools Tennis courts	Large parks, zoo Museum Concert hall Stadium
Schools	Elementary Secondary	Community colleges Vocational schools
Libraries	Small Bookmobiles	Central reference Interlibrary cooperation
Health	Clinics	Hospital
Development	Local planning and zoning Urban renewal Code enforcement	Broad planning Standards for development
Housing	Public housing management	Housing subsidy allocation

Figure 6–7 Some examples of local and areawide services.

controversy head on and playing hardball politics for keeps. A loss on the governmental power issue may also destroy good will and effectiveness for the existing planning/advisory organization.

Pressure for regional planning to become more effective has come largely from the federal level as a condition for continued funding. As a result of such pressures, a few federal aid programs have given substate regional councils virtual veto power over project funding decisions in those programs. State law also can provide similar regional decision-making authority over projects funded without federal dollars and has done so in a few cases. Evolution in this direction probably must come from outside the regional organizations themselves (and from outside member local governments), because the organizational incentives within the region work toward maintaining the present voluntary structure.

Consolidate or link regional organizations serving the same regions?   The Advisory Commission on Intergovernmental Relations has recommended that there be only a single multipurpose regional organization for any given region, or that if there is more than one, the multipurpose one should be made a policy body authorized to supervise the operations of single purpose ones.[35] The urge behind this recommendation is to achieve coordination among all functions assigned to the regional level. Short of consolidation or authoritative provisions for supervision, which would have to come largely from state law, federal aid rules could require that any regional planning funds approved for a given region be consistent with a single overall work program negotiated among the various regional bodies. Such a policy was enunciated administratively by the federal government,[36] but proved difficult to implement because it was perceived as limiting the independence of the various federal aid programs. The reduction in federal aid for regions made this provision even less effective, and it was dropped in 1983 when OMB Circular A-95 was replaced by new state-specified intergovernmental consultation processes under Presidential Executive Order 12372.

The move toward a generalist perspective at the substate level of regions has been paralleled at the multistate level by proposals that the economic development regions and the standard federal regions for federal regional councils should be made coterminous, and that the cochairman for the economic development commission should be designated as the chairman of the federal regional council. This would put a full-time presidential appointee with his own staff in charge of two of the three types of multistate regional organizations. The third type—river basin commissions—could be specifically added to the federal regional councils (although many federal agency members already are represented on the FRCs in other capacities). This would close the circle, encompassing all the multistate regional organizations in a single forum. A beginning on this was made in 1979 when the economic development commissions were added to the membership of the federal regional councils.[37] However, with the demise of the Title II and Title V commissions in 1981, the means for federal leadership in this movement are no longer available.

The final link in this generalist/functional coordination network could be made by following the lead of the Appalachian Regional Commission in systematically using substate regional councils to aggregate local planning and feed it into state planning, which in turn is reflected in multistate plans and programs. Through these mechanisms, presidential policies embodied in executive orders and circulars administered by the U.S. Office of Management and Budget could filter down to the federal regional councils where they would move out into the multistate economic development commissions and river basin commissions, the state A-95 clearinghouse agencies, and the substate regional councils. Such a network, the basic elements of which were largely constructed during the 1960s and 1970s, would allow a two-way interchange between the policies of the President, the governors, the mayors, and the county executives of the nation— offering the opportunity to balance the generalist view of public policy and management against the demands of individual functional programs. Unfortunately, the dismantling of multistate regions, the withdrawal of federal support for substate regions, a reduction in the size and responsibilities of the FRCs (by Executive Order 12314), and the rescinding of A-95 in 1981 and 1982 removed much of the potential for this concept. The FRCs, then, were abolished in 1983.[38]

Reevaluate the federal government's support for regions? Until 1981, the main issue with respect to federal support for regions was whether it should be more coordinated. There was a great deal of federal support, but it was fragmented. Since 1981, the federal support issue has shifted dramatically to the question of whether there is any federal role at all in most regional activities. The general position of the Reagan administration is that regionalism is primarily a matter for the states to decide. The withdrawal of federal funding, planning requirements, and organizational structures has been swift, with Congress salvaging only a few provisions for orderly transition to state responsibility. The immediate issue for most regional organizations in 1982 became how to survive a massive loss of federal funds and federally endowed regional planning roles long enough to make the transition to new forms of regional activity. By mid-1984, it was apparent that most regional councils had survived, but their staffs had become considerably smaller and their work programs had shifted from long-range planning toward much greater emphasis upon direct services to local governments and private interests—often to services generating fees to help offset the loss of federal funding.[39] State and local funding—on the average—has increased somewhat to compensate for loss of federal funding.

Linking together the various regional organizations, as discussed above, would have had the effect of coordinating the federal government's influence on them. And, even if those linkages did not come about—or until they did—progress could have been made toward the same ends by consolidating existing federal aids for substate regional organizations into fewer, broader grant programs and by more consistently designating the multipurpose regional councils as the preferred recipients. Federal interagency agreements to accept basic regional planning documents prepared for one program to satisfy planning requirements in others was another route being tried to reduce the burdens of multiple federal programs while achieving greater consistency among them. Changing federal requirements for the composition of regional organization governing bodies also was being worked on as a necessary step in some programs to allow regional council designation, even though this would take amendments to federal legislation in certain cases. These steps were being addressed only piecemeal, however.

Strengthen and broaden the plan and project review process? Presently, most regional organizations review only those projects funded wholly or partially with federal funds, and usually the review results only in advisory comments. Even this established process is not followed faithfully by all federal agencies (some of which approve projects before the required review period has ended) or funded adequately to allow the substate regional councils to provide meaningful comments in all appropriate cases. The Advisory Commission on Intergovernmental Relations (ACIR), as well as OMB itself, and others, have proposed improvements in this federally established process. In some cases, these proposals suggest that the comments should carry greater weight than more advisory opinions, holding up funding until regional concerns have been resolved. ACIR also has proposed that states, by legislation, extend this same type of review process to all projects of regional significance, whether or not they involve federal funding. For any regional organization whose major responsibility is planning, the review process is the mainstay of its influence. By expanding the scope of what is reviewed to include long range plans and multiyear programs as well as immediate projects, and to include state and locally funded projects as well as federally funded ones, and then to increase the weight of these comments, is to significantly increase the regional organization's influence. Nevertheless, the rescinding of A-95 by the Reagan Administration in 1982 and uncertainties about

The future for regional planning organizations   Two years ago, . . . I noted at a conference on regional planning at Princeton University that the nation's 2,000 regional planning organizations were facing a major crisis. After two decades of heavily promoting regional planning, the federal government had terminated or begun to phase out many of its supporting grant programs and regional planning requirements.

These shifts in federal policy created a severe test of the innate support for regional approaches at the state and local levels of government. It can be reported now that most regional organizations have survived this test, although not without significant transformation.

Only five of the nation's more than 600 substate regional councils went out of business in 1982, compared to the 30 that had been predicted in a 1983 survey of 335 regional agencies by the National Association of Regional Councils. But, at the same time, their federal funding receded substantially, from 76 percent of the typical regional council budget (as reported in the 1977 Census of Governments) to 48 percent in 1983.

The most important question, then, is not whether regional councils will survive, but what form they will take.

It's clear, first, that the scope of activities of regional agencies has broadened. Over the past decade, many of them have added economic development, transportation, housing, human services, management assistance, and computer services to their basic roster of land-use planning and environmental protection concerns.

The new role of fee-for-service contracts may be the most significant feature of the newly defined regional councils. These contracts call for packaging data about the region for local governments and the private sector; providing customized data and administrative services to both public and private clients; supplying professional planning and other consultant services; and delivering major public services (like transit or solid waste disposal) to local governments.

In short, as the work programs of regional organizations drift toward ad hoc activities that can be self-supporting, areawide planning and coordination tasks lose out. There is a very real danger that through neglect, the nation's

---

what will take its place suggests that fewer programs will be subject to review and that federal requirements for review may be withdrawn.

Increase state support for regions?   The states have within their power to legislate stronger, more self reliant and independent substate regions and to play bigger roles in multistate regions. Such legislation could substantially step up state financing for these organizations as well as develop stronger linkages between regional planning and state planning, policy making, and budgeting. A few states have done a great deal along these lines, but overall the states have let the federal government play the principal roles in financing and setting the agenda for regional planning—both substate and multistate. Many observers believe that there is no need for this, and that in fact it is undesirable. The structuring of substate units, particularly, is the Constitutional responsibility of the states, but they have been slow to exercise it. Now that the federal government is withdrawing both its financial support and the regional planning requirements that went with it, state legislation is more essential than ever.

Increase local support for regions?   Federal matching grants for regional organizations have stimulated local contributions to regional programs, especially

regional planning councils will lose their public planning functions, thereby becoming indistinct from private consulting firms. Areawide strategies, multifunctional coordination, and intergovernmental consultation may take a back seat.

Since the need for regional planning is as strong as ever, and since most of the regional organizations created in recent decades continue to exist, the present question is, "What roles will, can, and should these units play in the future?" . . . Three potential roles should be considered: the state partnership role, the member government service role, and the honest broker role:

State partnership. Until 1981, the federal government sought to make regional organizations its partners in achieving national goals. In the aftermath of the cuts, the states may choose to take on regional responsibilities and form partnerships with regional organizations to carry them out. In turn, regional agencies can help the states allocate federal block grant and state aid funds.

Member government services. In exchange for modest dues from member governments, regional organizations could continue to provide secretariat services to their governing bodies and to policy and technical committees. They could maintain regional forums for the discussion of common problems as they arise and support intergovernmental consultation on proposed federal-aid projects. Regional organizations could also provide a variety of services by contract, on a fee basis.

Honest broker. With state aid, a modest tax base of their own, or substantial dues from member governments, regional organizations could pursue a variety of policy analysis and mediation tasks, offering a forum for bringing the major parties together in support of common goals.

My bottom line as it was in that 1981 Princeton speech when I predicted, "Regional planning organizations will survive . . . but they no longer will be supported in the style to which they have grown accustomed. Most will have to scratch out their existence in much less fertile fields than before."

Source: Bruce D. McDowell, "Regions under Reagan," *Planning*, Vol. 50, No. 8 (August 1984), pp. 25, 26, 28, 29.

---

substate ones. As federal funding is withdrawn, it would be hoped that such voluntary local support would be maintained. One price of this, however, may be a reorientation away from areawide planning tasks toward specific services to individual local governments. To a certain point, this may be a useful movement toward building greater local support. Nevertheless, local support for more general planning tasks also is needed. To help ensure local support, states could require local participation in regional organizations, mandate payment of dues, and/or establish a separate tax base for the regional organization. A few states have taken such steps, but most have not. Ultimately, continued and enlarged local support, as well as state action requiring it, depends upon planners being able to demonstrate that regional planning provides benefits that are worth the cost of the plans.

Conclusion

In 1980, regional organizations covered the nation almost completely at two levels—substate and multistate. But, at both of these levels, regional activities were fragmented among several different organizations. This fragmentation placed limits on creative problem solving and coordination of recognized functional responsibilities at the regional level. Federal withdrawal from many regional support activities in 1981 and 1982 almost certainly will reduce the geographic coverage of regional organizations, but also may reduce some of the functional fragmentation. of course, it surely will also reduce the total amount of regional planning, at least in the short run.

Although membership in regional organizations is largely voluntary, federal incentives to join and remain in these organizations have been great. Only a few regional organizations have lost membership, and usually the loss has been temporary. Nevertheless, the threat of losing members is enough to encourage most regional organizations to avoid major controversies. Now, with the loss of many federal incentives, defections may increase.

Regional organizations perform largely planning and advisory functions. However, they also have established major new channels of intergovernmental communication which never existed before, and they have carved out some other important functions for themselves including technical assistance and the provision of noncontroversial services. Few regional councils are performing up to their full potentials, because they lack solid linkages to decision-making processes.

Regional organizations at both the substate and multistate levels have been highly (almost exclusively) dependent on federal aid and subject to federal rules and regulations. This stimulated some parallel state and local efforts, but made it unnecessary until now to rely upon and cultivate state and local support to the maximum extent feasible. This great federal reliance also has made it difficult to establish stable and independent work programs and staffing.

Such limited powers as regional organizations do possess have been conferred almost exclusively by the federal government. Substate regions were given federal aid allocation powers for certain transportation, waste water, and health facilities programs, while multistate commissions were given authority to allocate certain federal grant funds for economic development purposes and to influence priorities for federal water resource projects.

State support for regional organizations, although varying greatly from state to state, generally has been encouraged by federal initiatives. Nevertheless, this state support, while significant and growing modestly, is still quite minor compared to past federal support. If the vacuum created by the withdrawal of federal funds and program authority is to be filled, state legislation will be needed.

The work programs of regional organizations differ considerably one from another. At the substate level, metropolitan councils have built fairly balanced programs encompassing several different functions and leaning heavily toward a planning and coordination role. Nonmetropolitan councils have tended to concentrate their efforts in fewer fields, and have leaned more toward the provision of services, with less emphasis on planning and coordination. Multistate commissions have exhibited very different program priorities from one to another, based upon their unique economic and natural resource situations.

Almost all regional organizations face major difficulties in implementing their plans. They could use greater authority, more stable organizational structures and financial resources, stronger linkages with other regional organizations, more consistent support from a wide variety of federal aid programs, and stronger support from and linkages to state governments. But all of these are hard to come by. Still, great progress was made between 1965 and 1980. Regional problems and needs occur everywhere, and they are not to be denied. Regional planning and regional organizations are likely to become even more important and more effective in the decades ahead, despite the federal withdrawal from regional activities.

1 For further information on these local government frameworks, the reader is referred to Frank S. So, *et al.*, editors, *The Practice of Local Government Planning* (Washinton, DC: International City Management Association, 1979).

2 For further information, see Martha Derthick, *Between State and Nation: Regional Organizations of the United States* (Washington, DC: Brookings Institution, 1974), Chap. 2.

3 National Association of Regional Councils, *Regional Council Representation and Voting* (Washington, DC: March 1979), Table 8, p. 12.

4 Ibid., Table 9, p. 10.

5 U.S. Bureau of the Census, *Regional Organizations*, vol. 6, no. 6, 1977 Census of Governments (Washington, DC: U.S. Government Printing Office, August 1978), p. 7.

6 Bruce D. McDowell, *Most States Support Regional Councils, All Could Do More*, Report No. 42 (Washington, DC: National Association of Regional Councils, September 1979, Table 9.

7 U.S. Bureau of the Census, *Regional Organizations*, vol. 6, no. 6, 1977 Census of Governments, p. 4.

8 Advisory Commission on Intergovernmental Relations, *State and Local Roles in the Federal System*, chap. 5, "Area-wide Organizations" (Washington, DC: U.S. Government Printing Office, 1982), Tables 5-3 and 5-20.

9 For further information, see Derthick, *Between State and Nation*.

10 Ibid., chap. 6.

11 Jerome M. Stam and J. Norman Reid, *An Overview of Federal Programs Supporting Multicounty Substate Regional Activities*, ESCS Staff Report (Washington, DC: U.S. Department of Agriculture, May 1980).

12 Advisory Commission on Intergovernmental Relations, *State and Local Roles in the Federal System*, Chap. 5, Table 5-23.

13 Ibid.

14 McDowell, *Most States Support Regional Councils*.

15 Center for Social Analysis, State University of New York at Binghamton, *Title V Regional Commissions: An Evaluation* (Washington, DC: U.S. Department of Commerce, Office of Regional Economic Coordination, circa 1978), unpublished paper, pp. 14-15.

16 Advisory Commission on Intergovernmental Relations, *State and Local Roles in the Federal System*, Chap. 5.

17 Ibid.

18 U.S. Office of Management and Budget, *Intergovernmental Affairs Division, Conceptual Outline of Proposed Revisions to OMB Circular A-95* (Washington, DC: August 1980, Attachment VII, p.1.

19 Advisory Commission on Intergovernmental Relations, *State and Local Roles*, chap. 5, Figure 5-5.

20 *The Regional Council Act of 1980, Chapter 160*, Florida Statutes.

21 McDowell, *Most States Support Regional Councils*, Table 11.

22 Harvey S. Perloff, "Key Features of Regional Planning," *Journal of the American Institute of Planners* 34 (May 1968): pp. 153–159.

23 William L. C. Wheaton, "Metro-Allocation Planning," *Journal of the American Institute of Planners* 33 (May 1967): pp. 103–107.

24 Charles M. Haar, "Budgeting for Metropolitan Development: A Step Toward Creative Federalism," *Journal of the American Institute of Planners* 34 (March 1968): pp. 102–104.

25 William L. C. Wheaton, "Operations Research for Metropolitan Planning," *Journal of the American Institute of Planners* 34 (November 1963): pp. 250–259; and "Metro-Allocation Planning."

26 Willard B. Hansen, "Metropolitan Planning and the New Comprehensiveness," *Journal of the American Institute of Planners* 29 (September 1968): pp. 295–302; see also Wheaton, "Operations Research for Metropolitan Planning."

27 Wheaton, "Metro-Allocation Planning."

28 Arthur Maass, editor, *Area and Power: A Theory of Local Government* (Glencoe, IL: Free Press, 1959).

29 For further information, see Advisory Commission on Intergovernmental Relations, *Governmental Functions and Processes: Local and Area-wide*, Report A-45 (Washington, DC: U.S. Government Printing Office, February 1974).

30 Advisory Commission on Intergovernmental Relations, *Factors Affecting Voter Reactions to Governmental Reorganization in Metropolitan Areas*, Report M-15 (Washington, DC: U.S. Government Printing Office, May 1962).

31 Advisory Commission on Intergovernmental Relations, *Pragmatic Federalism: The Reassignment of Functional Responsibility*, Report M-105 (Washington, DC: U.S. Government Printing Office, July 1976); and ACIR, *The Challenge of Local Governmental Reorganization*, Report A-44 (Washington, DC: U.S. Government Printing Office, February 1974), Chap. 3.

32 David R. Godschalk, *et al.*, *Constitutional Issues of Growth Management* (Chicago: ASPO Press, 1977), chap. 5.

33 Robert H. Freilich, John H. Bracken, and William A. Denny, "Recent Developments in Local Government Law," *Urban Lawyer* 8 (Fall 1976): pp. 602–605.

34 Committee for Economic Development, *Reshaping Government in Metropolitan Areas* (New York: The Committee, 1970).

35 Advisory Commission on Intergovernmental Relations, Regional Decision Making: New Strategies for Substate Districts, Report A-43 (Washington, DC: U.S. Government Printing Office, October 1973), Chap. 11.

36 U.S. Office of Management and Budget, Circular A-95, Part IV.

37 Executive Order 12149, July 20, 1979.

38 Executive Order 12407, February 22, 1983.

39 Bruce D. McDowell, "Regions under Reagan," *Planning* 50 (August 1984), pp. 25–29.

7 Techniques for implementing regional plans

Most regional planning agencies are not a part of a regional government. In fact, such agencies are typically created to compensate for the absence of regional government by providing a channel of communication among the various local governments that comprise the region. Consequently, although a regional planning agency is governmental in the sense that it is created and funded by governments, it is not a government *per se*. It typically has the authority to develop policies and plans, but not the regulatory, taxing, developmental, or operating powers necessary to carry them out. All final implementation decisions are made by somebody else: local, state, or federal agencies; special purpose authorities, or private enterprise.

This absence of regional governmental powers makes regional plan implementation much more difficult than it would otherwise be. The implementation of plans across local government boundaries is always cumbersome, usually difficult and sometimes frustrating. However, there are ways to get regional plans implemented. This chapter discusses 12 approaches:

1. Implementation by local governments.
2. Regional project and plan reviews.
3. Regional improvement programming.
4. Concentration on regional plan components with maximum leverage.
5. Special regional implementation mechanisms.
6. Technical assistance.
7. Intergovernmental staff contacts.
8. Implementation by state government.
9. Implementation by the federal government.
10. Public support.
11. Political and intergovernmental bargaining.
12. Improvements in regional systems of governance.

Individually, they are fairly modest—there are no magic solutions among them. But if they are orchestrated with persistence, care, and sensitivity, they can have a significant combined effect in moving regional plans into the stream of implementation.

Implementation by local governments[1]

Although regional planning agencies do not normally have the power to implement plans, the local governments they serve do have such powers. By making regional and local plans fit together it is possible to get local governments to implement regional plans while they are implementing their own plans, or at least to implement local plans in a fashion consistent with regional plans.

One way that local governments can implement regional plans is by providing public facilities such as parks, airports, sewers, and water systems in a fashion consistent with regional plan recommendations. A second way is by operating their service programs in accordance with regionally adopted policies, such as

Figure 7–1
Planning is only
half the story.

permitting the joint use of public libraries or developing cooperative emergency medical services. A third way is by regulating private development through zoning, subdivision regulations, and other local controls in accordance with regional growth policies. However, local governments cannot normally be expected to subordinate their own preferences to a regional interest. It is necessary to weave regional considerations into the development of local plans and programs in such a way that local governments will implement regional policies incidentally while they are implementing their own plans deliberately.

Therefore, it is very important to get local government officials to participate in the regional planning process so that they will be more likely to view the resulting plans as being their own. It is generally a good idea, for example, to have the local governments' elected officials—preferably the chief elected officials—serve on the governing board and committees of the regional planning agency. Of course mayors and their county counterparts tend to be busy people. Moreover, they are generally partisan and often controversial, and they can make the regional planning process less serene than it might otherwise be. These and other special factors have to be taken into account in any given situation, so no blanket statement can be made concerning the ideal composition of a regional planning board. But, other things being equal, the presence of high-ranking political officials in the very center of the regional planning process can give the resulting plans a relevancy that they would otherwise lack. The effectiveness of this technique, however, depends on the direct interpersonal contact of the elected officials themselves, and this effectiveness is virtually eliminated if the rules permit them to send substitutes or alternates to the meetings. Attendance at regional planning meetings can be a problem in any event, and elected officials like to deal with each other, not with staff or citizen surrogates. If they know their counterpart may send a substitute, they are inclined to do the same. On the other hand, the knowledge that their absence from a meeting will deprive them of their representation acts as a strong incentive for them to attend and participate in regional affairs personally.

In addition to getting local elected officials involved in the regional planning process, it is also important to get local technical and administrative officials similarly involved. This includes such people as city and county managers and planning directors as well as line department heads and their staffs, particularly those who are responsible for functions that may be important components of regional plans, such as streets and highways, transit, parks and recreation, water and sewer, and housing. Their participation can be either formal or informal. Formal participation often consists of their serving on technical advisory committees responsible for helping to develop regional plans or reviewing proposed projects for their consistency with regional plans. But informal participation can be just as important. There is sometimes a tendency for the regional and various local governmental staffs within a region to be aloof or even resentful or competitive toward one another. A regional planning staff can greatly increase the receptivity of local governments toward regional plans simply by being open, friendly, and helpful toward them.

Another factor that is important in getting local governments to use their implementation powers to carry out regional plans is the way in which the regional plan itself is developed with respect to the various local plans. If a regional planning agency takes a "top down" approach on the assumption that it has wisdom broader than or superior to that of the local governments and therefore proceeds to develop an independent and idealistic regional plan, this will generally lead to a situation in which the regional plan is ignored or even actively opposed by the local governments. If it takes the opposite approach of simply "pasting together" the local plans as it finds them and calling the result a regional plan, this might have the advantage of gaining the support or at least avoiding the alienation of the local governments toward the regional plan, but it does so at the expense of making any useful original contribution to the process such as reconciling differences among local plans or injecting a regional dimension, constraint, or concern that may be lacking.

Probably the most effective regional planning consists of blending these two approaches, always reflecting local plans in the regional plan to the extent possible and at the same time adding whatever innovative, corrective, or regional aspects are necessary to make it a viable regional plan. Needless to say, this approach requires much adjustment and compromise on all sides in order to reach a consensus, which is why the continuous participation of the local officials, as discussed above, is so important.

Unfortunately, while the above blending of approaches is to be sought as an ideal, the actual choices to be made in putting together a regional planning process will almost never be that simple. Both regional and local planning are continuous processes involving periodic plan adjustment and refinement, and the meshing of these processes is complicated by the fact that the various local and regional planning processes will almost never be in perfect synchronization at any given time. For example, a regional agency may be about to begin an update of the regional land use plan at the same time that one of the local governments has just completed its update and another one is in mid-process. This and other complications inherent in the intergovernmental planning process require a careful dialogue in the development of compatible regional and local plans, but the result can be a regional plan that is far more likely to be honored by the local governments in their respective implementation processes.

Regional project and plan reviews

One way of tying regional planning agencies closer to the implementation process without giving them the actual authority to implement or veto projects is to empower them with "mandatory referral," which is the right to review and comment on proposed projects before a decision is made by others to carry them out. This is an old idea which has been used by local planning bodies for many years with respect to proposed public works projects, zoning amendments, and other public actions. Under this concept a regional planning agency is given the responsibility of reviewing certain classes of proposed projects to determine whether they are consistent with regional plans and to make recommendations or take steps that would bring the proposed projects and the regional plans into agreement.

Mandatory referral can apply to proposed plans as well as projects. A typical project might be a proposed sewer installation, street widening, or fire station. A typical plan could be a transportation plan for a particular community or the regionwide water supply plan of a special purpose authority.

The proposal to be reviewed may be of strictly local significance (that is, of significance to only one local unit of government), or it may be of intergovernmental or regional significance. If it is of local significance only, the regional agency and the other local governments may have little interest in it except to be aware of it. If it is of intergovernmental significance, such as a local zoning decision in an area bordering on a neighboring municipality, it may be of major interest only to the localities immediately affected, and the regional planning agency's primary role then is to make potentially affected parties aware of each other's concern and bring them together to reconcile differences.

If the proposal is of regional significance (that is, of significance to the region as a whole or to a major part thereof), the role of the regional planning agency includes not only notifying and convening other potentially interested parties but also making a determination as to the proposal's consistency with regional plans.

The notification and convening functions are important parts of the regional project review process, because they enable potentially interested parties other than the regional agency itself to learn about projects that are up for review. Practice varies widely from one region to another depending on local conditions and experience. It is important to develop a notification system that reaches as many potentially interested parties as possible without wasting effort or unduly burdening people who are not interested. Similarly, the nature and frequency of conferences, hearings, and negotiating sessions that are held as a part of the review process will vary from one regional agency to another and with the type of project being reviewed.

A mandatory process of regional project review and advice is not a panacea, and it will not force coordination or cooperation among parties who are determined not to coordinate or cooperate. With or without such a process, good regional planners should work closely with those who must be relied upon to implement the plans. However, an established regional review system can serve to institutionalize this relationship and foster a climate of communication and negotiation well in advance of the final review, so that by the time the project is finally and officially submitted, the review for regional plan consistency is perfunctory.

In addition to strengthening opportunities for inter-local and regional-local coordination, a regional project review process also has the advantage of shedding the light of publicity on public decisions that may be important but would otherwise be made without public scrutiny.

Examples of the concept of regional project review are to be found in various federal aid programs. Although the specific provisions may vary from time to time, the federal government in the 1970s would not generally award grants for highways, mass transit, water quality management or housing, for example, unless a determination has first been made that the projects to be funded will be consistent with applicable regional plans.

A broader example of the federal application of regional project review is the so-called "A-95" process. Under this process the federal government, during the 1970s, recognized certain state and regional agencies, including certain regional planning agencies, as "A-95 Clearinghouses," and many federal actions, such as the funding of local government applications for certain types of federal aid, could not proceed until they had been submitted for review. The A-95 process provided local, regional, state, and some private organizations with an opportunity to give a federal agency its views as to the desirability of a proposed federal funding action.

The A-95 process was originally established by the federal government in an effort to reduce the risk of spending federal dollars on projects that were at cross-purposes with one another or that were contrary to official state, local, or regional policy.

In many instances, it has been effective in discovering and reconciling conflicts or duplications among individual projects. In one case, for example, it was discovered that two adjoining counties were applying for federal grants to construct duplicating sewer lines, one on either side of the county line. As a result of the A-95 review it was discovered that a pumping station could connect the two together at much less cost and serve both counties more efficiently.

Over the years, A-95 played a significant role in strengthening regional planning agencies by establishing them as a place for exchanging ideas and information about federally aided projects within the region and by increasing the probability that regionally developed plans and locally implemented projects would be consistent with one another. As with regional mandatory referral in general, the great value in the A-95 review process was not how often it produced a "negative comment"—that is, a criticism or a finding of project inconsistency—but in the contacts, cooperation, and coordinated thought processes it fostered.

Unfortunately, problems can arise with respect to project reviews in general and with the A-95 process in particular. Consequently, A-95 met with mixed success and was variously characterized as a "rubber stamp," "red tape," and an opportunity for mischief, vengeance or "politics."[2] In 1982 A-95 was succeeded by Executive Order 12372, "Intergovernmental Review of Federal Programs," which established a new federal policy for reviewing requests for federal funds. According to OMB:

The Order fundamentally alters the manner and nature of intergovernmental consultation in three major ways. First, the Order allows states, in consultation with local officials, to establish their own process for reviewing and commenting on federal programs and activities. Second, the Order requires federal agencies to accept state or local views, or explain why not. And lastly, it allows states to simplify the plans that are federally required, substitute state plans for federally prescribed plans, or consolidate plans.[3]

Because it places much more responsibility in the hands of the states, the effects of EO 12372 vary widely from state to state. Whether it will come to define a new era in state and regional planning remains to be seen.

The following practices can help to maintain the credibility and usefulness of the regional review process whether it is based upon federal or any other requirements.

1. The review and comment should be based on the merits of the project in question, not on whether the regional agency board or staff feels favorably or unfavorably inclined toward the applicant for other reasons.

2. Regional agencies should maintain an up-to-date codification of their formally adopted plans and policies so that project reviews can be based on a true comparison of the proposed project with official regional positions and not on an *ad lib* opinion with no basis in adopted policy.

3. There should be no confusion or misrepresentation as to who is making the official comment—the governing body, a committee thereof, the staff, or a person or group to whom certain review powers have been delegated. Controversial or extremely significant reviews should not be delegated and should be conducted at the highest possible policy level.

4. The reviews should distinguish between fact and opinion as much as possible. Hence, it may be possible to return a negative comment on a project (e.g., a proposed housing project that is in a flood plain or an airport flight zone) on the basis of fact, policy, or both.

5. The applicant should give reasonable consideration to the views of the regional planning agency before making its final decision, and it should advise the regional planning agency as to its decision and the reasons why the agency's advice was or was not followed. (Obviously, this situation is often beyond the control of the regional planning agency.)

There are many other examples of project review processes that provide regional planning agencies with an opportunity to monitor various proposals to determine their conformity with regional plans. The federally required Environmental Impact Statement (EIS) is one such example. California's Environmental Impact Review (EIR) and Florida's Development of Regional Impact (DRI) processes are examples at the state level. Two examples at the regional level are the Area Plan provision and the Metropolitan River Protection Act provision of Georgia state law, which provide the Atlanta Regional Commission with the power to review certain proposed activities for their consistency with regional plans. But even in the absence of review processes mandated by federal or state law, local governments can sometimes be persuaded to submit proposals for regional review on a strictly voluntary basis.

Even in regional agencies with an excellent project review process there is a good chance that an occasional project review will precipitate political difficulties, even to the point of angry debate, emotional personality clashes, and dramatic media coverage. This is to be expected because there can be a strong difference of opinion as to desirability of a given project. Each situation is unique and there is no one best way of handling such situations. On the other hand, a regional agency may not want to force a political rift simply for the sake of making a negative comment about someone's pet project, especially since, as discussed above, the final "official" comment may be the least important part of a project review. On the other hand, it may not in good conscience be able to avoid a difficult or unpopular stand if the situation clearly calls for one.

Before leaving the subject of regional project reviews, one final point should be made. As pointed out in the section "Implementation by local governments," the relationship between local and regional planning is a two-way street. Just because a locally proposed project is inconsistent with a regional plan does not automatically mean that the project is wrong and the regional plan is right. It may be that the regional plan is arbitrary or out-of-date in some respect and that it could reasonably be amended to accommodate the project. Or perhaps a mutual adjustment of plan and project is in order. The main service that a regional project review process performs is to establish an ongoing communication on the relationship between various plans and projects so that differences can be worked out.

Regional improvement programming

In recent years efforts have been made to carry the regional project review idea a step further by coordinating regional planning and plan implementation across local government boundaries not only on a project-by-project basis but on a programming basis as well. Essentially, this idea takes the project review concept one step further—projects are evaluated not simply to determine their consistency with a regional plan but also to evaluate their relative importance, urgency, cost, funding sources, and functional, spatial, and scheduling relationships to other projects.

A regional improvement program is somewhat like a capital improvements program of a local government except that it is prepared by a regional planning agency and on a regionwide, intergovernmental basis. It is an annual compilation of short-range projects that tie into long-range plans and that are scheduled to be constructed soon, typically within the next five years. Projects may include traffic and street improvements, water and sewer facilities, parks, airports, and other public buildings and facilities of various kinds. Each year the process is repeated: progress since the preceding year is monitored, priorities and linkages among the remaining projects are re-assessed, and one more year's worth of projects is added. Regional improvement programming is a systematic way of keeping up with what should be done, who is going to do it, and whether or not it has been done. In an inflationary period, the annual re-estimating of costs and reallocation of available funds is an especially important feature of regional improvement programming.

Sometimes it is possible to connect regional improvement programming with the regional project review function (discussed in the preceding section) so that multi-project programs can be reviewed annually instead of reviewing one project at a time.

The type of regional improvement programming described above is best suited to regional improvements whose implementation can be measured in terms of capital improvement projects, that is, physical, public projects. But there are other equally important regional plan components that are not measurable in these same terms. Housing is a good example. Most of a region's housing stock is constructed privately, not publicly. Moreover, the nature and extent of public participation in housing (e.g., mortgage guarantees, interest subsidies, rent supplements) vary as government programs change. Finally, regional housing planning may place great emphasis on nonconstruction goals and objectives such as a desired geographical distribution of housing units or their availability to, or suitability for, certain population groups. Regional improvement programming should be broad and flexible enough to accommodate the annual monitoring of progress in housing and other special aspects of regional planning.

Typically the projects included in regional improvement programs are those which involve some level of state or federal funding. In fact, regional improvement programming has been promoted by state and federal governments as a way of setting priorities for state and federal grants among the local governments within a region. However, it is very difficult for competing governments to allocate priorities among themselves when this amounts to a decision as to which localities will get what share of the limited funds available. One incentive for doing so has come from the federal agencies themselves, who have sometimes required it of local governments acting within a regional context as a prerequisite to receiving any funding at all or as an alternative to being left out of the decision-making process entirely.

Many of the attempts at regional improvement programming are limited to a single functional area such as transportation. More recently, however, there have been attempts to make regional improvement programming interfunctional as well as intergovernmental—that is, not only to encompass the entire region but to combine various functions as well, such as transportation, waste treatment, water supply, and recreation. This increases the complexity of the effort because, in addition to having to deal with the conflicting priorities of local jurisdictions, it also brings into play the conflicts among the funding procedures, formulas, uncertainties, and timing cycles of the various state and federal grant programs.

Even though regional improvement programming expands the opportunity for intergovernmental communication on the relationships between projects and regional plans, it is still a very rudimentary tool for the implementation of regional plans because regional planning agencies do not have the kind of binding decision-making authority that local governments have. Short of the actual merging of governments or governmental decision-making processes within a region, the whole field of regional programming has room for considerable experimentation and improvement.[5] (See also the later section on Political and intergovernmental bargaining.)

Concentration on regional plan components with maximum leverage

Regional planning agencies do not normally have the power to make land-use decisions. Decisions as to the type, location, and density of use permitted on a specific parcel of land are usually made through the zoning, subdivision regulation, and related processes within local governments. Moreover, regional planning agencies are not even routinely asked for their opinion or advice on land use matters unless it is done through some form of regional project review as discussed earlier.

However, a regional planning agency can and does influence land use patterns indirectly through its participation in the location of key region-shaping facilities such as freeways, major streets, interchanges, transit stations, open spaces, and major sewer and water lines.

Consequently, instead of trying to influence or even keep up with land use decisions at the detailed level, a regional planning agency can often have relatively more impact on land development patterns, and therefore on regional development in general, by concentrating on those major community and region-shaping factors that it can influence, recognizing that the real estate market and zoning will often follow these. This also means that whenever a regional plan for transportation facilities, utilities, open space, or some other region-shaping system is being developed, it should be viewed not only as a transportation or utilities or open space plan *per se* but also in terms of its effects as a major land use determinant.

Often regional planners can play a constructive role in shaping a region's development by opposing a key project instead of supporting it. An example comes to mind in which a proposed "outer loop" highway was being proposed around a major metropolitan area. As with many projects, the merits of the proposal were mixed: it would have benefited some interests and damaged others. Arguments against the proposal included the scattering effect it would have had on regional development and the speculation and uncontrolled growth forces it would have unleashed in areas not yet equipped or inclined to cope with them. For these reasons the project was opposed, successfully.

Special regional implementation mechanisms

Sometimes the only apparent way to implement a regional plan is through the creation of a new implementation mechanism. There are two common ways to do this: one is through the creation of a special-purpose authority, and the other is through the negotiation of intergovernmental agreements.

There are many different kinds of special purpose authorities. They can range all the way from a huge interstate authority, such as the bi-state Port Authority of New York and New Jersey, to a village school board. The creation of a special purpose authority is a tempting way to implement a regional plan, because such an authority can be given the power and independence to "get the job done." However, it runs the risk of further complicating what is often an already too complicated pattern of local government, and of isolating the authority's function from public scrutiny and accountability. One of the advantages of general purpose government—that is, a city or a county—is that it is more likely to take into account the inter-relationships among the various functions for which it is responsible, whereas a special purpose authority is more likely to make decisions that are in the interest of its own field of responsibility even though they may be to the detriment of others. A water authority, for example, can run an extremely profitable and effective water distribution system and at the same time encourage a pattern and density of land uses that are in conflict with local zoning or regional growth management policies.

Therefore, if it is necessary to create a special purpose authority in order to implement a regional plan, ways should be sought that will preserve a close relationship between the authority and the general purpose governments serving the same area. One approach is to provide for overlapping board composition—that is, to have elected officials from the local governments serve on the authority's governing board so that they will bring to the authority an awareness of and responsibility for the needs and problems of the local governments and their citizens. This approach is sometimes difficult, however, because of the dual demands it places on an elected official serving in both capacities. Moreover, some states do not permit a person to hold more than one public office at a time. Another approach is to give the local governments the power to review and amend the authority's program and budget. A third way is to withhold one or more critical powers, such as the power of eminent domain, from the authority, so that it must rely on the local governments for the exercise of such power.

Table 7–1   City and county service transfers to counties, cities, and other organizations, by service categories, 1983.[1]

Classification	Total number of transfers	To counties (No.)	(%)	To cities (No.)	(%)	To special districts (No.)	(%)	To regional organizations (No.)	(%)	To state (No.)	(%)	To private firms (No.)	(%)	To nonprofit organizations (No.)	(%)
Total, cities and counties	1,412	469	33	140	10	78	6	109	8	92	7	392	28	163	12
Services transferred by cities	1,168	436	37	75	6	67	6	84	7	68	6	330	28	107	9
Public safety and corrections	164	106	65	22	13	5	3	11	7	11	7	7	4	6	4
Public works and utilities	381	74	19	23	6	15	4	31	8	28	7	198	52	10	3
Health and welfare	257	127	49	16	6	10	4	12	5	13	5	26	20	57	22
Transportation	62	8	13	5	8	11	18	16	26	0	0	7	11	12	19
Parks and recreation	51	10	20	0	0	8	16	0	0	2	4	14	27	13	25
Education and culture	43	30	70	1	2	3	7	2	5	2	5	2	5	5	12
General government, finance	210	81	32	8	3	15	7	12	7	12	6	76	36	4	2
Services transferred by counties	244	33	14	65	27	11	5	25	10	24	10	62	25	56	23
Public safety and corrections	39	5	13	20	51	2	5	2	5	8	21	2	5	4	10
Public works and utilities	61	10	16	19	31	4	7	5	8	4	7	24	39	5	8
Health and welfare	92	15	17	13	14	4	4	8	9	11	12	17	21	34	37
Transportation	8	1	13	3	38	0	0	2	25	0	0	2	25	4	50
Parks and recreation	15	0	0	5	33	0	0	3	20	0	0	4	27	4	27
Education and culture	7	1	14	3	43	1	14	1	14	0	0	0	0	2	28
General government, finance	22	1	4	2	9	0	0	4	17	1	4	13	57	3	13

Source: Lori M. Henderson, *Intergovernmental Service Arrangements and the Transfer of Functions*, Baseline Data Report, Vol. 16, No. 6 (Washington, D.C.: International City Management Association, June 1984), p. 7.
[1] Percentages add to more than 100 because some transfers involve more than one recipient.

Another type of regional implementation mechanism is the intergovernmental agreement, which is a contract or other formal arrangement among local governments to carry out some public function cooperatively, but within the existing structure of government instead of through the creation of a new authority. One common example is an intergovernmental contract for sewage collection and treatment.

Similar agreements can be used to implement regional plans for medical facilities and services, solid waste management, libraries, and many other purposes.

A key ingredient in the successful negotiation of such an agreement is that it be perceived by all parties to be in their own self-interest, or at least not counter to their interest. It cannot be assumed that a locality will enter into an agreement for the good of another locality or of the region as a whole. For example, if one local government generates a large volume of solid waste but has no available land for a sanitary land fill, it might be able to persuade an adjoining locality to accommodate its needs but only by providing a sufficient incentive—either

---

Interlocal contracting   In the early 1970s five Texas governmental units, the city of Sherman, the city of Denison, Grayson County, and the independent school districts of Sherman and Denison, approached the Texoma Regional Planning Commission for help in establishing a shared data processing system. The Commission, using Comprehensive Planning Assistance funds, contracted with a private firm for a feasibility study, which found that data handling costs of the five governments were too high and dissemination of information was inadequate. The report stated that a joint data processing undertaking might be difficult to establish but would be justified if five conditions were met:

All five governments would have to participate since high machine use is necessary to achieve the desired economies.

Adequate funding must be available to sustain the operation.

Administrative support, including payroll, purchasing, and accounting, would have to be provided.

A written agreement defining responsibilities and costs would be required.

The system must be carefully designed before installation of hardware.

All five public entities approved the ideas put forward in the study, and in 1973 joined in an agreement covering: (1) policy making for the joint center, (2) sharing costs, (3) management of the center, and (4) review of requests by other governments that might wish to use the facility.

According to the agreement, which was still in effect as of 1984, the center is managed by a policy-making body consisting of four voting members: each government has one vote. (Since the center was established, the Sherman school district has withdrawn from the arrangement.) A manager is hired by the board to conduct the daily affairs of the center, and the Texoma Regional Planning Commission provides administrative support. The center is financed from funds deposited at the beginning of each year based on the anticipated use by each member government. Requests for use by other governments are considered individually.

Source: Based on Michael E. Meyer and David R. Morgan, *Contracting for Municipal Services: A Handbook for Local Officials* (Norman, Okla.: Bureau of Government Research, University of Oklahoma, 1979), pp. 29–30.

money or some other consideration. In the absence of such mutual incentives, sometimes the state or federal government can provide the necessary coercion or inducement to effect an intergovernmental agreement. The federal government has had some limited success, for example, in providing bonus grants to neighboring local governments who construct joint sewage treatment facilities, and in granting or withholding housing assistance to (from) local governments on the basis of their participation or lack thereof in region-wide housing opportunity plans and fair share housing agreements.

In the establishment of special regional implementation mechanisms, whether through the creation of special-purpose authorities, through intergovernmental agreements, or in some other manner, the opportunity for tying the regional planning agency into the implementation arrangement in some constructive fashion should not be overlooked. Normally, local governments will carefully guard their powers of implementation and oppose any transfer of these powers into regional hands. However, if a regional arrangement of some kind is to be created in any event, it is worthwhile to try to avoid the duplication or splintering of regional mechanisms and to give the existing regional planning agency an additional measure of responsibility and stability. One approach is to somehow tie the regional planning agency's governing board or a subsidiary thereof into the process, by giving it either policy making or review and oversight responsibilities, particularly if that board is already composed of responsible local officials. Another approach is to make the management of joint services a responsibility of a single regional staff or at least to place this responsibility under a single staff head, even though more than one governing body may be involved.

Technical assistance

In addition to developing regional plans, regional planning agencies often provide staff assistance to local governments within their region. Sometimes this takes the form of local planning assistance, such as assisting a city or county in the development of its land use, transportation, or community facility plans or capital improvement programs or in the administration of its zoning ordinance or subdivision regulations. The assistance should be strictly technical, in the sense that the regional personnel who provide it should not supplant the local policy makers but should instead be responsible to them in carrying out local policy. It might seem, therefore, that this work is neither regional planning nor regional plan implementation. However, if regional planning and implementation are viewed as being necessarily interwoven with local planning and implementation, as discussed earlier, it can be seen that local planning assistance can help to implement regional planning in at least two respects: first, by filling in the gaps that might otherwise exist in local planning capacity and competence; and second, by seeing to it that regional planning considerations, where appropriate, are reflected in the local plans and programs as they are developed.

In providing technical assistance, regional planning agencies should beware of situations in which regional and local policies or interests may be at odds, potentially putting the staff in a conflict of interest situation.

In addition to providing technical planning assistance, regional planning agencies can also be of general administrative assistance to local governments in such matters as preparing grant applications, joint purchasing, developing personnel systems, and budgeting. Even this kind of assistance, while it may not implement regional plans directly, helps to build credibility, staff contacts, and a reputation for useful service on the part of the regional planning agency, which can enhance the agency in the eyes of its local governments and thereby help to implement regional plans indirectly. This kind of service and development of mutual familiarity and respect is closely related to the earlier discussion regarding the

Figure 7–2   Too late! The plans for Arnold Road were not brought together.

of local officials in the section titled "Implementation by local governments," above.

Another form of technical assistance that can help to implement regional plans is the provision of reliable and timely data, maps, and information to private developers as well as to state and local governments. By becoming known as a source of useful population, and economic data—such as current estimates of housing units, population, and employment on a small-area basis—and by stocking an available supply of reports and maps from various sources, a regional planning agency can put itself in touch with public and private decision makers who need the data for their own purposes. By so doing, it acquaints the regional staff with the nature of such decisions and permits it to pursue, monitor, and coordinate various implementation activities. Moreover, population and economic forecasts can to some extent be self-fulfilling if they are linked to the planning process and made generally available.

Intergovernmental staff contacts

Planning and planners have become a target of criticism over the years because of the tendency of some to develop plans in a vacuum and to eschew the involvement of those who would be affected by the plans or who must be relied upon to carry them out. In city and county planning this "back room" approach has vanished to a great extent as the local planning process has become a more integral part of the decision-making process which includes extensive citizen participation. It is still a more serious risk in regional planning, however, because regional planning agencies must be circumspect about bypassing their local governments to deal with the citizenry directly, and because regional planners can fall prey to an "aloofness syndrome" in the belief that it makes them more objective or less contaminated by parochial concerns. This tendency should be resisted, and it should be counterbalanced by an active and deliberate attempt to keep in touch with the staffs of local governments and other implementation bodies. This can counteract any tendencies toward apathy or antipathy that may otherwise exist on the part of local governments toward the regional agency, and it can even build a sense of teamwork toward wanting to achieve common goals.

Various ways to do this through formal technical and administrative contacts have been suggested earlier in this chapter, under the headings "Implementation by local governments" and "Technical assistance." Informal methods are also desirable, through courtesy visits, telephone calls, exchanges of ideas and information, offers of assistance, an attempt to understand local viewpoints, and an open-handed attitude.

The sharing, exchange, and rotation of personnel can also further the implementation of regional plans by helping to establish mutual familiarity and trust between regional and local staffs.

Implementation by state governments

It was pointed out earlier that the implementation powers of local governments can sometimes be utilized to carry out regional plans. The same can be said of state government. Not only is the state (or states, in the case of interstate regional planning agencies) a government with all of the implementation powers that go with being a government—it is also a higher level of government that transcends local boundaries and can therefore take actions affecting the several local governments that the localities could not take individually.

One way for state government to implement regional plans is for the various departments within its executive branch to include regional plan components in their own capital improvement programs. Obvious examples include highways and parks, for which most states have active implementation programs. State regulatory activities can also be effective in carrying out regional plans. Certainly this is true in the case of state enforcement of water quality standards through inspections and the issuance of permits governing municipal and industrial waste discharges into rivers and streams, both within the region and upstream from it. State participation in the implementation of regional plans has been especially prevalent within those functional areas involving federal aid programs, such as transportation, outdoor recreation, and environmental protection.

There have been some recent attempts to bring state government into the implementation of regional plans by formally linking the planning and program efforts of regional planning agencies with those at the state level. One example has been in Georgia, where the state requires each substate regional planning agency to submit an annual *Area Development Plan*, which sets forth the region's plans and needed projects in a uniform format corresponding to that of the *Governor's Policy Statement* and *Budget Report*. A further refinement occurred when the state was successful in reaching an agreement with the various federal agencies that fund the regional planning agencies to the effect that a single annual report would satisfy all of their respective reporting requirements. This type of role by the state does not guarantee the implementation of regional plans by state and federal agencies, nor does it ensure the inclusion of projects pursuant to regional plans in the state budget and federal grant programs, but it at least advances the likelihood of such implementation by coordinating funding processes and creating a common focus of attention on needs, resources, and priorities among the regional, state and federal officials. It is also probably a necessary first step toward more formal linkages between regional plans and state and federal budgetary decisions.

The legislative branch of state government has many basic powers which it can use, if it wants to, in the implementation of regional plans. Usually the state legislature has an important role to play in creating or enabling the creation of special purpose authorities, discussed earlier. But state legislatures can generally go much further and play a leading role in literally changing the structure or powers of local government in such a way as to further the implementation of regional plans through such actions as annexation; creation, abolition or consolidation of local governments; changes in the powers of local governments; taxation policies; and the establishment of formal mechanisms for regional project reviews, such as those discussed earlier.

However, state legislatures often are reluctant to interfere with the status quo of local governments' jurisdictions or powers. One step toward overcoming this problem is to improve linkages between regional and state interests at the policy level by increasing state representation on the regional planning agency's governing body, specifically by the appointment of state legislators or executives to serve in this capacity.

Because of the powers that state legislatures have to pass legislation that can materially affect the implementation of regional plans, it is a good idea for a regional planning agency to maintain a constructive and open channel of communication with its state legislature(s). One way to do this is through the annual adoption of a "legislative agenda," that is, a set of recommended legislative priorities or actions that would strengthen sound planning and plan implementation within the region. (A variation of this is for a state-wide association of regional planning agencies to act in concert in working for desired legislation just as statewide municipal and county associations do.) Unfortunately, this may not be as easy as it sounds because of the intergovernmental and political rivalries that often exist between and among cities, counties, regions, and states. In any event, the objective should be to improve and maintain an atmosphere in which the state legislature will be aware of, and sympathetic toward, regional plan implementation.

Implementation by the federal government

The powers of the federal government can also be brought to bear on the implementation of regional plans. Such powers include taxation; the making of grants, loans, and loan guarantees; regulation; and direct implementation such as development and construction activities by the federal departments themselves.

However, these powers vary in the extent to which they are likely to be applicable to the implementation of regional plans. Although federal powers and resources are very great in comparison to those of state and local government, the structure of the federal government and its relationship to regional interests often are complicated, indirect, and confused, and many federal policies naturally have a national focus rather than one tailored to the needs or interests of a specific region, so it can often be difficult to design a federal action that will be responsive to the plan of a specific region. The national urban policy prepared by the President in every even numbered year, and the national rural policy report prepared annually by the Department of Agriculture, both could be vehicles for focusing national policies more directly toward the needs of regions, especially if regional representatives participate in national policy processes.

The tax policies established by the Congress, for instance, have an enormous effect on investment decisions that can affect the implementation of a regional plan. One example is the differential tax benefits available for various kinds of investment—e.g., new construction, rehabilitation, and historic preservation. However, these are national policies which may or may not be consistent with the needs and priorities of a specific region and could even conceivably be counterproductive to a particular regional plan. Congressional hearings provide an opportunity for regional officials to make these effects known.

Federal grants, loans, and loan guarantees to states, regions, local govern-

Figure 7–3   Federal policies can distort regional planning.

ments, and private organizations are, of course, a common use of federal powers. These types of federal aid can lend themselves nicely to the implementation of regional plans, especially if they are used in conjunction with federally encouraged or federally required regional improvement programming and regional project review processes, as discussed earlier. One problem here is that the priorities established by the federal government—in terms of the amount of money available, the uses to which it may be put, and the conditions under which it may be used—may not be the same as those of the region, and the regional planning agency should not inadvertently distort the priorities of its region or its local governments simply to maximize the receipt of federal aid. Federal agency regulation writing processes frequently provide an opportunity for regional officials to affect the conditions of federal aid.

A third kind of federal power available for the implementation of regional plans is regulation. Because of a growing national emphasis on protection of the physical environment, the use of the federal government's regulatory power has grown rapidly in recent years in such areas as water quality management, air pollution, coastal zone management, noise control, and solid waste management. Often the federal government has linked its interests in the planning, grant making, and regulatory aspects of environmental protection into single or related programs, generally on a regional basis, and this has given regional planning agencies a more direct role to play in the implementation of regional plans through environmental regulations.

Another way to use federal implementation powers to carry out regional plans is through the direct development, construction, and operating activities that are pursued by various federal departments as a part of their regular program missions. The U.S. Corps of Engineers, for example, constructs and operates dams and reservoirs; the National Park Service acquires and maintains national parks; and the General Services Administration provides all sorts of public buildings and facilities and disposes of federal surplus property for reuse by others. Such activities can be carried on in such a way as to be in fulfillment of the plans of the regions in which they occur, or they can be irrelevant to these regional plans, or—worse yet—they can be in conflict with regional plans. Typically, a federal agency will understandably be concerned primarily with its own priorities and interests over those of the region. However, there has been an increase in the number of statutory and regulatory provisions of the federal government—such as Executive Order 12372 and the requirements for Environmental Impact Statements—that either require or encourage federal consideration of regional and local preferences. The judicious combination of these channels of communication with the more traditional ones that exist through the offices of U.S. senators and congressmen can often result in the promotion, elimination, or revision of federal projects to conform to regional plans.

An interesting illustration of the use of a federal program to implement a regional plan occurred in the case of a major urban river corridor which was beset by conflicting pressures: developers wanted to capitalize on its real estate potential, environmentalists wanted to preserve it, and various demands were being made on the use of its water for recreation, fish and wildlife preservation, and so on. The regional planning agency led in the development of a study that carefully considered these conflicting interests, arrived at a community consensus through extensive participation in the planning process, and developed the various regulatory and implementation measures necessary to carry out the plan, which was designed to leave much of the land in private ownership. It was clear, however, that a critical portion of the land would have to be publicly acquired in order to make the plan workable, and the funds needed for buying it were not available from the state or local governments. A successful case was made to the federal government that this river corridor was a unique national resource as well as a local one. This led to the purchase of the land in question by the federal government as a national recreation area.

Public support

The development of public support can be a very important technique in promoting the implementation of regional plans, particularly in the absence of any governmental mechanisms available at the regional level to carry them out automatically. However, since regional planning agencies must generally rely on the good will of the local governments for their continued support or existence, it is important to seek public support in such a way that it will not appear to be competing with the local governments for the citizenry's attention and support. Local elected officials can be very protective of their direct contact with the voters who elect them, and they may resent an effort by a regional planning agency to compete for credit or attention. Consequently, attempts to gain public support for the implementation of regional plans should be pursued with care and sensitivity regarding the feelings and attitudes of the local governments.

It is usually a mistake, however, for a regional planning agency to completely avoid the cultivation of public support, both in the interest of maintaining its own favorable reputation and in developing support for the implementation of its plans. Often the regional planning agency is the only organization that covers or represents the entire region, and this creates a special opportunity and responsibility to cultivate a region-wide public awareness of common regional interests. It also enables the region to speak with one voice on appropriate occasions when the region's interests need an advocate.

Two of the most common ways to gain public support for regional plans are (1) through the mass media—newspapers, television, and radio, and (2) through direct contact with interest groups. These may be special interest groups such as those primarily interested in environmental protection, economic development, or the future of a particular geographic area, or they may be groups having a general interest in the region. As with most public planning efforts, it is important to seek people's involvement throughout the planning process and not simply as a last-minute effort to "sell" the plans.

One important way to gain not only public support but the support and understanding of participating governments and other key groups is the production of tangible products that grow out of the regional planning effort. So much of regional planning consists of processes—inventories, analyses, reviews, coordination, and meetings of all kinds—that it is sometimes easy to forget the importance of producing tangible products that can serve as visible "snapshots" of this process. Many of the implementation techniques discussed in this chapter lend themselves to the production of tasteful, useful, and timely publications. Some examples are: a regional project review manual that takes the mystery out of what may otherwise seem like an obscure bureaucratic procedure; annual publication of the regional improvements program, graphically portraying the projects and their fulfillment of specific regional planning goals; summaries of population and economic data describing the region and what is happening to it; and directories of special-interest groups involved in a particular regional goal such as historic preservation, housing assistance or economic development.

Public support for regional planning can depend to a great extent on the ability of the regional planning agency's staff to maintain a reputation for objectivity, fairness, competence, and thoroughness. This is especially important because the regional board members may often, and understandably, be viewed as controversial partisans and as advocates of local interests.

Timing is also very important in developing public support for the implementation of regional plans. Developing a feeling for when to plan, when to push for the implementation of a plan, and when not to, can be a valuable asset in regional planning.

An important part of the public support effort could center on the preparation and delivery of a "state of the region" report. Such a report would monitor the development and condition of the region, as well as progress toward achieving regional goals. Its presentation annually by the top elected officials of the regional organization would create a media event with the potential to focus citizen and official attention on important regional issues and regional opportunities.

Political and intergovernmental bargaining

Perhaps one of the least developed yet potentially most effective techniques in regional plan implementation is the bargaining process. Regional planning agencies typically exist in a situation where there is a common regional problem or a set of mutual problems and a need for joint action but with no single government capable of handling the problem alone and some governments either apathetic toward or suspicious of one another. In other similar situations, bargaining is often used as a way to reach accord: nations bargain through foreign policy; labor and management bargain with each other to reach agreements they both can live with; and businesses bargain all the time. Intergovernmental bargaining can also be an appropriate and effective way to achieve mutually desirable results.

One way to encourage intergovernmental bargaining is through the development of techniques to establish personal relationships between local representatives. This often occurs simply through the board and committee meetings that take place in the normal course of a regional planning program. Representatives of local governments who might not otherwise meet each other, or even know each other, can become acquainted through monthly meetings. Out of this can grow opportunities to discuss, debate, and sometimes resolve regional or intergovernmental issues. These can take place during the regional meetings themselves or they can occur outside of the meetings as a result of the acquaintanceships that began there.

Sometimes a regional planning agency's professional staff can take the lead in effectuating agreements between governments, somewhat in the role of an informal mediator. This is often the way in which differences brought to light through an A-95 or similar process are eventually reconciled (see the earlier section, "Regional project reviews"). One modest but interesting example occurred when both a county and the principal city within it wanted to proceed independently with the expansion of separate water supply systems. Each side viewed the control of its own water supply as important because it produced substantial revenues, it avoided the risk of depending on others for an assured continued source of water at a fair price, and it was a source of municipal pride. However, there were important regional arguments for developing a joint water supply system, including long-term economies and protection of regional water sources. The regional planning agency's executive director set up a meeting of the key political officials from both sides and quietly and patiently met with them for several hours, stressing the reasons for cooperation and offering ways in which both parties' interests could be protected. The result was a joint approach that was satisfactory to both sides and better for the region in the long run.

In addition to the bargaining that can result from such informal or incidental relationships, more structured bargaining opportunities can be scheduled as a part of the regional planning process. An example is a regional planning "retreat." This is a situation in which the people responsible for developing regional plans meet together for a day or two for the specific purpose of getting an in-depth briefing on one or more regional issues and freely exploring them with each other in a low-key environment devoid of the posturing and polarization that occur in highly visible, highly publicized settings. Often this kind of candid, person-to-person approach can produce a mutual understanding of positions and viewpoints that can set the stage for an eventual reconciliation of differences. However, care must be taken not to use this approach in a way that would violate legal or ethical requirements that the public's business not be conducted in secret. No votes should be taken nor private deals made, and the retreat should not be permitted to take the place of public meetings at which deliberations will occur and actual decisions will be arrived at.

Often intergovernmental differences have to do with distribution of limited state or federal funds among competing local governments. This has led to recent attempts to develop structured bargaining processes within which the federal, state, and various local governments concerned with public investments within a given region can bargain together in order to allocate funds in accordance with some overall policy or set of objectives.[6] Given the generally nonhierarchical nature of regional decision making and the inherent limitations therein, this is not something that regional planning agencies have generally taken the lead (see the earlier section, "Regional improvement programming"). However, it is a subject that offers promise for improvement as a technique for regional plan implementation, and it is one which regional planning agencies should not disregard or leave to others.

Improvements in regional systems of governance

One of the obvious ways to further the implementation of regional plans is to revise the existing pattern of local governments within a region to make them more capable of responding to regional needs. This can take many forms—annexation, merger, elimination or creation of local units of government, redistribution of resources or responsibilities among local governments, the establishment of regional authorities or special intergovernmental linkages, or the creation of a whole new regional government. It is sometimes possible for the regional planning agency itself to conduct or participate in studies of the need for better regional governance and recommendations as to how it should be achieved.

This is not necessarily an easy role for a regional planning agency to play, because the existing local governments that control the regional planning agency, and to whom it looks for sustenance, may be opposed to the idea of changing the existing structure of local government because it would threaten their status quo. Consequently, the extent to which a regional planning agency participates in a process of governmental change often depends, in part, on how it views its own vulnerability and its long- and short-term interests.

In some instances, a regional planning agency may actually go beyond planning and coordination and enter the service delivery field itself, by operating an intergovernmental solid waste management system, for example, or by delivering health, welfare, or other public services that would otherwise be delivered by state or local governments. This is tantamount to changing the regional system of governance because the regional planning agency itself begins to take on the characteristics of a government. Such a step is often controversial if it is viewed by local governments as a threat to their own prerogatives.

An example of an innovative approach toward intergovernmental planning and implementation linkages can be found in Broward County, Florida. Municipalities within Broward County are legally required to make their zoning conform to the county-wide land use plan. A procedure was established whereby municipalities would submit their zoning ordinances for review and approval to determine whether they were in conformance. In order to make this system work and to enable a determination of conformance to be made, a series of "flexibility zones" was established to allow local zoning to adjust to special local conditions and still adhere to the broader dictates of the county-wide land-use plan.

Conclusion

The fact that this book has a separate chapter on regional plan implementation should not be permitted to obscure the fact that the way in which a regional plan is to be implemented is an important consideration throughout the regional planning process and not something to be pursued as a separate effort after a plan has been completed. At every step of the way—in identifying and working with participants in the planning process, in gathering and analyzing data, in identifying and evaluating alternatives, and so on—the questions of how, when and by whom the plan is to be implemented should be given primary consideration.

Finally, it should be clear from this chapter that the implementation of regional plans is more an art than a science—and an evolving one at that. As long as there is a need to make plans and implement them across political jurisdictions, there will be a need for further experimentation in how best to do it.

1   For purposes of this discussion, "local government" includes not only general purpose governments such as municipalities and counties but also special purpose authorities such as transit, water, and sanitation authorities.

2   U.S. Office of Management and Budget, *Office of Management and Budget Circular No. A-95: An Assessment*, (Washington, DC: May 15, 1978).

3   Quoted from OMB's "Federal Rules for EO 12372, 'Intergovernmental Review of Federal Programs'," a summary of agency regulations, sent to the state-appointed "contacts" for implementation of the Order.

4   Bruce D. McDowell, "White House Casts a Cold Eye on A-95," *Planning*, 48, (January 1982), pp. 6–8.

5   National Association of Regional Councils, *Regional Capital Improvement Programming: An Evaluation and Analysis* (Washington, DC: February 1976).

6   Negotiating the City's Future: A Report on an Experimental Plan for Pooling Urban Investments and Bargaining to Coordinate Policy Goals," a special supplement to *Nation's Cities Weekly*, November 26, 1979. Douglas C. Henton, *et. al., Re-thinking Urban Governance: An Assessment of the Negotiated Investment Strategy*, (Menlo Park, California: SRI International, July 1981). *Mediation and New Federalism: Proceedings of a Roundtable on the Negotiated Investment Strategy*, (Dayton, OH: Charles F. Kettering Foundation, July 8, 1981). Charles R. Warren, *National Implications of a Negotiated Approach to Federalism*, (Dayton, OH: Charles F. Kettering Foundation, July 8, 1981). Donald B. Rosenthal, "Bargaining Analysis in Intergovernmental Relations," *Publius*, Summer 1980, pp. 5-44.

Managing regional planning organizations

Success in managing a regional planning organization begins with the recognition of the special nature of the organization. It is not a government with taxing, ordinance making, and eminent domain powers. In nearly every case, the organization is voluntary. This applies to its membership, local financial contributions, and the actions needed to implement the organization's plans and policies. As an intergovernmental association, it must be managed for the benefit of and to the satisfaction of its members. As a relatively new type of organization, its role is still evolving, untested to some degree, and not fully accepted within its political environment. It may also be relatively unknown within the region and at other levels of government.

This situation in which the typical regional planning organization finds itself, whether a substate regional planning council or a multistate commission, presents a complex challenge to management—involving the managers' own philosophies, capabilities, and practices; a major emphasis upon external affairs; the need to work with many policy makers and committees; equal attention to managing internal operations; and a formal process for periodically reevaluating the regional organization's role and performance. These topics are addressed in this chapter.

The manager

Management personnel in the regional planning organization, and particularly the chief executive, face a complex set of demanding roles—both within and outside their organization—which puts a premium upon developing a smooth working management team and developing each manager to meet the special challenges in regional affairs.

Managerial roles in substate regional councils

The chief executive of a substate regional council is not only the administrative head of the organization's staff, but also a community leader. In this dual capacity, he or she must see that equal attention is given to both internal and external affairs. The executive must see that the staff produces high quality work at reasonable cost, but must also ensure that this work is relevant to community needs and acceptable to community leaders. In addition, the executive must see to it that the regional organization is known and trusted within its region as a useful and reliable source of information and policy leadership.

To accomplish all of this simultaneously requires a great deal of skill and tact. The executive's role is probably clearest as the administrative head of the staff. However, even here, recent trends toward participative management (as explained in Chapter 2) leave most managers experimenting. No longer does the boss initiate and make all the decisions. Increasingly professional and highly qualified staffs demand and deserve to be listened to carefully before major decisions are made. There is much to be gained from this participation, both technically and in terms of morale and higher productivity. Generally speaking, better decisions result from wider participation.

With respect to external affairs, the top executive's job is probably even more difficult. He or she undoubtedly is a community leader and is looked upon as such. The role of the executive requires frequent contacts with the community, including both officials and private citizens. The executive often is called upon to be the chief spokesman for the organization.

This community role, however, raises difficult questions about the role of staff in relation to potential leaders. The successful executive must continually be sensitive to the need for working behind the scenes as a staff advisor to political leaders when appropriate, and stepping out front as a visible leader in his or her own right as the situation may require. This can be a very delicate determination by the executive, and it can be made properly only within a given region's own political environment.

While the executive inevitably will be involved in external affairs in both behind the scenes and out front roles, a "passion for anonymity" generally is appropriate. When in doubt, the executive should opt for the behind-the-scenes role. For example, the chair or president of the regional organization, rather than the staff director, usually should make public announcements, hold press conferences, and so on. This puts political leaders out front in the visible roles where they should be. While staff sometimes may play this role on behalf of elected leaders, staff should never do so in competition with the political leadership of the organization.

Of course, the role of the staff director may vary considerably with respect to external affairs from one region to another. Where that individual's qualifications, experience, and stature in the community are recognized as outstanding, and where this person is perceived as being in step with the needs and desires of the community, a larger direct role in external affairs may be appropriate. This may more often be the case in smaller regions where there are fewer highly qualified leaders. In major metropolitan areas, the regional council executive is more likely to be numbered among many highly qualified leaders, and a role which is more behind the scenes may serve better. In the final analysis, though, the biggest factor in determining the chief executive's role may well be the interplay of personalities between the executive and the political leadership on the governing body of the regional council.

Managerial roles in multistate regional commissions

Most of what has been said about staff versus political leadership in substate regional councils also applies to multistate regional commissions, committees, or corporations. The same dual responsibilities for internal management and external affairs apply to the top management in these multistate organizations.

Nevertheless, there are some significant differences. The staff versus political leadership patterns are less clear in these bodies than in the typical substate regional council. Except for TVA, where the three-member commission very largely turns over staff functions to a general manager, the other multistate organizations involve governing body members in their staff functions. The Title II River Basin chairmen were full-time presidential appointees who headed the commission staffs. The Title V Economic Development Commissions sometimes have been staffed through an appointed executive director, but other times the staff was headed by the full-time presidentially appointed federal cochairman. Even when the executive director format has been followed, providing a neutral staff funded cooperatively by all participating governments, the federal cochairman headed a separate staff of his own, and the various gubernatorial members of the commission designated certain portions of their own staffs to work on commission affairs. The Appalachian Regional Commission has a staff headed by an executive director, but also a full-time federal cochairman and a full-time state's representative chosen by the governors to look out for their interests between commission meetings. With full-time federal commission members chairing or cochairing these multistate organizations, staff roles were more limited to the affairs of internal management, while external affairs were handled by the politically appointed policy makers.

Developing a management team

Whether or not the chief executive of an organization plays a politically visible role in community affairs outside the organization, he or she is equally responsible for both the organization's internal and external affairs. Often, the executive is not equally good at both roles, or in the larger organizations there may be too much work involved in keeping close tabs on both jobs at once. Therefore, depending upon the size of the organization, the basic top management tasks may be split with a deputy director, or perhaps with two—one for internal affairs and one for external affairs. Internal management then may be further divided among a series of departments and offices with directors reporting to the chief executive or his or her deputy. The external affairs staff would be concerned primarily with serving members of the regional organization's governing body, policy and advisory committees, and the press, as well as with public information and citizen participation tasks.

If internal management is slighted, work schedules will not be met, work will be of poor quality, cost controls may break down, morale may nose-dive, and insolvency has been known to occur.

If external affairs are neglected, the organization may remain unknown, its work may go unused and unappreciated, damaging rumors about the dangers of regionalism may spread, support by local governments and the community in general may dissipate, some members may actually drop out or cease paying their dues, the organization's effectiveness may decline, and ultimately its very existence may be threatened.

Regional organizations, as voluntary associations, must produce worthwhile services of high quality and must market them effectively if they are to prosper. The chief executive is responsible for this whole process, yet he or she cannot do it all alone. Thus, there is a need to develop an effective management team to cover all the bases, and a need to enlist the full support of the political policy makers in the organization.

Not all executives have the same style of management, but they all have the same broad scope of responsibilities. Therefore, they need to ensure that the way they manage will not neglect any of the major elements of their responsibilities. Some managers are just naturally more interested in external affairs than internal ones. Others have a creative/intuitive style of operation rather than a systematic one. Some tend to be more authoritarian, while others are naturally more inclined toward participative processes. Some tend to motivate their subordinates with the fear of failure, while others motivate more by example, encouragement, and counseling. While each of these styles may have strengths in certain situations, no one of these styles is likely to bring overall success to a regional organization. A properly developed management team can bring the balance which the organization needs to be successful in many different situations.

Management training and education

The ability to be a successful manager does not come automatically to most people. It needs to be learned, practiced, and honed to a fine point. With nontraditional organizations like substate regional councils and multistate commissions, the need for management excellence is magnified by the uncertainty and complexity of roles and the need for innovation. Therefore, managers in these organizations should assess their own management capabilities and weaknesses, and set out deliberately to grow into and grow with their jobs. They should take advantage of appropriate opportunities for training and continuing education.

Three general topics deserve the manager's attention in developing a sound program for growth in the job. The first is a better understanding of the type of organization being managed, and its general situation in terms of regional needs, regional roles and resources, and political acceptance. The second topic is an understanding of the tasks of management—both generally and within the particular organization. The third is the myriad of management techniques.

Various chapters in this book offer some understanding of these topics, but managers may need to get more information on some points. The footnotes and bibliography in this book are one point of departure, but there are others as well. For example, the publications and annual conferences of the National Association of Regional Councils can be an important continuing resource for the growing manager. Other membership organizations which may be helpful include the International City Management Association (particularly its annual editions of municipal and county yearbooks), and the American Planning Association (particularly participation in its Metropolitan and Regional Planning Division). The U.S. Office of Personnel Management published useful newsletters and magazines on intergovernmental management activities and methods of productivity improvement in the 1970s—and, it is hoped, will do so again sometime in the future. It also supplied training opportunities for state and local officials (including regional organization personnel). Basic management courses can be picked up at almost any nearby college or university, and the National Training and Development Service for State and Local Governments (located in Washington, DC) provides more specialized training opportunities. The really serious manager may also wish to consider membership in the American Management Association. Good management books (including many paperback editions) are available at most bookstores, and the literature on regional planning continues to grow. Book reviews in APA publications, and periodic visits or nearby college or university libraries, can alert the manager to current sources.

Managing external affairs

Regional organizations depend upon outside forces, to a very large extent, for their survival, success, and expanded roles in solving regional problems and being useful to the other levels of government. Regional planning staffs need to pair up with policy makers in the region to strengthen their organizations. Even so, there remains the question whether *regions*, as opposed to regional organizations, really can be managed. These are the topics of this section.

Institutional survival and success

The success and survival of regional organizations might be viewed in terms very similar to the success and survival of a business corporation. Neither has been mandated to stay in business. Both are at the mercy of a market for their products or services. Thus, their success and survival depends heavily upon identifying the products and services which will sell in their market, finding the means to produce these products and services, and successfully marketing them.

Identifying what the region needs   Speaking now within the framework of responsibilities and authority already possessed by the regional organization (by enabling legislation, intergovernmental agreement, or federal aid programs already obtained), there is still considerable latitude as to the products and services which the organization actually will provide to the region, and the precise forms which these products and services will take. There is also some latitude to tailor the products and services to individual local jurisdictions or subregions within the overall area. Satisfaction with the products and services actually produced very well may hinge upon their precise form and geographic or jurisdictional flexibility.

The first step, then, is to assess the pulse of the community. This means that in starting off a new program, viewpoints about what should be produced should be sought throughout the region from representatives to the regional organization, from individual local governments and established citizens' groups, and from others. The response is likely to be greater to the degree that the regional organization habitually operates in an open, aboveboard, accessible, and responsive manner. State and federal officials who may have something to do with this program also should be consulted at this stage to find what would satisfy them most. In addition, laws and court decisions bearing on the program should be reviewed to avoid later surprises concerning restrictions upon what may be done legally.

The happiest situation, of course, would be one in which the products and services desired by all factions are compatible with one another and feasible to produce. Nevertheless, it is unlikely that this will be the case completely. After reviewing the results of this survey from the viewpoint of the community at large, the local governments, state and federal officials, and applicable court decisions, alternative means of proceeding which would meet various combinations of needs should be developed and reviewed again from the various viewpoints. The regional organization's governing body, then, should make the decision about how to proceed.

Funding the program Funding may already be available for certain projects from a federal grant or the regional organization's own funds, although later detailed work programming may change the funding requirements somewhat. For other projects, funding may not already be available, so a federal grant may be sought, or the organization's budget may be reallocated to meet the need. If additional funds are needed as the work program evolves, the possibilities are to seek amendments to existing federal grants, a reallocation of the organization's present budget, authority to charge a fee for resulting products or services, and additional financial contributions from member governments to enable program modifications of specific interest to them. Occasionally, a private foundation or other interested organization may be interested in funding a part of the program which may help to meet its own program needs.

Usually, this funding process, which is essential to the survival of the regional organization, is very largely a matter of intergovernmental relations. Federal grants, state financial support, and local government contributions account for virtually all of the average regional organization's revenues. Thus, products and services especially tailored to the needs of the contributing governmental units encourage a smooth funding process.

Obtaining federal funds involves the "grantsmanship" process. This begins with the identification of federal grant programs for which the regional organization may be eligible and continues with research into the specific purposes and conditions that must be met under the program. The next step usually is to contact the federal office administering the programs to discuss preparation of an acceptable and effective application for funds. Preparing the application may be a major task involving the identification of nonfederal matching funds, demonstration of the regional organization's eligibility for the grant, revision of the

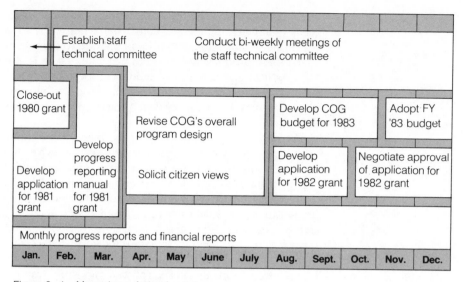

Figure 8–1   Managing a federal grant.

organization's existing goals and work program to reflect federal program requirements, development of political agreement in the region to participate in the federal program, and resolution of any other issues of concern to the federal agency. Sometimes the applications for federal funds must be submitted through an appropriate state agency. This may be the case increasingly if the federal government shifts more fully to the use of state oriented block grants in the future.

Obtaining state funds is a matter of convincing the governor and legislature to either include adequate amounts in the state budget or to authorize a dedicated local source of revenue. Generally, the local source would be either the required payment of local government dues to the regional body or authority for the regional organization to levy an additional millage on the local property taxes. In states where the regional organizations play roles of direct relevance to state goals and programs, it is easier to make the case for state financing actions of these types.

Local contributions of a voluntary nature, which are the most common means of raising regional planning funds within the region itself, must be secured by persuasion. Important factors are (1) involvement of local elected officials in developing the regional planning work program and budget proposal, (2) making sure that past accomplishments of direct value to each local government are well publicized, and (3) putting forth special efforts to explain the new budget to each local government in such a way as to emphasize specific benefits that can be expected in the coming year. In other words, these contributions should not be taken for granted. In addition to the positive approach, penalty provisions of the regional planning act or bylaws may "enforce" the payment of dues by withholding members' privileges to vote on regional issues or to hold office in the regional organization when dues payments are seriously delinquent.

Serving the region   As the regional organization's program moves ahead and begins to produce products and services, the regional organization should give particular attention to "marketing" them. This is the point at which well developed technical assistance, public information, and policy negotiation efforts are needed. A sound network of intergovernmental contacts is essential to the success of such efforts. The products and services are there to be used, and the objective is to increase their utilization. Whether the product is a new information report, a plan, a policy, a "state of the region" report, a regional improvement program, a set of legislative objectives, a newsletter, a computer program, a computer tape, a map, a telephone information service, or whatever, it will not be utilized unless potential users are aware of it, know how to get it, and are assisted in utilizing it to their fullest advantage. The form of the product may need to be tailored to the specific needs of different users, and some users may need more assistance than others to take full advantage of what the regional organization has to offer. Where the product is a policy or plan, specific implementation activities may need to be negotiated, with individual governments and agencies responsible for particular aspects of it.

Only when the regional organization's products and services are actually used is the organization really on the road to success. Therefore these marketing, technical assistance, and policy negotiation efforts should not be neglected.

Creating new roles for the regional organization

In many ways, creating new roles for the regional organization is similar to pursuing institutional success and survival through existing programs. The need is to identify possible and acceptable new roles, to find new resources to support them, and to get new authority to pursue them. At that point they become existing responsibilities in which the precise nature of products and services, the particular means of producing them, and the need to market them successfully become the next steps (as explained above). Here, the concern is with identifying the new roles and finding the new resources and authority to pursue them.

Identifying new roles New roles for the regional organization may be identified within the region as a consequence of pursuing established programs or by consciously initiating special consultations with participating governments and citizens. Other possibilities might come to light with the passage of new federal or state aid programs. Still others might be suggested by learning what other regional organizations are doing, either by direct contact with them, or by participation in a variety of relevant associations. Three such organizations are the National Association of Regional Councils, the individual state associations of regional councils, and the Metropolitan and Regional Planning Division of the American Planning Association. All of these organizations provide opportunities for contacts among peers in the regional planning movement. If a state does not have a state association of regional councils (37 states did by 1979), it would be advantagous to develop one there.

Finding new resources and authority If a new regional role is suggested by the establishment of a new grant program (either state or federal), the obvious means of obtaining that role for the general purpose regional planning organization is to qualify for that program. Sometimes, that could mean changing the organization's legislative basis and/or organizational structure. This might be quite difficult or relatively easy, depending upon the program specifics. If the necessary changes may be made within the organization's own bylaws, the decision may rest largely within the region itself. However, quite often changes in state legislation or a designation by the governor may be required to qualify. If this is the case, working closely with state government may be essential. The regional organization will be in a good position to do this if it has a past record of working with the state reliably and cooperatively. Alliances with other regional councils through the state association and with cities and counties through state municipal leagues and county associations also may be quite valuable.

Often, obtaining designation as the recipient for a new aid program results from competition. The new program may prefer establishment of a separate regional organization, and if state law and the sympathies of the governor do not strongly favor the existing regional councils, they may easily lose the designation. Some federal aid programs also allow the states to do the planning themselves for regions outside of the major metropolitan areas. This so-called "balance of state" planning might be quite attractive to many state agencies unless there is a strong state policy promoting the use of substate regional councils for such purposes. Again, a strong and congenial working relationship with the state should prove advantagous to the regional councils and benefit the state by giving it an easy means of tapping grass roots support for the program.

The more often that regional councils successfully work with the states to compile local plans and organize local support for programs for which there is a state interest, the more likely it is that the state will look to the regional councils to perform additional functions. Demonstrated usefulness is the key to obtaining more important roles for regional councils.

This same principle of success breeding further success applies equally in the case of multistate organizations. When real benefits are perceived by participating states, it is likely that the states will participate more fully and derive even greater benefits from these bodies.

If simple changes in bylaws are not sufficient to give a regional council the new authority and resources it may need to perform a new role, it may be possible to make the necessary provisions by negotiating an intergovernmental agreement or contract among the participating local governments in the region. This may involve all of the local governments active in the regional council, or only some of them, depending upon the scope of the new role and/or the desires of individual jurisdictions to participate or not. These agreements and contracts may be executed by local governments in almost all states, although the authority to do so may be broader in some states than in others. Frequently, states allow these agreements among localities located in two or more states.

Spinning off established regional operations　There is a debate about whether substate regional councils should undertake major regional operations themselves, or spin them off into separate operating organizations. Most regional councils are primarily planning and policy development bodies. Their stock-in-trade is coordination of policies among diverse jurisdictions and programs within a single regional community. In terms of organizational theory, this is a broad legislative and chief executive type of decision-making function, rather than an administrative function such as would be found in an operational line agency.

Many observers of regional organizations argue that major operations—such as operating a transit system, a sewage treatment plant, or a solid waste landfill—might soon drain so much of the organization's managerial energies that the planning and coordination functions would suffer neglect.

The Metropolitan Council of the Twin Cities (Minneapolis and St. Paul, Minnesota) has met this problem by leaving such operations in several separate regional organizations, each operating under the general supervision and policy control of the Metropolitan Council. These separate functions include water quality, parks, airports, and mass transit. Nevertheless, Metro Council itself acts as a metropolitan housing authority, allocating housing assistance funds among the various local housing authorities where most of the operations are concentrated.

This Twin Cities example shows the possibilities for different arrangements in different functional fields. A number of regional councils do perform operating functions themselves, and many provide technical assistance to local governments. These activities may have relatively little to do with overall planning and coordination of the region, but often strengthen the organization in the eyes of its members. So, it does not necessarily follow that all operations should be separated from the regional council. Nevertheless, there may be cases where this is desirable. If a separation is to be made, however, consideration should be given to the maintenance of basic policy control by the regional council.

Policy maker roles in external affairs

Deciding on the types of products and services to be produced by the regional organization, and determining which new roles the organization should undertake, are decidedly political choices. They should be made, and often must be made, by political leaders. The staffs of regional organizations should not move very far toward such decisions without involving their organization's political leadership. Acquainting these leaders with the issues as early as possible lets them help to shape their form and develop the background they will need to make their own decisions and to urge the decisions they want from state and federal officials. Without this type of political support, regional staffs usually are incapable of developing needed external support for their organizations.

Can the region be managed?

Managing the regional organization and managing the region itself are two quite different tasks. Quite clearly, the organization can be managed—though this may not always be easy as roles and resources shift and the relationships between staff and policy makers waver. Nevertheless, the structure of the organization is known, as are the rules under which it is to operate.

On the other hand, the region itself is much larger, much more diverse, very largely controlled by the actions of the private sector, and not organized as a single entity. Thus, it is an oversimplification to view the role of a regional organization as that of "managing" its region. Yet in layman's terms, that is the typical expectation. How close the regional organization can come to meeting this expectation varies greatly from one region to another, depending upon how committed the region is politically to reaching this goal and how much support it gets from state government for strengthening the role of the regional organization. State action which channels all or most regional activities into a single regional organization brings the goal closer than actions that allow numerous regional organizations to operate in the same area. Concerted actions by local governments supporting the coordinated implementation of regional plans goes much further in this direction than parochial attitudes of "every locality for itself." Consolidation of local governments in the area goes further than the minimal interlocal cooperation required to maintain eligibility for federal aid in the region. In other words, there are some relatively effective ways of "managing" or significantly influencing key elements of regional development. While this may fall far short of making the region run like clockwork, the best efforts now available can make a significant contribution toward this goal. More on this topic can be found in Chapter 7.

Working with policy makers, governing boards, and committees

Success in working with the regional organization's governing body, as well as with other policy makers and committees, begins with a sound relationship between the staff and policy makers. It also involves the proper use of meetings, the adoption of meaningful plans and policies, and the use of committed policy makers in advocating the actions required to implement regional plans and policies. These topics are examined below.

Staff–policy maker relationships

The governing body of the substate regional council or the multi-state commission is the essence of the organization. Its political leadership in the region holds the key to success or failure. The staff's function is to serve that governing body and facilitate its activities. A good staff will make the governing body's task easier and more effective, but it cannot substitute in place of the governing body.

The staff should cultivate sound personal relationships with individual policy makers and work hard to develop the organization's governing body and committees into smoothly functioning teams of policy makers who are well informed and willing to pull together in common causes. This is especially necessary in substate regional councils where most members are likely to be part-time local government officials with more than enough to do in their own jurisdictions, families, and businesses. Their participation in the regional council is likely to be squeezed in between other important tasks that demand their primary attention. Of course this is the case also with governors serving on multistate commissions, although governors are likely to be better staffed than most local officials.

Staff should see to it that all newly elected officials in the region are welcomed into the region's official family with at least a letter and a packet of basic information about the regional organization. New members of the governing body also should be contacted personally by the chief executive (and probably also the governing board's chairman and other important members). These new board (or commission) members also should be offered personal briefings about the nature of the organization, the issues it faces, and the procedures it uses in its activities. Even such small details as arrangements for reimbursement of costs incurred in attending board meetings or other activities of the organization, and any other compensation which may be offered, can help to ease the burdens of participation. A 1978 survey by the National Association of Regional Councils showed that at least 171 substate regional councils reimbursed their members for costs of board meetings, while 45 provided compensation beyond expenses. At least 98 substate regional councils also carried liability insurance for their public officials. Expenses were also reimbursed for committee meetings, including meetings of advisory committees, in 122 regional councils. Red carpet treatment of policy makers and advisors is important not just in practical terms, but also as psychic compensation for their sacrifices. The feeling of importance and respect generated by this treatment can return significant dividends in the form of support.

While some governing body members (as well as other elected officials in the region and members of advisory committees) will be involved with the regional organization over a long period of years, others will come and go much more quickly. This constant turnover (resulting from elections, appointments, and other circumstances) means that the welcoming and briefing process may well be almost a continuous one. Seasoned members also must be kept up to date, and former members should continue to be cultivated. All of these present and former participants represent a potentially growing body of support for the organization within the region.

Personal and working relationships between the staff and policy makers, and among the policy makers themselves, may be enhanced by holding special annual meetings which are at least partially social, by taking board members and key committee chairmen to national conferences, and by holding occasional working retreats for policy makers and advisors. The informal and less hurried atmosphere of these occasions helps to build "team spirit."

It is most important to avoid staff dominance of the organization. Many

Figure 8–2   "A properly developed management team can bring the balance which the organization needs." This photo shows the U.S. Army Parachute Team, Fort Bragg, North Carolina.

regional organization staffs have been accused of dominating. This condition can occur easily if care is not taken to develop the governing body and the organization's policy and advisory committees as the central mechanisms of the organization. Staff members need to be good listeners, and need to present their findings and analyses objectively and dispassionately. Boards and committees should be presented with alternative policy choices based upon various sets of explicitly stated assumptions and political value judgments. It is not the staff's place to make these judgments, only to point out the likely consequences of each. Policy makers should understand the consequences of various options, and they then make the political judgments themselves. Effective citizen participation in the various steps of the planning program will help to alert the staff and policy makers to the wide variety of assumptions and value judgments which should be considered. A sound planning program should broaden the options available to the policy makers, but at the same time it should clarify the likely effects of each action so that a public decision, once taken, is less likely to produce unexpected results. The staff's responsibility is to spell out the options competently and faithfully, while the policy makers' responsibility is to make the political choices.

Meetings

Regional organizations are, first and foremost, meeting places.

Multistate organizations have relatively small memberships. The economic development ones had a federal cochairman until 1981, when federal participation was withdrawn, plus the governor of each state—a total membership of perhaps half a dozen to a dozen or so. River basin commissions were perhaps double that size, with about one dozen federal agency representatives and one or more representatives from each of the participating states. The Tennessee Valley Authority has three commission members. Thus, the size of these commissions was kept manageable. For most purposes, their meetings involved their full membership.

In contrast, the substate regional councils have memberships which vary greatly from just a handful to several hundred members. In the larger councils, the full membership may meet only once or twice a year, delegating most of its business to a smaller board of directors or executive committee and a series of policy committees. Most regional councils also have a number of advisory committees, some composed of citizens, and others composed of technical staff representatives of the region's governments. Thus, committee meetings of one sort or another are going on almost continuously.

Whether the regional organization has only quarterly meetings (as with the Appalachian Regional Commission) or several meetings a week (as with a major metropolitan regional council), meetings represent a primary opportunity for involvement of diverse interests and the interchange of views among staffs, policy makers, and advisors. Meetings should be looked upon as learning experiences, as well as decision-making points.

In most cases these meetings should be conducted in the open under state open meetings laws and the federal Sunshine Act. Press coverage probably should be invited and facilitated in most cases, and the opportunity should be taken to let the whole region in on regional issues and activities through news reporting on these events and the ability of interested parties to observe directly what is going on.

One constructive use of committee meetings by the Twin Cities Metropolitan Council (Minneapolis–St. Paul, Minnesota) was reported in a 1976 series of HUD sponsored reports. In developing its metropolitan growth policy, the Metropolitan Council's physical development committee, composed of council members and chaired by the Council's chairman, met weekly in open session with its staff for a period of about a year to work out the best development options and implementation procedures for incorporation into the adopted growth policy. The committee held 70 open committee meetings and 200 public contact meetings, along with three cycles of formal public hearings which were widely publicized and recorded in 1800 pages of testimony. During this period, the committee sent weekly bulletins on the process to 3000 persons, including all local government officials in the area. Some special advisory committees and task forces also were used, but direct liaison with already organized groups was emphasized.[2]

As this process of intensive evaluation of community reactions to earlier staff studies and proposals unfolded, the staff supplied the physical development committee with policy-oriented discussion papers for each committee meeting. These were based upon discussion and feedback at preceding meetings. The whole process was observed and reported on in the metropolitan press and by other means. The whole region—officials and others alike—learned a great deal about itself and its future during this process.

Adopting plans and policies

Too often, regional plans are prepared by the staff and adopted by the regional organization's governing body with little discussion, simply to meet the requirements of some federal aid program. Without this formal adoption, federal funds would cease to flow. But simply meeting the letter of the law, and maintaining eligibility for federal funding, does not necessarily mean that the region has a plan to which its major decision makers are committed. Official rubber stamping of this staff-prepared, federally required "paperwork," usually under tight federally specified deadlines, frequently has little political meaning.

The Twin Cities example of intensive meetings and political bargaining over an extended time to arrive at acceptable planning policies to meet the region's own perceived needs (rather than just the need to keep federal funds flowing) shows how meaningful plans and policies reflecting real political commitment can be developed. The adopted document is not nearly so important as the development of political commitment among the policy makers. The visibility of the process also educates the community about the policies chosen, and the reasons why others were rejected. Thus, community commitment reinforces policy maker commitment. As such a process continues, year after year, the region becomes more planning conscious, and the community at large becomes to expect higher standards of regional planning and coordination.

Policy makers and implementation

The policy maker's job does not end with adoption of the regional plan. The plan and other regional policies are political statements that have little value without commensurate political action. While staff may help to keep track of potentials for such action and proposals which might be at odds with the regional plans and policies, only the political policy makers can effectively advocate the local government actions, state legislation, and the state and federal funding needed to achieve the region's goals. Effective lobbying for the region's interests needs political support from committed policy makers.

Managing internal operations

Managing the regional organization's internal operations involves what is more traditionally recognized as management functions. These involve setting the organization's goals, programming and scheduling appropriate staff work, coordinating policy, organizing and developing the staff, supplementing staff capabilities when necessary, using systematic management techniques, and providing sound financial management. These traditional functions of management—addressed in most management books—take special forms in regional organizations. These are examined below.

Setting the organization's own goals

While the region's future and the organization's future are closely related, the organization is likely to be most successful if its management focuses some of its attention directly upon the organization's own goals as distinct from the goals of the region. This organizational planning is comparable to the strategic planning processes now firmly established in many business corporations.[3] Of course, the private sector is most interested in evaluating those strategies that will contribute most to the financial profitability of the corporation. In the regional organization, the emphasis is upon identifying those strategies which will contribute most toward the political survival of the organization and improved effectiveness in solving regional problems and serving regional needs. But the strategic planning process can be pursued in very similar ways in both types of organizations. The success of such planning depends upon involving the top policy makers as well as top management and usually can benefit substantially by involving lower levels of management as well. The process involves evaluating the organization's situation from all angles, developing the organization's basic purposes and missions, translating these into long-range planning objectives, formulating appropriate strategies and functional programs, and converting the strategies into current decisions.

Specifically, in the regional organization, strategic planning can help to answer such questions as which grants to accept, which new roles (if any) to undertake, and which types of new authority (if any) to seek. Most private corporations practice strategic planning on an annual basis in conjunction with their budgeting cycles. This makes sense for regional organizations also, enabling them to incorporate their grant-seeking strategy into the new budget each year and provide for any new roles being sought. If any new authority is to be sought, the organization's strategies in that regard could be reflected in an annual legislative program which sets forth the organization's goals and priorities for establishing or revising inter-local agreements and contracts, memoranda of understanding, state legislation, and federal laws and regulations.

With respect to grant strategies, two points should be made. First, many federal grants can be quite expensive to apply for and administer. Therefore, if the amount of funds likely to be available to the regional organization is small, the grant may not be worth applying for. The other major consideration concerns the nature of the grant. The federal purposes involved should be such that they are capable of being meshed with the goals of the regional organization and acceptable to the regional community. In addition, grants that are designed to stimulate regional activity beyond what is financed by the immediate project should be evaluated for their long-run impact. Some grants begin with a larger federal share of funding that gradually reduces in future years, and others are temporary—designed to create a new activity and then turn it over in later years completely to the region and its own resources without further federal participation. If such grants are to be accepted, provisions should be made for their future continuation, since it is likely that a constituency for them will have developed under the grant program.

Work programming and scheduling

There have been many federal requirements for work programming that regional planning organizations have followed as prerequisites to their grants. This has been a major consideration because of most regional organizations' heavy reliance on federal grants.

These work programs and schedules have constituted the major substance of the federal aid applications. Usually, they lay out a fairly comprehensive view of the organization's full work program and then place the specific activities to be funded by the particular grant within that context. For grants from the Department of Housing and Urban Development, the concern has been to show how planning for the overall region would promote the revitalization of deteriorating neighborhoods and central cities and provide for housing the poor and minorities. For the Department of Transportation, the concern has been to show how overall planning would provide for the coordinated use of transit and highways in relation to development patterns, while at the same time conserving energy and controlling air pollution. For the Environmental Protection Agency, the concern has been to relate provisions for improved air and water quality, and the disposal of solid wastes, to overall regional growth and development. For the Economic Development Administration, the concern has been to show how the development of public facilities would help to promote and provide for economic development and jobs.

There are numerous common elements running through all of these concerns. Population and economic projections for the growth of the region, land-use inventories and plans, and basic physical and demographic characteristics of the region all are basic. Yet, the natural tendency of federal agencies has been to require a separate explanation of the regional organization's overall work program in a particular format for each separate grant program. This, of course, requires duplicate efforts by the regional organization. The organization's objective should be to reduce this duplication as much as possible.

Part IV of the U.S. Office of Management and Budget's Circular A-95 has called for memoranda of understanding among regional planning organizations which would provide for the use of common data and basic studies to the greatest extent feasible, and various federal agencies, from time to time, have had interagency agreements in effect among themselves providing that certain types of planning done for one grant program would be accepted as satisfying the requirements for another. It is to the regional organization's advantage to be familiar with such OMB provisions and interagency agreements, and to take full advantage of them. Regional organizations frequently band together through their state and national associations to lobby for the simplification and unification of work programming requirements.

Systematic techniques for work programming　During the 1950s, program management techniques evolved from the rather crude use of bar charts which showed work activities on a time scale, into a much more precise program evaluation and review technique which shows the functional interrelationships between a group of interrelated activities required to complete a project. This new technique, commonly referred to as PERT, uses a flow chart which shows which activities must be completed before others, and which can go on simultaneously. All activities required to complete the project appear on this diagram and can be assigned time, manpower, and cost estimates. It becomes clear, then, by analyzing this diagram which set of interconnected tasks will take the longest to complete. That particular path through the diagram (or network) is referred to as the "critical path." That path, then, controls the schedule of the whole project. Often it can be seen that the overall project can be speeded up by applying more manpower or greater resources to particular activities on the critical path. Likewise, it may be seen that reassigning manpower and funds from the other parts of the project to speed up those on the critical path would advance the overall project completion date. However, if the critical path is speeded up substantially, it may be that a different path becomes critical to the overall schedule. In that case, further balancing of the resources and activities may be considered until all reasonable options have been exhausted. At that point, the most effective and efficient work program and schedule will have been attained.[4]

Originally devised for the management of complex projects to develop military weapons systems rapidly, PERT has been applied much more widely to both complex and simple projects. It is not necessary to use all features of the technique in order to gain benefits from the general concept. The key element is the flow diagram (or network) itself. Developing such a diagram represents a systematic analysis of the tasks involved in a project from beginning to end. Even if the project is not complex enough to make it worthwhile to estimate

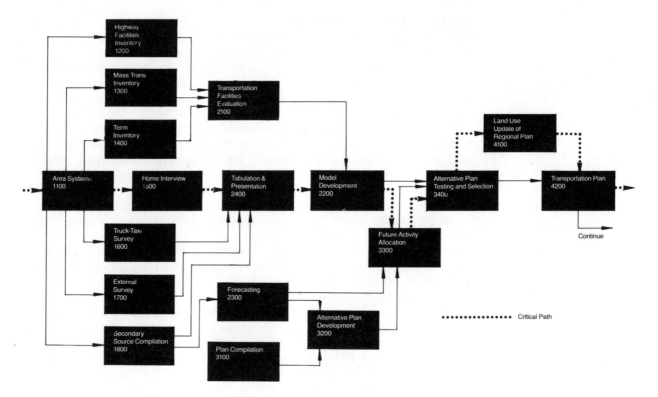

Figure 8–3 Simplified program flow diagram.

the time, manpower, and cost of completing each activity, the diagram clearly communicates to the manager and all those working on the project the importance of each individual activity and the consequences of not completing it on time. Periodic progress reporting on the basis of this diagram will show clearly when delays in certain activities threaten to delay completion of the overall project. This allows remedial action to be taken to protect the overall project schedule. While a computer may be needed to apply this technique completely to complex projects, nothing more than paper and pencil is needed to gain the most basic benefits. Figure 8–3 shows a simplified program flow diagram, with a dotted line marking the critical path.

An easily understood work program, for use with policy makers and the community at large, as well as within the staff, should include a statement linking regional problems to the regional organization's role and work program, followed by the work programs for individual projects (some of which may be a year or less in length, but others of which may go on for several years), and an indication of which activities will be funded by the current budget. A tabulation of regional goals and objectives in relation to prior years' activities, the activities' results, and related community characteristics to be monitored in the budget year, along with projected activities in future years is one way to connect program activity details to the broader purposes of the organization.

Work programming along with narrative explanations and specific budgets have been used to meet federal aid requirements and, at the same time, to provide a sound basis for managing the regional organization's staff and maintaining the support of the region's policy makers. Still, there is no formula which guarantees meeting all these needs at once. Careful consultations with federal funding agencies, regional policy makers, and others will be required to develop the type of work programming best suited to each region.

Scheduling citizen participation and regional decision making processes

Work programming in many regional organizations (and other governmental bodies as well) frequently tends to underestimate or undervalue the time and resources required for citizen participation and the adoption of regional plans and policies. Work programs tend to be developed by staffs for staff purposes. Consequently, they often emphasize the data collection and technical analysis tasks which are the primary responsibility of staff people. Citizen participation may be thought of in terms of a public hearing or two at appropriate times, and occasional contacts with advisory committees. Adoption processes may be considered very largely as a series of informational briefings, provided as staff work progresses, and a final meeting at which policy makers accept what the staff has prepared. In both cases, these are greatly oversimplified concepts of what should be involved.

Citizen participation, as explained in Chapter 12, should be viewed as a major source of information about the region and its attitude, applicable at all stages of the planning process—from the perception of problems, to the development of regional goals and objectives, the precise definition of needs of the various segments of the region's population, the creation and evaluation of alternative proposals for future action, and the evaluation of effects emanating from the implementation of adopted plans or policies. The need to adapt planning proposals to the specific needs and attitudes of a region has been clearly identified in working with underdeveloped nations,[5] but greatly underemphasized by most planners within the United States. Politically wise planners, of course, have been taking this need into account informally for many years, but formal planning theory and citizen participation techniques for making this a more formal part of the planning process are relatively recent.[6] The point to remember is that meeting this need takes time and organization resources which should be reflected in the work program and budget.

With respect to adopting regional plans or policies, developing a community consensus and political commitment to major statements or regional policy may take equally as long as producing the staff studies upon which such a debate may be based. The Twin Cities example of adopting a major new metropolitan growth policy, mentioned earlier in this chapter, shows how extended and intensive this process may become. If extensive political debate is not generated during the adoption process, chances are that there is very little content in the policy or very little political commitment represented by formal adoption. The work program and budget should anticipate that the adoption process will be more than the rubber stamping of staff recommendations.

Avoiding federal dominance of work programming

Whenever a regional organization receives a federal grant, chances are that the organization becomes responsible not only for fulfilling the directly enacted purpose of the grant, but also for assuring that those funds are administered in such as manner as to:

1. Redress past discrimination and prevent present and future discrimination on such bases as sex, age, race, and national origin.
2. Provide equal opportunities to jobs, education, housing, public accommodations, and any other benefits of the grant program.
3. Provide equal access by the handicapped and disadvantaged to government benefits and opportunities.
4. Protect and enhance the quality of the environment.

5. Protect relocatees against loss due to project activities.
6. Ensure prevailing wages for any construction workers who might be under contract in the project.
7. Ensure the use of qualified public employees who are appointed and treated according to "merit principles" rather than political patronage.
8. Bar financial kickbacks and corruption.
9. Facilitate intergovernmental and interprogram coordination.
10. Ensure project compatibility with local, regional, and state planning.
11. Freely provide information about the program to the public and involve citizens and appropriate public officials in program development and implemention.
12. Protect the privacy of information concerning individuals associated with or affected by the program.[7]

In addition, overarching presidential policies have been developed which have applied quite broadly to federal aid programs from time to time. For example, President Carter's 1978 and 1980 urban policies, and his 1979 policies for small communities and rural development, provided a series of administrative priorities for managing federal grants to emphasize national policies on such matters as revitalizing urban areas, targeting federal resources on distressed communities and disadvantaged people, conserving energy and environmental quality, and providing an improved climate for business and economic development.

Thus, there may be a great deal of policy already made for a regional organization's work program before the organization's management begins its work programming process. Nevertheless, the ways in which these broad policies are applied within a given region often may be affected quite significantly by the regional organization itself. The staff should be especially sensitive to opportunities for reflecting local priorities and desires, special concerns of its own region, and state concerns in the work program. There should be "something for everyone" in the work program to keep any available state and federal funds flowing, to satisfy local government members, and to meet real regional needs in tangible ways.

Policy coordination

A primary mission of regional organizations is policy coordination. This coordination needs to take place among levels of government as well as among diverse functions of government. Thus, the regional organization's work program will have many coordination projects within it. The organization's policy structure also will be designed to bring together disparate interests so that they can consider and, it is to be hoped, agree upon, common policies.

However, coordination is one of the most difficult tasks. If the regional organization's governing body is not careful to protect its primary policy adoption prerogatives, individual policy committees and member governments will pursue disparate positions. If the organization's chief executive does not maintain his or her position of final review over staff work, individual departments and staff members may pursue diverse and possibly inconsistent goals. If skill in negotiating compromises and mediating disputes is not exercised both by top management and top policy makers, proponents of diverse policies may harden their positions and create impasses.

For these reasons, it may be wise for regional organizations to make use of professional negotiators and mediators when major controversial issues are being worked out.

Once regional plans and policies have been agreed to, the primary means for bringing about consistency with them is the regional review process. In this process, the plans of other levels of government are reviewed by the regional organization, as are specific implementation projects which would affect the region. These reviews produce comments about the relationship of the reviewed plans and projects to regional policies. This process is a key to the primary mission of the regional organization; it should be given a prominent place in the work program, and it should be budgeted adequately.

To facilitate the review process, regional organizations should inventory their current policies and compile them into a review manual available both to the review staff and to governments and agencies that are likely to be submitting plans or projects for review. The mere fact of having such a compilation abroad in the community will familiarize many officials with regional policies that might otherwise go unnoticed, and it is likely to encourage voluntary compliance with them by those desiring quick and painless reviews from the regional organization. According to a 1978 survey by the National Association of Regional Councils, nearly 350 substate regional councils publish a guide to their review process to help facilitate this key element in their work programs.[8] Since this review process has applied only to federal projects or federally assisted projects for many regional organizations, expansion to cover nonfederal plans and projects may be one of the additional types of authority which regional organizations may wish to acquire.

Organizing and developing the staff

The staffs of regional organizations are made up very largely of professionals from planning and a variety of other disciplines. They may include engineers, economists, social scientists, and others.

These employees can be expected to be highly creative if given stimulating and satisfying conditions under which to work. Many of them will wish to participate in managerial and political processes, and most are likely to want good equipment to work with and opportunities for professional growth. Oppressive management, political climates that leave little room in which to try new ideas, and lack of opportunities for professional growth are likely to result in high turnover rates.

Some of the professional opportunities frequently sought are paid-up memberships in professional organizations, the opportunity to attend professional meetings and national conferences, and encouragement for taking continuing education courses. Adequate clerical support and up-to-date equipment for word-processing and computing also are major incentives for superior staff performance and creativity. Large regional organizations should consider offering career development, counseling, and training programs to give their employees a sense of recognition and progress.

The 1978 NARC Survey, mentioned earlier, reveals that nearly 400 substate regional councils have formal personnel systems, and that 350 have retirement systems. Those regional organizations which do not offer such benefits should consider doing so.

There is no one best way to organize the staff of a regional organization. Probably the most common way is to establish special staffs for each major program—such as transportation, housing, environmental protection, community and economic development, social services, health, and public safety. Others organize around major functions such as planning, policy coordination, and technical services. Of course, it is also possible to have a combination of these two types of units. Still another approach is to organize special project teams which stay together for the duration of a particular project, but then have their members dispersed among other projects as the work program shifts. This flexible approach might be especially useful in smaller organizations where staffs are less specialized. Recent experiences with rapid shifts in federal aid priorities have emphasized the advantages of hiring professionals who are flexible enough to work on a variety of different projects. As federal aid priorities and regional organization roles change, management should stay alert to the need for reorganization of the staff.

Supplementing staff capabilities

The regional organization's staff may not embody all the technical capabilities and manpower needed by the work program from time to time. Most regional organizations have technical advisory committees composed of personnel from participating governments who work in the same fields as those included in the regional work program. Frequently, these committees can be called upon to supplement the regional organization's staff work. This may be done either by having certain components of the regional work program performed by other governments, or by having other governments loan staff to the regional organization for specific tasks and periods of time. The regional organization also may hire consultants from time to time, and engage universities or other research organizations to perform special tasks for them.

The major consideration in using these outside sources for portions of the regional work program is that the regional organization should have the competence to direct, monitor, and make use of the work produced by others. If this is not ensured, the work may be out of step with the regional program, or may simply be unusable and a waste of effort.

Using systematic management techniques

There are several different management systems from which to choose. Some are based more upon strengthening supervisory relationships throughout the organization, while others are based more upon broadening and strengthening the budget system.

In the first case, the primary example is management by objectives. This type of management relies upon "a process whereby the superior and subordinate managers of an organization jointly identify its common goals, define each individual's major areas of responsibility in terms of the results expected of him, and use these measures as guides for operating the unit and assessing the contribution of each of its members."[9] Intermediate checkpoints are set up through the year, and progress is reported as these points arrive. If circumstances change or performance is not as expected, adjustments are made by mutual consent. Objectives are related to budgeted resources, and year-end performance is judged against goal achievement and budget allocations. A process which is working successfully keeps the various levels of management close to one another in a mutually supporting relationship and should avoid unexpected results at the end of the year.

In regional organizations, where most of the work program is under the direction of federal aid contracts, a contract monitoring system may come very close to using a process of management by objectives. The application for the grant generally includes a work program proposal jointly developed by the various levels of management and policy making within the organization. When the grant is made, perhaps after some further refinement of the work program in consultation with federal officials, this work program becomes a contractual obligation to be filled by the regional organization. Internal management then becomes responsible for seeing that it is carried out on time and within budget. If changes are needed as the contract period progresses, the regional organization's management must go back to the federal agency to making the grant to get a formal change. Regular progress reporting throughout the budget year alerts management to the need for such changes. The federal agency involved often requires progress reports also, and a final project report always is required for federal purposes.

Budget-based management systems are based upon program budgeting—a concept which has been in existence for nearly 70 years.[10] The concept is that the budget should be presented in terms of program objectives, and then debated and acted upon as a program policy document. Concerns about spending efficiency and effectiveness would be handled through expenditure reports and audits. This type of budgeting was accepted slowly in government, but became fairly common during the 1960s, and it is now the normal practice. (Previously, of course, budgeting was done by objects of expenditure such as personnel, equipment, contracting, interest on debt, and the like.)

As program budgeting has gained acceptance, variations upon it have been developed. In the mid-1960s, the planning, programming, and budgeting system (PPBS) was popular. The concept was that long-range planning for public program options should be linked to shorter range programming of governmental resources for a three to five year period in support of alternative program options, and budget year implications should be spelled out all within a single system. Costs and benefits (or program effectiveness) were examined, and the evaluation of past program effectiveness became an important consideration. Budget offices and planning offices became much more closely linked, and they spawned program evaluation units. The system required not just budget analysts, but also planners, economists, and program evaluators. While the concept made sense, and it enjoyed a great deal of success in the Defense Department, it proved too burdensome to be administered throughout the federal government. Instituted government-wide in 1965, it was abandoned in 1969. Nevertheless, multiyear budgeting, program evaluation staffs, and management by objectives were left in place in the wake of this experiment. There is a much greater realization now, than there was before the planning, programming, budgeting system was tried, that sound program budgeting rests upon multiyear considerations and economic analysis. Thus, in a conceptual sense, much of the planning, programming, budgeting concept remains with us.

The zero-based budgeting concept was the contribution of the 1970s. Its basic concept is that every budgeted program should be reevaluated each year in terms of its objectives, its past success, its future prospects, and its value in relation to alternative programs which might be adopted instead. The idea is for the budgeting process to ask what would happen if the program were discontinued, or funded at part of its previous level, funded at the same level as before, or funded at increased levels. It is a multiyear process like planning, programming, and budgeting, and it also relies upon program evaluation. But more than any budgeting system before it, zero-based budgeting emphasized the need to look at the whole budget, not just requested increases. *Thorough* planning, programming, and budgeting systems or management by objective systems would do this, but often in actual practice they did not—so the zero-based budgeting system emphasized the point.

Whatever its specific form, program budgeting now is a standard part of management processes. Linked up with a process of management by objectives, it ties together program planning, budget controls, and a systematic supervisory management network. Such a system should serve regional organizations well.

In large regional organizations, formal progress reporting systems probably are necessary to keep top management abreast of significant events and lapses in the work program. The Metropolitan Washington Council of Governments, for example, has a monthly progress reporting process in which each project manager or department head fills out a standard form for each project under his or her control. These reports are gathered and analyzed by a central management staff which meets with the department heads and senior program managers individually to explore any problems or questions which may surface. A progress report summary is then prepared and submitted to the executive director who may meet with his or her own management staff and/or particular department heads and program managers with respect to any unusual situations demanding personal attention. The progress report summary and any follow-up actions which may be taken on it by the executive director are made available to all department heads to keep them abreast of major accomplishments and problems. This early warning system allows remedial actions to be taken before problems become serious.

Financial and administrative management

Because regional organizations have relied so heavily upon federal financing, they have devoted a significant amount of time to preparing and negotiating applications for federal grants, administering these grants in accordance with federal financial and administrative rules, and submitting to audits of these programs. In past years, most federal aid programs had their own separate requirements with respect to these matters. More recently, however, the U.S. Office of Management and Budget mounted a significant effort to simplify and standardize these requirements. Standard application forms, reporting and auditing requirements, purchasing and personnel procedures, and cost eligibility provisions were developed. Congress passed a joint funding simplification act under which federal agencies are encouraged to waive certain requirements for the sake of allowing federal aid projects to be funded by two or more federal grants from different agencies under agreements by which they are administered by only a single federal agency and audited only once. Substate regional councils have been the most frequent users of this procedure.

Certain overhead or administrative costs of regional organizations also have been funded by some programs under a simplified procedure by which the organization qualifies for an indirect cost rate, rather than a procedure in which the organization would have to detail all such activities in an explicit work program. An indirect rate approval by one federal agency may be accepted by others.

Substate regional councils have been in the forefront of helping the federal government to develop a number of these techniques and have used them extensively. For example, NARC's 1978 survey showed that 211 regional councils had a single consolidated audit system designed to meet all federal audit requirements, while 345 used private certified public accounts to audit their total program. Two hundred fifty-seven regional councils had federally approved indirect cost rates, and 336 met the matching requirements of federal aid programs at least in part with in-kind services rather than cash provided by themselves or others in their region.

The financial management of substate regional councils has been particularly complex because of the large number of separately earmarked grant programs which had to be accounted for individually. Each grant had to be considered a separate revenue source to be spent only on activities approved in the work program authorized by the grant contract. Thus, auditing (as well as bookkeeping) became a matter of determining contract compliance for perhaps a dozen or more revenue sources each year. Thus, without joint funding, single audits, and other simplification measures, administrative burdens became quite high. With a number of different federal agencies auditing their books, many regional councils found it necessary to set aside an auditing room which got nearly continuous, year-round use. For these reasons, it was important for regional councils to support federal aid simplification measures and make maximum use of them.

Evaluating regional organizations

Every few years, regional organizations should evaluate their own performance and the way they are viewed in the region. In many respects, this is similar to the annual strategic planning process discussed above, in which the regional organization sets the organization's own goals for purposes of budgeting and establishing its legislative program. However, there are some differences. This evaluation is more exhaustive than the annual process, places much greater emphasis upon evaluation by those outside the organization, and is less frequent.

To be successful, this periodic evaluation process must be undertaken with a major commitment by the organization's staff and policy makers to cooperating in the process, learning as much as they can about the organization in objective terms, and avoiding a defensive posture. The purpose is to recognize and continue those activities in which the organization is successful while identifying problem areas and improving them. Major changes in the organization may not result from this process, although it should not be surprising if some do.

The evaluation process recommended by the National Association of Regional Councils[11] requires a substantial commitment of time by both the organization's staff and policy makers, and should be backed up by a designated item in the budget. The steps in the process include:

1. Establishing an evaluation committee of the organization's governing body;
2. Assigning staff and retaining any consultants which may be needed for supplemental work;
3. Contacting and organizing an outside team of experts in regional affairs to help with the evaluation process;
4. Developing a questionnaire and surveying all segments of the regional community—including public officials from all levels of government, private sector leaders, organized interest groups within the region, the press and other media, and others;
5. Bringing the outside evaluation team into the region to interview key staff members of the organization, members of the governing board, and a representative sample of those surveyed by questionnaire;
6. Preparation and submission of a report by the evaluation team giving its findings concerning the organization's performance and the perceptions of it in the region;
7. Submission of recommendations by the team calling for any changes needed in the organization's program and procedures;
8. Review of the evaluation team's report by the regional organization's staff and governing board and scheduling of a weekend retreat away from telephones and other distractions for full and frank discussion of the findings plus any needed changes; and
9. Preparation of a program of specific organizational improvements by the staff and board.[12]

According to the 1978 survey by the National Association of Regional Councils, referred to several times previously, 74 substate regional councils regularly carry out some sort of periodic evaluation process such as this.

Summary

Regional organizations are difficult to manage because they are relatively new types of organizations with evolving roles and few powers. Typically, a great deal is expected of them in comparison to the tools they have to work with. Their success depends very largely upon creative and sensitive management. Important elements of such management include:

Adjusting the manager's style and philosophy to the special needs of regional organizations;

Developing a management team capable of addressing both external and internal affairs affecting the organization;

Working hard to identify the special needs of the region, find the means of funding a program which will address these needs, and promote the use of the regional organization's policies and services by others;

Identifying and establishing new roles for the regional organization;

Involving the political policy makers in the management of the organization's external affairs;

Developing solid relationships of mutual respect and assistance between the staff, the policy makers, advisers, and citizens' groups;

Using meetings of committees and the governing body constructively and productively;

Ensuring that the adoption of regional plans and policies reflects political commitment, rather than a rubber stamping of staff work;

Using politically committed policy makers to help in the implementation of regional plans and policies;

Managing the internal operations of the organization with due regard for setting the organization's own goals and strategies for success, using systematic work programming and scheduling procedures, emphasizing the prime mission of policy coordination, developing effective organization and staff, supplementing staff capabilities when necessary (through the use of consultants, technical committees, loaned staffs, and outside research organizations), using systematic management and budgeting techniques, and using simplified and standardized procedures as much as possible for financial and administrative management; and

Periodically evaluating the organization's performance and reputation, using outside evaluators, in part, and a broad survey of community leaders to bring some objectivity to the findings.

Management should take special steps to avoid:

Financial insolvency (which has plagued a number of regional organizations in the past);

Staff domination of the organization's activities;

Staff isolation from and insensitivity to the community and the organization's participating governments;

Lagging staff productivity resulting from lack of clear goals and leadership;

Lapses of coordination within the staff;

Lack of openness, availability, objectivity, and a sense of perspective on the part of the staff as perceived by policy makers and/or citizens in the region; and

Conflicts of interest on the part of the organization's staff members and/or policy makers.

These are demanding tasks. Few managers come into regional organizations fully equipped to cope with them. Continuing education and training opportunities should be sought out for staff as well as for policy makers. Such opportunities are available without great sacrifice.

1   This is a phrase and philosophy popularized by Louis Brownlow, one of the early leaders in the fields of city management and public administration; Louis Brownlow, *A Passion for Anonymity: The Autobiography of Louis Brownlow*, 2 vols. (Chicago: University of Chicago Press, 1955–1958).

2   The Metropolitan Council of the Twin Cities Area, *The Politics and Planning of a Metropolitan Growth Policy for the Twin Cities: An Executive Summary* (St. Paul, MN: September 1976), pp. 7–8.

3   George A. Steiner, *Strategic Planning: What Every Manager Must Know* (New York: Free Press, 1979). See also Susan M. Walter, editor, *Proceedings of the White House Conference on Strategic Planning* (Washington, DC: Council of State Planning Agencies, 1980).

4   For further explanation of this technique see, for example, Robert W. Miller, *Schedule, Cost, and Profit Control with PERT: A Comprehensive Guide for Program Management* (New York: McGraw-Hill, 1963).

5   Glynn Cochrane, *The Cultural Appraisal of Development Projects* (New York: Praeger, 1979). See also Cochrane's earlier book entitled *Social Soundness Analysis*.

6   See, for example, John Friedmann, *Retracking America: A Theory of Transactive Planning* (Garden City, NY: Anchor Press/Doubleday, 1973); and

Advisory Commission on Intergovernmental Relations, *Citizens Participation in the Federal System* (Washington, DC: U.S. Government Printing Office, 1980), especially Chapter 3.

7   Adapted from Advisory Commission on Intergovernmental Relations, *Categorical Grants: Their Role and Design, Report A-52* (Washington, DC: U. S. Government Printing Office, 1977), p. 233.

8   Advisory Commission on Intergovernmental Relations, *State and Local Roles in the Federal System* (Washinton, DC: U.S. Government Printing Office, 1981), p. 322.

9   George S. Odiorne, *Management by Objectives: A System of Managerial Leadership* (New York: Pitman Publishing Corp., 1965), pp. 55–56.

10 David Novick, editor, *Program Budgeting: Analysis and the Federal Budget* (Cambridge, MA: Harvard University Press, 1965), p. 30.

11 Robert E. Sellers and Burton Spaier, *Evaluating Your Regional Council* (Washington, DC: National Association of Regional Councils, 1978).

12 These steps are adapted from Sellers and Spaier, *Evaluating Your Regional Council*, and from Minnesota Association of Regional Commissions and Minnesota State Planning Agency, *Self Evaluation Guide for Minnesota Regional Development Commissions* (St. Paul, MN: January, 1979).

Part two:
Analysis and information

9 Policy analysis

This chapter is intended to introduce planners and students of planning to the practice of policy analysis and to the range of activities engaged in by policy analysts. A comprehensive view of the field of policy analysis is presented, but special emphasis is placed upon the types of analysis and techniques most useful to state and regional planners. Case examples are included to illustrate policy analyses of both specific programs for particular locales and policy analyses of programs that might be applied in various settings.[1]

What is policy analysis?

So many definitions of policy analysis have appeared that there is no generally accepted one. As presented in this chapter, policy analysis is the medium through which one identifies and evaluates alternative policies or programs that are intended to lessen or solve a particular social, economic, or physical problem. This activity includes several critical components: problem definition, specification of evaluation criteria, generation of alternatives, evaluation of alternatives, identification of side effects, ranking of alternatives, specification of implementation procedures, and the identification of next steps, including procedures for monitoring, evaluation, and reassessment.

Policy analysis is more than a single entity, however. In one form, it is a *product*, the outcome of an analysis: the conclusion that results from the intellectual act of policy analysis. But it is also the *process* that produces the conclusion. Since planners and analysts need to inform their clients about alternatives and implications, policy analysis is oral or written persuasion.

Policy analysis is also more than the technical tools used to help make a decision. These techniques, both quantitative and procedural, may be given great attention in the policy analysis process, but they alone are not policy analysis. Rather, policy analysis is a mechanism for examining complex problems that provides insights about the appropriateness of alternative policies or programs that might be applied as solutions to these problems. As such, policy analysis can provide planners with information about the feasibility of alternative plans, about strategies for implementation, and about the consequences of plan implementation.

Differences between planning and policy analysis

Planners do practice policy analysis, yet there appear to be differences between the orientation and professional approach of planners and that of full-fledged policy analysts. These differences can be examined in relation to the role of the political official, a primary client of both the planner and the policy analyst, and in the context of the basic problem solving process.

Planners, policy analysts, and political officials have different orientations toward problem solving and policy development. The political official is adaptive, pragmatic, and oriented toward a constituency. The planner, typically operating

Science and the systems

approach   The idea that the dispassionate and yet clear mind of the scientist can aid in decision making is an old-fashioned one. Plato had it many years ago when he thought he could begin to design the underlying model of a city-state, as he did in his *Republic*. Down the ages, every so often a writer has set down what in his opinion are the essential ingredients in a messy situation in order to untangle the various factors and set the matter straight in a scientific and objective fashion.

A very fascinating development of this kind occurred in World War II, when the British Admiralty asked teams of scientists to consider some of the pressing problems that Britain faced during the first bombings by the Nazis. What is especially interesting about this story is that the scientists kept asking stupid questions. For example, the British were having a good deal of trouble knocking out the German submarines in the English Channel. The scientists noted that the depth charges dropped from aircraft were set so that the charge did not go off until at least 35 feet below the surface. The scientists asked the stupid question: Why not try to set the charges so they go off at a shallower depth? Once you've asked a stupid question, then you have to defend your right to ask it, and the scientists pointed out some of the weaknesses in the assumptions that were made by the military in the manner in which the aircraft was approaching its target. Eventually some experiments were run, and sure enough, the submarine kill went up significantly as a result of setting the charges at a shallower depth.

The success of the scientific teams in the military in World War II was outstanding both in Great Britain and in America. As a consequence after the war there was a rush to apply the same kind of thinking, which then was called "operations research," to various non-military problems, and in particular to industry. At first the problems considered were rather small. The scientists studied production as well as some minor problems of marketing and finance. A few sporadic attempts were made to solve some problems in transportation, e.g., the design of roadways. But luckily along came a computer that was an enormous aid to the scientist.

As the scientist's perspective widened, he began to think of his approach as the "systems approach." He saw that what he was chiefly interested in was characterizing the nature of the system in such a way that the decision making could take place in a logical and coherent fashion and that none of the fallacies of narrow-minded thinking would occur. Furthermore, using his scientific knowledge he expected to be able to develop measures which would give as adequate information as possible about the performance of the system.

In time the decision makers, both in industry and in government, began to see the possible values of the so-called systems approach. For example, Governor Brown of California in the early 1960s proposed to the aerospace industry that they submit to him four systems science designs for crime, sanitation, information and transportation. Governor Brown's idea was that people who are well trained in the design of complex hardware systems, such as space missiles, should be able to apply their thinking to the critical decision-making problems of the state. In practically every office of the government there are operations researchers, management scientists, system scientists, all attempting to look at the problems of the United States government from the so-called systems approach.

Source: C. West Churchman, *The Systems Approach* (New York: Dell Publishing, 1968), pp. viii–x.

in a cognitive-rational mode, seeks change, is prescriptive, and tends to view the general public as the consumers of his or her work. The policy analyst shares both the cognitive-rational perspective of the planner and the adaptive perspective of the political official.

Each of these actors plays a different role in developing and implementing policy. The political official is oriented toward policy adoption and implementation, while the policy analyst is concerned with policy identification and evaluation. The planner is primarily concerned with policies to guide plan development. While the planner's ultimate client is often the political official, his or her immediate client sometimes may be the policy analyst working for the political official.

Planners and policy analysts (and policy planners) approach the basic problem solving process—inventory, plan making, and implementation—in different ways. The differences are not clear cut, however, and the analytic activities of planners and policy analysts certainly overlap. Those planners who have incorporated policy analysis into their work may especially object to the use of the comprehensive planning paradigm to describe today's planning. The pure paradigm most likely does not exist, and the distinctions made in this chapter become less clear each day. Nonetheless, the comprehensive planning paradigm provides an appropriate comparative framework for the purposes of this chapter.

Inventory

Since planning is a continuous process, planners develop data sets, update them on a regular basis, and serve as a source of information for political officials and others involved in planning and governmental activities. Policy analysts, on the other hand, tend not to engage in general data collection, but rather collect specific data with which to address problems as they arise. Even more often, policy analysts attempt to use existing data collected by others.

These variations are due to the types of problems with which the two fields deal, the different time horizons within which the two groups operate, and the types of agencies in which the two types of professionals are located.

Plan making

Planners often conduct their activities within a 10- to 20-year time horizon, usually prepare comprehensive plans, and prepare plans for functional areas and for specific locations (for example, housing, transportation, or land use plans for specific regions). In producing such plans, planners attempt to consider all alternatives and evaluate these alternatives in relation to the goals of "the public at large."

The time horizon considered by policy analysts is much shorter. The analyst typically focuses upon immediate problems. In the case where the analyst works for an elected official, the time horizon may extend to the next election. (Policy researchers, discussed elsewhere in this chapter, may deal with broader issues over longer time periods.) Quite often the policy analysis is prepared as a reaction to a problem or issue rather than in anticipation of a problem or as a result of a need or desire identified through a goal setting process.

Since policy analysts are usually focusing upon immediate problems within a short time horizon, they often are preparing issue papers or memos, perhaps are drafting speeches, and many times are preparing draft legislation. Rather than focusing on a broad substantive issue, policy analysts may be dealing with a specific problem, such as the feasibility of increasing transit fares. Furthermore, policy analysts narrow the scope of their analysis to a search among "feasible" alternatives, rather than evaluating "all possible" alternatives. This limitation of alternatives is due in part to the shorter time frame of policy analysis but also to the narrower definition of the policy analysts' clients, e.g., specific agencies, politicians, or interest groups, rather than the public at large.

Implementation

Planners recognize the need to have plans implemented but have largely adopted an apolitical stance, preferring to leave the implementation to other units of government, politicians, or interest groups. Some policy analysts have become more political in mode of operation, not only including political factors in their analyses, but also advocating their preferred alternative and taking other actions to see that their policy proposals are implemented.

These distinctions are being attempted with the full knowledge that the line between the actions of some planners and some policy analysts is quite blurred, and that, for example, planners located in community development departments may be working with time horizons of considerably less than 10 or 20 years, and that some policy analysts are engaged in the development of inventories and data files upon which future analyses will be based.

Concern for generalization

Planners frequently deal with the analysis of a policy for a given time and place: that is, the analysis of a specific program or event, for the purpose of immediate application, with no intent to generalize to other settings. Although some policy analysts also engage in this type of analysis, others do not. Many policy analysts, economists, or political scientists, for example, tend more to be concerned about policies across times and places. They concentrate on the systematic analysis of policy variables and relevant dependent variables, while controlling for other variables such as city size or density.

This difference results in part from the location of planners in organizations that serve specific, somewhat limited jurisdictions, especially at the local level. In these situations the question is whether a given policy is good for a particular town, metropolitan area, region, or state. Policy analysts in other social sciences may be seeking the preferred policy for school districts, for prison systems, or for transportation systems, of various sizes in various parts of the country, and under alternative forms of governance. Planners at the state level, though, may analyze the relative effectiveness of, say, alternative transportation policies within the state for counties of different sizes, with different degrees of urbanization, and with different levels of affluence.

Another distinction might be made between the terms "policy analysis" and "policy research." "Policy analysis" would refer to analyses by practitioners, agency personnel, or consultants of a specific policy for a given organization for immediate application. "Policy research" would define studies by researchers, practitioners, or academics that attempt, through information collection and analysis, to identify the relative appropriateness of a general policy (and versions of that policy) for various types of entities under various conditions. This second type of analysis may include relatively large-scale, longer term data collection activities, a longer time frame for analysis, and experiments or trial programs.

Although planners conduct policy analyses as part of the planning process, policy analysis is more often done by other professions and by professionals located in different types of governmental units, most often in governmental units that deal with day-to-day issues. These units include budget bureaus, governors' offices, offices of city managers, public aid bureaus, departments of finance, boards of education, legislative committees, and federal departments and agencies. Policy analysis as a profession is still developing, more and more organizations are seeking policy analysts, and increasing numbers of policy analysts are being hired for positions traditionally filled by planners.

Types of policy analysis

Like planning, the field of policy analysis draws from many other disciplines. This mixed parentage has led to terminology problems and, to some extent, to philosophical problems about the proper nature of policy analysis. Should it be positive (descriptive) or normative (prescriptive)? Many planners (those who view their role as including the making of suggestions and recommendations about future actions) would quickly dismiss this debate. To be useful to them, policy analysis must be normative or prescriptive. While it is important to understand what led to the adoption of certain policies in the past, the political scientist's positive (descriptive) view of the policy process would be too confined for the planner using policy analysis techniques. To be useful to planners, policy analysis must identify the consequences of alternative courses of action. These outcomes must be evaluated, or weighed in relation to a set of criteria, so that value judgments can be made about the proper action to take.

Positive policy analysis

Positive policy analysis has been defined to mean both the analysis of policy events over time and the evaluation of the results of a given program or set of policies. Under both types of activities, the policy analyst is mainly involved in describing and interpreting the impact of given policies. By examining past policies, the analyst attempts to describe which policies led to certain outcomes. Although both types of analysis are descriptive, their results can be used in designing future policies and programs.

Program evaluation, a type of descriptive analysis, is already widely used in planning. Often planners are called on to determine whether conditions have improved or worsened as a result of a given policy or program. The question in this context is whether to continue existing policies. Are they causing the desired outcome? Program evaluation units or their equivalent can be found in state budget or legislative offices, under the jurisdiction of city or county managers, or within local budget or finance offices. Quite often, outside organizations are retained to provide these services, in order that the results of the evaluation are not unduly influenced by the unit responsible for the program or policy being evaluated.

Normative policy analysis

Normative analysis also can be divided into two categories: forecasting and prescription. Under forecasting, the analyst predicts what might happen by means of projection techniques. Statistical techniques can be used in these predictions, but often analysts must rely upon less quantitative methods such as interviewing experts and scenario writing. Although some writers would classify this approach as descriptive, the reliance upon a set of assumptions and one's view of future events makes this type of forecast at least quasi-normative in nature.

The truly normative type of policy analysis is that which prescribes the future, that which makes a recommendation about a set of actions to be taken, and that which predicts the impact or outcome of the actions taken. This level of analysis incorporates the other levels of policy analysis. The rationale and impact of past policies must be understood, estimates of future conditions under certain

Figure 9–1
Policy analysis shows
the potential side
effects of policy
implementation.

assumptions and policies must be made, future conditions that would result from a continuation of current policies must be considered, and this information is used to suggest particular policies and to estimate the impact of each policy.

A policy analysis can be conducted only when there is a disagreement about the way in which government is dealing or proposes to deal with a particular problem or issue and when there are alternative ways to deal with the problem. A story is told about an Israeli statesman being quizzed about the future of East Jerusalem. The statesman replied that this was not a problem, explaining to his stunned audience that, "in politics, if you don't have a solution, you don't have a problem. What you have is a condition, in the medical sense of the term. You live with it as best you can."[2] If there is no problem, no disagreement, and no action that might be taken, there is no need to conduct a policy analysis. Coplin and O'Leary have argued that all three of these conditions must exist for there to be a public policy issue.[3] Their checklist also highlights the key components of policy analysis: problem definition (what is the issue or condition affecting society), identification of relevant actors (which side of the issue do key actors support), and identification of possible alternatives (what action should government take).

From a planner's perspective, the primary purpose of policy analysis may well be to convince someone (a policy maker) to take a particular action. A given action is recommended because a specific result or outcome is expected. The client is shown the causal link between an action and a particular outcome. When an argument is made for an action that is expected to have a particular outcome, the value-laden nature of policy analysis becomes evident. The benefit of a particular policy can be identified only in light of a set of values. They might be the client's values, explicit development values of a community, or the values of a majority of voters. No matter the source of values, policy outcomes can be predicted only in the context of those values. It should be noted, however, that some writers have argued that policy analysis is *not* advocacy.[4] Others have taken the opposite position, most notably Wildavsky.[5] The question, it seems, is whether the policy analyst can be truly neutral or objective.

The issue of objectivity

Policy analysis necessarily involves the interpretation of problems, issues, and actions; bias will likely enter most analyses. Rather than pretend to be objective, analysts must state their biases and assumptions, cite their sources, keep accurate records, use multiple sources of information, and clearly state the components of any model used. Since policy analysis is also a form of persuasion, analysts may put these data in the form and sequence that best supports their argument.[6] This is not to say that analysts should manipulate their methods or that they should deceive, but facts and values cannot be kept separate in real-world experience. Wildavsky has spoken to this issue:

Analysis, which is in part rhetoric, should be persuasive. Presenting a preferred policy in the most persuasive manner, by finding arguments that will appeal to others, is not only personally permissible but also socially desirable. One promise of policy analysis is that through repeated interactions, common understandings (though not necessarily, of course, common positions) will grow, so that action will be better informed.[7]

Another approach involves the assembly of a series of alternative policies and alternative political views (social values), and the development of the pros and cons of each. The results are presented without staff recommendation. This approach recognizes that policy choices are based on political judgment and responds to the belief that the choices should be reserved for politicians. Staff, in this setting, takes pains to represent all views and refrains from advocating its own policy choices.

The policy analyst is concerned with the wide range of policy impacts, negative as well as positive. Therefore, an important element of policy analysis is the prediction of externalities or unintended consequences. If the client is to decide that a certain action should be taken, he or she must also be convinced that other events caused by the policy do not result in problems worse than that addressed by the policy, or that if worse problems result, he or she is willing to accept them. Along the same line, the client must be advised of the alternative policies that might have been pursued, and the probable consequences of adopting those policies.

The policy analysis process, one might argue, is a variation of the planning process, with perhaps more emphasis given to the beliefs and roles of actors, and, depending upon one's training in planning, more attention to the generation and qualification of alternatives. Yet another distinction, and one that also depends upon one's planning education, experience, and personal philosophy, is the emphasis in prescriptive policy analysis that is placed upon the selling of one's findings or recommendations. In this view of policy analysis, the figures do not speak for themselves. Policy analysts speak for them, they become advocates for a particular policy, and they see their roles as that of identifying or designing alternatives that link goals to action.

Values and goals play key roles in policy analysis. In order to select among alternatives, policy analysts must understand the goals and values of their clients and of the relevant actors involved. Most policy arguments will involve many actors and many policy alternatives, if the issue is significant and the fight is important. Although policy analysts can be assisted by quantitative techniques, they must base much of their analysis on an understanding of the client's goals and objectives. From this they can develop a set of criteria to use in selecting among competing alternatives on the basis of expected impacts. The policy analysis process, then, involves a recognition of the goals and values of the relevant actors (units of government, citizen groups, politicians, and individuals), an understanding of the issue being debated, a specification of the criteria that will be used to evaluate the policies, the generation of alternative policies, a prediction of the outcomes of the implementation of those policies, and the development of an argument to adopt a particular alternative.

Examples of policy analysis, and a discussion of the tools and methods used in policy analysis, are the subjects of later sections. First, an approach to policy analysis is sketched which recognizes that there is no one way to do policy analysis, as the many books on the topic surely attest.

An approach to policy analysis

Students of policy analysis often are told to define a problem in such a way that it can be solved and then to redefine the problem during analysis. Situations change, and analysts must ask whether the problem for which the analysis is being prepared still exists. In effect, this defines policy analysis as backward problem solving—to first analyze the best available data about the issue, to determine criteria that would be used to judge alternative solutions, to concoct alternatives, and then to redefine the problem. The problem is purposely reformulated in such a way as to permit its solution. This policy analysis process is described in Figure 9-2 and the steps in the process are summarized below.[8]

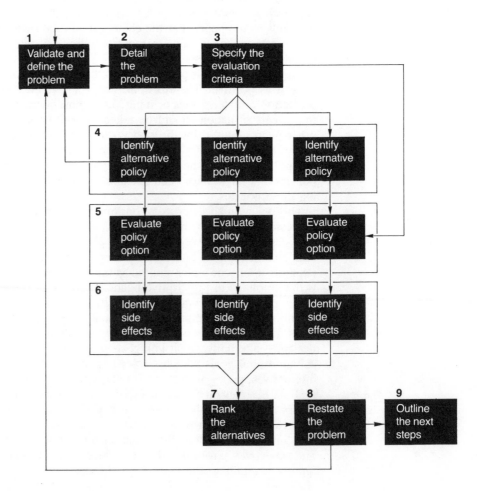

Figure 9–2   The policy analysis process.

Step one: define the problem

What is the issue? The initial problem description should rarely be accepted without question. The analyst must revise or restate the problem to be sure that it can be addressed by a policy change since policy analysis must involve variables over which decision makers have control. The cynic may argue that the problem is redefined so that it fits a solution on hand, but what is intended is an effort to validate the existence and extent of a problem that can be addressed by a policy change.

Step two: detail the problem

What are the details of the problem? What parties are concerned about it? Why are they concerned? What are their goals and objectives? What do they stand to win or lose? What power do they possess? The problem detailing process involves descriptive policy analysis. What have been the effects of past policies? Who was affected and how?

Step three: specify the evaluation criteria

How will the various alternatives be compared? What are the more important decision criteria (cost, equity, efficiency, administrative ease, political acceptability)? This step addresses the questions, "What do the various interests want?" and "Can it (they) possibly be obtained through public policy?" Specifying the evaluation criteria causes the analyst to clarify further the goals and values of the interested parties and to make explicit what are considered desirable and undesirable outcomes.

Step four: identify alternative policies

Having decided what the wants are, or at least having decided how to evaluate the acceptability of various outcomes, alternative policies are identified. Generating policies is difficult, and it is easy to make mistakes in the identification of alternatives and miss real options.[9] The status quo is always an alternative, and the experiences of others provide some guidance. Alternatives might also be identified through experiments, simulations, and brainstorming. The failure to consider appropriate alternatives, and the tendency to analyze favored alternatives, could result in the adoption of suboptimal policies. Changes in assumptions or changes in values of participants must be considered when alternatives are generated and while they are being evaluated.

Step five: evaluate the policy options

After possible policies are identified, they must be evaluated. What are the expected impacts of each policy? To what extent does each policy satisfy the evaluation criteria? Depending upon the problem, the analysis might involve a number of analytic techniques (qualitative as well as quantitative). An economic cost-benefit analysis of the alternatives might be performed, a political feasibility analysis might also be conducted, and a survey of community attitudes could be carried out. Given sufficient time, an experiment could be conducted. Depending upon the analyst's relationship with his or her client, the result of the analysis might be presented as a sequential enumeration and evaluation of alternatives, or a strong argument might be advanced for the preferred alternative. Sometimes the result of the analysis is presented in the form of a scenario, providing a

Figure 9–3   The status quo is always an alternative.

concise description of the alternatives, an accounting of the costs of the alternatives, and an identication of who benefits, who loses, and how difficult or easy it will be to implement the alternative. Since the growth field of policy analysis is in flux, it will be important to learn from the experience of others.

Step six: identify side effects

Most policy analyses are incomplete. All variables cannot often be analyzed; best estimates of impacts, outcomes, and possible side effects must be made; and recommendations must be derived under conditions of uncertainty. The "best" alternative in a technical sense may not be politically acceptable or may have political consequences understood only by the policy maker. Rarely does an analyst have access to all the critical information about the political relationship of the person for whom he or she works. This and similar uncertainties must be identified in order that policies can be modified when conditions do not materialize as expected.

Step seven: rank the alternatives

The evaluation may reveal alternatives that can be discarded and others that should be examined more closely. Additional evidence may have to be gathered. Merely identifying the preferred alternative may not be sufficient. In certain settings the option must be argued for and defended. Others may have to be persuaded to make related decisions. Implementing a given policy may require the cooperation of several units of government (perhaps several units of separate governments). Do the relevant decision makers have the influence and inclination to implement the policy? Would a less comprehensive policy that could be carried out by an individual department have a greater likelihood of success?

Step eight: restate the problem

Before making an argument for adoption of an alternative, it is useful (and essential) to restate the problem. Was the proper problem identified? Has an important aspect of the problem been ignored? Policies are not end states. The best alternative for particular conditions is sought. When conditions change, when new options become available, new alternatives should be considered.

Step nine: outline the next steps

What needs to be done to cause the preferred policy to be implemented? Who should be responsible for specific tasks? What plans should be made for the monitoring and evaluation of the policy after implementation?

This section was intended to give the reader a feeling for the process of policy analysis. Specific analytic techniques will be discussed later, although a full exposition of all techniques is beyond the scope of this chapter. To help provide an overview of the practice of policy analysis, the following section describes situations in which policy analysis techniques were applied at state and regional levels.

Policy analysis in practice

What types of problems have been addressed by policy analysis? When is it used? What methods are applied? In this section, examples of policy analysis applied to problems at other than the national level are presented.

Policy analysis has been institionalized at the federal level, and a body of literature has been produced about these efforts.[10] Although policy analyses have been conducted outside the federal level, few of them have been reported in publicly available sources.[11] Examples relevant to state and regional planners are becoming available, however. Alexander has reported about a policy analysis of public transit systems in Connecticut, several examples exist in the Intercollegiate Case Clearing House series, and cases have been included in works by Sawicki, Lynn, and MacRae and Wilde.[12]

In order to illustrate the use of policy analysis in state and regional planning practice, four examples have been selected from the literature. For each case, the problem is identified, the alternatives considered are described, and the analytic method is identified. The first two cases deal with policies for specific locations at a given point in time. The second two cases deal with policies for various conditions in a range of settings. The cases themselves illustrate concepts rather than provide the basis for generalization.

The cases describe relatively large-scale policy analyses involving the examination of substantial data bases. A great deal of day-to-day policy analysis involves smaller scale problems, limited data sets, and quickly derived estimates. Bardach, Fulton and Weimer, Hederman and Nelson, and Patton might be consulted for case examples and instruction about how to conduct such analyses.[13]

Case one: fourth airport for the New York metropolitan area

The problem   Air traffic in the greater New York area had increased dramatically during the 1960s, suggesting that a fourth jetport was needed. The New York Port Authority's proposed site for a new jetport generated opposition from persons concerned about ecological damage. The proposed location was adjacent to a suburban site that included 3000 homes and a vast natural preserve. The proposed jetport was supported by persons and groups concerned about economic and industrial decline that might result from lost air travel.[14]

The Port of New York Authority, the FAA, and aviation industry groups were proposing two sites in northern New Jersey. The governor of New Jersey, the legislature, and citizen groups were proposing sites in central New Jersey. The debate between the groups centered on whether a site should be selected on the basis of existing air traffic patterns and the location of air traffic generating populations, or whether it should be selected with consideration for social, economic, and ecological impacts on the state of New Jersey.

Both groups proposed alternative sites. The Port Authority prepared another study that confirmed its earlier study. The FAA prepared a study that recommended a site in the northwest quadrant of New Jersey. Opposition continued from various organizations. The need for a fourth airport was challenged by regional planners. Conservationists continued to pressure state and federal authorities. Alternative sites were proposed but were rejected by the FAA which again called for a fourth jetport to be located in the northwest part of the state where it would interfere the least with existing air traffic patterns. New Jersey residents thought these criteria favored New York City.

Proposals and counterproposals were made. Wishing to avoid the cost of equipping and staffing new terminals, the Aviation Development Council (representing 10 major airlines) proposed the expanding of existing facilities and the relegating of general aircraft to peripheral airports. The conservationists managed to have the Port Authority's favored site (Great Swamp) declared a national monument. New York's Governor Rockefeller proposed a site on Long Island. New Jersey's Governor Cahill opposed the Port Authority's now favored site (Solberg). The Port Authority then announced that it would meet the increased demand by further expansion of existing facilities.

With both sides deadlocked, a policy analysis was conducted by researchers at New York University to see if strategies might be found that would lead to a resolution of the conflict.

The analysis Political and technological analyses were conducted. An individual citizen's utility model was derived with preferences and power functions for each major participant. An analysis of technical alternatives to increase capacity other than through new construction was undertaken. The analysis indicated that no site would be suitable to all major participants and that the need for a fourth jetport could be postponed if the existing three airports were modified.

A mathematical model was developed to identify the utility of various sites to residents. Utility was measured as a function of travel time and population density. New York residents were essentially neutral toward sites in New Jersey, while New Jersey residents were neutral with respect to sites in New York. This was augmented by an analysis of decision maker preferences.

The analysis indicated that a site in central New Jersey would be politically feasible since New Jersey could unilaterally implement such an alternative. Furthermore, technical improvements could allow it also to serve New York and Philadelphia. An economic analysis was also conducted. It showed no negative near-term impacts from abandoning the idea of a new jetport.

Lessons learned This analysis is instructive because it incorporates an understanding of the political positions of key actors with a technical analysis of alternatives. It also illustrates the need to avoid a bias toward alternatives that are modifications of a preferred option (here, for example, a bias toward construction). Earlier Port Authority analyses had focused on alternative sites for the construction of a new jetport. This analysis examined other options such as expansion of other airports, development of new guidance systems that would increase capacity at existing jetports, and other concepts to increase efficiency at existing jetports. The case also points out the need for reevaluation of analysis. The introduction of jumbo jets and SSTs affected the timing of demand, and thus earlier analyses were no longer accurate. Perhaps above all, this analysis shows that seemingly technical problems have elements that must be examined through qualitative techniques.

Case two: pollution control in Lake Michigan

The problem Water quality in Lake Michigan has long been a concern of communities relying upon the lake for recreation. Abatement of phosphorus discharges into the lake has been in effect since 1973, but it has not been evaluated. Are the abatement orders working? Specifically, is the wastewater treatment efficient and equitable? This case discusses a regional policy analysis conducted by university researchers and a private consulting firm.[15]

In order to control eutrophication of Lake Michigan and reduce algal blooms along the shoreline, experts determined that a reduction in either nitrogen or phosphates entering the lake would be required. Reduction of phosphates was determined to be less costly than nitrogen reduction. The bordering states were to reduce the annual point-source inflow of phosphorus by 80 percent, and each was given a maximum discharge level.

Wisconsin had to be in compliance for the policy to work since drainage and population patterns cause Wisconsin to account for the bulk of phosphorus discharges into the lake. Wisconsin's plan to meet the 80 percent removal level included 85 percent treatment in 53 larger communities and exemption of 124 smaller communities where removal would be expensive. For a variety of reasons, only a 73 percent average removal level was reached at the 53 communities. In 1975, an effluent concentration limit for phosphorus replaced the removal standard.

It is difficult to determine whether abatement is worth the costs. Recreational benefits to lake users are limited, swimming is available elsewhere when algal blooms are present (which is not often), and the benefits to fishermen are limited. The principal benefit of abatement is the maintenance of clean water for use in the future. Since data are not available for measuring consumer valuation of clean water in the future, the analysts assume that benefits exceed costs and ask whether there is a more cost-effective way to abate the phosphorus discharge.

The analysis Using data from 50 treatment plants, the researchers were able to determine a way to reduce the daily treatment costs by allocating treatment to the more efficient plants. Using a dynamic programming model, the combination of treatment processes with the lowest state-wide cost was determined. The results showed a cost savings by using efficient removal, rather than uniform treatment, up to the 89 percent level where all plants would have to operate at full capacity.

The analysis indicates that there is a financial cost to a community from the setting of a basin-wide standard. Furthermore, people in the small towns and rural areas exempted from the order are able to use whatever portion of the total load they desire. The rest of the population has to share the balance of the permissible discharge, and this remainder is shared equally only to the extent that per capita wastewater flow is equal among the 53 treatment facilities.

Inequities exist since small communities are not paying for abatement, and some communities pay more than others for abatement because of varying marginal costs. The authors argue that these equity problems can be overcome by adopting a system of transferable discharge permits so that all dischargers contribute to the cost of treatment by a few efficient plants.

Lessons learned Not only did the analysis reveal that the overall cost of phosphorus abatement could be reduced when uniform treatment is not required, but it also pointed out the need to bring the real cost of abatement to the attention of those who can affect the level of pollution. These groups are households and industries in the region.

The case also illustrates the need to reevaluate policies after implementation and to examine alternative policies. Furthermore, it illustrates that policies need to be designed in light of regional variations.

Case three: public versus private refuse collection

The problem Local and regional governments provide a number of highly visible public services such as fire and police protection, garbage collection, education, and ambulance service. In many communities these services are provided by private firms. The argument has been made that private firms can provide these services at lower cost than can government. On the other hand, it has been argued that government can provide services cheaper because "it does not make a profit."

Refuse collection, provided both publicly and privately under many alternative arrangements, is an appropriate subject for policy analysis intended for generalization.

Researchers at Columbia University examined alternative arrangements for residential refuse collection. The options included municipal collection where a unit of local government provides the service, contract collection where the local government hires a private firm to collect the refuse, franchise arrangements where private firms are granted an exclusive right to provide refuse collection and to charge customers directly, private collection where the household contracts with any private firm, and self-service where the household delivers its refuse to a disposal site.[16]

The analysis The Columbia team conducted a telephone survey of governmental jurisdictions within 200 Standard Metropolitan Statistical Areas (SMSAs), using a sampling procedure that produced a range of cases from 1378 communities that included alternative collection methods for cities ranging in population from 2500 to 750,000.

On average, contract collection was found to be the least costly arrangement, followed by franchise and municipal collection and then by private collection. Municipal collection appears to cost 15 percent more than contract collection. However, the costs of each alternative varied widely. Within one alternative the most expensive arrangement was eight times that of the least expensive. Level of service also varied, as did collection frequency and labor costs.

An econometric model was constructed to isolate the effects of total quantity of refuse, quantity of refuse per household per year, wage rate, density of households, temperature variation, frequency of collection, and location of pickup point. Cities were divided into those with and without mandatory service. Details can be found elsewhere.[17] Savas reports the following:

No significant difference was found between municipal and private collection for cities with less than 20,000 or more than 50,000 in population, nor between municipal and contract collection for cities with less than 50,000. But for cities of more than 50,000, contract collection was significantly less expensive than municipal collection.[18]

Apparently government cannot collect refuse at a lower cost than private firms in cities with populations greater than 50,000. Savas believes the higher cost of municipal services can be attributed to higher municipal employee absentee rates, larger work crews, fewer households served per shift, more time spent serving each household, and less use of labor-incentive systems. For cities in the size range where service under private arrangement is more expensive than contract or mandatory franchise service, the difference is due in part to overlapping collection routes.

Lessons learned   This study provides useful information for improving the efficiency of municipal services, but it also illustrates the need to reexamine current practices and conventional beliefs. Beyond the lessons regarding adequate data collection and an analysis that recognizes the effect of multiple variables, including those of city size and density, this analysis also provides policy information to cities and regions. Cities of less than 20,000 in population could possibly lower their per-household collection costs by forming larger markets up to 50,000 in population served by one collection agency, either public or private. The cost will likely be lower if the service is financed by taxes.

Cities with private collection could lower costs by switching to contract collection.

Cities over 50,000 can reduce costs by contracting with a private firm.

Cities larger than 100,000 in population might be divided into service districts of at least 50,000 in population.

Before cities implement these policies, they will have to conduct local policy analyses, since the range of cost of services is wide, and the generalizations may not apply to all cases.

Case four: reducing injury and death rates in robbery

The problem   A large proportion of injuries and deaths that occur during robbery (theft accompanied by assault) are unprovoked. Even when the victim offers no resistance whatsoever, he or she may be harmed. In an attempt to reduce the amount and seriousness of crimes, state criminal sentencing statutes are being revised so that indeterminate sentencing provisions are being replaced with "price lists" that specify mimimum and maximum penalties.

Setting these determinate sentences requires the allocation of types of punishment among different types of criminal defendants. Choosing an effective punishment requires a knowledge of the way in which crime rates respond to marginal changes in the chance of being punished and the severity of that punishment. Although economic and social science research has been conducted on this topic, the data provide little information about the effects of alternative sanctions on various crime types.[19]

Cook hypothesized that more severe punishments for robbers who injure their victims would reduce the injury rate and that a "gun emphasis" policy in prosecuting and sentencing would reduce the robbery murder rate, but would increase the robbery injury rate.

The analysis   As an alternative to econometric analysis, Cook makes inferences about the potential effects of policy changes by combining an intuitive view of human motivation and information processing with a statistical description of existing crime patterns. Cook used this method to analyze issues in setting priorities for the prosecuting and sentencing of robbery defendants based on the type of weapon used by the robber and the degree of injury to the victim.

Criminal victimization studies from 26 cities, the Washington, D.C. Prosecutors Managment Information System research files, unpublished FBI data, and homicide files from Atlanta, Georgia and Dade County, Florida were examined to determine the possible outcomes of treating gun robberies that result in victim injury as more serious than other robberies. The key question is whether the victim injury rate in robberies can be reduced by prosecution and sentencing.

The empirical data suggest that the current injury rate in robbery results primarily from gratuitous violence and not from victim resistance. Cook argues that there is a real possibility of lowering the injury rate in robberies by giving prosecution and sentencing priority to defendants in injury cases. Giving priority to robbery with injury cases would encourage violence-prone robbers to control their bent toward harm and would keep convicted violent robbers off the street for longer periods of time.

Current policies that give priority to prosecuting robberies with guns are intended to reduce the robbery murder rate, but this policy may be increasing the injury rate since robbers wielding guns are less likely to harm their victims than robbers armed with other weapons. Cook's statistics on victim deaths during robbery show that the bulk of fatal attacks were unprovoked.

Although the severe punishment of robbers who murder their victims is widely accepted, a policy that relates the severity of the sentencing to injuries has not been widely accepted or implemented. Cook's data show that sentencing decisions are not noticeably affected by whether the victim was injured.

The "recreational" nature of robbery violence is supported by the finding that the likelihood of injury increases with the number of robbers in an attack, even though the victim is less likely to resist. Cook's examination of rearrest rates shows that violent robbers tend to be rearrested for other violent crimes rather than for robbery.

Cook believes the data support an injury-related prosecution and sentencing policy, but he also examined alternative policies. He argues that an alternative (but not necessarily conflicting) policy would assign high priority to cases that have characteristics of robberies in which there is a greater likelihood that the victim would be injured or killed; for example, robberies by two or more persons. Cases would be assigned priority whether or not injury or death occurred. Gun emphasis, as an alternative policy, is expected to cause a shift to non–gun robberies, with the result that deaths from gun robberies would decline, but deaths from non–gun robberies would increase, although there would be a net reduction in deaths from robbery. Furthermore, assuming fixed total court and correctional resources, emphasis on gun robbery defendants would result in lower conviction rates and less severe sentences for other robbery defendants.

Were a gun emphasis policy to be implemented, the net effect would depend upon the extent to which there was a substitution of non–gun robberies for gun robberies. Cook estimates that there would be no effect on the overall robbery rate. The shift to non–gun robberies, however, would result in an increase in injuries but a reduction in deaths, a tradeoff society would likely accept. The injury cost of a gun emphasis policy could be reduced if it were coupled with an injury emphasis policy.

Lessons learned   This case illustrates the use of a variety of sources of observational and statistical data as evidence in a logical analysis of alternative policies. Earlier analyses of crime prevention measures were hampered by a lack of reliable econometric data, so the author used an alternative approach for analyzing possible outcomes of alternative policies. Since observations about the effects of actual changes in policy are not available, the estimates developed in this manner provide guidance to policy makers. The findings should be of use to states that are now involved in redrafting criminal sentencing codes.

The case also illustrates the use of multiple sources of data, the estimation of the unintended consequences of current and proposed policies, and the need to define the problem clearly. In this case the problem was transformed from being a question about policies related to weapons to one of policies dealing with injuries to victims.

Tools of policy analysis

The case studies in this chapter are intended primarily to illustrate the content, structure, and logic of policy analysis, but they also provide an introduction to some of the tools used in the process of policy analysis, including modeling, survey research, economic analysis, and statistical analysis. However, many other tools are also employed. This section deals with the particular quantitative and qualitative policy analysis tools applied during the larger process of policy analysis. The reader should note that these tools are incorporated into the process or logic of policy analysis described earlier. They alone are not policy analysis.

The analytic method or technique selected depends upon the complexity of the issue, the availability of data, and the time frame for analysis. Many of the examples of policy analysis cited in the literature are partial analyses because few alternatives were examined, the roles of political actors were not always considered, political consequences were not always spelled out, marginal data were sometimes used, and implementation issues were not always resolved because time and resources were not available. Had a complete analysis been done, it may not have been available in time to be useful. Policy analysts must therefore "satisfice"—do the best they can in the time available with the best data and methods at hand.

The ability to decide when and how to analyze a problem is probably the most important skill a policy analyst can possess. Problem selection is a matter of experience and talent rather than of formal procedure.[20]

A methods cookbook will be of little help if analysts do not understand the problems with which they are faced, the political issues involved, and historical precedent. Once these factors are understood, then a number of quantitative and qualitative techniques can be usefully applied. This section is intended to introduce the reader to the primary policy analysis techniques—not to teach the reader how to do them—and to suggest sources for future self-study.

The tools of policy analysis trace back to systems analysis, network scheduling, modeling, simulation, operations research, microeconomics (cost-benefit analysis), and experimental design. To a degree, these techniques are used by policy analysts because the analysts come from fields in which these are the tools of the trade. Simply learning these techniques will not make one a policy analyst.

What tools does the policy analyst use? Qualitative political theory, for refining our picture of where we want to go; quantitative modeling, for systematizing guesswork on how to get there; microeconomics for disciplining desire with limited resources, and macro-organization theory, for instilling the will to correct errors: each has its place. Policy analysis, however, is one activity for which there can be no fixed program, for policy analysis is synonymous with creativity, which may be stimulated by theory and sharpened by practice, which can be learned but not taught.[21]

The following brief descriptions should provide a feeling for many of the tools or methods that can be used in analyzing policies. The tools might be used individually or in combination, and some of the methods encompass one or more of the other methods. However, these distinctions will not be dwelt upon.

Quade provides a framework for thinking about policy analysis methods.[22] He classifies the major techniques as operations research, cost-effectiveness analysis, cost-benefit analysis, and systems analysis. He admits that this classification is somewhat arbitrary, that a particular study might be classified under any one of the headings, and that they all draw from the same set of tools such as linear programming, queueing theory, simulation, and gaming. While their groupings are different, Stokey and Zeckhauser also cover the key techniques used by policy analysts, including difference equations, queueing, simulation,

Markov models, benefit-cost analysis, linear programming, and decision analysis.[23] The authors of both books warn against the indiscriminate application of these techniques.

The many techniques can be classified as those used for analyzing alternatives *before* a decision is made and those used for evaluating programs or policies *after* they have been implemented.

The first group contains the mathematical methods used for quantifying basic relationships and for combining inputs in an optimum way when an objective is known. Quite often policy analysts must deal with multiple and conflicting objectives. In this case, the goal of the analysis may be to meet the various objectives simultaneously or to adjust the relationships among them. This situation may require the use of quantitative techniques that permit the analysis of interactions among a number of variables under conditions of uncertainty. Among the pre-program qualitative tools are such techniques as political analysis and scenario writing that can help us to analyze a process and the interaction among actors. Postprogram policy analysis techniques involve versions of program evaluation and experimental design.

Preprogram tools

Operations research   Operations research is used to help decision makers get the "biggest bang for the buck." If the components of a system are well understood, the resources or inputs to that system can be combined in such a way as to result in the most efficient operation. Using mathematical and logical analysis, alternative approaches to production decisions or other management actions are evaluated. The analysis incorporates estimates of past experience and expected risk in order to predict outcomes.

Linear programming   Linear programming is a widely applied type of operations research. Used to allocate limited resources, linear programming identifies the best combination of scarce resources that will achieve a stated objective. For example, linear programming can help determine the combination of a given amount of bricks, lumber, concrete, insulation, etc. that will result in the construction of the greatest number of housing units of a given square footage.

Systems analysis   Systems analysis has been described both as a higher form of operations research and as a type of policy analysis. However, some systems analysis "does not emphasize the distributional consequences of costs and benefits and pays insufficient attention to implementation and to political and organizational effects."[24] Quade also suggests that the term "operations research" be reserved for efficiency problems, and that "systems analysis" be used to describe problems of "optimal choice." Operations research then refers to analysis when the objective is clearly understood, and systems analysis describes the process of assisting decision makers in the identification and selection of alternatives.

Cost-effectiveness analysis   Cost-effectiveness analysis, a type of systems analysis, involves the comparison of alternative actions in terms of dollar costs and effectiveness. The effectiveness of the alternatives is judged by the extent to which a specified objective is attained. Costs are measured in dollars or sometimes as units of a particular resource. The alternative selected is that which results in the greatest effectiveness at a given cost, or when a specific level of effectiveness is sought, the alternative which produces that effectiveness for the least cost. In the area of health care, a particular treatment for a given group of persons might be identified, and cost-effectiveness could be used to determine the least expensive way to provide that treatment. On the other hand, a fixed amount of money may be available for a given program, and the benefits of the alternatives may be compared in units of output. In the area of housing, for example, this may be the largest housing unit for a given cost. Stokey and Zeckhauser give this guidance:

> Because benefits and costs are measured in different units, cost-effectiveness analysis provides no direct guidance when we are unsure whether the total benefit from an undertaking justifies the total cost, or when we are trying to select the optimal budget level for a project. But if we know what we have to achieve, or what we are allowed to spend, it is an appropriate criterion that reduces the complexity of choice.[25]

Cost-effectiveness analysis can be useful when comparing alternatives that address the same goal, but it cannot be used to compare alternatives that address several goals. In this case a common denominator is needed to permit choices between or among policies. Cost-benefit analysis fills this need.

Cost-benefit analysis   By measuring costs and benefits in the same units, different types of alternatives can be compared. Cost-benefit analysis, then, is a form of cost-effectiveness analysis where the costs and benefits that would be experienced by competing alternatives during the life of a program are measured in dollar amounts. The alternative with the greatest net benefit is selected. Cost-benefit analysis must be done with care. The analyst must be aware of such errors as counting an item as both a cost and a benefit, must accurately convert future costs and benefits to their present value, must choose the appropriate discount rate for doing this, and must consider externalities or side effects of the program. A number of texts provide assistance.[26]

Fiscal impact analysis   Fiscal impact analysis, a type of cost-benefit analysis, is being used by governmental units. This technique addresses the costs and benefits to the governmental unit, rather than the costs and benefits to society as a whole. The focus of the analysis is on the difference between the cost of a particular policy or project to a governmental unit and the benefits to the governmental unit.[27]

Modeling   Planners and analysts simplify complex issues in order to understand them. Mathematical or verbal models can be constructed to describe, analyze, and test a problem or system. To be useful, and understandable, the model must incorporate the important components of the system, but not so many variables that it becomes unclear which ones are policy-sensitive. There are many types of models, from relatively simple models, such as a road map or topographic map, to complex computer-based mathematical models. Policy analysts tend to use mathematical models to describe the impact of alternative policies. These models might describe the impact of such options as alternative tax policies, changes in bus ridership because of a fare increase, and political consequences that might result from a policy choice.

Much of the benefit in modeling is the process of thinking about relationships, reexamining basic assumptions, and building and rebuilding the model. Modeling makes explicit what has been left out as well as what has been included. Like the architect who builds a model of a proposed building, policy analysts can use models to test alternative proposals without incurring the major expenses associated with implementation. Sensitivity analysis, changing various assumptions and parameters of the model, can inform us about the viability of various options.

Simulation   Unable to develop a mathematical model that accurately describes a system because the computations are too complex, analysts simulate the action of a system. The testing of an airplane design by examining the operation of a model airplane in a wind tunnel is a typical example. Policy analysts use a computer simulation where a mathematical model describes a situation, and then the process is run many times over to investigate the outcomes generated by policy changes in the model. The simulation could be done by hand, but the speed of the computer allows many more combinations to be tested. In essence, the simulation is an experiment conducted in a laboratory setting. Instead of building a crosstown expressway link and then observing how many people divert to the link, the simulation could estimate the behavior of the many motorists traveling across town between various origins and destinations at different times of the day for various purposes before and after construction of the new link.

Decision analysis Sometimes a series of decisions must be made where a given decision depends upon the outcome of the preceding decision, and the decisions are clouded by uncertainty. For example, the decision to purchase a more fuel-efficient car today depends upon such factors as the future price and availability of fuel and the future cost of automobiles. Decision analysis, the process of constructing a treelike description of the decision process and estimating the probability of outcomes at each step along the way, demands that we fully understand the problem. That is one of its major advantages. Constructing a decision analysis tree requires that each step in a course of action be identified, that options be specified, and that probabilities for each decision be estimated. The decision maker selects the course of action with the best (highest or lowest, depending on the situation) expected value. Conducting a decision analysis requires the consideration of many analytic issues beyond the basic ones discussed here.[28]

Political analysis The attention paid to political factors is a distinguishing characteristic of policy analysis. Political factors can be incorporated in policy analysis at several stages: during problem definition, during the search for alternatives, and during the evaluation and implementation analysis phases.

When defining the problem, the following questions are asked. How did the policy problem arise? What local factors caused the problem? Is the problem the result of a crisis or has it long existed? How do the origins of the problem affect the nature of the analysis that should be done? What are the motives of the client? Who are the other major actors? What does each believe about the issue? How do these beliefs provide opportunities and constraints for the analysis? The client may give only a general idea about his concerns, so boundaries must be set around the problem.

The political objective might not be (and need not be) identical to the policy objective. From previous studies, the preferred technical policy may be known, but the immediate concern might be to explore the political feasibility of the means to that end. Furthermore, the client and the target of the analysis are often, perhaps usually, not identical. Will the recommendation be supported by superiors, by outside groups, by the city council, or by whom else?

During the evaluation of alternatives, an issue is divided into its important parts, information is sought on each part, and the components are combined into the final statement. What will the major actors win or lose if a particular policy is adopted? What resources does each actor have at his disposal? Which actors are likely to use their resources to secure political support for their preferences? This information is assembled into predictions of possible outcomes, to help determine which alternatives are politically feasible, if other policies should be examined, or if additional analyses are needed.

Political maps may be constructed to link the major actors to the basic elements of the policy alternatives. Supporters, opponents, and the undecided are identified for each alternative. Areas of consensus, compromise, and coalition-building are located, as are the sites where critical decisions will be made. This information is used to predict the likely outcome for each policy alternative, and it may reveal new, politically viable alternatives that also satisfy the policy objective(s). Sources for guidance to this type of analysis include work by MacRae and Wilde, Meltsner, and Coplin and O'Leary.[29]

Scenario writing Scenario writing is a nonquantitative technique that is sometimes used in the evaluation of alternatives. Scripts are written to estimate how a number of alternatives would fare, if they were to be implemented. Sometimes analysts write scenarios for their own use, to help them think about alternatives. Other times scenarios are used as a means of presenting the analysis, a way to describe why certain alternatives are rejected and why another is superior. Scenarios are also useful in describing the political consequences of certain actions.

Several scenarios are usually composed. An optimistic scenario, in which the typical rules of the game are followed, and in which the proposal is eventually accepted, is usually prepared. Another version is the so-called "bail-out" scenario, in which the proposal is defeated but the proponent is able to cut his or her losses and avoid political damage. Another scenario may result in the defeat of a proposal but placement of the proponent in a better position for future offensives.

These descriptions of possible outcomes can be used in the modification of proposed alternatives, and they help analysts consider factors that might not have been part of the quantitative modeling but that nonetheless have an effect on policy outcomes. Like model building and decision analysis, scenario writing can help the analyst better understand a complex situation and the interrelationships among components of that system.

Survey research Survey research techniques are used quite often by planners and analysts to generate information needed in the application of the other methods discussed here. Survey research can provide information about citizen opinion on given issues, can measure the demand for public goods and services, can provide benchmark data for longitudinal studies, and can be used to update basic data collected earlier.[30] With the use of proper sampling techniques, all of this can be done quickly and relatively inexpensively.[31] Some communities conduct citizen opinion polls on a regular basis as a way of evaluating existing policies and as a means for collecting information about problem areas. Of course other methods such as public hearings may also be used to obtain citizen opinion, but survey research, conducted properly, can provide information that closely reflects the attitudes and beliefs of virtually all citizens, not only those who choose to attend a public meeting, for example.

Structured interviewing is also used to collect data from a sample of the population,[32] and elite or specialized interviews are used to collect information from public officials, analysts, or other persons who may be part of the policy-making network.[33]

Thinking quickly Policy analysts are not constrained by the methods identified above. A good analyst will select a technique appropriate to the problem at hand. In some cases simple descriptive statistics may be all that is needed. In other cases a verbal analysis might be appropriate. Sometimes the analyst must conduct a quick, basic analysis, a first approximation using available or quickly collected data. Thinking while on the run, and doing it well, is a necessary skill. Analysts often know more than they realize. Teasing out this information and interrogating others for policy information is another skill policy analysts find indispensible. Bardach has provided instruction about these methods,[34] and Patton has described how a policy analysis was conducted in a short period of time.[35]

Postprogram tools

The methods discussed above are those expected to be useful to planners because they deal with the anticipation or prediction of possible outcomes. The tools help us decide what policy to recommend. But planners also need to analyze the impact of implemented policies. Some of the preprogram tools, for example, cost-benefit analysis, cost-effectiveness analysis, and survey research techniques, can be used in postprogram analysis. However, postprogram analysis also involves the concepts of program evaluation and experimental design.

Program evaluation/experimental design A number of approaches can be taken when evaluating implemented policies or programs.[36] A distinction is often made between the goal model and the systems model. The goal model approach measures achievement or change in a target group acted on by a program. Well-defined criteria are measured before, during, and after program intervention in order to determine whether a stated objective has been achieved through the program. The systems model is used when objectives are difficult to specify, when change is difficult to measure precisely, or when multiple goals are sought through a program. Such goals might include not only change in the target population but also goals regarding system operation and organizational or political survival. With this model, shortcomings in one area might be traded off against successes in another area.

When policy or program impact is sought to be measured, experimental or quasi-experimental designs can be helpful. This is not the place to explain experimental design concepts,[37] but the policy analyst must be aware of the basic rationale for the use of randomly selected control and experimental groups (to isolate and permit measurement of program impact), pretesting and posttesting (to check the equivalency of experimental and control groups before the experiment and to measure their differences after), and the many threats to the interpretation of program impact (for example, the famous Hawthorne effect in which a change in behavior of factory workers was brought about as a result of the attention they received by being studied).

Since policy problems in the real world do not usually lend themselves to true experiments, quasi-experimental methods have been developed that recognize the compromises that must be made in real world experiments when participants cannot be randomly selected and when treatments cannot be withheld from a control group.

Statistical analysis Statistical analysis plays an important part in both preprogram and postprogram analysis. In both cases the target population is usually described statistically, historic changes are reported in these terms as well, and conditions in various locales may be compared. In conducting postprogram analysis, the concerns of the analyst also include determining whether the policy or program had an impact (made a difference) and whether the policy or program is transferrable to other settings. Therefore inferential statistics are used to help determine whether apparent changes are indeed changes or whether the apparent differences are due to chance, and whether the results obtained through a sample apply to the population from which the sample was drawn.

Statistical techniques can be used to describe the strength of association among variables, to identify possible cause and effect relationships, and generally to inform analysts about the interrelationships among variables. Path analysis, factor analysis, regression analysis, and analysis of variance and covariance are a few of the statistical techniques that the policy analyst may use to assess the impact of policies after they have been implemented. A number of texts provide an introduction to the application of these statistical concepts.[38]

Like any classification scheme, this preprogram/postprogram categorization implies distinctions that do not hold in all instances. Many of the preprogram techniques may be used in postprogram analyses, and the results of postprogram analyses can be used in later preprogram analyses.

Other tools

It is impossible to cover all the tools used in the practice of policy analysis, and many of the tools or methods used in policy analysis are already used in planning practice. It is also not possible to say which methods are most often used, since most policy analysis is not published. The quick, basic methods, based largely upon descriptive statistics and tabulations of out-of-pocket costs, are probably most common. This is not to say that these are the preferred methods, but rather to suggest that quality analysis requires good, hard thinking, not necessarily difficult mathematical techniques. To be useful, policy analysis must enlighten, not overwhelm.

Conclusion

What are the components of a successful policy analysis? Success requires quality technical analysis, but it also depends on the analyst's ability to define problems clearly, to generate alternatives, to cope with political factors, and to conceptualize implementation strategies. Wildavsky has provided a succinct summary.

Good analysis compares alternative programs, neither objectives alone nor resources alone, but the assorted packages of resources and objectives, which constitute its foregone opportunities. Good analysis focuses on outcomes: what does the distribution of resources look like, how should we evaluate it, and how should we change it to comport with our notions of efficiency and equity? Good analysis is tentative. It suggests hypotheses that allow us to make better sense of our world.

Good analysis promotes learning by making errors easier to identify and by structuring incentives for their correction.

Good analysis is skeptical; by disaggregating the verifying process—evaluations should be external, independent, multiple, and continuous—no organization is required or allowed to be sole judge in its own case.

Good analysis is aware of its shortcomings and so it hedges its recommendations with margins of sensitivity to changes in underlying conditions.

Good analysis works with historical contexts so that error stands out ready for correction.

Most important, good analysis remembers people, the professionals in the bureaus who must implement the programs as well as the citizens whose participation in collective decision-making can be either enlarged or reduced by changes in the historical structure of social relationships. . . .

It would be a mistake to look at good policy analysis as if it were already here instead of what we would like it to be when it does get here. Do not ask 'What is policy analysis?' as if it were apart from us. Ask rather 'What can we make analysis become?' as if we were a part of this art and craft.[39]

Few planners would argue that policy is not an important aspect of planning practice. Indeed, practicing planners are formally called upon to assist in policy development and implementation.[40] Planners prepare policy plans; policy planning is taught in our planning schools and discussed at national planning conferences; and special meetings are even held on the topic. This is not to say that all planners should practice policy analysis or become policy analysts. However, planners should recognize the roles played by policy analysts since both groups often operate in the same arena and on similar problems. In some instances planners and policy analysts may share data bases and engage in cooperative studies. In fact, one is often hard pressed to distinguish between the work of planners and policy analysts. The two activities are not necessarily in conflict, and neither should the two fields be. Planning can profit by adopting the mind set and political orientation of policy analysts. Furthermore, planners already use many policy analysis techniques and will be adding others to their repertoire.

The planner interested in conducting policy analysis will need to keep abreast of the expanding literature of the field and to attend the growing number of policy conferences where contacts with other analysts can be made. The practice of state and regional planning would benefit from the active involvement of planners in the field of policy analysis, and the expanding field of policy analysis would gain from the involvement of planners, many of whom already have substantial experience in the practice of policy analysis.

1 Barry Checkoway, William Goodman, Peter May, Bruce McDowell, Stuart Nagel, David Sawicki, and Frank So provided helpful comments on this chapter.

2 Irving Kristol, "Where Have All the Answers Gone?" in *Policy Studies Review Annual*, Vol. 4, ed. Bertram H. Raven (Beverly Hills, CA: Sage Publications, 1980), p. 126.

3 William D. Coplin and Michael K. O'Leary, *Analyzing Public Policy Issues*, Learning Packages in the Policy Sciences, no. 17 (Croton-on-Hudson, NY: Policy Studies Associates, 1978).

4 Thomas R. Dye, *Policy Analysis* (University, Alabama: University of Alabama Press, 1976), p. 3; and Edward S. Quade, *Analysis for Public Decisions* (New York: American Elsevier, 1975), p. 21.

5 Aaron Wildavsky, *Speaking Truth to Power: The Art and Craft of Policy Analysis* (Boston: Little, Brown and Co., 1979), p. 10. See also: Giandomenico Majone, "The Uses of Policy Analysis," in *Policy Studies Review Annual*, Vol. 4, ed. Bertram H. Raven (Beverly Hills, CA: Sage Publications, 1980), pp. 161–180.

6 Ralph S. Hambrick, Jr. and William P. Snyder, *The Analysis of Policy Arguments*, Learning Packages in the Policy Sciences, no. 13 (Croton-on-Hudson, NY: Policy Studies Associates, 1976).

7 Aaron Wildavsky, *Speaking Truth to Power*, p. 13.

8 For additional discussion about this process and the individual steps described below, see: Duncan MacRae, Jr. and James A. Wilde, *Policy Analysis for Public Decisions* (North Scituate, MA: Duxbury, 1979); and Harry Hatry, Louis Blair, Donald Fisk, and Wayne Kimmel, *Program Analysis for State and Local Governments* (Washington, DC: The Urban Institute, 1976). For an important discussion of errors in the process of analysis see: Giandomenico Majone and Edward S. Quade, *Pitfalls of Analysis*, International Series on Applied Systems Analysis, Vol. 8 (Chichester, Great Britain: John Wiley & Sons, 1980).

9 Peter J. May, "Hints for Crafting Alternative Policies," *Policy Analysis*, 7 (Spring 1981):227–244.

10 Arnold J. Meltsner, *Policy Analysts in the Bureaucracy* (Berkeley: University of California Press, 1976); and Walter Williams, *Social Policy Research and Analysis: The Experience in the Federal Social Agencies* (New York: American Elsevier, 1971).

11 Ernest R. Alexander, "Policy Analysis: Approaches to a 'State of the Art'," *Journal of the American Planning Association* 45 (April 1979):200–204; Thomas R. Dye, *Policy Analysis*, p. 59; and Robert L. Lineberry, "Policy Analysis and Urban Govern-

ment: Understanding the Impact," *Urban Analysis* 5 (no. 1, 1978):143–154.

12 Ernest R. Alexander, "Policy Analysis," in *Introduction to Urban Planning*, eds. Anthony J. Catanese and James C. Snyder (New York: McGraw-Hill, 1979), p. 141; Jean Burleson, ed. *Intercollegiate Bibliography: Selected Cases in Administration* (Boston: Intercollegiate Case Clearing House, 1977); Laurence E. Lynn, Jr., *Designing Public Policy: A Casebook on the Role of Policy Analysis* (Santa Monica: Goodyear, 1980); Duncan MacRae, Jr. and James A. Wilde, *Policy Analysis for Public Decisions*; and David S. Sawicki, "Lessons Learned in Teaching and Practicing Planning and Policy Analysis," paper presented at the symposium on the Role of Policy Analysis in the Education of Planners, Cambridge, Mass., Department of Urban Studies and Planning, Massachusetts Institute of Technology, 11–12 October 1979.

13 Eugene Bardach, "Gathering Data for Policy Research," *Urban Analysis* 2 (April 1974):117–144; Arthur D. Fulton and David L. Weimer, "Regaining a Lost Policy Option: Neighborhood Parking Stickers in San Francisco," *Policy Analysis* 6 (Summer 1980):335–348; William F. Hederman, Jr., and Terry A. Nelson, "Cost Analysis: Some CBO Experience," *Policy Analysis* 4 (Spring 1978):227–260; and Carl V. Patton, "A Seven-Day Project: Early Faculty Retirement Alternatives," *Policy Alternatives* 1 (Winter 1975):731–753.

14 Arie Y. Lewin, M. F. Shakun, D. R. Hortberg, J. F. Hyfantis, F. J. Iarossi, and J. C. Miles, II, "The Fourth Jetport for Metropolitan New York: A Case Study," in *Policy Sciences: Methodologies and Cases*, eds. Arie Y. Lewin and Melvin F. Shakun (New York: Pergamon, 1976), pp. 131–196.

15 Martin H. David, Erhard F. Joeres, and J. Jeffrey Peirce, "Phosphorus Pollution Control in the Lake Michigan Watershed," *Policy Analysis* 6 (Winter 1980):47–60.

16 E. S. Savas, "Policy Analysis for Local Government: Public vs. Private Refuse Collection," *Policy Analysis* 3 (Winter 1977):49–74.

17 Barbara J. Stevens, "Scale, Market Structure, and the Cost of Refuse Collection," Research Paper No. 107 (New York: Graduate School of Business, Columbia University, 1976), cited by E. S. Savas, in "Policy Analysis for Local Government," pp. 64–68.

18 E. S. Savas, "Policy Analysis for Local Government," p. 68.

19 Philip J. Cook, "Reducing Injury and Death Rates in Robbery," *Policy Analysis* 6 (Winter 1980):22.

20 Duncan MacRae, Jr., "Concepts and Methods of Policy Analysis," p. 17. See also: Giandomenico Majone, "An Anatomy of Pitfalls" in *Pitfalls of Analysis*, eds. Giandomenico Majone and Edward S. Quade, pp. 10–11.

21 Aaron Wildavsky, *Speaking Truth to Power*, p. 3.

22 Edward S. Quade, *Analysis for Public Decisions*.

23 Edith Stokey and Richard Zeckhauser, *A Primer for Policy Analysis* (New York: W. W. Norton, 1978).

24 Edward S. Quade, *Analysis for Public Decisions*, p. 25.

25 Edith Stokey and Richard Zeckhauser, *A Primer for Policy Analysis*, p. 155.

26 Edward J. Mishan, *Cost Benefit Analysis* (New York: Praeger, 1976); Edward S. Quade, *Analysis for Public Decisions*; and Edith Stokey and Richard Zeckhauser, *A Primer for Policy Analysis*.

27 Robert W. Burchell and David Listokin, *The Fiscal Impact Handbook* (New Brunswick, NJ: Center for Urban Policy Research, Rutgers University, 1978).

28 Howard Raiffa, *Decision Analysis: Introductory Lectures on Choices under Uncertainty* (Reading, MA: Addison-Wesley, 1968).

29 William D. Coplin and Michael K. O'Leary, *Analyzing Public Policy Issues*; Duncan MacRae, Jr. and James A. Wilde, *Policy Analysis for Public Decisions*; and Arnold J. Meltsner, "Political Feasibility and Policy Analysis," *Public Administration Review* 32 (November/December 1972):859–867.

30 Earl R. Babbie, *Survey Research Methods* (Belmont, CA: Wadsworth, 1973); Kenneth D. Bailey, *Methods of Social Research* (New York: The Free Press, 1978); and Claire Selltiz, Lawrence S. Wrightsman, and Stuart W. Cook, *Research Methods in Social Relations*, 3rd ed. (New York: Holt, Rinehart and Winston, 1976).

31 Leslie Kish, *Survey Sampling* (New York: John Wiley and Sons, 1965); and Seymour Sudman, *Applied Sampling* (New York: Academic Press, 1976).

32 Herbert H. Hyman, *Interviewing in Social Research* (Chicago: University of Chicago Press, 1975); and Robert L. Kahn and Charles F. Cannell, *The Dynamics of Interviewing* (New York: John Wiley & Sons, 1967).

33 Lewis A. Dexter, *Elite and Specialized Interviewing* (Evanston: Northwestern University Press, 1970).

34 Eugene Bardach, "Gathering Data for Policy Research."

35 Carl V. Patton, "A Seven-Day Project."

36 Harry P. Hatry, Richard E. Winnie, and Donald M. Fisk, *Practical Program Evaluation for State and Local Government Officials*, 2nd ed. (Washington, DC: The Urban Institute, 1981); and Carol H. Weiss, *Evaluation Research: Methods of Assessing Program Effectiveness* (Englewood Cliffs, NJ: Prentice-Hall, 1972).

37 Thomas D. Cook and Donald T. Campbell, *Quasi-Experimentation: Design and Analysis Issues for Field Settings* (Chicago: Rand McNally, 1979); and Donald T. Campbell and Julian C. Stanley, *Experimental and Quasi-Experimental Designs for Research* (Chicago: Rand McNally, 1963).

38 Frank M. Andrews, Laura Klem, Terrence N. Davidson, Patrick M. O'Malley, and Willard L. Rodgers, *A Guide for Selecting Statistical Techniques for Analyzing Social Science Data* (Ann Arbor: Survey Research Center and Institute for Social Research, University of Michigan, 1974); Hubert M. Blalock,, Jr., *Social Statistics*, 2nd ed. (New York: McGraw-Hill, 1972); and G. David Garson, *Handbook of Political Science Methods* (Boston: Holbrook Press, 1971).

39 Aaron Wildavsky, *Speaking Truth to Power*, pp. 397–398.

40 Ernest R. Alexander, "Policy Analysis"; Herbert J. Gans, "From Urbanism to Policy Planning," *Journal of the American Institute of Planners* 36 (July 1970):223–226; Kenneth L. Kraemer, *Policy Analysis in Local Government: A Systems Approach to Decision Making* (Washington, DC: International City Management Association, 1973); Dennis A. Rondinelli, "Urban Planning as Policy Analysis"; Michael B. Teitz, *Policy Evaluation: The Uncertain Guide* (Berkeley: Institute of Urban and Regional Development, University of California, 1978); and Jacob B. Ukeles, "Policy Analysis."

10 Environmental impact analysis

Impact assessment is not a new idea. Almost all decisions are based upon the evaluation of possible impacts or outcomes. An important change involves the explicit consideration of environmental impacts in planning and the role of statutes.

For a long time, planning decisions were based mainly upon economic and political criteria, almost to the exclusion of other factors. Natural resources were even viewed in economic contexts as constraints on land development. This contributed to significant resource degradation, accompanied by unanticipated adverse social effects and hazards to life and property. Examples of environmental problems arising from urban development include: frequent floods, water pollution by sewerage, losses of farmlands, and the destruction of wetlands. However, organizations are developing an environmental awareness, as reflected in plans dealing with erosion, toxic substances, and endangered species.

Effective environmental impact assessment requires an appreciation for the meaning of environment, the role of environmental impacts in planning, concepts and techniques of impact analysis, and governmental policies on environmental assessment.

A broad view of environment

Environment has many connotations. For the bedridden invalid, it may mean room furnishings. To city dwellers, it may include subways. For many persons, it is the natural world of plants and animals. These diverse viewpoints have one common aspect—surroundings. *Environment means surroundings.* In most planning, environment includes such natural factors as water and wildlife and such economic and social features as employment and housing. Meaningful environmental impact assessment thus involves just about everything. Economic or political matters are not enough.

Although some persons still think that environment is limited to concerns such as energy and air pollution, most governmental agencies now take a broader view. For example, the environmental assessment guidelines of diverse federal agencies such as the United States Department of Transportation, Housing and Urban Development, the Corps of Engineers, and the Environmental Protection Agency all require the analysis of economic and social impacts in addition to physical impacts.

Impact categories

Environmental impacts may be categorized in three groups: physical, economic, and social factors. The placement of factors in particular categories is somewhat arbitrary.

Physical factors   These constitute a large group from both the natural and built environments. Natural factors include: climate, air quality, land, water resources,

Figure 10–1 Environmental impact did not start with EPA. The top photo shows an approaching dust storm in Colorado, 1935; next, a flooded farm in Missouri, 1937; finally, stumps, snags, and a stump farm in Idaho, 1939.

biota, and considerations such as wetlands and earthquake zones. Features of the built environment include: land use, noise, vibrations, solid wastes, infrastructure such as roads and sewers, and special conditions such as rights-of-way.

Economic factors   These pertain to the resources directly or indirectly associated with the goods and services of an area. These factors include: income, employment, economic base, housing, land tenure, and considerations such as govermental finance.

Social factors   These primary relate to community goals and nonmonetary values. Some overlap with factors in other categories. These factors include: population (e.g., density, mix, displacement, and mobility), community cohesion, housing, services such as education and health care, aesthetics, historical sites, and aspects of psychological well-being such as the fear of physical harm.

Organizations usually address all three broad categories of factors. However, because of different perspectives and priorities, agencies emphasize particular environmental factors to different extents. As a result, impact assessments performed by the Corps of Engineers are likely to excel in the analysis of physical impacts, while those of Housing and Urban Development usually exhibit a sensitivity for social impacts.

These impact assessments do not occur in a vacuum. They are associated with proposed programs or projects, which are the result of the planning process.

Environmental impact assessment in the planning process

All planning, from charting a vacation to designing an urban renewal project or developing a water quality management plan, has the same principal elements. They are as follows.

1. Identifying problems and goals.
2. Specifying objectives.
3. Compiling an inventory of conditions and resources.
4. Developing and evaluating alternatives.
5. Selecting a plan.
6. Implementing and revising the plan.

Environmental impact assessment applies to all the planning elements, especially the latter ones. Impact assessment has particular utility in evaluating alternatives and selecting a plan. It aims at avoiding, reducing, or mitigating any adverse effects of implementing a program or a project. It is more than the coverage of economic, physical, and social concerns in the planning process. Impact assessment involves the detailed analysis of specific action proposals— the planning alternatives.

Although environmental impact assessment is most useful in the latter stages of plan formulation, it is not an activity that is handled apart from other planning functions. This separation can result in formulating alternatives of a restricted environmental scope, and can cause subsequent implementation problems. It also can waste resources by collecting data that are unsuitable for impact analysis. It is ironic that the U.S. Environmental Protection Agency inadvertently encourages this practice by requiring the preparation of environmental information documents that are separate from plans for wastewater treatment facilities.

At the main impact analysis stage, following the development of alternatives, the planning focus shifts from the central purpose of a plan to its effects upon other public and private goals and activities. For example, a highway proposal to relieve traffic congestion may increase noise and air pollution, stimulate economic development, contribute to urban sprawl, and disrupt ethnic neighborhoods.

Impact assessment deals with this entire range of possible impacts, from traffic improvement to neighborhood disruption.

An urban planning proposal has a myriad of goals that it must satisfy. The proposal should *not* do the following:

1. Damage the physical environment by causing erosion, air pollution, the extinction of species, or other detrimental effects.
2. Waste energy or other natural resources.
3. Adversely affect the job opportunities or civil rights of persons.
4. Contravene the President's urban, rural, or small community policies.
5. Increase inflation.
6. Distort intergovernmental functions and revenue patterns.
7. Destroy significant historical sites.
8. Break up families or their community support groups.
9. Lead to increased crime or juvenile delinquency.

The federal government is looking to state, areawide, and local planning processes to help resolve these problems. Impact analysis of planning alternatives is a means for achieving this goal.

Phases and methods of impact analysis

The various types of environmental factors are unique. Each may have its own impact analysis methods. For example, entire books are written about fiscal and water quality impact assessment. Book chapters feature the analysis of noise, aesthetic, and biotic impacts. A newsletter is devoted to social impact assessment. Although such kinds of environmental impact assessment have their differences, they share certain analysis phases, concepts, and techniques.

Impact assessment essentially consists of three phases:

1. Identification of the types of environmental impacts that warrant assessment.
2. Prediction of the future course for the identified impacts.
3. Evaluation and display of the forecasted impacts.

These activities apply to the proposed program or project, which usually is an array of alternatives.

Identification of impacts

The identification of impacts is largely dependent upon a knowledge of the existing environment and past occurrences. Much of the same information that goes into the development of planning alternatives is also used in the identification of impacts. The efficient use of these data and additional information requires an understanding of study boundaries, assessment criteria, and impact sequence.

Study boundaries Boundaries refer both to the geographical area and the study topics. The geographical area must be large enough to cover all potential environmental impacts. For example, it must include the entire area that might receive growth induced by projects such as roads and wastewater treatment plants. Similarly, it must be sufficiently large to consider cost-effective alternatives. Since assessment boundaries may cross town borders, especially in regions, political and legal tugs-of-war may occur among communities. This conflict may be held to a minimum by making sure that all relevant interests actively participate in the planning. Since state and local groups are especially sensitive to area priorities and values, their views can be invaluable in setting a course of impact assessments.

The U.S. Department of Housing and Urban Development (HUD) studied but did not implement impact assessment on an areawide basis where changes are occurring in either urban or rural settings. This broadened scope was to have helped HUD field offices in identifying broad, especially cumulative impacts, and in avoiding redundant assessment efforts. Other agencies and levels of government can also benefit from this approach (e.g., communities in block grant applications, coastal zone management programs, and the environmental evaluation of comprehensive plans). Of course, the areawide focus is not new to the federal scene. The Water Quality Management Planning Program of the U.S. Environmental Protection Agency has long had an areawide planning orientation.

Another type of assessment boundary is the scope of studies. Although some organizations, including the U.S. Environmental Protection Agency, require considerations such as population projections, other factors not explicitly named in regulations are pertinent. For example, in some areas the ethnic composition and location of residents may be just as important as the overall population size. The direction of the studies also depends, in part, upon the anticipated impacts and their value to the community. Every aspect cannot be studied to the last degree. Just as decisions must be made on the scope of studies, similar decisions must be reached on the scale and level of detail.

Assessment criteria   Environmental criteria, the rules for making judgments, must be fitting and explicit. The use of appropriate criteria at the various points in the process—from data collection to plan selection—is extremely important. While agencies may adopt some criteria such as those for cost-effectiveness analysis, other criteria may not be delineated. Sometimes, because of complex situations or a rush to get the work done, inappropriate data measures are adopted. A solution to this problem is having criteria that suit the subjects. While numerical data are extremely useful for factors such as physical resources, not everything can be meaningfully quantified. For example, aesthetics may not lend itself to quantitative assessment. Yet, some analysts use numbers to compare all factors, including aesthetics. It is important to undertand why certain assessment criteria are chosen, why others are ruled out, and what ramifications these choices have for assessment of the proposed program or project.

Impact sequence   An appreciation for impact sequence is crucial to environmental assessments. Plans always result in unexpected effects. Sometimes, these effects are significant, such as diminished bird populations following the widespread use of DDT. According to sequence, there are two basic kinds of impacts: primary and secondary. This designation refers to the occurrence of the impacts, rather than to their relative importance.

Effects directly related to the location, construction, and operation of projects or programs are called *primary impacts*. Depending upon the viewpoint of the planner, they can be either beneficial (positive) or adverse (negative). For example, the primary beneficial impacts of a proposed dam project may include the control of floods and the generation of electric power. Negative impacts may involve the loss of forests and agricultural land. Similarly, the benefits of a regional wastewater treatment facility include the removal of harmful pollutants from wastewater. Negative primary impacts of regional significance can involve the loss of open space, and the transfer of water out of an area. Primary impacts are important, but another kind of impact—secondary impact—may be even more important, especially for state and areawide plans.

Indirect effects that are induced by a program or project are called *secondary*

Figure 10–2 This aerial photo of a portion of Seattle, taken in 1922, shows the early development of infrastructure with the major street near the center and the bridges connecting both sides of the waterway. Bridges, often the most readily overlooked and widely neglected part of the infrastructure, profoundly affect the direction of growth.

impacts. They arise from the subtle, often long-term changes in location, density, timing, and type of development brought about by programs or projects. Secondary impacts often involve population, economic growth, land use, and physical factors such as air quality. For example, a dam project for flood control often leads to the establishment of vacation cottages and commercial businesses such as restaurants and service stations. These are secondary impacts.

There are numerous secondary environmental impacts associated with urban growth and sprawl. Traffic-related noise and air pollution may result from new suburbs, shopping centers, and industrial parks. Built-up areas usually increase stormwater runoff and nonpoint source pollution. Developments may infringe upon open space, historical sites, and agricultural lands. The ethnic or economic character of an area even can be altered by these forces. For example, regional interceptor sewers often lead to dense residential developments such as apartment complexes. A change in the type and quantity of housing in an area, as well as the people who can afford it, may indirectly result from these facilities.

Certain secondary impacts are given special attention by federal law. They include construction in wetlands, destruction of habitats for endangered species, and development in flood-prone areas.

Identification techniques Impact identification involves the determination of both the relevant environmental factors, and their systematic relationships. Numerous techniques are employed. Three have widespread use: checklists, matrices, and networks.

Checklists are commonly used in identifying impacts. These catalogs of items can be sources of ideas for types of environmental impacts. Checklists generally are easy to use. However, their simplicity is also a drawback. In addition to possibly omitting potential impacts, checklists have a static format. Their scope is limited to direct and individual effects. Further, this format does not show relationships among specific factors.

Matrices function as both checklists and display relationships. Matrices, tables of items, are organized into rows and columns. In a cause-effect matrix, actions that cause environmental impacts are usually listed in a row, while the potential impacts are placed in a column. A matching of rows to columns then can identify related causes and impacts. This approach also can be quantified, such as assigning relative values for the importance and magnitude of impacts.[1] Matrices rely heavily on in-house judgments. They share some limitations with checklists, including restricted use in comparing alternatives.

Networks consist of diagrams or webs of related components. They are useful in disaggregating a complex situation into its constituents, and in revealing explicit relationships. Networks give exposure to indirect effects, and show both joint and individual impacts. As illustrated by the Sorenson "stepped-matrix,"[2] a procedure for assessing conflicts among resource users in the coastal zone, networks also trace the sequence of impacts. A problem with networks is that linkages often are arbitrary and oversimplified. Networks also are usually unidirectional without feedback loops.

Impact identification techniques such as checklists and checklist-type matrices identify factors through increasingly comprehensive inventories, but they do not clarify system relationships. Systems description is rarely performed by most of the currently used impact assessment approaches. This is a serious lack because many impacts such as Dutch elm disease and carcinogenic poisoning are the result of multiple interrelationships. More work is needed on this problem. Simulation models such as K-SIM[3] appear promising. Simulation models also have roles in impact prediction and evaluation.

Prediction

Impact prediction is the central element of the impact assessment process. Known effects and anticipated impacts are the cutting edge by which alternatives are compared and evaluated. Therefore, it is ironic that this phase of environmental assessment receives so little attention and remains relatively underdeveloped. Major factors that contribute to the problem include the uncertainty of future events, and deficiencies in prediction methodologies.

Uncertainty   It is unreasonable to assume that current or past trends will automatically continue. Similarly, it is unlikely that presently held social and political values will remain unchanged. However, it can be argued that decisions must be based upon present information and judgments. Speculations about the future can go only so far. It is a difficult dilemma for which only partial solutions are available.

If the analyst has experience with the potential impact, the probability of its occurrence may be estimated. However, this approach may have planning limitations. Many decision makers are uncomfortable with mathematical probabilities. Another approach is to perform a kind of sensitivity analysis in which the range of possibilities is considered. Then, hopefully, plans based upon these studies can be made flexible for adjustment to future conditions.

Prediction methodologies   The diverse types of environmental factors require many different prediction methodologies. They range from broad frameworks such as matrices, to specific approaches such as income multipliers used in the assessment of regional economic impacts. As pointed out by Andrews[4] most of these methodologies seem to emphasize impact identification and display formats, rather than prediction processes. Many approaches do not account for the criteria and procedures used in making predictions. In addition to approaches such as networks, many predictive methods involve intuitive judgments or consist of quantitative techniques.

Networks, workshops, and *Delphi surveys* are examples of techniques that involve intuitive predictions. They rely either upon the professional judgments of individual analysts, as with networks, or upon the collective consensus of workshop participants or a Delphi panel of experts. These techniques can have local relevance, serve as vehicles for dialogue among impact assessment parties, and provide bases for the broadened identification of impacts. Their main drawback is their vulnerability to the bias and subjectivity by analysts and participants.

Principal quantitative methods used for impact prediction include *quantitative models* and *statistical correlation techniques* such as regression analysis and trend extrapolations. These techniques can simultaneously relate many variables and are amenable to mathematical manipulation. A problem with models is that although they simplify complex systems, they may omit or distort crucial elements and relationships. The main drawback of the statistical correlation techniques is that they often lack a strong supporting rationale for particular computations. For example, trend patterns and ratios are simply extrapolated and projected forward, based upon the blind assumption that the future will be like the past.[5]

Of all these approaches, those that usually have the greatest value for predicting impacts are those that identify system linkages. This is an essential requirement of a reliable and effective impact assessment technique.

Impact evaluation and display

The evaluation and display of forecasted impacts is the last phase of impact assessment. It leads directly to the task of comparing alternatives and selecting the final plan. One alternative usually involves taking no action or postponing action pending further studies. In addition to this alternative of doing nothing, other options include structural approaches of physical options such as sediment detention basins for stormwater runoff, and nonstructural measures such as land use ordinances and construction schedules. In evaluating the impacts of the alternatives, several considerations are in order. Some are even required by federal and state laws.

Tradeoffs   In focusing upon the benefits, drawbacks, and risks of each alternative, it is easy to lose sight of broad relationships and cumulative, long-term effects. Accordingly, the tradeoffs between short-term gains and long-term losses should be explored. For example, disruptions during a construction project should be compared with the probable impacts of induced growth and area development. Likewise, the development of an area for tax revenues should be assessed against the loss of wildlife or the disturbance of community cohesiveness. The extent to which a proposed plan would foreclose future options, what economists call "opportunity costs," also should be evaluated.

Furthermore, the impact assessments typically should identify commitments of resources which are irreversible or irretrievable. Especially appropriate during times of dwindling supplies, the assessment should determine which alternatives would result in the loss of irreplaceable natural areas, resources, or unique properties.

Evaluation and display techniques   Impact evaluation techniques can be classified into three categories: direct display, constraint setting, and weighting procedures.[6]

The diverse array of alternatives and study topics requires many different evaluation methods. One research effort[7] lists 77 techniques that can be used in forecasting and evaluating social impacts! Of course, only a few could be used in a given situation. The trick is to choose methods that can accomplish several tasks: identify and specify impacts, reveal areas of potential conflict, and provide a framework for evaluating alternatives efficiently and equitably. In a large area such as a state or a region, it is important that analysis methods be compatible throughout. For example, two techniques that are often used to estimate storm-water runoff in a watershed are the traditional rational method, and the newer soils cover complex method. Depending upon the analyst, these methods can give vastly different estimated volumes of runoff. Great differences in costs and stormwater control strategies can result. The potential chaos of various techniques used in an area thus becomes obvious.

Direct display approaches include the techniques that directly compare the impacts of the planning alternatives. These techniques range from matrices to the computer graphics of simulation models. An approach that has wide use is the *accounts sheet*, a technique employed by agencies such as the U.S. Environmental Protection Agency and the Nuclear Regulatory Commission. An accounts sheet is a type of table for showing the impacts associated with the various alternatives. It provides disaggregated technical information for an easy determination of the tradeoffs. It also breaks down complex actions into their causative components. It can even list assessment criteria, references, and other information. Its main drawbacks are associated with the data disaggregation. The technique does not deal well with the composite impacts and system interrelationships of the environmental factors.

Another assessment approach, *constraint setting*, involves the use of criteria and standards in making the evaluations. This approach requires that all actions meet the specifications that are agreed upon by all interests in the evaluation process. If each alternative can meet the standard, then tradeoffs among other factors must be the basis for reaching decisions. The approach has several difficulties. In addition to possibly hiding important differences among the alternatives, it requires criteria or standards that have universal acceptability, a tall order. Several constraint-setting techniques incorporate environmental constraints into land use planning. This *suitability mapping*, as popularized by McHarg,[8] involves the use of transparent overlay maps of physical and social factors. Some of these techniques also involve weighted factors, which overlap into the next category of techniques.

Weighting is the basis of another category of impact evaluation techniques. These procedures usually involve the quantification of all factors and apply multipliers to the factors for use in mathematical manipulations. Weights are involved in a spectrum of methodologies, including relatively simple cause-effect matrices[9] and complex computer-operated models such as the Environmental Evaluation System for Water Resources Planning sponsored by the Bureau of Reclamation.[10] Weighting techniques may involve several layers of value judgments. Proponents claim that the approach makes explicit the value judgments inherent to all planning. However, in practice the mathematical computations and summation totals tend to conceal the relationships among the factors and to obscure the tradeoffs among them.

None of the methods, even the commonly used checklists and simulation models, alone accomplish all that is required. Most methods are useful in describing the environment or in displaying the findings and tradeoffs of alternatives. In many areas, methods for evaluating alternatives are still being developed. No single analysis procedure automatically leads to all that is needed for planning decisions.

Mitigation of impacts

An important adjunct to impact evaluation involves ways to mitigate (reduce or remedy) the adverse effects of planning alternatives. The consideration of mitigative measures is required by federal agencies such as the U.S. Department of Housing and Urban Development. Some states, including Montana and Wis-

Figure 10–3   Primary and secondary impacts. This 4,200-foot bridge near Yaupon Beach, North Carolina, was built on pillars so that sunlight and tidal flooding would protect the salt water marshes.

consin, explicitly require mitigative techniques to minimize the adverse impacts of development. Maryland even demands the consideration of measures to maximize potential *beneficial* environmental effects.

Most primary or secondary impacts can be mitigated by several different techniques. Since both the measures and the local situations vary, it is important to select the measures that best meet the needs of a particular area. Factors for choosing the measures include technique feasibility and implementation responsibility.

Techniques feasibility   Primary impacts such as erosion associated with highway projects are generally short-term impacts. They usually can be mitigated through site planning, the control of construction activities, and program operations and management. Many problems can be avoided or kept to a minimum, in part, through thoughtful site planning. An example of mitigative site planning is the use of vegetation as a buffer against nonpoint source pollution. Another strategy is the control of construction impacts by providing sedimentation basins for road runoff and scheduling earthmoving activities for periods of expected low rainfall. An additional approach involves maintenance procedures such as periodic street cleaning.

Secondary, or indirect, impacts can have long-term consequences that are difficult to avoid or correct. Since these impacts are often related to growth, many mitigative approaches involve land use controls such as zoning and subdivision regulations. This is a situation where area-wide solutions may depend upon coordinated actions at the local level. In addition to appropriateness, technique feasibility is also dependent upon monetary costs and timing.

Implementation responsibility   Another important matter concerns the responsibility for mitigative measures. The final mitigative responsibility often is borne by the organization that sponsors the program or project, but the efforts of many organizations and individuals are usually involved. For example, the facility contractor may build erosion control structures such as sediment detention basins. The local government usually conducts an inspection and generally has the responsibility for such implementing mitigative measures as land use controls. However, the state may retain enforcement powers.

Although the coordination of various parties may be difficult, areawide arrangements may be troublesome. One community or organization may plan on the behalf of several others. If several jurisdictions are involved, no single organization may have the authority to implement mitigative measures outside its own area. The planning agency also may have powers that are insufficient to carry out mitigative actions. Therefore, this situation may require an inter-jurisdictional authority with powers for implementing mitigative measures. Substate agencies possibly can play this role.

Mitigative actions, in addition to other aspects of impact analysis, are proposed in most environmental impact statements.

Impact assessment procedures and process

In many states and regions, environmental assessments are roughly parallel in content to those required for federal environmental impact statements. This pattern was given an impetus by the National Environmental Policy Act of 1969 (NEPA), a landmark piece of legislation for enhancing the consideration of environmental factors in decision making. NEPA is only one of numerous federal laws enacted during the 1970s that have environmental significance. A few others include the Clean Air Amendments of 1970, the Federal Water Pollution Control Act Amendments of 1972, and the Housing and Community Development Act of 1974. In addition to effects upon the subsequent legislation, NEPA has led to environmental regulations written by dozens of federal agencies.

After years of implementation, a need for streamlining and standardizing the environmental process became necessary. The environmental impact statement, the main instrument of NEPA, suffered from the sundry regulations and procedures of the agencies. Statements were found to be ponderous and insufficiently analytical. Revised guidelines developed by the Council of Environmental Quality were developed to reduce paperwork, to accelerate the assessment process, and to promote better decisions. These revisions resulted in a uniform process with standard terminology for the first time. These aspects include: the categorical exclusion, the environmental assessment and/or environmental impact statement, a Finding of No Significant Impact, a scoping of issues, and process monitoring.

Procedures and terminology

The assessment process proceeds through a number of decision points. First, it may be determined if the proposed actions may be excluded from the assessment. Typically, routine agency actions that have no significant impacts fall into this category. For actions that are not excluded, two choices are possible: conduct an analysis to determine if an environmental impact statement (EIS) is required, or immediately begin EIS preparation.

In studying the necessity for an EIS, agencies evaluate planning information for environmental impacts, and determine ways of avoiding or minimizing the adverse effects of the actions. The resulting public document, called an *environmental assessment*, provides data and analyses on the significance of the environmental impacts. If no significant adverse impacts are anticipated, agencies issue a *Finding of No Significant Impact*. However, if significant impacts are anticipated, and they cannot be sufficiently reduced or eliminated, an *environmental impact statement* is prepared and released. The impact statement is a report which identifies and analyzes in detail the environmental impacts of proposed actions and feasible alternatives. The statement differs from the

Figure 10–4   A small plan can produce a big impact.

environmental assessment in the level of detail and the scope of analysis. It is more comprehensive than an environmental assessment and concentrates upon areas with potential for significant environmental degradation. Impact statements are prepared where programs or projects will cause significant changes in land uses, or other resources will be seriously altered.

Process streamlining

In addition to standardizing the procedures and terminology, other changes were adopted to streamline the assessment process. These changes include: restrictions on the number of pages of statements, time limits, a scoping mechanism, and monitoring actions. *Scoping* pertains to early decisions by the various parties involved on important issues to be addressed in the EIS, the length of the statement, and the responsibilities of the participants. Scoping reduces the possibility of overlooking crucial issues and encourages agencies to concentrate studies on significant rather than peripheral areas.

Initially, there was no followup on impact statements. Mitigative measures described in the EIS often were not implemented. In contrast, the current regulations make federal agencies responsible for mitigation. To accomplish this task, agencies are encouraged to monitor their decisions, and to enforce directives through means such as permits.

Changes to the impact assessment process, therefore, are largely procedural. The content of the statements remains essentially the same:

1   Discussion of impacts.
2.   Adverse effects which can not be avoided.
3.   Alternatives to proposed actions.
4.   Relationships between short-term uses and long-term production.
5.   Irreversible or irretrievable commitments of resources.

The statements also must be circulated for review and comment among all pertinent agencies and individuals. In addition to federal agencies, relevant state and local environmental agencies are involved in the review process mainly through the A-95 clearinghouse.

Environmental review by A-95 clearinghouses

Federal assistance to nonprofit organizations and state and local governments increased dramatically in recent decades, more than thirty-fold in the last quarter century.[11] Administrative conflicts and inefficiencies accompanied this growth, and it is useful to trace efforts to solve these problems.

In response to the need for better intergovernmental cooperation and communication in the federal assistance programs, Congress passed two pieces of legislation. Section 204 of the Demonstration Cities and Metropolitan Development Act of 1966 required the submission of public works plans to metropolitan planning agencies for review and comment relative to local plans and programs, prior to funding by the federal agencies. The Intergovernmental Cooperation Act of 1968 extended the review requirement to nonmetropolitan areas and a broader range of federal programs. These acts were implemented through administrative circulars issued by the Bureau of the Budget (now called the Office of Management and Budget). Circular A-95, issued in 1969, guided the comment and review process. Following revisions in 1971, state and local environmental agencies became involved in the review process.

Environmental involvements   Circular A-95 prescribed the administrative process for state and local governments through designated clearinghouses, to assess the impact of proposed federally funded projects and programs on state, areawide, and local plans and programs. The bulk of the review and comment workload was handled by the Project Notification and Review System. This review process was carried out by organizations at two levels: state clearinghouses and areawide clearinghouses which often were regional (substate) planning agencies. In addition to other functions, this system provided some of the input that was needed for compliance with the National Environmental Policy Act. Since a proposal was generally reviewed, under Circular A-95, *prior to* the preparation of an environmental assessment or impact statement, the system was an ideal means for producing information about the impacts of proposed projects on programs very early in the planning process. These clearinghouses notified other organizations about the existence of draft environmental statements and provided them an opportunity to help assess projects and programs in relation to concerns such as urban impacts. Furthermore, the clearinghouses prepared their own reviews and comments concerning impact statements.

The A-95 process continues to undergo change. While the President's 1980 National Urban Policy Report sought to strengthen urban impact analysis through the A-95 process,[12] the Reagan administration changed A-95. Under Executive Order 12372, "Intergovernmental Review of Federal Programs," states can establish their own review processes and federal agencies must still consider state reviews, or explain why not. Also, states may simplify plan requirements. While there has not been any systematic study of state actions since the executive order went into effect, in many states the review process seems to have remained essentially unchanged.

Although the A-95 process has been described as ineffective and ponderous, it has been a primary tool for promoting awareness and cooperation among all levels of government on developmental projects and programs. Federal aid applicants and the A-95 clearinghouses accepted the process as necessary and desirable.[13] Even where state clearinghouses have been abolished, as in Pennsylvania, agencies continue to conduct local reviews on an ad hoc basis. Without the impetus of a federal program, however, such efforts could decline over time.

States and environmental assessment

The National Environmental Policy Act (NEPA) is a federal law that applies only to federal agencies and users of federal funds, but many states have followed the federal lead through an environmental impact assessment process based somewhat upon the federal model.[14]

The state legislation often mimics NEPA, especially in the language of environmental policy. For example, Maryland considers its state agencies as "environmental stewards of the air, land, water, and living resources." Washington views itself as a "trustee of the environment for succeeding generations." It is state policy in Indiana to "encourage productive and enjoyable harmony between man and the environment." Most states have similar provisions, but differences exist in scope and assessment requirements.

Environmental assessments in some states have a limited scope. For example, Idaho requires environmental analyses when critical areas such as flood plains and sites of historical significance are involved. Nebraska requires environmental studies for state funded road projects. Such approaches are fragmented, but they have potential for improved decision making.

Regarding specific requirements, state directives are similar to the federal law, requiring an impact statement to be prepared for significant actions affecting the environment. The five provisions of NEPA such as irreversible and irretrievable commitments of resources are generally covered in most state statutes, but a few states omit some items and emphasize others. For example, Connecticut expressly requires the assessment of primary and secondary ecological impacts. California, New York, and Montana direct attention to the growth-inducing impacts of development. North Carolina authorizes local governments to require impact statements from special purpose districts and the private developers of major projects. In Florida, an EIS is prepared for a proposed development that is of an areawide scale. Heavy industries in the coastal zone of Delaware are required to file an EIS; however, while the consideration of secondary and irreversible impacts is required, no discussion of alternatives is mandated. A few states, including Connecticut and Michigan, explicitly require the use of benefit-cost analysis in the evaluation of planning alternatives.

Environmental assessments and reviews undergo different administrative arrangements in the states. Offices of planning develop the impact analysis guidelines and procedures in California and Delaware. The governor has these responsibilities in Florida, North Carolina, and Wisconsin. Environmental quality control councils or boards take the lead in Hawaii, Montana, and Puerto Rico.[15] In general, the states fail to provide these agencies with strong overview and regulatory powers.[16]

Problems

The main difficulties with the environmental impact assessment process at the state and local levels have to do with procedures and resources. NEPA and NEPA-like legislation do not effectively apply to many private projects. Even where state statutes require local governments to prepare impact statements on zoning or permit-issuing activities, hindrances exist. In states such as California, where large housing developers are required to file an EIS, private parties may be reluctant to disclose their plans to the public at an early time for legitimate business reasons. The openness and early involvement in planning sought by NEPA is progressing, but not at a fast pace.

The scarcity of resources for environmental impact assessments is another problem that is especially acute for state and local governments. The Housing and Community Development Act of 1974 requires localities to prepare the EIS

for community development projects, and some funding for environmental reviews is provided. Similar resources for environmental impact assessments are lacking both in NEPA and most state laws. This fact is alarming since the delegation of federal responsibilities to the states is likely to continue. The only major amendment to NEPA in the 1970s involved a transfer of the federal impact statement responsibility to state agencies.

Despite such procedural and funding problems, the environmental impact assessment process has made a substantial contribution to planning, especially in promoting better information gathering and in broadening the basis for making decisions. Furthermore, as more environmental considerations are integrated into planning on a regular basis, the costs of the environmental assessment will be provided for like any other factor in planning.

Summary

Because environment means surroundings and surroundings vary, the word *environment* has different connotations for various persons. It can mean just about everything. Environmental assessments, therefore, can evaluate jobs, housing, and aesthetics, as well as water quality, animals, and other natural resources. A broad perspective helps to avoid overlooking potential impacts.

All planning has the same basic elements. These steps involve: identifying problems and goals, specifying objectives, compiling data, developing and evaluating alternatives, selecting a plan, and implementing and revising the plan.

Impact assessment is more than the coverage of economic, physical, and social concerns in the planning process. Impact assessment involves the detailed analysis of the planning alternatives.

Programs have different regulations and terminology to describe the impact assessment steps. However, the same basic elements are involved: impact identification, impact prediction, and impact evaluation and display.

The early steps of impact assessment involve the identification of impacts. Problems at this stage can be avoided or held to a minimum through the consideration of study boundaries, assessment criteria, impact sequence, and identification techniques such as checklists, matrices, and networks.

Impacts can be either beneficial (positive) or harmful (negative). They also are classified as either primary or secondary, terms which do not reflect their importance, but show their relationships to actions. Primary impacts are due directly to project or program activities. Secondary effects, such as growth, are induced or caused indirectly by a project.

The prediction of future effects is at the heart of the impact assessment process. This step is underdeveloped because of data uncertainty and deficiencies with prediction methodologies which usually involve intuitive judgments or quantitative techniques.

The evaluation of alternatives involves various considerations. In addition to environmental effects and monetary costs, other factors such as legal constraints are involved. The assessment addresses both short-term impacts and long-range effects, and irreversible or irretrievable losses of resources. Impact evaluation and display techniques can be classified in three categories: direct display, constraint setting, and weighting procedures.

Figure 10–5 Environmental problems arising from economic development. When land use is changed, and resources are exploited, resource degradation or depletion usually follows. The top photo shows a housing development near Seattle that preempted prime agricultural land. The next photo shows farm land in West Virginia that was ravished by surface mining and is now being restored with funds from the Abandoned Mine Lands Program of the U.S. Office of Surface Mining. The last photo shows technicians covering soil excavated from a hazardous waste site in Maryland.

Successful projects require the mitigation of adverse impacts. The choice of mitigation measures depends upon technique feasibility and implementation responsibility. Secondary impacts, as compared to the primary (direct) impacts, are generally more difficult to mitigate.

Environmental assessments may lead to the preparation of environmental impact statements—reports which identify and analyze in detail the environmental impacts of proposed actions and alternatives. The statements of various agencies have similar formats and procedures, but they can have different emphases.

Many states have adopted environmental assessment and impact statement guidelines. Although differences exist between the federal government and the states, the environmental assessment policies and provisions are similar. The main problems at the state and local levels center around scope, procedural, and funding difficulties.

1   Luna B. Leopold, Frank E. Clarke, Bruce B. Hanshaw, and James R. Balsley, *A Procedure for Evaluating Environmental Impact*, Circular 645 (Washington, DC: U.S. Geological Survey, 1971).

2   Jens C. Sorenson, *A Framework for Identification and Control of Resource Degradation in the Multiple Use of the Coastal Zone* (Berkeley: Department of Landscape Architecture, University of California, 1971).

3   Julius Kane, Ilan Vertinsky, and William Thompson, "A Methodology for Interactive Resource Policy Simulation," *Water Resources Research* 9 (no. 1, 1973).

4   Richard N.L. Andrews, "Elements and Methods of Impact Assessment," in *Environmental Analysis: for Land Use and Site Planning*, ed. William M. March (New York: McGraw-Hill Book Company, 1978), Chap. 9.3.

5   John G. Rau and David C. Wooten, *Environmental Impact Analysis Handbook* (New York: McGraw-Hill Book Company, 1980).

6   Andrews, "Elements and Methods of Impact Assessment."

7   Kurt Finsterbusch and C.P. Wolf, *Methodology of Social Impact Assessment* (Stroudsburg, PA: Dowden, Hutchinson, and Ross, Inc., 1977).

8   Ian L. McHarg, *Design with Nature* (Garden City, NY: Natural History Press, 1969).

9   Leopold et al., *A Procedure for Evaluating Environmental Impact*.

10 Norbert Dee, Janet K. Baker, Neil L. Drobny, Kenneth M. Duke, and David C. Fahringer, *Final Report on Environmental Evaluation System for Water Resource Planning*. Prepared by Battelle-Columbus Laboratories, Contract No. 14-06-D-7182 from Bureau of Land Reclamation, U.S. Department of the Interior, 1972.

11 Advisory Commission on Intergovernmental Relations, *Regional Decision Making: New Strategies for Substate District*. Volume 1, A-43 (Washington, DC: U.S. Government Printing Office, October 1973).

12 Glickman, Norman J., editor, *The Urban Impacts of Federal Policies*. Prepared for the U.S. Department of Housing and Urban Development (Baltimore: Johns Hopkins University Press, 1979).

13 Advisory Commission on Intergovernmental Relations, *Categorical Grants: Their Role and Design*. A-52 (Washington DC: U.S. Government Printing Office, 1978).

14 Ibid.

15 Thomas G. Dickert and Katherine R. Domeny, editors. *Environmental Impact Assessment: Guidelines and Commentary* (Berkeley: University Extension, University of California, 1974).

16 Kenneth Pearlman, "State Environmental Policy Acts: Local Decision Making and Land Use Planning." *Journal of the American Institute of Planners* 43 (January 1977): 42–53.

11 Basic studies for state and regional planning

The purpose of this chapter is to provide the reader with a general understanding of the data needs of state and regional planning agencies for basic population, housing, and employment studies—"basic studies." At some point in time, every state and regional planning agency recognizes the need to organize a research unit (or person) to be responsible for data maintenance, expertise, and analysis. This unit may not be involved in making plans per se, but it will serve as an integral part of the planning process. The unit may respond to inquiries as simple as "What is the population of the region?" or as complex as "Enterprise zone legislation is being proposed for the state. What types of data are available to analyze the impact of this legislation on the state's economy?" This chapter presents four steps in the operation of a basic research unit:

1. The organization of a basic research unit.
2. The basic data elements that need to be assembled.
3. The recent trends of these data with which the unit must build expertise.
4. The techniques that will be needed to generate extensions and projections of the data.

The basic research unit: some general considerations

The size of a basic research unit can range from a single person to a large staff. In general, the demands on such a unit often exceed its resources. Therefore, it is particularly important that the state or regional planning agency attempt to examine its resources in some detail prior to organizing its research unit. What funds and how much are available? Monies are needed not only for salaries and general office support, but for duplication of output. Are computer facilities present? If so, costs are necessarily increased, data resources increase, and someone with computer expertise will be needed. How much space is available? Since data maintenance is a large part of the basic research unit's responsibilty, and because data require storage, consideration must be given to where the data can be kept securely. Who is the unit to serve? The research units of the Tri-State Regional Planning Commission in the New York metropolitan region and the Delaware Valley Regional Planning Commission in the Philadelphia region, for example, serve not only their own commissions, but the public in general. When possible they do so free of change; however, special requests for special services are filled on a cost-reimbursable basis. The effect of serving the general public is twofold: (1) it increases the demands on the research unit and (2) it defrays some of the costs incurred. How large is the planning region? A key indicator of this is not only population size, but also population growth. A region of small population size would need less of all of the above than a larger region, but a region which is experiencing growth needs to plan for expansion of its basic research unit.

The services and needs of a basic research unit are dependent also upon the particular type of planning agency—regional or state? There are several different kinds of regional agencies. Some service parts of several states such as Tri-State

The industrial revolution and the information age   In industrialized nations, the transition from heavy manufacturing, rail and ship transportation, and fixed-site commerce has been under way for a generation.

The change first came to general attention in the 1960s when students of social trends pointed out that we were entering the post-industrial society. Among the dozen or more characteristics of the post-industrial society, two of them—the trend from production-oriented toward service-oriented economic activities and cybernation —portend the information age.

Precursors of the information age can be traced back for at least two hundred years, from the development of simple counting machines to the telephone and telegraph in the 19th century to the latest in communication satellites, lasers, fiber optics, optical disks, and, of course, the computer.

The hardware is intriguing, but the real revolution lies in the ways that the information age can transform the world around us.

Cybernetics means regulation and control through monitoring and feedback of information. Data bases mean almost infinite capacity to compile *usable and accessible* information in huge quantities. Information access means rapid, almost instantaneous, ability to pull out and correlate pieces of information to find patterns and profiles. Information security means the protection afforded individuals and organizations if the information systems are working the way they should work.

In the information age it is possible to use computer models and other information tools for forecasting, trend analyses, qualitative comparisons, and both micro and macro reviews of science, literature, and the arts.

Regional Planning Commission which services parts of New Jersey, New York, and Connecticut. Others serve some subarea within a single state. These boundaries may prove troublesome for several reasons. Particular data items may be available only for a state in total. If the region encompasses several states, data may not be comparable from one state to another. In this latter case, a service of the research unit would be to recognize these differences in the data series and, when possible, develop new data to fit the region. State planning agencies, on the other hand, need data for the entire state for which they are responsible and often provide data services to regional agencies which have the state or part of the state in their jurisdiction.

More specifically, state and regional planning agencies may differ in focus. For example, an agency may be involved in housing plans only. Thus, its data needs would revolve around not only geographic considerations, but also data relevant to housing. Population data would be needed, but to a lesser degree than in an agency which is involved in comprehensive planning.

Thus, there are three main issues which must be considered prior to and during the development of a basic research unit for a planning agency:

1. The budget, personnel, and equipment resources available.
2. The geographic jurisdiction of the agency.
3. The problem and policy focus of the agency.

These three issues are interdependent. The larger the geographic area (and population) and the more numerous the policy interests of the agency, the more resources will be necessary.

What the basic research unit provides

What does a basic research unit do? What are its products?

Data assembly and maintenance If the unit is to serve as support for population, housing, and economic studies and planning, at a minimum, the unit should be familiar with the sources of those data, their limitations, and availability. It should maintain data for its planning region and the surrounding areas if possible. There should be a mechanism for distributing new data as they become available and/or informing the planning agency's staff of data availability. This may take the form of inhouse memoranda or regularly published newsletters that present recent trends in key indicators. It may either consist of a listing of data available or a detailed analysis of the data.[1] In New Jersey, for example, the Department of Labor publishes a statistical source directory which lists all of the publications produced by all of the state's agencies, how they can be obtained, and what phone number to call for further information on each publication.[2] The State of Delaware, on the other hand, publishes a statistical abstract which reproduces data on varying subjects.

Data expertise In addition to data maintenance, the research unit should have expertise in the data themselves, what their limitations are and how they can be used. There are probably no data which are perfect. For example, rarely does a survey result in error-free data. Every 10 years the U.S. Bureau of the Census conducts a census of population. Millions of dollars are spent to collect data on every single person residing in the United States. However, the bureau recognizes that it misses persons. Persons are not counted for several reasons: among them, the fact that some people simply do not want to be counted. In addition, a major portion of the data gathered during the census is collected on a sample basis, i.e., only a percentage of the population is asked certain questions which are not asked of the entire population. These answers are then "inflated" or assumed to represent the entire population. The tabulations from the sampled responses have statistical validity in varying degrees. Despite these "imperfections" in census data, censuses remain among the most important sources of data for planning. What must be recognized in using census data, or any data, is that all data have limitations. Knowledge of those limitations is the business of a basic research unit.

Other important characteristics of all data are the assumptions made in the process of developing the data. Some data are derived not from censuses or surveys, but from mathematical procedures or techniques. Equations are designed to produce estimates or projections based on various theories. While the theories may be sound, they are always based on assumptions about the relationship of past to future trends, and reality does not necessarily follow assumptions. This does not mean that data derived from mathematical procedures are unsound, but that the data must be used within that framework of assumptions in which they were developed.

Another common limitation is the definition of terms or concepts. There are many sources of employment data, for example. Not all of them are comparable. It is very important that the differences be recognized. Does the data source present data on the number of jobs in an area, the number of people employed

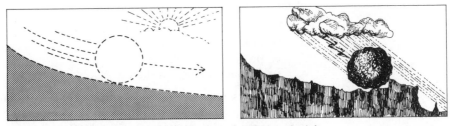

Figure 11–1   In the absence of reliable data, the plan on the left may turn out to be the reality on the right.

in an area, or the number of working people who all live in the same area, but do not necessarily also work there?

In conjunction with providing files, a responsibility of the basic research unit is to be knowledgeable of demographic, housing, and economic trends in general and for the planning agency's geographic jurisdiction in particular. This involves keeping abreast of the literature in professional journals and, again, examining data as they become available. A later section of this chapter will briefly overview demographic and economic trends at the national level as an example of some of the general knowledge that a basic research unit should have in its repertoire.

Data analysis and projection   The basic research unit's function also extends to knowledge of the technique of data analysis and projection. The following exchanges are typical:

Planner 1:   There are so many data available; how can I use them?
Researcher 1:   What do you want to use them for?

Planner 2:   I'd like all the population data you have.
Researcher 2:   What is the question you are trying to answer?

Obviously, no one person can know all of the ways data can be used, but the best approach is for the planner and the researcher to discuss the planning project. Through a give-and-take process the researcher can assist the planner with data needs. By discovering what the planner is attempting to do, the researcher can suggest the best data sources, explain their limitations, and provide guidance in their analysis.

Finally, depending upon resources, a basic research unit may be involved in producing new data where they do not presently exist. This was mentioned previously in connection with data limitations. For example, data may be available only from decennial censuses and/or only for a geographic region larger than the planning region. Techniques have been developed, ranging from simple to complex, for producing data estimates. Many have been well documented and can be operationalized via either hand calculation or computer modeling. Some of these techniques are described more fully later in this chapter.

In summary, the major responsibilities of a basic research unit are: data assembly, maintenance, and dissemination; knowledge of data limitations and trends; and skills in data analysis and data development. The next section will discuss a national program already in existence in the United States—the State Data Center program. Although this program is not a complete example of a basic research unit, its functions parallel those of one, and in several states it operates through a state planning agency.

The state data center program

The State Data Center program is a federal-state cooperative program that was initiated in the late 1970s by the U.S. Bureau of the Census. Not all of the states are presently involved in the program, but a majority are. The primary objectives of the State Data Center program are:

1. To increase the awareness, accessibility, and uses of census products.
2. To provide technical expertise.
3. To provide data anlaysis.
4. To conduct training in the use of census products.

Several states are attempting to go beyond census data and incorporate other data sources, including state produced statistics, in their programs.

Organizationally, the programs vary by state. In general, there is a lead agency,

Statistics and the computer   The broad river of thought that today is known as theoretical statistics cannot be traced back to a single source springing identifiably from the rock. Rather is it the confluence, over two centuries, of a number of tributary streams from many different regions. Probability theory originated at the gaming table; the collection of statistical facts began with state requirements of soldiers and money; marine insurance began with the wrecks and piracy of the ancient Mediterranean; modern studies of mortality have their roots in the plague pits of the seventeenth century; the theory of correllation in biology, the theory of experimental design in agriculture, the theory of times series in economics and meterology, the theories of component analysis and ranking in psychology, and the theory of chi-square methods in sociology.

Highly structured data gathering, based on reliable methods for constructing and testing survey samples, has come to the fore in recent decades for many uses, including public opinion polling, market projections, estimates of employment and unemployment, and the Consumer Price Index.

Statistics is the essence of the inductive method, of drawing inferences from data. The greater and more complicated the data, however, the more difficult it is to sort them out, apply appropriate measures, and draw out probabilities that are valid and reliable—that is, that can be trusted. This is where the computer has remade statistics in the past generation.

The computer takes the data input, often itself highly automated; places the data in storage/memory; applies control through stored programs; processes the data by arithmetic, logic, and control (the stored program); and produces printed reports and other kinds of output. The speed and capacity of the computer are well known, but it is the ability to perform complicated sequences with huge masses of data under the control of a stored program and memory that distinguish the computer from the calculator.

In essence, "Because the computer can compare, it can make decisions; using prescribed criteria, it can select from programmed alternatives."

Source: First paragraph excerpted from David L. Sills, ed., *International Encyclopedia of the Social Sciences,* Vol. 15 (New York: The Macmillan Company & The Free Press, © 1968, Crowell, Collier and Macmillan, Inc.), p. 224; balance abstracted from *Encyclopaedia Britannica*, Macropaedia (Chicago: Encyclopaedia Britannica, Inc., 15th ed., 1981), Vol. 4, pp. 1047–53, and Vol. 17, p. 615.

often within either a state planning agency or a university research center, which could be considered a basic research unit. There may be secondary participants, such as university computer centers and/or state libraries, which attempt to serve and coordinate the needs of particular data users. A network of affiliates distributed around the state is established to serve the local data user. These affiliates are already existing agencies, such as county planning boards. Federal depository libraries and regional planning commissions may also be a part of the program.

The lead agency receives all census data for its state directly from the Bureau of the Census and is responsible for disseminating them to its affiliate network, which in turn disseminates them to local users. Depending on the capabilities of members of the network and on the nature of the data, the data are distributed on computer tape or hard copy, automatically or upon request, and free or on a cost-reimbursable basis. Sometimes the lead agency selects summary data items from massive data files and repackages them for general distribution. The selection is based on the agency's awareness of data demands.

Most State Data Centers issue periodic newsletters. The frequency and content of these vary, but they tend to include information on data availability, as well as brief analyses of data and trends. Some State Data Centers are involved in demographic and/or economic research, the basis of which are published and usually available upon request.

Data requests received in writing, by phone, and in person are answered by all State Data Center network members, as are requests for technical assistance. Training in the uses and applications of data is provided by State Data Centers in conjunction with the Census Bureau in the form of workshops and on a one-on-one basis. Some State Data Centers also sponsor conferences which focus on demographic and economic issues in the state.[3]

Although the State Data Center program may be independent of many regional and state planning agencies, its usefulness to these agencies, particularly to these agencies' research units, is considerable. State Data Centers can not only provide data, but they can provide the technical assistance which planning agencies may need.

The remainder of this chapter is dedicated to presenting the reader with a general background in the three areas which are of importance to any basic research unit within a state or regional planning agency:

1. Data sources.
2. Population, housing, and economic trends.
3. Analytic techniques.

Sources of data

Among the major responsibilities of a planning agency's basic research unit are the maintenance of data and expertise in data sources. This section will describe several data sources which should be part of such a unit's library. It is recognized that the list is not definitive, but if a collection of all or most of the sources described is maintained, the research unit will have a good basic collection of data for planning purposes.[4]

Almost all of the data sources presented are federal sources. The decision to select primarily federal sources was based on several criteria. Utilizing federal sources, where possible, alleviates the problems of comparability. A data item for one state, chosen from a particular federal source, will be comparable in definition, concept, and derivation to the same data item from the same source for a different state. In many cases data published at the federal level are developed in cooperation with varying types of state agencies. The states themselves may also publish these data, but because these data may differ by state, the best approach, at first, is to consult the federal publications. In addition, federal data sources are readily available, usually for a charge, often on an individual or subscription basis, and many times single copies can be obtained at regional offices of the issuing agency located around the country. Federal data sources can also be reviewed at all federal depository libraries.

With few exceptions, the sources suggested are available in printed form. Additional information on each source can be obtained by contacting the issuing agency.

Population data

The major sources of population statistics are the U.S. Bureau of the Census and the state agencies. State and regional planners should not only become familiar with these sources, but should maintain a collection of the data. All of the data discussed below, while potentially representing a substantial library, are recommended as basic references.

The most vital source of population data is probably the Bureau of the Census, which conducts a decennial census of population, a monthly population survey, a program of population estimates and projections, and a number of other periodic surveys related to population characteristics.

The 1980 census of population and housing   The U.S. Constitution provides for a census of the population every 10 years, initially established as a basis for apportionment of members of the House of Representatives among the states. The census of population is a complete count. That is, an attempt is made to account for every person, for each person's residence, and for other characteristics (sex, age, family relationships, etc.). Since the 1940 census, however, some data have been obtained from representative samples of the population rather than from a complete count.

Recently the 1980 census was undertaken. Because data from this census will be released probably throughout the years of 1980 to 1984 and because the data from this census will be heavily relied upon by planners and policymakers, it is appropriate to discuss this census in some detail.

Figure 11-2 lists the subject items included in the 1980 census and delineates them by whether the data were collected on a 100 percent or sample basis.

Three major media will be utilized to disseminate the data: printed reports, magnetic computer tapes, and microfiche. The major portion of the results of the 1980 census will be provided in a set of five summary tape files (STFs) or tabulation counts. These STFs are designed to provide data with much greater subject and geographic detail than is possible or desirable to publish in printed reports. These tapes will not provide information on individuals but will consist of tabulations of responses by geographic areas. The first two STFs contain the subject items collected on a 100 percent basis in the census. STF3, STF4, and STF5 contain the subject items collected on a sample basis in the census and will also generally include sample data on the 100 percent items for purposes of cross-classification.

A substantial amount of data will be available in printed reports. A listing of the printed reports available from the 1980 census is given in Figure 11-3.

The Bureau of the Census will produce microfiche of some data tables that will not be printed. Others will be printed. As of this writing, two types of microfiche are being planned: (1) microfiche of selected reports, e.g., Block Statistics, Detailed Population Characteristics, and Metropolitan Housing Characteristics: and (2) microfiche of selected summary tape files, e.g., STF IA and STF IC.

Other census population products   Many statistical studies are undertaken each year by the Bureau of the Census which result in valuable references for state and regional planners. Among them are the Current Population Survey (CPS) and the Federal-State Cooperative Program for Population Estimates (FSCPE).

The CPS is a monthly survey, conducted largely to produce labor force data for the Bureau of Labor Statistics. However, the March CPS, which is also known as the Annual Demographic File, includes additional information on demographic characteristics of the nation's population. While every month's CPS data are available on computer tape, the Bureau of the Census produces a series of demographic reports from the March CPS. These reports are commonly referred to as the P-20 publication series and are available on an individual or subscription basis. Most of the data are for the nation, but some data are presented for regions and states.

The Federal-State Cooperative Program for Population Estimates was the first cooperative program established between the Bureau of the Census and the states. States join on a voluntary basis with the Governor of each state appointing

100 percent

Population	Housing
Household relationship	Number of units at address
Sex	Access to unit
Race	Complete plumbing facilities
Age	Number of rooms
Marital status	Tenure (whether unit is owned or rented)
Spanish/Hispanic origin or descent	Condominium identification
	Value of home (owner-occupied units and condominium)
	Contract rent (renter-occupied units)
	Vacant for rent, for sale, etc.; and duration of vacancy

Sample items*

Population	Housing
School enrollment	Type of unit and units in structure
Educational attainment	Stories in building and presence of elevator
State or foreign country of birth	Year built
Citizenship and year of immigration	Year moved into this house
Current language and English proficiency	Acreage and crop sales
Ancestry	Source of water
Place of residence five years ago	Sewage disposal
Activity five years ago	Heating equipment
Veteran status and period of service	Fuels used for house heating, water heating, and cooking
Presence of disability or handicap	
Children ever born	Costs of utilities and fuels
Marital history	Complete kitchen facilities
Employment status last week	Number of bedrooms
Hours worked last week	Number of bathrooms
Place of work	Telephone
Travel time to work	Air conditioning
Means of transportation to work	Number of automobiles
Number of persons in carpool	Number of light trucks and vans
Year last worked	Homeowner shelter costs for mortgage, real estate taxes, and hazard insurance
Industry	
Occupation	
Type of employment	
Number of weeks looking for work in 1979	
Amount of income in 1979 by source	

*For most areas of the county in 1980, one out of every six housing units or households received the sample form. Areas estimated to contain 2,500 or fewer persons in 1980 had a 3-out-of-every-6 sampling rate, which is required in order to obtain reliable statistics needed for participation in certain federal programs.

Figure 11-2   Items included in the 1980 Census.

the cooperating state agency. The objective of this program is the development and publication of estimates of the population of local areas for intercensal periods using uniform procedures standardized for data input and method. These data are published in the P-26 series of the Census Bureau, and most cooperating state agencies also publish the data.

Population data sources in brief   A brief list of population data sources is given in Figure 11-4. Not all of these have been previously described because in some cases their relevance to planning is not as consequential as the other sources.

Title of publication	100% data	Sample data
Preliminary Population	●	
Advance Population	●	
Census Tracts	●	●
Summary Characteristics of Governmental Units	●	●
Characteristics of the Population	●	●
Number of Inhabitants	●	
General Population Characteristics	●	
General Social and Economic Characteristics	●	●
Detailed Population Characteristics	●	●
Characteristics of Housing Units	●	●
General Housing Characteristics	●	●
Detailed Housing Characteristics	●	●
Metropolitan Housing Characteristics	●	●
Subject Reports	●	●

Figure 11–3   1980 Census printed reports.

These additional sources can usually be found in libraries, and the need for a research unit to maintain them, particularly if there are space limitations, is minimal. However, they are useful at times, and planning researchers should be familiar with them.

Housing data

Sources of housing data that are useful to policy makers, planners, or researchers for planning programs will be described in this section. These include federal sources as well as information available from private companies. Detailed information about national housing characteristics, trends, and the operation of the national housing market is available from many sources. At the national or regional level, major sources of recent housing data are the 1970 and 1980 censuses and the Annual Housing Survey. The decennial census was described in some detail earlier in this chapter and should be consulted for coverage of housing data items.

Annual housing survey   Current housing data are available from the Annual Housing Survey. This survey, initiated in 1973, includes two separate data collection efforts in which generally the same questions are asked. The first is a national level survey; the second is a survey of a sample of housing units in 60 metropolitan areas. The national level reports present data on urban and rural characteristics for the United States and regions and financial characteristics by indicators of housing and neighborhood quality, cross-classifying housing quality items by value, rent, and income categories. National level reports are issued annually in the H-151 series.

Data source	Issuing agency	Availability
1980 Census Data	U.S. Bureau of the Census	contact Census Bureau
P-20: Population Characteristics	U.S. Bureau of the Census	subscription
P-23: Special Studies	U.S. Bureau of the Census	subscription
P-25: Population Estimates and Projections	U.S. Bureau of the Census	subscription
P-26: Federal State Cooperative Program for Population Estimates	U.S. Bureau of the Census	subscription
Statistical Abstract of the United States	U.S. Bureau of the Census	annual
United States Life Tables	National Center for Health Statistics	single issuance
Series 20: Mortality Data	National Center for Health Statistics	irregular
Series 21: Natality, Marriage, and Divorce Data	National Center for Health Statistics	irregular
Vital Statistics of the U.S.	National Center for Health Statistics	annual

Figure 11–4   Population data sources.

Current housing and construction surveys   Current information on housing characteristics, vacancies, and construction is available in several Bureau of the Census reports. These reports are based on data collected through the Housing Vacancy Survey, the Survey of Market Absorption, and several construction surveys. Data from these surveys are usually published only at the national and regional levels.

Mortgage lending and commitment surveys   This national level survey conducted by the U.S. Department of HUD provides monthly information on the number of mortgage transactions for construction and long-term loans by five property types: one- to four-family homes, multifamily homes, multifamily properties, nonfarm nonresidential properties, and farm properties.

Private mortgage insurance activity survey   This survey, also conducted by the U.S. Department of HUD, covers all private mortgage insurers and provides monthly information on the number of applications, new loans, and their dollar amount. No data below the national level are reported.

Private sources   Besides federal government sources of data, many national associations and private sources can also provide further information about the national market. Often there is a charge for the information or a subscription fee for the service. In some cases the statistics are derived from actual surveys or current records. In other cases the data are based on national trends and projections of census data.

Several private firms, known as summary tape processing centers, provide automated census data services and prepare updates of census data. A list of summary tape processing centers and the services they offer can be obtained from the Census Bureau's Data User Services Division.

Housing in brief   All of the data sources suggested in Figure 11-5 are available on a single issue or subscription basis. Most of them provide data only for the nation as a whole. If the planning agency's resources are small it may choose not to purchase these publications, and rely instead on regional Census Bureau offices or federal depository libraries as the need arises to consult these sources.

Employment data

The primary types of employment data used in economic studies are: historical employment trends in an area, historical employment trends in the larger region or state, and employment projections for the larger region. The data should be disaggregated to at least the Major Divisions of the Standard Industrial Classification (SIC) code. The SIC code is a data filing scheme that classifies all different kinds of economic activity in the United States and periodically publishes counts of employment and other measures of economic activity for each category in the system. In the SIC Manual, published by the U.S. Office of Management and Budget, all activity is first divided into 11 Major Divisions. Each Major Division is divided into subareas called Major Groups. Each Major Group is assigned a two digit code number. Each Major Group is then subdivided into Groups, each assigned a three digit code, and each Group is then subdivided into Industries. Each Industry is assigned a four digit numerical code. All economic establishments fall under one on these Industry designations. These four levels of detail in the SIC code can be summarized as follows: Major Divisions

Data source	Issuing agency	Availability
1980 Census Data	U.S. Bureau of the Census	contact Census Bureau
C20: Housing Starts	U.S. Bureau of the Census	subscription
C21: New Residential Construction in Selected SMSAs	U.S. Bureau of the Census	subscription
C22: Housing Completions	U.S. Bureau of the Census	subscription
C25: New One-Family Houses Sold and for Sale	U.S. Bureau of the Census	subscription
C27: Price Index of New One-Family Houses Sold	U.S. Bureau of the Census	subscription
C30: Value of New Construction in Place	U.S. Bureau of the Census	subscription
C40: Housing Authorized by Building Permits and Public Contracts	U.S. Bureau of the Census	subscription
C45: Housing Units Authorized for Demolition in Permit-Issuing Places	U.S. Bureau of the Census	subscription

Figure 11–5   Sources of housing data.

Levels of classification	Range of letter or numerical code	Examples:	
		Code	Short title
Major divisions	A through K	B	Mining
Major groups	01–99	10	Metal mining
Groups	011–999	104	Gold and silver ores
Industries	0111–9999	1041	Gold ores

Figure 11–6   The Standard Industrial Classification (SIC) code.

(A through K), Major Groups (01–99), Groups (011–999), and Industries (0111–9999). Figure 11-7 presents a complete list of the Major Divisions and Major Groups.

The number of jobs in an area is not equivalent to the number of workers. A count of jobs represents the number of employment positions; and, more than one position may be held by one person. On the other hand, a count of workers is the number of people working; and, a worker may have more than one job.

Establishment data are usually obtained via required reporting forms, such as U.S. Treasury Form 941, or direct surveys of establishments. Establishment data usually represent, therefore, a count of jobs. In contrast, household data are usually compiled from sample questionnaires sent to residents of an area (who indicate type and location of their employment) and represent the number of workers. Some sources provide separate tables covering each of these, while others provide information covering one type. For example, *County Business Patterns* contains the number of jobs at establishments located in a county; however, *Employment and Earnings* provides both the number of jobs at establishments located in various geographical delineations (counties and labor market areas) and the number of workers in such areas. Figure 11-8 briefly describes the major sources of published employment data.

Other economic data

Measures of economic activity other than employment can be secured from the sources listed. For example, *Employment and Earnings*, as the title implies, contains data on earnings. In addition it contains, for most of the geographic areas delineated in Figure 11-8, data on the labor force: participation rates, unemployment rates, occupation, and industry.

Another indicator of economic activity is income. Income statistics take several forms. The two major sources of income data are the Bureau of Census and the Bureau of Economic Analysis. For the most part, and with the exception of decennial census data, income data are published in detail for the nation but in less detail for the states. The Census Bureau publishes various types of income data—household, family, individual—in its P-60 series, which is available on a single issue or subscription basis. Additional data for more geographic areas are available on computer tape. The Bureau of Economic Analysis publishes its data in the periodical *Survey of Current Business*. Substantially more data are available on computer tape than are published.

The analysis of trends in population and employment

As we suggested at the beginning of this chapter, simply having lots of data on the shelf or on file does not represent sufficient service for a basic research

SIC code	Major division Major group (2-digit code)	SIC code	Major division Major group (2-digit code)
A	**Agriculture, Forestry, and Fishing**	**G**	**Retail Trade**
01	Agricultural Production—Crops	52	Building Materials and Garden Supplies
02	Agricultural Production—Livestock		
07	Agricultural Services	53	General Merchandise Stores
08	Forestry	54	Food Stores
09	Fishing, Hunting, and Trapping	55	Automotive Dealers and Service Stations
B	**Mining**		
10	Metal Mining	56	Apparel and Accessory Stores
11	Anthracite Mining	57	Furniture and Home Furnishings Stores
12	Bituminous Coal and Lignite Mining		
13	Oil and Gas Extraction	58	Eating and Drinking Places
14	Nonmetallic Minerals, Except Fuels	59	Miscellaneous Retail
C	**Construction**	**H**	**Finance, Insurance, and Real Estate**
15	General Building Contractors	60	Banking
16	Heavy Construction Contractors	61	Credit Agencies Other Than Banks
17	Special Trade Contractors	62	Security, Commodity Brokers and Services
D	**Manufacturing**		
20	Food and Kindred Products	63	Insurance Carriers
21	Tobacco Manufactures	64	Insurance Agents, Brokers and Service
22	Textile Mill Products		
23	Apparel and Other Textile Products	65	Real Estate
24	Lumber and Wood Products	66	Combined Real Estate, Insurance, etc.
25	Furniture and Fixtures		
26	Paper and Allied Products	67	Holding and Other Investment Offices
27	Printing and Publishing	**I**	**Services**
28	Chemicals and Allied Products	70	Hotels and Other Lodging Places
29	Petroleum and Coal Products	72	Personal Services
30	Rubber and Miscellaneous Plastics Products	73	Business Services
		75	Auto Repair, Services, and Garages
31	Leather and Leather Products	76	Miscellaneous Repair Services
32	Stone, Clay, and Glass Products	78	Motion Pictures
33	Primary Metal Industries	79	Amusement and Recreation Services
34	Fabricated Metal Products	80	Health Services
35	Machinery, Except Electrical	81	Legal Services
36	Electric and Electronic Equipment	82	Educational Services
37	Transportation Equipment	83	Social Services
38	Instruments and Related Products	84	Museums, Botanical, Zoological Gardens
39	Miscellaneous Manufacturing Industries		
		86	Membership Organizations
E	**Transportation and Public Utilities**	88	Private Households
40	Railroad Transportation	89	Miscellaneous Services
41	Local and Interurban Passenger Transit	**J**	**Public Administration**
		91	Executive, Legislative, and General
42	Trucking and Warehousing	92	Justice, Public Order, and Safety
43	U.S. Postal Service	93	Finance, Taxation and Monetary Policy
44	Water Transportation		
45	Transportation by Air	94	Administration of Human Resources
46	Pipe Lines, Except Natural Gas	95	Environmental Quality and Housing
47	Transportation Services	96	Administration of Economic Programs
48	Communication	97	National Security and International Affairs
49	Electric, Gas, and Sanitary Services		
F	**Wholesale Trade**	**K**	**Nonclassifiable Establishments**
50	Wholesale Trade—Durable Goods	99	Nonclassifiable Establishments
51	Wholesale Trade—Nondurable Goods		

Figure 11–7   The 1972 Standard Industrial Classification (SIC): major divisions and major groups.

Source	Publishing agency	Technique	Coverage		
			SIC-level	Geographic scale	Type of employment
County Business Patterns (CBP)	U.S. Dept. of Commerce, Bureau of the Census (annual)	U.S. Treasury Form 941 and special multi-unit survey	1,2,3,4-digit for all	Nation, state, county, SMSA, large cities	Nonfarm wage and salary, federal civilian government
Employment and Earnings	U.S. Dept. of Labor, Bureau of Labor Statistics (monthly)	Employment reports, household interviews, administrative, statistics	1 and 2-digit for U.S.; 1-digit for all others	Nation, state, SMSA, labor market areas	Nonfarm wage and salary, civilian government
Employment and Wages	U.S. Dept. of Labor, Bureau of Labor Statistics (quarterly)	Employers tax reports	1,2, and 3-digit for U.S.; 1-digit for states	Nation, state, region	Nonfarm wage and salary, civilian government
Economic Censuses	U.S. Dept. of Commerce, Bureau of the Census (quinquennially)	Employer survey and sample of tax returns	1,2,3 and 4-digit for Business and Manufacturing; 1,2,3,-digit for Mineral Industries	Nation, state, SMSA, counties, large cities	Nonfarm wage and salary
Monthly Labor Review	U.S. Dept. of Labor, Bureau of Labor Statistics (monthly)	(See Employment and Earnings)	1 and 2-digit	Nation	Nonfarm wage and salary, civilian government

Figure 11–8 Comparison of employment data sources.

effort. Intimate knowledge of the data is required if they are to be used intelligently when they are needed. The best means for gaining that knowledge is through a continuous or periodic program of general data analysis to discover and keep track of trends and patterns in the data that apply to your state or region. The dissemination of these general trend studies is an important service to the larger audience of which the research unit is a part as well as to the general public. We turn now to an examination of these general trends in population and employment at the national level in order to demonstrate what we mean.[5]

Population growth patterns

The major features of population growth patterns over the past 30 years are a deceleration of the growth rate and subnational population redistribution. Redistribution has taken place among the nation's four regions (Northeast, North Central, South, and West), between metropolitan and nonmetropolitan areas, and within metropolitan areas. Within these 30 years, the decade of the 1970s has been one of trend reversal.

National population growth and regional redistribution Over the entire 30 year span, from 1950 to 1980, the population of the nation increased by more than 75 million. However, the pace of growth has been far from constant. The rate

Table 11–1   Total resident population of the United States: 1950 to 1980 (in thousands).

Year	Decade	Population	Population change Number	Population change Percent
1950		151,326		
	1950–1960		27,997	18.5
1960		179,323		
	1960–1970		23,889	13.3
1970		203,212		
	1970–1980		23,293	11.5
1980		226,505		

Note: As of April 1. Not adjusted for undercounting.   Source; U.S. Bureau of the Census, U.S. Census of Population: 1950, 1960, 1970, and 1980.

has steadily declined. Table 11-1 shows the total resident population of the United States from 1950 to 1980, as well as the changes for each of these periods.

Traditional growth areas—the Northeast region, metropolitan areas, and particularly, the large metropolitan centers—have, in the last decade (1970–1980) experienced a slowdown in population growth, if not a decrease in population size. Table 11-2 shows the population changes that occurred on a regional and divisional basis between 1950 and 1980. Between 1950 and 1960, population growth was relatively evenly shared (in total numbers) among the major regional clusters, with the exception of the Northeast. Between 1960 and 1970, regional

Table 11–2   Regional growth patterns: 1950 to 1980.

Region and division	Population (in thousands) 1950	1960	1970	1980
Northeast region	39,478	44,678	49,061	49,137
New England	9,314	10,509	11,847	12,348
Middle Atlantic	30,164	34,168	37,218	36,788
North central region	44,461	51,619	56,590	58,854
East north central	30,399	36,225	40,263	41,670
West north central	14,061	15,394	16,328	17,184
South region	47,197	54,961	62,813	75,349
South Atlantic	21,182	25,959	30,679	36,943
East south central	11,477	12,050	12,808	14,663
West south central	14,538	16,951	19,326	23,743
West region	20,190	28,053	34,838	43,165
Mountain	5,075	6,855	8,290	11,368
Pacific	15,115	21,198	26,458	31,797
U.S. Total	**151,326**	**179,311**	**203,302**	**226,505**

Note: As of April 1.   Source: U.S. Bureau of the Census, U.S. Census of Population: 1950, 1960, 1970, and 1980.

Table 11–3   Metropolitan–Nonmetropolitan growth patterns: 1960 to 1980.

Classification	Population (in thousands)		
	1960	**1970**	**1980***
Metropolitan	128,841	150,883	165,183
Over 3,000,000	45,766	52,861	53,707
1,000,000 to 3,000,000	32,403	39,341	44,007
500,000 to 1,000,000	19,386	22,548	25,054
250,000 to 500,000	15,838	18,262	21,335
Less than 250,000	15,448	17,870	21,080
Nonmetropolitan	50,470	52,419	60,296
U.S. total	**179,311**	**203,302**	**225,479**

*Figures in this column are preliminary; the final tabulations were not available as of this writing.

Source: U.S. Bureau of the Census, "Population Profile of the United States: 1980," Current Population Reports, Series P–20, No. 363 (Washington, D.C.: U.S. Government Printing Office, 1981).

disparities began to come into focus, with the Northeast and North Central regions differentiated from the South and West. Most population growth since 1970 has been in the sunbelt.

The movement away from an agricultural nation to an industrialized one resulted in the metropolitan areas becoming the major growth areas over the past 50 years. However, data for 1960 through 1980 (Table 11-3) show how the nonmetropolitan areas have become the foci of population growth.

The nation's major cities have been the center of attention during the 1970s, among other reasons because of their population losses. For the first time, the central cities in total are not gaining population (Table 11-4). While nonmetropolitan growth rates have moved above those of metropolitan areas, the suburban rings, although being pressed hard by nonmetropolitan areas, still represent the fastest growing territories of America.

Components of population change   While total population growth and redistribution have implications of their own for planning, the three components of population change—births, deaths, and migration—have important ramifications as well.

Table 11–4   Intrametropolitan growth patterns: 1970 to 1980.

Classification	Population (in thousands)		Change 1970–1980	% change 1970–1980
	1970	**1980**		
In SMSAs (318)	153,694	169,405	15,711	10.2
In central cities (429)	67,850	67,930	80	0.1
Outside central cities	85,843	101,475	15,631	18.2
Nonmetropolitan	49,608	57,100	7,492	15.1
U.S. total	**203,302**	**226,505**	**23,203**	**11.4**

Note: Numbers in parentheses represent the total number of SMSAs and total number of central cities, respectively, as defined in 1981 by the U.S. Office of Management and Budget.

Source: U.S. Bureau of the Census, "75 Percent of Population Now Lives in Metropolitan Areas," Press Release CB38–113 (12 July 1981).

Year or period	Rate
1940–44	2.523
1945–49	2.985
1950–54	3.337
1955–59	3.690
1960–64	3.459
1965–69	2.636
1970–74	2.106
1975	1.799
1976	1.768
1977	1.826
1978	1.800
1979	1.840
1980	1.875

Table 11–5   U.S. fertility rate: 1940 to 1980.

Source: See Table 11–3.

By examining a time series of any one of these components, certain trends become readily apparent. (See Tables 11-5 and 11-6.) In particular, considering total fertility rates (this rate is the sum of the age-specific birth rates of women over their reproductive life-span) as observed from 1950 to the present indicate two major historical phenomena: the baby boom of the 1950s and the baby bust of the mid-1960s and later.

The number of births reached a low in 1973 and then began to increase, with the most rapid increase occurring since 1976. The recent increase in numbers of births has been much more rapid than the increase in the total fertility rate, with the 1976–1980 rate of increase in births being twice the increase in the fertility rates. The increasing number of births is the result of both a slight upturn in fertility rates and a larger number of women who are currently in their childbearing years. It is interesting to note that, even if the present below-replacement birth rates were to persist for some time, the population of the United States would still continue to grow by natural increase until well into the twenty-first century.

The decline in death rates is a continuance of the trend in death rates all through the twentieth century. On the other hand, the reduction or slowdown in the number of deaths is relatively new and, in part, is accounted for by the slowdown in population growth.

Migration is the third component of population change and has been playing an increasing role in producing population differentiation across the country. Birth and death activity does vary by area; however, there has been a trend of convergence to the national averages. As birth rates and death rates become more similar, the growth of one area vis-à-vis that of another (the area's change in population, both in terms of direction and in terms of scale) becomes more contingent upon migration. The recent patterns of population growth away from the Northeast and to the South and West, for example, have in large part been caused by migration. The turnaround in metropolitan versus nonmetropolitan growth can also be accounted for by migration, as more persons moved *from* metropolitan areas than *to* them in the five-year period from 1975 to 1980.

Migration is a highly selective process; that is, people of certain characteristics have a tendency to migrate more or less than people of other characteristics. It is often induced by transitions from one stage of the life cycle to another. Migration rates vary sharply and with great regularity according to age groups. Historically, males have had a tendency to migrate more than females. However, as women participate more actively in the labor force, this may change.

Year	Deaths	Death rate
1950	1,452	9.6
1955	1,529	9.3
1960	1,712	9.5
1965	1,828	9.4
1970	1,927	9.4
1971	1,930	9.3
1972	1,965	9.4
1973	1,974	9.4
1974	1,935	9.1
1975	1,894	8.9
1976	1,910	8.9
1977	1,900	8.8
1978	1,925	8.8
1979	1,908	8.7
1980	1,984	8.9

Table 11–6   U.S. Deaths: 1950 to 1980 (in thousands).   Source: See Table 11–3.

Understanding the motivations for migrating and the types of people most likely to move is important for planners and policymakers. If certain trends in population growth of an area are to be maintained or changed, a planner needs to understand what is happening and to identify its causes in order to develop the appropriate plans.

Births, deaths, and migration also create structural changes in an area's population which have impacts on almost all phases of an area's economy and social well-being. At the national level, birth activity has played the major role in formulating age structure changes. It is this topic which is next addressed.

Age structure changes   The three major phenomena that have shaped the last 25 years and whose implications will be a basic part of the future are the baby boom, the baby bust, and the growth of the elderly population. The post–World War II baby boom began in 1945 with an approximate 20 percent increase in the number of live births over the number recorded in 1945. A steady increase in the annual number of births continued to 1957, the peak year of the postwar era. It is this group that has inserted a permanent but moving bulge into America's age structure, flooding the nation's school systems in the 1950s and 1960s, its higher education system in the 1960s and 1970s, and its job and housing markets in the 1970s and (we expect) 1980s. The subsequent baby bust, foreordained by definition, trails in the wake of the baby boom as it works its way through the country's age cohorts. Finally, the elderly—those 65 years of age and over—are increasing in number and significance, virtually doubling over the last 25 years. These phenomena tend to dominate the age structure shifts that have taken place in the United States from 1950 to 1980 and will continue their influence into the future.

The major patterns of change in population growth have important information implications in the area of housing. With large population growth comes increased housing demand. The implications of population change for the housing market become even more apparent when household size and family size changes are considered.

Household and family size changes   The total number of *households* increased by approximately the same percentage from 1960 to 1970 and from 1970 to 1980. For the same time periods, the number of *families* also increased by about 14

Year	Household size	Family size
1950	3.37	3.54
1955	3.33	3.59
1960	3.33	3.67
1965	3.29	3.70
1970	3.14	3.58
1975	2.94	3.42
1980	2.75	3.28

Table 11–7   Household and family size: 1950 to 1980.

Source: See Table 11–3.

percent. These increases were substantially greater than the total population increase and can be accounted for by the declines in both household and family sizes. As can be seen in Table 11-7, the size of households and families has decreased dramatically from 1950 to 1980. Changes in living arrangements, delayed childbearing, lower fertility, and higher divorce rates are among the factors accounting for these decreases. The increasing pressures on the housing market are caused by these changes. The baby boom generation entered its prime household and family formation stage during the 1970s and this pressed housing supply even further.

Of course, demographic phenomena are but one area of expertise with which a research unit should develop. Because it is an area of widespread import, substantial emphasis has been placed on it. Employment trends are of significant importance also and will be briefly highlighted.

Trends in employment

While the greatest number of jobs in 1975 was still in the manufacturing industries, by 1980 the wholesale and retail trade sector had taken the lead. As Table 11-8 reveals, the manufacturing sector has been losing its prominence steadily over the 1960–1980 period. And although the wholesale and retail trade sector has increased its share of total employment considerably, it is the service industries that have shown the most rapid rate of increase.

Within the nation there have been regional shifts in employment, as in population. Historically, the Northeast and North Central regions have been the nation's employment centers. By 1970, the South had captured the largest share of the nation's employment. Throughout the decade, the shares of the Northeast and North Central regions continually declined, while the South's and West's shares expanded.

Other economic trends

Employment, of course, is but one measure of an area's economic activity. Others include labor force patterns. In terms of labor force, there are three prominent patterns which deserve a planner's attention and of which a planning agency's research unit should be aware:

1. The labor force participation rates of women.
2. The trend toward early retirement.
3. The unemployment rate, particularly of youths and minorities.

Since 1950, the labor force participation rate of females has increased substantially from over 31 percent to 52 percent in 1980. During the same time period, 1950–1980, this rate for the total U.S. population fluctuated around 59

Table 11–8   U.S. nonagricultural employment: 1960 to 1980.

Classification	1960	1965	1970	1975	1980
	Numbers in thousands				
Mining	712	632	623	752	1,025
Construction	2,926	3,232	3,588	3,525	4,469
Manufacturing	16,796	18,062	19,367	18,323	20,361
Transportation and public utilities	4,004	4,036	4,515	4,542	5,156
Wholesale and retail trade	11,391	12,716	15,040	17,060	20,573
Finance, insurance and real estate	2,629	2,977	3,645	4,165	5,162
Services	7,378	9,036	11,548	13,892	17,741
Government	8,353	10,074	12,554	14,686	15,612
U.S. total	**54,189**	**60,765**	**70,880**	**76,945**	**90,657**
	Percent distribution				
Mining	1.3	1.0	0.9	1.0	1.1
Construction	5.4	5.3	5.1	4.6	4.9
Manufacturing	31.0	29.7	27.3	23.8	22.5
Transportation and public utilities	7.4	6.6	6.4	5.9	5.7
Wholesale and retail trade	21.0	20.9	21.2	22.2	22.7
Finance, insurance and real estate	4.9	4.9	5.1	5.4	5.7
Services	13.6	14.9	16.3	18.1	19.6
Government	15.4	16.6	17.7	19.1	17.8
U.S. total	**100.0**	**100.0**	**100.0**	**100.0**	**100.0**

Source: U.S. Department of Labor, Bureau of Labor Statistics,
   Employment & Earnings, annual.

and 60 percent, until the late 1950s, when it began to slowly but steadily increase to just over 64 percent in 1980. Of the females, the most dramatic increase in labor force participation rates was exhibited by married women, increasing from approximately 25 percent in 1950 to over 50 percent in 1980.

Referring again to labor force participation data, the patterns of early retirement can be documented. Participation rates for all males have decreased with the exception of a few age groups. However, the most significant declines in these rates have been for males aged 55–64 years and 65 years and over. For the former group, the labor force participation rate has dropped from 85 percent in 1960 to about 72 percent in 1980; for the latter group, the comparative decrease has been from 32 percent to 19 percent. Females 54–65 years of age, on the other hand, have experienced an increase in labor force participation from 37 percent to 42 percent, while females 65 years of age and over have declined in labor force participation from 11 percent in 1960 to slightly over 7 percent in 1980.

Unemployment has fluctuated since 1950, with a low of 3 percent in the early 1950s to a high of 8.5 percent in 1975. Unemployment of the young, particularly those under 20 years of age, and of minorities has steadily increased during the recent past. Additional indices of economic activity include various measures of income—total personal income, disposable income, household income, family income, per capita income, etc. Trends in these measures will not be discussed here.

These economic patterns—employment, labor force participation patterns, unemployment—while briefly overviewed only in a national setting, play a significant role in planning. For example, consider a state planning agency that is attempting to attract industry to the state. Before locating or relocating in an area, an industry needs to know about the area's labor force. In particular, how does it compare to the nation and the surrounding area? A planner should be able to confer with a research unit and learn how the labor force of interest is faring. The research unit must have at its fingertips a general knowledge of these economic patterns and the data to substantiate these trends.

Techniques of projection and data extension

When needed data are not available, the staff of a basic research unit may be called upon to develop new data from existing sources. This is particularly the case when the need is for intercensal population estimates and projections of future population and employment levels.

Population estimates are produced by the U.S. Bureau of the Census for the nation, states, counties, and subcounty units. For many states, these estimates are produced in conjunction with states agencies through the Federal-State Cooperative Program for Population Estimates (FSCPE).[6] A research unit in a state planning agency should be familiar with the techniques used for two reasons: (1) it may be the agency assigned to work with the Bureau of the Census or (2) it may be called upon to utilize the resulting estimates and to evaluate them for reasonableness. A research unit in a regional planning agency, on the other hand, should be acquainted with these procedures for an additional reason—the planning region may not be coterminous with areas for which estimates are available; therefore, it would need to develop the estimates appropriate to the region's boundaries. These estimates (those produced by a regional planning agency) should be consistent with those developed through the FSCPE.

Population projections, as well as employment projections, are produced by a variety of public and private agencies. Future levels of either are often referred to as predictions, forecasts, or projections. However, most researchers tend to reject the terms "prediction" and "forecast." Rather, they prefer "projection" which reflects the extension of past trends, based on reasonable assumptions. Projections of population and employment are used by all planning agencies. Some examples of their use include capital facility planning, such as water treatment plants; transportation planning; housing; educational planning; and health care planning. As with estimates, a research unit may be assigned the task of either analyzing or producing projections. Thus it is essential to be familiar with the state of the art of projection techniques.

Population estimation methods

The four methods most frequently used for estimating population are: (1) the housing unit method; (2) ratio correlation; (3) component method II; and (4) administrative records.

Housing unit method This method begins with the permanent year-round housing inventory from the Census as a base and estimates annual postcensus changes in year-round housing units through the use of reported building permits (adjusting for units authorized but never constructed) and demolition data; surveys of mobile-home parks; and adjustments for segments of public housing and conversions, such as from seasonal to permanent units, that are not covered by building permits. Occupancy rates and population per household from the decennial census are modified in accordance with observed changes as reported in U.S. Bureau of the Census surveys. These rates are then applied to the estimated current year-round housing inventory to arrive at household population.

Ratio correlation   This method employs a multiple correlation equation to relate changes in four data series to changes in population distribution. Typical variables used are passenger car registration, a two-year average of resident births, employment covered by unemployment insurance, and housing units.

Component II   This method utilizes reported births and deaths to determine the increment of natural increase, and elementary school enrollment to determine net migration of the under 65 year old household population. Special populations and those 65 years of age and over are estimated in a similar manner to the administrative records method described below.

Administrative records method   This is a component procedure developed by the U.S. Bureau of the Ceneus in which postcensus births, deaths, net migration, and special populations are estimated separately. Reported births and deaths, by residence, are used to estimate the natural increment. Migration rates are determined through federal income tax 1040 returns. Individual returns are matched for successive time periods to arrive at in-migrants, out-migrants, and nonmigrants by area. A net migration rate, which is developed from the difference between the in- and out-migration of taxpayers and their dependents, is then applied to the base year population to yield an estimate of net migration for all persons in the area. Adjustments for special populations, whose changes cannot be adequately reflected by the above components, are then made. Such special populations include in-migrants from abroad, members of the Armed Forces living in barracks, residents of institutions, and college students.

Population projection methods

While population estimates are crucial to analyzing what is currently occurring in an area, population projections are generally used to plan for the future. Estimates are usually the data base for projections. They are also used in the evaluation of projections.

National population projections, developed by the Bureau of the Census, are produced by a method which projects each of the components of population change—births, deaths, and migration. The Census Bureau includes a detailed discussion of method in its projections publications.

State population projections are prepared by many agencies—federal, regional, and state. Both the Bureau of the Census and U.S. Bureau of Economic Analysis prepare state population projections, using two different techniques. Some regional planning agencies prepare state level projections. And, many states prepare population projections of their own. Methods vary extensively, and the result can be confusing. To deal with this problem the Census Bureau initiated the development of a federal-state cooperative program for projections similar to the one for estimates.

This program includes the Bureau of the Census, the Bureau of Economic Analysis, and the states. The states are playing an active role in deciding the appropriate approaches for developing state population projections, who should be producing state projections, and the use to which population projections should be put.

The methods to be discussed here need not be restricted for use to any particular geographic area. All of these techniques can be and, in most cases, have been, used at the state level. In a few cases they have also been used at the national level. Often analysts find it useful to utilize the results of the simpler methods of analyzing the results of more complex models. In addition, many of the procedures to be described can also be employed to develop intercensal population estimates. With the aid of a computer, and in some cases, a hand calculator, a large number of alternative population projections can be produced for an area in a single day.

Some of the most frequently used models will be presented:

1. The linear model
2. The exponential
3. The modified exponential
4. The Gompertz curve
5. The comparative method
6. The ratio method
7. Cohort-component.

The linear (straight-line) model   This model is used when the population of the area being studied has exhibited a history of nearly equal absolute increments of population growth per year, decade, or other unit of time. The assumption is made that this pattern will persist into the future. There are two simple ways the data can be fitted to a straight line. One is simply to graph the data, to observe that, indeed, the historical trend is linear (not significantly curved or irregular), and to take a straightedge and a pencil and extend the line. The other approach is to calculate the numerical differences in absolute growth for the historical periods, to determine if they were equal, or nearly so, and then to add these increments in future time periods.

Exponential curve projections   This technique assumes that population tends to grow at a geometric rate. The exponential curve portrays this idea. Growth is at a constant rate or percentage, which means that with each successive unit of time the absolute addition to population gets bigger. While often accurate in the short run, growth conditions seldom pertain where this exponential assumption can hold true in the long run. It leads to predictions of fatal overpopulation in the very long run.

The modified exponential   A sometimes more reasonable curve of the exponential family of mathematical functions is one with a declining pace of growth approaching an upper capacity limit. The projection formula states that the population in a future time is found by taking the maximum limit and subtracting from it some portion of the unused capacity. The further in time one projects, the smaller the amount that is subtracted from the limit. The model uses a predetermined ceiling for potential total population and forces projected growth rates to decrease continually so that the ceiling capacity is never reached. Maximum population levels are typically determined via zoning and land use development controls that affect population density.

The Gompertz growth curve   This curve is also of the exponential family and has an S-shape, having both a lower limit and an upper limit. The assumptions implied are that growth begins slowly, increases momentum until it reaches an inflection point, and then slows to increments of continuously decreasing size.

The comparative method   The above four techniques each assume that future growth is predictable on the basis of knowledge of past growth trends within an area, a tenuous assumption in many cases. The comparative technique asserts that future growth of an area is predictable on the basis of historical trends in a different area. The latter area is called the pattern area. It is assumed that the origins of the two areas are similar and that their histories form a similar pattern but that one area is ahead of the other, and thus the leader can be used as a pattern to predict the future of the follower.

Projections with ratios The basic idea of the ratio technique is represented in the following example. It is assumed that population growth in the study area, say a community, is highly dependent on what happens to population in its surrounding region, say the state in which it is located. If it is assumed that the nature of this real interdependence is likely to persist into the near future, and if population projections are available for the state, then by assuming that the ratio between the two populations will remain constant, the community's share of the state's projected total can be calculated.

Cohort-component The cohort-component method is premised on the recognition that population change is a function of natural increase and migration. The term "cohort" indicates that the computational procedure is applied to age categories (rather than gross population totals), with the identity of each age group retained as it is carried forward through time. For example, the 1975 cohort comprising population 15–19 years of age is projected to 1980 by accounting for deaths (employing survival rates) and migration, at which time the cohort's population will be between 20 and 24 years of age. Typically, the cohorts span five years and contain four subpopulations—the male and female sectors of the white and nonwhite populations. In order to retain the identity of the age cohorts, the projection periods must be similar to, or multiples of, the width (in years) of the age groups.

Cohort-component analysis is the descriptive term for the overall model. The natural increase component (particularly the survival portion) is often called cohort-survival analysis.

The migration component of the model can be structured in several ways. Simple migration rates can be used. However, the trend at the state level has been to develop more complex variations tying migration flows to employment opportunities. The assumption of this method is that population and employment growth are related. The difficulty lies in defining the exact relationship between population and employment, i.e., to what extent do people follow jobs, jobs follow people, or both? Additionally, people migrate for other than employment-related reasons. These factors include climate, educational opportunities, retirement, and others.

Employment projection methods

Many agencies are involved in projecting employment. At the national level, the two most relied upon are the Bureau of Labor Statistics and the Bureau of Economic Analysis. Each agency projects national employment using its own technique and provides detailed technical documentation in its publications that should be consulted prior to utilizing the data. In general, BLS tends to project a shorter time into the future than BEA. Both agencies, however, are continually revising their models and updating their projections. At the subnational level, techniques for developing employment projections vary considerably. An overview of the models in use is provided below.

Trend extrapolations Models that simply plot the progress of a variable over time and extrapolate the trend into the future are called trend extrapolations and are, of course, not peculiar to employment studies. They are applied to population, as previously discussed, and widely used throughout the social and physical sciences. They fall under a general category of curve-fitting techniques. The particular curve selected to represent a set of data can vary from a straight line to various exponential curves, cyclical patterns, and to an almost infinite variety of geometric shapes.

Market share models There are many relatively simple models that have been developed to project employment at the substate level. These models avoid the many data requirements and the expense of some of the more complex models described below. Often these market share models are called step-down models because, for example, county projections are derived from multicounty, state, and national forecasts, with the latter serving as the exogenous input. Most of the models assume that the growth of the county is based on the growth of its multicounty region, which is based upon the growth of its state, which in turn is based upon national growth. Different models execute these assumptions via alternative procedures. In addition, some approaches involve regression of the historical trends of an area's employment growth or regression of an area's changing shares of total employment activity over time.

Many of these methods are of a family called shift-share techniques. Shift-share models, for the most part, consist of two components: (1) a share or ratio of county employment to state employment (or any larger region); and (2) a shift or competitive component. This second component can be derived either explicitly or implicitly. An explicitly determined shift component is one that is directly calculated from historical data of two periods and presumably reflects the differentials between a county's economic growth and regional (or state) growth, for that time frame. The explicit variable can be population, the tax burden, labor force skills, income, or any other factor that causes the competitive component to change over time. It is, however, often unstable over time and, therefore, should be used with caution.

Alternatively, a shift increment that is executed implicitly is ascertained usually via a regression of historical employment series data against time, where the derived slope represents the shifting difference between county economic activity and regional (or state) growth. If the shift component is greater than zero, then the implication is that the economy (or industry) is growing faster in a particular county than in the region (or state), and vice versa.

Three market share models have been chosen for further discussion: constant share, population/employment, and OBERS. The constant share model projects, for example, county employment at the same rate that the state's employment is expected to grow. The population/employment model, a modification of the constant share model, is based on a ratio of a county's population change to a state's population change. OBERS is technically the only true shift-share model. The competitive component is derived through a regression of the logarithm of the county share of state employment against the logarithm of time. These models are discussed more fully below:

Constant share Of the models described, constant share is perhaps the simplest in terms of assumptions, calibration, and data requirements. Statistical testing of this model indicates that in some cases it has produced results superior to those of more elegantly designed alternatives.

The assumption of the constant share model is that an area's current share of regional employment will persist over time. This assumption implies that an area will grow at the same rate as its larger region. The method is a step-down technique in that exogenous national projections are used to calculate state projections, which in turn provide the bases for county projections.

Population/employment Another model is a constant share model modified by an area's relative population change. It is a step-down technique and again is easily calculated. The difference between this model and alternatives is that population plays a role in its operation by weighting the constant share results. Specifically, if the smaller political entity is projected to increase its share of the larger political unit's populations, then the constant share employment is adjusted upward to reflect its increased market share.

The basic assumption of population/employment goes beyond that of constant share. It is assumed that the changing market size affects an area's employment growth. The market is assumed to be an important factor in the growth of local market-oriented industries. Because this technique relies on exogenous employment and population projections, its errors may be greater than those of the two previous methods.

OBERS   The OBERS shift-share model was developed by a research group drawn from the Office of Business Economics (now the Bureau of Economic Analysis) and the Economic Research Service of the U.S. Department of Commerce in 1974. Its purpose was to project employment activity at the regional level of the United States. It is a modified double exponential model whose "competitive" or shift component is implicit. The model combines the step-down character of constant share and the trend extrapolation device of simple regression.

The OBERS model modifies the assumption of the constant share model via the shift component. This component measures the difference between the proportional growth accounted for by the constant share term and the attained level of economic activity. In other words, an area is assumed to grow faster or slower than the rest of its region with respect to the industry in question because of differences in the area's relative attractiveness to economic activity.

The technique yields a trend extrapolation of an area's historic percentage share of the regional employment total for a given industry. This is accomplished by fitting a least squares regression line to the logarithm of regional percentage shares versus the logarithm of time. The use of the logarithm of percentage shares converts the data to a ratio scale (where the slope of the line expresses the growth rate) so that the projected rate can be compared to the historic rate by observing the comparative slopes. The logarithm of time is used to smooth the slopes of rapidly rising or falling curves.

There are several advantages to the OBERS model. One, of course, is that the data inputs are manageable. Another is that with the use of large-scale computers its calculation is not overly time-consuming and its cost is minimal.

Models of sectoral interdependence   The most common, easily understood model of sectoral interdependence is called the economic base model. It supposes that we divide all economic activity (measured as either product, employment, income, or value added) into two sectors: that which produces for export consumption and that which produces for local consumption. A constant ratio between the amount of activity in each of these sectors is assumed to endure into the future. The model then depends on the availability of an exogenous forecast of demand for the export products. Local production in those export sector activities is then projected to change in response to the projected exogenous demand forecast for exports. Income brought into the community as a result of these export sales is then assumed to generate local consumption activities as it circulates through local buyers and sellers in cycles that multiply the initial export dollars. This "Keynesian" multiplier or ratio of export to local activities is the heart of the economic base model. The multiplier is estimated for current and historical periods and then held constant for projection purposes and applied to alternative forecasts of export activity.

A difficult technical problem in using this model is estimating, for past and current periods, which activities are export and which activities are local. There are basically two approaches to this problem. One is to survey every economic establishment to determine the sources of all of their purchases and the destinations of all of their sales. This information is extremely costly to gather, but yields such a full picture of the workings of the economy that, indeed, much more than employment forecasts can be determined from these rich data. In fact, the analysis of such a table of data is subject to a whole branch of economic analysis called input-output analysis. If all one wanted was employment projections, the use of input-output analysis might be doing it the hard way.

The other approach to sectoring activities into export and local sectors is to use one of several short-cut techniques, such as location quotients and minimum requirements techniques. These techniques try, for each industry or group of industries, to determine an ideal or standard proportion of a community's activity that is needed to meet local consumption needs. Any excess over that minimum proportion is presumed to be excess for export. The location quotient bases its standard on national averages. The minimum requirements techniques bases its standard on a national minimum or near minimum proportion.

Input-output analysis is in fact also a kind of multiplier model but one so much more elaborate and detailed than economic base analysis as to be of a different kind. There are yet other models of sectoral interdependence employed to study metropolitan, regional, and state economies for planning and projection purposes that fall under the general rubric of econometric models. Mathematically, these models take the form of a set of linear equations, seldom fewer than 10 equations, sometimes more than 100. Complex linear regression models are used to calibrate the parameters of these equations, so that the many dependent variables might be simultaneously projected with a minimum of error. While they do sometimes have in their results a forecast of future employment, they tend to focus more on short-run policy variables such as rates of return, levels of taxes, business investment, aggregate unemployment rates, bank deposits, etc.

Summary

This chapter has attempted to accomplish several objectives:

1. To describe a basic research unit of a state or regional planning agency in terms of what issues need to be considered in organizing one and what it does.
2. To overview some basic data sources which should be part of a research unit's library.
3. To present recent trends in some of these basic data series.
4. To summarize some techniques for extending and projecting data series.

The main factors to be considered in developing a basic research unit are:

1. Resource availability.
2. Geographic coverage of the agency.
3. The policy focus of the agency.

The major responsibilities of such a unit include:

1. Data maintenance.
2. Data dissemination.
3. Knowledge of data limitations and uses.
4. Data analysis.
5. Data development.

Primary sources of population, housing, and economic data are U.S. Bureau of the Census publications, which are not limited to decennial census data. Housing data are also available from the U.S. Department of Housing and Urban Development. The U.S. Bureau of Labor Statistics is another major source of economic data.

Trends in population, housing, and economic activity were examined and can be gleaned from an examination of the tables in the chapter.

Procedures for estimating and projecting population, housing, and employment range from simple to complex, both in computational and data needs. Many states in cooperation with federal agencies prepare demographic and economic estimates and/or projections using some of the techniques described.

1   An excellent example of a regional data sources directory is the Tri-State Regional Planning Commission's *Tri-State Data Resources* which includes aerial photography and maps, census data, computer models and programs, forecasts, monitoring, and surveys and data files.
2   See Division of Planning and Research, Department of Labor and Industry, *Statistical Source Directory for New Jersey State Government*.
3   More information including names and addresses of the lead agencies of State Data Center programs throughout the nation can be obtained by contacting Data User Services Division, U.S. Bureau of the Census, Washington, DC 20233.
4   We have limited our discussion here to numerical data. Another important form of data, often used

to supplement these sources, is found in mapped and photographic forms. An excellent guide to these data is the U.S. Department of Interior, *Map Data Catalog*.
5   A fine discussion on trends in national and regional housing data is found in Sternlieb and Hughes, "Housing in the United States: An Overview," a small book within a book. An excellent example of housing analysis at the state planning level is C. Theodore Koebel's *1979 Housing Report for Kentucky*.
6   A listing of states and their respective cooperating agencies can be obtained from the Chief, Population Branch, U.S. Bureau of the Census, Washington, DC 20233.

12 Citizen participation

Citizen participation is a curious element in the democratic decision-making process. While its roots can be traced to ancient Greece and colonial New England, its growth in the last two decades reflects a contemporary recognition that American government is simply too remote to be truly "of, by, and for the people" without some help. Public involvement is an effort to ensure that citizens have a direct voice in public decisions.

Unfortunately, citizen participation programs often are viewed with skepticism by decision makers, who charge that they are monopolized by obstructionist special interests; by planners, who resent interference in decisions they believe to be technical in nature; and by citizens, who fear that they are merely tokens in a process where all the decisions have been made already. In many cases, of course, all of the above are correct. In others, the process works very well and converts even the most cynical skeptic. It is not the purpose of this chapter to persuade the reader that citizen participation is a panacea. Rather, we accept it as a way of doing public business in the latter part of the twentieth century, describe the planner's role, and discuss ways to make it more effective and satisfying.

Citizen participation is a process which provides private citizens an opportunity to influence public decisions. Though it has been an informal part of the democratic decision-making process since the beginning of the Republic, it was institutionalized with President Lyndon Johnson's Great Society programs in the mid-1960s. At the present time, citizen involvement requirements are a requirement of countless federal, state, regional, and local programs. While many of these have been eliminated or reduced during the Reagan Administration, some form of public participation still is required in most large-scale planning efforts, and many citizen activists demand involvement even where none is required. Implementation often is placed in the hands of the professional planner, who may not be given training, guidance, or support in directing this important activity.

At the local level, citizens often become involved spontaneously in having an effect upon decisions because they are close to home and readily understood. Issues confronting state and regional agencies, however, tend to be more abstract and distinct from the citizen's everyday life. An attempt at participation in decision making at those levels usually is by more sophisticated individuals who represent well defined viewpoints or organized groups. While the task of the local planner is to manage citizen involvement effectively, the challenge to the state or regional planner is usually more fundamental: to stimulate involvement in the first place and to manage its integration into the decision-making process.

Many planners grudgingly go through the motions of involving the public because it is a requirement for a grant or loan. This need not be the only reason. Citizen participation can provide a number of tangible benefits to the entire planning process:

1. Information and ideas on public issues.
2. Public support for planning decisions.

Alexis de Tocqueville on citizen participation   The political activity that pervades the United States must be seen in order to be understood. No sooner do you set foot upon American ground than you are stunned by a kind of tumult; a confused clamor is heard on every side, and a thousand simultaneous voices demand the satisfaction of their social wants. Everything is in motion around you; here the people of one quarter of a town are met to decide upon the building of a church; there the election of a representative is going on; a little farther, the delegates of a district are hastening to the town in order to consult upon some local improvements; in another place, the laborers of a village quit their plows to deliberate upon the project of a road or a public school. Meetings are called for the sole purpose of declaring their disapprobation of the conduct of the government; while in other assemblies citizens salute the authorities of the day as the fathers of their country.

Source: Alexis de Tocqueville, *Democracy in America*, Vol. I, Chapter XIV.

3.   Avoidance of protracted conflicts and costly delays.
4.   Reservoir of good will which can carry over to future decisions.
5.   Spirit of cooperation and trust between the agency and the public.

There are real costs associated with public participation. Decision making becomes more involved. Additional financial allocations for staff training and implementation may be required, and there is a danger that one point of view may be allowed to dominate the citizen group. Careful planning is necessary if the planner is to realize the most benefits from citizen participation at the minimal cost.

This chapter begins with discussion of the differences in citizen participation at the state, regional, and local levels. A discussion of public involvement from both the citizen's and planner's perspectives follows. The next section describes techniques of citizen participation. Finally, criteria for an effective program are suggested.

State, regional, and local differences in citizen participation

Federal, state, regional, and local citizen participation programs vary in responsibilities and functions. Generally, federal and state governments develop policies and allocate resources, while local governments implement the resulting programs. Regional agencies most often assume neither legislative nor operational responsibilities but provide planning and coordinating functions. Of all levels of government, they have the fewest direct links to the public. This creates special problems for those regional agencies which attempt to identify and develop citizen constituencies affected by their land use, transportation, wastewater management, and other planning decisions.

Relationship to planning

In the broadest sense, the planning process involves a related series of actions which include goal setting, policy identification and analysis, policy making, administrative rulemaking, program operations, and evaluation. Implicit to all these actions is the generation, appropriation, and allocation of resources.

Within this context, public involvement opportunities range from substantial to minimal. Citizen participation is an appropriate goal for every part of the planning process, but the potential contribution of the public varies for different

Figure 12–1   Potential contribution of citizen participation in the planning process: a comparison.

Planning actions	Levels of government			
	Federal	State	Regional	Local
Goal formulation	○	●	●	●
Data collection and analysis	—	○	○	○
Alternative policy definition	○	○	●	●
Alternative policy evaluation	—	—	○	●
Policy selection	—	—	—	●
Policy implementation	—	○	○	●
Monitoring and evaluation	○	○	○	●

Potential contribution
● = High
○ = Moderate
— = Low

activities and governmental levels. The quality of participation varies also and is influenced by the planner through the allocation of resources and the creation of expectations among participants. Figure 12-1 shows the potential contribution of citizens to various steps in the planning process at different levels of government.

Public involvement is most appropriate and effective in the stages of goal formulation and policy definition. In general, after goals and policies are determined, there are fewer opportunities for citizen contributions and greater technical roles for planners. The specific level of involvement often depends on the aggressiveness and sophistication of the citizens.

When policies originate at the federal and state levels, the opportunities for regional and local citizen participation often are severely restricted. These also vary, and block grant and revenue-sharing programs offer greater opportunities for local influence than categorical programs. Regardless of their inherent constraints, however, some degree of citizen participation is required for most programs initiated at the federal level.

State and regional agencies generally focus their efforts on policy development, interpretation, and application, relying on local institutions for implementation. They also are involved in functional planning and resource allocation and serve in a passthrough/coordinating/clearinghouse role to ensure that local actions are consistent with federal, state, and regional requirements. These functions limit citizen participation to oversight activities, e.g., clearinghouse review processes.

Regional agencies are more limited in purpose and scope than state governments, and generally do not have the power to initiate policy. One notable exception is the Portland (Oregon) Metropolitan Service District, whose elected legislative body and executive officer operate under state authority to provide selected direct services.

Citizen participation in state and regional planning

The state performs functions ranging from broad policy development to specific site oriented activities, and thus provides numerous opportunities for citizen participation. However, a few individuals have direct contact with their state governments, and citizen participation tends to operate through traditional political means—the electoral process and lobbying by professional, trade, and single-purpose associations. It is necessary to develop additional involvement techniques if the full benefits of citizen participation are to be realized by the government as well as the governed. Members of the executive branch of most states respond to this need through formal participation mechanisms, such as boards and commissions. Unfortunately, these tend to attract a narrow range of citizens with specialized knowledge or well-defined interests who are known to the appointing bodies, i.e., governor or legislature.

Regional agencies, most commonly councils of government (COGs), usually are composed of representatives of local governmental units. Most COGs have difficulty identifying their constituencies, since few people view themselves as regional citizens.

The policy or technical advisory committee is the most common form of citizen participation at the regional level, though hearings and conferences are commonly used, as well. Individuals who serve are selected because of their knowledge, position, or constituency; they may be involved to protect a local governmental interest, to support the concept of regional planning, or to share their particular knowledge in a functional area such as transportation or solid waste. Within these general parameters, the inherent roles and responsibilities of regional planning agencies constrain citizen involvement activities, even for the few regional agencies which have directly elected governing bodies. Most often, state and federal regulations require a certain framework through which participation efforts must be organized. Regional agencies need to institute special means and techniques if they want to expand citizen participation efforts beyond the advisory committee approach, because they usually do not have direct contact with the citizenry. This is due to several factors:

Management responsibility for problems which may not be perceived by citizens as affecting their daily lives.

Delegated responsibility from other authorities.

Involvement of laypeople who have definite technical, experiential, or ideological viewpoints, rather than general interest.

Representational rather than direct citizen participation.

With state and regional agencies providing general policy guidance, administrative rules, or resources, the responsibility of operating programs commonly is passed on to local government. The former play an important oversight/evaluation role to ensure that these programs are managed in a manner consistent with their policies and administrative guidelines. Even if the development of their own policies lacked citizen participation, federal and state programs frequently require such participation at the local and regional level.

In summary, state and regional planning is more removed from the electorate than local planning efforts. The former tend to be more functionally oriented and lack the ongoing type of citizen relationships more commonly found in local situations, e.g., wards or established neighborhoods. Federal and state policies often require functionally oriented citizen participation, e.g., criminal justice, solid waste, wastewater, and transportation planning, which require agencies to confer with constituencies at various levels—political and technical representatives of local governments as well as informed citizens.

Figure 12-2 identifies some of the key characteristics of the intergovernmental system and associated citizen participation issues and problems.

Figure 12–2 Characteristics of citizen participation.

Government level	Planning functions	Constituency	Citizen participation problems
Federal	Policy setting Resource generation/allocation Rulemaking Policy evaluation	Organized interest groups Political activists	Remoteness Insensitivity to local differences
State	Policy setting Resource generation/allocation Rulemaking	Organized interest groups Political activists	Remoteness Insensitivity to local differences
Regional	Coordination Functional planning Resource allocation Policy oversight	Local governments Special interest groups Technicians	Defining constituency General nature of issues
Local	Policy implementation Service delivery Resource generation	Individual citizens Wards/neighborhoods	Political differences Parochialism/factionalism

Perspectives of the participant and the planner

While public involvement often is a requirement for the planner, it is optional for the citizen. Individuals choose to participate probably because they expect a satisfying experience and hope to be able to make a difference.

Participation can offer a variety of rewards to the citizen. These may be either intrinsic to the involvement (deriving from the very act of participation) or instrumental (resulting from the opportunity to contribute to the shaping of public policy). Planners should attempt to incorporate both in the program. Ignoring the intrinsic could lead to burnout; ignoring the instrumental can result in tokenism.

The planner's own expectations also are important, and an effective citizen participation program can contribute to the planner's job satisfaction as well as the quality of the planning process and product. Too often, however, public involvement causes only complications and constraints of time and money so that planners naturally feel degrees of frustration and skepticism.

In a well-planned program, the expectations of participants and planners should be related. Arnstein's well-known "ladder of citizen participation" illustrates this (Fig. 12-3).[1] Aside from its obvious normative implications, the ladder can help the planner to assess his or her perception of the program's purposes and compare this with the likely perceptions of citizen participants. In a successful program, the disparity is minimal. For example, if both planner and citizen expect the process to involve primarily information and consultation, their expectations are likely to be realized. However, if the planner expects consultation while the citizen anticipates some degree of power, or if the citizen expects consultation while the planner aims for manipulation, conflict is inevitable.

Such conflict is damaging to the planning process, to future public involvement efforts, and to the relationship between planners and citizens. Most importantly, it is avoidable. Its source is not in conflicting demands but rather in conflicting

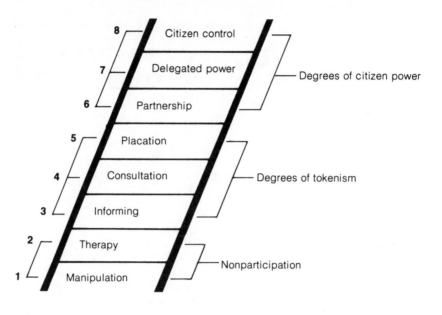

Figure 12–3 The ladder
of citizen participation.

expectations. The planner can help to guard against this conflict through honest
and clear communication at the onset of the process.

Citizen perspective

Models of public involvement at the local level are inappropriate for regional
and state planning. Common situations in which neighbors organize to demand
that city hall put a stop sign on their corner are not transferable or helpful in
understanding participation in decisions about state and regional issues which
often are more abstract and remote from the lives of most citizens. State and
regional agencies themselves are more distant and less accessible to citizens.
These factors usually discourage spontaneous grassroot involvement. There are
dramatic exceptions where the agency's decisions do have a direct community
impact, such as for landfills, highways, or other large-scale public facilities. In
these cases, demand for direct citizen involvement should not be a surprise.

In general, however, the state or regional planner often is confronted with
the problem of stimulating participation. A simple conceptual model is useful
in illustrating why citizens choose to become involved:

$$
\begin{aligned}
\textbf{Instrumental} \quad & \begin{bmatrix} \text{Perceived} & & \text{Expected} \\ \text{importance} & \times & \text{influence} \\ \text{of issue} & & \text{on outcome} \end{bmatrix} \\[2pt]
\textbf{Intrinsic} \quad & + \begin{bmatrix} \text{Expected} & & \text{Perceived} \\ \text{personal} & - & \text{inconvenience} \\ \text{benefits} & & \end{bmatrix} \\[2pt]
& = \text{Degree of participation}
\end{aligned}
$$

The more importance the citizen attributes to the issue, the more influence on
the outcome he/she expects to have, and the more satisfaction expected from
the act of participation, the greater the degree of participation. By the way in
which the process is structured, the planner can influence every element in this
equation.

In the model, the relationship between the perceived importance of the issue and the expected influence on the outcome multiplies in importance rather than simply being additive. This indicates their close relationship. Regardless of an issue's importance, citizens will not participate in the planning process if they realize they will have no influence on the final decision. Conversely, they will hesitate to participate in a process which accords substantial influence on a trivial issue.

Some public issues are obviously important, while others require public education efforts to demonstrate their value. The role of public education in citizen involvement is discussed in the next section. These efforts should not only generate greater public information but also enhance the public's perception of the issue's importance.

The planner is directly responsible for designing a public involvement process which plays a key role in shaping the final decision. Consequently, the citizen's influence on the outcome is largely in the hands of the planner who also is responsible for explaining to citizens their role in the overall planning process. Candor and mutual trust are essential. While he/she should not underestimate the value of the citizen, the planner also must not overstate the contribution citizens can expect to make to the final decision; both actions can lead to ill will and mistrust. The fear of tokenism is one reason many citizens are reluctant to become involved in public issues.

The intrinsic factors in the citizen's decision to participate are shaped even more directly by the planner. Inattention to personal benefits provided by involvement is an important cause of early burnout of citizens. Those who volunteer their time and energy in planning efforts deserve recognition. This may take the form of news releases, receptions with important officials, or other expressions of appreciation such as letters, certificates, plaques, etc. In addition, these citizens should be provided with timely information on the progress of the overall project. The planner should see that each element of the participatory process is comfortable, appealing, or supportive for citizens.

Citizens are more likely to respond to an attractive, well-written survey than to a dull and unattractive one. People respond better if a meeting is in comfortable surroundings. Refreshments also contribute to a relaxed atmosphere. Advisory committees should be provided access to staff members, photocopying, and other forms of support. The planner should make involvement as convenient as possible for participants. For example, mailed questionnaires should include prepaid return envelopes and meetings should be scheduled for convenient locations and times. Large regions and states should plan to hold meetings in more than one location so that citizens will not have to travel long distances. For some individuals, child care, travel allowances, handicapped access, or bilingual facilities may be necessary for their participation.

The individual balances these factors in deciding whether to become involved, and for a particular citizen, one factor may outweigh the others. For example, participation by people representing trade associations, environmental organizations, and other special interest groups invariably results from their perception of the importance of the issues. Other individuals view participation in terms of personal, professional, or political benefit to themselves.

Timing is a key element in developing a public involvement program. The planner should recognize that the perceived importance of an issue may change radically over even a short period of time. As the time for decision approaches, the perceived importance tends to increase. The planner who may have had difficulty finding anyone to participate in the early stages may be overwhelmed by interested citizens later on. On the other hand, a process which seems to go on interminably may burn out enthusiastic participants.

Planner perspective

Public involvement provides incentives and disincentives for the planner as well as for the citizen. These should be carefully considered, since many planners seem to be at least as skeptical concerning citizen participation as the public.

Advocates of citizen involvement often reject the concerns of reluctant planners as merely "protecting their turf." Although many of these objectives should not be taken seriously, some must be recognized.

There is no doubt that public involvement complicates a planning process and requires additional time, budget, and staff. However, attempting to save time and money by avoiding public involvement often represents a false economy. It also exposes the agency to criticism and possible obstruction to which it need not be vulnerable. Lack of participation may increase the possibility of obstruction through the courts or ballot box. On the other hand, the so-called dilemma of citizen participation[2] may arise; opportunities for involvement sometimes fuel opposition rather than result in cooperation.

The planner should view this as an opportunity rather than a problem. Opposition expressed in the context of a public involvement program can be addressed more effectively than opposition expressed in political and legal arenas. It is far less costly in time and money to resolve differences as part of the planning process rather than later in protracted lawsuits, administrative delay, and political battles. An open process confers on the outcome a degree of legitimacy which may be very important to ultimate implementation.

It remains true that public involvement complicates the agency's planning process and increases the cost. While savings in time and money if there is no public involvement may represent false economies, the costs of public involvement are nevertheless real.

A second major concern of many planners is that public involvement is not appropriate for problems with technical solutions. As John Friedmann points out in *Retracking America*,[3] the nature of classical allocative planning tends to separate the role of planners as technicians from the citizens and elected officials as people who impart values to the process. In his analysis, Friedmann identifies these two areas as processed knowledge and personal knowledge and suggests the inherent potential for conflict. Because planners perceive this danger, they often delay citizen involvement until technical solutions are developed, and then seek only citizen concurrence. In these instances, it is not uncommon for citizen groups to emerge in opposition to the recommended technical solution—resulting in angry confrontation and long delays.

An obvious solution is to expand the planning process to consider both personal and processed knowledge views in the formulation of goals and objectives and the selection of recommended solutions. A politically unacceptable technical solution may not be "better" than a less perfect but politically supportable resolution. The open public involvement process provides a means for identifying solutions which are technically and politically acceptable.

A third issue for planners is the confidentiality and objectivity of information. Certain types of data, such as personal interviews, cannot be shared. This raises the issue of credibility and trust between planners and citizen participants. The cloaks of confidentiality or objectivity need not be used to separate citizens from information needed to make a decision.

Planners often view citizens as incapable of understanding technical issues or believe that citizen views may "pollute" their inherent objectivity. Planners also can develop a proprietary interest in data; this may limit their willingness to share it with citizens and block the level of their interaction. Whenever possible, information should be shared with citizens, who can be expected to understand where confidentiality needs to be guarded.

The Metro tie-down For six years the residents of Yuma Street [in Washington, D.C.] waged steady warfare, filing four lawsuits, testifying before Congress and jamming three public hearings to express the fear, as one of their leaders put it, that the subway would "vandalize our street and make it unlivable." Subway noise and vibrations would disturb their tranquility, the homeowners said. The air vents . . . would disfigure their front walks. As a result of their protests and court victories, the vents were moved from curbs to vacant lots. Otherwise, the tunnel . . . was built . . . according to Metro's original plan.

Construction of the subway line . . . was delayed for more than a year, raising its cost by $6 million. According to Metro officials, the new, more elaborate planning procedures ordered by the U.S. Court of Appeals in the case added about $120 million to the total cost of the transit system.

As Metro officials predicted, noise from the trains has barely been noticed since the Red Line opened. . . . "I have not detected any noise but we just didn't trust them at all," said Joseph J. Saunders, [who] spearheaded one of the homeowners' main court cases against Metro. "I think Metro had to be taught an expensive lesson, and we had to do it. They have to take citizens' concerns into account. They said we were standing in the way of progress. We felt they were riding roughshod over our rights."

The homeowners' chief foe during most of their battles was Jackson Graham, . . . Metro's first general manager. He excoriated the Yuma group as obstructionists. Later, after retiring to Palm Springs, Calif., Graham headed a homeowners' association there that battled plans for a new highway.

What made him different from the homeowners on Yuma Street? "I felt they were unreasonable," Graham replied in an interview. "We were never unreasonable. . . ."

"It's all in the eyes of the beholder," Saunders remarked last week.

Source: *The Washington Post*, September 4, 1984, C1. Line cut by Charles E. Brock, originally published in Jonathan Swift, *Travels into Several Remote Nations of the World* [*Gulliver's Travels*] (New York: Macmillan and Company, 1894). Reissued in facsimile by University Microfilms, Ann Arbor, Mich., 1967.

Another concern of planners is the difficulty of achieving agreement between the staff and their supervisors and gaining concurrence from the decision making body about the appropriate level and type of participation. In many state and regional agencies, staff planners responsible for public involvement receive little support from their supervisors. Such support, however, is essential throughout the involvement process in order to avoid false expectations and attendant conflicts. Compromises are required at every stage in the citizen involvement process, including the design of the program. Agreement concerning the role of citizens must be reached before the process is presented to the public.

In spite of these concerns, citizen participation offers the planner a number of incentives. One of the most obvious is the necessity to meet requirements for citizen participation in nearly every federal or state funded planning program. Moreover, citizen participation as an end in itself can make the planner's job more satisfying and effective by means of the following:

Reducing isolation of the planner from the public.

Generating a spirit of cooperation and trust.

Providing opportunities to disseminate information.

Identifying additional dimensions of inquiry and research.

Assisting in identifying alternative solutions.

Providing legitimacy to the planning effort and political credibility of the agency.

Increasing public support.

Techniques of citizen participation

Forms of public involvement

Numerous techniques are under the rubric of citizen participation. They range from simple regulations requiring open meeting to the sophisticated Delphi method of developing consensus; from commonplace public hearings to experimental cable television. With few exceptions, a successful public involvement program incorporates several techniques. Our purpose in this chapter is to provide the reader with an overview.

Citizen participation techniques may be arrayed on a continuum based on the degree of passive or active involvement, ranging from publicity to public partnership.

Publicity techniques are designed to persuade and thus gain public support, relating to citizens as passive consumers.

Public education programs present relatively complete and balanced information so that citizens may draw their own conclusions.

Public input techniques solicit ideas and opinions from citizens. They are most effective when combined with feedback mechanisms which inform participants of the extent to which their input has influenced ultimate decisions.

Public interaction techniques facilitate the exchange of information and ideas among citizens, planners, and decision makers. When these techniques are effectively utilized, each participant has the opportunity to express his/her views, respond to the ideas of others, and work toward consensus.

Public partnership offers citizens a formalized role in shaping the ultimate decisions.

More active citizen participation is not necessarily better in every situation. While a program which includes only support building and information dissem-

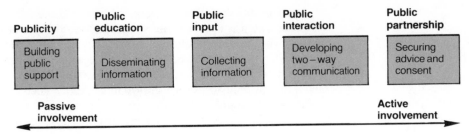

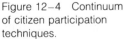

Figure 12–4 Continuum of citizen participation techniques.

ination is hardly participatory, both elements should be part of a thoughtfully designed program.

Many techniques do not fit neatly into a single category. For example, while it is designed principally to collect information, a public hearing also may be a means to disseminate information and facilitate two-way communication.

The number of citizens who can be involved in any process is inversely related to the level of active involvement. Public relations efforts can reach thousands of citizens through the mass media, while public partnership limits participation to a few. A more definitive discussion of each type of technique follows.

Description of techniques

Publicity Without public relations efforts, governmental officials risk isolating themselves from their constituencies. The information disseminated must be relatively straightforward and may be through a simple device such as a distinctive slogan or logo which is transferred to posters, bumper stickers, buttons, T-shirts, and/or billboards; the Forest Service's Smokey the Bear campaign is an excellent successful example of this technique. Brochures, displays, and exhibits can transmit more substantive information. Professional quality radio and television public service announcements are other effective means of publicizing governmental activities.

Notices of participation opportunities also are a key part of the publicity function. They should be attractively designed as well as informative. The typically required legal notice usually is not effective.

Public education Press conferences, news releases, newspaper articles, newsletters, documentaries and slide shows, handbooks, information centers, speakers bureaus, and public meetings are means of educating the public on specific subjects. Agencies thus can inform the public about governmental policies, programs, and decisions which would benefit from citizen participation. State and regional agencies, which the public may consider complex and remote, can utilize information programs to demonstrate their openness to the needs of those they serve.

The following rules are important to designing an effective public information program:

Carefully select the channels by which information is to be transmitted in order to reach the desired audience.

Use a variety of communication techniques.

Design the message specifically for the medium which is used.

Tailor the message to the targeted audience.[4]

All materials should be understood easily. If the information is too technical or relies extensively on professional jargon, the public may misinterpret the message or become suspicious of the sponsoring agency's motives. A citizen advisory committee may be useful in reviewing the materials to assure that they are clear, concise, and understandable. Timing also is critical; citizens must be given ample time to absorb information before decisions are made, especially if the issues are unfamiliar or complex.

Public information techniques are essential to a comprehensive citizen participation program. Used with other elements, they can provide a foundation of public trust in state and regional decision making.

Public input   Information about the characteristics, needs, and attitudes of the citizenry is essential to effective governmental planning and political decision making. Far too often, planners assume that they know what the public needs and wants. Public input programs encourage citizens to express their own opinions and possibly influence public decisions.

These efforts can be formal or informal, designed either to gauge the attitudes of a cross section of the population or provide concerned citizens a chance to voice their opinions. Like most citizen participation techniques, they are valuable because they both contribute to decision making and create a spirit of mutual trust. If the information collected from such efforts is not analyzed and utilized effectively by the agency, the exercise is futile for citizens and an unnecessary burden for policy makers.

Any controversial issue is likely to generate some expression of public opinion, through direct communication with the agency, letters to local newspapers, radio and television talk show discussions, petitions, participation at public meetings, or demonstrations. While public hearings are a common means of responding to an aroused citizenry, they rarely are entirely satisfactory to either citizens or officials. (Public hearings are discussed at some length below.)

The opinion poll can provide an opportunity for interested citizens to express their views and permit decision makers to formulate an accurate profile of public attitudes, although complete fulfullment of either function requires some sacrifice of the other.

A broad opportunity for individuals to express their opinions is provided through simple questionnaires widely distributed through mass mailing, the printed media, or handouts. It is important to note that in this type of survey respondents represent a self-selected and biased sample who are likely to have higher incomes and be better educated than the general population. Seniors, young adults, and minorities are likely to be underrepresented. A disproportionately greater number of persons with strong views will respond to a questionnaire than their actual representation in the population justifies. If these biases are recognized, such surveys still can be useful in eliciting broad public response; they do not permit precise statistical inferences.

If the planner's goal is to develop an accurate portrait of public opinion, more sophisticated polling techniques are required, such as a survey administered to a carefully selected sample of the targeted population. Selected citizens are interviewed by telephone or in person, or questionnaires may be sent through the mail accompanied by prepaid return envelopes and perhaps followed by reminder postcards. Careful design ensures the polling of a representative sample from which inferences about the population may be drawn.

A survey can accomplish one or more of the following:

Collect data on the demographic characteristics of the population.

Invite citizens to express their needs and concerns.

Present new ideas and elicit citizens' reactions.

Assess the public's knowledge, attitudes, or opinions at a point in time.

Measure changes in attitudes and opinions over a period of time.

Polling techniques offer the potential for reaching all segments of the population, including those who customarily do not attend hearings, meetings, and workshops. Furthermore, surveys alone can provide representative information about the entire population, although ensuring statistical validity can be costly and time consuming. However, because of the quality and quantity of information which can be gathered, the well-designed survey is often a cost-effective technique.

Respondents to surveys may doubt their effect on the decision making process unless the purpose and uses of information gathered are described clearly and the results disseminated widely, particularly to the respondents themselves.

Other more simple polling techniques may be used to foster citizen involvement. For example, written questionnaires may be distributed to persons attending hearings, meetings, or workshops, thus providing decision makers with a written record of citizens' concerns and impressions.

A specialized public input tool is the Delphi technique, a complex reiterative survey process. Respondents are anonymous. Initially, a group of individuals representing diverse positions and information on specific policy issues is selected. Each participant completes and returns by mail a detailed questionnaire. The results are incorporated into a second questionnaire which also is sent to each respondent, along with a summary of the group's responses to the first round of questioning. In some cases, participants meet at the end of the process to discuss results. The Delphi method results in a set of thorough, thoughtful, and tested opinions, and can involve thousands of people. In the state of Washington, for example, a three-round Delphi questionnaire format was used to obtain the opinions of 2400 citizens regarding current and future trends affecting the state's development. The results were incorporated by a state-wide task force into its Alternatives for Washington futures program.

Public input techniques are a valuable foundation for decision making. They provide opportunities to obtain contributions from carefully selected respondents, and invite active—though not interactive—participation. While a great deal of information may be disseminated and collected, only limited opportunities are provided to exchange and synthesize different viewpoints.

Public interaction All the techniques discussed above involve one-way communication. Interactive techniques encourage citizens and planners to share ideas, react to one another's views, ask questions, and formulate and test alternatives.

The key to effective public interaction is the elimination of the "we/they" dichotomy often present in public meetings and hearings. A number of techniques foster cooperation rather than confrontation.

For example, the Florida Division of State Planning utilized a participatory public hearing format to develop the state's comprehensive plan. In a series of two-day meetings, staff presentations of pertinent issues were followed by question-and-answer periods. An extensive publicity campaign resulted in the participation of approximately 1200 citizens.

In Oregon, the workshop technique was used successfully to formulate state-wide land-use planning goals and guidelines. Twenty-eight workshops were conducted around the state. In addition to mailed invitations, television and radio stations carried public messages from the Governor to all citizens inviting them to attend the workshop in their area. In all, it is estimated that more than 3000 citizens participated directly in the process.

A public workshop offers citizens the opportunity to interact directly with agency staff and elected officials. A cross section of citizens can be expected to attend if time and location are convenient, the topic affects them or is of direct interest, and they are notified and invited personally. Small group discussions in which every participant has an opportunity to express ideas and opinions promote interaction and discourage the domination of a few vocal participants.

A conference is another means of fostering interaction among concerned citizens, agency staff, and decision makers. Typically lasting one or two days, this technique includes speeches, presentations, general and small group discussions, and workshops, frequently concluding with the adoption of recommendations for future action. Although they require substantial planning and coordination, these meetings promote cooperation and mutual understanding, command media attention, and may result in regional or national recognition.

Public partnership   In most cases, citizens involved in ongoing state and regional planning serve in an advisory capacity. We use the term "advisory committee" to include several types of groups:

General advisory.

Technical and scientific.

Research commissions.

Special clientele, e.g. industry, consumers.

Special task forces.

Advisory committees usually are composed of 10 to 15 individuals selected either from a cross section of professions, interests, and geographic locations, or from a more narrow special purpose range. The use of advisory committees is especially common in regional planning. Frequently, in highly technical areas such as transportation or solid waste, regional agencies involve citizens in both policy and technical advisory committees. Such committees serve an important role, especially in an agency which has a tenuous relationship with its constituency.

An advantage of the advisory committee is that lay individuals work together over a period of time and learn to know each other and the particular issues which they are addressing. They also can provide fresh perspective to the more technical staff. Single-purpose committees or task forces should be disbanded after their assignment is completed. It is unwise for the agency to perpetuate the group's existence by finding other projects. The advisory committee can function as a sounding board for the agency and help bridge the gap between government and the public by sponsoring workshops and hearings.

To ensure state or regional representation, individuals appointed to these bodies should have a broad range of interests or represent specific constituencies. Clearly defined objectives and agency/committee roles are necessary to assure the successful fulfillment of the committee's functions, which can be educational, advisory, program development, or support building.

An interesting variation is the futures program, such as developed in a number of states, which involves citizens and governmental officials in forecasting and shaping future development. Participants set goals and objectives and explore medium- and long-range implementation strategies.

Unlike most other involvement techniques, the futures concept has gathered momentum without any particular impetus from the federal government. These commissions generally have larger memberships than the typical advisory committee, and in some cases they are constituted and funded privately. They use a variety of techniques to involve the broader public in their work, including media presentations, questionnaires, and conferences.

Additional techniques *The public hearing* is the technique employed most often to include citizens in the planning process. Often required by federal or state legislation, public hearings are used in both the legislative and executive branches. They are scheduled usually in the last stage of decision making, just prior to the announcement of a new or modified public policy. Because citizens may sense that they have little real opportunity to affect the outcome, hearings often erupt in hostility, anger, and bitterness.

Rarely do decision makers have a real opportunity to evaluate public testimony judiciously. They may be confronted with a seemingly endless parade of people who appear to be ill-tempered, irrational, and unrepresentative. Even well-intentioned citizens and public officials may have difficulty rising above the constraints of the circumstances.

In the typical agenda of a public hearing, the sponsoring agency presents its proposal and then allows for public testimony. The customary physical arrangement of the hearings chamber, with officials on a dais and the audience at some distance in rows of chairs accentuates the distance between officials and the public, promoting rigid communication and an adversary relationship.

The traditional hearings process has inherent limitations, which include the following:

Inhibiting two-way communication.

Providing inadequate opportunity for citizens to express their goals, values, and opinions when they can have an effect on the planning process.

Not allowing extensive exchange of information or providing equal opportunity for each participant to be heard.

Fostering emotionalism and hostility.

The underlying atmosphere of a hearing often is one of basic mistrust: citizens do not trust officials to respect their views; officials do not trust citizens to distinguish the public interest from their own narrow self-interest. Individuals may have to wait hours to speak and then find they are limited to a few minutes; officials may have to sit through hours of testimony which drains their energy and patience. The hearing format is not conducive to discussion in depth or to resolution of conflicts.

The most serious obstacle to improvement in the hearings process is the attitude of many planners and public officials who believe that the least public participation is the best. This attitude is narrow, though understandable if their experience with citizen participation has been limited to acrimonious and unproductive public hearings.

Because they involve minimal expenditures of time and money and are required by law in many cases, public hearings will continue to be the most widely used technique of citizen involvement. Therefore, within their limitations, agencies should strive to improve them as much as possible. For example, an agency may schedule hearings at an early stage in the planning process when public opinion can have a meaningful impact on decisions. Careful summaries and analyses of the hearing record, along with clear statements of resulting actions, also are constructive. However, a program which includes only public hearings and perhaps some publicity or public information activity invites citizen participation only in the narrowest and most legalistic sense.

Cable television deserves special note because of its potential for expanding and enhancing the nature and extent of citizen participation. Cable television can revolutionize the public education process. Unlike commercial television, it makes available to communities a considerable number of channels with few programming limitations. Public meetings, presentations, discussions, speeches, and debates may be televised for interested citizens to view and evaluate conveniently in their own homes.

In addition, the capability for viewer response is available. The use of this technology as a component of public decision making in Columbus, Ohio, has elicited both praise for broadening the political process and criticism for limiting participation to citizens who subscribe to pay TV.[5] These experiments may be the forerunner of citizen participation efforts elsewhere.

Selecting program components

As noted earlier, usually a successful citizen participation program requires a combination of techniques. While legal requirements for public involvement must be met, they should be considered minimum guidelines. For the most part, federal and state laws and regulations require specific details such as a hearing agenda and specific committee composition but rarely provide guidance regarding approaches. A successful citizen participation program must be: integral to the planning process and focused on its unique needs; designed to function within available resources of time, personnel, and money; and responsive to the citizen participants. A number of efforts have been made to relate specific techniques to the objectives they serve most effectively.[6] Figure 12-5 summarizes our assessment of the purposes served by selected techniques.

Figure 12–5　Objectives served by selected public involvement techniques.

Techniques	Maximum exposure	Reach specific publics	Minimum funds	Minimum time	Minimum staff effort	Broad public input	Specific public input	Generate new ideas	Build support	Resolve conflict	Set goals	Political acceptability	Access/convenience
Mass media	●	○	—	—	—	—	—	—	●	—	—	●	●
Open meetings	—	—	●	●	●	—	—	—	—	○	—	○	—
Public meetings	—	●	○	○	○	—	●	—	○	—	—	○	○
Surveys	○	○	—	—	—	●	●	—	○	—	●	○	●
Delphi	—	●	—	—	—	—	●	●	○	●	●	—	○
Workshops	○	●	—	—	—	○	●	●	○	●	●	—	—
Conferences	●	○	—	—	—	○	●	●	○	○	●	—	—
Advisory commissions	—	○	○	—	○	—	●	●	●	●	●	●	—
Public hearings	○	○	●	●	●	—	○	—	—	—	—	●	—
Cable TV*	○	—	●	●	—	●	—	—	●	—	●	○	●

*Based on assumed general availability and acceptance
● Strong potential for meeting objectives
○ Some potential for meeting objectives
— Limited potential for meeting objectives

Criteria for an effective citizen participation program

Each citizen participation program must be designed to fit the unique needs and resources of the sponsoring agency. While we cannot offer rules which are applicable in every circumstance, in this section we identify the elements of a well-designed participatory process and suggest evaluation criteria.

Elements of an effective program

Although citizen participation efforts vary greatly, experience indicates a number of common elements which characterize successful programs. The program must do the following:

Meet legal requirements.

Clearly articulate goals and objectives.

Command political support.

Be an integral part of the decision making structure.

Receive adequate funding, staff, and time.

Identify concerned or affected publics.

Delineate clear roles and responsibilities for participants.

Meet legal requirements Citizen participation efforts frequently are required by federal or state legislation and may be accompanied by detailed regulations. The first criterion, of course, is to comply with these guidelines. However, these requirements are viewed too often as definitive rather than minimal. For example, a program has not necessarily succeeded because its advisory committee has the required number and proportion of minority, elderly, and low-income members.

Each citizen participation program should be designed to meet its particular situation, integrating legal requirements into the overall goals and objectives of the agency's planning process.

Clearly articulate goals and objectives The public involvement program should be related as closely as possible to the goals of the overall planning process. Its specific role may be derived by identifying the nature and extent of public information, support, or input required to meet these goals. For example, if one goal is to develop a profile of general public opinion on an issue, a survey may be in order. A conference or advisory committee may be more appropriate if the goal is to understand the specific needs of identifiable interest groups.

Command political support Just as citizen participation is part of the overall planning process, both are components of the larger political system and are effective only to the extent that they command political support.

Effective citizen participation provides decision makers with information about public needs and attitudes, permitting the adoption of plans, policies, or programs which are politically feasible, economically desirable, and socially acceptable. Thus, public involvement can be a valuable political resource.

Each program must gain the support of the necessary political leaders, who should be identified and involved in the process as early as possible. On the state level, the attitude and position of the governor can be critical to the effective involvement of citizens in decision making. Support from other elected officials and agency administrators also is important, since they often have the authority to allocate needed resources and determine whether citizen input will be incorporated into agency policies. Finally, successful citizen involvement requires the support of influential members of the public, particularly if the participation of organized interest groups is necessary. To ensure a sense of identification and commitment, these individuals should be included in the earliest stages of the process.

As previously noted, citizen participation is valuable not only for its own sake but also for its contribution to the planning process. A well-designed program allows political leaders to make more informed, responsive, and justifiable decisions. For this reason, the needs of decision makers should be taken into account as the program is designed. For example, public input can help them define problems, establish priorities, or improve communication with citizen groups. A program designed to meet needs such as these will command support.

The program's techniques, as well as its purposes, must command support. Some decision makers may be skeptical of surveys, advisory committees, or workshops. To ensure the acceptance of the results of citizen participation as an integral part of the planning process, such misgivings should be addressed prior to the program's implementation. Planners should expect to have to change or modify some program elements if these elements are objectionable to decision makers.

Integral to decision making structure   Citizens must be assured that their efforts are integrated into the planning process and linked to the decisions that result. They can contribute to the decision making process at every stage including the investigation of facts, formulation of goals, development and evaluation of alternative courses of action, and selection of the optimum alternative.

However, if citizen participation efforts are tangential to decision making, opportunities for creating public goodwill and adding a valuable dimension in planning are lost. This occurs when the findings of an advisory committee are ignored or a public hearing is held after a decision has been made. Every step should serve the planning process, and citizens should be informed explicitly how their participation contributes to the final outcome.

Although citizen opinions should be considered seriously, it should be made clear that other factors also will influence the final decisions; tradeoffs and compromises are part of the political process.

Adequate funding, staff, and time   These are valuable resources which must be budgeted carefully. Although some agencies appear to espouse the goals of public participation in the planning process, the resources they allocate for implementing programs are limited or nonexistent.

A successful citizen participation effort usually requires a substantial investment of staff and calendar time to permit citizens to formulate and incorporate their ideas into the planning process. Specific program elements must be commensurate with time constraints. For example, a brief telephone poll, which may be completed more quickly than a more sophisticated survey, might provide sufficient information.

Moreover, the planning and management skills required for effective public involvement programs often are underestimated; either experienced personnel should be hired or existing staff should be trained to deal with the public. These skills include knowledge of the following:

Role of public involvement in planning.

Group dynamics and human relations.

Involvement techniques.

Meeting facilitation.

Conflict resolution.

Resources required for effective public involvement.

Individuals who possess these skills cannot function at maximum efficiency without adequate material and staff support. For this reason, some training in these areas is important for program administrators and technical staff who may be required to make public presentations.

The inclusion of a public involvement program as a line item in a budget may be nearly as important as the amount appropriated. A budget category to which time and expenses associated with the program are allocated is a useful means of evaluating the cost effectiveness of different involvement techniques, such as expensive media productions versus publications prepared in the agency print shop.

The amount of resources allocated should reflect the scale of the program and goals of the agency. A modest program with an adequate budget is preferable to an ambitious program with an inadequate budget. The likely failure of the latter may jeopardize future citizen participation efforts. However, a large budget alone does not assure a successful citizen participation program.

Concerned or affected publics Although some situations require involvement of the public at large, frequently it is necessary to identify groups particularly affected by a proposed decision. Citizen participation efforts should be designed thoughtfully to suit the special needs of these groups.

As stated above, convenience is a critical factor in facilitating participation. For certain groups, the noon hour is best for meetings, while others are not available until evening. The availability of child care is important to some people, while others can participate only if provided with honoraria, transportation costs, or per diem allowances. In large regions and most states, finding meeting sites convenient to a majority can be a serious problem, but care must be taken not to exclude any known groups. For example, public transportation and/or adequate parking facilities should be convenient and nearby.

The method of presenting technical information should fit the sophistication level of participants. While sufficient material should be provided so that citizens can understand issues and make informed judgments, some technical information should not be oversimplified. The level of understanding required for effective participation will determine the range of techniques used in the participation program.

Roles and responsibilities of participants In order to avoid conflicting or unfulfilled expectations on the part of citizens, planners, and decision makers, the program agenda and roles and responsibilities of participants must be defined clearly. This includes clarification of the planning context, the nature and extent of citizen involvement, and the manner in which public input will be integrated into the final decision.

Effective participation programs demonstrate to citizens that government is accountable and responsive. However, since it is impossible to please everyone, the process cannot be expected to be entirely free of conflict. Nevertheless, if decision makers demonstrate that publicly expressed concerns have been seriously considered, the goals of the process have been satisfied. Even those opposed to the final outcome may acquiesce in the decision if they believe it has been formulated in a fair and open manner.

Figure 12–6   Citizen participation can take many forms.
The challenge is to stimulate
citizen interest without pro-
voking a war. The swastika
painted over a U.S. government car is a crude reminder
of the stormy reaction to the
initial planning work of the
National Park Service in the
Upper Delaware River Valley
that separates New York and
Pennsylvania. Negative citizen reaction may also take
the form of angry testimony
at public hearings, seldom a
productive kind of citizen
participation from the planner's point of view. The third
picture shows a more positive form of participation, a
commuter Ride Match Fair
arranged by the Southeast
Michigan Council of Governments.

Evaluating a citizen participation program

While it is an important dimension of every planning effort, program evaluation is especially necessary for citizen involvement. Participants need and deserve feedback regarding the impact of their involvement. Moreover, a successful program helps create a favorable climate for future public involvement efforts.

From our discussion of the elements of an effective citizen participation program, a number of evaluative criteria can be suggested, including the following:

1. Legal requirements:
    Did the program meet all legal rules and regulations?
    If requirements constrained the program, were these constrained unavoidable?
2. Goals and objectives:
    Is there widespread support for the final decision?
    Has public understanding of the issue increased?
    Does the final decision meet the agency's or program's articulated goals and objectives?
    Were significant conflicts aired and resolved?
    Did planners and decision makers receive an accurate portrayal of public opinion?
    Were all interested parties provided access to the process?
3. Political support:
    Were important individuals and groups identified and contacted early in the planning process?
    Was their input considered in designing the involvement program?
    Were these individuals informed of all developments in the program?
4. Decision making:
    Was the program an integral part of the planning process?
    Were the form and timing of its outputs compatible with the requirements of decision making?
    Were the outputs of the program used in the decision making process? If not, why not?
5. Adequate resources:
    Was sufficient time given to each step of the process?
    Was sufficient staff assigned?
    Were staff members adequately trained for their roles?
    Were sufficient funds allocated for support services and materials?
6. Publics:
    Were concerned public groups and individuals adequately identified?
    Were they all notified of meetings and offered opportunities to participate?
    Was participation convenient for targeted publics?
    Did the targeted public(s) participate fully? What could have been done to encourage fuller participation?
    (Note that "body counts" are inadequate. The evaluation must analyze the breadth of participation as well as the number of persons and groups participating.)
7. Roles and responsibilities:
    Were participants given adequate information upon which to base their expectations of the process?
    Were these expectations reasonably met?
    Did participants influence the process and/or ultimate decision? How?

In addition to these elements of the program, the satisfaction of participants also should be measured. Involvement may be rewarding to participants even when they are not particularly influential in the decision-making process.

By measuring levels of satisfaction of participants through discussions, interviews, or questionnaires, these efforts themselves will contribute to the participants' satisfaction with the process.

Opinions of planners and decision makers also should be assessed. As we have noted, a frequent obstacle to meaningful citizen participation is the negative attitude of some public officials.

A final measure of program success concerns the degree to which results of the process have been reported fully and accurately to the public:

1. Did interested citizens receive an accurate report of the program's results?
2. Were they made aware of how these results were used in the overall planning process?
3. Did these reporting mechanisms help build agency credibility?

The most important measure of success will emerge in the political arena. An effective program may encourage the governor or local executive to take a strong leadership role in the implementation of a policy or facilitate controversial legislative action. In some cases, the ultimate measure of success will come at the ballot box, as voters express opinions which may be based largely on information or impressions derived from the public involvement process. The outcome may affect tax levies and bonding measures essential to the agency's operation, as well as the future of elected officials.

Conclusion

There is a tendency for planners to view their professional roles as purely technical, and therefore removed from the public whose input they judge to be value laden and political. One of our purposes in this chapter has been to demonstrate that this dichotomy is false and counterproductive. Not only is planning far from an objective science, but the public often has opinions and insights which can be helpful to the planning process. Moreover, people will become involved in issues which affect their lives, regardless of what planners do. Citizen participation should be welcomed as an opportunity for productive cooperation rather than angry confrontation.

While it can be argued that public involvement is desirable in a democratic society, it is more to the point for our purposes that it provides practical benefits to the planner and the planning process. Citizen participation can be a source of information, ideas, public support, and goodwill; it sometimes can prevent costly legal and political delays; and it can help to transform the siege mentality unfortunately present among many planners into a spirit of cooperation and trust.

While an effective public involvement effort demands time, money, and specialized skills, it also requires a climate of flexibility, candor, and mutual respect. That is not possible if planners approach citizen participation as a threat, a burden, or an unnecessary impediment to technical planning activities.

The planner who is committed to public involvement as a constructive part of the planning process must begin by understanding why individuals volunteer to participate in oftentimes arduous and thankless jobs; it is important also to ensure that there is consistency between the public's expectations and his or her own.

There is no recipe which can be used in constructing an effective program, though we have provided a list of essential ingredients. The most critical element is the commitment of the planner to an open, cooperative, and constructive planning process.

1   Sherry Arnstein, "A Ladder of Citizen Participation," *Journal of the American Institute of Planners*, 35 (July 1969):216–244.

2   Robert Seaver, "The Dilemma of Citizen Participation," in *Citizen Participation in Urban Development*, Vol. 1, ed. Hans B. C. Spiegel (Washington, DC: Center for Community Affairs, NTL Institute for Applied Behavioral Science, 1968).

3   John Friedmann, *Retracking America: A Theory of Transactive Planning* (Garden City: NY: Anchor Press/Doubleday, 1973).

4   Transportation Research Board, *Tranportation Decision-Making: A Guide to Social and Environmental Considerations* (Washington, DC: Transportation Research Board of the National Research Council, 1975).

5   See Robert Jacobson, "Cable's Fuzzy Image" and Leo Murray, "QUBE Answers Back," *Planning* 46 (October 1980):3–4.

6   Two notable efforts may be found in Judy Rosener, "A Cafeteria of Techniques and Critiques," *Public Management* 57 (December 1975):16–19; and Advisory Commission on Intergovernmental Relations, *Citizen Participation in the American Federal System* (Washington, DC: The Commission):chap. 3. Our own effort in Figure 12-4 owes much to these.

Part three: Development policies and strategies

13 Urban development

Either we stand by and continue to tolerate the loss of decent homes and jobs in our city and town centers, the random dispersal of sprawl development, the waste of existing public facilities and the exorbitant costs of providing new public facilities, the loss of thousands of acres of prime farmland every year, and the needless degradation of fragile natural resources and of the unique character of individual regions and communities, *or* we come to grips with the fundamental choices that must be made if this state of affairs is to be changed.

> *City and Town Centers: A Program for Growth.*
> Massachusetts Office of State Planning, 1977.

Faced with the realization that urban development issues are too serious and complex to be managed by local governments acting alone, many states and regions have recently awakened to their responsibilities for urban development policy. These responsibilities have been stated in differing ways, but certain basic concerns appear consistently. Central issues are lagging economic growth and deteriorating physical plants in older urban areas, leapfrogging patterns of suburban building, spiraling costs of public facilities and services, urban encroachment on productive agricultural lands, and destruction of the natural environment by spreading urban development.

Policy and strategy elements

To cope with these concerns, a number of state and regional planning agencies have encouraged the formulation of *urban development policies and strategies—* explicit statements of goals and objectives designed to address issues of growth, development, or decline affecting local communities, coupled with specific programs and actions to reach the policy goals and objectives. A distinctive feature of these urban development policies and strategies is their pragmatic joining of long-term plans with the immediate proposals for institutional change needed to achieve the planning goals. Use of the term "strategy" in connection with urban development policy implies both an emphasis on implementation and a concern with selective action that focuses on those critical initiatives which will have the most leverage for change. In the following discussion, "policy" and "strategy" will be used interchangeably to refer to the longer phrase, "urban development policies and strategies."

According to a recent study by the National Academy of Public Administration,[1] an urban strategy should contain three basic elements:

Goals: Statements of the purposes and objectives of the strategy.

Programs: Activities which will be used to reach the stated goals.

Processes: Methods and approaches to be used in program implementation, including the organizational and managerial methods by which individual programs will be coordinated with other programs and activities, and the methods of monitoring and evaluating progress in reaching strategy objectives.

That study observed that state-level urban strategies offer the governor a way to balance competing claims for increasingly scarce state resources and to use existing state programs more productively.

State and regional strategies compared with local comprehensive plans

The development strategy at the state level can be viewed as the analog of the comprehensive plan at the local level. A recent discussion of city development plans[2] characterized them as "the cornerstone of American planning theory and practice since the early 1900s" and identified their consistent aspects: (1) physical focus; (2) long-range time span; (3) comprehensive coverage, both functional and geographic; (4) statement of desired growth policy; and (5) use as a guide to decision-making. While early state planning attempted to emulate city planning practice, it soon became clear that important differences had to be recognized.

Key differences stem from the need for state strategies to include economic and social factors with physical factors, to operate on a shorter time horizon that accords with the terms of office of governors and legislators, and to deal with a limited number of issues which can be politically negotiated and supported. While retaining the growth policy statement and the decision guide elements of city plans, contemporary state strategies thus differ in several major respects from their urban cousins. They usually are not limited to a physical focus; they typically are not structured around a long-range time span; and they are not necessarily designed for comprehensive coverage, either in terms of all development functions or the entire state territory. As strategies, they are "strategic" in their choice of the crucial targets for action; their target areas may range from major metropolitan areas to sparsely populated rural districts and from critical environmental areas to problem industrial sites, and their target objectives may range from economic development to environmental protection and from growth management to revitalization of declining areas.

It has been argued that neglect of these differences caused early state plans, conceived as city plans written larger, to be ignored by decision-makers. One comparison of these two conceptions defines them as:

1. The Civic Model, which embodies a perception of the State as an organic community capable of pursuing state goals under a comprehensive development plan to be implemented by state government, but willing to accept planning only as an advisory process.
2. The Management Model, which casts state planning as a staff function of the Governor's office, charged with the clarification and transmission of gubernatorial goals through a planning system that encourages effective management throughout the organization, and furnishes more rational basis for execution of the Governor's program, evaluation of performance and problem solving.[3]

In practice, the sharp differences between the civic and management models are rarely found, and in fact, most states combine features of both models in a synthesis that has come to be known as policy or strategy planning. Under this combined approach, long-range goals and policies are joined with an effective management plan that includes more immediate priority and program directives and serves as a vehicle for intergovernmental coordination. The strengths of both the civic and the management models are brought together in a form that is both practical and visionary.

At the regional level, differences with local comprehensive plans are not as pronounced as at the state level. Because most substate regions covered territories that are closer in size to large metropolitan areas than to entire states, the regions can make use of physical development plans that include their entire jurisdictions. The usual practice is to prepare these plans in a more general fashion that those prepared for cities, however, and to view them more as guides and coordination devices than as regulatory devices, since more regional agencies lack the legal authority to regulate development. When regions plan for capital facilities, such as highways and water systems, these plans usually represent compilations of state and local plans, since these governments possess the taxing and spending powers that regional agencies lack. Regions, like states, must stress their management capacities in order to compensate for their lack of control over the development projects of the private sector and of other governments.

State and regional urban development strategies thus are hybrids. They draw certain elements from the long experience of cities in preparing comprehensive development plans, but they also add management features called for by their own unique political and institutional environments.

Necessary conditions

Urban development policies and strategies depend on three key conditions. First, there must be a commitment by leadership to create and support such policies and strategies. Second, a planning staff must be available to handle the necessary analytical and design tasks. Third, authority and resources must be assembled to carry out the action proposals selected.

At the state level, the governor's commitment to formulating an urban development strategy and to pressing for its acceptance by the state legislature and its implementation by the state bureaucracy is the single most essential condition. Gubernatorial politics played the central role in launching state strategies in California, Massachusetts, and North Carolina, for example. Often the issues are highlighted during the governor's campaign for election. To back up the chief executive's leadership, a central policy/planning staff directly responsive to the governor is needed to develop and coordinate the strategy. Not only must this staff be technically capable, but it also must be organizationally and politically adept to manage the tasks of welding diverse agencies and functions into a smoothly coordinated urban policy process. Finally, an urban strategy depends upon the right combination of authority and resources in order to be effective. Formal authority typically is granted by the state legislature in the form of enabling legislation providing for the preparation of an urban policy and of legislative acts to carry out the policy. While either the legislature or the governor may initiate the urban policy process, the legislature will nearly always need to enact new programs and allocate new resources to implement the policy goals. In Michigan, for example, the legislature produced six major pieces of urban strategy legislation: State Revenue Sharing, Detroit Equity Package, Property Tax Circuit Breaker, Downtown Development Act, Plant Expansion Act, and the Michigan State Housing Authority Act.[4]

At the regional level, there is no chief executive counterpart to the governor at the state level. Leadership tends to be more diverse, including both influential individuals and coalitions of public and private sector organizations. For example, the impetus for the formation of the Metropolitan Council of the Twin Cities came from a broad-based group representing civic, business, government, and labor organizations, who were willing to "think metropolitan."[5] The regional planning agency itself, typically governed by representatives of local governments, takes the lead role in bringing together support for an urban development strategy, as well as providing the research, analysis, and public information necessary for strategy formulation. Regional agencies must look to the federal government and to state legislatures for formal program authority and to local governments for cooperation and support. As brokers and middlemen, the regional agencies rely extensively upon persuasion and coordination in carrying out their urban development strategies.

Types of urban development strategies

Depending on the situation in the state or region, urban development strategies can take many forms. Three characteristics are useful in distinguishing among the various strategy types: overriding concerns, organizational linkage, and implementation approach.

A study of state urban development strategies by the Council of State Planning Agencies assumed that the *overriding concern* of such strategies is problems of older central cities. This study "begins with the basic premises that city governments and the special districts which serve them are creatures of state governments, and that the States have the necessary legal powers in their constitutions and statutes to change the powers, boundaries and governments of the cities. It further recognizes that central cities are valuable resources which must be supported and that the welfare of a central city and its residents is inextricably intertwined with the welfare of the State."[6] The overriding concern of the study is the effect of an urban policy on helping or hurting central cities, and it sorts policies into three types:

1. *Neutral* policies do not favor or penalize governments or individuals because of their urban or non-urban location.
2. *Help the hinterlands* policies restrict the powers of major metropolitan areas, offer special assistance to nonmetropolitan areas, and locate new state facilities outside of urban areas.
3. *Save the central city* policies promote the interests and welfare of central city governments and residents through targeting economic development, transportation investments, new state facilities, tax advantages, and grants and investments to central cities, while regulating business and industry moves and investments so as to strengthen central city economies.

In this instance, problems of older central cities are paramount concerns. In other cases, the concerns may be fiscal efficiency as influenced by the urban services pattern of a region on environmental protection as affected by management of land conversion or various other concerns. In most situations, there will be more than one overriding concern, as the complexity of the politics and problems involved dictates a multiple-objective strategy.

Organizational linkage refers to the intergovernmental relationships focused upon by the strategy. These relationships may be of the "picket fence," the "layer cake," or the "marble cake" variety. The "picket fence" approach relies upon *vertical* coordination of government agencies at various levels. For example, Oregon's urban strategy involves both state and local governments in growth management policy formulation and implementation. The "layer cake" approach relies upon *horizontal* coordination of the agencies at a single government level. California, for example, developed its urban strategy primarily through the state Office of Planning and Research and focused it upon a state-level urban action program. The "marble cake" approach *combines* vertical and horizontal coordination in a mixed pattern that depends upon the particular state context. North Carolina's coastal area management program, for example, involves both horizontal coordination of local governments in the coastal region and vertical coordination of development permits. Because of our history of intergovernmental relationships based on functional programs, such as transportation or housing, it is often simpler to coordinate vertically around a single function, such as growth management or environmental protection, than to coordinate horizontally across several functional areas.

Implementation approach distinguishes between strategies that are carried out by voluntary coordination and those that are based upon mandatory regulations. Nearly all regional strategies are forced to depend upon voluntary coordination of the local governments in the regional jurisdiction in order to achieve strategy goals. This is because the majority of regional planning agencies do not have the right to use the police or taxing powers of general purpose governments. State governments, on the other hand, have the option of using both coordination and a full range of taxing and regulatory powers. The types of implementation available are critical in selecting the objectives of an urban strategy. Some objectives require the force of regulation if they are to be achieved, while others can be reached through cooperation, information sharing, and joint planning.

Common concerns

A recent analysis of the urban strategies of ten states found four major themes or concerns which were addressed: (1) economic development, (2) growth management, (3) urban revitalization, and (4) fiscal reform. Under each major theme were several supporting objectives:

Economic Development: Job creation and retention; Industrial development; Business attraction and expansion.

Growth Management: Anti-sprawl; Agricultural preservation; Environmental protection.

Urban Revitalization: Improve housing supply; Improve public facilities; Improve public services.

Fiscal Reform: Increase state aid; Improve equity; Balance revenue with needs.[7]

Each state emphasized at least two of the major concerns, but there was considerable variation in the individual strategies.

Economic development was one of the most popular concerns of the ten state strategies. This emphasis appeared both in those "Frostbelt" states suffering from loss of jobs and population during the 1970s, such as Connecticut, Massachusetts, Michigan, New Jersey, Ohio, and Pennsylvania, and in the growth states of the "Sunbelt" and West Coast, such as California, Florida, North Carolina, and Oregon. Across the country, attraction of new businesses and industries was seen as the primary way to solve urban problems through providing higher incomes, which would support better housing, reduce demand for social services, and increase local tax bases. In Frostbelt states, retention of existing industry was an equally serious concern.

Urban revitalization was an equally popular concern. Even the cities of the Sunbelt and West Coast face problems of deteriorated housing, streets, sewage systems, and other public works in older core neighborhoods and inner suburban rings. Shifts of higher income residents and jobs to the suburbs have reduced urban tax bases and private plant, equipment, and maintenance expenditures. Apartment buildings and warehouses have been abandoned in a process of "disinvestment" when it becomes significantly cheaper to build in undeveloped areas than to operate in a declining city center. Urban revitalization attempts to channel public and private investments back into existing built-up areas, to counter decline and disinvestment, and to increase and improve housing and neighborhoods.

Growth management, with its concern for guiding new development into existing urban areas so as to make optimal use of the existing infrastructure and public services while conserving prime agricultural lands and fragile environmental areas, seeks to accomplish some of the same goals as urban revitalization and economic development. Growth management, however, relies more heavily on land use regulation and development management to influence the location, amount, rate, type, and quality of future growth.[8] For example, the California strategy calls for a commitment to more compact urban areas, stating that new urban development should be located according to three principles:

1. Renew and maintain existing urban areas, both cities and suburbs.

Figure 13–1 "Transfer
of equity to suburbs."

2. Develop vacant and under-utilized land within existing urban and suburban areas
    and presently served by streets, water, sewer and other public services. . . .
3. When urban development is necessary outside existing urban and suburban areas,
    use land that is immediately adjacent.[9]

By bringing residences and work places as close as possible, the California
strategy seeks to save energy, reduce freeway congestion, clean up air pollution,
and provide more leisure time. By "infilling," or developing vacant and underutilized land within cities, it seeks to make more efficient use of existing facilities
and services and to reduce public expenditures for new capital-intensive infrastructure. By containing urban sprawl and providing tax incentives to agricultural
enterprises, it seeks to protect productive crop and rangelands from premature
or needless conversion to urban uses.

Fiscal reforms were recognized as needs by the state strategies but were not
usually accorded primary concern. These reforms, where included, sought to
increase equity of local tax systems and fiscal capacity of local governments.
They reflect the impact of the property tax revolt spearheaded by passage of
California's Proposition 13 in 1978, which halved the property tax base available
to local governments. A public attitude of hostility to tax increases and a legislative mood of fiscal restraint have dictated a concern for making sure that tax
burdens are equitably allocated and that budgets are balanced. Among the ways
of addressing fiscal reforms are increased state funding for mandated programs,
state revenue sharing, legislation controlling property taxes, and balanced budget
requirements.

Regional concerns have tended to focus on two major concerns: (1) growth management, and (2) urban revitalization. Without the powers of general purpose governments, most regional planning agencies have not been able to initiate fiscal reforms nor to make public investments to attract economic development. They have attempted to coordinate land-use regulations and capital improvements programs of state and local governments into regional growth management programs. They have also used planning and review powers granted by the federal government under its functional programs, such as housing, water quality, and transportation, and under its A-95 clearinghouse requirements for regional review of local grant requests, to guide public investments toward urban revitalization needs.

Common methods

With their heavy emphasis upon implementation, urban development strategies actively seek out methods or tools to reach the goals they set. These methods range from catalogs of existing programs to proposals for new legislation or regulations. They can be categorized as: (1) program coordination, (2) regulatory policies, (3) tax incentives, (4) growth and land-use policies, (5) fiscal assistance, and (6) review procedures.[10]

Program coordination is a popular method for obvious reasons. It involves no new expenditures, but instead it seeks to make more effective use of existing programs to achieve urban policy goals. In order to make program coordination something more than a paper exercise, it must be tied to some concrete action, such as a budget or a construction project. For example, the state planning office can review agency budget requests against the urban goals, as in California, or state agencies can be required to file Capital Development Impact Statements, as in Connecticut. A high level coordinating committee or interagency "development cabinet" can be formed, as in Massachusetts under Governor Dukakis, to coordinate the actions and expenditures of state agencies in contributing to the implementation of the urban strategy. At the regional level, an areawide capital improvements program can be used to bring together into one coordinated program all capital improvements expenditures with regional significance which are proposed by the state and local governments within the region. Also at the regional level, a fair share housing program can be used to coordinate federal, state, and local projects for low and moderate income housing to ensure an equitable distribution of housing opportunities throughout the region.

Regulatory policies seek to improve opportunities for economic growth and urban revitalization through recasting laws and procedures affecting banking, insurance, environmental quality, land use, and urban development. State-level examples are proposals by California to prepare a model building rehabilitation code, to enforce strong anti-redlining policies prohibiting geographic discrimination in mortgage lending, to increase efforts to reduce air pollution from stationary sources, such as power plants and petroleum operations, and to amend safe drinking water regulations to give preference in allocation of funds to areas whose development is consistent with urban strategy priorities. Regional-level examples are the regulations for requiring development permits in areas of critical concern, as in the North Carolina coastal area.

Tax incentives include tax exemptions, abatements, and deferrals as a means of encouraging private developers and employers to assist in meeting urban strategy goals, as well as tax sharing to reduce unnecessary competition among communities within a region for property tax revenues generated by major new commercial and industrial development. Among tax incentive approaches are abatements for housing rehabilitation, exemptions for industries locating or expanding in urban areas, tax increment financing to pay for redevelopment of blighted areas, tax credits for new job creation, and industrial revenue bonds to provide facilities for new plants. The "enterprise zone" concept is a way of encouraging private investment in a specified urban area, so as to meet development goals and needs.

Growth and land-use policies seek to influence both state actions that trigger development and local decisions on policy, planning, and regulation of growth. At the state level, for example, North Carolina's Balanced Growth Policy called for the designation of local "growth centers" to be targeted for federal and state resources to enhance their attractiveness to industrial and residential growth. Local areas seeking designation as growth centers had to show willingness to pursue orderly development, potential to expand their industrial or economic base, capacity to support additional growth, and livability factors that make them attractive as locations for new people and jobs. Oregon and Florida have required local governments to prepare comprehensive plans, which must be in accordance with state goals. At the regional level, North Carolina has provided for the preparation of land classification plans to provide serviced land for ten-year development needs.

Fiscal assistance methods seek to relieve local fiscal problems. Examples of these approaches are state revenue sharing and block grant programs, state assumption of local service costs for mandated programs, and direct funding to urban areas for programs of assistance in housing, water and sewer, and transportation facilities.

Review procedures are used by both state and regional agencies to evaluate local government plan and project proposals. Under the federal A-95 clearinghouse requirements, all local applications for federal grants had to be reviewed by state and regional agencies for their consistency with existing plans and policies. While reviewing agencies could only comment on applications, their comments had to be taken into account by the federal agency responsible for the grant program. After the phaseout of the federal A-95 program, states will need to work out new review approaches.

Historical overview

To put current urban development policy initiatives into perspective, it is helpful to look at their historical antecedents. Even without a comprehensive survey of history back to the time of Jefferson's *Notes on Virginia* in 1784, we can find considerable effort devoted to shaping urban development during the present century. This historical overview will touch briefly on state and regional planning for urban development during the era of the National Planning Board, later the National Resources Board, in the 1930s and then skip to significant activities during the 1960s and 1970s.

Urban strategies during the 1930s

While the urban strategies of recent years appear to break new ground, a brief review of fifty years of American urban history turns up many of the same problems and proposed solutions. In a report by the National Resources Committee to President Franklin D. Roosevelt published in 1939, Harold Buttenheim identified the pattern of the typical American city as declining central area slums, abandoned factories, and congested commercial districts ringed with unused or unplanned mixtures of land use and outer bands of residential subdivisions and new industries.[11] He cited the problems preventing rational urban development as wildcat speculation and frenzied city growth, speculation in outlying areas, premature subdivisions, poorly planned subdivisions, speculation in improved lands, underuse and overuse of land, peripheral growth and urban blight, lack of neighborhood planning, difficulty of assembly of large urban land areas, and inadequate use of land in private and public ownership. Buttenheim believed that the source of the problem lay in a failure to use effectively municipal government's instruments of control: planning, zoning, assessment, taxation, eminent domain, and land transfer procedures. Clearly the issues of urban development policy have been with us a long time.

Buttenheim's analysis was commissioned by the National Resources Board, the federal agency which promoted and supported the creation of state planning boards in nearly 46 states as of 1935. These boards surveyed natural and human resources, analyzed trends, and prepared recommendations for public works, transportation, land use, housing, and other functional areas. While many of the concerns were similar to those of modern urban development strategies, there was one important difference. State planning was defined as an "*advisory*, not an administrative activity."[12]

Regional plans of that period also were viewed as advisory in nature. For example, the Regional Plan of the Philadelphia Tri-State District, published in 1932, sought to ensure cooperation among the localities of eleven counties in Pennsylvania, New Jersey, and Delaware in planning the physical facilities requirements of the region's projected growth between 1930 and 1980. The plan focused on housing, transportation, sanitation and water supply, and park facilities, forecasting requirements for them on the basis of population and land-use trends. While the forecasts underestimated the actual growth of the region, the plan highlighted the major issues of urban development strategy, including suburbanization trends, farmland conversion, shortage of water supply, and need for modernizing transportation facilities.

Recent urban strategies

Frustration with the ineffectiveness of advisory urban development approaches and with the intractable persistence of urban problems addressed by local government programs led to the call for new development *management* approaches and for more *activist* roles by state governments and regional agencies. These changes came together in the urban development strategies of the 1970s, but the groundwork for them was done in the 1960s.

New York State under Governor Nelson Rockefeller's leadership prepared a development policy in 1964 which foreshadowed later efforts in several respects. *Change/Challenge/Response: A Development Policy for New York State* offered a broad-gauged vision of a 60-year development plan for orderly growth.[13] A metropolitan and regional planning institutional framework was proposed to bring the state's population growth into balance and to distribute development across the state. While it did not prepare a capital improvements program, the policy did recognize the importance of guiding future capital construction through public and private planning. The policy also recommended a number of basic action steps, including designation of development regions served by Regional Councils appointed by the Governor, formulation of statements of statewide development needs, annual preparation by the Budget Director for the Governor of a physical and financial program for meeting state development needs, and establishment of a state regional development fund as a public benefit corporation to channel private investment into regional programs. However, it differed from recent urban strategies in its inclusion of specific land-use elements, which made it appear similar to a regional land-use plan *writ large*.

Implementation of the New York policy proposals ran a mixed course.[14] The state retreated in the face of local opposition on the matter of the Governor's appointment of the regional councils, which became locally appointed regional planning boards. Other proposals moved strongly ahead, with state efforts to integrate planning, programming, and budgeting, to reorganize the agency struc-

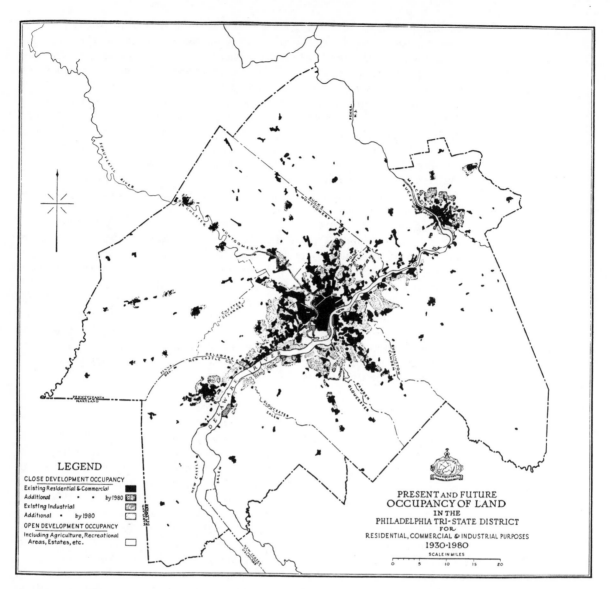

Figure 13–2 Present and future land occupancy, Philadelphia
Tri-State District, 1930–1980.

ture of state government along programmatic lines, and to establish a number
of public benefit corporations to expedite state capital projects and assist localities
and private enterprise in achieving development objectives. The most famous
of these corporations, the New York State Urban Development Corporation,
compiled a remarkable record in housing and commercial development projects
before it ran afoul of state and local politics and the mid-1970s' recessions and
was sharply cut back.

The quiet revolution Also during the 1960s and early 1970s, several states and
regions had begun to enter the land-use planning and regulation arena, which
had formerly been the province of local governments. This "quiet revolution in
land use control" was described as:

The ancient regime being overthrown is the feudal system under which the entire
pattern of land development has been controlled by thousands of individual local

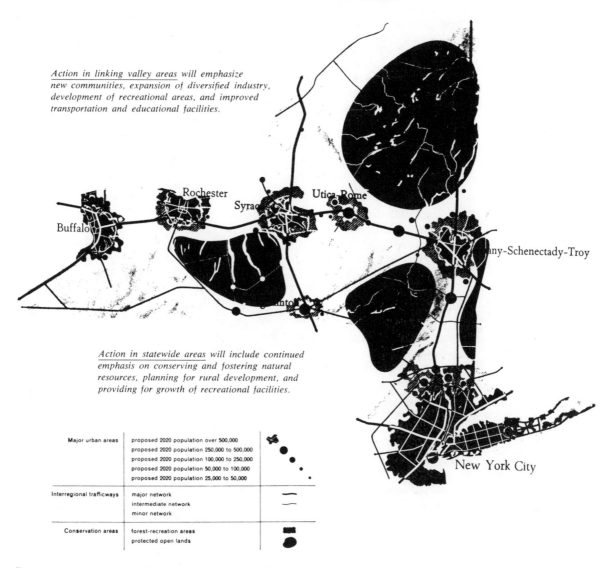

Action in metropolitan areas will emphasize open space and new and enlarged communities in the suburbs. In the city centers non-residential renewal projects will be increased.

Action in linking valley areas will emphasize new communities, expansion of diversified industry, development of recreational areas, and improved transportation and educational facilities.

Action in statewide areas will include continued emphasis on conserving and fostering natural resources, planning for rural development, and providing for growth of recreational facilities.

Major urban areas	proposed 2020 population over 500,000	
	proposed 2020 population 250,000 to 500,000	
	proposed 2020 population 100,000 to 250,000	
	proposed 2020 population 50,000 to 100,000	
	proposed 2020 population 25,000 to 50,000	
Interregional trafficways	major network	
	intermediate network	
	minor network	
Conservation areas	forest-recreation areas	
	protected open lands	

Figure 13–3   New York state development policy, 1964.

governments, each seeking to maximize its tax base and minimize its social problems, and caring less what happens to all the others.

The tools of the revolution are new laws taking a wide variety of forms, but each sharing a common theme—the need to provide some degree of state or regional participation in the major decisions that affect the use of our increasingly limited supply of land.[15]

The nine main programs in the "revolutionary" cadre included the following:

Hawaii's Land Use Law, passed in 1961 to preserve agricultural land from urban development pressures by dividing the state into conservation, agriculture, rural, and urban districts;

Vermont's Environmental Control Law (Act 250), passed in 1970 to provide a state and regional framework to protect the state's rural character from a recreational resort and second home boom;

San Francisco Bay's Conservation and Development Commission, created by the California legislature in 1965 to prepare a plan to control the filling of the Bay by developers.

Minneapolis—St. Paul's Metropolitan Council of the Twin Cities Area, established by the Minnesota legislature in 1967 to plan and implement regional public facilities and land use programs;

Massachusetts' Zoning Appeals Law, approved in 1969 to use state land use control powers to attack zoning by local governments which excludes low income housing projects;

Maine's Site Location Law, passed in 1970 to require approval by a state agency of large commercial, industrial and residential developments by a state commission;

Massachusetts' Wetlands Protection Program, a series of statutes adopted starting in 1963 to control development of coastal and inland wetlands;

Wisconsin's Shoreland Protection Program, enacted in 1966 to require counties to adopt regulations for protection of shorelands in unincorporated areas; and

New England's River Basin Commission, created in 1967 under the provisions of the federal Water Resources Planning Act to provide coordinated interstate water resources planning.[16]

The observers of the quiet revolution found a new concept of land emerging that weighted its value as a *resource* equally with its value as a *commodity*. The resource concept grew from the spread of an ecological understanding of the contributions of wetlands and other formerly ignored "marginal" areas to human welfare through valuable service in flood protection, waste absorption, water purification, and wildlife habitat provision. They also found a change in the accepted roles of state and local governments in the land planning and regulation process, which took the form of reviewing development decisions of "state or regional significance" at a level higher than the local level. While more recent commentators have argued that the changes were more of a gradual metamorphosis than a revolution, they do acknowledge the impact of the new concepts and roles.

We now see that what actually took place during the past two decades was an increase in development management activity at *all* levels of government. The new federal, state, and regional programs did not reduce local development management responsibilities, which in fact increased at an unprecedented rate during the same period.

The ALI model code Along with these reforms in development management practice came a new interest in reforming the law of development management. Most state and local laws and ordinances prior to this time were conceptual offspring of the model planning and zoning enabling acts published by the U.S. Department of Commerce under Secretary Herbert Hoover in the 1920s. In 1963, the American Law Institute, a legal study group with offices in Philadelphia, began preparation of a new model statute to update the legal framework for land use planning and regulation.

The Institute assembled a blue ribbon group of land use lawyers, who set to work to create a new approach to development management that recognized contemporary concepts and roles. This group decided that existing enabling acts failed to guide local public officials, land developers, planners, and lawyers and judges in decision-making for rational allocation of land resources. Their new approach, the American Law Institute *Model Land Development Code*,[16] spelled out a new system of government institutions, procedures, and tools.

Unlike the earlier model codes, the ALI Code has not enjoyed sweeping acceptance. Perhaps most states were not yet ready for comprehensive reforms of their existing laws and agencies or felt that the aims of the ALI Code could be met by already available means or had shifted their concern from environmental protection to economic development by the time the ALI Code was published in the mid-1970s, after most of the major new state land use laws had already been passed. Only Florida has adopted major parts of the ALI system, although Colorado and several other states, especially those with fragile natural environments, have accepted one or more of its tools in modified form.

The tools of the ALI Code are genuine innovations, fundamentally changing the traditional concepts of land use regulation. These new tools attempt to regulate:

1. *Areas of Critical State Concern*—those areas which affect major public facilities; historical, natural, or environmental resources of regional or state importance; proposed new communities; and jurisdictions of local governments without their own development regulations.
2. *Developments of Regional Impact*—those proposed projects which present issues of state or regional significance, in terms of environmental problems, traffic generation, amount of new population, size of site, potential for generating other new development, or particular unique qualities.[17]

In Areas of Critical State Concern, special regulations are established and development permits are required to protect types of land or geographic locations, while in Developments of Regional Impact special regional agency review procedures are set up for those types of proposed development projects which meet certain threshold criteria of size or impact.

Many states have included procedures for designation of Areas of Critical State Concern in their coastal area management programs under the federal Coastal Area Management Act. National land use legislation based upon the ALI Model Code, however, was introduced and actively debated in the early 1970s but never passed Congress.[18] Changes in the political and economic climate forced a shift from comprehensive state program reforms to legislation dealing with particular areas or resources.

National urban policy   Most national development policy enacted by Congress has dealt with single functional programs, such as environmental quality. The Coastal Zone Management Act, the Clean Air Act, the Clean Water Act, and the National Environmental Policy Act, are examples of this singular approach. However, in the Housing and Urban Development Act of 1970, Congress called for a biennial report by the President on broader aspects of National Urban Policy.

Early Policy Reports dealt mostly with trends and analysis. However, in 1978, the Carter Administration announced a comprehensive management-oriented urban policy to conserve communities. The President's 1980 National Urban Policy Report reviews accomplishments in carrying out the 1978 policy objectives, summarizes urban development trends and problems, and presents an updated policy statement.[18]

Objectives of the 1980 policy are to strengthen urban economics, improve job opportunities and mobility for the long-term unemployed, promote fiscal stability, expand opportunity for those disadvantaged by discrimination and poverty, and encourage energy-efficient and environmentally sound patterns of urban development. To carry out these objectives, a broad range of coordination, tax incentive, fiscal assistance, and growth and land use policies is proposed. These policies are justified in the 1980 Report by reference to six key trends expected to cause the urban changes of the coming decade:

1. Spreading out of urban America, due to continuing movement of people from central city to suburbs and from the Northeast and North Central regions to the South and West.
2. Decline of manufacturing jobs in most central cities, despite overall job increases in the nation as a whole.
3. Increasing concentration of poverty and unemployment in central cities.

4. Shrinking tax bases and increasing service demands that put fiscal pressure on city budgets.
5. Rising costs and diminished production of housing which has priced many families out of the housing market, despite a general improvement in housing and neighborhood conditions.
6. Increasing importance of energy conservation and environmental quality concerns in urban development patterns and policies.[19]

Despite an optimistic tone in the 1980 Report, and a number of successful administrative actions, many of the legislative reforms proposed to Congress by the 1978 Report failed to pass. The first management-oriented federal urban policy resulted in only moderate implementation reforms. One of the casualties was proposed legislation for State Incentive Grants, designed to encourage states to prepare urban strategies.

Under the Reagan Administration a broad policy of cutting back on federal programs and funding appeared in 1981, along with specific proposals for minimization of federal regulations, reductions in financial assistance to state and local governments and regional organizations, and devolution of authority and responsibility from the federal to the state and local levels. The 1982 decision to discontinue A-95 review and the 1982 Urban Policy Report's emphasis on economic recovery continued these policy thrusts. It appears that the federal role in urban development policy under President Reagan will be limited to defining and paying for specific minimum programs of housing, employment, transportation, and environmental quality, while leaving state, regional, and local agencies to prepare more comprehensive strategies to cope with problems of urban developments.

One of the targets of the federal cutback in 1981 was the 701 program of the Department of Housing and Urban Development (HUD). Under HUD's 701 incentive funding for state and regional strategies, two objectives had been stressed:

1. *Community Conservation*: conserve and improve existing communities by addressing existing conditions of distress or decline, including inefficient and disorderly growth.
2. *Expansion of Opportunities*: provide greater housing and employment opportunities and expand access to such opportunities for minorities and the poor.[20]

Actions eligible for federal support included policies for managing the amount and location of growth, public capital investment programs, public service delivery and financing, tax base sharing, promotion of fair and equal housing opportunities, and others. Without the 701 program, states and regions will have to rely on block grants and state funds to support these efforts.

Urban strategies of the 1970s Even without national legislation encouraging states to prepare urban strategies, a number of state governments forged such strategies during the 1970s. A 1980 study by the National Academy of Public Administration analyzed ten states, whose population was 40 percent of the total U.S. population as of 1977, and found nine with active policies, the majority of which were published between 1977 and 1979.[20] The *1980 National Urban Policy Report* also identified a number of recent state actions to assist distressed communities.

The Academy of Public Administration study concluded that the state strategies they analyzed either preceded or paralleled, rather than derived from, the National Urban Policy effort initiated by President Carter in 1977. In this field, no one level of government has been the consistent leader. While all of the strategies were undoubtedly influenced by the actions of other governments, the problems and politics of their own jurisdictions were more important than outside

Figure 13–4 Summary of state actions to assist distressed communities.

Field	Action taken by states	Number of states taking action
Housing finance	Provide financial assistance to lower income households	44
	Geographic targeting in home rehabilitation aid	19
	Targeted home rehabilitation tax incentives	17
	Fair housing statutes	30
Economic development	Targeting site development aid to underdeveloped communities	15
	Promote commercial and manufacturing facilities in distressed communities	11
	Tax credits to stimulate industrial development in designated needy areas	12
	Tying small business aid to community need indicators	8
	Customized job training	23
Community development	Authorize creation of local renewal agencies	48
	Targeted community development aid	18
	Preferential siting of state facilities in distressed communities	4
Fiscal reform	Targeted state-local tax and revenue sharing	21
	New school finance equalization plans (since 1970)	25
	Cutting per-pupil expenditure disparities within the state (since 1970)	17
	State assumption of at least 90% of local welfare costs	30
	Authorization of local sales or income taxes to reduce reliance on property taxes	36
	Reimbursement to localities for state-mandated expenses	16
	Authorize local tax base sharing	1

influences in leading them to devise a new way of doing business in urban development policy.

Selected innovative strategies

To grasp the nature of changes proposed by recent state and regional strategies, it is useful to review a selection of the prominent efforts. The following examples are drawn from the most innovative state and regional strategies. It should be noted that these selections represent the leading edge of current practice, rather than its center.

California

California's urban strategy is one of a series of government actions to manage urban development in this rapidly growing state. Earlier in 1972, the state's voters approved Proposition 20, a citizen-originated ballot initiative to "save the coast." This coastal management program, which gave powerful state and regional coastal commissions control over nearly all forms of construction along the entire 1072 mile coastline, has been described as:

the boldest effort to date in state land use regulation. Endowed by the original ballot initiative with an exceptionally strong legal and political position, the coastal commissions—particularly the state commission—aggressively implemented the law. California courts, traditionally tolerant of innovations in planning, allowed the commissions great flexibility. The volume of development permits processed and the diversity of land use issues that were raised and dealt with are unrivaled by any other state land use program, coastal or noncoastal.[22]

The 1972 initiative set up six regional coastal commissions under a state coastal commission. They were charged with: (1) issuing development permits for all proposed projects in the coastal area, and (2) preparing a plan for long-term management of the coast to be submitted to the 1976 session of the state legislature. Not only did the commissions decide on over 25,000 development permits between 1972 and 1976, but also they produced a plan whose major principles successfully weathered strong attacks by business and local government lobbying to pass the legislature. The resulting California Coastal Act of 1976 created a new state-local partnership for coastal management, with state policy goals to be implemented by regional review and certification of local land use plans and regulations. The coastal commissions have been credited with making a major difference in the amount, location, and quality of development and with demonstrating that coastal development raises issues of greater than local concern, including public access to beaches, view protection, retention of farmland and low-cost housing, prevention of sprawl, and location of energy facilities and state infrastructure.

California's success in coastal management set the stage for its urban strategy, published in 1978. The legislative authority for the strategy stems from a 1970 state law directing the governor to prepare and regularly revise a State Environmental Goals and Policy Report. Staff capacity was provided by the 1970 Act, which created the Office of Planning and Research to prepare the environmental report.

A 1973 environmental report, largely technical and advisory, was the forerunner of the 1978 action-oriented strategy. Governor Brown provided the leadership commitment to the new strategy during his campaign for a second term, using it to demonstrate his commitment to the cities.

Guiding urban development appears as the overriding concern of the California urban strategy. The dominant focus is on a more compact urban environment.

Both horizontal and vertical organizational linkages are proposed. The state took the lead in preparing the strategy and the state's responsibility for overall goal setting, air and water quality, and infrastructure investment is recognized. But the strategy is designed to be carried out by a "partnership" of the state, local government, regional agencies, citizens, and the private sector. Proposed implementation approaches include administrative regulations or policies, executive orders, budget act approval, new legislation, and constitutional amendments.

Forty-five specific actions are recommended as first steps toward meeting fourteen broad urban goals. Action steps are grouped under three main directions:

1. Improve existing housing and encourage new urban development.
2. Improve urban social and economic conditions.
3. Resolve interjurisdictional conflicts.[23]

Examples of innovative actions proposed are investment of public retirement system funds in California housing mortgages; requiring cities, counties, and special districts to prepare five-year capital improvement programs; creation of a builder's surety bonding company for small and minority contractors; and requiring formal assessment of region-wide development needs and resources by local governments in cooperation with the councils of government in the large metropolitan areas.

The long-term effect of the California urban strategy, unlike the state's influential coastal management program, is uncertain. It has not received major attention from the legislature nor the governor since its publication. Perhaps its major impact will be realized through its highlighting of important urban development issues and resulting incremental changes in state government operations.

Florida

After a colorful history of promoting laissez faire, boom and bust, freebooting urban development, Florida's government finally recognized the need for growth management early in the 1970s. Spurred by an "explosion" of growth in which as many as 25,000 new residents moved into the state each month, coupled with a severe drought in south Florida, the governor and legislature created a state development policy. Prior to the first of the new laws setting forth and implementing this policy, the Environmental Land and Water Management Act of 1972, neither the state nor local governments had done much growth management. More than 50 percent of the state's land area was without development controls.[24]

Florida's first growth management act followed the approach of the ALI Model Land Development Code, preferring an emphasis on regulating strategic projects or sensitive environments to the preparation of a comprehensive state land use plan. Two of that Code's major tools, developments of regional impact and areas of critical state concern, were incorporated into the Environmental Land and Water Management Act.

Developments of regional impact, those projects that affect the citizens of more than one county, include such things as airports, large manufacturing plants, shopping centers, and housing developments that meet specified threshold sizes. A developer who applies for a permit, called a "development order," for a project that meets the development of regional impact criteria must submit detailed information about the environmental, economic, and fiscal impacts of the project. The local government holds a hearing on the application, after receiving a recommendation on it from the regional planning agency. Local decisions can be appealed to the governor and cabinet, acting as the Land and Water Adjudicatory Commission. The resulting process combines the devel-

Figure 13–5   Goals of California's urban strategy.

California's urban strategy envisions as its goal a society in which people live in harmony with the land: where urban areas are exciting, safe places to live; where the air and water are clean; where work places are close to homes; where crops and animals thrive on the state's best agricultural lands; where areas of great scenic or fragile nature are set aside for permanent protection. To accomplish this California must commit itself to more compact urban areas, to the revitalization of its existing cities and suburbs, to the continued production of its best agricultural lands.

The actions included in this strategy are based on a set of broad goals:

1   increasing employment through environmentally sound industrial and commercial growth;

2   improving the quality of public schools;

3   providing an adequate supply of affordable housing in both cities and suburbs;

4   curbing wasteful urban sprawl and directing new development to existing cities and suburbs;

5   protecting the state's natural environment, particularly the land and air and water quality;

6   revitalizing central cities and neighborhoods and eliminating urban blight;

7   protecting the most productive agricultural lands;

8   encouraging land-use patterns in a manner to stimulate necessary development while protecting environmental quality;

9   improving the efficiency of government and limiting taxes to the lowest practical level;

10   encouraging effective local law enforcement;

11   providing an adequate transportation system, includng both public transit and well-maintained streets and freeways;

12   providing recreational and cultural activities;

13   guaranteeing needed social services, such as health care, job training, and adequate unemployment and other financial assistance to those in need;

14   ensuring full participation of citizens in decisions affecting the future of their cities and neighborhoods.

oper's initiative with local control, regional evaluation, and state review. The number of applications was greatest in the first years of project review and has fallen off since, leading some to believe that the start of the process coincided with the peak of Florida's second great land boom and that review of developments of regional impact is a tool of the last war.

Areas of critical state concern can be designated by the cabinet or legislature. Three types of areas are eligible, including environmental and historical areas, areas with a significant effect on a major public facility, and proposed new community sites. Three areas of critical concern have been selected—Big Cypress Swamp and the Green Swamp, both major aquifer recharge areas, and the Florida Keys, where rapid and uncoordinated development was threatening fragile environmental resources. However, the critical areas program has been hampered by constitutional challenges and by lack of capacity to plan and manage the designated areas, and its future is uncertain.

Other parts of the Florida development policy package include:

1.   The State Comprehensive Planning Act of 1972, which named the

governor as chief planning officer and provided for preparation of a state comprehensive plan for long-range guidance of the social, economic, and physical growth of the state.

2. A growth policy statement, passed by the legislature in 1974, which declared that it shall not be the state's policy to stimulate growth generally, but to plan for and distribute such growth as may develop and the desired kind, rate and extent of growth shall be primarily determined by the carrying capacity of natural and man-made systems of an area.

3. The 1975 Local Government Comprehensive Planning Act, which required local governments to prepare and adopt Comprehensive plans by July, 1979. Local governments that fail to prepare plans will have them prepared by the state, at local expense. After plan adoption, all land development regulations must be consistent with the plan.

4. The Florida Regional Planning Act of 1980, which strengthened the state's regional planning councils and provided for the development of comprehensive regional policy plans.

The Florida State Comprehensive Plan, prepared in 1978, is completely devoted to policy. It contains no land use maps or capital programs. What it does contain are broad goals, more specific objectives, policies to achieve these objectives, and recommended implementing actions for fourteen functional areas ranging from agriculture to water.[25] For example, the Land Development section of the plan declares that future growth should be guided to uplands areas of the state, rather than to those parts of the coastal zone and wetlands with resource constraints; it directs state agencies to include this policy in coastal zone and economic development plans, and in the identification of "areas of major development potential," those locations with high growth tolerance and few environmental limitations on development.

A recent strategy effort, published in 1979, stresses "community conservation"—improvement of the fiscal capability, economic resources, and physical conditions of developed areas. This strategy began as a demonstration by the Department of Community Affairs, but was taken over by the governor after the creation of a new Office of Planning and Budgeting within his office. Proposals in the strategy include establishment of a state housing finance agency and revisions in distribution of state revenue sharing funds.

Florida exemplifies a case of innovative response to the impacts of heavy growth pressure on a state with serious environmental limitations. Rather than relying upon a single policy or tool, Florida has adopted a broad range of goals and methods to guide its development. Each level of organization is involved in planning and growth management. Local governments have a mandate to adopt comprehensive plans and to issue development orders for large scale projects. Regional planning councils also have authority to prepare comprehensive policy plans and to review developments of regional impact. The state government has drawn up a comprehensive policy plan and has the power to designate areas of critical state concern. Florida has squarely faced the challenge of intergovernmental development guidance, while boldly testing new concepts of policy implementation.

Massachusetts

Publication of *City and Town Centers: A Program for Growth* in 1977 marked a new phase for growth policy in Massachusetts. It was the state's first comprehensive statewide growth policy. It was the first state policy process that was shaped from the bottom up. And it was the state's first attempt to substitute a "public learning" approach for the traditional rational planning model.

Local governments in Massachusetts traditionally have enjoyed a great deal of autonomy in land use and growth management, under home rule legislation. The state had enacted some nonlocal legislation, such as the 1969 Zoning Appeals Law that gave the state power to overrule local exclusionary zoning, a number of wetlands protection statutes between 1963 and 1972, and a 1973 Environmental Policy Act requiring environmental impact statements for projects involving state funds or approval. In 1974, it established on Martha's Vineyard the nation's first regional land use commission with power to overrule local zoning laws. However, no action had been taken to coordinate various state and local programs into a unified development policy prior to the enactment of the Massachusetts Growth Policy Development Act of 1975.

In a unique departure from the top-down growth policy processes of other states, Massachusetts created a one-year participatory process giving citizens, communities, and regional agencies an opportunity to send a message to the state government regarding growth issues they wished to see addressed. Not only did this broad public participation process bring to the surface the critical development issues, but also it initiated community discussions in order to encourage public learning on a broad scale about the problems and values involved. As the growth report declares, "The overall purpose of the growth policy process has been to prepare the people of Massachusetts for the difficult choices that must be made if the benefits of continued growth and development are to be enjoyed".[26]

Leadership for the growth policy process began with a study commission created by the legislature in 1973. In 1975, Governor Dukakis joined with legislative leaders in supporting the proposed legislation, which gave an important role to his Office of State Planning. After intensive debate, the bill passed in 1975, and the involvement process began. Localities had six months to establish local growth policy committees and to prepare statements of problems and priorities in response to a questionnaire from the Office of State Planning. Regional planning agencies then had two months to summarize local statements and identify regional growth problems and priorities. After public hearings, the reports were submitted to the Office of State Planning for analysis and incorporation into a report to the Special Commission on the Effects of Growth Patterns on the Quality of Life.

As indicated by its title, the primary theme of the Massachusetts policy report is to conserve and develop existing city and town centers. Local growth policy committees were particularly concerned with the preservation of community character, with the need for economic development, with housing cost and supply problems, with a state and local tax system seen as regressive and burdensome, with public facilities, and with local control of growth. Regional agencies, ranging from metropolitan Boston to the smaller and less-developed regions, took differing positions on the issues of housing, industrial development, center revitalization, transportation, and environmental preservation, depending upon the regional context—urban, suburban, or rural. The state identified six areas of consensus based on the need for the following:

1. Increased economic development.
2. Revitalization of city and town centers.
3. Maintenance of environmental quality.
4. Property tax relief.
5. Preservation of farm land.
6. Improved sensitivity to differences in community character.

To articulate the overall policy, a number of statewide growth policies were recommended:

1. Growth should be channeled primarily into developed rather than outlying areas, especially into city and town centers, and discouraged in critical environmental areas, consistent with individual communities' willingness and ability to accommodate growth.
2. Future growth and development shall be designed to complement the natural and man-made environments.
3. The level of future growth will be sufficient in quantity, quality, and distribution, to provide job and housing opportunities for all citizens.
4. Growth shall be phased so as not to strain the community's ability to provide public facilities and services, not to disrupt the social fabric, and to be in keeping with the community's desired rate of growth.
5. Responsible and effective growth management will be promoted to ensure consideration of relevant impacts, participation by affected parties, consistency with adopted policies, and timely decisionmaking.
6. Land use and growth decisions shall remain principally a local prerogative, and shall be supported, not preempted, by higher levels of government.
7. Viewpoints of each region shall be given increased significance in decisions which affect their growth and developed.
8. State government shall ensure that all of its actions support the desires of its citizenry for future growth and development.[27]

The growth policies were to be carried out by means of some 36 action recommendations, including state legislation and program changes as well as encouragement of local revitalization growth management. Among the proposed state actions were anti-redlining legislation, revision of the State Building Code to encourage rehabilitation, formation of development finance organizations, establishment of a farmland development rights acquisition program and an agricultural transfer of development rights program, requiring the state to size and locate sewer facilities in compliance with local growth plans, enabling legislation for regional planning agencies to control development of regional impact and/or areas of critical environmental concern, and provision of state assistance to communities to control local expenditures.

Massachusetts presents an example of a unique vertical strategy to build consensus for government action to meet problems of economic decline and urban revitalization. Its bottom-up policy formulation process resulted in a primary local government role, and the governor created a "development cabinet," chaired by the director of the Office of State Planning, to coordinate state agencies. However, one of the major strengths of the Massachusetts policy, its strong connection to Governor Dukakis, turned into a liability when the next governor succeeded to office. There was some continuity in antisprawl policies, and plans and legislation adopted under the policy are in place, but the policy lost momentum with the change in governors. With the passage of Proposition 2½ by Massachusetts voters in 1980, cutbacks in revenues from local property taxes forced further reductions in public resources for development. Despite these conditions, new private investments continued in 1981, leading to comments of "public sector bust and private sector boom."

North Carolina

The economic and urban landscape of North Carolina differs from other states with growth policies. Instead of dominant metropolitan areas with high density "peaks" of urban population, North Carolina's population spreads much more evenly across the state in a low density "sheet" of small towns, medium-sized cities, and rural-agricultural centers. The economy depends on both farms and factories. In 1970 North Carolina's total cash crop value was sixth in the United States. In 1975 it ranked eighth in total manufacturing employment, though last in average hourly wages of production workers. Not surprisingly, development policy focuses on concerns of low density settlement patterns and low wage employment.

Major problems addressed by the current development strategy include the following:

1. Reaching a higher standard of living all across the state by bringing more and better jobs to where people live.
2. Providing adequate public services equitably for all of the state's people at an efficient cost; and
3. Maintaining the natural environmental heritage while accommodating urban and agricultural growth.

These concerns are not new; they also show up in earlier growth policy statements.

The roots of present policy go back to the creation by statute of the Council of State Goals and Policy in 1971 and the publication in 1972 of the North Carolina *Statewide Development Policy*. The goal of the 1972 policy was to seek a jobs-people-public services and environmental balance, based upon dispersal of population centers. Basic tools to be used were measurement of regional jobs-people balance and designation of growth centers—urban clusters which have the capacity to attract a larger population base through expanding job opportunities and public services. Many of the people involved in this early policy formulation, including the present Governor who was then Lt. Governor, later returned to positions of authority in state government. However, the change from a Democratic to a Republican governor in 1973 shelved implementation of this policy in favor of more current planning and problem solving by the State Planning Office.

A major legislative initiative resulted in another important element of development policy with passage of the Coastal Area Management Act in 1974. This bill, whose beginnings go back to a legislatively mandated study of coastal conservation in 1969, established a Coastal Resources Commission to develop guidelines for mandatory local planning in the coastal area, to designate areas of environmental concern, and to develop growth policy. The 20 coastal counties are required to prepare plans based on a five category "land classification" system, designating areas as developed, transition, community, rural, or conservation. Planning assistance funds are provided through the federal Coastal Zone Management Act. Within fragile coastal areas designated as areas of environmental concern, all major and minor development projects must obtain permits in order to proceed. North Carolina's coastal management program is considered one of the more effective in the nation.

Also passed in 1974 was the North Carolina Land Policy Act. The purpose of this new law was to develop land policy recommendations and an information system. It created a Land Policy Council of state and local government officials and a citizens' Advisory Committee on Land Policy. However, no implementation powers were provided. The primary products of the Land Policy Council have been a state land classification system, which is required for use in coastal areas and recommended for use in other parts of the state, and a computerized Land Resources Information System. The proposed land policy, which included not only statewide land classification similar to that of Hawaii but also a critical areas and issues of greater than local concern approach similar to that of Florida, was not adopted.

With the inauguration of Governor Hunt in 1977, the proposals of the earlier 1972 policy came back into the spotlight. The new format, entitled Balanced Growth Policy, arose during preparations in North Carolina for the 1978 White House Conference on Balanced Growth. Under the governor's direction, it was prepared by a new Division of Policy Development, which replaced the Office of State Planning and Intergovernmental Relations in the Department of Administration. Passed by the legislature in 1979, the North Carolina Balanced Growth Policy Act charged the governor with the designation of growth centers and developing measures of balanced growth in partnership with local government. It provided a policy advisory role for the State Goals and Policy Board and established an Office and Council of Local Government Advocacy to represent the interests of local governments in the balanced growth policy process.

The Balanced Growth Policy was both a response to existing growth patterns and a strategy to promote decentralized growth. It covered both growth in population and in jobs. Primary concerns were attacking the underdevelopment of the state's economy while maintaining the livability of its small towns and the viability of its natural environment. To influence the location of growth, the policy relied on two major tools: (1) designation of communities or areas as "growth centers," and (2) measures of "regional balance." Growth centers were to be targeted for state and federal resources to enhance their capacity to attract industrial and residential growth. Each county was to contain at least one growth center. Regional balance measures, to be developed for each of the 18 multi-county regions, were to evaluate both economic activity and adequacy of public services. The Act required the governor to secure the advice of local government officials and citizens in both growth center and regional balance decisions. In fact, almost half the text of the Act was devoted to provisions for a "state-local partnership," in recognition of the strength of local governments in the state.

Ten program area guidelines were specified by the Act:

1. Diversified job growth, especially for those groups with high unemployment, to provide work opportunities at high wage levels where people live.
2. Development of transportation systems linking growth centers.
3. Expansion of family-owned agriculture, forestry, and seafood industry.
4. Wise use of natural resources.
5. Availability and accessibility of human development services.
6. Expansion of early childhood, elementary, secondary, and higher education opportunities.
7. Technical training for high skill jobs.
8. Availability of cultural opportunities where people live.
9. Expansion of local government growth management capacities.
10. Conservation of energy resources.[28]

At the start of the 1980s, the centerpiece of North Carolina development strategy was the Balanced Growth Policy. As has been pointed out, North Carolina already has balanced growth, and the policy essentially sought to maintain and enhance it. In 1981, however, attention shifted to a new development initiative by the Hunt Administration to recruit major microelectronics firms to North Carolina through creation of a state-funded Microelectronics Center in the Research Triangle Park.

Twin Cities Metropolitan Council

Among substate regional planning agencies, the most well known is the Metropolitan Council of the Twin Cities Area. Created by the Minnesota legislature in 1967, the Metropolitan Council has responsibility for coordinating the development of the seven counties containing Minneapolis and St. Paul, whose population is over half the state's total population. While the substantial powers conferred on the Council by the legislature make it atypical of regional planning agencies in general, the principles of its planning process offer a model for strong regional development management.

Regional planning and development commissions with advisory powers were

Figure 13–6 Development framework, Twin Cities Metropolitan Council, 1975. The development framework to the right shows the keys for various kinds of development from 1975 to 1990.

A series of adopted policies state the council position about development in the general areas indicated on the map (left). Local planning will define the areas more specifically.

Urban Service Area 1975, 1980, 1990

Fully Developed Areas. Central cities and more developed first ring suburbs.

Area of Planned Urbanization, 1975. The area where most new growth will occur.

Urban Service Area Additions. General area and time frame for access to metropolitan interceptors:

1976-1980.

1981-1990.

Freestanding Growth Centers. 14 existing designated centers with public service and economic base as a basis for policy supported growth.

Rural Service Area

Commercial Agricultural Regions. Area where agricultural is viewed as the long range land use.

General Rural Use Region. More mixed, agricultural is viewed as priority use where soils and other conditions permit.

Rural Town Centers. Existing towns within rural area with less service and economic base than the freestanding growth centers.

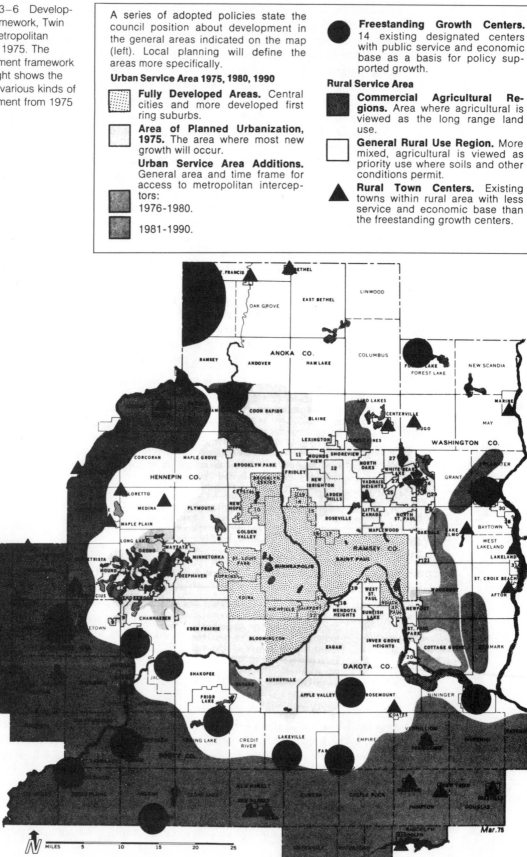

established in the Twin Cities area in 1957. An environmental health crisis which showed the need for intergovernmental cooperation to construct regional sewer facilities led to creation of the Metropolitan Council by the legislature in 1967. Because Council members are appointed by the governor, a regional perspective has been fostered.

Successive legislatures have increased the powers of the Metropolitan Council, which is now the areawide planning agency for housing, transportation, airports, water resources, wastewater management, parks and open space, comprehensive health care, criminal justice, cable communications, and aging. The Council is supported by its own regional tax base, as well as by state and federal grants. Its local governments are required to make plans, which it has authority to review and to require them to modify. It approves the capital programs and budgets of the municipal waste control commission and the transit commission. It serves as the clearinghouse for A-95 review of applications for federal funding, and it has the power to review proposed developments of "metropolitan significance," which it can cause to be delayed or amended under certain conditions.

The major tool for coordinating regional growth is the comprehensive development guide, an integrated policy, plan, and program provided for in the state statute establishing the Council. The guide consists of separate functional planning chapters covering sewers, solid waste, open space, housing, transportation, and others, along with a comprehensive regional growth policy entitled the Development Framework:

Starting from an overall goal of maintaining and improving the quality of life for the residents of the region, the development framework articulates goals and policies for urban development and redevelopment, social improvements, citizen participation, and the reconciliation of regional economic expansion with protection of the natural environment. These policies are expressed both in prose and through regional maps which show the council's projections for staged urbanization by two increments covering the period from 1975 to 1990. The area in which development and redevelopment are to be encouraged, the urban services area, was made as compact as possible while providing enough area to prevent an artificial shortage of available land. Development beyond the urban service area is to be discouraged with the exception of the 14 freestanding growth centers identified throughout the region.[29]

The Development Framework is the benchmark against which the Council reviews functional plans for regional services and development plans of local governments and service districts. It identifies an "urban service area" and "freestanding growth centers" in which growth is encouraged. The urban service area contains the "metro centers" of Minneapolis and St. Paul central business districts, a "fully developed area" covering the inner suburbs, and "areas of planned urbanization" adjacent to the existing built-up area. The "rural area" is planned to remain in agricultural or conservation uses, and will not receive metropolitan services of facilities. Development policies for each of these areas have been adopted.

Implementation of the Development Framework depends on public facility planning and coordinated capital improvements programming. According to the Framework, metropolitan investments that encourage urban development will be made only in the urban service area, and urban reinvestment will have priority over new investment unless the new investment is needed to open land for development. Chapters in the development guide provide the regional commissions that operate sewer, transit, airport, and park systems with plans and policies. Also required local government plans must include five year capital improvement programs which are consistent with metropolitan system plans.

A 1971 act passed by the Minnesota legislature is designed to reduce competition for tax base increases among localities in the region. The Fiscal Disparities Act's objectives are to provide for sharing of the resources generated by growth, to increase the likelihood of orderly urban development by reducing fiscal considerations in business and service facility location decisions, and to encourage all parts of the area to work for growth of the region as a whole. Under the Act, 40 percent of the net growth in commercial and industrial assessed valuation in each community is shared with the entire metropolitan area.

The Metropolitan Council stands out as an example of what a progressive regional development policy can accomplish. It has been effective in influencing the orderly distribution of growth, the efficient location of public facilities, the equitable allocation of low and moderate income housing, the preservation of farmland, and the protection of natural systems and open space. At the same time, the Council has initiated widespread citizen participation, developed a regional consciousness, and built up a consensus supporting regional growth management.

Metropolitan Washington Council of Governments

The Metropolitan Washington Council of Governments (COG) relies upon planning, coordination, and review powers to carry out development policy for the urban area of the nation's capital. Lacking the regulatory and taxing powers enjoyed by the Twin Cities Metropolitan Council, the Washington COG exemplifies the voluntary approach to regional development guidance which constrains the majority of U.S. regional planning agencies. Despite a complex intergovernmental situation involving both interstate and federal relationships, it has proven effective in working with the resources at its disposal.

Jurisdictions within the Washington COG include four Virginia counties, two Maryland counties, eight cities, and the District of Columbia. Its counties have considerable planning capacity and sophistication. Montgomery County, Maryland, for example, has a planning staff and budget larger than those of the COG.

Planning for the Washington region goes back to the work of the National Capital Park and Planning Commission, formed in 1926. A predecessor agency published in 1961 the development concept which has captured the imagination of government officials; the *Policies Plan for the Year 2000* proposed a regional pattern of transportation and development corridors separated by wedges of open space. This structure of wedges and corridors was accepted by the agencies in the area and incorporated into their plans.

In 1966, the Metropolitan Washington Council of Governments was formed and assumed responsibility for all regional planning functions. After a review of regional development goals and a reexamination of the Year 2000 Plan, COG adopted its *Metropolitan Growth Policy Statement* in 1977. This policy calls for:

1. A compact development pattern to conserve the region's air, water, land and energy resources with development promoted in growth centers, especially those served by mass transit.
2. Efficient use of existing public service capacities and limits on extension of new public services to support more compact development patterns, with expansion targeted on growth centers.
3. Programs and development patterns to help remove barriers to equal opportunity and access to jobs and housing.[30]

To carry out the policy, which is seen as consistent with the previous wedges and corridors approach, the area is divided into "growth centers" and "conservation areas" to be designated by local government after consultation with neighboring jurisdictions and with the COG. Four types of growth centers are defined:

1. The Metropolitan Center contains the built-up area of Washington with its concentrations of government, business, residences, and visitor facilities.

2. Transit Centers include those station areas on the Metrorail system outside the Metropolitan Center, where growth increases are forecast.
3. Outer Suburban Centers are those locally planned communities, such as new towns or corridor cities outside the Metropolitan Center, which might not have large mass transportation capacities but offer desirable locations for future development.
4. Rural Centers are growing communities in the rural area of the region, which are to be expanded in order to reduce development pressures on farmlands.[31]

Conservation areas are divided into two types. Urban Conservation Areas are those areas outside locally designated growth centers which have been developed at urban or suburban densities. Rural Conservation Areas are those not currently urbanized but containing agriculture, parks, and large residential estates, which are not to be provided with urban services.

In addition to the Growth Policy Statement, COG devised other innovative tools. Their "cooperative forecasting process" is a method of achieving consensus among COG member governments over the official forecasts for population, households, and employment in the region, by cooperatively reconciling local and regional forecasts. Their "impact assessment" program analyzed the implications of the forecast growth for regional land use, air quality, energy, transportation, water resources, and housing, highlighting the problems anticipated from a dispersed growth pattern. Their "action program" focused on drafting and gaining agreement on the metropolitan growth policy statement. Their "fair share housing formula" has been used to equitably allocate federal housing subsidies among member jurisdictions.

Resources available to the Washington COG have been largely provided by federal programs. It must use these resources as the basis for a negotiated regional consensus among its member governments who possess implementation powers. It is generally agreed that the COG has done an exceptional job of bringing together these governments in an influential growth management program.

Other states and regions

The development strategies of the six states and regions described here give a sense of the similarities and differences found in current practice. Many other examples could have been drawn upon to do this. Hawaii, the prototype for the Quiet Revolution, adopted the first statewide land classification policy. Vermont has had over a decade of experience with one of the nation's most comprehensive state land use laws, the Vermont Environmental Control Act of 1970. Oregon's Land Use and Growth Management Act of 1973 has gone perhaps the furthest toward building a strong state role in development control by mandating that local governments plan within a state framework. The Portland Metropolitan Services District has a unique elected regional council with the requirement that local plans must be integrated into the regional plan. New York's Adirondack Park Agency uses development permits to implement its land classification system. The Tahoe Regional Planning Agency's regional land use ordinance is based upon a land capability map which identifies permitted amounts of land coverage for each district.

While the specific details of the situations vary in each case, the development policy and strategy goals and methods overlap a great deal. Nearly all areas seek to reconcile urban development, economic growth, and environmental preservation. Many use techniques of program coordination, plan review, capital facilities programs, and development permits to carry out their objectives. While the variations are interesting, it is not necessary to analyze each individual case to understand the major problems and prospects for state and regional urban development policies and strategies.

Problems and prospects

Urban development policies and strategies have proven their value in coping with contemporary urban issues. Still, those attempting to use these policies and strategies in the future need to recognize some persistent problems, along with anticipated positive prospects.

Changing leaders dilemma

Recent state examples, such as Massachusetts, highlight the problem of leadership turnover. This dilemma centers on the need of urban strategy for strong support from, and identification with, the governor; yet because governors often serve only one or two terms, that support for a specific policy may turn into a liability when the next governor takes over. Legislative leadership can provide some continuity, although policy leadership is often difficult within legislative constraints, and leadership turnover remains a problem. Embodying policy in legislation is another way to attempt to ensure continuity across administrations, but even this approach is no guarantee that a policy and institutional structure will not be ignored or bypassed. Another means of bridging political generations is through non-governmental organizations, such as California Tomorrow or the New York Regional Plan Association, although such groups lack the budgetary and legal authority to carry out public policies. To meet the problem of leadership turnover, it is important for urban policy designers to provide for continuing constituencies as well as for flexibility so that succeeding leaders can modify policy to meet changing agendas.

Conflicting goals dilemma

Few urban policies can afford to pursue only one goal. The dilemma of the multiple-objective policy is how to resolve conflicts between equally important objectives. Presently, the conflict between economic development and preservation of environmental quality is the clearest illustration of this dilemma. Achievement of air quality standards has been delayed to allow for necessary economic growth and energy development, for example. Future conflicts may arise between the desire of people and businesses for suburban locations and the desire of governments to revitalize older urban areas. Recognition of these conflicts is behind the frequent use of the term "balance" in urban policies, and pragmatic compromise is often used to resolve them on a case-by-case basis. When compromise is not feasible, then the courts are called upon to determine the outcome of these conflicts.

Intergovernmental control dilemma

Every state and regional development policy must confront the desire of local governments to retain their traditional autonomy in development decision making. The dilemma here revolves around asserting larger state and regional interests without disrupting the day-to-day process of deciding on local matters. This problem has been especially acute for the newest member of the intergovernmental group: the substate regional council. Some states, such as North Carolina, have tended to bypass their regional agencies in urban policy approaches; others, such as Florida, have continually strengthened the roles of their regions in development planning and management. The desired solution is a partnership, but the nature of responsibilities depends upon acceptance of new partners.

Preventive planning dilemma

Democratic governments find it difficult to reform themselves without the spark of a crisis to justify proposed changes. Even though the medical profession is coming to realize that a preventive approach to "wellness" is wiser than simply trying to cure illness, that lesson has not been widely appreciated in public policy. The dilemma is one of building public and political consensus for action on a problem before the problem is widely recognized as serious. State and regional agencies try to use persuasion to educate the public and technical studies to convince political leaders that advance action is necessary.

Simplistic solutions dilemma

Before urban development policies can become truly effective, we must gain a deeper understanding of the underlying causes of urban growth and decline. Too often in our zeal to convince people and politicians of the need for strategic action, we fall back on "quick fixes" and simplistic concepts, such as urban sprawl as a villain or permit simplification as an easy solution to complexity or deregulation as the answer to complaints about government intervention. Future urban policies must be willing to establish long-term learning processes which systematically evaluate the impacts of their actions and seek to build up an operational theory of the workings of our urban development system.

Area-wide prospects

As urban systems grow more interdependent, it is increasingly difficult to solve their problems solely within local jurisdictions. Clearly there are problems whose area-wide nature requires a state or regional solution, such as air and water quality, transportation, and economic development. The recent concern over hazardous waste disposal is another convincing example of the need for broader than local solutions. The federal government has long supported area-wide planning and development management; many states have taken a similar course. As area-wide problems increase, other states may be forced to recognize that regional problems require regional solutions.

Federal delegation prospects

During the 1970s the U.S. Congress turned down a national land use bill and a state urban development strategies bill. The message for states and localities was that this was their problem. Under its New Federalism Initiative the Reagan Administration seeks to turn many current federal programs back to state and local governments. It seems likely that states, regions, and local governments will be expected to bear the primary responsibility for comprehensive urban development strategies in the future. One trend of the 1980s is increased reliance on the block grant as a favored form of transferring funds from federal to state and local governments. If this trend continues, more discretionary resources should become available to prepare and implement state comprehensive strategies for integrating separate programs. Without unified federal policy, however, individual states may become preoccupied with competing against each other while losing out to the comprehensive development programs of other countries.

Management capacity prospects

Since the 1960s state and regional development management capacities have taken a quantum leap. This movement seems likely to continue given new management technology, such as computer information processing and communications systems, improved management methods, and an increase in the number of skilled people attracted to careers in state and regional public service. One way to express this prospect is in terms of the growth in anticipatory capacity of state and regional agencies. By developing sensitive early warning systems, these agencies can alert governments to negative trends and developing problems in economic, social, and environmental systems before these reach a crisis stage. Building anticipatory indicators into urban development strategies can provide them with the credibility and forward-looking nature needed to ensure that they become mainstays of public policy, rather than passing trends.

The future challenge

No one expects the state and regional urban development policy field during the coming decade to imitate the past decade. Serious efforts by the Reagan Administration to deregulate, decontrol, devolve, and defund public development programs pose the greatest challenge to state and regional planners in many years. Without federal support, many valuable existing institutions and policies will be lost. In order to continue, a new style and philosophy of urban development management will have to evolve, based upon new public/private sector roles and relationships and upon creative planning by state and regional officials. It is possible, however, that the fresh approaches that are forged in response to this challenge will constitute a renaissance of state and regional policy. Released from federal dominance and forced to build local support, state and regional development strategists could well find more effective solutions to our age-old urban problems.

1   Charles R. Warren, *The States and Urban Strategies: A Comparative Analysis* (Washington, DC: U.S. Department of Housing and Urban Development, 1980), p. 3. Much of the first section of this chapter relies upon Warren's excellent analysis.

2   Frank Beal and Elizabeth Hollander, "City Development Plan," in *The Practice of Local Government Planning*, ed. Frank So *et al.* (Washington, DC: International City Management Association, 1979), pp. 153–182.

3   Lynn Muchmore, *Concepts of State Planning*. The State Planning Series, Number 2. (Washington, DC: Council of State Planning Agencies, 1977).

4   Warren, *The States and Urban Strategies*, p. 19.

5   John E. Vance, *Inside the Minnesota Experiment: A Personal Recollection of Experimental Planning and Development in the Twin Cities Metropolitan Area* (Minneapolis: University of Minnesota, Center for Urban and Regional Affairs, 1977), p. 66.

6   Harold A. Hovey, *State Urban Development Strategies* (Washington, DC: Council of State Planning Agencies, 1977), p. 1.

7   Warren, *The States and Urban Strategies*, p. 25. The ten states analyzed were California, Connecticut, Florida, Massachusetts, Michigan, New Jersey, North Carolina, Ohio, Oregon, and Pennsylvania. Each of these was described in a separate case study in *The States and Urban Strategies* series.

8   David R. Godschalk *et al. Constitutional Issues of Growth Management* (Chicago: Planners Press, 1979), p. 8.

9   Office of Planning and Research, *An Urban Strategy for California* (Sacramento, 1978), p. 10.

10 See Warren, *The States and Urban Strategies*, p. 34, for a list of categories of state-level methods.

11 Harold S. Buttenheim. "Urban Land Policies," in *Urban Planning and Land Policies*, Vol. II. Supplementary Report of the Urbanism Committee to the National Resources Committee (Washington, DC: Government Printing Office, 1939).

12 National Resources Board. *State Planning: A Review of Activities and Progress* (Washington, DC: Government Printing Office, 1935).

13 New York State Office for Regional Development. *Change/Challenge/Response: A Development Policy for New York State* (Albany, 1964).

14 Vincent J. Moore. "Politics, Planning, and Power in New York State: The Path from Theory to Reality," *Journal of the American Institute of Planners*. 37 (March, 1971): 66–77.

15 Fred Bosselman and David Callies. *The Quiet Revolution in Land Use Control*. (Washington, DC: Government Printing Office, 1971), p. 1.

16 Ibid.

17 American Law Institute. *A Model Land Development Code*. (Philadelphia: The Institute, 1976).

18 Noreen Lyday. *The Law of the Land: Debating National Land Use Legislation 1970–75* (Washington, DC: The Urban Institute, 1976).

19 Department of Housing and Urban Development. *The President's National Urban Policy Report: 1980* (Washington, DC: Government Printing Office, 1980).

20 Department of Housing and Urban Development. *The President's National Urban Policy Report: 1982* (Washington, DC: Government Printing Office, 1982).

21 Warren, *The States and Urban Strategies*, p. 5.

22 Robert G. Healey and John S. Rosenberg. *Land Use and the State*, 2nd ed. (Baltimore: Johns Hopkins University Press, 1979), Chap. 4, "California—Saving the Coast," p. 119.

23 Office of Planning and Research, *An Urban Strategy for California*, p. 13.

24 Healy and Rosenberg, *Land Use and the States*. Chap. 5, "Florida—Harnessing the Growth Explosion," p. 133.

25 The Florida State Comprehensive Plan's 14 sections include agriculture, economic development, education, employment and manpower, energy, growth management, health, housing and community development, land development, recreation/leisure, social services, transportation, utilities, and water. Many of the Plan's recommendations were controversial, and the Florida legislature refused to approve it, leaving the governor to attempt to implement it as "executive planning policy."

26 Massachusetts Office of State Planning. *City and Town Centers: A Program for Growth*, The Massachusetts Growth Policy Report (Boston, 1977), p. i.

27 Ibid.

28 Deil S. Wright. *North Carolina's Balanced Growth Strategy* (Washington, DC: U.S. Department of Housing and Urban Development, 1980).

29 Godschalk *et al., Constitutional Issues of Growth Management*, Chap. 27. "Metropolitan Council of Minneapolis—St. Paul Twin Cities, Minnesota."

30 Metropolitan Washington Council of Governments. *Metropolitan Growth Policy Statement*, adopted 1977 (Washington, DC: Metropolitan Washington Council of Governments).

31 Ibid.

14 Rural development

Rural America is very different from urban America in a number of ways. Rural development is sparse, while urban development is dense. Rural governments are small with limited capacities to govern and to supply services, while urban ones usually are larger and better equipped. Rural people tend to think of themselves as being more self-reliant and less inclined to ask government to help meet their needs. Governmental planning is much newer in rural areas than in urban ones, and it responds to different needs. For all these reasons, and more, planning for rural development is distinct from planning for urban areas, and the roles for regional organizations and state governments also differ for these two types of development.

Since public planning is relatively new in most rural settings and since most planning education has dealt with urban concerns to the exclusion of rural ones, this chapter begins with an examination of the nature of rural America as it exists today and the diverse ways in which it grows and changes. Then, the chapter describes how the concept of rural development planning evolved through policies and programs of the federal government and has taken form at regional and state levels.

The nature of rural America

Most of the nation's land and water resources, and most of its local governments, are outside the major urban centers where most of the nation's population lives and works. The concentration of population in metropolitan areas—each having at least 50,000 people in a densely urbanized setting—is a relatively recent occurrence in the nation's history.

The urban population—including small urban places—did not outnumber the rural population until 1920, and the population living in large urban areas (designated "metropolitan") did not pass the 50 percent mark until 1940. The rural population declined in actual numbers as well as percentages in the next three decades, accounting for only 26.5 percent of the nation's people by 1970. Since that time, however, the number of rural people has begun growing again in absolute numbers and at a rate (10.5 percent for the decade) nearly equal to the rate of growth in urban areas and places (11.8 percent). This new trend has been such a startling reversal that it attracted a great deal of analysis during the latter part of the 1970s. Unfortunately, most of the discussion was in terms of nonmetropolitan versus metropolitan growth rates without regard to the potential for growth to change these areas' boundaries. What was seen as more rapid growth in nonmetropolitan America became the justification for increasing the number and land area of metropolitan areas in 1980. Thus, the percentage of the nation's population living in metropolitan areas continued to increase during the 1970–1980 decade despite the substantial "return to the countryside" movement.

The observed increase in population of the 1970 nonmetropolitan areas took place in the open country and unincorporated hamlets as well as in small urban and nonurban places.[1] It was accomplished, despite a declining birth rate, by a shift in migration favoring nonmetropolitan counties. A number of factors supported this trend. One was that more than half of the new jobs in manufacturing in the 1970s were in nonmetropolitan areas. Another was the willingness of individuals to commute long distances to work in return for rural residence opportunities. Third, many Americans preferred small town and open country living as a lifestyle over city living, according to various polls. A fourth factor contributing to nonmetropolitan growth was the movement of retired people to these areas.

Characteristics of rural America

There are several ways of differentiating rural America from urban America. These include census counts of people by their place of residence, measures of the density of development, the attitudes and beliefs of rural people and officials, the nature of rural local governments, and patterns of rural development. Each is examined below.

Determining "rural" by place of residence   The U.S. Department of Commerce Bureau of the Census provides data on the nation's population by place of residence. It does this by two statistical means: officially differentiating between (1) urban and rural populations, and (2) metropolitan and nonmetropolitan populations. The urban population includes all persons residing in contiguously built-up areas of 50,000 population or more (urbanized areas) and, outside these areas, all persons residing in incorporated or unincorporated communities of 2500 or more inhabitants (urban places). By this definition, urban territory is that area occupied by the urbanized areas and urban places. Rural population consists of those individuals living elsewhere. Rural territory thereby comprises unincorporated territory and those places not defined as urban.

The census delineation of the nation into metropolitan and nonmetropolitan areas designates those individuals living in counties included in Standard Metropolitan Statistical Areas (SMSAs) as metropolitan residents; all others are nonmetropolitan residents. An SMSA consists of one or more counties which contain a central city of at least 50,000 inhabitants, or "twin cities" with a combined population of at least 50,000 plus any contiguous counties that meet certain criteria indicating social and economic integration with the central city or cities.

The rural/urban dichotomy results in several thousand urban places of varying population and geographic size being distributed across the nation's landscape. The metropolitan/nonmetropolitan dichotomy divides the nation into fewer but larger geographic areas more easily distinguished as either one or the other. However, all metropolitan areas contain population that is classified as rural, and most contain substantial amounts of such sparsely developed territory. Some counties in multicounty SMSAs are definitely more rural than urban in character except for the social and economic linkage characteristics that prompted designation as part of their SMSAs. In turn, nonmetropolitan areas contain many small urban places in the 2500–50,000 range.

The metropolitan/nonmetropolitan dichtomy has quite often been used as a basis for making distinctions between urban and rural due to the ease of utilizing census data and identifying geographical areas. However, the continuing addition of counties to existing SMSAs, the designation of new SMSAs, and the change in the criteria for designating SMSA counties has resulted in metropolitan designation for individuals who did not experience any change in the condition of their lives. The metropolitan designation did alter the availability of some federal programs in those areas, but did not alter the rural-urban census counts.

The "Fourth Annual Report of the President to the Congress on Government Services to Rural America," submitted in 1974, pointed out that "the true picture of the American population today is one of degree along a rural to urban continuum." To provide for such a continuum, the President's report divided the SMSA counties into three groups; *large, medium*, and *small*, with the large group being further divided into *core* and *fringe* counties. The nonmetropolitan counties were also divided into three groups: *urbanized, less urbanized*, and *thinly populated*, and these three were further classified as being *adjacent* or *nonadjacent* to metropolitan counties. Thus, 10 groups of counties were identified in the President's report for the purpose of discussing federal per capita expenditures by selected programs for each of the county groups. With this degree of refinement, the metropolitan/nonmetropolitan dichotomy provides effective distinctions for program purposes.

In the final analysis, however, there is no universally satisfactory definition of rural. To place rural in a reasonable perspective, it is necessary to recognize an urban-rural continuum with high density population and intensive urban activities representing one extreme and the open country with few people and a low level of occupational activity at the other extreme. Where urban ends and rural begins along the continuum is artificially marked by a line differentiating metropolitan from nonmetropolitan. This nonmetropolitan statistical delineation of people and area will be referred to as rural in this chapter on rural development.

Density of development   A further way to distinguish rural America is by population density and land area. In 1970, the SMSA population occupied only 388,000 square miles or about 11.0 percent of the nation's land area. The remaining 3,149,000 square miles of land or 89.0 percent of the total was occupied by the nonmetropolitan population. The population density for the SMSAs was 360 persons per square mile and for nonmetropolitan America 20 persons per square mile. However, the population density for the urban portion of the SMSAs averaged 2760 persons per square mile and only 15 persons per square mile for rural territory *within* the SMSAs. In 1970, 58.3 percent of the nation's population lived in urbanized areas within SMSAs and occupied 1.0 percent of the land area.

Rural people and officials   Several generalized characteristics can be attributed to people living in nonmetropolitan America. Many are cultural differences that are difficult to measure. Although modern technology and communication have the capability of moving America toward a homogeneous way of life, there is evidence that a number of patterns of traditional rural social and economic behavior, values, beliefs, and attitudes persist.[2] The 26.5 percent of the nation's population that is rural may have significantly influenced the survival of cultural patterns often associated with farming, even though less than 10 percent of the rural population is engaged in farming or farm related activities.

One characteristic is individualism, which persists and dominates in much of the rural United States. Many rural citizens still believe that the application of governmental police power to control use and development of land is a limitation on constitutionally guaranteed freedoms. Some citizens live in small communities and the rural countryside specifically to escape not only the more crowded urban environment but also the more formalized controls and higher taxes found in the larger urban places. Many of these individuals look upon governmental planning and development initiatives as a threat to their way of life and thus oppose governmental efforts to influence community development. Vocal and occasionally violent opposition in many areas of the country to the introduction of federal, state, or area-wide rules in land-use planning continues to occur.

Seventy-five percent of the nation's land—mostly in rural areas—is not subject to local planning and zoning controls.[3]

Many rural residents do not have an understanding of planning and development issues. They reason that since the crossroads hamlet of today will not become a metropolis tomorrow, planning for development has no useful function. The leaders of small communities may have had little exposure to planning and development concepts or to the need for restructuring local government. Consequently, they may not recognize the important benefits that may be derived from such programs. These and similar attitudes limit both the local desire to undertake planning and development programs and the degree of local involvement once programs are initiated.

Moreover, residents of rural America seldom see their community from the perspective of system planning or community-wide development. They do not think in terms of generalized land use, street systems, private versus public facilities, or community decision making, but are more likely to identify each parcel of land with the present owners, its price, and its actual or "expected" use.

Local governments Another way to differentiate rural America is by the number and character of its local governments. There were 20,768 incorporated and unincorporated places in the nation in 1970. The Census Bureau delineated boundaries for closely settled population centers without corporate limits. The minimum size of unincorporated places reported outside urbanized areas was 1000, compared to 5000 within urbanized areas. Of these, 6211 were in SMSAs, and the remaining 14,557 were in nonmetropolitan counties. Of the nonmetropolitan places, 3042 were over 2500 population, while 11,515 were under 2500 population.

In 1967, three out of four, and in 1977, two out of three, local governments in the nation were located in nonmetropolitan America. There were 60,045 local governments consisting of counties, municipalities, townships, school districts, and special districts in nonmetropolitan America in 1967 and 56,993 in 1977 compared to metropolitan figures of 20,703 local governments in 1967 and 25,869 in 1977. The decrease in the number of nonmetropolitan local governments and the increase in the number of metropolitan local governments was mainly due to the increased number of counties designated as metropolitan in 1977.

One of the most notable characteristics of nonmetropolitan America is the tremendous number of local governments, many with little population and most with limited social, economic, fiscal, physical, and political resources. The nonurban incorporation (of which there are more than 11,500), whatever its form of government, typically lacks full-time, trained officials. The mayor may be an undertaker, a druggist, a garage mechanic, or a farmer who devotes only a token amount of time to the affairs of the community. Fortunate is the incorporation that has a retiree as mayor or alderman with a career experience that can be transferred to local governance. The typical nonurban incorporation has no full-time employees as city clerk, water superintendent, city attorney, or city engineer. Such employees as do exist often have only a technician's or laborer's level of experience and little management capability.

Development patterns Structurally, the typically nonurban place is not as complex as larger urban places. Single-family residences predominate, the central business district serves as the dominant retail and service center of the community, and industries are few. Because land uses in the nonurban places are at low densities, some uses, such as grocery stores and service stations, are tolerated in residential areas when such might not be permitted in larger cities. Sprawling development is not a significant problem (though the continuing impact

Figure 14—1 Cultural differences. Although technology has brought much of America together, there are still distinct differences in the ways people live. Shown here are breakdancers in Arlington County, Virginia, a suburb of Washington, D.C., and a sack race at a fall festival in Clio, Iowa.

of the automobile often leads to commercial and residential uses locating indiscriminantly along major streets and roadways, usually state highways.)

Growth in a nonurban place frequently does not have the same impact as growth in an urban place. For example, an increase of 50 persons in a place of 500 persons may not have as great an impact on community facilities and services as an increase of 10,000 persons in a city of 100,000 persons, though both places experienced a 10 percent growth. The nonurban place may be able to absorb its 10 percent growth without new subdivisions, new water mains, new schools, and the like, while the city of 100,000 must provide considerable infrastructure for the new population. But on the other hand, an influx of 500 people to the small community in the example above would constitute a "boom town" crisis of major proportions, while that number of new residents in the larger community hardly would be noticed.

Many nonurban places may be compared to the suburbs of a central city; that is, they are bedroom communities, with many residents employed in nearby larger nonurban or urban places. Frequently, people living in a town of 250 may commute 30 to 50 miles or more to work in a larger place. Often, the nonurban place is dominated by an urban place, which, in turn, may be dominated by an urbanized area many miles distant.

The nonurban place usually offers a limited variety of goods and services to its inhabitants. (This limitation often extends even to such staple items as groceries.) At the same time, good transportation and communication have lessened the dependence of residents on local services, and external factors play a significant part in determining the level of services within the nonurban place. For instance, a modern hospital in a nearby city reduces the chances that the nonurban place will maintain a medical clinic or even attract a physician.

Quality of rural development   There is a wide variation in the quality of life in nonmetropolitan America. This variety may be due in part to differences in regional and local economies. Some communities and open countryside have an economy capable of supporting a wide range of public facilities and services. Other areas, at or near the poverty level, are unable to provide community facilities necessary for modern living. Those who live in the unincorporated or rural territory look primarily to the nonurban and urban places to provide for their needs.

In addition to the numerous nonurban places, there are over 3000 urban places in nonmetropolitan America ranging in size from 2500 to 50,000 population. Even these nonmetropolitan places vary significantly as to available resources. Generally, the smaller urban places may reflect many of the characteristics described for nonurban places. On the other hand, many larger urban places have professional staffs and command fiscal resources necessary to serve the public needs of inhabitants.

Many places with inadequate financial resources find it virtually impossible to sustain future-oriented planning and development programs or even to hire the technical and professional services necessary to formulate ad hoc programs competently.

The dispersed population in nonmetropolitan areas, the large number of small governmental units, the social and cultural differences, and the limited social and economic resources all help to account for the difficulties local political units face in planning for and providing contemporary services and facilities. This situation indicates the need for a regional or state-assisted approach to many nonmetropolitan problems. A broader resource base is needed to provide both the expertise and the resources to meet many of their problems and needs.

Over the years, as the concept of rural development has evolved and broadened to include that large land area known as nonmetropolitan America, the number of public policy areas being given attention has increased. Special attention has been given to the rural aspects of poverty, employment, health and health services, transportation, and housing.

In brief, nonmetropolitan America has a higher incidence of poverty, experiences poorer health, and has more substandard housing than its metropolitan counterpart.[4] Residents in nonmetropolitan America also have lower median family incomes, lower educational attainment, and a lower participation rate in the labor force.[5] Furthermore, nonmetropolitan America has a larger proportion of its population over 65 than metropolitan America. Since all of these factors indicate planning problems to be met in rural America, they are elaborated upon somewhat below.

Poverty Rural America has 34 percent of the nation's total poor. The roughly 9 million rural poor are not uniformly distributed across the nation. Nearly two-thirds of them are concentrated in the South. Poverty falls disproportionately on the minorities in rural America (as it does in urban America) with 38 percent of the blacks and 27 percent of rural Hispanics being in poverty as compared with 12 percent of the whites. The rural poor are located in areas generally lacking community facilities and individual job opportunities. The low incomes of many rural people result from welfare status, relatively low wages, the part-time and seasonal nature of many jobs available in rural America, and the limited training, skills, and education of rural workers.[6]

Employment Less than one in ten rural residents works solely or primarily in agriculture. Nearly one out of four is employed in manufacturing. Of the nearly 2500 nonmetropolitan counties in 1974, more than 1000 had less than 10 percent of their employment in agriculture. Counties with over 30 percent of their labor force in agriculture were concentrated in the thinly populated Great Plains and in the Central and Western corn belts. The countermovement of people into nonmetropolitan America in the 1970s brought individuals in professional services, work-in-trade, and manufacturing, in that order.[7]

Health and health services Rural people experience poorer health than urban people. They experience more days lost from work due to illness or incapacity and suffer from a higher incidence of chronic disease. Every county that has infant mortality rates double the U.S. average is rural. The shortage of health manpower (doctors, dentists, pharmacists, registered nurses) and inability to pay for adequate health care are the principal health problems facing nonmetropolitan residents. Rural America has proportionately more older and poor people requiring more medical care than the general population. Rural areas do not have a shortage of hospital beds, however, because of federal hospital construction funds received during the period 1948–1971. Most rural people feel that they have adequate access to health services.[8]

Transportation Nonmetropolitan America has a number of transportation problems. These problems include:

1. Prospects for rail abandonment for low traffic lines as authorized by Regional Rail Reorganization Act of 1973.
2. Deterioration of rail freight service and physical deterioration and/or abandonment of rail lines.
3. The elimination of a large portion of the rural road system from the federal aid secondary system.
4. The large number of narrow and dilapidated bridges, blind curves, unprotected railroad crossings, etc.

Figure 14–2 Farming, then and now. The photo of the man behind the plow was taken in 1937, but it could have been taken in the 1880s. The lower picture, showing a powerful, eight-wheel tractor with air conditioning and AM–FM radio, suggests how agriculture has changed in two significant ways: the pace of the work has increased dramatically, and the acreage than can be handled by each farm employee is much greater.

5. Increasing cost of motor fuels.
6. Lack of public transportation especially for the young and the elderly.

The impact of rail abandonment on rural America is difficult to measure. Rail abandonment generally has a negative impact on economic activities. Changing rail technology, such as larger and heavier freight cars, require better tracks and road beds which in turn require higher maintenance costs. Thus, low-volume

Table 14–1   Trends in number of farms and farm population, 1910–1982. The table shows the number of farms, total and 1,000 acres or larger, and the farm population, total and ratio to U.S. population. On the graph below, these data were converted to an index base of 100 to show that the number of large farms has more than tripled while the total number of farms and population on farms have shriveled.

Year	Number of farms[1]		Number of people living on farms	
	Total (000)	1,000 acres or larger (000)	Total (000)	% of total U.S. population
1910	6,362	50	32,077	34.9
1920	6,488	67	31,974	30.1
1930	6,289	81	30,529	24.9
1940	6,097	101	30,547	23.2
1950	5,388	121	23,048	15.3
1959	3,711	136	16,592	9.4
1969	2,730	151	10,307	5.1
1982	2,241	162	5,620	2.4

1 Part of the decrease in the number of farms from 1950 to 1959 and from 1969 to 1982 was caused by adoption of more restrictive farm definitions.

Source: U.S. Department of Commerce, Bureau of the Census, *Historical Statistics of the United States*, vol. 1 (Washington, D.C.: Government Printing Office, 1975), pp. 8, 457. Data for 1982 from unpublished Census compilations.

lines serving low-density rural areas become unprofitable and railroads seek to, or actually, abandon them by nonmaintenance.

Similar problems face rural roads. Larger and heavier trucks place greater stress on the roads, increasing construction and maintenance costs. These costs must be borne by state and local governments. Of the 3.9 million miles of roads in the nation, 3.2 million miles are in rural America. Much of this mileage is in unincorporated areas. Unlike railroads, the mileage cannot be abandoned as it must exist to provide access to property and to move the products of agriculture, forestry, mining, and manufacturing. This enormous system must be maintained and the cost of maintenance keeps increasing due to increasing loads and costs.[9]

Housing   The incidence of substandard housing in rural America is more than three times that of metropolitan America, and 1.9 million rural households live in overcrowded housing or housing lacking some or all plumbing. In 1970, it was estimated that nearly 4 million families in nonmetropolitan America were living in dwelling units considered to be substandard (without complete plumbing facilities) and overcrowded. The Census Bureau's annual housing surveys initiated in 1973 confirmed that nonmetropolitan housing failed to achieve the quality of metropolitan housing in all categories measured except one (breakdowns in heating equipment).[10]

Patterns of rural growth and development

A portion of the growth in nonmetropolitan America in the decade of the 1970s can be attributed to individual and family preference.[11] There was a high preference on the part of individuals and families to live in the open country and small urban places for such reasons as less crime, better quality of air and water, better life for children, and lower cost of living. Rural people desire to remain in rural America. The major push for those leaving rural America was economic (lack of job opportunity). This was reflected in the 20–24 age group which had a net loss of 381,000 persons in the 1970–1975 period, even though job opportunities in rural America increased significantly after 1970, and outmigration of this age group slowed considerably.

There are a number of ways in which rural America can handle growth of people and activities. These include growth in open countryside, growth of existing nonurban places, growth of existing urban places, and establishment of new places.

Growth in open countryside

The unincorporated open countryside offers one opportunity for accommodating rural growth. Urban uses can economically displace the traditional rural activities of agriculture and forestry. Rural growth can take place along the numerous existing roads with single-family dwellings including manufactured homes situated on parcels of varying sizes, small retail and commercial establishments as well as commercial-type agri-business including grain elevators, feed lots, and broiler houses appearing in what may be considered random locations.

As development takes place in the open countryside, there is an increasing demand for basic urban facilities and services such as public water and sewer systems, police and fire protection, and solid waste and garbage disposal. Providing these kinds of services is costly due to the low density development, and many open countryside inhabitants just must make do without many of these facilities and services.

Residents of the open countryside often derive the benefits of cleaner air and privacy at a cost of inconvenience in obtaining retail and professional services and of increased transportation costs. County governments are hard pressed to maintain a county road system. The young and the elderly are isolated due to lack of accessible transportation. In the open countryside, the least is also done in the way of planning or in growth management. Since much of the nation's unincorporated area is not subject to formal local planning, land use and development regulations are nonexistent. This situation fosters uncoordinated decisions by federal, state, and local governments in their efforts to provide facilities and programs for people living in the open countryside.

Growth of existing nonurban places

Many nonurban places of under 2500 persons provide opportunities as settlement sites for a significant portion of the nonmetropolitan population. As previously noted, there is considerable evidence that many people wish to live outside of large urban centers, either in small places within commuting distance of those centers or in semi-rural environments if certain types of urban amenities are available. Many of these nonurban places are underbuilt or of such low density that additional population can be accommodated without the necessity to extend or add services and facilities, although some facilities may need increased capacities. Many of these communities may have underpriced real estate (due to earlier outmigration and lack of maintenance) that may be attractive to new residents.

One might ask "What about the future of those places *under* 2500 population in the rural territory? Should these places continue to exist or should they be planned out of existence?" These small places might provide centers for regional community networks. Such networks could be primarily residential in character with the population engaged in farming and farming-related activities, or in commuting to jobs at urban places nearby. These communities would resemble large subdivisions found in urban places and would provide water, sewage disposal, and public utilities. Basic retail services to meet the daily needs of the residents would be provided, but the typical nonurban community would not and should not support such facilities as hospitals and clinics, technical schools, cultural facilities, airports, industrial parks, and the like. Such a community setting provides an alternative to so-called urban living for those who cannot tolerate the number and intensity of interpersonal relations required of metropolitan living.

Supporting growth in existing nonurban places has the advantages of small-scale operation and of lower demand for capital investment. However, these nonurban places many times lack the management and maintenance capability necessary for efficient or effective operations. In any given nonurban place, one would likely have the advantage of fairly compact development, but without all the services and facilities of larger urban places. This concept of growth in nonurban places, therefore, is necessarily predicated on a good (cost- and energy-efficient) transportation-communication network and linkage with urban places offering a greater variety of services and facilities and providing employment opportunities.

Growth of existing urban places

The continued growth of urban places (2500–50,000) in nonmetrpolitan areas could take place through increasing densities in the existing urban places or by geographically expanding such places through annexation—or by a combination of these two methods. Most urban places have a number of special purpose districts designed to broaden service capabilities. These governmental units with varying resources and capabilities result in significant differences in service and facilities among urban places. Many small urban places in rural areas have the professional and technical skills and fiscal resources needed to handle increased populations. Most already will have made significant capital investments for many urban services relating to medical care, sewage treatment, solid waste disposal, fire protection, education, and the like.

There have been efforts to select or designate specific urban places as growth centers or nodes and to provide these with special support or inducements for growth and development. The growth center concept has been fostered by the Public Works and Economic Development Act of 1965 that provided for designation of one or more communities in each multi-county district which already had a sufficient mass of professional and technical skills and fiscal resources to provide a logical base for accommodating additional growth with relatively little difficulty and with positive overall results. These growth centers, varying in initial population size, have been given a favored status as the recipients of federal funds for highways, health care facilities, and other public investments that would foster additional growth. The rationale for this concept is relatively straightforward—accentuate existing successes and "ripple" economic benefits to outlying areas.

However, accentuating growth centers for economic development does not necessarily produce regional networks. This is due to the inability to translate regional plans into regional projects. Most projects are community specific. Most communities undertaking projects do so with little concern for building a regional network.

Establishment of new places

Generally speaking, the establishment of new places is not a practical way to accommodate significant growth in rural areas and is not likely to become practical in the foreseeable future. The development of new places has not become an integral part of United States development policy and thus has not had any significant impact on America's growth patterns, rural or urban.

Since World War II, a small number of new places have appeared in rural areas, designed primarily to attract retirees. Such retirement places have appeared on large tracts wholly controlled by developers and generally quite some distance from large urban areas. These places are usually designed to satisfy a number of housing preferences and make provision for retail sales and services and recreational opportunities. Few provide employment opportunities in basic industries.

The establishment of new places requires massive expenditure of investment funds in a very short period of time. It is an expenditure on which a return is not quickly attainable. Land must be acquired, the basic service facilities (water, sewer, storm water drainage, streets, parks, open spaces, etc.), housing, retail, and commercial buildings must be provided and built. All this takes time and poses problems if initial investment capital is not in hand. Funds must be borrowed and interest payments made without any substantial return on investment for several years. Private enterprise is not likely in the immediate future to initiate the establishment of any significant number of new places in rural areas, nor is there any likelihood that the federal government will provide long-term financial commitments to encourage new place development.

Exceptions to this general proposition are most likely in the case of energy development. Indeed, some major new mining and energy generation sites did open up in several western states during the 1970s to help replace expensive foreign oil sources with coal. Boom town conditions accompanied several of these activities, and embryonic state and federal assistance programs, along with private energy company efforts to accommodate workers, were established.

Governmental policies for rural development

Rural development in the United States cannot be said to have been planned in accordance with any grand design, yet it has not been totally unplanned. For many years, the planning process has been applied to rural problems little by little as a fuller set of public development policies and planning institutions has evolved in rural America. In the following sections, the rural development planning process and the evolution of rural policies and programs are described.

The rural development planning concept

As a planning process, rural development involves need identification, determining a course of action, marshalling the resources, and then executing an agreed-upon plan of action. This is basically a problem-solving mechanism. Various structures, public or private, utilize the process in achieving program objectives.

The application of this process has been a major concern of the Cooperative Extension Service of the states and the U.S. Department of Agriculture as it undertakes educational activities that are practical, problem-centered, and situation-based. The Extension Service is, and has been for many years, extensively involved in providing training for agency personnel and community leaders in the process of social action and resource development. Its programs generally place emphasis on developing motivation and leadership as well as understanding in applying the development process.

Probably no two states have the same approach and philosophy for applying this process. In states like California, where a higher overall level of development leadership skills in rural areas has resulted from highly scientific and professional management of agriculture (as well as manufacturing and other business), the problem-solving process has become increasingly oriented toward improving linkages among organizations to address already defined needs rather than toward concentrating on the traditional upgrading of personal skills. The emphasis that state programs place on personal versus organizational upgrading must inevitably reflect the general availability of management skills and the sophistication of rural institutional organizations that exist in a particular state.

The expanding scope of rural development policies

Rural development is commonly described by public policy goals. This practice recognizes the disproportionate share of the nation's problems that reside in nonmetropolitan America, coupled with the low level of resource potential there, and seeks to solve rural problems by allocating the necessary resources on a nationwide basis.

Rural development efforts in the early 1900s were concerned more with the economic well-being of farmers at a time when they represented a much larger segment of the population and the work force. Early attention was focused on the betterment of agriculture and forestry and the related supportive services and industries that were spread throughout the nation. There was also concern about farm and small town living and about the relationship of farmers with town dwellers. Prior to World War II, the major federal actions affecting rural America were creation of the Cooperative Extension Service in 1914, establishment of the Federal Land Bank in 1917 to provide farm credit, and the "New Deal" legislation of the 1930s providing for the development of rural electric and telephone services, for farm subsidy payments to the farmers, and for soil conservation districts.

Since the mid-1960s, rural development as a concept has implied that the federal government, as a part of its national development policy, must provide special services to nonmetropolitan America to increase opportunities through location of industries and commercial services (economic opportunity) and through the provision of adequate public services and facilities, housing, education, transportation, and health services. It further implies that the federal government's motivation for such action will result from recognition that the total land and population resources in rural areas constitute national resources in dire need of conservation and rehabilitation. This concept of rural development was the response of those who believed that the nation's resources should not be targeted toward solving solely urban problems.

Logically, rural development requires that the locational decisions for economic activities and investments in public services and facilities be "directed" or "influenced" by national policies. Historically, however, major industries and

---

Joseph Cannon on the Country Life Commission This country life commission has been trying to uplift the poor farmer with theories. They have been dishing out literature on the subject, carloads of it. Heavenly Father, I'll take oath that they don't know what they are talking about. There are several excellent gentlemen on the commission, but what they have compiled is pure rot, if what I have read of it is a fair sample. The country life commission is a flat failure, because it has dealt with conditions that didn't require

dealing with by theorists and because its members don't know what they are talking about.

Source: Joseph G. Cannon, Speaker of the House of Representatives, at the banquet of the First National Conference on City Planning, Washington, D.C., May 22, 1909. Originally published as Senate Document No. 422, 61st Congress, 2d Session, 1910. Reprinted by the American Society of Planning Officials in 1967.

businesses making locational decisions for new investments used statistical projections, including population distribution, generated by federal agencies. Both those who did the projecting and many of those who used the projections tended to view them as "inevitabilities." The credibility attached to these projections by businesses and industries strongly biased private location decisions to take advantage of future manpower and market expectations developed from such projections. Fortunately for rural America, not all decision makers accepted governmental population distribution projections as inevitable, and the historic trend of depopulation of countryside and continued concentration of people in metropolitan centers experienced a reversal in the 1970s.

The first major recognition in the twentieth century on the part of federal government of the need to improve rural life was the creation of the Country Life Commission by President Theodore Roosevelt in 1908.[12] The Commission's Report included comments on two aspects of rural life. One was the role of science in helping to better understand and value the problems of farmers. The second aspect was that farmers had to be self-reliant, but the commission did point out that there was a function for state and federal governments to safeguard the inherent rights of the farmers.[13]

One result of the Commission's work was that Congress provided in the Smith-Level Act of 1914 provision for the Cooperative Extension Service within the U.S. Department of Agriculture. The report of the House Committee on Agriculture in submitting the bill included these guidelines:

The theory of the bill was to extend this system to the entire country by providing for at least one trained demonstrator or itinerant teacher for each agricultural county, who in the very nature of things must give leadership and direction along all lines of rural activity—social, economic, and financial. . . . He is to assume leadership in every movement, whatever it may be, the aim of which is better farming, better living, more happiness, more education, and better citizenship. (U.S. H. Rept. 110, 63d Cong., p. 5)[14]

Approximately 10 years after the report of the Country Life Commission, the American Country Life Association was organized, and its first national meeting was held in 1919. This Association focused on many of the concepts of the Country Life Commission by bringing together individuals, people with leadership possibilities, and representatives of national and statewide organizations and agencies concerned with development of people and institutions in rural America.

During the 1920s and 1930s, the Association provided one of the principal public forums on rural life and development. At its meetings, public and private leaders discussed many areas of concern to rural residents including public health, community conflict, improving the rural village, redistribution of population, community adult education, rural-urban area planning, and rural land use.[15]

The Tennessee Valley Authority (TVA) was established by Congress in 1933 to provide for the resource development of the Tennessee River watershed, a poverty-stricken, predominantly rural area. The TVA utilized a regional resource development process to socially and economically revitalize the area.

The National Resources Planning Board, established in 1934 by President Franklin Roosevelt, encouraged creation of state planning boards. The state planning boards were encouraged to consider basic social trends, rural land use, transportation systems, water resources, power production and distribution and industrial location, the suburban trend, stranded population, public works programs, and social resources and requirements. All of these areas had implications pertaining to the vitality of rural areas. State planning agencies were looked upon as being a coordinating, stimulating, and guiding mechanism providing two kinds of services. First, they would provide essential information in all fields of public endeavor. Second, they would provide the governor, the state legislature, and state departments with information that would aid in program development and delivery.[16]

As the nation recovered from the depression of the 1930s, interest and concern about rural life by the federal and state governments diminished, and it was not until a decade after World War II that there appeared to be an increased concern with the problems of rural America. At that time, 1955, the Secretary of Agriculture established a pilot rural development program.

In 1966, President Lyndon B. Johnson, by executive order, established the National Advisory Commission on Rural Poverty which made its report in 1967. The report titled "The People Left Behind" focused on current conditions in rural America and on the urgent need for action. The Commission established a relationship between rural and urban poverty and took the position that urban poverty could not be solved without also solving rural poverty. The Commission examined specific rural problems and suggested changes in current programs as well as new programs to fight poverty. The Commission addressed the rural problems of unemployment, health, education, deteriorating communities, and existing governmental programs.[17]

In 1967, a second major articulation of a concept for rural development was stated in *Communities of Tomorrow*, a document prepared by Secretary of Agriculture Orville L. Freeman. Secretary Freeman said:

For too many years too many people have crowded themselves into central cities— people attracted by the hope, often the illusion, of greater opportunity.

As a result, our metropolitan areas have more people and problems than they can cope with. All around us they are exploding with violence. At the same time, many villages, small towns, and their surrounding countryside are being drained from people and economic vigor.

This document outlines in broad terms the solution to this imbalance of people and opportunity: A new type of community, neither urban nor rural, but possessed with the highest values of both; a functional, multicounty Community of Tomorrow that blends the economic and cultural opportunities of affluent Metropolitan life with the space and beauty of the countryside.

These Communities of Tomorrow will make possible in both city and countryside a quality of civilization that fully reflects man's aspirations and inventiveness. Rural improvement will make the urban improvement job easier.[18]

The document envisioned that communities of tomorrow would offer an alternative to metropolitan living.

The shape and nature of the Communities of Tomorrow will vary with the needs and desires of the people.

However, they will have certain basic characteristics.

First, the Community of Tomorrow will cover a much larger geographic area than today's community. It may extend over several counties. It will include a large or small city or two and a number of towns, villages, shopping centers, with open country in between. Together they will provide the economic, social, and cultural facilities for the area.

Second, the Community of Tomorrow will be natural in its geographic structure. Each of its components—villages, towns, cities, and counties—will be bound together by roads, rivers, and other physical and resource features that enable it to be a dynamic and fully functioning economic, social, and cultural unit.

Third, the Community of Tomorrow will offer a wide range of industrial jobs as well as a full range of employment in business, research, professional, and trade services. Other jobs will be available in government, in the field of public recreation, and in the arts. A wide variety of jobs will be filled by people simply providing services for other prople.

How will all this differ from the troubled big cities of today?

Communities of Tomorrow will use space as an asset for a better life.

Rather than build ever larger, more impersonal cities, we will help people build communities where each individual can find a place, where each person can make a more important contribution to his community.[19]

To support the development of communities of tomorrow, U.S. Department of Agriculture programs would focus on programs in twelve areas: planning, farming, business and industry, community facilities, elimination of poverty, education and job training, housing, outdoor recreation and natural beauty, natural resources conservation and development, health and welfare, food, and transportation.

In 1969, President Nixon created a Task Force on Rural Development which submitted its report to the President in March 1970 in response to his charge to recommend "what might be done in the private and public sectors to stimulate rural development."[20] The Task Force saw "the purpose of rural development is to create job opportunities, community services, a better quality of living, and an improved social and physical environment in small cities, towns, villages, and farm communities in rural America."

The Task Force had this to say about rural development:

Rural development does not "give" people anything except the encouragement and tools to work together and the promise that their effort will be rewarded.

Rural development is not:

A new agency of government
A new appropriation to spend money in rural America
A new set of directives from the Federal Government
A program handed down and run from above.

Rural development is, however, many things:

1. Rural development is aimed at those with low income and the underemployed, but it is not just a poverty program—however, dealing with poverty is a no. 1 challenge.
2. Rural development is a "people" program to lift up those in greatest need, whether disadvantaged for economic or social reasons—but it is not a civil rights program or a rural slum program. However, by creating greater opportunity for all, those who will be helped the most are those who have been the most disadvantaged.
3. Rural development is aimed at job creation, but it is not just an industrialization program—although jobs through private enterprise is the key to long-lasting economic opportunity.
4. It is aimed at improving rural America, but is not just a farm or rural program that benefits only those in the rural countryside—although this is where the work will be done.
5. Rural development is built on local initiative, but it does not depend solely on local resources and local leadership—nevertheless, local initiative is the key to the success of rural development.
6. Rural development is aimed at a better quality of life, but rural development is not just a social program—even though quality of life and better society is the end product of rural development.
7. Rural development is aimed at population and industrial dispersion, but it is not just a land policy or settlement program—however, physical surroundings and environmental development are vital for clean air, clear water, open space, scenic beauty, recreation and "room to live."

Rural development, then, is a combination of specific programs directed toward a broad horizon—all intended to help create a nation of greater beauty, deeper satisfactions and expanded opportunities for all Americans, now and in the future, both in urban and rural areas.

Rural development will build a new rural countryside America; and by building a new and better rural America we will build better cities and a better America—a new life for the country. This report from the Task Force on Rural Development will tell how.[21]

The Task Force submitted recommendations for rural development under the following categories: national policies for growth; streamlining federal programs; strengthening state and local participation; building rural America through private enterprise; financing rural development, education, nutrition, and welfare; housing and health; and developing natural resources, transportation, and research.

The National Advisory Commission on Rural Poverty Report, the Communities of Tomorrow document, and the Task Force on Rural Development Report served as the basis for much of the program development in the 1970s, including the rationale for the Rural Development Act of 1972.

The next major synthesis in rural development was the "Small Community and Rural Development Policy" enunciated in 1979 by President Jimmy Carter. The President stated "this policy provides a clear purpose and a clear program of action for addressing important small community and rural needs, and for managing the profound demographic and economic changes that are taking place in rural America.[22]

The President's policy was committed to work toward:

meeting the basic human needs of rural Americans;
providing opportunities for rural people to be fully and productively employed and providing a favorable climate for business and economic development;
addressing the rural problems of distance and size; and
promoting the responsible use and stewardship of rural America's natural resources and environment while preserving the quality of rural life.[23]

President Carter also proposed an action agenda as outlined below:

1. Meeting the basic and human needs of America
       Housing
       Health
       Water and Sewer
       Education
       Income Maintenance, Social Services and Legal Aid
2. Job creation and business and economic development
       Job Creation
       Economic Development
       Energy
3. Addressing the rural problems of distance and size
       Transportation and Communication
       Capacity Building
4. Promoting the responsible use and stewardship of America's natural resources and environment.[24]

Treatment of the above included actions that the federal government already was undertaking as well as those additional actions the President felt were necessary to properly address the problems of rural America.

President Carter's policy statement provided for coordination of efforts by the executive departments and agencies in the delivery of programs and in identifying needs of rural America as authorized by Section 603 of the Rural Development Act of 1972.

Since the turn of the twentieth century, the federal government has increasingly pursued policies aimed at optimizing most desirable social and economic characteristics of the population which can be reported statistically. It has, however, done little toward formulating comprehensive national policies specifically intended to affect distribution of the population.

Federal programs affecting rural development

Since 1955, there have been both legislative and administrative efforts on the part of the national government to address rural problems. The first 15 years of the effort centered on activities of the Department of Agriculture, the Department of Commerce, and the Appalachian Regional Commission, and at the end of the period, on the Department of Housing and Urban Development.[25] These early departmental efforts are described next.

Department of Agriculture   In 1955, a rural development program was established by the Secretary of Agriculture to address the problems of low-income farming areas. The program focused its attention on promoting voluntary community development in "pilot" counties of low income farming states. In the early 1960s the Office of Rural Areas Development (ORAD) was established by the Secretary of Agriculture. An objective of the office was to establish RAD county committees. One of the responsibilities of the RAD committee was to prepare the county's overall economic development program (OEDP). For those eligible, this was a requirement for participation in the Department of Commerce's area redevelopment administration's (ARA) program. The RAD program provided technical and financial assistance to county RAD committees, but program initiative was a local responsibility. The assistance provided by the RAD program was in the form of technical action panels (TAP) staffed by the Farmers Home Administration, the Soil Conservation Service, and the Agricultural Stabilization and Conservation Service, all units of the U.S. Department of Agriculture.

A "rural renewal" program (the rural counterpart of urban renewal) was authorized by Congress in the Food and Agriculture Act of 1962. However, only two states responded with rural renewal enabling legislation. Six years after authorizing the program, only five rural renewal areas had been designated in the nation.

The Food and Agricultural Act of 1962 also provided for a resource conservation and development (RC&D) program which was the responsibility of the Soil Conservation Service (SCS). The SCS built its program around natural resource planning and development in multi-county areas and at the end of the six-year period had projects in 39 states.

In 1963 a cabinet-level rural development committee was established by the President with the secretary of agriculture as chairman. This committee was charged with a coordinative function for rural development program functions and related activities. By 1965, ORAD was converted into the Rural Community Development Service (RCDS) within the USDA.

The first major housing program for rural America was authorized by the Housing Act of 1949 when programs for homeownership and housing repair loans were made available to farmers. The Farmers Home Administration (FmHA) in the Department of Agriculture was designated as the agency responsible for administering the program. The Housing Act of 1961 authorized the FmHA to make direct loans to eligible nonfarm rural families. Additional rural housing program followed including: farm labor housing loans (1961); rural rental and cooperative housing (1962); farm labor housing grants (1964); self-help housing loans and technical assistance (1968); rural housing site loans (1969); a rural rental assistance payments program (1974); and a deep subsidy homeownership program (1978). Congress has maintained a population limit on nonmetropolitan towns eligible for benefits under this act. In 1965 it was set at 2500 but it has since been raised to 10,000. Towns and cities over 10,000 population are eligible for the same housing programs as available to metropolitan residents. The major focus of rural housing programs has been low- and moderate-income families and farm labor.[26]

Department of Commerce   In 1961, Congress passed the Area Redevelopment Act which made economically depressed areas eligible for federal community facilities and other assistance where counties in depressed areas had an economic planning body and an OEDP. The planning body was to be representative of all interested groups in the depressed area. The OEDP was envisioned as an action program to attack the economic problems of the depressed areas. The requirement for a planning body was to encourage local people to analyze local problems. While this requirement did not always achieve its objective, several thousand individuals did serve on local economic development committees.

In 1965, Congress adopted the Public Works and Economic Development Act of 1965 which converted the Area Redevelopment Administration created by the 1961 act into the Economic Development Administration (EDA). To be eligible for assistance under this act, the recipient was required to maintain a currently approved OEDP for its area. While the Area Redevelopment Administration recognized the county as the basic unit in area redevelopment, the 1965 act authorized the establishment of multicounty economic development districts and provided financial assistance for 75 percent of the cost of a full-time professional staff for such districts. The EDA was a strong supporter, in principle, of a comprehensive community development planning process. The multicounty district concept also was encouraged by the Appalachian Regional Commission, and all but one of the 13 member states participating in its economic development programs had local development districts in place by the end of the 1960s.

The approach of the Department of Commerce to economic development planning for depressed areas resulted in a large segment of rural America organizing multicounty planning organizations for addressing their economic development problems and applying federal, state, and local resources to development and to meeting local community needs, especially in the area of public facilities that would promote local economic growth.

Department of Housing and Urban Development In January of 1969, the Department of Housing and Urban Development (HUD) made its first 701 planning assistance grant to a nonmetropolitan district (NMD) under provisions of a 1968 congressional amendment to the Housing Act of 1954. The amendment authorized HUD to make grants to nonmetropolitan districts with concurrence of the Secretary of Agriculture and to EDDs with concurrence of the Secretary of Commerce. The amendment to the act made possible the expansion of the program by the USDA to all of nonmetropolitan America. USDA was authorized to provide technical assistance to nonmetropolitan planning districts.

By the early 1970s, the three federal departments, USDA, Commerce, and HUD, were involved in supporting development activities for rural America.

Major legislative initiatives since 1970 In 1972, Congress adopted the Rural Development Act of 1972. The act defined rural development as follows:

"Rural development" means the planning, financing, and development of facilities and services in rural areas that contribute to making these areas desirable places in which to live and make private and business investments; the planning, development, and expansion of business and industry in rural areas to provide increased employment and income; the planning, development, conservation, and use of land, water, and other natural resources of rural areas to maintain or enhance the quality of the environment for people and business in rural areas; and processes and procedures that have said objectives as their major purposes.[27]

The act contained six titles, each dealing with a different aspect of rural development. Title I dealt with a number of substantive areas. Section 106 of the act stated in part that "no loan under this section shall be made that is inconsistent with any multijurisdictional planning and development district area-wide plan of such agency." The Secretary of USDA was required to deny a grant due to nonconformance to an area-wide plan. The Title provided for grants to nonmetropolitan planning agencies as well as for water and waste disposal construction grants, an agricultural credit insurance fund, insured watershed loans, industrial assistance (loans and grants), rural housing loans, and small enterprise operation loans.

Title II dealt with conservation and utilization of land, land use and water quality, and municipal and industrial water supply. Title III was concerned with rural community water supplies being included in reservoir projects of the Soil Conservation Service. Grants-in-aid were authorized for rural community fire protection under Title IV.

Title V covered rural development and small farm research and education. This Title had as one of its purposes "to enhance the capabilities of colleges and universities to perform the vital public service roles of research, transfer, and practical knowledge in support of rural development." Colleges and universities were to carry out rural development programs in extension, research, and small farms. All public and private colleges and universities were eligible to participate in these programs.

Title VI provided that the Secretary of Agriculture exercise "leadership and coordination within the executive branch and shall assume responsibility for coordinating a nationwide rural development program" and provided further that the Secretary of Agriculture "report annually prior to September 1 to the Congress on progress toward achieving rural development goals." The Title also provided that other executive agencies locate their offices having a rural development mission in the appropriate USDA offices in the field.

Implementation of programs authorized in the Rural Development Act of 1972 has been varied. Section 111 providing for grants to nonmetropolitan planning organizations was not funded until 1978. The Title V program has been in annual jeopardy since initial funding, with the executive branch frequently recommending nonfunding and Congress providing annual appropriations. Some programs have never been funded, while others have had erratic funding. There did not appear to be a serious effort on the part of the executive branch to ensure USDA leadership in rural development until late 1979 when President Jimmy Carter enunciated his small community and rural development policy.

In 1980, Congress adopted the Rural Development Policy Act of 1980. One feature of the act was the addition of Section 607 to the Rural Development Act of 1972. Section 607 set forth three responsibilities for the Secretary of Agriculture pertaining to rural development policy. One responsibility of the Secretary of Agriculture was to provide the leadership within the executive branch for coordinating a nationwide rural development program. The second responsibility was to undertake a systematic review of federal programs affecting rural areas and to determine the benefits being received and to identify factors that are restricting availability of federal programs to rural areas.

The third portion of Section 607 directed the Secretary of Agriculture to prepare "a comprehensive rural development strategy based on the needs, goals, objectives, plans, and recommendations of local communities, substate areas, States, and multistate region" to ensure that federal resources are effectively utilized to improve opportunities and meet needs in rural America. Also included was the charge "to improve State and local government management capabilities, institutions, and programs related to rural development and expand educational and training opportunities for State and local officials, particularly in small rural communities."

The Rural Development Policy Act of 1980 also provided for the establishment of an Undersecretary of Agriculture for Small Community and Rural Development as well as increasing the fiscal authorization to make grants for rural development technical assistance, rural community leadership development, and community and area-wide rural development planning.

The Reagan administration has initiated steps to implement the Rural Development Act of 1980. An Undersecretary for Small Community and Rural Development was appointed, an Office of Rural Development Policy establishment and staffed, and the National Advisory Council on Rural Development appointed in 1982. Secretary Block, in a progress report to Congress in January 1982, indicated the Department would "prepare a strategy that will provide for (1) identifying emerging rural issues and needs on an ongoing basis; (2) strengthening State and local government roles in rural development; (3) contributing to strengthening local economic viability and improving community resources through encouraging the private sector to expand its role in rural development; and (4) developing and implementing policy guidelines that can provide sound government program direction for service to rural America."

While the Reagan administration is responding to the intent of Congress to develop and coordinate a nationwide rural development program, indications are that there will be a wide gap between the legislative intent and the programs proposed by the Executive Branch calling for significant federal fiscal commitments for rural development.

Federal programs in the 1980s With the inauguration of President Reagan in 1981, budget cuts in virtually all domestic programs of the federal government became a top priority. As a result, the HUD planning grants were terminated; community development funds for small communities were routed through the states with very little federal guidance and the proposal that they should be phased out; the whole EDA program was proposed for termination; the same was true of the Appalachian program; and the Department of Agriculture's rural development programs were seriously crippled and proposed for extinction. While Congress may not accept the President's full set of budget proposals, it seems certain that a significant federal withdrawal from rural development activities is occurring.

Multicounty structures for rural development

The characteristics of rural America along with the increasing availability of federal programs applicable to meeting rural needs resulted in the development and utilization of multicounty organizations. A few states established and provided financial support for such organizations early. A good example is Georgia, with its area planning and development commissions provided for under the state's General Planning Enabling Act of 1957. However, the impetus for creating most multicounty organizations came from federal recognition of the need for a broader structure that could both coordinate governmental efforts and provide the professional and technical expertise otherwise unavailable to the majority of small governmental units in rural America.

The original ORAD program sponsored by the USDA in the 1960s was unable to provide the specialized professional and technical staff support needed by the county ORAD committees. But, as noted earlier, it was reinforced by additional federal programs from EDA, HUD, and USDA that began promoting multicounty planning structures in the late 1960s. EDA encouraged creation of planning and development districts for economic development; HUD aided the establishment of nonmetropolitan districts for community and land use planning; and USDA, through the SCS, supported the organization of resource conservation and development districts for soil and water conservation projects. While the multicounty organizations sponsored or required by these three agencies had specific federal objectives, once they were established, many moved quickly to fill local voids in leadership and technical skills in general.

The early multicounty organizations fulfilled three main roles: grantsmanship, planning, and coordination,[28] as explained below.

Grantsmanship

With the increase in the number of federal grant programs and available funds starting in the 1960s, small communities were in need of assistance in the grant application process. In addition, the federal requirement that specific applications for grants had to be reviewed by an area-wide planning body under the provisions of Section 204 of the Demonstration Cities and Metropolitan Development Act of 1966 and Title IV of the Intergovernmental Cooperation Act of 1968—in accord with Circular A-95 of the U.S. Office of Management and Budget—resulted in much of nonmetropolitan America establishing multicounty planning and development structures for such reviews.

These multicounty planning and development organizations became the focal point for providing information to local governments on grant programs. They also assisted local governments in preparing applications, then reviewed and commented on those applications' conformance to local and area-wide plans, and finally represented the local governments in follow-through with federal agencies in seeking grant approval. Such roles by the multicounty bodies made it possible for small governmental units to compete for grants with larger communities with more resources. The multicounty organizations partially justified their existence on the number of grants awarded to local governments within their districts.

Planning

Most federal grant programs required some kind of "plan" as a prerequisite for project applications. These requirements resulted in multicounty organizations preparing a variety of plans for specific activities. One of the early requirements for public facility grants was the OEDP required by EDA. Multicounty agencies prepared the needed OEDP strategy documents. While some critics questioned the value of the OEDP in making grant decisions, the process of developing such documents often was fruitful in identifying and building local consensus. The continued retention of this EDA requirement has resulted over time in more careful preparation of the OEDP, allowing it to become a basis for a broader strategy in multicounty economic development.

With the increase in the number of federal programs that could be managed or handled by a multicounty organization, many such organizations became involved in a number of program activities ranging from traditional public facility grantsmanship to programs concerned with the environment, manpower training, services to the elderly, public transit, criminal justice, health services, housing, rail abandonment, and public management. All these programs normally required some kind of plan or strategy and, in nonmetropolitan America, the responsibility for accomplishing this fell on the multicounty organizations.

Coordination

Multicounty planning bodies have provided unique mechanisms for coordination. They brought together the public and private sectors and indicated how a number of separate projects could be coordinated. For example, the desire of a number of small nearby communities to have a public water system could be realized with combined or more efficient coordinated projects replacing individual community efforts that would not have been economically possible by themselves.

Another multicounty coordination role has been that of aiding local governments with efforts to meet an impact situation. For example, the location of large employment enterprises in a rural setting normally created both problems and opportunities for local governments. The multicounty organizations have offered technical expertise to local governments in evaluating the impacts of such enterprises and suggesting ways to mitigate them with public programs for better roads, more housing, larger water supply or wastewater treatment facilities, solid waste disposal, and the like.

These three roles were vital to the multicounty nonmetropolitan agencies in the late 1960s and early 1970s. They remain an important aspect of their ability to survive in rural America. The growing number of federal programs with planning requirements and the necessity for regional clearinghouse A-95 review substantially increased the scope of activities that most nonmetropolitan organizations became involved in.

White River Planning and Development District[29]

To make this brief history of rural regionalism come alive, a specific example is useful. The one chosen is the White River Planning and Development District (WRPDD) in Arkansas. It is one of many nonmetropolitan multicounty planning and development organizations established by local governments in response to the opportunities presented by the federal program incentives and requirements in the late 1960s. The WRPDD, originally known as the North Central Arkansas Economic Development District, Inc., was organized as a nonprofit corporation in April of 1967. The articles of incorporation stated:

The general purpose of the corporation shall be to advance and improve the economic, commercial, educational, civic, social, general business opportunity and growth in North Central Arkansas, . . . and the improvement and location of all character of highway facilities, public recreation facilities, public health and sanitation facilities, together with such other facilities as may tend to improve the economic opportunity of the area, including the promotion of research studies of the methods and feasibility of accomplishing such objects and purposes.

The district was recognized as an Economic Development District by EDA in May 1968, under provisions of the Public Works and Economic Development Act of 1965.

In 1969, the Arkansas General Assembly passed Act 118 which recognized as planning and development districts the eight economic development districts that covered the entire state. The governing boards of the economic development districts were recognized as the representative organizations of the planning and development districts. This made the two entities one and the same. The purpose of the act was to encourage multicounty planning and development organizations "to promote economic development, to assist local governments and private organizations in obtaining federal grants and loans, to prepare comprehensive regional plans for economic development and improve government services, to enlist private support for these activities, and to coordinate private and public programs in the multicounty districts." Act 118 also authorized state funds to support planning district operations in accordance with the purposes of the act. The Arkansas General Assembly has appropriated funds continuously since 1969 to support district operations. In 1970, the district adopted its present name—the White River Planning and Development District—in recognition of its statutory role.

The WRPDD area consists of ten counties located in north central Arkansas. Its southern boundary is approximately 20 miles north of the city of Little Rock and extends northward to the Missouri border. The ten counties had a 1970 population of 142,725. No city in the district had a population in excess of 10,000 in 1970, and only three had a population between 5000 and 10,000. In 1970, the district's rural population was 79.3 percent of its total. Population densities ranged from 11.2 persons per square mile in the least populated county to 37.7 persons per square mile in the most populous county.

The district had its offices at Batesville, a community of 7209 in 1970. The governing body of the district has continuously had at least two-thirds of its membership drawn from elected county or municipal officials. The remainder of the membership is drawn from the private sector.

Upon its organization, the WRPDD program consisted of creating employment opportunities through industrial projects funded by the EDA. As a result of WRPDD initiatives and grantsmanship, many local communities in the district received grants for various economic development projects including water and sewer facilities, rail and road access to industrial sites, regional health and medical facilities, and recreational and cultural facilities.

The WRPDD had three cities designated as economic development centers by the EDA, these being the three cities over 5000 population in the district. All three cities were targeted for concentrated economic development programs. At the end of ten years of economic development efforts, approximately 3000 new jobs had been added in the district, another 3000 saved, and $50 million in federal and state funds invested in the ten-county area.

In the early 1970s the district became involved in comprehensive health planning and in "701" nonmetropolitan planning assistance. WRPDD also soon became involved in the emergency medical services program, nutrition, health care and transportation for the elderly, a small business development program with special emphasis on assisting minorities, and housing. The WRPDD was instrumental in creating the White River Housing Authority and was responsible for administration of the Section 8 housing program funded by HUD.

More recently, several new activities were undertaken by WRPDD. With financial assistance from the Farmers Home Administration under provisions of Section 111 of the Rural Development Act of 1972, the district has provided technical assistance to local governments on fiscal management, revenue sharing, and handicapped regulations. It has also been active in assisting rural communities in establishing rural fire protection districts, water and sewer service districts, and recreational parks and programs.

Another district activity was a special project under Title VI of the Comprehensive Employment Training Act. This project provided definite job skills to long-term unemployed persons through training, instruction, and on-the-job training.

The district also worked on a regional transportation program and rural mass transit needs with financial and technical assistance from the Arkansas State Highway and Transportation Department.

The WRPDD undertook a major update of its OEDP in 1977. This update served as the basis for preparation in 1979–1980 of the White River Regional Investment Strategy. The WRPDD was one of nine area-wide planning organizations in the nation to receive a "701" comprehensive planning assistance program grant to be used to develop a format to utilize the strategy for evaluating the potential impact of all federally funded projects in the WRPDD. This reenforced WRPDD's long-time service as an A-95 regional clearinghouse.

The WRPDD also prepared a Housing Policy Plan and a White River Regional Housing Opportunities Plan. The latter was one of ten in the nation approved by HUD in 1979–1980.

Finally, the district has been actively involved in promoting the HUD Community Development Block Grant program. In 1977, it had 22 active CDBG grants in the district amounting to nearly $8 million. The district provided administrative support to receiving local governments.

By 1980, the district grouped its activities for regional planning and development into eight categories. These were employment development; community development; natural resources, environmental enhancement, and energy; transportation; institutional development and government services; agricultural development; transportation; and human resources. This shows how much WRPDD had expanded its scope of activities since its inception in 1967. During this period, most of the new activities were initiated in response to federal initiatives and opportunities. Some activities were spun off as separate entities, including emergency medical services and the housing authority. The Office of Aging founded by the district was made a separate entity by state directive.

In 1980, the WRPDD had a staff of 34 persons involved in its eight project categories. By December 1982, due to less federal funding, the staff numbered 16, with no decrease in project categories. Local governments, municipal and county, were calling on WRPDD for additional technical and management assistance. More was being accomplished with less. Funding for district programs was from federal agencies, state agencies and state appropriations, and local government membership dues.

By necessity, the activities of the WRPDD were programmatic and short range. Most were dependent upon continued federal and state funding. Little attention was given to long-range planning or strategies. This was a situation that existed with nearly all multicounty organizations in nonmetropolitan areas.

State government and rural development

The major initiatives that have been specifically directed to rural development have been provided by the federal government. However, numerous state governments have developed their own efforts that have aided in the development of their rural areas. In most instances state efforts were statewide economic development efforts and were not designed specfically to be "rural" in nature.

The Council of State Planning Agencies, in its publication on "State Development Strategies for Rural Communities,"[30] noted that state efforts in rural development usually fell into one or more of three categories. One category of activities was concerned with advertising, promotion, and the identification and development of prospective employers. The emphasis was on selling the state as a good place to visit or for a business to locate, and involved state participation in identifying those interested in investing in new facilities and in attracting firms to locate within the borders of the state.

The second kind of state activities involved direct financial support for industrial sites, buildings, and equipment. This had generally been accomplished through the issuance of industrial revenue bonds by local governments or industrial development agencies under provisions of state legislation. States have also provided tax incentives for new economic development within a state's borders.

The third set of state activities with potential to aid rural development has involved subsidies for local physical, social, and institutional infrastructure. States have offered grants and loans to local governments for basic utilities to serve new industries and expanding populations. The state itself has aided in rural development by providing highway access to new sites and in developing recreational and cultural facilities that serve rural populations.

As indicated earlier, many state activities that encourage rural development were not designed as rural development initiatives *per se*. They were initiatives designed to enhance the economic development of the entire state, and many also have been utilized by the larger urban centers of the state to great advantage.

There has been a growing awareness by states that economic and technological changes have had adverse impacts on them. For example, in the field of transportation, the changes in railroad technology and the increased costs of maintaining trackage have resulted in low use lines being abandoned. Most of these serve rural areas and many have been used to move agricultural, forestry, and mineral products. In addition, the deregulation of the airlines has resulted in loss of scheduled airline service. Bus companies faced with rising costs also have ceased to serve small communities with passenger and package service. Truck companies, as well, have been reducing or eliminating their services to low use areas. Rural and small town residents are finding themselves increasingly isolated and immobile—especially the young, aged, and poor. State governments, many unwillingly, find that they must address these transportation problems.

State governments are being pressed to address the problems of the rural areas. In addition to transportation, states are concerned with water resources—especially allocation of water for municipal, industrial, and agricultural purposes. There also are special problems in rural education, rural health, rural housing, and manpower development.

As states have endeavored to deal with the problems of rural development, they often have sought to use federal resources. Although most federal programs for this purpose have been provided directly to recipients such as local governments, the states have endeavored to have these funds funneled through them, or at least made available through a process that gives state governments some influence over how the federal resources are used within the state.

Historically, the states have not targeted rural development as a policy issue. This may, in part, be because of the view that rural development involves little more than farming, invoking the historical link between the federal government and the independently operated cooperative (agricultural) extension service and other federal USDA programs such as those offered by the Soil Conservation Service and the Farmers Home Administration. Another factor has been the unwillingness of state government itself to specifically target rural development when urban areas are constantly pressing for special attention.

Illinois Rural Development Council

With the federal government encouraging states to take a coordinated approach to rural problems, several states responded by creating some type of state rural development coordinating mechanism. Illinois is a good example. It responded to this encouragement by creating the Illinois Rural Development Council (IRDC) in late 1978.[31]

The IRDC consisted of approximately 60 members representing all levels (federal, state, and local) and branches (executive and legislative) of government; major rural, agricultural, and other interest groups; educational institutions and service organizations; and others. The council membership was subdivided into four principal committees to focus on major components of the rural development program. These components were housing and community development; natural resources and the environment; economic development, employment, and training; and human and social services. Each of the four committees or task forces were to identify problems to be addressed, the data and the statistics needed to quantify and analyze those problems, and possible solutions or implementation strategies to overcome the problems utilizing available resources.

The four task forces completed their work in late 1979 and reported to the full IRDC. As the council was only a study and reporting mechanism, implementation was left for others to initiate. This was the pattern followed by most state rural development efforts. As might have been expected, therefore, little was done specifically about rural development in Illinois as a result of the IRDC efforts.

State resources for rural development

Many agencies and institutions exist in the states that can focus their efforts on rural development opportunities. It must be remembered that most of these resources are also available to urban clients as well. These resources include:

1. Cooperative Extension Service. This is a long-established federal, state, and local government partnership that provides a variety of capabilities and expertise to local individuals and governments.
2. State universities and colleges. Many institutions of higher education have public service and outreach programs that can be brought to bear on rural development needs and problems.
3. State departments of local or community services. This type of agency may provide technical assistance as well as take administrative responsibility for a number of grant programs that local governments may use.
4. State department of economic development. This type of agency may provide a number of services and functions to local communities seeking industries and economic opportunities.
5. Substate planning and development districts. Substate districts often receive state appropriated funds and can be instrumental in carrying out state policies and programs.

Alternatives for achieving rural development

The very nature of nonmetropolitan America, with its numerous local governments and their limited resources, indicates that there is a need for a better governmental structure or structures if rural America is to improve its conditions and provide a viable alternative to metropolitan or urban living. To date, there has been no serious sustained nationwide effort to focus on how best to build a nonmetropolitan America.

There are alternatives that may be considered for use in improving rural America. Three of these are regionalism, county modernization, and special districts.

Regionalism

Regionalism as a concept for meeting problems and needs was recognized in an article by Alfred Bettman in 1927 that noted "there is need of developing both regional planning and regional government, in other words, first the making of regional plans and, second, the creation of regional legislative and executive organs for carrying them out."[32] Regionalism acknowledges that area-wide problems and their solutions transcend the boundaries and capabilities of local governments—in terms of expert assistance, authority, and fiscal resources required. Regionalism calls for broader governmental arrangements than area-wide planning organizations or councils of government have exhibited to date.

The application of regionalism to rural America was the focus of a paper titled "The Regional Community—A Concept for Nonmetropolitan Planning and Development."[33] The regional community concept implied a geographic and political entity incorporating a number of smaller units. It was conceived as a socio-economic phenomenon and a multigovernmental, decision-coordinating organization.

The concept envisioned that two types of authority needed to be made available to a regional community organization; one was economic, and the other was regulatory. The economic authority was to be over the utilization of federal and state resources for regional and local needs and purposes. Thus, decisions on where, when, and how to invest governmental resources within regional communities would become largely regional decisions. The second authority to be granted—regulatory—would provide the regional community with powers to implement plans. The application of regulatory authority was generally conceived in terms of preventing the occurrence of specified actions by local governments that would conflict with regional goals.

County modernization

The modernization of county government is considered less drastic and more acceptable by those who do not desire a new "layer" of government between local governments and state government as conceived by the regionalism concept. Counties originally were formed as geographic subunits of the state for the purpose of carrying out state functions in close proximity to the people. With modern communication and transportation, both centralization of state government and increases in local powers have taken place. As a result, counties are less identified with state functions. As the urbanization of the countryside and the increasing demand for services and facilities has occurred, counties in many states have been left without the statutory authority and the resources needed to meet the modern demands placed upon them.

The Advisory Commission on Intergovernmental Relations (ACIR) developed "An Agenda for County Modernization" which contained several suggestions, including authority for counties to perform urban services; provision for transfer of services from municipalities to counties; encouragement of local government consolidation including city-county consolidation; and the provision of authority to plan, zone, and control the subdivision of land and to assume planning authority within smaller municipalities. These and other proposals by the ACIR for modernizing county government would permit a more effective response on the part of local governments to rural development.[34]

Usually, the modernization of county government requires both constitutional and statutory actions. There is evidence that states are beginning to respond to this need. Arkansas provides a good example. In 1977, Arkansas voters adopted a constitutional amendment that provided county government with potentially greater authority than granted the municipalities of the state.

By expanding both the authority and the ability of counties to provide for the needs of their population, counties in rural America will be better able to meet the challenge of planning and development.

Special districts

Still another way to meet the needs of rural development is through the use of special districts. State legislatures are more prone to adopt permissive legislation to establish special local districts for a single function or limited set of functions than to reorganize general purpose local governments.

The special district concept permits establishment of a function or facility that serves a number of local government units. Generally, the districts are established in response to a need or for solving a problem. If an area needs a water supply source and individual governments do not have the economic capability to establish it, the special district may be the most easily available mechanism to meet the need.

Special districts have been utilized in rural areas for drainage, roads, bridges, fire protection, water supply and distribution, solid waste disposal, and the like. Special districts are a piecemeal approach to rural development—but it is an approach that is acceptable in light of political realities in most rural areas.

The future

Despite apparent changes in federal government policies, the basic means for meeting rural needs and solving the problems facing rural America are not likely to change radically in the near future. Rural America will need to make do with existing governmental structures—placing its emphasis on modernization of local governments, interlocal cooperation, area-wide planning and policy building, and the undergirding activities of state government.

1   David L. Brown and Calvin L. Beale, "The Sociodemographic Context of Land Use Change in Nonmetropolitan America in the 1970s." Paper prepared for Conference on Land Use Issues in Nonmetropolitan America, College Park, MD. June 24–25, 1980, mimeographed.

2   Thomas R. Ford, "Contemporary Rural America: Persistance and Change," in *Rural U.S.A. Persistance and Change*, ed. Thomas R. Ford (Ames: Iowa State University Press, 1978), pp. 3–4.

3   Task Force on Natural Resources and Land Use Information and Technology, *Land: State Alternatives for Planning and Management* (Lexington, Ky.: The Council of State Governments, 1975), p. 5.

4   [David L. Brown and Kenneth L. Deavers] *Social and Economic Trends in Rural America* (Washington, D.C.: The White House, 1979), p. 1.

5   Anne M. Smith, "Some Social and Economic Trends in Nonmetropolitan America," in *Rural Development: An Overview*, prepared by the Congressional Research Service, Library of Congress (Washington, DC: Government Printing Office, 1979), pp. 21–30.

6   [Brown and Deavers] *Social and Economic Trends in Rural America*, pp. 4–12.

7   Ibid., pp. 17–21.

8   Herman Schmidt, "Health of and Health Services for Rural Poor," in *Rural Development: An Overview*, pp. 31–34.

9   Leon M. Cole, "Transportation in Rural America," in *Rural Development: An Overview*, pp. 139–148.

10 Robert Eprile, "Federally Assisted Housing in Rural America," in *Rural Development: An Overview*, pp. 149, 150.

11 James J. Zuiches and Edwin H. Carpenter, "Residential Preferences and Rural Development Policy," in *Rural Development Perspectives* (Washington, DC: Government Printing Office, November 1978), pp. 12–17.

12 Bryan M. Phifer with Frederick List and Boyd Faulkner, "History of Community Development in America," in *Community Development in America*, ed. James A. Christenson and Jerry W. Robinson, Jr. (Ames: The Iowa State University Press, 1980), p. 18.

13 Charles Josiah Galfin, "When Fortune Favored the Farmer," in *National Planning and Rural Life*, proceedings of the Seventeenth American Country Life Conference, Washington, D.C., November 16–19, 1934 (Chicago: The University of Chicago Press: 1935), p. 28.

14 Phifer with List and Faulkner, "History of Community Development in America," pp. 19–20.

15 Nat T. Frame, "American Country Life Planning," in *National Planning and Rural Life*, pp. 7–23.

16 R. A. Mann, "Developments in State Planning," in *National Planning and Rural Life*, pp. 72–95.

17 *The People Left Behind*, A Report by the President's National Advisory Commission on Rural Poverty (Washington, DC: Government Printing Office, 1967).

18 U.S. Department of Agriculture, *Communities of Tomorrow* (Washington, DC: Government Printing Office, 1967), p. 1.

19 Ibid., p. 7.

20 *A New Life for the Country*, Report of the President's Task Force on Rural Development (Washington, DC: Government Printing Office, 1970), p. 1.

21 Ibid., pp. 7–8.

22 *Small Community and Rural Development Policy* (Washington, D.C.: Government Printing Office, 1980).

23 Ibid., p. 6.

24 Ibid., pp. 11–42.

25 James L. Sundquist in collaboration with David W. Davis, *Making Federalism Work* (Washington, DC: The Brookings Institution, 1969) pp. 132–166.

26 Eprile, "Federally Assisted Housing in Rural America," in *Rural Development: An Overview*, pp. 151, 152.

27 U.S. Congress. House. *Rural Development Act of 1972*, Pub. L. 92-419, 92nd Cong., 2d sess., 1972. H.R. 12931.

28 Sundquist in collaboration with Davis, *Making Federalism Work*, pp. 185–198.

29 Information on the White River Planning and Development District was secured from numerous annual reports, OEPD and updates, regional strategy, and personal knowledge.

30 William E. Bivens, III, *State Development Strategies for Rural Communities*, State Planning Series 6 (Washington, DC: Council of State Planning Agencies: 1977).

31 *The Illinois Rural Revitalization Planning Program* (Springfield, IL: Department of Local Government Affairs, December 1978).

32 Alfred Bettman, "How to Acquire Parks and Other Open Spaces," in Harvard City Planning Studies, Vol. III, *City and Regional Planning Papers* (Cambridge: Harvard University Press, 1946), p. 80.

33 William S. Bonner and Robert K. Middleton, *Regional Communities: A Planning and Development Concept for Nonmetropolitan Areas* (Washington, DC: American Institute of Planners: 1972).

34 Advisory Commission on Intergovernmental Relations, *State Legislative Program, Part 2—Local Government Modernization* (Washington, DC: Government Printing Office, November 1975).

15 Economic development

Economic development planning is the process through which a government defines goals for the nature and extent of its economic growth and designs a strategic program of actions for the achievement of those goals.

Such governmental "intervention" can be regulatory or budgetary. Through regulations, governments determine procedural actions and product characteristics of individuals and firms. Governmental budgets intervene in the economy in three ways: (1) they tax persons and private enterprises; (2) they grant funds directly to private firms and individuals and to other levels of government; and (3) they buy services and goods for consumption. The overall effect of regulatory and budgetary actions is to reallocate private resources in order to achieve societal goals. When government enters the marketplace, it does so for two reasons:

To correct imperfections in the free market system, so that the system works more efficiently. For example, the federal government has had a continuing interest in discouraging monopolies, because they inhibit competition and innovation in industries necessary for national growth such as railroads, steel production, and more recently, information processing.

To minimize the adverse effects of private sector activities which are contrary to the public good. Federal, state, and local programs to control air and water pollution are examples.

Economic development addresses one or both of the following objectives:

Broad economic development seeks to stimulate private economic activity which is judged to be beneficial to any part of an economic area. The so-called "all ships rise with the tide" philosophy assumes that in this nation opportunities to share in economic prosperity are equally accessible to all persons, firms, and areas. When the overall economy prospers, the benefits of prosperity "trickle down" to those at the "bottom" of the economic system.

Targeted economic development seeks to stimulate *specific* private sector activity in order to benefit *geographic areas of* economic decline or stagnation; *sectors* of the economy, sometimes industry specific, which are in decline, or which government hopes to protect or encourage; and *persons* who are economically distressed, such as those who are unemployed or underemployed, those whose income is low, and those who have difficulty accessing economic opportunities.

Philosophies of economic development

The history and practice of economic development in the United States have been marked by continuing tensions between "free market" and "interventionist" attitudes. Attitudes have changed as the economy has become more complex and as prosperity has waxed and waned, but attitudes of the past generation have been colored by the growth of the federal presence in all areas of national and local concern.

Free market philosophy

There are those who believe it is inappropriate for government to intervene greatly in the private economy. They contend that the economic system in this nation should rely primarily on the "free market" where enterprises and individuals are rewarded on the basis of efficiency and productivity, and where all compete on an equal basis.

This view assumes relatively pure competition where:

All actors in the economy have adequate information to make rational economic decisions. Consumers know the competitive advantages of products to be purchased. Producers know all pertinent facts about the market and production costs essential to compete equally with other producers. Workers are knowledgeable about competitive employment opportunities and select the jobs with the best wages.

No producer or consumer in the economy has the ability to dominate the market. (There are occasions, however, when a monopoly of a product or service is necessary, such as telephone service or space exploration.)

There are no substantial barriers to entering or exiting the market by producers or workers. Competing entrepreneurs have equal access to capital, land, and labor.

Proponents of this philosophy do not emphasize public infrastructure necessary to support private economic activities and contend that such imperfections as do exist in the economy are attributable to government intervention. If the government were to reduce its participation in the economy through reduced regulation and expenditure, they contend, the free market system would be able to return to satisfactory operation.

There are, of course, many examples of government intervention that have had an adverse effect on the natural functioning of the economy. Perhaps the most striking is the body of federal programs that has encouraged the financing of new housing in suburban areas, which, coupled with the development of suburban road systems, has caused widespread abandonment of urban housing by the middle class. Savings and loan associations were chartered by the federal government to channel savings into mortgage capital which created a demand for housing in suburban areas, particularly aided by the Federal Housing Administration and the Veterans Administration and stimulated by direct federal investments in highways and water and sewer systems. More striking evidence of the costs of governmental intervention are the proliferation of environmental controls during the 1970s. These regulations resulted in direct costs to firms for equipment, personnel, and procedures, costs which would not have occurred without government action.

The interventionist philosophy

Belief in the unfettered competitive nature of the free market economy is tempered by those who support government intervention in the economy in order to improve the performance of the overall economy and in order to achieve societal goals. This viewpoint contends that the market does not operate satisfactorily in the American economy without some government involvement. The more rational and knowledgeable such intervention is, the better the economy will work. This philosophy is based on several beliefs:

The economy is the basis of societal well being   The economic system provides the framework on which society functions and is closely related to the form and function of government. Economic prosperity is the key element to the strength and stability of a democratic society, particularly in the United States where an expanding economy has fostered population growth and geographic expansion which have supported the basic national belief in the availability of economic opportunities for all citizens.

A healthy economy supports and expands government services   As economic expansion occurs, the tax base increases, thus increasing income to the federal treasury. This makes more funds available to government to provide basic services and to expand government activities in general.

The size of the federal budget makes government a major actor in the American economic system   Growth in federal expenditures, often mirrored in state and local budgets, has made government a participant in the economy for better or worse. Many actions of government which involve enormous expenditures, such as national defense or transportation, are undertaken with goals appearing not to be related to the economy. However, their magnitude has a significant impact on the way the economy functions. It is important for government to understand the economic impacts of all of its actions, because it is often possible to ameliorate adverse impacts and to capitalize on positive impacts in order to achieve economic goals.

Government can intervene to minimize market imperfections   The classic "pure competition" model does not exist in the national economy. There are several market imperfections which government has chosen to address:

Industry concentrations, the control of production and marketing within certain industries, has been a long-term concern of the federal government. Beginning in the nineteenth century when action was taken against the large petroleum monopolies, public policy has espoused open competition and free entry in the marketplace. Such policy has also advocated small businesses of all types as well as the family-owned farm, a particularly threatened component of agri-business.

Social differences among workers and entrepreneurs have been addressed by governments during recent years. Such programs seek to raise skill levels and develop awareness among the poor and minorities in order to place them in a more competitive position for jobs and entrepreneurial opportunities.

Geographic differences place firms at various levels of advantage in accessing markets and acquiring labor, land, and capital needed for production. Within virtually any economic system there are subareas that lag behind others, and behind the whole, in economic prosperity. The federal government has taken an active part in encouraging growth and/or revitalization of newly acquired territory, such as the American West, or of depressed areas such as Appalachia.

The free market does not include societal costs in its actions   Government, as the representative of society's interests, must minimize societal costs of private sector actions. When a manufacturing firm produces a harmful chemical by-product as waste, there is no economic incentive for the firm to dispose of that waste in a responsible, and usually more expensive, manner. Government has taken on the responsibility for correcting the adverse effects of the improperly disposed waste in the absence of the market taking such action. Recently, government has begun to insist that the private sector ameliorate the adverse societal effects

The rise of big business and the role of government The line cut, dated 1881, shows "Monopoly" threatening Miss Liberty while Puck asks Uncle Sam, "What are you going to do about it?" The bands on the serpent are mostly railroads and senators. The following quote from two highly respected historians, Nevins and Commager, points out that governments were very kind to the special interests of the day.

Throughout the generation after the Civil War the business interests were in charge not only of the national, but also of state legislatures. The system of protective tariffs, established during the war as an emergency measure, was continued, and the iron, steel, copper, marble, woolgrowing, textile, and chinaware industries were particularly favored beneficiaries. The Congressional grant of subsidies to railroads was imitated by states and local communities, until altogether the railroads reaped a harvest of some three quarters of a billion dollars in land, stock, tax exemptions, and other gratuities. Government authorities took a complacent attitude toward land grabbing, and toward timber cutting, and cattle grazing on the public domain; numerous fortunes were founded on exploitation of the property of the nation. Congress showed little inclination to regulate private enterprise, and the courts gave substantial immunity to restrictive legislation coming from the states. Not until after the turn of the century was the philosophy of "rugged individualism" effectively challenged.

Source: Allan Nevins and Henry Steele Commager, *A Short History of the United States*, 6th ed. (New York: Alfred A. Knopf, 1979), p. 298. Line cut from Library of Congress.

of its actions. Amelioration usually entails private investment in capital equipment and/or labor for pollution abatement, safety inspection, or information dissemination. Such investments may prove to be more cost effective than subsequent public costs to correct measures.

Government intervention in the U.S. economy

Ever since colonial times this nation has pursued policies and activities that today we would label as "economic development." Economic expansion has been at the heart of the American political ethic. Colonial governments practiced free land distribution for selected enterprises, gave bounties to selected industries, and regulated certain industries.

During the first hundred years after independence the federal government acquired additional land and exploited natural resources. The states had the responsibility to develop the infrastructure of the era: railroads and canals. Both federal government and the states pursued policies aimed at constructing a national economy, with a mixture of business promotion and regulation. States even promoted banking services. The federal policy of opening up the west by granting land to railroads is well known. (see Figure 15-1).

During the first two decades of the twentieth century, the rapid growth in the number of automobiles brought about state and federal programs to build roads to connect farm with city and one city to another.

The paradox about the connection between government and economic activity during most of our history is that while government did promote economic development, business and government talked as though they believed the philosophy of laissez-faire. Up until the Depression the conflict was simply papered over with the notion that the government only intervened to make the economy more efficient.

The 1930s brought the worst economic depression in the nation's history. The New Deal signaled a profound change in public expectations of the role of government in the economy. President Roosevelt's administration took a series of programs that would influence the course of government involvement in the economy for the next fifty years.

Since this period of our history is so extensively covered in typical history courses at the secondary and college level, and because some of this history, as

Figure 15-1   Site of the future city of Perry, Oklahoma, on the Cherokee Strip in 1893. Population on September 15, 0; on September 16, 20,000. Population in 1980, 6,000. The building is the U.S. Land Office a day before the land was opened for settlement.

applied to the planning field, is covered in Chapters 2 and 3, we will move on to the post-war period to the present since it is less well-documented for the student. Two excellent books[1] are comprehensive studies of this period with particular emphasis on topics of interest to planners, for example the National Resources Planning Board, which promoted state and local economic planning agencies.

Post World War II to 1960

After World War II the nation turned away from activist federal leadership in economic development. Until the 1960s attention was focused on foreign policy issues, as the Cold War between the United States and the Soviet Union intensified and the role of the U.S. as a world power necessitated more sophisticated approaches to relations with foreign nations. The economy generally prospered; population increased rapidly; income rose; technology adapted readily to peacetime enterprises. It became clear that government intervention, so welcome during the economic crises of the 1930s, was less welcome during times of economic prosperity.

The period 1945 to 1960 was marked by a single federal action which is of more significance in philosophy than in fact. The Employment Act of 1946 declared a role for the federal government in creating an environment for "maximum employment, production, and purchasing power."[2] The Act states a philosophy which requires no specific programs, only an annual economic report by the President to the Congress.

The Act created the Council of Economic Advisors (CEA), an advisory group to the President. Although the role of the CEA has varied under different Presidents, it has provided a useful surveillance mechanism over the economy and can be a focal point for economic policy. The Employment Act of 1946 is of greatest significance for its declaration of the legitimacy of government concern and action in the maintenance of a healthy economy. The Act has been the philosophical basis of virtually every federal economic program since, from full employment efforts to public works programs and wage and price controls.

Public works expenditures reflected the return to normalcy after World War II. Although both public and private construction grew during the prosperity of the late 1940s and 1950s, its composition did not match the 1930s. Conservation and water resources development continued to be federally financed, but state and local expenditures for sewer, water, and school construction dominated public building. The 1950s saw the beginning of the largest public works project in American history, the interstate highway system, with the federal government financing a large portion of costs.[3] That program has proved to be a remarkable federal-state-local partnership in planning for capital expenditures. The impacts of its implementation are surely as profound as any governmental development project in history, changing the settlement pattern of the nation and drastically altering the nation's attitude toward mass transit, housing, and their relation to place of work.

Two decades of federal development activism: 1960–1980

By 1960 it had become clear that the federal government was unwilling to formulate a national development policy such as had been discussed by the National Resources Planning Board and the framers of the Employment Act of 1946. However, there was increasing attention in the Congress to the problems of specific geographic regions of the country that were suffering high rates of unemployment and which had escaped the remarkable economic growth of the postwar years.

In 1955 the Economic Report of the President, written by the Council of Economic Advisors, viewed the problem of depressed areas as one that "should be carried out by the local citizens themselves." But only one year later, in the next report, the CEA revised itself to say, "the fate of distressed communities is a matter of national as well as local concern."[4] From that time until the early 1960s, there was increased concern for both urban and rural areas in economic decline, and from that time until the 1980s whenever the Administration or the Congress considered programs to address the economic problems of such areas, the debate centered on the familiar theme of the appropriateness of government intervention in private sector economic concerns.

The debate in Congress leading to the first federal program to address the problems of distressed areas produced comments by two senators who were leaders of the opposing viewpoints.

Senator John F. Kennedy of Massachusetts, acting as the floor manager for the first bill introduced on the subject in 1956, stated:

The responsibility of the Federal Government to aid such areas is commonly acknowledged. The responsibility is in the interest of the areas which are subject to chronic unemployment and underemployment, and coincides also with the interests of the Nation. The fact is that these less fortunate areas exert a general drag upon the economy, and the Federal Government, in order to assure full prosperity for the Nation as a whole, should do all it can to eliminate pockets of unemployment and underemployment.[5]

At the same time, Senator Barry Goldwater of Arizona acknowledged the existence of such areas but found them to be a part of the inevitable cycle of boom and bust in American communities. In the past, such areas had not sought federal assistance, but had faced their dilemma "with stout hearts and strong backs." Goldwater felt that the movement to aid such areas was "a phobia afflicting certain politicians and pseudo-liberal left-wing theorizers, who would substitute for our free enterprise system the awful spectre of the planned super-state." The problems of depressed areas would disappear, concluded Goldwater, if the central planners in Washington would not continue to insist upon thwarting the free enterprise system.[6]

And so the debate continues into the 1980s.

The Democratic victories of 1960 and 1964 created an environment in both the Congress and the White House which was favorable to Senator Kennedy's viewpoint. The 1960s saw the greatest activity by the federal government to address physical and economic problems since the 1930s, but with an important difference—instead of addressing a current human and economic crisis, federal programs were to deal with long-term structural social and economic problems with hoped for near-term results to be gained within the context of fundamental corrective actions directed to the long-term.

During the 1960s there were three major federal programs designed to stimulate sub-national economic development:

The *Area Redevelopment Administration* (ARA), later evolving into the *Economic Development Administration* (EDA), provided (at various times) public works grants and loans, business development loans, and planning grants. Recipients were state and local governments, sub-state regional planning and development organizations, and private groups and individuals. The purpose was to address the problems of economic distress in specific areas of the nation qualified by high rates of unemployment, low income, or out-migration.

The *Appalachian Regional Commission* (ARC) was created to address a broad spectrum of human needs within the specific geographic area of the

Appalachian Mountains, including all or part of thirteen states. ARC investments are in construction projects and technical assistance for transportation (primarily highways), community services, natural resources, environment, energy, and human development. Although such programs are not usually classified as economic development, they are critical to the development of the human capital, infrastructure, and physical environment critical to an area's economic well-being.

The so-called *Title V Commissions,* formally designated the *Regional Action Commissions* in Title V of the Public Works and Economic Development Act of 1965, share EDA's authorizing legislation but have had relatively little connection with EDA's purpose or administration. The President was empowered to create multi-state commissions to address common economic development issues. Federal funds were made available for projects consistent with issues of common interest.

A discussion of the similarities and differences of these programs would be a too lengthy addition to this chapter. Suffice it to say that all three evolved considerably over time, changing emphasis according to Presidential, Congressional, and administrative mandates and maturation of the state-of-the-art in economic development.

The economic development programs of the 1960s arose from an emerging body of issues and philosophies that survived remarkably unchanged during the ensuing twenty years:

1. Recognition of diverse communities, sub-state areas, and multi-state areas where economic conditions warrant federal intervention to stimulate private sector economic activity. The difficulty has been in deciding which places warrant assistance and at what point in time. The need to secure legislative approval has usually meant that distressed areas have been defined so broadly as to preclude narrow targeting of assistance.
2. Definition of economic distress on the basis of simple indicators: employment rate, income, and, to a lesser extent, migration. Although underemployment appears often in legislative histories and program descriptions, it is difficult to quantify and so has seldom been used as an indicator. The statistical basis on which areas might be qualified for targeted programs is an inherently complex issue. Differences among regions of the nation and between urban and rural areas raise issues of equity about virtually any formula. In the 1970s the Congressional Budget Office and the Department of Housing and Urban Development constructed complex indices of economic distress using a variety of data elements such as municipal finance capability and the age and condition of housing stock. Also during the 1970s, the federal government's capability to collect and analyze data of all kinds grew markedly. However, with more sophisticated indicators, unemployment rate and income data continue to prevail as the leading indicators of economic distress.
3. Reliance on the "growth center" concept of regional economic analysis. Regional analysis came into its own in the 1960s. One of its basic tenets is the concept that public investments in a region should be placed where opportunities for stimulating private sector investment are maximized. Even in a lagging region, there are geographic points where opportunities for growth are maximized; the benefits of such growth will then accrue to the distressed population of the region. This concept remains controversial in practice as interjurisdictional rivalries within regions compete for federal investments, making it difficult to define and maintain a growth center.

4. Realization that local development efforts are best implemented through an intergovernmental process of coordination and planning. This commonsense belief rarely encounters doubters in theory, but in practice they abound. Federal development programs have espoused planning and intergovernmental cooperation from their beginning. Creative processes have been designed which have emphasized different activities and different actors at various times, to varying degrees of success. The growth of state and local government during this time is largely attributable to the federal mandate to increase the nonfederal role in local development. Federal requirements for planning processes prior to receipt of funds hearkened back to the intentions of the National Resources Planning Board to set up a multi-state and state framework for planning public works projects and other economic development activities.

5. Conviction that private sector growth was the ultimate objective of all public development efforts. All federal development programs of this period had as their primary objective the creation of permanent private sector jobs. In fact, job creation, both primary and secondary, became the ultimate criteria for the success of development projects. Since the number of such jobs created and the cost per job created are difficult to determine, debates concerning the relative success of federal investments based on these criteria continued into the 1980s. Programs also sought to form partnerships with private sector leaders and to involve them in the planning and implementation of development efforts. Evidence of the success of this objective was clear when substantial local private and public support came forward as the programs were threatened in the late 1970s.

The antirecessionary public works programs

The New Deal conviction that large infusions of federal funds for public works projects was a useful and appropriate way to create private sector employment during national economic downturns did not disappear with the Great Depression. It has continued to remain in the minds of public policy makers, and twice since 1960 the concept has resulted in large-scale public works programs. There also have been efforts to grant the President standby authority to mobilize a public works program quickly, triggered by some specific level of unemployment over a given period of time. There is a lag time, sometimes extending to several years, between legislative consideration of public works expenditures and final payment of wages in a community. Sometimes these wages were paid long after the recession is past. Standby authority would enable such programs to be implemented immediately, *during* the economic crisis.

There is an interesting contrast between discussions accompanying Congressional authorization for a standby public works program in the 1960s and 1970s and similar discussions during the New Deal. In the 1930s and early 1940s, the National Resources Planning Board was active in establishing an intergovernmental network to plan for public works on a long-term basis, with the goal of establishing a "shelf" of projects ready to be implemented immediately when economic conditions warranted. Planning was a prime component of those discussions even during the early 1940s when it was anticipated that high unemployment would exist immediately after the war. In contrast, such discussions in the 1960s and 1970s do not include planning at any level of government.

Standby authority for the President to approve public works programs has never been enacted, perhaps because of Congress's perpetual reluctance to relinquish its annual appropriation process and also because of disagreement about exactly what unemployment rate or other economic conditions ought to "trigger" such a program. However, Congress has been willing to enact two specific public works programs duing recessionary periods.

Following the moderate recession in 1961–1962 the Public Works Acceleration Act authorized $851 million over a two-year period to speed up public works expenditures in communities with substantial unemployment. Eligibility was limited to communities already qualified for grants from the Area Redevelopment Administration and additional places with a nine-month unemployment rate of at least 6 percent. This added about 150 communities with a population of 22 million to ARA eligible areas which numbered 1000 and included 37 million people.[7] Eligible areas include about 33 percent of the total United States population.

Again, following the recession of 1974–1975, Congress passed the Local Public Works Capital Development and Investment Act of 1976 over President Gerald Ford's veto. This was followed in 1977 by the Public Works Employment Act, part of President Carter's economic stimulus package. These measures came to be referred to as LPW I and LPW II. Approximately $2 billion was appropriated in LPW I, and $4 billion in LPW II. Their stated goals were to stimulate national and regional economies; to create employment, particularly in construction and related industries and services; and the construction or rehabilitation of public facilities.

The LPW legislation contained the unprecedented requirement that the administering agency, the Economic Development Administration, approve or reject projects 60 days after submission, and that each approved project begin within 90 days. There was also a set-aside of 10 percent of total expenditures which was to go to minority-owned firms.[8]

Selection processes were substantially modified in LPW II, alloting target funding amounts to states and eligible local areas, allowing them project selection discretion according to their own priorities. This process revealed an interesting pattern among state and local governments. Those places where economic development programs were facilities oriented and supported by a vigorous capital budgeting process captured their fair share of funds early with viable projects. There were notable differences among states and communities in their ability to generate projects that were economically and architecturally viable. Those with the strongest economic development planning processes tended to fare best.

The Kennedy tax cut

There was one additional federal economic stimulus initiative during the 1960s. It was not targeted to economically distressed areas, but rather it was to stimulate recovery from the national recession of 1961–1962. The Council of Economic Advisors under President John F. Kennedy recommended a reduction in personal income taxes, an act consistent with the Keynesian theory in vogue at the time. The tax cut would stimulate aggregate demand, reversing the basic course of the recession. The recession was brief, followed by resumed economic expansion; Keynesian theory seemed to work again.

The urban 1970s

The 1970s saw a change of focus in federal policies on economic development, as the nation rediscovered its urban poor. Continued national economic growth had resulted in massive population shifts away from rural areas and small towns to large urban centers. Enormous federal attention and resources were turned to community development, housing, education, manpower training, and job creation. There were ambitious federal requirements as well as financial support for planning and analysis prior to the expenditure of project dollars. These analytical techniques and planning processes advanced the art of economic development considerably. They also resulted in the creation of a cadre of urban economic development professionals and citizens who were successful in turning public attention to the "urban crisis" and sparked interest in the revitalization of America's cities as places to live, work, and play.

The participation of states and regional planning agencies in urban economic development soon was precluded by two facts.

Federal aid to cities bypassed states almost entirely for two reasons. First, the political alliances which had created Congressional interest in the revitalization of cities wanted no outside interference with the delivery of federal resources. The Congressional tendency to want to deliver projects directly to the home community not only prevailed, but it was also reinforced by a large body of public interest groups who lobbied for federal legislation, shaped the nature of its implementation, and participated in its delivery. Second, states were seen as contributing to the problems of urban America, not the solutions. State legislatures were in the hands of rural interests in 1970; by the end of the decade they were controlled by suburbanites—in both instances the cities would lose. States had a reputation in Washington as being controlled by parochial, political interests and lacking in professional development expertise.

Regional planning programs in urban areas were not given program responsibility for economic development. Their work program emphasis was in transportation, environmental quality, and land use—financed by the federally selected agenda. The two primary sources of federal support for urban economic development were manpower training under the Comprehensive Employment and Training Act (CETA) and planning assistance under Section 302(a) of the Public Works and Economic Development Act administered by the Economic Development Administration (EDA). Bot CETA and EDA were committed to a regional approach in rural areas but chose to give planning and program assistance directly to the central city in urban areas, ignoring the existence (and significant staff expertise and political clout) of regional planning agencies. It is interesting that federal programs in housing, land use, environmental quality, and transportation appreciated the need for both municipal and regional components to the urban planning process, but those in economic development did not. In a few cases EDA did fund Economic Development Districts in urban areas, but they were usually apart from the comprehensive regional planning agencies with a program focus on the rural area of the region. Amendments to the CETA legislation continued not to encourage regional cooperation among local prime sponsors in a region.

Final events of the 1970s were to strike a devastating blow to federally supported economic development programs of the previous two decades.

First, evaluations of the economic effects of the programs of EDA, CETA, the Title V Commissions, and ARC raised serious questions about their cost effectiveness. Allegations of "pork barrel" projects in response to political pressure heightened the argument.

Second, the nation's economic problems became more complex. Inflation, the cost of short- and long-term borrowing, deteriorating infrastructure, and changing export/import conditions called for new approaches to economic development.

Third, public sentiment shifted away from the 50-year trend toward government intervention in the economy. Government came to be seen more as the cause of economic problems, not the solution. This led to three actions by the federal government which were to reverse the course of economic development followed since the New Deal.

First, there were massive cutbacks in nondefense domestic expenditures, causing reductions in virtually all development programs.

Second, Congress and the Administration of President Ronald Reagan sought to reduce government presence in the private sector by reducing regulation of banking, energy resource production, transportation, environmental quality, and health care.

Third, under President Reagan's "New Federalism" the government moved to return programmatic responsibility to the states and local governments for a myriad of programs previously aided and guided by federal aid.

The evolution of current structure and process

State and regional economic development programs in the 1980s are shaped by four circumstances.

First, state and local development programs have a long history dating back to colonial times, with a recent emphasis on industrial development.

The relative leadership of federal, state, and local governments in economic development has varied throughout United States history, but each can claim a long tradition of public initiatives to encourage economic growth in the private sector. The emphases of each of these programs have changed over time, and since World War II state and local development programs have a tradition of industrial development in a well-defined sense of area promotion, recruitment of firms, and financial assistance to new and expanding enterprises.

Second, state planning does not have a tradition of involvement in economic development. The same can be said for regional planning in urbanized areas. However, regional planning in rural areas has its roots in economic development theory and practice.

State planning and regional planning in urban areas focused on land use, environmental quality, and transportation issues in the twenty or so years prior to 1980. It was not until the economic dimensions of these issues became important during the 1970s that state and regional planning programs began exploring economic concerns through research and policy development activities. Regional planning programs in rural areas, however, had been conceived and designed to address primarily economic problems of lagging areas.

Third, economic development planning programs at all levels of government have been shaped by federal program philosophy and design and by the availability of certain types of federal implementation dollars.

State and regional economic development planning programs were created and maintained through participation in one or more of the three major federal development programs run by the Appalachian Regional Commission, the Title V Commissions, and the Economic Development Administration. Requirements of those programs for staff and advisory organization structures, planning processes, and documentation continue to color state and regional economic development planning. Throughout the 1960s and 1970s, such programs also reflected federal initiatives in such areas as civil rights, affirmative action, energy conservation, and intergovernmental coordination.

Unfortunately, some of the weaknesses of federal development efforts were mirrored in these programs. The proliferation of distinct and uncoordinated federal development programs perpetuated similar fragmentation, particularly at the state level. Such tunnel vision encouraged state and local development-efforts to focus separate planning programs on distinct sources of implementation funds, rather than encouraging comprehensive planning for the use of all available development resources. Federal largesse also created a dependency which allowed economic development planners to grow independent of local political power structures which did not fund or design the program. As federal support wanes, planners are having to scramble to gain the confidence of local decision makers whose resources and priorities they have had the luxury to ignore.

Fourth, many states and regions turned their attention to economic development issues in the late 1970s, in creative and innovative ways.

There have been many important initiatives taken recently by states in economic development, apart from the structure and activities of the federally supported programs. There is a new awareness among governors and legislators alike that most public policy decisions have an economic dimension that must be understood and considered in their deliberations. In fact, many recent successful election campaigns have been waged on a platform of economic development—or more simply the creation of new jobs or the saving of existing ones.

State economic development planning

The traditional state development program

After the brief experiment of the 1930s under the leadership of the National Resources Planning Board, many state planning programs went out of existence until at least the late 1950s. The activities of the New Deal state programs relating to economic development did not entirely die, however. After the war, particularly in the South, some vestiges of the industrial development programs survived in a new form—promotion. Many states put together programs to attract expanding enterprises or to encourage relocation from other areas. Such programs were typically located in a state department of commerce and usually included *promotion, industrial recruitment,* and *financial assistance.* The objective was to capture investments and jobs for the state. Those programs were seldom targeted to specific locations in the state nor were they selective in terms of encouraging types of economic activity aimed at the solution of a particular economic problem. These efforts continued to be the basis of most state economic development programs until the late 1970s, and in some states, remain so today.

Promotion focuses on advertising the state's overall quality of life and its unique natural and human resources. In the 1950s and 1960s, states in the Southeast advertised their inexpensive, non-union labor force. Appalachian states touted their coal and mountain water. Northeastern states claimed advantages because of proximity to markets and transportation. Western states, to the extent that they still push for in-migration, note their recreational resources and clean environment.

These programs promote tourism to a great extent. Postwar affluence has brought a significant increase in the proportion of disposable income that most Americans spend on leisure, and vacation travel has opened markets for many types of leisure expenditures. States have been active in developing historical sites, national scenic areas, recreational facilities, and cultural amenities aimed at the long-distance or neighboring tourist.

Many states have engaged in aggressive *recruitment* campaigns to lure enterprises away from current locations or to capture expansions. These programs usually target specific industries and are vigorously led by ambitious political and business leaders. They involve "prospecting," often through middlemen such as industrial location consultants, and usually result in the state's "packaging" of certain incentives such as tax abatement, site preparation, or financing.

Financial assistance has traditionally taken the form of programs either to reduce the cost of capital or to abate taxes. These tools of state economic development programs have evolved into varied and sophisticated devices to stimulate economic growth and will be dealt with in detail in the next section. However, three early state programs are notable for their foresight and innovation.

In 1936 Mississippi inaugurated the Balance Agriculture with Industry program (BAWI), establishing a state agency to conduct a coordinated effort to attract new industry and to authorize communities to float their own bonds to finance site acquisition and construction for industries which the state agency found to be desirable. After decades of local initiative in industrial promotion, the BAWI program was the first state effort to provide public funds to subsidize plant construction in response to local initiative, but under overall state direction. The BAWI program accounted for a substantial amount of the industrial jobs produced in Mississippi into the 1950s.[9]

Beginning with Maine in 1949, states began to establish development credit corporations to provide low-cost credit on a statewide rather than a local basis to firms locating in the state. The corporations were privately chartered, capitalized by private sources, to guarantee loans made to firms locating in the state by conventional lending agencies. Such guarantees lower the interest charged by the lender and thus lower the firm's cost of location.[10]

In 1956 Pennsylvania established its Industrial Development Authority (PIDA) with an appropriation from the state legislature, making PIDA the first statewide public development corporation. Its purpose was the same as the privately chartered development credit corporation, except that PIDA targeted its loan assistance to firms locating in depressed areas of the state.[11] PIDA remains a particularly successful venture in this area.

Financial assistance has also taken the form of abatement, exemption, defferal, or reduction of local or state taxes, usually over a set period of time for firms locating in that state. Tax incentives are either (in the case of local taxes) authorized by the state and granted by local governments or (in the case of state taxes) granted directly by the state.

The traditional state economic development programs do not have a planning component. They are based on the experience and intuition of political leadership and practitioners and usually have no relationship to state planning programs. Programs respond to perceived economic needs and usually reflect the general state-of-the-art in other states rather than an outgrowth of research, analysis, and complex decision making processes. Although traditional state development programs are usually located in departments of commerce where federally-supported economic development planning programs are sometimes housed, they are seldom well integrated with the planning components of those programs except where the use of federal funds can contribute to a state-sponsored development project.

Federally supported state economic development programs of the 1960s and 1970s

This discussion focuses on the three major federal economic development programs which involved states and regions during the 1960s and 1970s; the Applachian Regional Commission (ARC), the Economic Development Administration (EDA), and the Regional Action Commissions created under Title V of EDA's authorizing legislation. Although they are not the only such programs, they have been chosed for emphasis here because of their relative longevity among federal assistance programs, the consistency of their philosophies and requirements over time, and the continuity of the state and local institutions they created.

Three of the more minor programs are worth mentioning before going on to describe the major ones. The Department of Agriculture's Farmers Home Administration created a limited program of assistance to states and sub-state areas in the late 1970s under Section III of its authorizing legislation. At various times during these two decades, HUD's 701 assistance to states emphasized economic development issues. The Department of Labor's manpower planning program also was an important state and local development program during this time.

States have had an uncertain role in recent federal development programs. Throughout the several decentralization initiatives of the 1960s and 1970s there has been lip service paid to an increased role for states in the development process, but that role has never been defined. The federal government has done a particularly poor job of articulating its expectations for state involvement in development and has seldom been willing to hand over responsibilities for oversight of local development programs. In the budget reduction discussions of 1980 and 1981, economic development programs were particularly elusive to block grant enthusiasts. Congressmen appreciate being associated with popular local development projects back home. The hometown-Washington link is too valuable to them to be discarded easily.

In the early days of ARC, EDA, and the Title V's, the role of the states was relatively clear. They were to draw the boundaries for sub-state districts and provide enabling legislation or executive orders for the creation of sub-state regional development agencies. Many also provided important technical assistance to the new agencies.

In the ARC and Title V programs, states became increasingly active in the administration of sub-state programs and in the coordination of their plans at the state level. Both programs emphasized the programming of a relatively predictable amount of money for given types of local development projects, with very little non–project-related planning required. Both programs were usually administered by a small staff in the governor's office or in a line agency such as a commerce or community affairs department.

The ARC and Title V programs were particularly popular with governors for several reasons. First, funds were relatively predictable. Second, projects were consistent with their states' development needs, having been selected according to criteria set among the governors of a region, not in Washington. Third, state administration of the program gave governors valuable project selection oversight, relatively free of federal intervention.

Over the years, the Appalachian Regional Commission refined a project selection system that is a model of intergovernmental cooperation. It is strong on established structures and on processes of goal setting at the local and state levels and strategic programming of ARC and other development funds. The Title V Commissions, although diverse in their specific planning processes, share with ARC similar goal setting and project selection exercises.

States were far less involved in the EDA program. An early requirement that states approve regional development plans faded over time; no allocations were made by states; and states played no role in the administration or coordination of regional or local programs. In 1975, EDA began a new program of assistance to states for economic development planning under Section 302(a) of its authorizing legislation, but it did not include a role for states in EDA supported planning programs or projects, which continued to go directly to local governments and Economic Development Districts. Section 302(a) assistance was a program setting broad objectives within the framework of the state's comprehensive planning program; it was intended to increase the state's capacity to deal with economic issues through a technically proficient staff close to the governor having powers to coordinate state and sub-state development activities.

The EDA program for state economic development planning assistance is an interesting contrast to the ARC and Title V programs. EDA sought a comprehensive approach to planning, realizing that states needed a foundation of research and analysis of their economic problems before planning could begin. EDA also gave states no monetary rewards for establishing a good planning process or development strategy. EDA largely ignored issues of intergovernmental coop-eration and sub-state coordination of development programs, finding that most states had to spend several years establishing their programs before tackling such sensitive issues.

ARC and the Title V Commissions were supporting planning programs pri-marily to prepare capital programs for their funding allocations. Until very recently they largely ignored other development resources. The planning process, with strong intergovernmental processes, properly followed, became its own reward. All three programs were structurally located close to the governor, but the ARC and Title V programs enjoyed far more gubernatorial attention: They were tied to distinct projects in a given time period which could be directly attributable to state action. EDA objectives of building solid capacity for overall economic development planning in the governor's office were appreciated by most governors, but the rewards for a job well done were difficult to perceive, and even more difficult to explain.

State initiatives in economic development planning

In the 1970s, states began to realize that their economic interests were not well served by their fragmented, federally supported economic development pro-grams or by their traditional industrial development programs. There was much room for innovation and initiative.

The political climate was right. Economic development had become an accept-able, and desirable, government activity. Governors and legislators became concerned with the growing limitation of resources for economic growth. In the Midwest and Northeast, concerns were for job creation in a declining industrial base and for retention of firms migrating to the Southeast and West. In the West, politicians sought a balance between environmental quality and continued economic growth. In the South, attention turned to continued low incomes in rural areas and to the economic concerns of an aging population.

State planning itself contributed to this climate in several ways. In an effort to be more relevant to gubernatorial concerns, state planning agencies began to explore their own development priorities, rather than those of the federal gov-ernment, and economic issues were a recurring concern. State planners had begun to see the economic implications of the other programs they were con-ducting, and they saw the dangers in defining economic development too narrowly.

Local development programs also stimulated state interest in economic devel-opment. Regional and municipal development programs mushroomed during the 1970s. Even if states could ignore the economic implication of their own actions, they could not ignore the pleas of local development planners to help facilitate the new programs they were designing. States responded with technical assistance programs, enabling legislation, and training for local development initiatives.

Today there is no set place in the organization chart for the actors in the state economic development planning process, nor is there a model set of actions. Much depends on the nature of planning in the particular state. Where a cen-tralized planning program exists close to the governor, chances are that the lead economic development function will be there. Where planning is distributed among line agencies, a department of economic development or commerce more typically houses such a planning program. With the growing trend to merge community affairs and commerce departments, an economic development plan-ning function is likely to be in the new department.

With its roots in so many different programs, state economic development planning is a diverse discipline in practice. Virtually no state has had the luxury of establishing an economic development planning program without many actors on the scene believing that they already constitute such a program, and, as always, it is difficult to separate the planners from the implementors.

A word about planners versus implementors is in order. Economic development is one area of public policy which *can* exist without planning. There are always immediate actions that can be taken by government to aid private sector growth. In an environment where the nature of growth does not matter, then planning is unnecessary. Economic development planning can only be practiced where elected officials are willing to affect the nature, timing, and location of growth according to the community's expectations for its future. In such cases, economic development planning becomes the process of selectively intervening in the economy to achieve certain defined societal goals. Economic development planners, newer on the scene than economic development implementors, have the burden of proof for the effectiveness of planning. The implementors have been successful according to their own standards, and they can be expected to reject other standards.

Organizing for state economic development planning

Although there is no agreed upon model for the organization of a state economic development planning program, there are characteristics which should be present for success.

Strong support of the governor   As with most programs in state government, the confidence and leadership of the governor are crucial to a sound development planning program. The governor must understand planning programs and be willing to allow a rational planning process to take place in his/her administration. He/she must be willing to place economic planning in the hands of someone who is technically competent and in whom he/she has confidence. Most important, the governor must be willing to orchestrate the tedious, and usually frustrating, process of coordinating actions within the executive branch, with the legislature and with others in a way which satisfies local constituents. The governor must understand that the implementation of the plan is his/her responsibility.

Strong technical and political leadership   Economic issues tend to be complex; their discovery, analysis, and interpretation must be, at once, thorough, competent and easily understood by decision makers. The person designated by the governor must be technically competent to manage such a process. That person must be equally astute at the politics of managing the development process. He/she must have the full confidence of the governor to coordinate the input of key actors including:

1. *Executive branch leaders and their staffs* whose involvement in the planning process is crucial for their knowledge of policy issues in their area of responsibility, because of the need to sensitize them to the economic implications of their programs, and in order to win their confidence in the program changes and initiatives that will implement the economic development plan.
2. *Local political leaders, planners, and development practitioners* who will be the ultimate beneficiaries of the development plan. Virtually every state action results in the occurrence of an event at a specific local place. Local involvement is critical throughout the planning and implementation process in order to ensure that state actions are responsive to local needs and are well received when put into effect.
3. *Legislators,* as budget designers and performance appraisers, are

important actors in state policy. Their involvement throughout the planning process is absolutely critical to the development program.

4. *Capacity and authority to participate in the state's budgeting process.* Most actions taken to implement a development plan require adjustments to the receipt or expenditure of state resources. Economic development planners must participate in the decisions that formulate both capital and operating budgets. Ideally, their participation would be in setting the economic framework for the design of the budget, contributing to cost-benefit analyses during budget formulation, and evaluating program performance according to economic development standards.

5. *Permanence.* The organization with lead responsibility should be a permanent part of state government, housed in the governor's office, with financial and political support to ensure its long term survival.

The state economic development planning process

Planning for economic development parallels the classical steps in any planning process. Its stages can be described as follows (remembering, of course, that planning is always a continuing process):

Information and analysis   Among the substantial gains in state government in recent years have come programs to create comprehensive information systems. Data processing systems for administrative purposes are in place in most states; however, such systems seldom exist for policy analysis, particularly for economic issues. In the late 1970s many states experimented with econometric models and other forecasting techniques, exercises which proved costly and difficult to maintain. Information systems for the analysis of economic issues should adhere to several simple principles:

Have a plan and keep it simple. Design a plan for the acquisition and analysis of information within given resources. It is not necessary to know every fact in a state's economy. Concentrate on the *discovery* of major economic forces and *understanding* their causes.

Design the plan in cooperation with other state agencies and sub-state development programs. Create a market for your information program by meeting the needs of others as well as your own program. Others' familiarity with your data will enhance its credibility. Also be certain that information can be disaggregated into sub-state units.

Gather and analyze information uniformly over time. Economic development planning is, in large measure, planning for adjustments to changing economic conditions. It is important to study economic conditions over a period of several years in order to fully understand trends and also to detect early warning signs of changing conditions.

Make information relevant and understandable to decision makers. Even the most enlightened public official does not have time for lengthy, complex presentations of economic data. It is important to keep reports and presentations brief and simple, and to pose issues which are directly related to the high priority concerns of decision makers.

Draw on already available resources. Few state development planners have the luxury of designing and maintaining data systems. Many state agencies have information of value to planners—revenue and budgeting offices, transportation departments, education and manpower programs, and state data centers. Public and private universities, federal agencies, and private sources such as banks, industrial realtors, and large corporations that do market research can be valuable sources of information, analysis, and research.

Understand the context of the state's economy. The state's economy should be studied in the context of national and international trends.

Goal setting   Once the state has a clear understanding of economic conditions, it is prepared to approach the issues of where the economy *can* be directed, the practical considerations of what the opportunities for growth are. From these the state can decide where the economy *should* go, identifying choices for the nature and degree of economic growth and selecting goals consistent with the expectations and desires of the state's citizens.

Development goals may address a variety of development issues, some of which may conflict with others. Where maintenance of environmental quality is of importance, it may still be necessary, and desirable, to develop natural resource based activities that may threaten the environmental status quo. With proper information concerning the costs of developing such enterprises under a variety of environmental constraints, decision makers can select a course of action that achieves both, environmental quality and economic growth, though such choices are seldom politically easy to make. The role of the economic planner is to present the best information possible on economic issues, and to relate that data to non-economic issues wherever possible.

Programming   After goals have been established, a set of actions can be laid out to achieve these goals. Such actions should be as specific as possible and should identify resources needed to take action and those who are responsible for doing so.

Where employment generation is the focus of economic development, programming might be framed by four concerns: *level* of employment, geographic *location* of employment, *who* is to be employed, and *type* of employment.

Evaluation   As with all planning functions, evaluation of the economic development planning program is critical. Programs should be designed with quantifiable objectives that can be examined over time in order to fine tune programs and to make future programming decisions.

State economic development strategies

There are a variety of actions states can take to implement an economic development strategy. Figure 15-2 categorizes and explains these actions. Only the rare economic development program will have the mandate, opportunity, and capability to affect state policy in this full range of activities. However, a strategy that is based on sound analysis and has clear goals will point to several of these actions as effective tools for implementation.

The coordination role   These actions suggest the primary role of the state economic development program—coordinator of resources to achieve economic goals. The state economic development program is unlikely to be given vast resources for its direct use, but state government itself is such an economic force that simply ensuring that the business of state government is conducted with sensitivity to its economic impacts is a laudable achievement for the state economic development program. If additional resources can be allocated to specific state initiatives to stimulate desired economic activity, so much the better. But one emphasis of the economic development program should be in persuasion and information which marshals existing state programs to achieve economic goals.

Figure 15–2 Development strategies and tactics.

Strategy	Tactics
Overall growth	Managing availability of capital for new firms
	Changing business taxes
	Assisting entrepreneurs
	Changing regulatory policies
Targeting of growth to refined areas	Environmental regulation
	Targeted tax incentives
	Location of public infrastructure
	Fiscal assistance to distressed areas
	Targeted capital subsidies
	Land purchases
Helping the disadvantaged	Improving education, work experience, and training programs
	Incentives to firms for hiring the disadvantaged
	Improving transportation access
Improving job quality	Safety and health regulation
	Reducing cyclical instability
	Subsidies to on-the-job training programs

Targeting Unless a state's development goals are simply to increase economic growth in its broadest sense, they will be targeted at specific people and firms, usually in certain geographic places. Targeting is a central element to the strategy; choices must be made about who will receive the benefits of government intervention. This implies that some, probably most, firms and people will *not* be beneficiaries. Since economic development programs depend on legislatures for their existence, and legislators are seldom willing to vote for measures that do not benefit their constituents, targeting has been an elusive accomplishment in economic development, as in other government programs.

Not only is targeting politically difficult, it is technically difficult as well. It requires excellent information concerning the costs and benefits to the targeted people or firms as well as to those who will not be beneficiaries. Targeting also requires that the effects of the assistance be measured and compared to similar conditions of nontargeted firms and persons.

Geographic targeting is usually done on the basis of economic distress as measured by low income and unemployment rate. Targeted population groups can include women, minorities, native American Indians, and certain labor groups. Firms are targeted by size and by type of economic activity, usually those experiencing cyclical or structural decline, sometimes those with promise of growth in the state's economic environment.

The small business ethic There is a recurring theme in state economic development programs, echoing a long-held American value—the special place of small business in the United States economy. Small business is a symbol of the individually (or family) held enterprise where the owner's presence assures honesty and efficiency and where potential growth is unlimited. Small business, and its rural counterpart, the small family farm, have been protected by public policy throughout American history. While opposing monopolies and industry concentration, government was championing small business.

In recent years this attitude has been bolstered by growing awareness of the contribution of small business to economic growth. The work of David L. Birch of the Massachusetts Institute of Technology and others has revealed that small businesses account for 98 percent of all United States firms, 43 percent of GNP, 75 percent of new jobs, 60 percent of existing jobs, and over half of technological innovation.

Before the 1970s, states spent most of their development energies on "smokestack chasing"—luring major industrial giants to locate within their borders with tax relief, low cost financing, infrastructure, and other incentives. Today states understand, in theory if not in practice, that their energies are better spent in maintaining the healthy firms already within the state, and in facilitating business formation and expansion wherever possible. Increasingly, this means targeting development resources to small business.

Local government capacity building The rapid maturity of economic development programs at all levels of government has produced uneven levels of competence among jurisdictions and levels of government. There is no clear pattern of capacity among regions of the nation or types of local governments. In the past, states have reacted primarily to local initiative in designing economic development programs; in a few cases the availability of federal program dollars also caused state actions. In light of the likely shift of resources and responsibilities away from federal programs to the state and local level in the 1980s, states should develop a clearer sense of their leadership role with respect to enhancing the ability of local governments to deal with development issues. The absence of federal leadership in this area leaves states free to creatively design strategies that address unique local development problems and opportunities.

State implementation actions

Figure 15-3 is a summary of the specific actions a state can take to implement its economic development strategy. It is divided into three major categories: government operations, assistance to business, and assistance to local governments.

State government operations These reflect the coordinative role of economic development planning, discussed above. Government *revenues* come from firms and individuals; they are a cost of doing business. Thus, the nature and extent of government revenues, particularly taxation, can be significant determinants of consumer and business behavior. Government *expenditures*, both capital and operating, are investments which stimulate further expenditures in the private sector. *Management* of the financial resources of government is related to expenditure policy: how a state invests funds in both the long-term and short-term affects private sector capital markets. State *regulation* of business and consumer activities has profound economic costs which must be understood by state planners and adjusted to maximize economic benefits in light of regulatory goals.

State assistance to business This is a rapidly evolving area in economic development. There is a tradition of state assistance to large industrial projects, but recent innovative actions have centered on smaller business, often in economically distressed areas. Such assistance is often provided through a business development corporation—a quasi-public body supported by the state but with

Figure 15–3　State and regional actions to implement economic development strategy.

	STATE GOVERNMENT OPERATIONS
Revenues	Taxation: Taxes are one element of personal and business expenses that can be totally controlled by government, particularly at the state level. States design their own tax systems (sadly, very few states consider their fragmented tax code to be an integrated system), and they decide the taxing authorities of local governments. Many states have altered their tax code to provide incentives to business, primarily to locate or expand within the state! These incentives have come under a lot of fire recently; their effectiveness, matched against losses in revenue are questionable unless they are fine-tuned.
	Fees: States charge for services and facilities from professional licensing to camp site rentals. The price of such services affects the demand for them. Fees can be used to encourage exclusivity in professions or to simply cover the costs of state services. Their interest relative to economic development is largely in their ability to inhibit the creation, or add to the cost, of an economic activity.
	Federal funds: Most Federal funds flowing to, or through, states require some kind of plan. States have varying degrees of discretion in the use of such funds, but the "block grant" trend would indicate that state and local flexibility is the wave of the future.
Expenditures	Capital budget: Long recognized as the ultimate implementation device by planners, the capital budget is of particular value to the economic development strategist because of the impacts of facilities siting on economic activity.
	Operating budget: This is where much of the Federal pass-through appear as program dollars. Here is the opportunity to impact the non-facilities expenditures which greatly affect the location decisions made by both firms and consumers—manpower training, education, welfare, and health programs.
Financial management	Procurement: States themselves consume millions of dollars of goods and services every year. The process through which such purchases are made is usually complex and can be difficult for the private firm to tap into. Some states attempt to assure that a certain minimum amount of state procurement goes to targeted firms, usually small and/or minority owned.
	Investments: Apart from the investments made consciously and directly in programs and infrastructure, states also invest large sums of money held in trust such as employee pension funds. Such funds can be invested in certain enterprises and locations not only to maximize investment return but to achieve state economic development goals.
Regulations	Although the Federal government has come under fire in recent years for its overzealous regulation of personal and corporate actions, it is states which are the primary regulators of business activity in this nation. States regulate banking, business licensing procedures, workplace health and safety, fair labor standards, and transportation among many other activities.

Figure 15–3   (continued)

	STATE ASSISTANCE TO BUSINESS
Access to capital	Direct loans: States make direct loans to businesses, not to reduce the cost of borrowing, but to provide funds where they would not otherwise be available. In fact, such loans are usually at above market interest rates. A few states make loans from a revolving loan fund, where an initial state or federal appropriation is recycled as payments are made on loans. Direct loans can also be part of a loan package, serving the partial capital needs of a firm where private sources provide some but not enough of the needed capital.
	Industrial revenue bonds: These are the most widely used state vehicles for stimulating investment capital. They are intended the cost of borrowing money. IRB's are issued by a public agency on behalf of a private firm. The facilities constructed by the bond proceeds are either leased or sold to the private firms for an amount sufficient to cover the interest and the amortization of the bonds. IRB's are exempt from federal and most state income taxes, so they cost the state very little (only administrative fees and default costs) and are attractive to investors while providing capital to private firms at below market rates.
	Guarantees: A number of states offer guarantees for loans or bonds, making the project more attractive to the private lenders, as the state accepts liability if the borrower defaults. Loan guarantees require less initial state investment than direct loans, because they have lower reserve requirements.
Formation and expansion of enterprises	This area is of only recent interest to states, and only a few have programs to address it. States can target capital assistance programs to new ventures and to research and production of innovative product ideas.
Market development	During the 1970's, it became fashionable for states to open offices in Europe and the Far East to encourage foreign investment in the home state and to link state enterprises with foreign markets. State funding cutbacks in the early 80's have caused the closing of several of these offices.
	Delegations of top state elected officials and private sector leaders to foreign countries to sell the state's products and locational advantages are also popular. They are usually privately financed.
	States also promote their businesses in the domestic market through advertisements on behalf of specific business sectors such as tourism.
Small business assistance	By 1980, 46 states had programs targeted to small businesses, most through "state SBA's" supported by the U.S. Small Business Administration. Their programs include: General assistance and advocacy: Through offices of small business development, often in the state's economic development agency, serving as the state's policy and program focus for small business. Procurement: Through procedures for state expenditures of goods and services that set aside or encourage some degree of purchase from small business.

Figure 15–3 (continued)

	Direct financial assistance: As part of the growing involvement of states in capital formation, at least half of states offer direct, subsidized, or guaranteed loans to small business.
	Ombudsman: In response to the proliferation of state regulations which affect business several states have "one-stop" contact points for businesses, providing information and assistance in getting through state regulatory processes.
	Minority business assistance: Over half the states target small business assistance to minority-owned firms; some seek to introduce minority business development concerns to economic development policy. The U.S. Minority Business Development Agency has had a major role in stimulating such state programs, similar to that of SBA's relationship.

STATE ASSISTANCE TO LOCAL GOVERNMENT

Enabling legislation	Local governments receive their legal authorities from the state. Particularly when municipalities want to take initiatives in economic development that involve subsidizing business development through access to capital or tax and regulatory relief, they must turn to the state for the power to do so. Planning and land use enabling legislation should be sensitive to economic concerns. Requirements should include economic development components to comprehensive plans and consideration of economic impacts in development reviews. Local taxation can be used to stimulate development in the form of abatements, tax increment financing, and special assessments. Local development authorities sometimes exist apart from local government in order to participate in private business enterprises as lenders, partners, or developers. Enterprise Zones are a new and controversial tool for local governments to set aside a geographic area in which relief from some taxation and regulation can be offered to business as an inducement to locate within the zone.
Local capacity building	States have assumed an increased role in helping local governments improve their performance. Although departments of community affairs usually have primary responsibility in this area, state planning offices and departments of economic development have much to contribute to enhancing the capacity of local governments to manage economic development through: research and information which is of use and regularly disseminated to local governments; direct planning assistance grants that have a strong economic development component; and technical assistance and training in economic development.

REGIONAL COORDINATION

Coordination of existing regional program for economic development perspective	Most regional planning agencies have completed comprehensive plans with various functional elements, including economic development. Such plans are most effective when the elements are fully integrated. This is a two-step process: 1) each element is made sensitive to the goals of the others and 2) trade-offs have been made to achieve a comprehensive set of planning goals.

Figure 15–3 (continued)

	The existence of an economic development strategy assumes the basic knowledge to bring economic considerations to bear on other functional areas of planning; it also assumes courage on the part of the regional agency to make difficult choices among various functional development goals. The comprehensive planning agency also has an important role in coordinating the activities of other groups concerned with economic development at the regional and local levels, including regional business groups, manpower and education programs, and industrial development corporations.
Coordination of local economic development programs	Where local economic development programs exist, primarily in metropolitan areas, the regional agency can serve a valuable role in coordinating their efforts to minimize interjurisdictional tensions and to provide a common base of information for all programs.
Leadership through planning and implementation	Regional Promotion: A good economic development strategy will identify a region's strengths so that they can be marketed to potential investors. Many regions have successfully "packaged" themselves and advertised particular attributes, most often the areas of tourism and industrial development. This effort involves identifying economic advantages, linking local development opportunities, mobilizing local leadership to "think regional," packaging a promotion campaign, and assuring local and regional ability to respond to inquiries.
	Regional Issue Forum: The regional economic development strategy, like any plan, is a dynamic program; from the beginning it will be clear that not all development issues can be addressed at once. Most will require further research and discussion. The regional agency's role in selecting, expanding, and addressing issues is one of its prime mandates.
	Small Area Development: A strategy can include development plans for two types of areas within the region: 1) sites with development potential of benefit to the entire region, such as ports, airports, tourist attractions, and industrial corridors; and 2) economically distressed sites with need for coordinated initiatives to stimulate their own renewal or to link up with economic growth in other parts of the region.

LOCAL CAPACITY BUILDING

Information, research, and training	The regional agency will be one of the best sources of data analyses of regional economic issues. This expertise should be marketed for several purposes: Information to businesses, local governments, and local development programs which is simple, accurate, and places local issues in a regional, state, national, and where necessary, international context. Research into development issues of interest to local governments and businesses without the resources or expertise to pursue them. Training in regional and local development issues for local elected officials, local planning/economic development groups, and business.

Figure 15–3 (continued)

Technical assistance	Regional staff expertise can also be marketed to local governments to provide technical assistance in local economic development strategy formulation and/or in specific development project assistance.
Legislative coordination	The regional agency is often in an excellent position to mobilize both sound issue analysis and local political/ private leadership to provide state and federal legislators and administrators with a clear voice on regional development issues. A continuing agenda for such a role can make the regional agency a valuable resource to the state or federal official for information on the local economy and development attitudes.

BUSINESS ASSISTANCE	
Capital access and cost	A few regional planning agencies have assumed this emerging public development role through the creation of revolving loan funds which make loans available to targeted firms, sometimes operating in specifically designated areas. A limited number of regional agencies also participate in the Small Business Administration's 503 Development Operation Program.
Site development	Regional agencies coordinate development on major sites in several instances: Sites of regional significance such as airports and harbor facilities which have regionwide development benefits. Interjurisdictional sites, which lie adjacent to or within several local municipalities and where coordination of local incentives and permitting are required. Other large parcels on development areas where local governments are unable or unwilling to undertake development responsibilities.
Technical assistance	Technical assistance to firms takes two forms: Management assistance, a rare activity, providing management advice to firms, usually small and often targeted to type, ownership, and location. Development assistance, a common activity, providing assistance to firms in identifying sources of capital and government assistance, and in dealing with local and state government regulators.
Market development	Promotion activities discussed above are the primary form of market development by regional agencies. However there are potentials in the establishment of foreign trade zones and in linking regional marketing programs with state and federal overseas prospecting efforts.

powers to develop and finance projects. State business assistance focuses on lowering the *cost* of *capital* and providing lending to enterprises without *access* to funds regardless of cost. A few states give assistance through equity financing and loans to *new and expanding enterprises*, usually targeting particular types of firms. Most states engage in *market development* programs, primarily in export promotion in Western Europe and the Far East. Many states operate *small business assistance* programs modeled after the U.S. Small Business Administration.

State assistance to local governments In its infancy, this form of action focuses on two areas: state *enabling legislation* to ensure that local governments can be creative in development initiatives and local operating procedures, and state programs to inform, aid, and train local governments to *enhance the quality of local development* efforts.

Regional economic development planning

The theory and practice of regional economic development planning is based in regional economic analysis which contends that economic systems ultimately are not constrained in fundamental ways by political boundaries. The underlying factors defining an economic region operate largely apart from geo-political considerations and are based, rather, on three markets existing in any economic system:

Labor markets define the area in which workers reside and work.

Consumer markets define the area in which shoppers reside and purchase goods and services.

Factor markets define the area in which producers obtain the resources for their production activities, including raw materials, financing, and equipment.

The literature of regional economic analysis makes it clear that there is no such thing as a wholly self-contained economic region. Obviously, communities and nations are enormously interdependent, and trade among them has produced the only true economic region, the world itself.

Somewhere between the theoretical concept of the economic region and the reality that there can never be a perfect one lies the discipline of defining and analyzing regional economies. In the United States there are three units of measure for doing so. *Multi-state areas* are composed of groups of states with homogeneous, and sometimes interdependent, economies. In recent years such regional analysis has been done to identify common problems and to coalesce elected leadership to articulate and advocate regional economic concerns in Washington. *States* sometimes define themselves as economic regions to study their economy and treat its symptoms of distress. Multi-state areas and states as distinct economic, political, and cultural regions, date back to colonial times. *Sub-state economic regions* are a newer device for defining economic systems; they are the subject of this discussion as it refers to regional economic development planning.

Sub-state regions as they exist in the United States today are primarily defined by labor and consumer markets. Such markets areas are defined primarily by commuting patterns, newspaper advertising areas, and branch banking. Producer markets, however, usually extend far beyond sub-state regional economies because of firms' market areas, commercial transportation and communication networks, and the complexity of production inputs.

There are important distinctions between rural and urban regions. Urban regions tend to be economically complex systems experiencing overall economic growth where problems center on the distribution of the benefits of future growth and the disparity between distressed and prosperous communities within the same region. Rural regions tend to experience overall economic stagnation in a simply structured economy where development objectives seek economic growth in any one area of the region in order to improve the entire regional economy. The discussion that follows reflects this dichotomy.

Rural economic development planning

Federal programs to stimulate regional development began in the 1960s. Most notably, the Appalachian Regional Commission and the Economic Development Administration shaped the form of regional economic development planning. At the same time that the start-up of planning for urban highway systems was creating regional transportation planning agencies in metropolitan areas, national attention on rural development created economic development agencies in non-metropolitan areas. Unlike state economic development planning programs, regional programs were—from the beginning and even now—heavily dependent on federal support for planning and implementation. That dependence has also shaped their organization and operation.

Rural development agencies were created to fill a void in local leadership capability. Technical expertise was required to analyze regional economies and plan appropriate projects to ameliorate poor economic conditions. In the absence of strong local political lealdership, federal agencies required the participation of private sector leaders in the planning and implementation process. A planning document was required which described the regional economy and proposed projects for stimulating economic growth. Whether or not there was direct federal support for the preparation of the document, its maintenance was required in order to qualify the region for project funding from the federal agencies. As described earlier, the state's role in this process was to delineate sub-state regions, assist in the establishment of an organization, and in the case of ARC, to coordinate regional plans into a state development agenda.

From 1960 to 1980 there were four agencies offering direct support to regional agencies for economic development: the Economic Development Administration (EDA), the Appalachian Regional Commission (ARC), the Title V Commissions, and the Farmers Home Administration (FmHA). These agencies cooperated in their requirements for boundaries, organization structure (notably the composition of the governing board), and documentary requirements. Although each federal agency directly funded only a portion of the total number of local agencies, such cooperation produced a remarkable homogeneity in agency characteristics and produced a cohesion among the agencies that resulted in a formidable lobbying effort in Washington.

With the growth of the regional comprehensive planning movement in the 1970s, most of these development agencies grew to encompass the full range of planning responsibilities delegated by the states and the federal government to rural regional agencies.

The economic development programs have been popular with rural leadership for several reasons:

First, the planning requirements were not extensive and did not require the technical studies and citizen participation procedures that many other federal planning programs did.

Second, implementation funds were available for projects which were politically pleasing to award. Infrastructure projects improved the climate for business; loans and loan guarantees were of direct benefit to business. Projects seldom had the social stigma attached to the products of some other planning programs.

Third, the involvement of private sector leaders in a public planning effort proved enormously successful. Private leadership is critical to the success of most local development projects, and their early participation often enabled projects to truly "take off."

Urban economic development planning

There has been no permanent federal funding available to regional planning agencies in urban areas for economic development planning. Although EDA and ARC funded a number of agencies in large metropolitan areas, their activities were expected to concentrate in the rural portions of the region.

During the 1970s, metropolitan planning agencies began to recognize the economic issues emerging in their programs. Most developed a capability in sophisticated statistical analysis as part of their transportation and environmental quality projects, and the economic dimension to those studies became increasingly evident. Several agencies began activities, apart from their regularly funded work programs, which gave an economic development dimension to their programs.

Although EDA had an active planning assistance program in urban areas, such funds went directly to cities and urban counties. It was not until 1978 that EDA initiated a demonstration program to explore the potential role of metropolitan agencies in economic development planning. At the height of the demonstration, 18 agencies were funded to conduct a variety of programs in research, data analysis, site development, regional policy development, technical assistance to local governments, coordination of local manpower activites, and special projects.

Organizing for regional economic development planning

Although there are no organization models for regional economic development planning, there are some principles to guide the organization designer:

Economic development planning should be practiced within the organizational framework of the comprehensive planning process. Economic development is too clearly related to transportation systems, environmental quality, manpower training, and land use to exist outside of their planning structure and practice.

Depending on the local institutional setting, economic development planning is likely to operate differently in urban and rural areas. In the *rural* area, the organization might be unique in its staff expertise, its political leadership, and its private sector alliances. As such, it will have the freedom, and the burden, of designing its own agenda and operating procedures. In the *urban* setting, there are numerous actors already having technical expertise and political power in economic development. The planning agency that enters the field must do so with sensitivity to existing turf and with a spirit of inclusiveness in setting an agenda that serves a variety of needs.

There must be commitment from the private sector that there is a need for a public/private regional approach to economic development; that they will share their knowledge and information about the regional economy; that they will support a planning process which is very time-consuming by private sector standards; and that they will participate in the implementation of a development strategy.

There must be staff expertise in economic analysis and in communicating analysis to decision makers in the public and private sectors. Staff experience in the private sector is indispensable.

The organization should have a clear view of the distinction between planning and implementation functions in economic development. Very few implementation actions will take place in the planning organization. Implementation will not automatically happen. Outside actors should be a part of the planning process, with an early understanding of their potential role.

The regional economic development planning process

The steps outlined previously under the state economic development planning process are largely transferrable to the regional setting.

Actions to implement the regional economic development strategy

The regional planning agency defines its role in economic development through the actions it takes to implement the development strategy. That role must be consistent with the agency's established mission and operating style. If the agency chooses to depart from a style and mission born of experience and public acceptance, it must be prepared to lay a careful framework of staff expertise and member support before the new program begins.

The agency undertaking an economic development program will face three challenges missing in most traditional regional planning programs:

1. The private sector will be integral to the strategy and its implementation.
2. Economic development will be a program with local support for its basic goals, particularly in recessionary times, and in depressed areas.
    However, specific implementation efforts are likely to select certain jurisdictions for assistance to the exclusion of others. Interjurisdictional rivalries are familiar to regional planners, but when the stakes are economic, political tensions are compounded.
3. There will be no clear source of funding for implementing the strategy. The regional agency must be innovative and brave in its search for supporting public and private resources.

Figure 15-3 categorizes and explains the actions a regional planning agency can take to implement its economic development strategy.[6] Few agencies will have the resources or the mandate for the full range of activities, but a good economic development strategy will point to specific actions to implement its goals for the economic prosperity of the region.

Regional planning agencies are familiar, and comfortable, with *regional coordination*. Most agencies are already sensitive to the economic aspects of *existing regional programs* and have taken steps to introduce economic development coordination into comprehensive and functional plans. *Coordination of local economic development programs* can be more difficult, as the regional agency seeks to influence existing programs whose political acceptance is assured. The regional agency is also comfortable in the *overall leadership* position for economic development through *promotion, issue discussion,* and *small area development*.

Local capacity building activities are intrinsic to the success of regional planning. Most agencies are proven sources of *information, research,* and *technical assistance* for local governments. *Training* activities have potential in both urban and rural areas, particularly in conjunction with growing state interests. *Legislative coordination* can be a particularly effective means of lobbying state and federal governments as well as generating a sense of regional identification and commonality of concerns among local elected officials.

Business assistance is a rapidly expanding role for regional agencies, particularly outside of metropolitan areas. Following a long history of acting as a broker between business and government (local, state and federal) for *capital* and *site development*, some regional agencies are now direct providers of low-cost and/or difficult-to-get capital as well as site developers. *Technical assistance* to business can take one of two forms—management assistance, a rare activity, or more traditional broker activities. *Market development*, except for general promotional programs, is largely an untried activity.

The challenge of the 1980s

The 1980s seem likely to begin reversing the 50-year trend toward increasing government involvement in the operation of the United States economy, as the role of government is re-examined in relation to all aspects of American life.

The mood of the 1980s blames government for many of the nation's economic ills, while at the same time, it demands that government take action to pull the economy out of its worst recession since the 1930s.

Popular belief has it that government is largely responsible for the inability of the private sector to sustain its unbridled postwar growth. Taxes and the cost of regulations cut into profits, discouraging reinvestment and dwindling needed capital. Government expenditures are inflationary; interest rates are choking business expansion. Government's response to these sentiments has been predictable: cuts in domestic spending (coupled with schizophrenic increases in defense spending), tax cuts, and deregulation of business activity. Somewhere around mid-decade, the nation is likely to sift through domestic priorities and reach a balance of governmental participation in private sector activity, provided the international political scene does not overshadow such domestic reasoning.

States and regions fare differently under the 1980s version of the "New Federalism." While it suggests a greater role for states in traditional federal areas of concern, there is no mention of regional planning agencies, except to lessen their powers of review over local jurisdictions.

States probably will assume greater development responsibilities during the 1980s for several reasons. First, that would simply be the continuation of a trend begun in the mid-1970s. Second, local governments are likely to demand more leadership from states in this area. And finally, as the federal government withdraws from the development scene, states will find it easier to operate in the void than they did in the previously competitive environment.

The major impediment to this new state role is resources. State revenues are tied to economic performance almost to the extent that federal revenues are. In the face of economic recession and federal funding cutbacks, and limited in their capacity for debt, states are facing monumental resource constraints. If states are to play a greater role in economic development, they must *assume* that role, rather than having it delegated to them as in past delegations of authority and resources. That assumption must be a conscious allocation of resource priorities by governors and legislators who understand their potential for leadership in this area and the intrinsic importance of economic development to the well being of their states.

The atmosphere for an expanded role for regional planning agencies in economic development is less favorable. Regional planning itself is threatened by the political environment and governmental resources of the early 1980s. Those agencies that have proven themselves to be good brokers for interjurisdictional issues and are judged to be useful to member governments are likely to survive as viable regional bodies; economic development is a natural area of concern for them, given the availabilty of necessary resources for planning and implementation. Success is more likely among those agencies with established development programs; this will be a difficult time for public investment in unproven ventures.

For those states and regions that choose an active role in economic development, the issues are complex and challenging.

The economy of the United States is undergoing structural changes that affect both its role in the world economy and the function and distribution of domestic economic activity. Economic development planning must shift from accommodating, stimulating, and channeling economic growth to *adjusting* to the new structure of the United States economy. This task will be politically difficult as basic industries like steel and automobile production decline; government's role will be to smooth the transition of the economic base, to retain and strengthen existing viable enterprises, and to anticipate and stimulate new ventures in areas of economic advantage. It will be a difficult evolution for the traditional field of economic development, requiring an unaccustomed analytical sophistication coupled with difficult political innovation.

In the 1980s there are likely to be three constraints to development as the economy makes this difficult transition:

First, there continues to be a shortage of capital for business expansion, particularly among new ventures and small and medium sized firms. This problem has been recognized since the mid-1970s, and states, particularly, have been leaders in developing programs to provide access and affordability to capital to sustain and expand economic growth. Concern with capital markets has led to considerable recent discussion of the structure and function of private capital markets. This issue will reach maturity in the public policy arena in the 1980s, given proper political recognition.

Second, the United States has long recognized the importance of physical infrastructure to economic development. It is ironic, therefore, that during a period of severe economic strain the nation is less committed to infrastructure improvement than at any time in its history. The construction, financing, and maintenance costs of infrastructure have become prohibitive; the lead time necessary to plan and construct projects adds to costs to public resistance. The problem is equally severe in older industrial regions, where deterioration is the issue, as in expanding economic areas where new construction is needed to accommodate growth. Discussion of this issue has begun, but public awareness is slow in coming. Perhaps the best hope for attracting public attention to this issue lies in the example of the interstate highway system, whose construction proved far easier to finance than its maintenance.

Third, perhaps the most difficult challenge for the 1980s lies in the area of manpower development. There is widespread public dissatisfaction with the manpower programs of the 1970s, centering on the failures of public employment. Although there is a shift to dependence on private sector resources for job training, public discussion has not addressed the critical issues surrounding manpower development: public education as preparation for employment, retraining of older workers, worker relocation incentives, and training delivery mechanisms.

The economic development planner in the 1980s faces a complex and politically difficult economic condition. The game will go to those with a sound understanding of the economy, bolstered by enlightened political leadership, who are patient in designing a strategy to help their economy make the difficult adjustments necessary in the post-industrial twenty-first century.

1   See Otis L. Graham, *Toward A Planned Society* (New York: Oxford University Press, 1983); and Marion Clawson, *New Deal Planning* (Washington, DC: Resources for the Future, 1981).

2   As quoted in Graham, *op. cit.*, p. 89.

3   Mark Aldrich, *A History of Public Works in the United States 1790–1970* (Washington, DC: Economic Development Administration, US Department of Commerce, 1979) (mimeographed).

4   Sar A. Levitan, *Federal Aid to Depressed Areas* (Baltimore: The Johns Hopkins Press, 1964), p. 24.

5   As quoted in Levitan, p. 23.

6   As quoted in Levitan, p. 24.

7   As quoted in Levitan, pp. 152–160.

8   US Department of Commerce, Economic Development Administration, Local Public Works Program: Final Report (Washington, DC: December 1980), p. 1.

9   Alfred S. Eichner, *State Development Agencies and Employment Expansion* (Ann Arbor, MI: Institute of Labor and Industrial Relations, The University of Michigan—Wayne State University, 1970), pp. 17–20.

10   Eichner, p. 20.

11   Eichner, p. 20.

Part four:
Major types of
state and
regional plans

16 Housing planning

The federal government undoubtedly has been the prime initiator of public activities in the housing field. Beginning with slum clearance projects in the 1930s and progressing through formal public housing, urban renewal, and housing opportunities programs in the following decades, local governments and then, more gradually, the states were induced to become active. Area-wide bodies joined the field in the 1970s, at about the same time the states did, when area-wide housing planning requirements and incentives were enacted by the federal government.

This chapter describes how states and area-wide planning organizations affect or engage in the planning and delivery of housing services. However, the 1980 national elections, resulting in a new President and the emergence of a Republican majority in the Senate along with a generally more conservative House of Representatives, foreshadow important changes in housing policies and programs in the years ahead. The resources and tools available to state and local governments to deal with low- and moderate-income housing programs are changing.

Thus this chapter was written during a period of transition in national housing policy. While particular approaches to housing problems may vary with changes in the political climate, insights for the future may be gained by examining the evolution of state and regional planning activities over time. Planning, regulating, financing, and allocating resources in the housing sector will continue to be public concerns in some form in the future.

The chapter is organized into five sections. The first overviews state and area-wide planning activities related to housing. The second focuses on housing planning and program activity at the state level, including direct housing aid, regulation and control of housing developments, occupancy of housing, and housing credit. In the third section, regional and area-wide housing activities are discussed at length. Section four focuses on rural housing issues and regionalism. The final section draws some conclusions about the future.

Overview of state and area-wide planning for housing

The paths of state and regional agencies in the housing field have been quite different from one another, reflecting the distinct roles, powers, and responsibilities of each.

Area-wide agencies, with a few notable exceptions, remain voluntary associations of local governments, seldom having more than advisory responsibilities over the major functional, as well as comprehensive, planning components within their jurisdiction. Their review-and-comment powers over federal grants to member jurisdictions through the A-95 process have had mixed impact. In housing, the area-wide organization's role sometimes appears to have less standing than in other functional areas where a regional plan is a prerequisite to capital investment.

Zoning, market-rate housing development, and the provision of assisted housing all are key elements of regional growth that the area-wide organization may

Figure 16–1   The 1980 Census of Housing shows that the United States has a total of 86.8 million dwelling units. Almost 62 percent are detached, single-family houses. Four percent are attached, single-family houses in the form of row houses and other types of connected structures. Twenty-five million units are in apartments, ranging from two flats to buildings of 50 or more units; this group makes up 29 percent of the total. The remaining number is small—4.4 million units (5 percent) in trailers, mobile homes, and similar kinds of housing. The accompanying photos suggest the variety of housing within these statistical categories.

seek to influence, but it must do so through leadership rather than control. Moving toward the financing of housing and the promotion of fair housing practices in its region, the area-wide body typically must seek to facilitate and integrate the activities of others, rather than to fund, regulate, or enforce on its own.

In sharp contrast, states possess a wide range of authority that can be brought to bear directly on housing. Though limited by the 1980 Mortgage Subsidy Bond Tax Act (commonly referred to as the Ullman Bill), their continuing capacity to issue tax-exempt bonds allows them to infuse new capital into housing projects at a reduced cost to housing consumers. Regulatory powers over banking can

Figure 16–1 (continued)

The single family house that is pictured is typical of units built over the past generation in thousands of subdivisions. The row houses too are typical and show how construction in the seventies and eighties used varied exteriors to break away from the visual uniformity of older row house developments in many large cities. The term "row house," although accurate, has been superseded by "town house" or "town home." Apartment houses come in all sizes and shapes, but the one pictured above reflects the postwar trend toward buildings on open land with many amenities, including off-street parking. The manufactured home is the latest in the progression from trailers to mobile homes to manufactured homes. Since 1976, all manufactured homes have been built according to standards issued by the U.S. Department of Housing and Urban Development governing safety, quality, and durability. The one shown above has all of its landscaping in place.

be used to counter unfair withholding of mortgage funds from least-favored neighborhoods. Statutory provisions of fair housing potentially enable states to protect the civil rights of their residents. Ultimately, the states' taxing, financing, and capital investment policies could have greater impact on the changing urban and rural character of the country than could the efforts of area-wide councils.

Yet, the breadth of state concerns and authority, to say nothing of the complexity of state political leadership and coalition building, has generally created a more diffused, less focused image of housing activity at the state level than at any other level of government. It has been at the area-wide level that dramatic, though limited, innovations often have occurred. Area-wide housing planning achievements often have been possible because of a less diverse jurisdiction, a more limited potential base across which a bridge must be built, and the ability to focus on single issues.

Genesis of the mortgage business   The formation of the Federal Housing Authority and ancillary housing programs of the thirties revolutionized housing financing in the United States. Federal loan guarantees transformed the mortgage from a five-year renewable vehicle by providing for a low down payment, low monthly payments, amortization through level payments, and a long repayment period of twenty to thirty years. Prior to the thirties, the mortgage business was a small-scale operation. The following excerpt shows what mortgages were like before the federal government became a partner.

Mortgage lending as a U.S. industry was not to develop fully until the Twentieth Century. Earlier mortgages were simply affairs in which the owners of property (or lenders) agreed to take a buyer's note for a stipulated cost, interest rate, and term of repayment. The borrower, or mortgagor, took possession of the property and assumed full ownership under a lien until the mortgage, or pledge, was paid in full.

By the 1920s, the typical mortgage banker was an individual, a partnership, or a small, family-owned corporation that continued to sell mortgages to individuals. The more successful middlemen became local representatives for insurance companies; but mortgage banking was still conducted on a relatively small scale.

Usually, a loan for purchase of real property (land or home, or both) was made on only a part of the actual cost—rarely more than 50 to 60 percent of the price. Interest often ran at eight percent over a five-year term. At the end of that period the entire amount of the principal was due in one lump sum. Because of the low percentage loans, many people had to resort to secondary financing in which they borrowed the difference between the primary loan and the total cost of the property. The secondary loan had a substantially higher interest rate. This resulted in few people being able to make the lump sum payment, but the lender usually renewed the primary loan on the same terms. Investments in home mortgages were considered very safe, since defaults were almost unknown up until the Great Depression of the 1930s.

Source: U.S. Department of Housing and Urban Development, *HUD International Brief*, Program Report 10 (Washington, D.C.: Government Printing Office, no date), pp. 4–5.

There are exceptions to those general observations, however. For example, in New Jersey, as a result of the 1975 New Jersey State Supreme Court decision in *Southern Burlington County NAACP* v. *Township of Mount Laurel*, the state moved to require proportionate distribution of lower-income housing in every jurisdiction.[1] Thus, the state enhanced a traditional area-wide role in planning the distribution of assisted housing by using its legislative and constitutional powers—though with imperfect results thus far.

In Minnesota, for another example, the state created an area-wide agency with sufficient legal powers and authorities to enforce its housing and other functional plans. Jurisdictions of the state-appointed Metropolitan Council of the Twin Cities (Minneapolis–St. Paul) must follow the broad outlines of development patterns and major capital investments prescribed by the Council. In addition to developing and enforcing a far-reaching regional plan for distributing assisted housing, the Council also functions as a housing authority for the area outside the major cities. In this example of the differing roles of state and area-wide agencies, the state provided the key to area-wide effectiveness.

The Miami Valley Regional Planning Commission, in Dayton, Ohio, provides the more typical example. It possessed no powers greater than any other voluntary area-wide body. Initially, it used its A-95 advisory powers to enforce the nation's first assisted housing "fair share" plan. When the commission began operation in 1970, 95 percent of all assisted housing was in the city of Dayton; by 1976, such housing was divided evenly throughout the metropolitan area. The agency's director had made consistency of applications with the regional plan a virtual prerequisite to area-wide endorsement of federal funds, thus providing innovative housing planning with the necessary leverage to enforce it, even though the state had provided no legal authority to this end.

The single most important impetus to housing planning by states and area-wide agencies came in the 1968 and 1974 amendments to the federal "701 Section" comprehensive planning assistance program. These amendments progressively emphasized the importance of housing in the comprehensive plan. The 1974 amendments required that any ongoing comprehensive planning process funded by this program had to at a minimum include housing and land-use elements. The acceptable content of each plan was gradually spelled out in regulations and guidelines, backed up by additional statutory amendments in 1980 requiring that the plans further the following national policy objectives:

1. The conservation and improvement of existing communities, particularly the improvement of those communities faced with fiscal, economic, or social distress.
2. An increase in housing and employment opportunities and choices, especially for lower income and minority persons.
3. The promotion of orderly and efficient growth and development of communities, regions, and states, taking into consideration the necessity of conserving energy.[2]

The 1980 amendments also reflected a decreased interest in the comprehensive plan itself and an increased interest in the implementation of the plan. Under these amendments, Section 701 program recipients had to develop and work toward the implementation of a "strategy action program" that would further the previously mentioned national policy objectives. Moreover, the law required that the Secretary of Housing and Urban Development work with other federal agencies to encourage their use of the plans and strategies developed by Section 701 recipients.

This shift of emphasis in the law showed the natural evolution of the planning processes undertaken by state and area-wide agencies. Although the law had required that plans be updated and approved by HUD periodically, with the passage of time less attention had been paid to the actual plans, while more attention was given to specific implementation activities undertaken by the Section 701 recipients. Once they received approval for their plan, they turned their attention to a wide range of eligible implementation activities. It is these activities from which many notable state and area-wide achievements have arisen. Legislation for state housing finance agencies, fair housing ordinances, and rehabilitation programs have often been the products of Section 701 funded staff. Major structural reforms in state government, which often led to increased attention to housing needs and establishment of community affairs agencies, also have been attributed to the housing planning undertaken through Section 701.[3]

The Section 701 program itself, however, was terminated in 1981. At the time of passage of the 1974 amendments, the Section 701 appropriation exceeded $100 million; for a short period, metropolitan cities were eligible as direct recipients. However, funding declined precipitously from $110 million in fiscal year 1975 to under $35 million in fiscal year 1981 and to zero in fiscal year 1982. Cities were dropped as recipients in fiscal year 1977, thus dropping a major potential political constituency from a program that had largely failed to define a mission sufficiently focused to generate sustained and effective political support.

Housing planning is somewhat unique as a functional planning activity because it was supported by a federal planning program (Section 701) that was separate from the federal government's housing implementation programs. The consequence was the perception, only partially correct, that housing plans are simply "paper plans" prepared in order to retain eligibility for federal *planning* without any necessary relationship to the use of federal *housing* funds; thus, once prepared, they "sit on the shelf" unused. From the perspective of over a decade of housing planning funded by the federal government, it seems clear that, while a certain amount of effort has been wasted in the fulfillment of program requirements, states and regions have gradually shaped and molded their housing planning to meet immediate, practical needs with assured payoffs.

State housing activity

The role of states in housing is broad. It spans a wide range of activities from the direct financing of housing to code development and the enforcement of credit and fair housing regulations. Many different agencies within state government become involved in housing, and often act independently of one another, in the absence of strong executive leadership. In North Carolina, for example, a legislative study commission on housing found that at least 12 separate departments and agencies in that state share housing responsibilities; the commission has recommended that the General Assembly establish a Housing Commission in the Office of the Governor which would coordinate all state housing activities. The Housing Commission would also be responsible for preparing a state housing action plan for submission to the Governor who "will present it, with his recommendations and comments, to the General Assembly by the beginning of the regular legislative session."[4]

The housing planning function, howver, is often a starting point of state involvement in housing. Housing plans of states prepared under the comprehensive planning program typically contain an overall appraisal of housing trends and needs, identification of problem areas, and recommendations for specific actions. Implementation activities, however, vary widely. Recommendations reflect the policy and political climate of the state and generally emphasize programs and activities which are timely and likely to play to a responsive audience.

Direct state support

At first glance, it may not seem that states play a significant role in the housing sector. This is because the amount of direct state housing aid to local government is relatively modest overall and quite unevenly distributed across the country. Thus, the total amount of state aid to local housing and urban renewal activities in fiscal year 1976–1977 was just $291 million, equal to only 16 percent of all federal housing aid.[5] But, this relatively small amount of support was accounted for by just 20 states.[6] To put the direct state housing investment in perspective, it can be noted that housing aid in 1976–1977 equaled less than 1 percent of total state aid to local schools, one-thirteenth of the state investment in public welfare, and one-eleventh of the total state support for highways.

Although these data are somewhat old, it is unlikely that more recent statistics would alter the relatively low housing profile reflected in 1977. In fact, a recent survey carried out by the Council of State Governments of all 50 Governors indicated that housing ranked a relatively low fifth in priority in states' "problems" agenda, following energy, tax relief, road maintenance, and public employment.[7]

The modest amount of direct state housing support notwithstanding, it would be incorrect to assert that states are unimportant participants on the housing scene. More states are beginning to commit direct appropriations to housing at the same time that traditionally active states are becoming even more aggressive in their efforts to deal creatively with the growing problem of housing costs and affordability.

Among the more interesting state initiatives to keep home ownership affordable to as broad a segment of the population as possible is California's $100 million shared equity home ownership assistance program.[8] Under this pilot effort, the state will provide up to 49 percent of the purchase price of a dwelling unit for eligible households and share in the net sales proceeds proportionately to its financing commitment. The amount of the state interest in any given house will depend upon the household's income, housing prices, and the prevailing terms in the conventional mortgage market. If house prices and incomes are held constant, the state's equity share would be expected to increase as conventional loan terms become more stringent. Payouts to the state upon sale of dwellings financed in part under the shared equity program will capitalize a revolving loan fund to sustain the program over time. Another innovative effort has recently been mounted by the Minnesota Housing Finance Agency. Using $10 million from a $45 million single-family bond issued in late 1982, MHFA is providing loans to qualified buyers of houses owned by older persons so they can, in turn, move into smaller quarters.[9] MHFA has placed no maximum income limits on the "empty nesters" who it wants to encourage to sell their underutilized large houses to younger families with children who need more space but cannot afford new construction. The new borrowers must have incomes below $30,000.

Increasingly, states are engaging in a variety of energy-related activities. These range from the carrying out of energy audits for individual home owners and requiring the disclosure at time of sale of the energy efficiency of residential structures to a variety of energy conservation financing programs. With respect to disclosure, the Minnesota Energy Division now requires the energy efficiency of residential structures built before 1976 to be fully disclosed at the time of sale, with the information being based on the results of an energy audit.[10] The same regulations, adopted in December 1982, established mandatory energy efficiency standards that all rental structures constructed prior to 1976 had to attain by July 1, 1983. New Jersey's Residential Solar Hot Water System Program begun in 1980 provides below market interest rate loans for the purchase and installation of solar hot water systems. These loans have been made available to any home owner regardless of income.[11] Finally, Maryland's first state-wide energy conservation loan program, which was initially financed with $1 million in community development funds, financed energy improvements for home owners and owners of rental buildings with up to 20 units, without regard to the owner's income. A unique feature of the program is the participation of Baltimore Gas and Electric Company which provides loan application packages to its customers, conducts energy audits, reviews and processes loan applications, and originates and services loans across its service area.[12]

Another area of growing direct state support is rural housing. Texas, Florida, and Maine, among others, have developed special programs tailored to the unique needs of rural areas which suffer disproportionately from credit shortages, poorly organized housing delivery systems, and the lack of technical staff required to take full advantage of the available federal and state housing programs. In partial response to the problem, the U.S. Farmers Home Administration reached an agreement with the states of North Carolina as a test case for improving program approaches under which Farmers Home Section 502 (home ownership) and Section 515 (rental housing loan assistance) would be allocated in accord with the state's balanced growth and rural development policy.[13]

Some states also are making efforts to adjust a fixed and aging rural housing stock to the changing needs of their populations. While not operational at the time of this writing, New York State's Division of Housing and Community Renewal and the Maine State Housing Authority were seeking ways to convert large, old, and deteriorating Victorian single-family houses into congregate facilities for the elderly and cooperative or condominium units for small, nonelderly households. New York State has also established one of the first operational Neighborhood Housing Services (NHS) programs in a rural area. This public/private partnership brings together community residents, private lenders, and local governments in a three-county area to carry out a coordinated rehabilitation program. Organized community resident participation in the NHS program would not have been possible without prior assistance from the Rural Preservation Companies Program, also financed by the state, under which nonprofit groups engaged in housing and community preservation activities in rural areas are eligible to receive annual grants up to $100,000 for up to three years to cover administrative costs, planning, and program development activities.

To be successful, housing conversion and rural NHS efforts must be highly coordinated exercises in intergovernmental cooperation and public/private partnership—involving community-based organizations and private lenders as well as state planning and finance agencies. The kind of orchestration of the many actors involved in the housing arena, illustrated by these cases, suggests an important role in rural communities for the state.

State regulation and control

Even though there are some recent indications of increased levels of direct housing subsidy, states still legislate and regulate more than they appropriate. States play a very significant role in regulating and controlling a wide variety of local public and private behavior relating to the use and production of housing. Local housing markets may be substantially affected by the ways in which states regulate landlord-tenant relationships by the nature of enabling or other legislation controlling rents in the private rental housing stock, and by such other regulatory measures as condominium and cooperative conversion laws.

In addition to regulating lending activities of state-chartered banks, many states also limit maximum interest rates that private lenders may charge on residential mortgage loans and the terms and conditions under which mortgage loan assumptions may take place. These actions influence the cost and availability of mortgage credit. By virtue of the regulation of insurance companies, states may also affect the availability and cost of fire and liability insurance for home owners and rental housing investors in urban communities. In addition, states define the nature and character of mandatory insurance programs that provide coverage to high risk inner city properties that, by virtue of the deteriorated conditions of their neighborhoods, would not otherwise be served by the industry.[14]

Finally, states have substantial and direct impacts on housing through tax incentive laws and regulatory measures affecting land use, permit process, and building standards. Just about half of all the states have enacted rehabilitation tax incentive programs that include systems of tax credits, rebates, and exemptions. These programs, which are designed to encourage investments in home improvements, should not be confused with circuit breaker and other tax limitation measures such as Proposition 13 in California that several states have also enacted to lessen the impacts of rising real estate taxes, especially on elderly and low- and moderate-income home owners. These housing occupancy cost-containment measures vary widely, although a 1980 measure in Massachusetts which limits property tax valuations at 2.5 percent of full cash value is reasonably representative of the kind of legislation currently under consideration in several other states.[15]

With respect to activities to increase the supply of buildable land and to foster

Where are the nation's poor? It is often assumed that poverty is a problem primarily of minorities living in central cities, but this is a half-truth. The proportion of people living below the federally defined poverty line is indeed high in central cities (20 percent of these people), but the ratio is almost as high in the areas outside metropolitan areas (18 percent). The ratio falls sharply for the people living outside central cities but within metropolitan areas (9 percent).

Looking at the numbers and ratios from another perspective, in 1982, 34 million people in the United States were living below the poverty level, with ratios as follows: 37 percent in central cities, 25 percent outside central cities but within metropolitan areas, and 38 percent in the cities, towns, villages, and rural areas that make up the nonmetropolitan areas of the country.

When we look at the characteristics of people living below the poverty level, irrespective of residence, another picture emerges. The level of poverty is very high among blacks and Hispanics, but it also is high among female householders with no husband present, people under 24 years of age, unrelated individuals (both male and female), and persons living on farms.

Source: U.S. Bureau of the Census, Current Population Reports, Series P–60, No. 144, *Characteristics of the Population Below the Poverty Level: 1982* (Washington, D.C.: Government Printing Office, 1984).

responsible land-use controls, President Reagan's Housing Commission has urged state and local governments to review their policies with regard to the sale and transfer to public lands to the private sector for possible housing development.[16] The Commission's final report indicates that "some states . . . have undertaken comprehensive inventories and plans for the improved management and disposal of public lands to private control," and cites the example of Arizona's State Urban Lands Task Force which studied "the impacts of State lands on community development needs of Phoenix and Tucson and recommended lands to be assessed for disposal to meet these needs."[17]

The President's Commission also highlighted other recent state actions designed to increase the supply of buildable land. A recent California statute "requires local growth-control proponents to bear greater responsibility for justifying growth controls . . . while an amendment to the zoning enabling law requires . . . cities and counties to designate and zone enough vacant land for residential use to meet future as well as present housing needs."[18] Noting that delays in processing permit and related requests by developers add unnecessarily to building costs, the Commission praised an Oregon law which prohibits municipalities from "engaging in a pattern of conduct of failing to provide timely State building code inspections or plan reviews."[19] Finally, the Commission underscored the fact that not all creative initiatives in this area must be implemented through legislation. A 1979 Memorandum of Understanding between the Massachusetts State Executive Office of Communities and Development and the Executive Office of Environmental Affairs requires funding for local acquisition of conservation land to be "withheld unless a community has accepted its fair share of all housing growth."[20]

With respect to the regulation of building standards, three clusters of state activities are of direct interest. First, 23 states have enacted state-wide building codes to minimize the extent to which local communities can impose unreasonable and costly standards on new housing built within their jurisdictions and to eliminate the possibility of builders having to face patchwork quilts of different codes in the regional housing markets in which they operate.[21]

While these codes deal principally with conventionally built housing, HUD's manufactured housing code establishes a federal standard applicable to mobile homes and other manufactured housing systems.[22] There is no direct state regulatory role here inasmuch as any manufactured housing unit meeting the HUD code can be located in any community regardless of state or local code provisions. Indirectly, however, states have a potentially powerful influence on the extent to which mobile homes and manufactured housing are accepted and encouraged in local communities. Often subjected to discretionary zoning exclusion because of what some refer to as the "trailer mentality" of local officials, mobile homes and other forms of manufactured housing deserve wider utilization as an affordable alternative to "stick-built" housing. Not only can states encourage more progressive community attitudes toward manufactured housing by highlighting outstanding projects, they also could mandate the local adoption of inclusionary zoning ordinances that would require communities to provide for a "fair share" of affordable housing in their jurisdictions.[23]

Manufactured homes Going back to the 1920s, several terms have been used to cover housing that was not built on site, including "trailers," "prefabricated houses," "modular houses," and "mobile homes." In the Housing Act of 1980, Congress mandated that the term "manufactured homes" be used for all homes built in factories that comply with the 1976 National Manufactured Home Construction and Safety Standards, as amended. The manufactured home has been defined as follows:

"A manufactured home is a structure, transportable in one or more sections, which, in the traveling mode, is eight body feet or more in width or forty body feet or more in length, or, when erected on site, is 320 or more square feet. It is built on a permanent chassis and designed to be used as a dwelling with or without a permanent foundation when connected to the required utilities. The manufactured home includes the plumbing, heating, air conditioning, and electrical systems."

The industry comprises 185 companies with 410 factory sites throughout the country. There are approximately ten thousand retailers of manufactured homes in the United States and about twenty-four thousand manufactured home communities. Census data for 1981 showed that 46 percent of occupied manufactured homes were located within manufactured home communities with the balance on individual sites.

Source: Second paragraph excerpted and third paragraph abstracted from Manufactured Housing Institute, *Quick Facts about the Manufactured Housing Industry* (Arlington, Va.: Manufactured Housing Institute, 1984).

Mobile homes that are truly mobile—that is, not fixed to permanent foundations—are typically taxed as personal rather than real property. The occupants of such mobile homes therefore pay taxes that "do not generally go directly to the jurisdictions that must supply services to them, and the amount of taxes paid is generally lower than comparable real property taxes."[24] As a result, it has been argued, until the taxing issue is resolved, most local communities will continue to oppose mobile home developments that do not pay their way. Indeed, it has been asserted that mobile home zoning in California has become significantly easier to accomplish since passage of legislation changing the tax status of mobile homes from motor vehicles to real estate.[25]

When manufactured homes (the term used within the industry) are placed on permanent foundations, such properties are taxed as real property in 47 states.

The accompanying sidebars provide definitions and other information on production, location, costs, and demographic characteristics of manufactured housing.

The third kind of regulatory activity relating building standards to local housing market practices concerns the relationship between building codes and the rehabilitation of substandard housing. In March, 1978, Congressional hearings on this subject began with the consensus that "existing model codes and code enforcement techniques are designed for new construction, and contain neither the administrative, legal, nor technical mechanisms to properly deal with rehabilitation."[26] One outgrowth of the hearings was the fuller recognition that "current building regulations may force the upgrading of rehabilitated buildings to the level required for new construction which may impose unanticipated costs. . . ."[27] This led the Congress to direct HUD in Section 903 of the Housing and Community Development Amendments of 1978 to develop and promulgate a set of rehabilitation guidelines that would permit the upgrading of buildings to less than new construction standards. The first of a series of guidelines were published by HUD in 1980 and are intended for voluntary adoption by states and communities in conjunction with existing building codes in the inspection and approval of rehabilitated properties.[28] Although it is too early to tell how aggressively the states will move to adopt, build upon, and promulgate these new guidlines, it is certain that the level of state activity in this area will grow in the immediate future.

Does manufactured housing pay its way?   One of the most frequent complaints made about manufactured housing, especially in manufactured home communities, is that it does not carry its fair share of local government taxes in relation to local government services. No direct and clear-cut evidence was available as of 1984, but several ancillary indicators point toward financial stability and cost-benefit balance.

Manufactured homes built and installed since 1976, when the HUD standards were issued, have appreciated in value at 5 percent or more per year.

In 47 states—all but Connecticut, New Mexico, and Rhode Island—manufactured homes that are on a *permanent foundation* are taxed by local governments as real property.

The head of the household is over 50 years of age in 43 percent of manufactured homes.

There are only 2.3 persons per household in manufactured homes.

It takes 6 manufactured homes to produce 1 school child.

Both FHA and conventional financing are available for permanently sited manufactured homes, and there is a secondary mortgage market. This means that such housing can be financed just like conventional housing.

Source: Unpublished data from the Joint Venture for Affordable Housing, Office of Policy Development and Research, U.S. Department of Housing and Urban Development, 1984.
and Urban Development, 1984.

State housing finance activities

Though it is by far their largest housing role in dollar amount, most housing finance activities of state governments are not directly reflected in the state expenditure data discussed earlier. This is because the states' substantial financing role is largely accomplished indirectly through the activities of their housing finance agencies, which are state-created entities of a quasi-governmental character.

Within limits, housing finance agencies have been relatively successful in accomplishing their goals of lowering housing costs, increasing the housing supply and tapping new sources of long-term housing capital;[29] but not without some serious concern being raised by housing and other policy makers. With respect to the cost reduction goal, for example, HFA tax-exempt borrowing does produce savings on interest costs of around 20 percent for single family mortgages and potentially between 6 and 9 percent on the total capital and operating costs of federally subsidized rental housing.[30] Whether these latter savings are routinely passed on to tenants in the form of lower rents is not at all clear, however. Since project rents under HUD's Section 8 housing program are established with reference to local rental levels and HUD rent standards, they do not vary consistently with total development costs. According to Peterson, "while HFA cost advantages make it possible to build rental projects that otherwise would be economically unfeasible and open the possibility of higher quality construction, the cost savings may be dissipated in production inefficiencies."[31]

Their success in tapping a new source of housing capital is reflected in the fact that the collective appetite of HFAs was sufficiently great in 1978 to consume fully 10 percent of the total tax-exempt capital market.[32] Peterson estimates that "at recent market levels, each billion dollars of housing bonds adds 4 to 7 basis points to the overall tax-exempt rate."[33] At a $13 billion level of housing bonds in 1979, HFAs could have bid up long-term, tax-exempt interest rates for all borrowers by between one-half and nine-tenths of a percent.[34] Because of the upward pressures they exert on tax-exempt interest rates and the fact that a $13 billion level of HFA borrowing costs the federal government around $350–400 million in foregone income tax receipts,[35] it is entirely appropriate that the public purposes served and programs developed by HFAs be held up to careful scrutiny and be consistent with national housing goals. Indeed, Congressional scrutiny of the mounting costs "to the Treasury . . . and use by some municipalities of tax exempt funds to support neighborhoods and borrowers other than those most in need, the Federal government set limits and conditions on the issuance of single family mortgage revenue bonds at the end of 1980."[36] Among other provisions, the Ullmann Bill forbids new single family tax-exempt revenue bond issues after the end of 1983.

There are other problems on the horizon, as well. In the 1974–1975 credit squeeze, several agencies, most notably those in New York, Massachusetts, and Pennsylvania, were unable to convert some of their outstanding short-term construction notes to permanent mortgages financed with revenue bonds because they could not market these bonds. As a result, the states had to make good on their so-called moral obligations to back their agency finances and assisted their HFAs in working out debt repayment arrangements.[37] Since that time HFAs have been less casual in their use of short-term notes, while the bond market has further discounted the value of the moral obligation, preferring instead the more tangible support of agency operations such as direct state appropriations to HFA capital reserve funds.

Up until the end of 1980, the major policy concern involving HFAs had to do with their dramatic withdrawal from the multifamily rental market and their swift movement into the single-family home ownership market. Since then, of course, their problems and the policy issues which they raise have become even more complicated.

The HFA movement into the single family sector was spectacular in the latter part of the 1970s. Starting from a zero level of single-family financing in 1974, HFAs collectively issued one-half billion dollars in single-family bonds in 1978. In 1980, the aggregate volume of HFA tax-exempt single-family bonds had grown tenfold to $5 billion, or 78 percent of total HFA financing.[38]

The changing mix in the HFA bond portfolio is important because the relative emphasis on single-family home owners or multifamily renters has potentially significant income and spatial consequences. While most of their single-family programs serve households with incomes near the national median, at least half of all multifamily units produced by HFAs serve lower-income families by virtue of a deep federal subsidy added to the savings produced by lowered interest rates.[39] Moreover, HFA-financed multifamily housing tends to be more concentrated in central cities where housing problems are more severe. As of June, 1977, around three-quarters of all HFA-financed multifamily units were in central cities, compared to one-quarter in the suburbs and nonmetropolitan communities.[40] Although this figure drops substantially (to 43 percent) when New York state is excluded, it is still much above the 25 percent of all HFA-financed single-family housing located in the central cities.[41]

The shifting mix must also be viewed as a reflection of rapidly rising interest rates. As interest rates have climbed, demand for single-family financing has risen correspondingly. The federal subsidy required for lower income rentals financed by HFAs has climbed as long-term financing has risen in cost. The amount of HFA-backed new construction and substantial rehabilitation has been limited by federal subsidies overall and by growing concern at the cost of HFA-produced units. The residual, nonsubsidized, multifamily rentals, enjoying tax-exempt financing as a single-cost moderating factor, faces dollar levels generally higher than most HFAs find to be sound investments. This dilemma is, in turn, a reflection of the sustained demand for home ownership, which continues to be a higher priority for moderate- and middle-income households seeking tax shelter and insurance against inflation.

An overall assessment of the HFA track record to date would be quite favorable, although one would have to conclude that they have come as far as they have more by their brute strength than by finesse. Although they have provided low-cost financing for over 420,000 single-family homes and more than 360,000 low-income multifamily units since the late 1960s,[42] neither their program mixes nor the types and locations of the housing they finance generally have been products of carefully concerned state housing strategies. With several important exceptions, they tend to neither target their investments in capital-poor areas nor provide alternative housing delivery systems where the unaided private sector cannot or will not respond to latent market demands or housing needs. While they have pioneered in the development of a major and previously untapped source of long-term mortgage capital for development, until recently they have been reluctant to explore new mechanisms for financing inner city rehabilitation. Over the last few years, however, they have provided more than $1 billion in home improvement and energy conservation loans. Moreover, now that almost all of the states have assumed administrative responsibilities for the Small Cities Community Development Block Grant Program, it will be easier for them to create deeper subsidy rehabilitation loan programs in nonmetropolitan and credit-poor rural areas, by using CD funds to further subsidize the interest rates on HFA bonds.[43] While this kind of integrated financing will be further encouraged by the targeting and related requirements of the Mortgage Subsidy Bond Tax Act, increasingly unstable and deregulated credit markets and a revised national housing policy environment in which there will be few federal subsidies for new low-income housing construction, means that housing finance agencies are facing very uncertain futures.

Housing finance and pension funds

Another dimension of the state's indirect role in housing finance concerns the management and investment practices of trustees of state pension and retirement systems. Historically, managers of pension funds have been reluctant to invest in mortgages because of the nonstandardized nature of real estate investments, the difficulty in assessing the risks associated with mortgages, and the fact that the management of mortgage loans takes a different mix of professional skills than are required to manage more traditional kinds of investment portfolios. However, with the development of insured mortgages, standardized loan under-writing procedures, and the development of secondary mortgage market facilities like the Federal National Mortgage Association (FNMA) and the Government National Mortgage Association (GNMA), many of the problems that prevented pension funds from becoming an important source of housing credit began to disappear. The recent development of GNMA mortgage-backed securities has spurred pension fund investments in mortgages. This is because GNMAs are not mortgages at all but securities that are backed by pools of government-insured mortgage loans. Since the loans are insured and the payment of principal and interest on the GNMA securities is guaranteed by the federal government, even conservative pension funds may safely and conveniently invest indirectly in residential mortgage loans.

Another important reason that the development of mortgage-backed securities is important in the evolution of state pension fund support of housing is that many state retirement systems are prohibited by law from purchasing mortgage loans, although they may invest in certain kinds of securities which are backed by insured loans. Indeed, in 1981 North Carolina's state retirement system was the first to purchase conventional mortgage-backed securities issued by a private corporation created by the state's banking and savings and loan industries expressly for that purpose. The North Carolina Mortgage Investment Corporation (NCMIC) is nothing more than a corporate conduit that collects pools of mortgage loans originated by private lenders in the state and issues securities that are collater-alized by those loans. The securities are then purchased by the state's pension fund with the proceeds of the sale being funneled back to the participating lenders who can then make additional loans to home buyers.

While NCMIC was the first private sector corporate entity created to tap state pension funds as a source of mortgage credit, it is now not the only one. The Yankee Mortgage Assistance Corporation (Yankee Mac), a recently created secondary mortgage agency in Connecticut has also marketed mortgage-backed securities to that state's retirement system. In late 1982, the state's teachers and employees pension fund committed $40 million to purchase pass-through secu-rities to be issued by Yankee Mac which would be backed by new mortgage loans to be originated by lenders throughout Connecticut.[44] Although the loans will be originated at market rates, an innovative feature of the program is that half of the funds will be reserved for mortgage loans to state teachers and employees, with the balance to be made available to the general public. This represents one of the first times that the trustees of a state pension fund have declared the achievement of a specific state housing goal to be compatible with their fiduciary responsibilities as managers of the fund.

State fair housing efforts

Despite the fact that fair housing is the law of the land, a recent national study of housing market practices concluded that "significant levels of racial discrim-ination—both direct and indirect—still exist in America's housing market."[45]

In reflecting on the study's findings, former HUD Secretary Patricia Roberts Harris indicated that the nation's fair housing law and related civil rights acts "have failed to achieve the goal of equal opportunity in housing" and concluded that "the disadvantaged in our society are still waiting for a place at the table of opportunity."[46] The principal legislation to which Secretary Harris referred is the Civil Rights Act of 1968; in particular Title VIII, which prohibits most forms of discriminatory market practices such as blockbusting, steering, racially biased advertising, and unequal lending practices.

Title VIII designates the Department of Housing and Urban Development (HUD) as the federal agency responsible for administering the Fair Housing Act, while it limits the Department's powers to "the receipt, investigation, and conciliation of complaints . . . [and] . . . the authority and responsibility to make studies, publish and disseminate reports, and to cooperate with and render technical assistance to other public or private agencies."[47]

Although Title VIII defines the *federal* fair housing responsibility, it establishes two important links to the states. The first, alluded to above, concerns HUD's technical assistance and outreach efforts to state and local fair housing agencies, enabling them to strengthen their respective enforcement capabilities. The second and principal link between federal and state fair housing activities derives from Section 813(c) of Title VIII, which requires the HUD Secretary to refer all fair housing complaints to the appropriate state or local fair housing agency for initial processing where substantial equivalence exists between the federal law and relevant state or local statutes.[48] In 1980, 22 states were recognized by HUD as having substantially equivalent fair housing laws.[49]

While the enforcement provisions of most state laws are limited to receiving and investigating complaints and attempting resolution through conciliation, some have greater enforcement provisions. In a few states, after finding probable cause, the fair housing agency is empowered to enjoin the respondent from selling or renting the dwelling that is the subject of the complaint until the investigation and conciliation process has been fully played out.[50] Although Title VIII does not presently give HUD similar authority, several state agencies are empowered, following failure of the conciliation process, to impose cease and desist orders; to require the payment of actual and punitive damages to the injured parties by the respondent; and to require that the dwelling unit originally applied for (or the equivalent) be offered to the complainant.[51]

It is important that neither the strict enforcement provisions in a few fair housing laws nor the overall state fair housing record be exaggerated. For one thing, it must be remembered that 16 states have no fair housing legislation at all, and that "substantial equivalence" requires neither strong state enforcement powers nor their effective implementation in order to substitute state action for initial federal processing of complaints. With respect to their collective fair housing record, the National Committee Against Discrimination in Housing (NCDH) reported that the majority of "the state agencies are underfunded and understaffed, and in some instances, the state agency is deficient in competence as well.[52]

The combination of weak enforcement powers under Title VIII and the fact that "vigorous enforcement action by state agencies tends to be the exception rather than the rule[53] led NCDH to conclude that overall "while the broker, agent, or landlord who discriminates stands a chance of being caught and severely penalized, the level of risk in terms of probability is minimal. Clearly, if fair housing practices are to become a reality, that level of risk must become greater."[54]

To increase the likelihood of that reality, President Carter, in his State of the Union Address in January, 1980, made the enactment of the Fair Housing Amendments Act his highest legislative priority in the civil rights area. These amendments would have increased HUD's Title VIII enforcement powers by authorizing "administrative hearings in housing discrimination cases filed with HUD, with administrative law judges having the power to issue final orders to end discriminatory housing practices."[55] Although not enacted by the Ninety-sixth Congress, to the extent that some strengthening of Title VIII is ultimately achieved, HUD would be able to carry out a more vigorous fair housing enforcement program, while the test for "substantial equivalence" would likely be

Housing segregation and the politics of exclusion   Housing in the United States, especially the tens of millions of units built since World War II, follows a pattern of single-family dwellings that are grouped (segregated, if you will) by economic and social criteria, especially income and race. But it was not always so. Prior to the automobile and the suburban boom of the twenties, housing was dense and diverse to meet the practical needs of employment, commerce, social life, and residence in areas bounded by walking and horse-drawn vehicles. The following excerpt provides a historic overview of housing settlement patterns and the ways these patterns reflect economic, social, and governmental influences.

To a greater degree than in other modern societies, urbanization in the United States has separated people spatially along economic and social lines. Nowhere in urban America is the heterogeneity encompassed by a metropolis reproduced in its local jurisdictions and neighborhoods. Instead, the forces of urban growth and change have produced significant income, class, ethnic, and racial variations among the many disparate communities which comprise a metropolitan area.

Until well into the nineteenth century, social and economic differences were not markedly reflected in the residential pattern of most American cities. Since walking was the principal mode of transportation for all but the wealthy, city dwellers were forced to live close to their place of work. . . . This undifferentiated settlement pattern was radically altered by a succession of transportation innovations which freed residential development from the constraints imposed by the necessity to walk to work. By opening more and more land for housing, improvement in accessibility greatly accelerated the spread of urban development at progressively lower densities. Enhanced mobility combined with the vast increase in the scale of the metropolis to sort urban dwellers out along economic and social lines.

Reinforcing this pattern of income differentiation has been the widespread desire of urban dwellers to separate themselves from lower-income and minority groups. In the past as in the present, most of those moving outward have been seeking social separation from the lower classes as well as better housing and more spacious surroundings.

In sharp contrast to the waning significance of ethnicity is the persistence of race as a potent influence on urban settlement patterns. Black Americans have not been able to move out of the urban core in the same fashion, or with as wide a range of choices, as white ethnics. Instead, after half of a century of rapid urbanization of the nation's black population, blacks remain the most spatially differentiated group in the modern metropolis.

Underlying the racial bifurcation of the metropolis are income differences between blacks and whites, the reluctance of blacks and especially whites to live in integrated neighborhoods, and a ubiquitous set of discriminatory practices which exclude blacks from most white residential areas.

In response to white opposition to black neighbors, home builders, realtors, and financial institutions have systematically discriminated against blacks in order to maintain segregated housing markets.

Source: Michael N. Danielson, *The Politics of Exclusion* (New York: Columbia University Press, 1976), pp. 1, 5, 6, 7, and 9.

toughened accordingly. Whether the states' response to the higher equivalence threshold is likely to be a strengthening of their own enforcement powers or surrender of their equivalence certification cannot be determined before the fact. However, to the extent that tougher equivalency standards would increase staffing requirements and related costs to the states of carrying out their fair housing programs, it is likely that many would turn over the enforcement responsibility.

This possibility is implied in HUDs experience with respect to its last state fair housing law recertification effort in 1977. Disappointed by the fact that, in 1975 alone, more than half of the complaints it referred to state and local agencies were recalled because they were not being processed in a timely fashion, HUD decided it would continue making referrals only if the states agreed in writing that their processing of complaints would conform to federal standards.[56] For lack of funds to strengthen their fair housing efforts, virtually all the states chose not to strengthen their processing efforts and to decline further participation under Title VIII. In recognition of these real financial constraints and the fact that fair housing activities are unlikely to ever fare well in the intense competition for state funds, Congress enacted, in 1979, the Federal Fair Housing Assistance Program (FHAP).[57]

With fiscal year 1980 appropriations of $3.7 million, FHAP is intended to provide federal financial support and incentives to states that are willing to develop aggressive and innovative fair housing programs. FHAP contains four separate elements under which states may request funds:

1. General financial support to strengthen program operations and complaint processing capacity.
2. Training and technical assistance to fair housing staffs.
3. Support for fair housing data and information systems needed to inventory complaints, monitor progress toward resolution, and gather data on the extent and patterns of housing discrimination.
4. Innovative project support for potentially replicable pilot efforts which focus on the elimination of systemic or institutional rather than individual forms of discrimination.[58]

Congressional enactment of FHAP recognizes the necessary federal role in assisting states to carry out their fair housing responsibilities. Under FHAP, the states could increasingly become an important means by which higher quality fair housing enforcement services are delivered on behalf of minority households.

Anti-redlining efforts

States also have become active in promoting rehabilitation and reinvestment in older areas by attempting to ensure adequate financing for home improvements and purchase. In reviewing state achievements in so-called "anti-redlining," it is important to distinguish between reforms that are directed principally at *racial* discrimination, and those that are aimed at correcting lending abuses centering around specific *geographic* areas. While the two are related (e.g., it is common for a neighborhood to be "redlined" because it is changing racially), the concept of redlining rests on an arbitrary and unwarranted refusal to lend, or to offer less favorable financing terms, because the property is in a particular area (often, but not always, one showing signs of deterioration).

State activity in anti-redlining is directed principally at state-chartered financial institutions and may include requirements of disclosure of lending activity, as well as specific prohibitions against discriminatory practices that are not based on the actual risks associated with the prospective home buyers. Such legislation faces formidable political obstacles, because lending institutions generally oppose them as intrusions into their management. By 1980, only 11 states had adopted anti-redlining statutes or regulations. Seven of these are in the northeastern section of the country.[59]

The state of New York, through its regulatory authority, requires banks to submit to the State Banking Department extensive data on lending patterns including loan terms and delinquency and foreclosure status. The department has prepared aggregated reports, on a neighborhood basis, and has made these available to the public. These data are also used during bank examinations to help determine the lending institution's compliance with the Community Reinvestment Act. The state of California has particularly detailed statutory requirements, including those that not only prohibit redlining, but which also address appraisal, application, and advertising practices. California also has data collection requirements and makes annual reports (with full color maps) available to the public.

Notable federal complements to state anti-redlining reforms are the Home Mortgage Disclosure Act and the Community Reinvestment Act, which require, respectively, disclosure of mortgage lending activity and adequate deposit and lending service to a bank's primary service area before it is allowed to expand to other parts of the metropolitan area. These two statutes (especially the HMDA, which was strengthened and reauthorized in 1980) should provide the basis for increased state and area-wide anti-redlining activity in the future.

An example of this type of assistance is that provided by the Northeast Ohio Area-wide Coordinating Agency (NOACA) in Cleveland. This Section 701 planning agency collected HMDA data for institutions in the Cleveland SMSA, matched them with census data, and produced highly reputable analytic reports on lending patterns in the Cleveland area. As a result of the availability of NOACA's report, several community groups have been able to file challenges against applications by lending institutions for new branches or mergers, the city government has been able to convince several lenders to provide financial support to the city in its application to HUD for an Urban Development Action Grant, and a local hospital has even developed plans for hospital expansion.

Housing in state urban strategies

In addition to the direct federal funding of housing planning, states have also begun to promote more general urban concerns, including the development of broad-based housing strategies. While students of government have long recognized the potentially critical role states can play in coordinating resource flows and the potential for regional approaches to a range of urban problems, the National Urban Policy announced by President Carter in April, 1978, and its major follow-up in August, 1980, emphasized for the first time major urban policy roles for states and substate regional organizations. This heightened federal interest in the potential of state urban initiatives built upon the growing gubernatorial and/or legislative interests in attacking a wide range of land use and environmental problems, which, when pursued to their logical conclusions, have significant urban development implications.

In the early 1970s, a number of states (Massachusetts, Connecticut, Oregon, Florida, and California are most widely acknowledged) laid the groundwork for state urban policies. The relationship between growth and the condition of older urban areas became explicit in the states' efforts to establish policies to moderate and balance economic development forces. In Massachusetts, then Governor Michael Dukakis spearheaded an urban strategy that sought to deal with problems of economic decline rather than growth. Within the policy was a separate objective of revitalizing older urban centers. In the late 1970s, other states broadened their own growth policies to include urban revitalization; for those states, the political coalition of environmental and urban preservation provided a strong, but certainly not inviolate, basis for action.

In 1980, HUD identified 10 states that had developed urban strategies and analyzed their substantive and political content. In the context of urban revitalization, housing has played an important but not preeminent role. Housing themes are likely to appear in one of two areas. First, environmental concerns, and the desire to preserve agricultural land, have led to state policies that encourage infill within existing communities and discourage noncontiguous new development. California's urban strategy, for example, lays out three principles for growth management:

1. Renew and maintain existing urban areas.
2. Develop vacant and underutilized areas within built-up areas.
3. Use immediately adjacent land when additional development in necessary outside existing areas.[60]

Second, housing is even more explicit in the urban revitalization themes of the state urban strategies. According to a 1980 survey of state strategies by the National Academy of Public Administration, approaches to housing in a revitalization strategy typically consist of one or more of three themes:

1. Increased bonding authority for state housing authorities.
2. Better coordination and targeting of state housing programs.
3. Tax policies that encourage rehabilitation.

Illustrative of these are additional bonding authority in Massachusetts for public housing, greater urban emphasis by the New Jersey Housing Finance Agency, and California's new agency to provide rehabilitation funds.[61]

A key question of the impact of state/urban strategies on housing is their net effect after considering other state housing actions. Promotion of rehabilitation may have positive effects on the urban core, but widespread subsidies of suburban home owners through mortgage revenue bonds may negate that positive good by encouraging middle-income individuals and families to leave the city. Thus, the housing element of an urban strategy must be reviewed in the context of all state housing policies, not simply those put under the "urban" strategy label. Under the more decentralized national urban policy of the Reagan Administration, the states are expected to become even more aggressive partners in a "new Federalism." In the administration's view, "State governments have the authority to correct the imbalances in the fiscal capabilities of local governments within a state resulting from inappropriate boundaries, inequitable allocation of functions, and inadequate tax bases . . . [and] are in the best position to encourage metropolitan-wide solutions to problems that spill over political boundaries. . . ."[62] Whether the states have the political will to solve these problems or will receive the necessary financial assistance from the federal government to deal effectively with them, however, remains to be seen.

Summary

To recapitulate, state action in the field of housing is developing in a multifaceted way. The somewhat mixed record shows that:

1. Direct state housing subsidies are quite modest in amount and are accounted for by only 20 states.
2. State regulations affect housing markets by controlling landlord/tenant relations, rents, condominium and cooperative conversions, building standards, and the lending activities of state-chartered banks and

insurance companies. About half the states also offer tax incentives for housing rehabilitation.

3. The state housing role with the greatest dollar impact is that of the state housing finance agencies. They use the tax-exempt borrowing capacity of the state to provide low-cost loans for housing construction. Though successful in attracting new funds into the housing market, these activities have raised questions about unfair competition in the nation's money markets and certain other concerns.

4. Some state pension funds have begun to invest in housing mortgages to expand the supply of housing funds.

5. Although about two-thirds of the states have fair housing laws "substantially equivalent" to the federal laws, and take on the enforcement task, "vigorous enforcement action by the state agencies tends to be the exception rather than the rule." Only 11 states have anti-redlining laws.

6. By 1980 10 states had urban growth strategies with important, though not preemiment, housing elements.

Regional housing activity

Regional agencies are often strategically positioned to influence housing development. Their jurisdiction typically corresponds to a housing market area, whether metropolitan or nonmetropolitan. They also are commonly designated for other functional planning tasks in the same area, such as highways, transit, and water and sewage facilities. Finally, their A-95 review responsibilities give them an opportunity to guide and coordinate development investments and to assume a leadership role on behalf of the region in fitting together the plans for housing and other functions of area-wide significance.

Despite these advantages, the record of area-wide achievements in housing has been mixed. The most important reason for their lack of full success in systematically guiding growth has been their own status as voluntary associations of governments. In most regions, each local unit retains its own set of priorities (some of which may conflict with regional goals) as well as the basic development powers such as zoning and subdivision regulations. Efforts by area-wide agencies to guide and influence federal decisions often have been undermined by reluctance on the part of federal agencies to accede to area-wide housing policies and A-95 comments over the objections of local governments.

Against this backdrop, it is not surprising that area-wide achievements in housing often have entered not on control of the overall housing development process, but rather on activities for which political consensus can be developed, or where there is relatively less controversy or opposition. Only in limited instances of sharing political or persuasive leadership, or unusual structural features such as mandatory membership and actual growth management powers, have area-wide organizations been able to take a strong hand in shaping the character of development and housing patterns in their region.

Examples of important achievements[63] by area-wide organizations in housing include:

1. Development of plans for the allocation of assisted housing (AHOPs, described in more detail below).

2. Design of more flexible, less restrictive zoning ordinances to promote mixed use, compact development zoning by local governments (Cincinnati).

3. Development of model local building and housing codes and the regional administration of such codes in some cases.

4. Acting as housing authorities, or nonprofit housing development corporations (Twin Cities Metropolitan Council; Middle Flint Area Planning and Development Commission).
5. Providing technical assistance to local governments, nonprofit organizations, and developers.
6. Working with realtors to promote affirmative action (Metropolitan Washington Council of Governments).
7. Use of the A-95 process to anticipate any adverse urban impacts of proposed projects.

"Fair share" plans and area-wide housing opportunity plans

In the late 1960s and early 1970s a few pioneering area-wide agencies began the development of what were then called "fair share" plans: region-wide allocation plans for assisted housing, which shifted emphasis from concentration in the central city to increased housing in suburban jurisdictions. The best-known examples of these plans were prepared by the Miami Valley Regional Planning Commission (Dayton, Ohio), the Metropolitan Council of the Twin Cities (Minneapolis–St. Paul), and the Metropolitan Washington Council of Governments (Washington, DC).

The objectives behind the early housing distribution programs differed. The political support and rationale in metropolitan Washington lay in the realization that many suburban households, often public employees such as teachers and firemen, were having trouble in a high cost area and needed access to assisted housing. In Dayton, the improvement of housing choice for minorities then limited to central city locations was the principal goal of the "fair share" plan creators. At the same time, however, the leadership of the planning commission also recognized that more evenly distributed assisted housing would benefit the central city by reducing its traditional role as a "magnet" for the poor. Finally, in Minnesota, the strong management and housing planning owers given to the Metropolitan Council by the state were the base from which developed a strong regional role in allocating assisted housing.

In spring, 1976, HUD revived a policy first used by HUD Secretary George Romney to provide bonus assisted housing funds as an incentive to regions participating in "fair share" plans. Now called Area-wide Housing Opportunity Plans (AHOPs), the plans had to meet a structured set of requirements to be approved and compete for bonus funds. Once approved, the AHOP served as HUD's primary basis for allocating housing assistance among jurisdictions in the region. If selected for bonus funds, a region could receive up to 50 percent more funds than regularly allocated to the region, as well as special allocations of Community Development Block Grant and Section 701 funds.

AHOPs had to be approved by half the jurisdictions representing at least 75 percent of the population of the area served. According to HUD regulations, the plan also had to establish a system for allocating housing assistance that would provide "greater housing opportunities for lower income households outside areas of concentration of lower income households." Typically this meant increased numbers of assisted family housing in suburban jurisdictions. Numerical goals for assisted housing for all major communities were part of the plan, and the AHOP goals had to be consistent with one another and Housing Assistance Plans (HAPs) of each community. A strong emphasis was placed on helping lower income families to find housing outside areas of minority concentration and in working to reduce barriers to the provision of assisted and lower cost housing in such areas. Evidence that the plan could and would be implemented was required.

The concept of area-wide plans grew gradually, and adoption of plans accelerated during the late 1970s. By early 1980, 40 metropolitan planning agencies had HUD approved AHOPs. About a dozen nonmetropolitan AHOPS also had been approved.

The early regional "fair share" plans had a dramatic effect on the distribution of assisted housing to suburban jurisdictions, as compared to distributions in earlier periods. Before 1975, suburban areas received about 40 percent of total assistance, while under the new plans about two-thirds of the units were designated for suburban areas.

Implementation of Section 213 of the Housing and Community Development Act of 1974 threatened to reduce somewhat the relative redistributive effects of AHOPs as compared to the earlier "fair share" plans attempted under HUD Secretary Romney. Section 213 provides for a formula allocation of housing assistance based on existing need rather than redistribution principles, and communities desiring Community Development Block Grant (CDBG) funds generally had to use housing assistance funds allocated to them in order to remain eligible for CDBG. However, in five AHOP region studies in 1979, actual results did not reflect such a change. The suburbs contained 62 percent of all income-eligible households in these five regions, were calculated to receive 63.4 percent of all assistance under HUD's Section 213 allocation formula, and were targeted to receive 69.2 percent of all resources under the AHOP goals. Between 1977 and 1979, suburbs in the five study regions actually received 73 percent of all assisted housing approved in their regions. The added suburban units reflected both the continuing redistributive efforts of AHOPs and the effect of the bonus units that generally went to the suburban areas.[64]

The acceptance by suburbs of assisted housing as a prerequisite for community development program participation under the 1974 act, although reluctant, underscored the tenuous position of central cities as the heart of the area-wide plan. In many regions, bonus housing funds provided to AHOPs allowed the area-wide organization to maintain the central city's actual level of funds as the suburban portion grew. In the five regions studied in 1979, however, the absolute number of units going to central cities declined by 13.4 percent from 1975 to 1979. Only in the Puget Sound (Seattle) and Washington, DC regions were the total area-wide allocations sufficiently large to maintain previous central city levels.[65] As overall housing production levels have declined, the availability of bonus funds became even more tenuous. More importantly, the decreasing number of units makes competition for units within an area more acute, placing greater stress on the difficult negotiating process carried on by the area-wide agency.

It is important to recall, however, that central cities, because of the minimum population requirements for approval of AHOPs, have a virtual veto power over any AHOP. Dayton, for example, had a right of first refusal over any assistance allocated to the area, but for a number of years passed its housing on to the suburban jurisdictions. In other areas central cities used their bargaining positions to gain other urban development-related concessions within their regions.

The reduced effect of the AHOP as a straight redistributive tool shifted both its programmatic emphasis and its long-term prospects for the achievement of other goals.

In the early period of AHOPs (then called "fair share" plans), the regional plan had two principal objectives: to promote the acceptance of assisted housing in heretofore "closed" suburbs, and to prevent the concentration of assisted housing in other jurisdictions, often the central city, but occasionally older suburban areas facing economic and racial transition.

As the AHOP program evolved in the late 1970s, increasing emphasis was placed on implementation of the plans, and on the interjurisdictional mobility of lower income, especially minority, families, allowing them to relocate from racially segregated areas. Preference was given for bonus funding of AHOPs in which all locational restrictions were dropped, and where counseling and other housing search assistance was provided. Use of Section 701 and CDBG bonus funds emphasized activities designed to encourage the mobility of families into nontraditional areas. The area-wide organizations worked with cities, private developers, and HUD to facilitate construction and occupancy of assisted housing for younger families in these areas as contrasted with the more politically popular elderly housing that was relatively easy to locate there.

There are many examples of the types of outreach and mobility activities undertaken by regional councils through their AHOPs. The Metropolitan Washington Council of Governments (COG) is one. It worked with the public housing authorities in its area to develop procedures in the Section 8 "existing housing program" to avoid further buildups of assisted households in areas of minority concentration. COG prepared and disseminated brochures about the program to be used in outreach work that identified potential owners and managers of rental housing outside the areas of concentration who were willing to participate in the Section 8 program.

An even more ambitious program of activity was undertaken by the Metropolitan Council of Minneapolis–St. Paul using its broad state legislative authority for housing activities. The Council established an active landlord outreach program that publicized the Section 8 existing housing program. It actively discouraged any form of residency preference among the local public housing authorities (PHAs) and assisted housing managers in the area. As a result, no PHA in the area adopted residency preferences. The Council circulates assisted housing applications throughout the region so that families interested in housing in one jurisdiction of the area need not travel there to submit their initial applications.

The extent to which an emphasis on lower income mobility will be sustained— and remains politically acceptable at the local level—is uncertain. By shifting its goals from the relatively neutral one of allocating housing assistance among localities to the more controversial one of encouraging interjurisdictional mobility of residents, the AHOPs confronted a fundamental element of racial and economic segregation. In doing so, they risked losing support for improved regional housing coordination. As federal funds for housing assistance, comprehensive planning, and community development became increasingly scarce in 1980–1981, federal budget cuts eliminated Section 701 planning funds and reduced housing funds to the point that bonus funding no longer could be made available. Consequently, HUD proposed eliminating the AHOPs. It remains unclear the extent to which area-wide agencies, faced with the loss of resources to undertake housing planning and the HUD requirement to do so, will choose to sustain these activities.

Diverse approaches to rural housing

The literature makes frequent reference to the fact that the decade of the 1970s witnessed an unprecedented revival of rural and small town America, and the fact that "although agriculture is still the dominant influence in many rural economies, overall employment in manufacturing, trade, and professional services now exceeds direct agricultural employment."[66] As the Carter administration Small Community and Rural Development Policy statement pointed out, however, "notwithstanding the progress that has been made, a disproportionate share of the nation's poor still live in rural areas—about 40 percent of the total."[67] Not surprisingly, therefore, the problem of inadequate housing in rural communities is equally serious, both in absolute and relative terms. To wit:

1. Three times the proportion of rural housing units in comparison to urban units lack complete plumbing.[68]

2. Over 2 million rural Americans do not have running water in their houses; over 4 million have inadequate sewage disposal systems or none at all.[69]
3. Sixty-one percent of the housing units occupied by rural Blacks are substandard; 37 percent of all housing units occupied by people of Spanish heritage are substandard; 43 percent of all Indian housing is substandard.[70]
4. Overall, around 75 percent of all substandard rural housing is in communities of less than 2,500 population; this includes farm workers whose housing conditions are particularly poor.[71]

Both the federal and state challenges to improve housing conditions and the quality of life in rural communities are made more formidable by the "social, cultural and even programmatic isolation" of the rural poor.[72] Few would dispute the contention that existing government programs, even those specifically designed for rural settings, do not reach the most inadequately housed rural households. Fixed subsidies and rising costs, coupled with such problems as high site preparation costs, the frequent absence of basic public facilities and supportive services, the lack of established housing delivery systems, and lending institutions with insufficient supplies of mortgage capital all contribute to the difficulties of serving the housing needs of rural communities.

On the matter of available housing funds, for example, the General Accounting Office recently reported that the per capita assets of most rural banks in 1975 were about half that of those in the largest metropolitan counties.[73] These modest-sized institutions are called upon to serve the broad credit needs of their communities, including housing finance. Moreover, according to GAO, about 800 of the nation's 2,400 rural counties had no savings and loan associations at all; these are institutions that specialize in residential lending.[74] And even in those counties that did, although mortgage interest rates charged by rural savings and loan associations were similar to those levied by urban thrift institutions, down payments required in rural areas were higher and mortgage terms were shorter.[75]

The kind of isolation that characterizes rural areas is reflected in the urban lending bias of many state housing finance agencies (HFA). In part, these slights against rural lending are the result of a conscious policy by state HFA managers to target their lending programs to urban areas in part because rural lenders are much less likely than their urban counterparts to participate in such complex HFA programs as loans to lenders, loan purchasing, and forward commitments, involving the processing of government insured loans with which few of them have much experience.[76] Since relatively few rural lenders are FHA-approved, rural communities are bound to be underserved by these and similar programs which presuppose prior program experience, unless concerted efforts are made to lower the administrative barriers.

The special problems of small communities can be addressed in different ways. In hearings on this subject, the Advisory Commission on Intergovernmental Relations (ACIR) suggested that one way to improve service delivery in small communities was through the development of cooperation agreements among adjacent local governments.[77] According to ACIR, there are several hundred rural regional councils that are "providing basic professional services to small local governments; . . . local public services to areas where individual localities are too small to do so on their own; and they are helping to develop and carry through on community and economic development strategies which deal with the problems of both growth and decline."[78]

In these same hearings, North Carolina's Governor James Hunt, speaking on behalf of the National Governor's Association, argued for a different kind of regionalism; that which characterizes the interstate development efforts of the Appalachian Regional Commission (ARC). Noting that so great a proportion of federal funds flowing into the states are beyond the control of the Governors that it is virtually impossible to implement a state-wide development policy, Hunt argued for an extension of the ARC model because it embodies a state checkoff of local development projects before they are finally approved for federal funding.[79] According to Hunt, Governors have both the will and capacity to serve the development needs of their small communities but must be able to direct the flow of federal funds into their states in accord with their own area-wide development policies. Toward this end, Farmers Home Administration (FmHA), HUD, and EPA signed joint memoranda with ARC which would require local development districts (LDDs) within the 13 state ARC region to develop consolidated development plans that each federal signatory would consider in its own resource allocation decisions.[80]

Still other models for strengthening the delivery of housing and community development resources to rural communities are being tested by HUD sponsored projects. Rather than emphasizing either substate or multistate regionalism, these demonstration projects focus upon the removal of administrative and regulatory program barriers that prevent widespread use in rural areas, and upon the development of outreach methods and new program delivery systems.

As part of its Rural Assistance Initiative, for example, HUD devised a means of bringing its insured housing programs closer to rural communities. Under the delegated processing program, rural savings and loan associations and other approved mortgagees have been authorized to initiate most of the steps involved in processing HUD insured loans. Instead of having to do business with a HUD area office that could be a couple of hundred miles away, rural builders and consumers can continue dealing with their community lenders who offer them the benefits of HUD's insurance programs directly. To the extent that delegated processing increases rural lender interest in HUD programs and their familiarity with insured loan processing regulations, these same lenders are also more likely to become active in state HFA housing finance programs that make HUD insured loans.

Although as of this writing it is not clear whether they will be continued, these rural demonstrations are proving that states can package assistance programs for rural communities. This frequently requires placing teams of loan processors, rehabilitation specialists, and experts in community and economic development in remote communities, and utilizing where possible the expertise of agricultural extension personnel and other available resources. In some cases, these decentralized staffs might be attached to a regional council of governments (COG), and in some cases might "circuit ride" from community to community. Indeed, some federal and state personnel have been colocated with substate regional councils for mutual support.

The potential role of the area-wide agency in providing the institutional "missing link" for rural areas is exemplified by the accomplishments of a few area-wide agencies under the AHOP program. For example, the Southern Iowa Council of Governments, the first nonmetropolitan AHOP approved, was the catalyst for the formation of a regional housing authority to serve a multicounty area. Beginning with a small Section 8 "existing housing" program, the housing authority is developing the capacity to promote other assisted housing in that underserved area.

Future directions

The 1980s will prove to be a period of significant transition for area-wide agencies and states in the field of housing as well as other areas. For area-wide agencies, the precipitous decline in comprehensive planning funds and demise of the federal requirement for area-wide housing opportunity plans will probably result in a drastic reduction in the amount of housing planning activity, although many agencies will continue in operation using other federal programs and funding provided by state and local governments. For states, the loss of comprehensive planning funds will require a relatively minor adaptation compared to the changing federal emphasis in community development, housing tax policy, and assisted housing. The contrast between area-wide and state authority and responsibility mentioned at the beginning of this chapter showed the state's superior budgetary position. In a period of transition toward reduced federal funding and policy intervention, that superior position offers significant opportunities for adaptation.

To move aggressively in the housing sector in the 1980s, states should assume greater direct management control over their housing finance agencies and make them more complete and responsive instruments of state housing policy. Wisconsin is the first state to have taken affirmative steps to do just that. Under a bill signed into law on May 7, 1982, the Wisconsin Housing Finance Agency is prohibited from spending or obligating any surplus it might accrue without the prior approval of the Governor and then the legislature. Also, the law requires the state's Department of Development to prepare and revise biennially a comprehensive state housing plan which will guide the housing resource allocation decisions of all agencies with housing responsibilities, including the HFA. Finally, the bill creates a Council of Housing to advise the Department of Development in the preparation of the housing plan and to otherwise assist in the coordination of state housing activities. The integration of finance into the broader housing functions of state government does not mean that the bond ratings of HFAs must deteriorate or that the investment orientation of their operations must become subordinate to the achievement of social welfare objectives. While some have argued that HFAs must maintain their quasi-independent status from the executive and legislative branches of state government to insulate them from housing politics, the fact is that, unless they become part of the state housing function, the link between planning and implementation cannot be made effective.

Three recent developments that underscore the importance of bringing the diverse housing activities of state governments into closer harmony are the enactment of the Tax Subsidy Bond Act of 1980, the declining Congressional support for long-term subsidy of new construction for low-income families, and rising interest in housing block grants.

The Bond Act places several limitations on the ability of state and local governments to issue tax-exempt revenue bonds to finance single and multifamily housing. By capping purchase prices, imposing geographic targeting requirements on issuers of revenue bonds, and narrowing the profits finance agencies may make from their bond programs, Congress hopes to reduce the volume of bonds marketed and to more sharply define the public purposes served by state and local bond-financed housing programs. While the full implications of the act are not yet clear, the Bond Act does provide a basis for the states to gain better management control over their finance agencies. This is because the law specifies that targeting of bond monies may be defined in accord with the states' definitions of "areas of chronic economic distress," while limitations on the spread allowed between interest paid on housing bonds and interest charged on individual mortgages issued from the bond proceeds may make it necessary for some states to appropriate funds to subsidize HFA operations or to capitalize their bond reserve funds.

The decline of Congressional appropriations for the Section 8 "new construction" program and the growing interest in housing block grants both point to potentially expanded low-income housing roles for the states in the years ahead. Should the Section 8 program for new construction be eliminated, should no long-term construction subsidy program be enacted in its place, and should no further appropriations be requested by HUD for GNMAs below market-rate financing for multifamily housing beyond 1982, bond financing will become even more important as a source of multifamily credit than it already is. This means that state housing finance agencies' roles as sources of multifamily credit will grow in the years ahead and that their decisions about what to finance and in which communities and locations to finance it may largely determine the pattern of below market-rate housing development. To the extent that states will be called upon to subsidize the projects they finance either through front-end capital grants, interest write-downs, or in other ways to make them available to low-income families, the relationships between the housing planning and financing functions of state government will grow still closer.

Finally, the states' housing role is likely to become more significant should the Congress enact a Housing Assistance Block Grant program (HABG). Though a HABG could take many forms, it is likely that states would be called upon to administer that part of the program dealing with so-called nonentitlement communities—the cities, towns, and rural areas which are too small to receive direct allocations of housing funds from the federal government.

Among the important housing roles states would assume under a housing block grant are those of planning technical assistance, administration of housing assistance contracts, and allocation of housing funds. While the states already play each of these roles to some extent, a federal housing block grant, even with declining federal housing budgets, would substantially increase the flow of housing resources through the states. This means that most states' capacity to administer statewide housing programs would have to be expanded, encompassing better integrated planning and delivery systems.

1 The Mt. Laurel decision is the subject of intensive analysis as a planning and legal landmark. See, for example, the American Bar Association's *Housing for All under Law*, 1978, pp. 104–113 and 133–136.

2 Title IV—Planning Assistance, Housing and Community Development Act of 1980.

3 "Accomplishments of 701-Funding Planning," unpublished paper, Department of Housing and Urban Development.

4 *The House We Live In*, Report of the Commission to Study the Housing Programs in North Carolina, January 1983, p. 22.

5 *Recent Trends in Federal and State Aid to Local Governments*, Advisory Commission on Intergovernmental Relations, Report M-118, July 1980; Table 10, p. 11.

6 Ibid., Table A-20, p. 71.

7 *Journal of Housing* (March 1980): p. 157.

8 "California Homeownership Assistance Program," California Department of Housing and Community Development, Division of Community Affairs, July 3, 1980.

9 *Housing Development Reporter*, Bureau of National Affairs, January 3, 1983, p. 657.

10 Ibid., p. 659.

11 Michael A. Stegman, Jean Crews, and Susan Hyman, *Financing Energy Conservation in North Carolina's Housing*, prepared for the North Carolina Alternative Energy Corporation, July 20, 1982, p. 20 (mimeo).

12 Ibid.

13 *State-Federal Rural Development Coordination in North Carolina, Report of Progress*, November 1979.

14 *Insurance Crisis in Urban America* (Washington, DC: Federal Insurance Administration, 1978), pp. 7–24.

15 *Housing and Development Reporter*, 8 (November 10, 1980), p. 500.

16 *Report of the President's Commission on Housing* (Washington, DC, 1982), p. 105.

17 Ibid.

18 Ibid., p. 235.

19 Ibid.

20 Ibid.

21 *Impact of Building Codes on Housing Rehabilitation*, Hearing before the Committee on Banking, Housing, and Urban Affairs, U.S. Senate, March 24, 1978, p. 43.

22 Development Choices for the Eighties, *Council Newsletter*, no. 16, September 29, 1980.

23 Ibid.

24 Ibid.

25 Ibid.

26 *Impact of Building Codes on Housing Rehabilitation*, p. 1.

27 Ibid.

28 *Rehabilitation Guidelines 1980* (Washington, DC: Department of Housing and Urban Development, 1980).

29 George E. Peterson with Brian Cooper, *Tax-Exempt Financing of Housing Investment* (Washington, DC: The Urban Institute, 1979).

30 Ibid., p. xiii.

31 Ibid., p. 52.
32 Ibid., p. 2.
33 Ibid., p. xv.
34 Ibid.
35 Ibid., p. xvi.
36 *Report of the President's Commission on Housing*, p. 169.
37 Peterson and Cooper, *Tax-Exempt Financing*, p. xvi.
38 *Report of the President's Commission on Housing*, p. 170.
39 Peterson and Cooper, *Tax-Exempt Financing*, Table 1, p. 3.
40 Ibid., p. 44.
41 Ibid., p. 146 and p. 147, Table 2.
42 Thomas W. White, "Opinion and Comment," *Journal of Housing*, (March/April 1982), p. 38.
43 *Housing Development Reporter*, Bureau of National Affairs, December 20, 1982, pp. 598–599.
44 *Housing Development Reporter*, Bureau of National Affairs.
45 HUD News Release July 20, 1979 "Housing Discrimination Still a Major Factor in America."
46 Ibid.
47 Title VIII, 1968 Civil Rights Act, cited in *Guide to Fair Housing Law Enforcement*, National Committee Against Discrimination in Housing, prepared for HUD, July 1979, p. 5.
48 Title VIII, 1968 Civil Rights Act.
49 "Fair Housing Assistance Program: Eligibility Criteria and Funding Standards," *Federal Register*, part III, May 14, 1980, p. 31881.
50 *Guide to Fair Housing Law Enforcement*, p. 6.
51 Ibid.
52 Ibid.
53 Ibid.
54 Ibid., p. 7.
55 Senate Bill 506 and House Bill 5200, The Fair Housing Amendments Act of 1980.
56 Fair Housing Assistance Program, *Federal Register*, p. 31880.
57 Ibid.
58 Ibid., pp. 31881–31885.
59 *The States and Distressed Communities: Indicators of Significant Actions*, National Academy of Public Administration and the U.S. Advisory Commission on Intergovernmental Relations, p. 12.
60 *States and Urban Strategies*, p. 29.
61 *The States and Distressed Communities*, pp. 8–16.
62 *The President's National Urban Policy Report*, (Washington, DC: Department of Housing and Urban Development, 1982), pp. 4–35.
63 "Accomplishments of 701—Funded Planning."
64 *Assessment of the Impact of the Housing Opportunity Plan (AHOP) Program, Executive Summary*. (Berkeley Planning Associates, 1978), p. 2.
65 Ibid.
66 *The Carter Administration Small Community and Rural Development Policy*, December 20, 1979, p. 2.
67 Ibid.
68 Ibid., p. 3.
69 Ibid.
70 *Of the People, By the People, For the People: Cooperative Housing for Rural America*, Rural Community Assistance Cooperative, 1979, p. 27.
71 *Ways of Providing a Fairer Share of Federal Housing Support to Rural Areas*, CED-80-1, March 28, 1980.
72 *Of the People, By the People, For the People*, p. 21.
73 *Ways of Providing a Fairer Share of Federal Housing Support to Rural Areas*, p. 33.
74 Ibid., p. 37.
75 Ibid.
76 Ibid., p. 33.
77 Wayne F. Anderson, "Small Cities: How Can the Federal Government Respond to Their Diverse Needs?" in Hearings before the Subcommittee on the City, House of Representatives, May 16, 19, 26, 1978; p. 128.
78 Ibid., p. 132.
79 See note 77 above. Statement of Governor James B. Hunt, Jr., p. 98.
80 *Area-wide Action Program, A Guide to its Preparation and Use*, Appalachian Regional Commission, June 1978.

17 Transportation planning

Transportation is one of the most important and most pervasive functions of society. It consumes 22 percent of the gross national product (GNP) and over one-half of the nation's oil. Changes in transportation are reflected almost immediately in the personal welfare of every citizen and in the productivity of every business. Thus, the provision of transportation services, as well as its cost and impacts, are principal concerns of planning at every level of government, especially state and regional levels, and of a large segment of the private sector.

Although most of the nation's basic transportation system—i.e., waterways, freeways, rail lines, airports—is in place and relatively few major additions are likely to be required, there is still much planning to be done. Social, technological, economic, and other forces are creating major changes in the volume and types of travel which must be accommodated and in the conditions under which services and facilities can be provided. Moreover, substantial continued growth is forecast in the demand for travel. For example, the National Transportation Policy Study Commission (NTPSC) projects an increase in travel of 81–96 percent in person-miles and 165–226 percent in ton-miles between 1975 and 1990.[1] Thus, there will be a sustained pressure to improve or rebuild transport systems.

Although the interstate highway system is virtually complete, much future development will fill in areas already provided with transportation, and individuals will travel more carefully and efficiently; the scale and impact of changes and improvements to transportation will be substantial. In many ways, the challenges for transportation planning that lie ahead are far greater than those of the past. Many of these—and ways of meeting them—are described here.

Although some background and history is provided, emphasis is on the future—on issues, methods, techniques, organizational roles, and, most important, solutions which must be faced in the years immediately ahead.

Transportation planning requirements vary substantially from state to state, region to region, and between regions and states. It is difficult to provide a discussion of issues, methodologies, and organizational approaches which will be appropriate in every situation. However, the material here deals with those issues and conditions which are common to many or most states and regions and will indicate some of the variations in approach that will be needed. It focuses especially on the processes and techniques that are common in preparing plans at the policy, system, corridor, and project levels.

Transportation planning roles and responsibilities

Many agencies and organizations are involved in "planning" for transportation at state and regional levels. Cities (especially larger cities), counties, port and transit authorities, and even semiofficial neighborhood organizations each play a role. Private railroads, trucking firms, pipeline companies, as well as bus, taxi, and air carriers, also plan and implement services and facilities. At the state level, public utility commissions, departments of commerce, and other agencies

Figure 17-1 A chronology of U.S. transportation.

1775	James Watt perfects his steam engine	**1904**	New York City subway opened
1793	Lancaster Pike between Philadelphia and Lancaster—first turnpike in the U.S.	**1907**	Ford's Model T is first mass-market car
		1914	Jitneys begin operating in cities
1807	Fulton steams up the Hudson River to demonstrate commercial potential	**1916**	First federal-aid Road Act
		1918	First regular air mail service
1825	Erie Canal completed; first railroad—a half-mile line in Hoboken	**1927**	Lindbergh flies the Atlantic; first modern city bus is manufactured
1827	The B&O Railroad becomes first commercial railroad	**1942**	First U.S. jet plane flight
1832	First horse-drawn street car in New York City	**1956**	National system of interstate highways established
1859	Suez Canal construction begins	**1961**	U.S. Housing Act provides first federal assistance for mass transit
1869	First transcontinental railroad completed	**1967**	U.S. Department of Transportation established
1873	San Francisco's cable cars begin service	**1971**	AMTRAK established
1883	Brooklyn Bridge opened	**1972**	Bay Area Rapid Transit System (BART) dedicated as first high tech system
1886	First citywide electric trolley system in Montgomery, Alabama		
1890	Automobiles commercially available	**1975**	Boston and San Francisco order 275 "flight rail transit" trolley cars—first built since 1952
1892	Diesel engine patented		
1903	Wright brothers fly; Henry Ford organizes Ford Motor Company		

are often responsible for developing and implementing regulations and licensing, taxation, or financing programs. Thus, dozens—and perhaps hundreds—of organizations and individuals may perform significant planning of some aspect of transportation in every region and state.

Metropolitan regions

Major efforts have been made to extend and to improve and coordinate planning at both regional and state levels. In the early 1950s large, complex studies were initiated in several metropolitan areas primarily to develop highway plans on a regional basis. These studies pioneered the development of processes for planning and for the analysis and forecasting of travel demand. The Federal Highway Act of 1962 made the institution of such activities mandatory in all metropolitan areas with cities having populations of more than 50,000. Such planning was to be in accordance with the "3 Cs" process, "comprehensive, coordinated, and continuing."[2] To implement this requirement, most cities had to create new mechanisms for planning at both policy and technical levels.

As new areas of transportation concern have emerged and received federal funding—transit, airports, etc.—the roles of these regional agencies have been repeatedly reinforced by legislative and administrative direction and funding. Legislation related to environmental protection (National Environmental Protection Act [NEPA], 1969) and especially air quality, and to the overall coordination of federal programs (Demonstration Cities and Metropolitan Development Act, 1966) strengthened further the roles of agencies at the regional level, including many involved in transportation planning.

Despite considerable acceptance of the role of regional organizations in transportation planning, most are considered quasigovernmental, and their relationships to local and state government and to the implementation of transportation programs are sometimes weak and are not always clear. One of the last (1973) and strongest efforts to assure coordination and clarity was embodied in joing FHWA–UMTA regulations which provide for the designation of metropolitan planning organizations (MPOs) to receive and coordinate federal funds and programs emanating from the FHWA, UMTA, and (in part) FAA for every urbanized area. This has been done for most communities. However, in practice, actual responsibility for planning is often divided between many different agencies with coordination being achieved through cumbersome and elaborate review and committee procedures, and through interagency agreements and published plans and work programs.

States (usually highway departments or departments of transportation) are designated to perform the MPO role in two out of every five urbanized areas. Only two out of five designated transportation planning agencies also served as the designated comprehensive planning agency, and only one out of three had responsibility for "A-95" services.[3] Thus, to obtain coordination, to minimize duplication of effort, and to assure adequate participation in planning by all affected governmental units, elaborate procedures have been established. Most regional transportation planning is encompassed in several layers of committee activity and intergovernmental checks and balances which involve, if not active technical work, at least substantial reviews and participation in evaluation and decision making by representatives of state, regional, and local organizations.

States

Transportation planning (particularly multimodal) is a relatively new activity at the state level.[4] Until recently, most state transportation planning was concerned almost solely with the development of state highway systems. Cities (or special authorities) in combination with federal agencies assumed responsibility for air, water, and sometimes truck terminals, and rail and bus facilities were privately owned. A number of recent developments are expanding the range of state involvement. These include requirements and funding specified in several pieces of federal legislation, including especially the creation of a U.S. Department of Transportation (DOT), the Federal-Aid Highway Act of 1970 requiring the development of an "action plan" which assures consideration of environmental and multimodal issues, and the various acts aimed at railroad reorganization and revitalization.[5] With or without federal stimuli, states have become more concerned with such issues as maintaining rail service to rural areas, supporting economic development, and meeting the transportation needs of the rural poor and elderly. Efforts to clarify and strengthen the overall structure of state government also have been a prime factor in the creation of state departments of transportation.[6] The general "logic" of creating a single agency to deal with transportation as part of overall governmental reorganization is often as much of a factor in this decision as the need to obtain better planning and coordination.

Defining roles and responsibilities

Although state DOTs and MPOs have key roles in transportation planning, in practice the distribution and exercise of responsibility is much more complex. Responsibilities must be divided among governmental jurisdictions and private suppliers according to mode and often by the nature of the activity involved (e.g., planning for finance, construction, operations, regulation, etc.). Responsibilities must also be assigned for roles in relation to various levels of planning—policy, system, corridor, project, and operations—and steps in the planning process for each level of planning.[7]

Planning responsibility can be established by mode (air, water, rail, highway, etc.) or by activity. Each activity requires planning and organization. Some of this planning is long range and may be comprehensive (e.g., basic system plans, regulation, standards, methods of finance); other planning may be more closely related to current operations (e.g., vehicles, finance, maintenance, construction, and operation of facilities). Such classification and assignment helps avoid needless duplication and conflict and omissions in planning.

The task of defining responsibilities for planning is complicated by the fact that transportation planning agencies do not operate in a vacuum. Because they are usually direct creatures of state legislation and are also extensions of the office of the Governor, state DOTs may have rather broad and vaguely defined missions. A simple and common definition of their mission is that of "helping to move people and goods." However, it is plain that this activity is only a part of a DOT or MPO responsibility and that it is the servant of a larger mission which may entail responding to a whole range of transportation-related economic, environmental, and human needs. Thus, this definition is constantly being modified and extended by legislative and administrative directives—both state and federal. These directives call for transportation agencies to assume major responsibility for protecting the environment, developing the economy, and meeting social needs. This is particularly true where needs and issues related to land and economic development and conservation are not strongly articulated. Under these circumstances, transportation planners have a special responsibility to look beyond narrowly defined objectives, and to take the lead, if necessary, to assure a balanced and comprehensive approach to the solution of urban and state problems.

Although transportation agencies, at regional and, especially, state levels (MPOs and DOTs) are frequently the only agencies in their jurisdictions with a broad responsibility for most types, functions, and impacts of transportation; they cannot and should not attempt to be the sole or even primary suppliers of transportation facilities and services. However, because of their unique position, they have a very special mission and responsibility. This mission may be defined as follows:

The agency should do whatever is possible and necessary within the limitations of competing demands on available resources to help the people under its jurisdiction obtain the transportation services and facilities which they need and to meet the responsibilities and commitments of the jurisdiction for the achievement of national needs and objectives.

The agency should be prepared to take action in situations where there is, or may be, a need for transportation which cannot be or is not being met adequately by private individuals or enterprise or by other units of government.[8]

In making decisions about the nature and level of its participation, the agency should consider these factors.

1. The ability of a facility or service to generate sufficient income to attract necessary investment capital and/or to cover operating costs.
2. The ability and willingness of private enterprise or local governments to meet minimum standards required to assure safety and equity and to pay for and/or avoid indirect costs (negative impacts) which may be generated by a facility or service.
3. The need to avoid the creation of a private monopoly.

4. The need to capture benefits generated by a facility or service to the degree necessary to cover costs and assure equity.
5. The need to meet state and federal legislative and/or administrative requirements.
6. The need to achieve significant economies of scale and/or to enable the use of a necessary or advantageous technology.
7. The adequacy and availability of resources available to the region and/or state.
8. The overall impact of the action on the achievement of regional or state goals.

It is with this mission in mind that the description of issues, needs, tasks, processes, and organizational concepts of transportation planning contained here has been prepared.

Emerging issues and needs

The issues and needs of a particular time are the forces which tend to dictate what will be done and where the emphasis in planning will be. They are the "engines" which drive change, which in turn creates the need for decision (planning) and action.

The sheer complexity of the changes which must be met in the next years is so great that no one can predict their force or direction with great accuracy. Moreover, these changes are being generated by conditions which exist on a world scale which are well beyond the ability of the United States alone or in concert with others to control. In fact, this "loss of control" and strong interdependence by the United States relative to the balance of the world may be one of the most important new, overriding conditions which must be faced.

Conditions and trends will vary between states and regions. However, a number of needs and forces which are now evident or which are emerging will affect transportation planning and transportation investment in virtually every part of the country. Just as inexorable urban expansion and the building of a great national highway system dominated transportation planning throughout the nation for almost 30 years, so new objectives and needs will dictate most future planning, with some variations resulting from regional differences.

Six areas of change

Major areas of change include (1) efficiency and productivity, (2) existing investments, (3) technology, (4) environment, (5) social-institutional, and (6) growth in travel. They are discussed, in turn, below.

Efficiency and productivity There will be greatly increased emphasis on efficiency—efficiency in the use of energy, money, land, and other factors affecting productivity.

Energy Tremendous progress must be made in increasing the efficiency with which transportation uses energy if national targets are to be achieved. For example, the National Transportation Policy Study Commission (NTPSC)[9] calls for transportation's share of energy to be reduced from 1975 to 2000 by as much as a fifth, from 33 to 26 percent. This includes a 30 percent decrease in gasoline consumption. Major improvements must be achieved in the use of fuel and the efficiency of vehicle fleets if this condition is to be reached. Although much of the effort required must be generated by the private sector and at the national level, state, regional, and even local transportation programs must play a significant part.

Money   As long as the financing of transportation facilities could be tied to an ample, growing, dependable source (such as the gallonage tax), and inflation was not severe, problems of competition for scarce dollars could be minimized, or at least kept within the bounds of transportation planning and programming. However, a number of factors are emerging to create intense competition for available funds. These include:

1. Rapid inflation in construction and maintenance, which has been much higher than the consumer consumer price index in recent years.[10]
2. Increased competition for capital among transportation modes. The need to refurbish rail, water, transit, and other nonhighway systems is very great. For example, NTPSC estimates the shortfall in funds available to make needed improvements to rail systems between 1976 and 1985 to be from $3.6 to $21.1 billion. Similarly, the commission indicates that if highway expenditures are limited to projected user revenues, there would be little or no money available for capital improvements (even routine resurfacing) in the late 1990s. For Maryland the shortfall of funds for capital expenditures between 1978 and 1998 is projected to range from $240 million to $2.5 billion.[11] For Minnesota the shortfall of revenues is projected at $88 million for 1980–1981, $187 million for 1982–1983, and $263 million for 1984–1985.[12] Confronted with declining or stable revenue, many states have dramatically cut capital improvements.
3. Increased competition for capital with other sections of the economy. Society must make tremendous investments to develop sources of energy, to protect environmental resources, and to modernize industry. The need for such investments will make it increasingly difficult to obtain funding for transportation.
4. Weakening of traditional sources of revenue, particularly the gallonage tax on petroleum based fuels. Reduced vehicle travel and increased fuel efficiency of vehicles are already having a devastating effect on the budgets of most state departments of transportation. Shifts to nonpetroleum fuel sources, such as alcohol, will further aggravate this problem.

Land   Rural areas always have been viewed as a sort of endless frontier from which lands can be taken as needed to build highways, power plants, airports, shopping centers, and other urban and nonagricultural facilities.[13] However, concern for the loss of prime agricultural land as an economic resource as well as an environmental asset is now reaching a point where strong limits are being placed on further conversions to nonagricultural use in many locations. Positive programs to preserve agricultural land are underway in a dozen or more states, including New York, Maryland, Michigan, Wisconsin, Oregon, and others. These programs will doubtless become more widespread and will have a profound effect on the location of development which generates travel and on the development of transportation facilities themselves.

Existing investments   In the past century we have built several extensive transportation systems and have converted enormous areas to urban use. Between 1958 and 1977, the amount of land devoted to urban use increased from 51 to 90 million acres.[14] Three-quarters of this expansion occurred between 1967 and 1977. Much of this expansion was possible because of the existence of over 3.8 million miles of roads. Almost 700,000 miles have been added to this system in the past several decades.[15] In an earlier time, the nation built the world's most extensive railroad system, including a 200,000 mile network with over 300,000 miles of track and 181 terminals.[16]

There are two major results of this great construction of transportation and other urban facilities. One is that we now have an expensive and extensive physical plant in place, which needs continuing repair and maintenance. The second is that, in the rush to build new facilities, we often neglected those constructed earlier. Thus, we have acquired a tremendous backlog of work to be done in replacement, repair, and maintenance of both transportation facilities and urban development. This work includes the substantial rebuilding and upgrading of much of the nation's rail and waterway systems, an extensive bridge rebuilding program, and periodic reconstruction of heavily used highways. The demand for maintenance is dramatically increasing the share of budgets which must go to this purpose. For example, for the Maryland DOT, it increased from 31.3 percent in 1973 to 42.9 percent in 1977, with every indication that this trend will continue.[17]

Potholes, depressions, and washboards "Potholes . . . probably do greater damage to a community's reputation than bad politics."

And so does deferred maintenance of highways, streets, and bridges. The costs of neglect are real and very high—deteriorating reputation, loss of credibility, lawsuits because of negligence, and total resurfacing and replacement are some of the costs.

No matter how well built, bituminous pavements are subject to wear and tear which shows up in potholes, cracks, corrugations (washboarding), depressions, and raveling at the edges. Moisture is the enemy, and continual maintenance is the solution.

Concrete pavements, although costing more than bituminous, require very little maintenance provided that cracks and joints are sealed promptly. The long-run cost of concrete often is lower.

Concrete and steel bridges have different maintenance requirements, and both of course are heavily affected by types and volume of traffic, weather, location, and moisture. The minimum requirements are records with identifying information on each bridge, technical information on the physical structure and characteristics of each bridge, and annual inspections of every bridge by qualified engineers.
Source: William S. Foster, in William E. Korbitz, ed., *Urban Public Works Administration* (Washington, D.C.: International City Management Association, 1976), pp. 286–90, and William S. Foster, in William S. Foster, ed., *Handbook of Municipal Administration and Engineering* (New York: McGraw–Hill Book Company, 1978), pp. 2–8, 3–12, and 5–2 to 5–6.

Another example of the burden of maintenance and replacement is the cost of $150 million (in 1979–1980) for the reconstruction of 15 miles of the Edens Expressway in Chicago. This is six times the total per-mile cost of this route when it was originally built in the early 1950s.

There will be similar demands on resources to modernize, maintain, and support the infill of older shopping, industrial, institutional, and residential areas, including substantial costs to maintain and increase the productivity of existing transportation facilities. As a result, a much greater emphasis must be placed on planning for maintenance and reconstruction and relatively less on new construction.

Figure 17–2 "I think it would be cheaper to fill it with money."

Technology Technological developments have always had a strong impact on transportation and will have an even greater impact in the future. Although such developments are difficult to predict, some speculation is possible.

In most cases, state and regional agencies cannot greatly affect the development of technology. However, they may be able to play a major role in adopting regulations, facilities, and systems to its requirements. Changes in technology will generate significant planning needs.

Environment Protection and improvement of the environment has been a special concern of transportation planning since the early 1970s. It will be a continuing and growing factor in transportation decision-making, both for the location of new facilities and in efforts to rebuild and revitalize existing urban areas. Examples of the types of effort that will become more important include:

The reduction of noise and the development of noise barriers. Many transportation facilities were built in the past with little or no regard for the impact of the noise which they generate on nearby development. There is a substantial need to redesign and retrofit many existing facilities in order to protect existing development from the impact of noise. In some cases, such as airports, more dramatic solutions may be involved, including the relocation of land uses affected by noise.

The reduction of other conflicts between transportation and land use. Such conflicts exist along major arterial streets, within neighborhoods, in business districts, around freeway interchanges, and in other areas of concentrated traffic or activity. Small cities and towns are sometimes greatly affected by through traffic along state highways and on mainline railroads. Solutions in the past have frequently included building "bypass" or relief routes. Modern efforts include the development of "automobile-restricted" or "automobile-free" zones, the redesign of street systems to channel traffic where it can be best handled, and the introduction of improved traffic controls. As traffic volumes increase on existing systems (air, rail, and highway) ever greater concern will be generated in this area.[18]

The reduction of air pollution, especially in areas of concentrated development and traffic. Reductions in the overall pollution of air are being accomplished by reductions in fuel consumption. Further progress may be made in this area through greater shifts to small vehicles and alternative (electric, alcohol) energy sources. However, there will still be problems in central business districts and in other areas of high traffic concentration, particularly as reductions due to decreased use of fuel are offset by the growth in population and economic activity and by higher concentrations of development. Continued planning will be required to deal with this concern.

Social/Institutional   Some of the most pervasive changes affecting transportation and other types of planning may be labeled as social or institutional. Such changes also may be the most difficult to predict and from which to anticipate impacts.

Growth in travel   On top of all of these potential changes in the amount and nature of both the demand for and the supply of transportation services, the nation as a whole and most regions are faced with dramatic overall increases in the movement of both people and goods. The NTPSC report[19] provides the most recent effort to estimate these increases. Although these estimates may not reflect all of the trends listed above (some of which are contradictory), they are indicative of the magnitude of demand with which planning may need to deal.

In addition to all of the above, many issues and objectives of the past will continue to be important. For example, there will be a continuing need to minimize or reduce *congestion* and to maximize or increase *reliability, flexibility, security, comfort, freedom*, and *privacy*. However, new pressures and concerns will tend to increase the difficulty of making decisions which effectively balance all of these objectives in providing transportation facilities and services.

These changes and trends are making it necessary to reexamine many of the standards and guidelines for transportation planning and methods of providing transportation service which have been developed over the past 20 years. One of the tasks of transportation planning will be to follow these changes closely so that plans and programs can be adjusted in a timely fashion to take advantage of and to meet them.

The activities of planning

Activities in state and regional planning are affected by both concepts of classic planning and constantly changing demands related to emerging issues described in the preceding sections. For example, many agencies have had to take rapid and unanticipated action to adjust budgets to reflect the effects of inflation and declining revenues. Similarly, some agencies have quickly adjusted their programs to try to deal with the problems emerging from sudden fuel shortages, the abandonment of rail lines, the "discovery" of the problems of deteriorated bridges, emergencies such as floods, hurricanes, earthquakes, crises associated with the financing and operations of transit services, and even volcanic eruptions.

The steps and levels of planning

Despite the uneven and often unpredictable nature of the demands on transportation planning agencies, there is—or there can be—a pattern to their work. This pattern can be derived from the systematic application of the steps in the conventional planning process to the different types or levels of planning decisions which must be made.

The importance of work in each step of the planning process in specific state or regional programs will vary substantially depending on many factors, including the nature and urgency of local issues, the relative roles of state, regional, and local organizations, etc. For example, in some situations (such as Maryland) the state DOT provides both transit and airport facilities serving Baltimore and must plan for these at all levels from policy through operations. In other situations, airports and transit are handled on a strictly local—even subregional—basis.

Thus planning responsibilities of states and regions vary substantially and often overlap. Some indication of trends in the activity of each of these areas is provided in the discussion of steps and levels below.

A great deal of change in the emphasis being given different areas or levels of planning has taken place over the past few years, and more change is likely in the future. Some areas are becoming more important, some less. And changes in the attention being given to different modes strongly affect the nature and mix of the work involved. Each of the levels of planning and trends associated with them are discussed below.

Policy/program planning   Planning at the policy or program level usually deals with the most basic questions in the broadest or most general way. It is concerned with choosing among competing goals and demands for resources, as between transportation and all other needs and as between basic transportation solutions. Planning in this area usually operates at levels where difficult trade-offs in the use and allocation of resources must be made and where many people will be affected in important but often subtle ways. Hence, judgment, both political and technical/professional, is needed. This level of planning virtually always requires legislative or formal executive action and often depends on protracted debate and sometimes on public referenda.

The activity of policy planning has increased substantially in recent years. More alternatives are being considered and are allowed under federal programs. More people have become aware of the impacts of policy decisions and are demanding that they be made openly, with public debate, and with input of more objective data and analysis. Thus, more work is being done in this area than ever before.

Some of the types of questions that are addressed in the policy/program area include:

1.   What basic concerns—economic, social, environmental—should guide transportation investment? Redevelopment and revitalization of older areas? The opening of new areas to development? The restriction of access (development) in areas of environmental importance? The promotion of tourism? Industrial development? The development of energy resources? etc.
2.   What emphasis should be given to short- versus long-term investments? To capital versus operating expenditures?
3.   How should costs be distributed between users, the general public, and others who may be benefited?
4.   To what extent should transportation facilities and services seek to compensate for indirect costs or recapture secondary benefits?
5.   What levels or standards of service should be provided?
6.   What fundamental types of transportation should be provided in an area? Limited access highway? Public transit? Fixed guideway transit? Air terminals and service? Truck routes?
7.   Should restrictions or controls be used to limit demands on transportation systems? To limit secondary impacts?

Many aspects of policy planning can only be dealt with effectively in the context of strong executive or legislative involvement. If planning agencies do not have strong relationships in these areas, opportunities to do effective work, even in technical/professional areas, will be limited. However, when concern becomes critical and issues are complex, planning agencies may be in a position to make important contributions. Much will depend on their ability (and credibility) to focus and define issues, to analyze them, and to formulate and objectively evaluate alternate courses of action. As can be seen from the nature of the questions listed above, a wide variety of types of data and of analytical skills may be required. Many complex economic, social, environmental, and institutional/political issues are frequently involved. Thus, planning in this area can be difficult and complex as well as exciting and important.

Systems planning   Planning for entire systems (one or several modes) of transportation has been a much more important activity in the past than it is now or is likely to be, at least at the state or regional level. Programs growing out of the Highway Act of 1962 and the heavy flow of funds into highway construction during the 1960s and 1970s made it necessary to produce comprehensive system plans. In most cases, this work defined systems of state and regional highway routes in many areas which are more than adequate for the needs to be served.

The San Diego trolley   The San Diego trolley, a light-rail system that opened in July, 1981, has been operating with great success on its 16-mile route from the city center to San Ysidro at the Mexican border. The line is financed by state and local gas taxes and involves no federal funding.

The system is recovering a substantial part of its operating cost from the fare box—80 percent in 1982—and has had a 97 percent on-time record. Most of the route runs along an abandoned railroad line that was upgraded and rebuilt. The 64-passenger cars (124-passenger capacity with standees) are well-tested equipment built by a German manufacturer.

The operating agency is the Metropolitan Transit Development Board, which was created by the California legislature in 1975. The trolley has had such high public approval and financial success that a 6-mile branch line is under construction, to be in operation in 1986.

Thus, system planning, of the type common in the 1960s and early 1970s, is not likely to be a major activity in most states and regions. However, several new types of system planning will be required. In most cases these will involve planning for the upgrading and improvment of existing facilities, with limited new construction, as compared to the conception of major new systems and facilities. In fact, "system" planning will be required to determine which routes and facilities should be removed from existing plans, as in the case of railroad abandonment and decisions to not build elements of the interstate system.

Other types of systems for which planning may be required include:

1. Airports and air service, especially for smaller cities and nonmetropolitan areas.
2. Rail services and facilities to be retained and improved, at both state and regional levels.
3. Public transportation service, intercity and intraregional, and subregional.
4. Subregional road and other systems, to serve new growth as well as revitalization areas.

New physical system planning also may be required to accommodate demands in areas which will grow substantially, such as Florida or Arizona. However, most system planning will deal with incremental extensions and improvements to existing facilities and with modes for which there is a "new" public concern, such as those listed above. This means that for most state or region-wide system planning, the steps in the planning process will be exercised in only limited and specialized ways, often related more to corridor, small area, or project planning.

The one exception may be in data collection and analysis. A good understanding of demands for movement and of system characteristics is needed not only for the planning of systems, but in policy planning and in preparing detailed plans for corridors, projects, regulation, and operations, and in planning for new modes. Thus, continuing and perhaps in some cases, major new work may be required in the collection and analysis of information regarding existing and projected travel, the condition and capability of existing facilities, and related factors. New types and forms of data will be especially needed in such areas as greater attention is given to problems of intermodal coordination goods movement, rail system reorganization, and maintenance and operational planning and scheduling.

Corridor planning   The amount and type of corridor planning to be done will also depend very much on the amount of new construction and development which will take place. In many parts of the country, the low levels of construction which can be expected will greatly limit the amount of such work to be done. Most corridors in such areas have fully developed and "mature" systems of transportation, at least in terms of rights-of-way. However, there are still segments of freeway systems to be built, and some communities will be building new transit routes. In these situations, all of the steps in the planning process will need to be applied, and substantial attention will likely need to be given to related land use and environmental areas.

As congestion and other problems develop, another type of corridor planning will become more prominent. This will involve the comprehensive analysis of existing facilities and of all or several modes to identify ways in which they can be coordinated and used more efficiently and effectively. Such planning is being advocated as a part of a program called Transportation Systems Management (TSM).[20] In some situations this work will also include planning for the development or redevelopment of land and corridor beautification, buffering, and landscaping. Actions which will normally grow out of such planning include a wide variety of small-scale transportation improvements, such as the upgrading of traffic signals, the grade separation of selected intersections, the widening and redesign of roadways, and the provision of traffic lanes for the exclusive use of transit and multipassenger vehicles; and the restriction of parking on roadways, the provision of off-street parking, and the provision of special facilities for cyclists and pedestrians. In some corridors actions may include the provision of new or additional common-carrier service or the upgrading of rail or air service and facilities. Some of the types of existing corridors which need and are receiving attention are:

Old urban arterial routes   Many have become heavily congested with commercial and other development and attendant property access movement, or have become obsolete or deteriorated from changed or heavy demand. In many instances this work will be approached at a limited, "project" scale. However, at best it will include consideration of a wide range of modes (automobile, transit, pedestrian, cycling) and of relationships with parking and land use.

Freeways and highways which are yet to be built   In many instances these are extremely controversial and their planning may include consideration of abandonment or major modification of original design concepts and conversion of rights-of-way which may have been acquired to other transportation or non-transportation use. Plans emerging from this work should increasingly include or be linked to proposals for development or redevelopment or the enhancement of sensitive environmental features.

Proposed transit lines   This especially includes those involving exclusive travelways. Although the number of such corridors will be limited, proposals will require careful planning. The costs of such facilities are likely to be extremely high, and the generation of needed ridership quite difficult. In addition, problems of coordination with existing development are likely to be important.   Because transit ridership is highly dependent on proximity of services to higher densities of development, proposals for such development may need to be generated along with transit plans and, thus, rather detailed and comprehensive corridor planning—including land use—is likely to be required.

In some instances the planning of services—that is, making decisions regarding the types of vehicles to be used and their operations—may be the principal activity involved. (This may be considered to be *operational* as contrasted with *corridor* planning.) However, where extensive new rights-of-way, costly construction, and high technologies are being considered, planning must include very intensive analyses of costs, ridership, intermodal coordination, and similar factors on a corridor basis.

Intercity corridors   Metropolitan and regional growth and travel have become so extensive in some areas that severe problems of capacity and congestion have developed in corridors that have been traditionally regarded as "intercity." Although many of these problems are generated by heavy local use of long distance routes, solutions are sometimes sought in the upgrading of intercity and interstate facilities. In the Northeast Corridor, between Washington and Boston, emphasis is being placed on improvements to the rail system. However, in other areas a more comprehensive multimodal approach is being pursued. For example, in the 120 mile San Diego–Los Angeles corridor, all modes, includingg air and water, were examined to determine their most appropriate roles, and to develop plans both for individual modes as well as for intermodal coordination.[21] There are many other intercity corridors which will require or which could benefit from comprehensive planning. Many of these involve pairs or clusters of cities which are relatively close together, such as Washington–Baltimore, Toledo–Detroit, and Bay City–Saginaw–Midland (Michigan). Others involve connections between a linear series of communities such as Miami–Palm Beach or Chicago–Milwaukee. Because actions are so dispersed, planning in such situations must include participation by a wide range of governments and transportation providers, and the roles of state and regional agencies may be largely in the realm of supporting and coordinating the planning being done by others. However, the full range of planning activities will likely be required, from the identification of issues to providing for implementation and operation. Because most corridors will cross several jurisdictional lines, including two or more states in some instances, special planning and decision-making mechanisms will be required.

Resource transportation corridors   As patterns of resource production and consumption shift, certain corridors become much more heavily used for the movement of fuel, agricultural products, and other resources. Such movements are generating major transportation and land use conflicts in some areas. Such conflicts are being examined in several areas.[22]

Project planning   Roles of state and regional agencies in project planning will depend on the extent to which large projects are pursued and the relative overall roles of the agencies involved. For example, Departments of Transportation in Maryland and North Carolina can expect to be heavily and directly involved in project planning because of their substantial direct responsibilities in the provision of highways and air and port facilities. On the other hand, relatively few regional planning agencies have direct responsibility for project implementation, and many state agencies are confined to projects involving limited, designated state highway routes. The roles of regional and state agencies tend to be further restricted by the trend to smaller scale projects and to operational as contrasted with physical improvements, which often fall within the jurisdiction of local governments, special authorites, or private enterprise.

Still, good project planning is essential to the achievement of many state and regional objectives. To assure continuity and efficiency and to avoid conflicts, it is important that certain standards be observed and that the timing and location of improvements be coordinated. Many of these needs may be met at the level of corridor planning where basic decisions regarding standards, location, timing, and budgets can be made for subsequent application in a wide variety of projects.

Where staff and regional agencies are directly responsible for project planning, they will likely need to deal with all of the steps in the planning process from identification of issues and goals to implementation and operation. However, in the more likely case where project planning is the direct responsibility of others, state and regional agencies will probably concentrate their efforts in the support roles of providing data needed for planning and design and/or reviewing and helping to evaluate plans to assure that broader policies and standards are being met.

Management   An area which is often overlooked as a subject for formal planning is that of management. Yet, for many reasons it has become extremely important and will likely become a larger part of the planning activity of state and regional transportation planning agencies.

As used here, the term "management" includes the three broad areas of decision processes, financing and budgeting, and organization. With the growing importance and complexity of relationships between levels of government and between government and private enterprise, and with increasing competition for resources, all of these areas are more significant. This significance is recognized in federal requirements that call for the development of "action plans" at the state level, which spell out procedures for planning and decision making at various levels, for the designation of MPOs and A-95 review agencies and procedures, and the preparation of comprehensive work programs for planning called Overall Program Designs (OPDs). Growing problems of finance are also causing state and regional agencies to spend much more time identifying and evaluating sources of revenues and developing new financing systems. Increased participation of public agencies in activities such as the operation and management of transit systems, transportation terminals, rail facilities, car and vanpool programs, and emergency fuel allocation systems calls for increased attention to be paid to ways in which to organize staff and other resources both for planning and for implementation.

Operations planning   Operations planning covers a wide variety of activity including the provision of transit and other services, the administration of preferential lanes on major streets and highways, the operation of terminal, railroad, ferry, or other services, and the administration of carpool or vanpool services. Such planning is a relatively new function for most transportation agencies, at least in a formal sense. However, with the emphasis on transportation systems management (TSM) inaugurated by federal agencies in 1975, much greater attention has been given to this area of planning. Concern for energy conservation and air quality management has also provided a stimulus in these areas.[23]

Procedures and techniques

The body of procedure and technique associated with transportation planning is both very broad and very sophisticated. Since the mid-1950s, it is likely that more money, time, and skill have been devoted to transportation planning than to planning for all other aspects of state and regional development combined.

The complexity, cost, and volume of the work to be done and the assurance of steady financing have attracted talented people to this field in great numbers and have been the basis for the establishment and operation of teaching and research programs in transportation at many universities. As a result, the body of research and of resultant technique and procedure is very large. Many volumes would be required to contain all potentially relevant information on this subject.[24]

The range of activities for which techniques have been developed has steadily grown, and the emphasis is changing. An early and continuing concern was for the *estimation and forecasting of travel demand*. As transit has become more significant, *mode split analysis* has received growing attention. With passage of environmental legislation, ways of *measuring impacts* have become important. As difficult choices need to be made in fragmented political environments, *evaluation and decision-making techniques* need to be developed. As resources become more scarce, *cost and financial analysis, and modal coordination and management techniques* all must be developed and applied. And as the future becomes more uncertain, techniques for *projecting alternate futures* and for *sketch planning* come into use.

The biggest impetus to the development and dissemination of more complex and sophisticated techniques came from the passage of the Highway Act of 1962 which made "comprehensive, coordinated, and continuous" (3 Cs) planning a prerequisite of federal funding and which, through a number of implementing guidelines, indicated a range of subjects to be covered.[25] These guidelines, along with those related to the Urban Mass Transit Act and the National Environmental Policy Act, have been steadily expanded and refined. As a result, virtually every region is involved in many, if not all, of the activities listed above, and many use standardized techniques developed through federally financed research programs. However, because of differences in needs, capabilities, and resources, the range of techniques being applied is—and will remain—very great. In fact, with a growing relative emphasis on small-scale, short-term planning, they are likely to become even more numerous and varied.

The needs being addressed and the general nature of techniques being used in each of the activity areas listed above are briefly summarized below.

Estimation, forecasting, and assignment of travel demand

Work in the estimation and forecasting of travel demand is needed to provide information regarding the amount, location, and timing of the desire to travel, which is further used to project the location and capacity of service and facility needs. Much of the early work in transportation planning and research was devoted to developing reliable ways of making such projections. Rather early it was determined that travel behavior could be related to land use and so techniques were devised to measure and project this relationship. The principal techniques employed included:

Land use   Land-use surveys are conducted to identify the type and density of land use, numbers and types of households, etc.

Travel surveys   Travel surveys are made (principally the "home" interview) to measure the economic and travel characterisitics of households (income level, car ownership, family size, etc.), and the destinations, purposes, amounts, and types of trips taken by all household occupants.

Correlation of travel with land use   Data on travel and land use are correlated to develop factors which indicate the amount and type of travel which is generated by various land uses (including different household types). A number of early, major studies used sample sizes large enough to produce data on the amounts of travel between the various parts (zones) of a region. With smaller samples, such data are generated by applying travel generation factors to land-use information. In either case, "trip tables" are produced to show the amounts and types (purposes) of travel which exist or can be expected between zones. Projections are developed by applying travel generation to projected land use.

Modeling of the characteristics and use of the transportation systems A model of the transportation system is developed in terms of the capacities and speeds which can be generated on its various elements. Existing travel is measured on existing portions of this system. This, in turn, is compared to an "assignment" of travel demand from trip tables based primarily on the assumption that desired travel will follow the path of least resistance, usually measured in time, but sometimes reflecting cost and comfort. A number of mathematical models and computer programs have been devised to make such assignments (UTPS). However, these need to be tested (calibrated) in specific situations by determining how accurately they "predict" existing, measurable conditions. When reasonable levels of accuracy are reached or deviations can be explained, these models and programs can be used to estimate travel on all or portions of the system assuming changes in land use and with changes (additions, deletions, or modifications in access, speed, or capacity) in the system.

In many early studies, relatively large sample sizes (1–5 percent) were used in travel surveys, and massive amounts of data were collected and handled to provide a basis for estimating and forecasting travel. Subsequent work has indicated that, with careful design, much smaller samples, (e.g., 1 percent) can be used, and the process can be made much more efficient with no substantial loss in accuracy.

Many smaller regions have never developed the capability to use some of the more sophisticated, computerized models and techniques for predicting and assigning travel. However, in virtually all areas of any size, basic data are available for land use and the use of existing facilities, and factors which enable the estimation of travel generation by various land uses have been developed. In such regions manual methods of estimating and assigning travel are in use.

As attention shifts from planning for whole systems or large parts thereof, the need for travel forecasts tends to be more related to specific corridors or projects, or to areas of concentrated activity such as shopping centers, business districts, and transportation terminals. In such situations it is usually possible to obtain detailed information about the area in question which will permit an estimation of travel demand which is much more accurate than that which could be obtained from a data base and from models developed at the regional level. Good information about land use and population is still needed. However, the generation of travel to and from a concentrated area of concern may best be estimated through a detailed analysis of the land uses and activities involved and possibly small sample surveys to ascertain travel desires and patterns. Through traffic (if any) may be projected from regional or area-wide system forecasts. However, the assignment of traffic to specific routes will require a detailed analysis of features such as the performance and capacity of specific intersections, the location of parking facilities, and the effect of land use, transit, truck movement, and other frictions on the capacity and attractiveness of specific routes.

Computer and other models have been developed to assist in making traffic assignments at this level. However, in many cases hand analysis and manipulation of data will produce results that are more readily obtainable and that may possibly better reflect all of the variables involved.

The forecasting and assignment of travel at the state level is still handled with relatively simple techniques. A few states such as Wisconsin[26] and Colorado[27] are applying techniques that involve some measurement of travel behavior and are attempting to relate this to population and economic activity for prediction purposes. However, more common are techniques that rely on the translation of projections of population and economic activity into overall projections of travel volumes. As the difficulty of allocating scarce financial resources increases and as certain routes show signs of congestion, it may be necessary to use more refined techniques which can make meaningful distinctions between corridors and which take into account potentials for modal change. For example, the modified gravity model techniques are used in the preparation of the Colorado transportation plan; sample surveys of intercity travel demand were conducted in Wisconsin.

Mode split analysis

The way in which travel is distributed between types of transportation is called "mode split." In areas where a significant proportion of travel is by common carrier, e.g., over 5 percent, knowledge about the mode split is important not only for the planning of transit, bus, airline, and other public transportation facilities but in the planning of highway and street systems as well.

Yet in many instances the proportion of travel by common carrier is so low that it is insignificant in the planning of street and highway facilities on a regional basis and will make virtually no difference in system requirements. However, in situations where street and parking capacities are limited, such as around college compuses, central business districts, and major shopping centers, the movement of even small percentages of people by public transportation, in shared-ride situations or as pedestrians, can make a difference in levels of congestion and in the number and size of facilities required. Thus, there are substantial reasons for wanting to estimate the mode split under both present and projected conditions.

A tremendous amount of research has been devoted to developing reliable methods of estimating the mode split.[28] Although many refinements are possible, models used to do this tend to focus on the variables of (1) travel time, (2) travel cost, (3) economic status of the tripmaker, and (4) relative travel service. Most other variables have been found to be highly correlated with the above four.

In applying these models, the principal work involved is in measuring relative cost and time, and in establishing the relationship between the variables and the behavior of travelers. The latter is usually done through the use of regression analyses and computer programs developed by UMTA for this purpose. The determination of values for "economic status" is relatively straightforward. "Level of service" is determined by rather arbitrarily choosing a number to reflect time spent other than in actual travel (i.e., delays, transfers, etc.); the lower the level of service is judged to be, the higher this number is. A useful refinement is to estimate the mode split separately for work, shopping, recreation, and other trip purposes.

In general, computerized analysis of mode split is used in only the larger, more sophisticated, and "transit-oriented" regions. Estimation of mode split in other situations is most often done through simpler techniques involving the analysis and extrapolation of present travel behavior, sample surveys, and the transfer of experience from other situations. In some instances, the concept of "policy mode split" is applied, which sets a target for ridership in public transportation and shared-ride situations which is then used to shape the system of services, incentives, and disincentives to achieve the balance desired.

Impact analysis

It has always been recognized that transportation facilities and services generate strong secondary impacts, some of which provide the basic rationale for the development of the service or facility in the first place. Facilities provide access to a region, a community, or to a site, thereby attracting development, creating jobs, and generating a tax base. These have been traditional benefits and goals which have generated the transportation investment. However, such access may stimulate development or create pollution in an area of critical environmental concern, thereby generating problems of water or air quality, higher public service costs, increased energy consumption, the loss of desirable agricultural land, or other undesirable results.

Recognition of the importance of secondary impacts, and particularly of their costs, has increased dramatically in recent years. This recognition was reflected in the passage of the National Environmental Protection Act of 1969 and has become greater and more comprehensive since. As a result, in recent years much effort has been given to the development of techniques for the measurement, prediction, and evaluation of the impacts of providing facilities and services and even of *not* taking action.[29] State and regional planning must, accordingly, be prepared to support or to take the lead in impact analysis in several ways, and they must be able to understand and apply many techniques, many of which are still being developed.

Some of the techniques which are most fully developed and most widespread are described briefly below.

Air quality   The impacts of transportation on air quality are both very strong and pervasive. The effects of air quality on health are relatively well understood. Because both air and vehicles move freely from location to location, these impacts cannot be confined and air quality is clearly considered to be of regional significance. However, many effects of air pollution may be localized in topographic basins or areas of concentrated activity, such as central business districts where large numbers of people may be affected. Enough work has been done so that reliable techniques for evaluating the impacts of transportation on air quality are now available and in widespread use.[30] These techniques generally require that estimates of changes in fuel consumption be made as a basic point of departure in analysis. Many additional factors then come into play, depending on the scale of the analysis. These include the timing, location, and type of fuel consumption, climate conditions, the efficiency of engines, etc. Enough work has been done so that reliable techniques for evaluating the impacts of transportation on air quality are now available and in widespread use.[30] These techniques generally require that estimates of changes in fuel consumption be made as a basic point of departure in analysis. Many additional factors then come into play, depending on the scale of the analysis. These include the timing, location, and type of fuel consumption, climate conditions, the efficiency of engines, etc.

Noise   The importance of noise impact is receiving increasing recognition. Major steps have been taken to deal with the impacts in "high noise" areas, such as airport approach zones and along some crucial sections of freeway. In addition, noise standards have been applied to vehicles to reduce noise generation at the source. However, techniques for the measurement and analysis of noise impacts will need to be applied to more smaller and localized projects and actions, as well.

Energy   Impacts on the use of energy are becoming of critical importance. Transportation projects or actions have the potential to reduce or limit or to increase outgoing energy consumption. They can also have a substantial impact on the use of embodied energy—that is, on the consumption of energy associated with initial construction. Thus, many factors may be involved, including determining whether a specific action encourages or discourages travel, increases or decreases the efficiency of vehicular use and operation, changes the fuel source or modal mix, and/or the consumption of fuel in construction. The most ready index of energy use is fuel consumption. As a result, techniques for estimating travel demand, mode choice, and the conditions and efficiencies of vehicle operations, similar to those used in the study of air quality impacts, are most useful. Standard travel forecasting models are often used and modified and extended to determine impacts on vehicle use and mode choice, and resultant fuel use.[31]

Socioeconomic impacts   Some of the most far-reaching impacts of transportation are those which stimulate or deter economic development, increase or decrease the mobility of various elements of the population, or divide or help to unite communities. Although such impacts are often very strong, they are also often difficult to measure or predict to acceptable levels of certainty. Thus, techniques for the analysis of impacts in these areas are constantly being refined and improved, and often much work must be done to tailor-make techniques for individual situations.

Areas of impact which are frequently the focus of such work include:

1. The stimulation and support of economic development near or related to a transportation investment. This can be at a small, site-specific level or can deal with whole regions or industry types (e.g., tourism or resource extraction).
2. The attraction of economic activity away from areas where it is needed and desired, such as central cities, by improvements such as bypasses in other areas.
3. The disruption (or uniting) of the physical and social fabric of neighborhoods.
4. The provision of increased (or decreased) mobility to those who may be disadvantaged, such as the aged and poor.
5. Potentials for damage to features of unusual cultural, historic, or architectural value.
6. The effect on property values, public finance, and business volumes.
7. The loss of agricultural land and/or the impact on agricultural operations.

Natural environment   In addition to air and noise, other aspects of the natural environment may be strongly impacted by transportation investments. These include wildlife habitats, natural or rare and valued vegetation, and areas of scenic attraction and recreational value.

As can be seen by the above, the range of impacts is wide and the job of measuring them in ways that are meaningful and that can be compared can be very complex. Increasingly, however, secondary impacts provide critical rationale for making decisions about whether to make transportation investments, where to make them, and their nature or design. Thus, much of the technique employed in transportation planning at state and regional levels, must be in the areas of impact analysis listed above.

Evaluation and decision making

Several factors have made the work of evaluation and decision making increasingly complex. These include the growing involvement and interest of local public officials and citizens in transportation decisions, which increases the numbers of people who must be incorporated into the decision process. It also includes the increasing list of concerns (economic, environmental, social) which must be balanced in the decision process, and it includes greater restriction on resources (financial, energy, etc.) and rising costs which make it more difficult to meet all needs and satisfy all interests.

Elementary efforts to assure an adequate decision-making process consist primarily of trying to assure the creation of boards or committee which can equitably represent all of the important interests involved. These may be ad hoc groups designated to make or recommend decisions in limited situations involving a specific project or corridor. Or they may be bodies with ongoing responsibility for planning and programming for a state or region. The metropolitan planning organizations (MPOs) which the United States DOT requires be established are examples of the latter.

However, needs in evaluation and decision making have extended well beyond what can be handled solely through normal or "simple" group interactions. To meet these needs, sometimes elaborate "processes" have been defined to assure that all interests are heard, that all factors are considered, and that trade-offs and comparisons can be made in ways that are as objective and open as possible. For example, the FHWA requires that states develop and use a work program or "Action Plan" which describes the processes to be used in making decisions at system, project, and corridor levels. Such plans spell out the work to be done and the roles of the various levels of government and their interests in making decisions.

For example, the core of the transportation plan for the State of Minnesota[32] consists of four chapters which define planning and decision-making processes. These prescribe in considerable detail the steps by which proposals may be developed and translated into plans and programs.

Cost and financial analysis

A number of factors are serving to increase the importance of financial analysis as a planning technique. Principal among these is the relative (and in some instances absolute) decline in revenues available for the development and maintenance of transportation systems. A second is rapidly rising costs. A third is the greater involvement of transportation agencies in the operation and subsidization of services—as contrasted with facilities—which requires much greater attention to continuing costs and revenues. Additional impetus is provided by concern for the impact that regulation has on transportation costs.

As a result, transportation planning is increasingly involved in developing and using techniques in financial analysis. These techniques deal with several different and fundamental questions:

1. What is the potential of existing or proposed sources of revenue? How will these potentials be affected by changes in various factors such as levels of service, use of transportation, tax rates, etc?
2. How will costs change in the future? Costs to transportation agencies? Costs to users? Costs to the general public? How will they be affected by changes in resource availability and cost, by changes in the use and technology of transportation systems, changes in management and operation, etc.?
3. What are the economic effects of regulations? Of subsidies? Of different rates of taxation?
4. What is the value of the benefits of a transportation investment? Do they offset costs? Can they be "captured" to help offset costs?
5. What formula and techniques can be used to allocate funds between various regions and modes?

Ways must be found to answer these questions on a routine basis as part of the process of plan development—to reflect the results in individual modal plans as well as in policies and programs.

Modal coordination and management

As the need grows to use transportation facilities more efficiently and as more travel modes come into use, there is a growing demand for better management and coordination of transportation services. This demand is being met by the development of joint use terminals to facilitate transfers between modes (e.g., local bus to intercity bus, taxi to rapid transit, etc.) They include the design or redesign of travelways to separate or otherwise better accommodate and reduce frictions between modes (e.g., special lanes for bicycles and/or transit). They also include the application of techniques to assure that each mode is being accommodated and is being used most effectively to meet the particular needs of a corridor or region, including special incentives and disincentives, marketing programs, provision of "targeted" services to meet specialized needs, and selective capital improvements.

The programs that have emerged in this area are known as Transportation Systems Management (TSM).[33] The activity of TSM is in many ways in its infancy and, as such, is only beginning to accumulate the specialized techniques and methods which may be required for its success. However, it is clear that skills will be needed increasingly in areas such as the following:

Communication, in both the solicitation and dissemination of views and ideas regarding TSM actions needed. Many TSM actions require voluntary or at least willing and understanding participation on the part of many persons. Thus, the implementation of TSM strategies depends strongly on skills in this area. It may also require the development of a whole new concept of what a transportation "plan" must be

Monitoring to identify both problems and the effects of solutions. Because many TSM actions require a continuing commitment of funds or efforts or may be either reversed or replicated, the availability of accurate information on impacts can be very important in making decisions concerning the continuation or termination of an action. The need for monitoring will in many instances require that the activities of planning and implementation be closely integrated.

Coordination in the provision, design, or operation of services or facilities between different jurisdictions and agencies and between public and private entities will be critical. Not only must plans for coordination be developed, but measures for continuing implementation must be devised. These may require the development of solid facts regarding benefits or the application of inducements, penalties, or other means to obtain cooperation. In many instances these are tools which are new, untried, and unfamiliar to the transportation planner.

Evaluation, such as that discussed in a preceding section but applied on a highly decentralized basis and small in scale, will be important. Evaluation will need to balance both area-wide as well as local concerns. Because of the scale and number of the decisions involved, techniques will need to be relatively simple and easy to apply.

Budgeting will become much more important than in traditional transportation planning. Many more categories of action and "projects" will be involved, and many activities will need to be rebudgeted year after year. Moreover, to the extent that ongoing payments and/or revenues are involved, budgeting becomes a key tool in communicating, monitoring, evaluating, and coordinating programs and activities to assure that key goals are achieved.

Joint development will be more important in terms of joint planning, financing, and construction of facilities, for both different transportation modes and transportation and land use. Such development is the key to achievement of greater intermodal coordination and to greater integration of transportation and land use. Planning for joint development requires a much broader range of skills and knowledge than is required for planning in only one mode or for transportation alone. Persons in transportation who expect to become involved in joint development will need to broaden their range of knowledge and capabilities.

Sketch planning and the transportation plan

Uncertainty about the validity of long-term projections and plans plus emphasis on planning for projects and other short-term actions has produced a decline in the attention given to the preparation of comprehensive and long-range plans. Still, such plans are needed to provide a framework for short-term decisions both in transportation investment and in land and development planning. Several approaches have been developed to meet this need without becoming involved in massive data collection and analyses activities or making commitments to policies or plans which will be fixed for long periods of time. These include sketch planning, alternative futures planning, a continuing planning cycle with periodic plan updates, and other techniques.

One of the features which is common to these approaches is that they recognize the complexity of the content of planning decisions and, thus, of "plans." "Plans" contain six elements: projections, goals, standards, plans, programs, and procedures. These elements can provide general information, give external direction, provide a basis for coordination, and help meet federal requirements. With so many purposes and elements, it is increasingly difficult to think in terms of the development and publication of a "comprehensive" plan through a single major effort. Rather, the updating of the "plan" becomes an ongoing process which focuses on one or a few features at a time.

Another dimension of complexity is provided by the uncertainty about the future which has become widely recognized and which has caused much disillusionment about comprehensive or long-range planning. The concept of "alternative futures" has been developed to help deal with this problem. This concept calls for several basic, conceivable "futures" to be identified and the implications of these futures to be assessed. These assessments are then used as a basis for the development of alternative plans and programs. Policy makers then can make a choice based on a knowledge of the alternatives which lie behind the proposals. One concept which can be applied to reduce the risk of basing decisions on the "wrong" alternative is to implement only those improvement and program elements which are common to all futures.

1   National Transportation Policy Study Commission, *National Transportation Policies Through the Year 2000,* TTPSC, June, 1979.

2   Federal Highway Administration, *Planning Process Memorandum 50-9,* 1965; *Planning Process Memorandum 90-3,* 1974.

3   Advisory Commission on Intergovernmental Relations, *Toward More Balanced Transportation: New Intergovernmental Proposals,* ACIR, 1974.

4   Transportation Research Board, National Academy of Sciences, *Urban Transportation Policy Research: Workshop Report* prepared for U.S. DOT, December, 1979; Roy J. Harris, Jr., "Regional Air-

lines, Using Efficient Planes Over Short Hops, Outpace Trunk Carriers," *The Wall Street Journal,* Tuesday, July 22, 1980; Gilbert Castle, and Rodney E. Engelen, *Joint Transportation and Development Planning at the State Level: A Case Study,* presented to the Committee on Transportation and Land Development Policy, at the 55th Annual Meeting of TRB, January, 1976.

5   U.S. Government, *Railroad Revitalization and Regulatory Reform Act of 1976.*

6   See note 3 above

7   Rodney E. Engelen, and Darwin G. Stuart, *New Directions in Transportation Planning,* (Chicago,

American Society of Planning Officials, 1975); Barton-Aschman Associates, Inc., and Creighton Hamburg, Inc., *Development of a Transportation Planning Work Program for the Delaware Valley Regional Planning Commission* Work Papers numbers 1–10 and Summary Report, 1972–1973.

8   This definition of "mission" is derived from efforts to define the missions of DOTs in several states, including California, North Carolina, and Maryland. See note 7 above; *New Directions in Transportation Planning;* Maryland Department of Transportation, 1978, *Maryland Transportation Plan,* Maryland Department of Transportation, July 1978; Barton-Aschman Associates, Inc., *State-Wide Transportation Plan: — Phase One, Interim Report,* February 1975—*Phase One: Summary Report,* August 1976;—*Phase One: Technical Report,* January 1976.

9   See note 1 above.

10 See periodic reports contained in the *Engineering News Record* on trends in construction costs. Recessionary developments in 1980-1983 have lowered rates of growth in costs, but overall trend noted here is still correct.

11 See note 8 above; *Maryland Transportation Plan.*

12 Minnesota Department of Transportation, *A Transportation Plan for the State of Minnesota,* Minnesota Department of Transportation, July, 1978.

13 Max Schnepf, *Farmland, Food and the Future,* The Soil Conservation Society of America, 1979.

14 Ibid.

15 See note 1 above.

16 US DOT, *A Prospectus for Change in the Freight Railroad Industry,* October, 1978.

17 See note 8 above, *Maryland Transportation Plan.*

18 Barton-Aschman Associates, Inc. and Ernst & Ernst, *Alternative Solutions to Railroad Impacts on Communities in Minnesota and North Dakota,* MNDOT and North Dakota State Highway Department, 1979.

19 See note 1 above.

20 Transportation Research Board, Special Report 190, *Transportation System Management in 1980, State-of-the-Art and Future Directions,* National Academy of Sciences, 1980.

21 Barton-Aschman Associates, Inc., *San Diego/Los Angeles Corridor Study* California DOT, Southern California Council of Governments, Comprehensive Planning Organization of the San Diego Region, 1975

22 See note 18 above

23 See note 20 above; Barton-Aschman Associates, Inc., *Petroleum Shortage Response Program for the State of Illinois, Phase One: Thirty Day Actions,* prepared for the Illinois Institute of Natural Resources, June, 1979; Transportation Research Board, *NCHRP Report 209: Market Opportunity Analysis for Short-Range Public Transportation Planning, Transportation Services for the Transportation Disadvantaged,* National Research Council, October, 1979; *NCHRP Report 210: Market Opportunity Analysis for Short-Range Public Transportation Planning, Economic, Energy, and Environmental Impacts,* National Research Council, October, 1979; *NCHRP Report 211: Market Opportunity Analysis for Short-Range Public Transportation Planning, Goals and Policy Development, Institutional Constraints, and Alternative Organizational Arrangement,* National Research Council, October, 1979; *NCHRP Report 208: Market Opportunity Analysis for Short-Range Public Trans-*

portation Planning, Procedures for Evaluating Alternative Service Concepts, National Research Council, 1979; Harold M. Mayer, *Problems of Planning for Goods Movement in North Carolina,* January, 1975; Transportation Research Board, *Transportation Research Record 714, Impact of Air Quality Control Measures,* National Academy of Sciences, 1979; David R. Miller, *Equity of Transit Service Study: Volume Two,* W.V. Rouse and Company, June, 1977.

24 Edward Weiner, *Evolution of Urban Transportation Planning,* U.S. Department of Transportation, April, 1976; George E. Gray, and Lester A. Hoel, *Public Transportation: Planning Operations and Management,* Prentice-Hall, Inc., 1979; John W. Dickey, et al., *Metropolitan Transportation Planning,* Scripta Book Company, 1975; Transportation Research Board, *Special Report 187: Transportation Planning for Small and Medium Size Communities,* National Academy of Sciences, 1980; Marvin L. Manheim, et al., *Transportation Decision-Making: A Guide to Social and Environmental Considerations,* MIT, July, 1974; Transportation Research Board, *Research Record 723: Travel Behavior Methodology,* National Academy of Sciences, 1979; *NCHRP Program Report 217: The No-Action Alternative, Impact Assessment Guidelines,* National Research Council, December, 1979; *Research Record 707: Urban Transportation Planning, Evaluation and Analysis,* National Academy of Sciences, 1979; *Research Record 701: Applications and Use of Transportation Data,* National Academy of Sciences, 1979.

25 See note 2 above

26 Wisconsin Department of Transportation, *State Transportation Policy Plan,* January, 1980

27 Alan M. Voorhees and Associates, Inc., *Colorado State Wide Transportation Planning Project: Final Report,* prepared for the Colorado Department of Highways, AMV and Addp Associates, September, 1977.

28 See note 24 above: *Travel Behavior Methodology; Applications and Use of Transportation Data.*

29 See note 24 above: *Transportation Decision-Making; The No-Action Alternative;* Transportation Research Board, *Research Record 686: Effects of Transportation on the Community,* National Academy of Sciences, 1978; note 23 above: Impact of Air Quality Control Measures.

30 R.K. Jain, L.V. Urban, and G.S. Stacey, *Environmental Impact Analysis,* New York: Van Nostrand Reinhold Company, 1977.

31 Barton-Aschman Associates, *Petroleum Shortage Response Program for the State of Illinois,* Illinois Institute of Natural Resources, 1979; *Evaluation Manual: Energy Saving Traffic Operations Project,* Illinois Department of Transportation, August, 1980 (draft).

32 Minnesota Department of Transportation, *Minnesota Looks at Transportation: A Report on Phase One of the MN/DOT Plan,* Minnesota Department of Transportation, January, 1978; *Minnesota Moves Toward a State Transportation Plan: A Report on Phase Two of the MN/DOT Plan,* Minnesota Department of Transportation, January, 1978; *A Transportation Plan for the State of Minnesota,* Minnesota Department of Transportation, July, 1978.

33 See note 20 above.

34 See note 27 above.

18 Energy planning

The number and complexity of energy matters engaging the attention of the state planner have grown significantly since the early 1970s. Identifying effective and appropriate energy policies and programs to help maintain an energy equilibrium at the state level poses a tremendous challenge. The planning discipline has been forced to mature and adapt quite rapidly in order to respond to situations for which most states initially were poorly prepared.

Each state is unique in its energy resources, applications, and needs. Energy planners must tailor their efforts to best suit those individual circumstances, of course. But states do not exist in a vacuum, and the larger energy systems—those of the United States and of the world as a whole—significantly shape the energy environment in which each state must function. It therefore is appropriate to seek an integration between state-oriented planning and the larger energy circumstances.

An overview

Unfortunately for the planner, those circumstances are characterized by turmoil. The world's industrialized nations are finding themselves in competition with the less-developed nations for supplies of energy, and the effects of this competition extend down to the local level. In this section, we will examine the larger perspective within which state energy planning must take place.

Definitions of energy These excerpts help define the phenomenon of energy as a force in resource development and use.

Energy. The physical force which can manifest itself as heat, as mechanical work, as motion, and in the binding of matter by nuclear or chemical forces. The modern concept of energy was developed early this century following the work of Einstein, whose special theory of relativity made it clear that mass itself is a manifestation of energy, and the pioneers of quantum mechanics, which led to a vastly improved understanding of energy transfer at the microscopic level.

Conservation of energy. The physical principle that energy cannot be annihilated or created out of nothing; it can be converted only from one form into another. . . . The principle of the conservation of energy has nothing to do with *energy conservation*.

Energy conservation. Not to be confused with the conservation of energy, which is a law of nature, energy conservation is the careful and sparing use of energy with a view to conserving the natural resources from which energy is derived (especially fossil hydrocarbons) and minimizing environmental pollution.

Source: Martin Counihan, *A Dictionary of Energy* (London, Boston, and Henley: Routledge & Kegan Paul, 1981), pp. 49–50, 38, 51.

International context

The economies of the industrialized nations—and the welfare of their citizens—have become extremely vulnerable to disruptions in the world flow of petroleum and, to some extent, of natural gas. This fact is well understood by countries which export these premium fuels and has been used to advantage to promote political and ideological goals. The Arab Oil Embargo of 1973 startled many oil-importing nations; energy planners expect similar occurrences in the future.

The vulnerability of energy-importing nations is apparent in light of the fact that the 1973 shortage which caused such chaos involved the temporary loss of less than 10 percent of the world's oil supply. The economic and human impacts of the impacts of the event seem, in retrospect, far out of proportion to this degree of shortage. Much larger energy supply disruptions are conceivable, and the effects could be expected to be disastrous.

To understand why petroleum and natural gas have come to dominate energy concerns, it is useful to examine the process by which these fuels became key elements of the energy mix. In the nineteenth century, wood yielded its place as the chief energy source to coal. Coal's emergence occurred for several reasons: industrialization and centralized manufacturing required a high-heat energy source; wood was becoming increasingly scarce and expensive; and coal's nature permitted new activities.

It was coal's superiority over wood in these criteria, coupled with the fact that the nature of energy-consuming activities was changing both rapidly and radically, that made it possible and desirable for industry to adopt coal as the primary energy source.

The entry of petroleum and natural gas into the energy mix was similar in that these fuels had an inherent superiority over coal: convenience of handling was one primary factor. These fuels also arrived at a propitious time, when new fuels were needed: technology had reached a point where the internal combustion engine was a practical development. At the beginning of the twentieth century, oil and gas made possible a dramatic increase in the amount of available energy with a substantial decrease in the costs of obtaining it.

These shifts in energy sources—wood to coal, coal to oil and natural gas—took place in a favorable environment. Changes in fuel-using activities and fuel availability took place concurrently and were mutually reinforcing. Social, environmental, and economic considerations played a role as well, strengthening the impetus toward new energy sources.

Today, industrialized nations are going through yet another transition in energy sources. This time, however, the transition is occurring more because the old fuels—gas and oil—are causing a kind of inconvenience than because new fuels or fuel-using activities are exerting a pull. This, in turn, is creating a number of hardships for both governments and energy consumers.

National policies

In the United States, energy policy has swung sharply since the early 1970s. Soon after the events of 1973 there was a federal emphasis on energy self-sufficiency, with a great interest in the production of synthetic fuels.

However, the use of oil products had been encouraged, directly and indirectly, by the federal government for decades. The national highway system permitted easy mobility; it also encouraged the widespread ownership of private vehicles and fostered the shifting of freight transport from the more fuel-efficient railroads and inland waterways to the truck. In the desire to improve the quality of the environment, power plants and industry had been urged to convert from coal to oil to gas. Even in the aftermath of the 1973 oil embargo, which many argued

The energy base of the Industrial Revolution   The Industrial Revolution was made possible by fossil fuels, first coal, then petroleum, that fed the extraordinary development and expansion of railroads, ships, factories, mills, electric power, and the automobile.

In the 17th century, wood began to disappear in Europe as the industrial and commercial age was born. Coal—formerly regarded as a curiosity—was rediscovered as a cheap and abundant source of energy. England led the way in industrial development, fueled by coal.

Coal also became the energy base of development in the United States. Coal was abundant; it was cheap; and it brought a declining real cost of energy that provided economic and technological bases for the industrial age. The countries in the 19th century with abundant coal—Great Britain, Germany, and the United States—were the winners in industrial development.

Coal fueled the railroads and steamships that revolutionized transportation, opened up national and international markets on an unprecedented scale, provided new kinds of jobs for millions, and irrevocably changed ways of living. Above all, it freed many national economies from dependence on an extremely limited resource—firewood.

By the mid-19th century in this country, however, the discovery of petroleum, both oil and natural gas, presaged a change.

"If coal was good, oil was great. Its availability led to the *internal combustion engine* in the 1880s."

"Petroleum is much more complex in its makeup; cleaner, safer and easier to produce than coal; and much more versatile in use. Its chemical complexity is of paramount importance; the list of useful refined or processed products is endless."

Source: Abstracted and excerpted from Office of Conservation, Seattle City Light; and Institute of Public Service, Seattle University, *Urban Energy Management: A Course on the Administration of Public Energy Programs* (Washington, D.C.: U.S. Department of Energy and Public Technology, Inc., 1980), pp. 66, 67, 68, 70–71.

---

should have precipitated the imposition of taxes or other measures to work in tandem with higher oil prices against oil consumption, the federal government used its fiscal policies to keep petroleum prices at a level that encouraged, rather than discouraged, additional use.

By the late 1970s, under the Carter Administration, it became national policy to discourage the use of oil and natural gas by industry and utilities in favor of coal or other fuels; regulations prohibiting new fuel-burning installations from using premium fuels were imposed; strategies were developed to force to help existing plants to convert to coal or other energy sources.

Campaigns to encourage petroleum and natural gas conservation were waged; some focused on voluntary actions, ridesharing, for example, but others involved incentives, notably income tax credits for expenses incurred in improving residential energy efficiency. There also were regulatory efforts to bring about conservation, such as the ban on the use of natural gas for decorative lighting, and the creation of automobile fleet mileage requirements.

Crisis management programs—rationing plans, gasoline allocation, and the like—proliferated during this period. Profits of oil companies were taxed and the revenues were intended to stimulate the development of synthetic substitutes for oil and gas.

The essential character of our national energy goals at this time was one of reducing oil imports. Unfortunately, the effort was bound to fail since there was an unwillingness to decontrol prices and a lack of faith in the ability of the marketplace to allocate resources.

By the summer of 1979, when there was yet another petroleum shortage, the country at last seemed willing to recognize that the problem was serious and that it would not be solved by clinging to the status quo and maintaining artifically low prices.

The arrival of the Reagan Administration brought about a change in emphasis in national energy goals. During the early 1980s, petroleum was deregulated; energy conservation campaigns were cut back drastically; federal activities designed to hasten the commercial acceptance of new non-oil energy technologies were curtailed; and policies were implemented to stimulate greater efforts to find new reserves of domestic oil and gas. Gasoline prices have declined in the short term, but whether these policies will work over time is an open question.

Energy demand

The need for energy—quantities consumed and uses to which it is put—provides the framework within which energy policies and plans must be developed. The primary motivation for governmental intervention in regard to energy is to seek a balance between supply and demand. Population growth and increasing technological sophistication in the United States during the 30-year period between 1949 and 1979 led government generally to espouse policies designed to increase supply rather than to depress demand in order to maintain this parity.

The concern that arose in the 1970s over the uncertainty of imported oil offered the first serious challenge to the wisdom of relying solely on efforts to increase supply. Policy makers quickly grasped the complexities involved in any effort to radically alter patterns of consumption, however; in addition, the traditional sources of energy and ways in which they are used proved resistant to abrupt change.

Over time, various types of energy have become wedded to specific applications: gasoline, considered a waste product of the petroleum refining process early in the twentieth century, for example, became a crucial fuel for the emerging automobile.

A basic understanding of how much energy is used in the United States, for what purposes it is used, and in what relationship to population and economic activities, must be coupled with knowledge of the mix of available energy sources if realistic plans are to be made for affecting either fuel choices or total energy consumption.

In 1979, petroleum represented the single largest energy source in the United States, accounting for nearly half of the mix. Natural gas represented about 25 percent, and coal about 19 percent. The remainder was provided by nuclear and hydropower, with wind and solar energy growing and wood beginning a resurgence; geothermal and other unconventional energy forms had just begun to emerge. The residential and commercial sectors accounted for the largest share of energy consumption in 1979 at 37.7 percent; the industrial sector followed at 36.9 percent, and transportation consumed 25.3 percent. Transportation accounted for the largest share of petroleum use at 51.8 percent; nearly three-fourths of this total was in the form of gasoline, which is used principally by automobiles.

Energy supply

Supply is the other side of the energy equation. The United States has become increasingly dependent on foreign sources of energy to meet demand. Domestic, production has not kept pace with demand. Domestic coal production could be

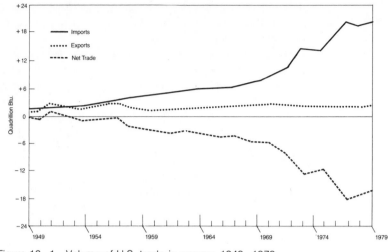

Figure 18–1 Volume of U.S. trade in energy, 1949–1979.

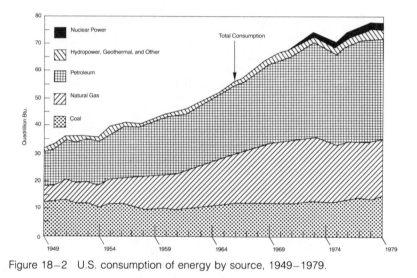

Figure 18–2 U.S. consumption of energy by source, 1949–1979.

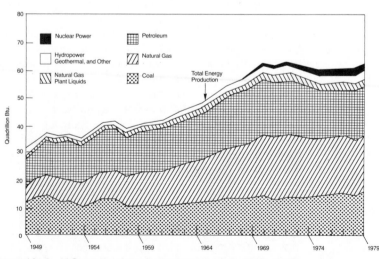

Figure 18–3 U.S. production of energy by source, 1949–1979.

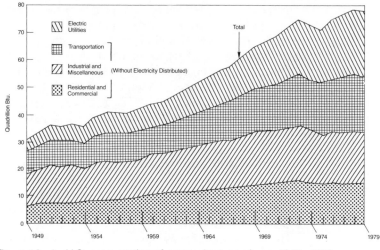

Figure 18–4   U.S. consumption of energy by type of use, 1949–1979.

increased substantially; in 1979, 775.8 million short tons were mined in the United States. In that year, coal represented 18 percent of all energy consumed in the nation, yet coal amounts to 90 percent of all domestic energy reserves. Oil production, on the other hand, probably cannot be increased significantly in the United States, although some dissenting opinions have been voiced. The 3.1 billion barrels produced in this country in 1979 were nearly matched by oil imports.

Coal and oil, finite and exhaustible   Before congratulating ourselves on industrial development and agricultural technology, we should remind ourselves of the good luck the United States has had in its natural resources of coal and petroleum. It was coal that literally and figuratively fueled the industrial explosion of the late 19th century, and it was petroleum that made the automobile possible. The following excerpts from a large-scale study conducted in 1962 for the National Academy of Sciences show that substantial portions of the world's coal and crude oil are within our boundaries.

The coal reserves of the world are far from equitably distributed among the world's people. The continent of Asia, for example, has 49.4 percent, or almost exactly one-half, of the world's coal reserves, nearly all of which are in the U.S.S.R. and China. North America has 34.4 percent, or about one-third; Europe has 13.0 percent; and the remaining 3.2 percent is divided among the three continents: Africa, South America, and Australia.

A fairly widespread delusion among the citizens of the United States is that this country owes its phenomenal industrial development, as contrasted with lack of development of regions such as Africa, South and Central America, and India, to the superiority of American personal and institutional characteristics. It may be well to remind ourselves that, but for a fortuitous combination of a large fraction of the world's resources of coal and iron in the eastern United States, the growth of which we are justly proud could never have occurred.

Source: M. King Hubbert, *Energy Resources*. A Report to the Committee on Natural Resources of the National Academy of Sciences–National Research Council. Publication 1000-D. (Washington, D.C.: National Academy of Sciences–National Research Council, 1962), pp. 36, 38.

This dichotomy led policy makers at least twice in the 1970s to call for national efforts to create synthetic petroleum fuels from coal, oil shale, tar sands, and biomass. But several million barrels per day of such fuels would have been needed by 1980 to alleviate the need for imported oil.

Other forms of energy, notably renewables including solar, wind, tidal, hydropower, and biomass energy resources, offer as yet unknown potential for decreasing the need for petroleum fuels. The resources are quite large in volume, but the degree to which they will be exploited will depend on a wide variety of unpredictable factors.

The states and energy: seeking an equilibrium

Defining a state energy policy is a challenging and perilous task. Energy is a new item on the public agenda, and there is little historical precedent upon which to draw.

The states traditionally have felt a responsibility for fostering their own economic and social well-being, with a particular emphasis on preparing for future growth. But energy affects the diverse economic and social elements within each state in so many different ways that conflicts and contradictions are abundant.

Four stumbling blocks

In particular there are four stumbling blocks that a state will face as it tries to define its energy policies: the private ownership of energy supplies, state interests versus national interests, energy losers versus energy winners, and the absence of reliable data.

Private ownership   Probably the most serious reality that state policy makers must face is that energy is a commodity that is bought and sold like grapefruit or washing machines. We have for too long seen headlines referring to the energy crisis and have forgotten what energy is. The word itself has taken on meanings associated with foreign policy, war, lifestyle, the economy, and other cosmic subjects.

But despite these moral and other connotations, energy at base is a commodity that is traded on the market. This seemed relatively insignificant when energy was cheap and available, but as prices rose and some forms became harder to obtain, we could not escape the impact it has had on household budgets, on business profits, and on ways of life.

It is true that the market for energy is regulated and influenced by governments. State public utility commissions for years have regulated the price and distribution of natural gas and electricity. The federal government has regulated the price of oil and natural gas, and a host of governmental agencies control the health and environmental hazards associated with producing or using energy. Taxes, too, are significant in shaping the market for energy.

Some will argue that there are energy sources that are "free," such as solar. There are two problems with this argument. First, any capturing of solar energy requires an initial capital investment which is a cost to someone. Second, a policy maker in the 1980s will recognize that solar is only a small but growing part of the total energy economy.

Basically, energy is privately owned, and the owners make a profit from its sale. For state policy makers the issue is: how much more should we intervene in the marketplace and in what ways?

State versus national interest   A second obstacle for the state policy maker is one of sorting out the conflicts between national goals and state goals. U.S.

energy problems should be divided into two categories —one worldwide, and the other domestic.

The worldwide problems are complex and multifarious. The worldwide issues that have an energy element include such things as Soviet influence in the Middle East, French cooperation with NATO, Arab-Israeli peace negotiations, and Chinese-Japanese trade relations.

The domestic energy issues include such things as auto emission standards, strip mine regulations, water rights, disposal of nuclear wastes, right-turn-on-red lights, and the 55-mile-per-hour speed limit. The only thing that really connects these two sets of problems is their involvement with oil imports. Except for that connection, the two sets of issues have little to do with each other. Some of the worldwide problems are of crisis proportion. Domestic problems are all problems of adjusting to rising energy prices. These problems are serious, but in the end are manageable.

Part of the confusion in energy policy development is the inability of policy makers to separate the worldwide from the domestic problems. Individual states have little to contribute to the solution of worldwide problems but have a great deal to win or lose as the nation attempts to solve its domestic energy problems. A few illustrations will make the point.

A simple law to limit speeds to 55 mph was met with great outrage by the western states, where travel distances are longer. A proposal to close gasoline stations on Sundays to conserve gasoline and protect short supplies was not welcomed by any state, but the states that are dependent on tourist traffic complained loudly and killed the idea.

The federal government wants everyone who can to shift from petroleum to coal; everyone agrees with the need for the shift, but the northeastern states, which are more dependent on petroleum, want more time, a subsidy from the federal government, and assurances against any negative environmental impacts. Meanwhile, Montana, with its vast coal reserves, is pleased with the new interest in coal and imposes a 30 percent tax on any coal mined in the state. Users of Montana coal, unsuccessfully sued the state, arguing that Montana's tax is a restraint on trade, thereby violating the interstate commerce clause of the constitution.

All the states—Montana, the tourist states, the western states, the northeastern states—surely agree that the country needs to curb its appetite for imported oil, but no individual state wants that goal accomplished at its expense. Everyone wants to let someone else pay the price.

The paramount example of this war between the states is the deregulation of oil and natural gas prices. Virtually everyone agrees that domestic oil and gas prices have been held artificially low and must rise to world market levels in order to send proper price signals through the economy. The southwestern states where the oil and gas is to be found are pleased. It would bring new jobs, a boost to their economies, and more state revenue through severance taxes. The states which lack their own energy are not pleased and expect the nation as a whole to subsidize the higher costs they will have to pay for energy in the future.

This war between the states will be fought in the Congress and in the courts as each state presses for its own advantage.

Winners versus losers   The problem of energy winners and energy losers exists within the state as well, thus raising a third obstacle to the design of a state energy policy. While everyone in a state might agree with the need to conserve energy as well as the need to develop new supplies, the specific actions necessary to accomplish those ends might help some but harm others. A coal-rich state might, for example, demonstrate its commitment to coal through a policy to install coal-fired boilers in all of its prisons, schools, and other public buildings.

Coping with boom-town growth   In the 19th and early 20th centuries, cities and towns in the United States and Canada were formed overnight with little planning when a gold strike occurred, a copper vein was located, rich coal deposits were exploited, or an oil pool was discovered. The results too often were dingy company towns with little to commend them except the nostalgia of a few saloons.

But state and local governments have learned a lot in recent decades about orderly growth and public and private responsibilities. Craig, Colorado, is a small city that provides an example of rapid and effective response to an energy boom that includes coal mines and construction of a large power plant and a coal-to-methanol synthetic fuel plant. The following excerpts show how the city government dealt with both the negative and positive aspects of rapid growth.

Craig was a quiet ranching community in northwest Colorado with a diminishing population in the late '60s and early '70s. Then the energy boom, fueled by coal mines and power plant construction, started and Craig grew from a population of about 4,000 people in 1974 to 9,405 in 1977 to approximately 12,000 in 1981.

The city's budget grew from $883,000 in 1974 to $15,432,043 in 1981. Much of this increase was for capital projects.

The effects of rapid growth such as Craig has experienced, especially the negative effects, have been extensively examined, studied and documented. Some of these negative effects include a rise in crime, child abuse, suicides, mental problems and drug and alcohol abuse; the overloading of public and private facilities; a rapid increase in the price of housing, which tends to exclude people from the housing market; and alienation between the new residents and the old residents. The cost of food, clothing, and services also increased at a very rapid rate. The negative effects of the boom were and are especially hard on the elderly and others on fixed incomes.

While the negative effects of boomtown growth are well known, the positive impacts tend to be ignored. The basic economy of the community has been diversified from its dependence on agriculture. The Craig economic base has been broadened to include mining and its support industries, recreation, and retail shopping for a large part of northwestern Colorado. The additional growth has fostered more

diversified merchandise in the stores, new services, and cultural activities. The youth of the community are able to find employment locally and are not leaving the area. This has reversed in Craig a trend which is common to many rural areas.

One of the questions the city council is grappling with is, "What does the future hold and how will the city meet its demands?" The city, which presently has a 12,000 population, is expected to grow to about 20,000 by the end of the '80s.

The city is preparing for future growth now by constructing water and sewer plants capable of handling a population up to 30,000. Service levels and staffing are also being geared to that target population. One major problem facing the city is how to finance this growth. Unfortunately, the revenue derived from energy development does not accrue as fast as the expenses generated by energy impact. Combined with the fact that most facilities generating the impact are located outside the city's boundaries and do not add to the city's tax base, this causes serious financial concern. Therefore, Craig has adopted a policy of pursuing grants actively and is determined to pay for growth as we go and not incur a debt which will become burdensome to bear.

Source: Donald B. Cooper, "Coping with Boomtown Growth," *Colorado Municipalities*, Vol. 57, No. 4 (July-August, 1981), pp. 4–7. The photo shows the Colorado–Ute power plant.

The coal miners will be delighted, but natural gas utilities and petroleum suppliers will not be. In addition, environmentalists will object because of the probable increase in air pollution.

So-called lifeline utility rates illustrate another kind of dilemma faced by the energy policy maker. These rates are designed to ease the burden of high energy costs for the poor. Utility rates would be set so that the first units of energy, whether electric kilowatt hours or gas therms, would be very cheap and the next units substantially more expensive. The big users of energy, such as businesses or families with large homes, would pay more, thereby subsidizing the poor. As desirable as this may be socially, it raises the question of whether energy policy should be used explicitly as an instrument of social policy. If the poor cannot pay their energy bills, perhaps the subsidy should come from tax breaks or direct grants rather than by skewing utility rates to make one class of customers pay more than another for exactly the same commodity.

Another problem with lifeline rates is that the lower rates protect people from reality—rising energy costs—and therefore do not provide proper incentivies to conserve. In fact, the biggest single failing of national energy policy following the 1973 oil embargo was the decision to keep prices artificially low through price controls rather than allowing them to rise to world market levels. The result was that no one really believed there was an oil problem and, more to the point, did not act as if there was one by buying more efficient cars, homes, or equipment. Consumption patterns have followed energy prices—for example, when gasoline is expensive, more smaller cars are sold than when gas prices decline.

The use of income or sales tax incentives to encourage purchase of solar systems is another example of having one segment of the population subsidize another. Solar users will receive a financial gain from a tax incentive. Those who do not choose solar will subsidize those who do through their relatively higher taxes. Policy makers who want to use this technique will welcome the praise of those who gain, but they also must expect to reap the criticism of those who lose.

Lack of data A final obstacle to effective energy policymaking is the lack of reliable data. Knowing where energy comes from, how it is transported, and how it is used is essential information. The lack of a comprehensive data base is not too surprising since energy is only a recent addition to the public agenda. When environmental protection became an important public issue in the late 1960s, there was little known about the character and quantity or effects of environmental pollutants. It took a decade of research, model-building, and data-base development to understand the complexities of the problem. Similar amounts of time and money will have to be invested in the field of energy information.

Despite all these difficulties, the states clearly do have energy responsibilities, and by and large the states have recognized this fact and have acted on it.

Organizing for energy planning

The state energy agency—as distinguished from the public utilities commission or from such regulatory agencies as those governing mining—has emerged to address many of the energy responsibilities of the states.

Prior to 1973, no state had an energy agency in the sense that the term now is used; currently no state lacks such an agency. The federal delegation of some fuel allocation powers to the states in the mid-1970s prompted the forming of the first generation of energy offices. The states subsequently expanded the duties and resources of these units, in many cases integrating the energy functions into either natural resource or economic development agencies.

There are four distinct organizational categories into which state energy offices tend to fit:

Department/Agency: Both of these similar forms enjoy cabinet-level status, with the director and agency accountable to the governor. They are line-item agencies in the state budget. Usually there are energy advisory boards with members from the public and from other agencies and the legislature to provide guidance.

Commission/Council: Accountable to the governor, these forms are governing bodies whose members are appointed from the public or are directors of state agencies. In the case of the council, legislators also are members of the governing body, which develops policy positions and programs to be carried out by state agencies. Both require support staff.

Office: Housed in the office of the governor or the lieutenant governor, this form of state energy office is headed by an office director appointed by and directly accountable to the governor. Often the head and staff are not under civil service. This was a common model for early energy offices.

Division: These energy units are part of, and under the direction of, a larger state department, such as those responsible for planning, commerce or natural resources.

Whatever its form, the state energy office represents one of the resources available to the state energy planner. In many cases, the office director assumes the task of energy planning. Regardless of where the ultimate responsibility for preparing the plan lies, the quality of the work will depend in some measure on the resources which are tapped in the process. These resources include both the human and inanimate sources of information, advice, and counsel.

The planner is looking into a range of matters which affect every individual and, every economic sector within a state. The broader the participation and the more diverse the information base, the more likely the plan is to fully integrate the needs and concerns of the whole of the state.

The planner needs accurate information on energy sources and supplies indigenous to, and imported into, the home state. There must be an understanding of how and where those supplies move. This information cannot be secured from only one source; rather, it must come from a collection of energy suppliers, utilities, business associations, and regulatory agencies. Utility commissions, environmental agencies, mining and drilling regulators, geologists, and revenue departments typically hold vital pieces of information.

For information on energy use and needs, the planner can turn to industry associations, interest groups, and state business development agencies, among others, in addition to the sources already mentioned. Energy issues involve all sectors of the economy, including limited-income and elderly citizens.

Unfortunately for the planner, there are some real difficulties in applying the laudable principle of obtaining the greatest possible input and the most accurate possible information. The state of New York, for example, found that petroleum suppliers tended to focus on regional, rather than state, areas, in their planning and found that coal suppliers had little information on the state's future coal needs.

Citizen and consumer groups often lack the expertise or the funding necessary to prepare and present their concerns. Additionally, it may be difficult, as in the case of petroleum suppliers, to gather particular groups together because of ingrained reluctance to divulge information that might competitively aid others in the same business.

However, efforts should be made to seek input, advice, and criticism from as wide a body of representatives as possible both prior to and after initial planning efforts are undertaken. The state of New York, for example, held hearings before planning was begun and again after a first draft of the plan had been prepared.

Defining energy goals

As policy makers search for an energy program that suits their states, they probably will give careful consideration to four basic goals. Although the weighting and emphasis will vary from state to state depending upon a number of factors, these goals can be expected to be shared in common: (1) to encourage conservation, (2) to promote the development of indigenous energy resources, (3) to ease the public burden of rising energy costs, and (4) to prepare for energy emergencies.

What will differ significantly, however, are the strategies and actions chosen to pursue these goals. Each state's economic and social characteristics, climatic and geographical circumstances, and energy resources available for use will to some degree dictate which tools are selected to shape an energy future. The following discussion, therefore, will focus primarily on objectives and cite as examples some of the strategies or actions that have been selected by energy planners at the state level.

Conservation

There probably has been more misinformation about conservation than any other subject of the energy debate. The topic seems to generate strong passion from those who think it unamerican to drive small cars or from those who think conservation is the only way to create some sort of utopian society.

The available evidence suggests that conservation is an important element of energy policy and need not carry the dramatic overtones ascribed to it by those who have taken ideological positions either for or against conservation.

There really are three kinds of conservation, although the boundaries between them inevitably blur. The first category of energy conservation is deprivation: it is the conservation that occurs when people want energy but cannot get it.

During the summer of 1979 when gasoline supplies were short, people walked to work or shared rides in order to "conserve" gasoline. They were successful but not necessarily pleased. This kind of involuntary conservation is not a reasonable long-term public policy. No state should plan on shortages as a way to force conservation.

It is true that when supplies are short everyone should be encouraged to conserve, or even required to do so, in order to avoid further disruption. However, this kind of conservation should be seen for what it is: an emergency response measure designed to solve short-term problems rather than a permanent public program.

The second kind of conservation is the conservation of sacrifice or denial. In this instance members of the public are told to give up what they want, can afford, and could get because it is good for them or for the country to do so. Ultimately this kind of conservation will fail.

In the absence of any clear and present danger the public is unwilling to "freeze in the winter and roast in the summer" for some abstract notion of the public good. Indeed, some of the U.S. Department of Energy's past policies and former President Carter's rhetoric did more to give conservation a bad name than to advance its cause.

Conservation need not—and should not—be equated with the giving up of something. It should connote the intelligent and efficient use of a resource which is expensive and limited in supply. This is the third, and most appropriate form of conservation. Here we are talking about how to use less energy to achieve the same outcome. People need not sit home and freeze when they can enjoy a comfortable home with more insulation and a better heating plant. There is

---

The myth of superabundance The most deadly aspect of American life is the profligacy growing out of the persistent myth of superabundance. . . .

In the Cumberlands, where the frontier lingered for a long generation as a reality and for another century as an unfading folk memory, the myth of superabundance took deepest root. Even as the land was running out, the myth provided a psychic escape, and farmers clung to failing practices rather than shift to rejuvenative new ones. When mining superseded tillage the myth said the coal veins were "inexhaustible." This fallacy was shared by all segments of highland society, from barefoot boys in creekbank schoolhouses to coal tycoons in the airconditioned offices of giant corporations. The conventional notion held that there was so much it could be prodigiously wasted or destroyed at the whim of the "owner," and that no one should ever be held to account for an action taken against one's own "private property."

These exaggerated manifestations of the neo-frontier produced in the Kentucky hills land use practices so irresponsible as to border on the maniacal. In the shattered valleys and their flood-harried, dependent people we discern the disastrous consequences of unleashing mineral hunters as laissez-faire entrepreneurs armed with dominant and dominating "rights" and legal powers. If lessons are to be learned anywhere in American about this crucial clash and its deadly consequences it is here, and from the Cumberland experience the rest of the country should derive guidance in what to avoid if men and mines are to coexist. At the same time and from the same experience we can derive an understanding that resources remain finite and that, when the storm that tears them from the soil has passed, there still remain people to fashion lives amid the wreckage.

Source: Harry M. Caudill, *The Watches of the Night* (Boston: Little, Brown and Company, 1976), pp. 269–70.

no need to give up toast; rather there is a need to design more efficient toasters. Gasoline consumption is down in the U.S. because people are driving more efficient cars at more efficient speeds, not necessarily because they are driving less.

There are enormously wasteful energy practices in this country, and these practices should be "sacrificed" immediately—but in favor of better practices. We do not need overheated buildings or offices lit so brightly it hurts the eyes; or new buildings built with single-glazed windows and no insulation. Energy conservation that stresses efficiency and avoids waste should be a part of every state energy policy; sacrifice should not be welcomed.

There is an argument that conservation need not be a public policy since the market will take care of the problem. When prices rise, people will conserve. It is true that consumers respond to prices, but there are two reasons why a state needs to pursue a policy of conservation. First, government can provide the knowledge, advice, information, and assistance needed by those who want to conserve but do not know how. Second, government can remove legal obstacles that might discourage conservation. For example, in most states certain motor vehicle laws discourage company-sponsored vanpooling programs, and those laws can be amended easily to encourage this conservation practice.

It is important to recognize the different motivations that support a conservation policy. The federal government is interested primarily in conserving petroleum in order to reduce dependence on imports, which are causing serious balance-of-payments problems, contributing to deficits, and threatening our stability and security.

States, on the other hand, are more interested in conserving all forms of energy in order to strengthen the state economy relative to the economies of other states. Families that are spending their money to heat a poorly insulated home are not spending as much on shoes, movies, or anything else that would help support the local economy. Similarly, a business that fails to conserve energy may find its cost rising faster than its competitors' in a neighboring state. If this

Figure 18–5 The oil and gas boom in the 1880s made it possible for the streets in Findlay, Ohio, to be extravagantly lighted by natural gas. But the boom only lasted a few years as the wells quickly ran dry.

Sources of energy for the United States and Canda   There are only three *major* sources of energy for the United States and Canada: coal, petroleum, and natural gas. There are only two more *major* sources that offer potential for development: solar energy and nuclear energy.

Coal, petroleum, and natural gas are fossil fuels that are nonrenewable. Coal will be widely available for hundreds of years. Both petroleum and natural gas are in good supply as of 1984, but the future is incertain. Both could be extremely limited by the last half of the 21st century.

Coal is the major energy source for generating electricity and for heavy industry, but it is expensive to mine and transport, a major source of air pollution, and with strip mining, a destroyer of the landscape.

Petroleum, compared to coal, is easily extracted and transported and is an efficient energy source. It is, however, a major source of air and water pollution. With limited reserves in the United States and Canada, and an unstable political situation in the Middle East, petroleum is a questionable source for the long run.

Natural gas is easily extracted and transported and is clean and convenient to use. Assuming current usage, however, the limited reserves will be gone within a few decades.

Many held that solar energy is the wave of the future, but that depends on the kind of solar energy. Most of us link the term with various devices that capture, store, and convert sun rays to heat, but the term is broad in definition and also includes biological energy (the best known form is wood), hydroelectricity (water power), and other forms.

Wood is a renewable energy source, assuming forest management, selective cutting, and reforestation. Wood has a few small-scale applications, but it is expensive to extract and transport and is a major source of air pollution.

Water power is fine where available— the Pacific Northwest, the Tennessee Valley, and a few other locations. It is efficient and low in cost.

In the 1950s and 1960s, nuclear energy was considered the energy source for centuries to come. Developments to date, however, have been disappointing. It is expensive to set up

---

persists, the business will fail, putting yet another strain on the state's economy. A school system that cannot, will not, or does not know how to conserve will be paying more to out-of-state miners or Middle Eastern princes than to teachers for the young.

In summary, as the price of all forms of energy continues to rise, the state must pursue a policy of conservation, in part as its own contribution to national conservation goals, but mostly to protect its own citizens and the health of its own economy.

Energy development

The second of the goals most states will adopt in trying to gain some control over their energy futures is to develop indigenous energy resources. Here again, the economic arguments are compelling and the differences with policy are telling.

Every state recognizes that it is in its own economic self-interest to use local energy resources, and, where possible, to enter the export market. In the Midwest the resource might be alcohol fuels. Along the volcanic belt paralleling the West Coast, it might be geothermal. Much of the Northeast is turning to wood,

the facilities and difficult to convert the energy to electric power. It is controversial and widely regarded as dangerous.

The graph below shows the historic trends in energy usage in the United States from 1850 to 1975. Note that wood was the dominant source in 1850, to be succeeded by coal from the late 1890s to the early 1930s, and then by oil and gas. The incipient trend toward nuclear energy seemed, as of the 1980s, to be on hold because of long-term safety problems both in generating plants and at disposal sites.

Source: Abstracted from Martin Counihan, *A Dictionary of Energy* (London, Boston, and Henley: Routledge & Kegan Paul, 1981), and Michael J. Meshenberg et al., *Guidebook for Establishing a Local Energy Management Program* (Washington, D.C.: U.S. Department of Energy, 1982; available from National Technical Information Services). Chart from Meshenberg et al., p. 62.

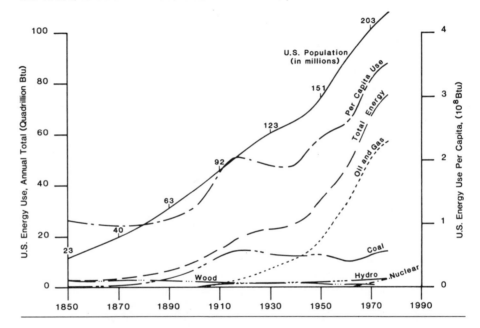

while the arid Southwest may be able to grow plants which yield oil substitutes. All states can to some extent develop solar energy, and many more can use wind.

A state that does not try to develop its own internal sources of energy will find more and more of its income going to support the economies of the energy-rich states. Alaska's good fortune resulting from the oil finds of recent years is well known: the wealth is so great that the state has eliminated its personal income tax, and there is a great debate over how to use the energy income. Alaska seems to be the luckiest in the energy sweepstakes, but others such as Louisiana, Texas, and Montana also are reaping rewards from their energy resources. Other states are not so fortunate.

In Illinois, for example, consumers were paying $100 million yearly in the early 1980s in the form of oil and coal severance taxes collected by other states. This figure is not the cost of the fuel, but the cost of the taxes; clearly, any development of indigenous energy resources in Illinois would help offset this drain on the state's economy.

Consumers, of course, will not switch to local energy supplies if they are more costly and less reliable. State governments, however, can do much to make local supplies more competitive. In the Midwest with its vast grain-growing capacity, many states have tried to stimulate alcohol fuel production by giving a variety of tax breaks to both consumers and producers. States also can help develop an energy source through research, technical assistance, and demonstration projects. Of course, the states are watching Congress to assure that the national policies favor their indigenous energy sources. As the nation realigns its energy system, every state will be pushing for its own self-interest—even if that is not congruent with national interests or policies.

Protection

A third common policy of the states will be one that tries to protect citizens and businesses from the negative effects of the changing energy picture. Higher energy prices have caused great pain and suffering in our society, and governments, including state governments, cannot be immune to the problem.

Stories about families having to choose between paying for food or fuel are quite real and more numerous than we would like to admit. The federal government has launched a variety of financial assistance programs to help low-income families in meeting their energy needs. The states, too, have tried to be responsive to the issue. Most states have reviewed their welfare service systems, provided emergency hotline telephone numbers for families unable to purchase fuel, rewritten the rules for cutting off utility service during winter months, given home insulation assistance to low-income families, and provide a variety of direct and indirect subsidies to pay energy bills.

But it is not only families who are suffering the effects of rising energy prices; businesses of all kinds are having to adjust. In particular, small underfinanced businesses as well as energy-intensive industries are being hit hard. For the most part the business community is coping on its own, but states would do well to help in order to protect their economic bases.

In designing policies to protect against the shock of higher prices, the state should keep in mind that these are welfare or income redistribution policies. As such they should be short-term in nature, designed to get through a transition period. If not, the programs will become permanent subsidies of energy costs which will distort responses to market trends. The best kinds of programs are one-time efforts that subsidize the costs of conservation; the worst are the continuous subsidies of monthly energy bills. The former will bring permanent and continuous benefits; the latter will place people on a self-defeating welfare program.

Emergency response

The fourth set of policies that will be common to the states will be those that deal with energy supply shortages or disruptions. Here the problem is one of preparing for an emergency.

Experience shows that energy emergencies can come in many different forms with different consequences for each. In just the last decade the nation has witnessed electrical system blackouts, coal strikes, oil import cutoffs, oil refinery fires, natural gas shortages, winters so severe they depleted energy stocks, and even the nuclear scare of Three-Mile Island.

Most experts agree that such energy emergencies will become rather more common than less. For most of this century, energy supplies were so abundant and cheap that emergencies were virtually unknown. Electric utilities at one time applied for rate decreases and had more than enough capital to finance reserve capacity. Oil companies once were not so dependent on foreign imports, and natural gas utilities had abundant supplies. Such security in our energy future can no longer be expected.

The states therefore must be prepared to respond to emergencies. They must review their legislation to see what authority they have to act in an emergency. They must establish data systems to see who supplies energy to whom and must build monitoring systems to provide early warning of impending emergencies. They must establish communications systems and be able to determine who in the state can provide assistance to whom. Finally, they must work with energy suppliers to determine when supplies are short and how one kind of supply can be substituted for another.

The states have employed a variety of means to conserve supplies which were available, allocate them fairly, and lessen the panic and chaos that accompanied shortages. The states in the nation coped, but in some cases barely. California, for example, was forced to allocate access to gasoline supplies in metropolitan areas during the 1979 event, setting an example that later was followed elsewhere in the nation. Motorists were divided into two groups, depending on whether their license plates ended in an odd or even number, and could purchase gasoline on alternate days. Essentially a means of quelling panic by cutting in half the length of lines which formed at service stations, the practice proved of doubtful merit but did challenge the ingenuity of motorists seeking ways around the restrictions and spawned a new part-time occupation— "line-sitting."

By the time the 1979 oil emergency occurred, most states had developed some type of contingency plans for dealing with emergencies. But the difficulties of contingency planning were illustrated repeatedly as unpredicted behavior, unexpected logistical problems, and unforeseen interstate communications failures persisted in occurring. These lessons have had to be incorporated in plan reviews and revisions.

But there are other constraints on state energy emergency planning, as well, and these pose significant challenges to the planner. Limits to state powers and authorities and reluctance to interfere in labor-management disputes serves as two examples. The state of Illinois, faced with a coal miners' strike, undertook careful negotiation with unions and employers to arrange for delivery of coal to provide heat for hospitals and homes where supplies had run out but stepped back from aiding industrial users of coal, for example. The state's contingency plan recognizes and discusses these limitations but leaves to each occasion the problem of deciding specific responses.

Emergency planning, at base, involves the attempt to foresee the widest possible range of potential situations and to extrapolate the consequences. This requires an understanding of how, where, and what energy is used, and from where it comes, as was discussed earlier. Then it is possible to determine what possible mitigating actions can be taken and to assign responsibilities.

Conclusion

The four goals which have been discussed here are common to virtually every state in the nation. Clearly, the specific strategies for attaining these goals will vary substantially from state to state. The state energy plan for one state may share goals with another state's program, but the implementing policies could be radically different or even contradictory. It is this variation that makes state energy planning so fascinating. There is no easy formula, and borrowing ideas from your neighbor may or may not add up to a viable national program.

Implementing energy goals

We now have explored the obstacles which can strain state energy policy making and have identified four energy goals common to most states. In this section we will examine the tools available to the states for achieving their goals. These tools are clustered into five categories: (1) tax incentives or disincentives, (2) the powers of the public utility commission, (3) regulations other than those imposed by utility commissions, (4) direct grants, and (5) advice, information, and technical assistance.

Taxes

In an age long since passed, taxes were imposed to raise revenues for government programs. Today, taxes are an instrument of social policy. They are imposed or reduced to achieve certain social purposes as well as to raise revenues. The system of taxation in this country is enormously complex with several layers of government taxing such things as property, goods, and services; labor income; and investment returns. The system constantly is being adjusted, not so much to generate new income as to make the economy function more effectively or to encourage some interest group to act differently by changing its economic circumstances. It is understandable that the nation's system of taxation would be looked upon as a means of altering energy production and consumption practices. Taxes are a powerful tool in shaping behavior and can help achieve goals, whatever they may be.

From a state point of view, we again confront the problem of reconciling federal action with state action. National policy, for example, should be designed to discourage petroleum consumption. One way to do this would be through some sort of rationing scheme. Another way would be to let the price rise, thus discouraging consumption. Decontrol may eventually have this effect, but it could be accelerated by taxing petroleum and driving its prices even higher.

When Congressman John Anderson was running for president in 1980 he proposed a 50-cents-per-gallon tax on gasoline as a way to reduce consumption. He further proposed that social security taxes be reduced by the amount generated by the gas tax, thereby protecting consumers from any increase in total taxes. There is considerable merit in former Congressman Anderson's proposal. Some variation of that idea may be enacted by Congress, but it is not an idea that can be adopted unilaterally by an individual state.

In general, energy consumption taxes are of limited value to a state, even though the nation as a whole should be taxing its nonrenewable resources in order to discourage their continued high rates of consumption. Whether or not the national leadership has the courage to take this step remains to be seen.

There is, however, much the states can do to shape energy policy through their tax structures even in the absence of a coherent federal energy tax policy. Principally, states can help encourage conservation and the development of renewable resources. These are more decentralized energy sources and therefore more subject to the influences of a state-imposed tax structure.

Prior to 1973 almost no state provided incentives for conservation or the use of non–fossil-energy sources. Since then, more than 40 states have adopted some type of tax change in order to encourage conservation and the use of renewable energy resources. The types of incentives fall into four main categories: (1) property tax reductions or exemptions, (2) sales tax exemptions, (3) income tax deductions, and (4) income tax credits.

Property tax exemptions are the most common form of state financial incentive. In most cases the exemption is for solar equipment. In some cases, the law provides that solar heating systems are to be assessed at no more than the value of a conventional heating system. The property tax exemption does not reduce the purchase price of solar equipment, but at least it guarantees the purchaser that there will be no tax penalty incurred as a result of his property improvement.

The sales tax exemption is increasingly popular, if somewhat symbolic. Since sales taxes are in the 3–8 percent range, an exemption is not likely to make much difference on large purchases, such as solar equipment.

However, the sales exemption (coupled with the elimination of gasoline taxes) does seem to have been a significant factor in encouraging the development of the gasohol industry in some of the midwestern states. Individual states give varying degrees of preferential tax treatment to gasohol, including waving state excise or sales taxes, or combinations. In Iowa, for example, the entire tax on gasohol in 1980 was only 3.4¢ per gallon, about 10¢ less than on regular gasoline.

Several states allow the purchaser of solar equipment to deduct the cost of the device from gross income when calculating income tax liability. This appears to be a cumbersome and not very effective approach to encouraging conservation or alternative energy development. Among the many problems is the fact that it favors those in the higher income tax brackets because they are the ones who itemize deductions and because the deduction is worth more to those in the higher income brackets. In addition, a consumer cannot really figure out his dollar savings at the time of purchase; he has to wait until tax time to see how much the savings amount to.

Tax credits are really much more effective than the tax deduction. Although the legislation is due to expire in 1985, the federal government allows a credit against taxes owed of 15 percent of money spent on conservation. One-third of the states have some kind of tax credit program for alternative energy devices or conservation investments. New York State, for example, created an additional 15 percent tax credit for solar equipment in 1981. Tax credits are equitable in the sense that they offer the same dollar savings to each user regardless of income. Additionally, they are simple to calculate at the time of purchase and are effective because they represent what amounts to a rebate on the purchase price.

It remains to be seen whether these kinds of tax incentives are really significant in promoting conservation or solar development, or whether they are mostly symbols of public support and encouragement. There have been stories of retailers raising prices in amounts equal to the available benefits. In addition, except for a few instances, the amount of savings is fairly small in comparison to the total cost of the product.

The decision to install insulation or an alternative energy device is a complex one and the initial cost of the device is only one part of the calculation. For major investments, the cost of borrowing money is usually more significant than any of the tax benefits that might be available; low interest rates could be a far greater incentive than most of the tax breaks currently available.

The four types of tax incentive packages described above do not in any way exhaust the possibilities for using financial incentives or disincentives. For example, license plate fees that are based on horsepower are a disincentive to buying big cars. Uniform fees, in contrast, provide no incentive for buying a smaller car. The list of possibilities is long, and a state that knows what it wants to accomplish would do well to look at all of its taxes, licenses, and fees to see whether they support or discourage the accomplishment of their energy goals.

Utility regulation

Public utility regulation is the most complex, controversial, and problematic aspect of state energy planning and management. One need only attend a rate hearing or read the testimony presented at a rate case to see how complex the subject really is. One need only read the daily newspaper to recognize how controversial it is.

Consumers are angry about rising energy costs. Utilities are faced with rising fuel costs, heavy capital investments, and a slowing demand for the product. The financial community is sending warning signals; bond ratings are dropping and investors no longer perceive utility stocks as the guaranteed blue-chip investments they once were. Finally, the state public utility commissioners are struggling to figure out what to do while the federal government hovers in the background trying to decide what, if anything, to do itself.

The times were not always so difficult. For most of this century, the public utility industry was one in which virtually everyone was a winner. Utilities across the country grew at an unprecedented rate as the nation's population and economy grew. As the utilities grew, they found that the unit cost of their product actually declined. As the cost declined, more and more people were using more and more of their product, thus contributing to more growth and more economies of scale which could be passed on as reduced costs.

The financial community viewed utilities as one of the safest investments possible. Utilities were a natural monopoly with their rate of return almost guaranteed by friendly state public utility commissions. The confidence of the financial market was an integral part of this happy time, since it provided utilities with ready access to investment capital at the cheapest possible rates.

The state public utility commissions were happy because they had little to do. Often their toughest assignment was to decide how much of a rate *decrease* they could give to utility customers. The customers never really complained because they were receiving efficient, reliable service at a very reasonable cost. It was clearly an American success story because what was good for the utility investor was good for the utility customer and vice versa.

All this began to change a few years ago. There is considerable debate as to the cause, or even the nature, of the change; but few doubt that the industry is going through a period of rapid and fundamental evolution. So important are these changes that more than one elected political leader has lost his job over his stand on a utility-related controversy.

If the interests of the stockholders and the customers are no longer congruent, that places public utility commissions in the middle of the problem, since it is their job to balance the competing interests of investors and consumers. Public utility is an art and a science. But mostly it is a political process. As the noted utility economist Alfred E. Kahn has indicated:

Governmental price fixing is an act of political economy, and, it bears repeating, this means that it necessarily and quite properly involves the striking of a balance between conflicting economic interests, influenced by political considerations in both the crassest and broadest possible senses, and informed by community standards of fairness.[1]

Since a utility does not operate in a free market, it is up to the utility commission to determine how much profit (or total earnings) a utility will make. It does this by establishing a rate base (RB) and a rate of return (ROR) on their investment. The relationship is as follows: Total earnings = RB × ROR.

The rate base is the dollar value established by a regulatory commission of a company's plant, equipment, and intangible capital used in serving the public. The rate of return can be any percentage figure that the commission determines. However, if the return is too high it will mean unnecessarily high costs to the consumer. On the other hand, if it is too low, the utility will not be able to attract investors, thereby depriving the utility of needed money for expansion, required maintenance, or both.

Since a utility's profit or total earnings can be increased by a rise in either the dollar value of the rate base or the rate of return, the commission scrutinizes very carefully what the utility puts into its rate base and questions any plans for expansion that might increase that base.

In theory, once the value of the rate of return and the rate base are agreed upon, the utility could be left alone to sell its product to its customers at a price that would cover its costs and earn the agreed-upon profit.

In practice, however, the utility commission further intervenes to stipulate the *rate structure*, that is, the prices the utility should charge to each class of its customers in order to get a fair rate of return. Electric utilities do not charge a uniform price for each kilowatt of electricity they sell. Instead, they charge different prices to different customer classifications and also offer reduced prices for buying in larger quantities.

In theory, the *price* charged each class of customer should be an accurate reflection of the *cost* to the utility of servicing that customer. As can be imagined, it is extremely difficult to attribute costs, which is why the arguments before commissions are so complex and protracted.

Determining rate schedules, rate of return, and components of the rate base are merely the tip of the iceberg for utility commissions. Volumes have been written on the subject, and it would serve no purpose to go into more detail here. However, it would be instructive to highlight two of the current issues since they illustrate the range of the problems faced by a public utility commission.

The first issue involves the fuel adjustment clause that most utilities now are permitted to include in monthly bills to their customers. This allows a utility to immediately recapture the cost of higher priced fuels without going back to the utility commission to ask for a rate increase, a process which usually takes months. For example, if the price of coal used to generate steam for electricity production goes up 10 percent, the utility may be able to pass all or most of that cost on to the consumer in the next bill. It sounds simple and equitable; however, the fuel adjustment clause does generate controversy. For example, some customers claim that by virtue of the automatic nature of the fuel adjustment clause, a utility will have little or no incentive to find the cheapest possible fuel.

In some Midwestern states, the fuel adjustment clause has opened up a bitter debate as to where the utility should purchase its coal. Some utilities, for example, import low-sulfur Western coal, even though their plants are close to vast amounts of higher-sulfur Midwestern coals. This has prompted state legislatures and utility commissions to propose that any utility using out-of-state coal not be allowed to pass on cost increases through the fuel adjustment clause; but if they used coal mined in the state, they could in fact use the benefits of the fuel adjustment clause. Utility rate making thus becomes the vehicle by which the state tries to promote the development of its coal fields. The utilities protest, arguing that the state should not be using its utility regulatory goals to pursue unrelated economic development goals.

A second issue for public utility commissions involves the controversy over construction work in progress (CWIP), a controversy which has been increasing for years. CWIP is the allowance added to a utility's rate base for the dollar amount of generating equipment under construction but not yet generating electricity. Utilities want their current customers to help finance plants that are being built for future use; customers want to wait until the plants are operating before they must pay for them.

The interest of utilities in getting CWIP in their rate base stems from the increasing difficulties they are having in financing new construction. Most utilities have serious cash-flow problems. In the early 1960s, electric utilities financed about 40 percent of their plant expansion through outside lending markets and the remainder through current earnings. Today, over two-thirds of all expansion funds have to come from the capital markets, and with interest rates higher than in the past, it is easy to see why the utilities want to add a little to everyone's current bill in order to assure them future plant capacity.

Opponents argue that they are financially "better off" by not paying for CWIP. They also argue that by allowing CWIP in the rate base, utility commissions will take away an efficiency incentive to complete plant construction expeditiously.

There also is an equity argument raised in CWIP cases: the elderly argue that they should not have to pay for something not yet built when they probably will not receive the benefits when they are produced. The same is true for customers who may move out of the service district.

Many public utility commissions are, in fact, allowing CWIP on a case-by-case approach where special circumstances can be used to justify it. The controversy, however, is far from over. The outcome will have a major economic effect on both utilities and customers.

The fuel adjustment clause and CWIP controversies are but two from a long list which includes such things as lifeline rates to subsidize the poor, how to treat taxes in the rate structure, who should pay for utility company advertising, and how much utilities should do to promote energy conservation.

All of this and more has thrust the state utility commission into the political limelight. Some commissions are rising to the challenge and doing everything they can to reshape the character of the entire energy system. Others are clinging valiantly to the notion that they are merely accountants and have little to do with the more complex social and environmental questions being raised by the consumers. In all probability, this latter group will be unable to resist the forces at work and will find themselves thrust into the middle of the energy debate.

Regardless of what a state government organization chart might look like, it is the state public utility commission that is the real energy office. Commissions, by virtue of their vast authority, will determine the rate at which solar, conservation, and alternative forms of energy are introduced into the state. They will determine the fuel mix a utility might use, and they will be responsible for the long-term economic health of the utilities as well as the availability and reliability of energy for the consumer.

Energy use regulation

In the course of one decade energy regulation proliferated enormously. Energy efficiency has been codified; certain energy uses have been proscribed, others required; and law which previously existed has been redrawn to incorporate energy considerations formerly disregarded or unrecognized.

State laws have been rewritten in the areas of housing, transportation, business, and agriculture; in many cases, the new laws force change, preempt discretion, and serve as the driving force in energy decisions for many classes of energy users.

The new laws range from vanpooling legislation, which may simplify this activity by dropping the requirement that the driver have a chauffeur's license, to building codes, which may prescribe in detail the construction materials and techniques to be incorporated in new housing, offices, hospitals, and factories.

Although some momentum had developed in the 1980s toward reducing regulation in general, there still is widespread concern that the marketplace alone cannot solve all of our energy problems. Despite the demonstrable fact that certain changes in energy matters are prudent and desirable, it also is a fact that we are burdened by resistance to change.

Experience suggests that state-mandated energy codes are the quickest way of making new buildings more energy efficient. Comparatively few communities have adopted such codes on their own, even though building codes traditionally have been the prerogative of local government in many states, and in any case community energy codes leave significant areas untouched.

The states are comfortable with regulating energy extraction activities, such as mining and drilling, but there is less precedent and experience in other areas. Most states have yet to pass regulations governing the collection of solar energy, for example. Ways have to be found to guarantee access to solar radiation or to treat the transfer of the right; windmill design, placement, and safety may require state attention; and consumer protection laws will need to be written or adapted.

Depending on the forms of energy used in a particular state, there will be different regulatory emphases. But the states' traditional roles of mitigating property disputes, guaranteeing access to common resources, and protecting consumers will be tested in new ways as energy circumstances change.

Thus more than a dozen states regulated solar access and easements by the early 1980s, which is consonant with the tradition of avoiding or settling property disputes, while California in 1980 was alone in having a rigorous energy-efficient building code which it had developed through a public hearings process.

Grants and subsidies

It often happens that the interests of society at large do not coincide precisely with the interests of particular segments of society, just as state and federal interests at times differ. It traditionally has been one of government's roles to reconcile such situations.

For example, subsidies have been paid to producers of goods which are necessary but whose production is unprofitable. In this area, the federal government has developed mechanisms for improving the business side of synthetic fuels manufacture, including price and purchase guarantees. There are instances in which the states may find it desirable to apply this principle in the area of energy, but the occasions probably will be somewhat limited by the fact of interstate trade—a state would not want to subsidize energy to be used in another state.

But when a state does determine that the best interests of its citizens on the whole are served by changing the way energy is used or by changing the form of energy which is used, the aggregate benefits may be accompanied by discrete disadvantage to some classes of energy users.

Grants offer one means of easing the costs imposed if a state concludes that a particular energy use sector should relinquish one form of energy in favor of another. The cost of new equipment can be offset partially on the grounds that the affected class of energy users would have had no cause to undertake the change in the absence of governmental dictate. In the event that a state mandated the use of solar energy in any newly-constructed housing, for example, it might be appropriate to offset higher construction costs through grants. The rationale would be that the buyers of the homes would, if left to their own discretion, have preferred to forego the added expense of the solar equipment. This class of energy users would be at a disadvantage, while energy users at large would benefit from reduced competition for supplies of conventional energy sources and would reap the added benefits later of improved solar equipment at perhaps lower prices. Application of this principle in the area of energy is not yet widespread at the state level, but it represents a potentially useful tool by which government can effect decisions which are not inherently of benefit to the individual energy user.

Currently the grant and subsidy programs that exist in the states tend to follow the pattern of Wisconsin, which offers a 15 percent rebate on the cost of solar equipment (the rebate is not tied to the tax system); or that of Illinois, which has a $70 million Coal and Energy Development Bond Fund used to provide grants as part of the funding package for research or demonstration in coal and alternative energy technologies; or that of Maine, which offers $400 rebates to purchasers of solar hot water systems.

However, many state officials are reluctant to institute such grant and subsidy programs as part of their energy programs because they see such financial aid as income transfers or a sort of welfare program. The issue here is much the same as the utility service issue, where conservation aid and payment of utility bills for limited-income consumers are feared to be counterproductive in various ways. The energy planner must balance the competing concerns if such grants and subsidies are to be used effectively, and if the technique is chosen must be prepared to face resistance.

Advice and information

Setting energy policy is but the first, and perhaps easier, step for the state to take, for energy users will not act in the desired ways if they do not know both why and how. Most states have in the past few years created energy agencies of one sort or another; these bodies usually focus much of their efforts on the spreading of information.

The Minnesota Energy Agency, for example, was formed in 1974 when that state's government decided Minnesota energy users needed more accurate information to cope effectively with the existing energy circumstances. The agency sends personnel out to business, industry, agriculture, and the communities to present the state's energy policies, to give advice, and to provide technical assistance. There are staff experts in energy conservation, alternative energy technologies, and consumer protection, among other areas. Although these endeavors are not unlike those found in other states, Minnesota's energy programs are tailored to the conditions which exist in Minnesota. They reflect the forms of energy used in the state; the climate; the range of economic activities pursued; and the standard of living.

A state's energy circumstances help shape state energy policies, which then define the character of the state's energy programs. Thus, content and emphasis should and do vary from state to state.

A state which obtains most of its energy in the form of petroleum reasonably could be expected to stress energy conservation with great emphasis. Expert help would be provided to homeowners, business firms, and commuters who want to use energy more efficiently, since such a state logically would perceive conservation as a necessary first step to remedying its energy problems. If it were practical for the state to ease its oil dependence by shifting to other forms of energy, such as coal or alternative energy resources, the state's government could be expected to direct energy agencies to focus resources and activities toward this area as well. Indeed, the actual responses in states with such energy circumstances do tend to fit this pattern. Vermont, for example, aggressively promotes energy conservation and urges the adoption by energy users of wood, solar, water, and wind systems, all of which are available options in Vermont, given its resources and character.

However, persuasion and assistance are most useful in situations where relatively rapid action and comparatively easy responses are possible—conservation, for example, and in some cases fuel switching. The states increasingly are finding it necessary to go a step beyond and commit resources to efforts which may not bring a rapid return. Energy reseach is one such area.

Utilities in a state may be willing to convert oil-fired boilers to coal when those boilers originally were designed to burn this fuel and if the cost is perceived as reasonable. But while a state may be able to stimulate this response through persuasion and perhaps the provision of some type of technical assistance, it well might have to do far more to guide the utilities into adopting coal-derived synthetic fuels or advanced coal-combustion technologies. The state might find it necessary to carry out development and demonstration of the applicable technology in partnership with the utilities.

It is widely accepted that state government has a responsibility to provide services to its citizens, to offer protection where possible. But the movement by many states into energy research and development represents a significant extension of the traditional role of the state.

University-based applied research has, of course, long been supported by state government. However, a growing number of states have created research funds which may be granted to the private sector. It is not unusual for research grants to be distributed to the very classes of energy users who will most directly benefit from the products of the research.

The motivation for this kind of state initiative may be easily perceived on one level: development of an energy technology particularly suitable to an individual state may yield benefits which outweigh the associated expenditure of public funds. Other, less apparent stimuli play a part as well: if the development of new technology stands to benefit the broad elements from which the state is composed, there may at the same time be a significant risk of failure. In this case it is appropriate for the risk to be shared through the office of the state. The state of Kentucky has created an Energy Development and Demonstration Trust Fund of $55 million as a means of stimulating research in technology areas that otherwise might be neglected or pursued at a slower pace in the absence of state support. Much of the emphasis is on energy advancements which involve coal or otherwise meet needs basic to that state.

Conclusion

State energy planning is less than a decade old. In a few short years, all 50 governors had an established energy office to analyze and plan for their states' energy futures. The events of this tumultuous period have kept the planners slightly off balance as one crisis blurred into another and governments tried one instant solution after another.

The energy planner has faced two major petroleum shortages and two national coal strikes. Natural gas once was treated as a fuel on the way out; now we have a glut. The price of all energy rose at an unprecedented rate, higher than the already high rates of inflation. Families had, in some instances, literally to choose between food and fuel. The accident at Three Mile Island scared nearly everyone and further delayed construction of nuclear power plants. Synthetic fuels were seen as *the* answer, but they no longer are. State energy planners listened as one President said that the energy struggle was the "moral equivalent of war" and to yet another who said there is no energy problem that the marketplace cannot solve. The only thing one could expect during these years was the unexpected.

Generalizing about this period is, of course, difficult, and predicting the future of state energy planning is even more of a risk. One thing is clear, however: the function of state energy planning is here to stay. It might be downgraded, rearranged, or renamed, but someone in state government will continue to be concerned with the problems of energy consumption, production, availability, and cost. The amount of state wealth spent on energy is far too great to be ignored, and the effect of rising costs on the citizens of the state is too significant to be left only to the workings of a marketplace. State energy planning does, in fact, have a future.

1 Alfred E. Kahn, *The Economics of Regulation: Principles and Institutions* (New York: John Wiley and Sons, 1971), Vol. 1, p. 42.

19 Environmental protection

Recent years have seen a major growth in environmental protection programs at all levels of government. Congressional legislation created many of these programs, but the states also adopted environmental legislation on their own initiative. These new programs have enlarged the role of state and regional planners in environmental protection.

This chapter examines the state and regional role in state and federal environmental protection legislation. Federal legislation covered includes the National Environmental Policy Act (NEPA), the Clean Air and Water Acts, and the National Coastal Zone Management Act (CZMA). The chapter also considers state legislation which establishes state and state-approved controls for the protection of natural resource areas.

The governmental interest in environmental protection

An awakening environmental movement took form in the late 1960s and spurred new government programs in which state and regional agencies play leading roles. Many observers believe that 1969 was an important transitional year. A series of environmental events, including a serious oil spill off the California coast at Santa Barbara, focused attention on environmental problems. A key national commission also reported early in 1969 on the need for national coastal legislation. Congress authorized a series of major federal environmental programs in the years that followed.

The first of these new environmental statutes was the National Environmental Policy Act (NEPA) enacted late in 1969.[1] NEPA addresses a problem environmentalists considered serious in federal programs—the lack of attention environmental issues were receiving in federal agency decision making. NEPA corrected this problem by requiring all federal agencies to prepare environmental impact statements for all major federal actions significantly affecting the environment.

Federal programs had been weak or nonexistent in other areas of environmental concern. No federal coastal zone management program existed prior to enactment of the National Coastal Zone Management Act in 1972.[2] Enactment of the CZMA reflected congressional concern that state participation in coastal management was necessary in order to protect coastal resources. The congressional response in the CZMA was a federal coastal management program which provided a major role for the coastal states.

Pollution control also received congressional attention during this period. The weak federal pollution control programs in effect during the 1960s proved inadequate. Congress left their implementation primarily to the states, which were unable and unwilling to carry out the congressional mandate. Congress responded in the early 1970s with tougher clean air and water acts.[3] These acts placed explicit pollution control responsibilities on the states, strengthened the federal government's role, contained important technology-forcing requirements, and imposed strict pollution cleanup deadlines.

The miners' environment in the north of England As you walk through the industrial towns you lose yourself in labyrinths of little brick houses blackened by smoke, festering in planless chaos round miry alleys and little cindered yards where there are stinking dustbins and lines of grimy washing and half-ruinous w.c.'s. The interiors of these houses are always very much the same, though the number of rooms varies between two and five. All have an almost exactly similar living-room, ten or fifteen feet square, with an open kitchen range; in the larger ones there is a scullery as well, in the smaller ones the sink and copper are in the living-room. At the back there is the yard, or part of a yard shared by a number of houses, just big enough for the dustbin and the w.c. Not a single one has hot water laid on.

The majority of these houses are old, fifty or sixty years old at least, and great numbers of them are by any ordinary standard not fit for human habitation. They go on being tenanted simply because there are no others to be had. And that is the central fact about housing in the industrial areas: not that the houses are poky and ugly, and insanitary and comfortless, or that they are distributed in incredibly filthy slums round belching foundries and stinking canals and slag-heaps that deluge them with sulphurous smoke—though all this is perfectly true—but simply that there are not enough houses to go round.

Source: George Orwell, *The Road to Wigan Pier* (New York: Berkeley Publishing Corporation, 1961), pp. 53, 54. Originally published in England in 1937.

The need for national uniformity in environmental programs also explains the new wave of congressional activity in this period. Pollution controls affect economic and development opportunities. Competition between states for new development could lead many states to adopt weak controls in the hope of attracting new industry. The national pollution control statutes eliminate this opportunity by providing uniform pollution control standards applicable nationwide.

Congress considered national uniformity less essential in environmental programs, like coastal management, which govern important but localized environmental resources. The national CZMA contains a set of national coastal management policies but allows the states to determine their own implementation policies in state coastal programs.

During this period, many states also adopted environmental resource protection legislation not related to federal programs. States with critical environmental areas pioneered in this development, and many states adopted legislation protecting inland and coastal wetlands and floodplains. Through voter initiative California and Washington adopted coastal legislation before the national CZMA was adopted.

This introduction shows that environmental protection legislation serves a number of purposes. Much of this legislation is intended to prevent environmental degradation. Environmental impact statements (EIS) prepared under NEPA disclose the impact of governmental action on environmental resources. The CZMA funds state coastal programs intended to protect coastal areas. State wetlands and floodplain legislation prevents environmental degradation through strict controls over development in these environmental areas.

The national Clean Air and Water Acts prevent degradation of the air and water environment through controls that reduce air and water pollution to tolerable public health limits. These programs focus on pollution control as an environmental problem.

Environmentalism and social issues A social reform movement is still needed to alleviate major twentieth century health problems. But many environmentalists fail, at least publicly, to see to the *social* ramifications of their work. For this reason, the response of minority communities to environmentalism is usually disinterested or disdainful. Environmentalism is often perceived by minorities as a predominantly conservative force, a movement which reverses natural resources and ignores the human problems of black, red, brown and yellow people. Too often, environmental reforms have been focused inordinately on wilderness preservation, while inner city children who suffer from elevated blood lead levels and resulting neurological damage and death, have hardly received commensurate attention.

Environmental groups, even those who are involved in conservation, can improve their effectiveness and broaden their constituencies by engaging also in struggles that directly improve the quality of life in urban settings. Municipal services, sanitary conditions, housing and community problems, as well as urban health difficulties, are environmental issues. . . . Environmental measures can improve garbage collection, reduce lead levels, control the number of rats, and at least curb the high incidence of diseases associated with air and water pollution. Yet even these changes are contingent on changing attitudes and institutions that affect low income, inner city minority communities.

Source: Ellen Hall. *Inner City Health in America* (Washington, D.C.: Urban Environment Foundation, 1979), p. 3.

The role of planning

The role of planning in environmental protection programs varies. The environmental impact statement required by NEPA provides a comprehensive full disclosure of the environmental impacts of government projects and programs. This comprehensive environmental review resembles the review of problems and issues carried out in the comprehensive planning process, especially since NEPA covers urban as well as natural environmental impacts. Like comprehensive plans, the environmental impact statement also considers alternatives.

NEPA's environmental review differs from planning in that it simply discloses the environmental impacts of the government action and does not produce a policy. The environmental impact statement also is prepared for individual projects at the proposal stage. These projects often reflect commitments made earlier in the planning process. The environmental impact statement also is limited to individual projects, although federal agencies must consider their cumulative impacts. They must also prepare "program" impact statements on groups of related projects.

Coastal management planning that provides coastal policies to be implemented in state coastal programs is the heart of the coastal management program. Water quality management planning required by the Clean Water Act is likewise intended to produce policies that guide the implementation of the water pollution control program. The Clean Air Act does not contain a comparable comprehensive planning program but does require a transportation control planning process. Transportation controls adopted in that process are intended to reduce dependence on the motor vehicle for transportation.

Figure 19–1   The environmental impact statement must deal with impacts on the total environment, not just on the project interest, for example, transportation in this drawing.

Environmental control options

Federal environmental protection legislation either requires a review process which considers environmental impacts but does not apply environmental standards, or enacts standards that limit environmental degradation. NEPA's environmental impact statement requirement illustrates the environmental review process. Government agencies need only consider the environmental impacts of their actions in their impact statements. No standards in NEPA determine the outcome of this environmental review.

The Clean Air and Water Acts differ from NEPA because they provide air and water quality standards which polluters must achieve. There are two types of standards. One type imposes limits on the amount of pollution allowable in the air and water. A second type limits the amount of pollution produced by individual polluters. The relationship between these two types of standards varies in the two programs. The Clean Water Act relies principally on standards applied to individual polluters. The Clean Air Act makes compliance with air quality standards the dominant pollution control technique.

Implementation measures also are necessary to assure compliance with standards adopted in environmental protection programs. Permit requirements are the implementation technique these programs usually employ. The Clean Air and Clean Water Acts require permits for new and existing sources of pollution. State coastal management legislation frequently requires permits for new development to assure compliance with state coastal policies, and permit requirements are common in state wetlands legislation.

Environmental permit programs differ from the implementation techniques commonly used in land use controls, such as zoning. Zoning establishes land-use districts for compatible land uses. It employs some administrative techniques, such as the zoning variance, but the local governing body authorizes most land-use changes through legislative amendment of zoning district maps. Zoning should and in some jurisdictions must be consistent with a locally adopted comprehensive plan. Environmental permits ensure compliance with statutory environmental standards and may not implement the policies of a comprehensive plan.

The federal environmental programs also make use of federal financial assistance to achieve environmental protection goals. As compared with federal permit programs that directly apply environmental standards, federal influence in assistance programs is indirect. Federal assistance is made available to state and regional agencies if they comply with federal statutory program requirements.

The national coastal zone management program illustrates a federal environmental program which relies on federal assistance to achieve environmental protection objectives. There are other examples of federal environmental assistance programs. The Clean Water Act provides federal assistance for water quality management planning as well as federal funding for wastewater treatment systems.

Federal environmental legislation providing financial assistance necessarily confers considerable autonomy on state and regional agencies. In the CZMA, for example, Congress indicates the federal policies the states must implement, but the states enjoy considerable autonomy in defining the content of state programs.

Federal agencies exercise more control over those assistance programs that fund state or regional projects. An example is the federal program for funding wastewater treatment plants. The Environmental Protection Agency (EPA) which administers the Clean Air and Water Acts must approve federal statutory policies for treatment plants through its control of the federal funding process.

State and regional roles

Most federal environmental programs contemplate an important role for state and regional agencies. Some federal legislation which does not appear to include these agencies, such as the National Environmental Policy Act, can also apply to their programs. NEPA's environmental impact statement requirement applies under the statute only to federal agencies, but it also includes state and regional projects which have a "federalizing" link. Federal financial assistance for a state or regional project may provide a federalizing link. State highway projects receiving federal aid are one example. NEPA also authorizes impact statement preparation by state-wide agencies such as state highway agencies. The federal agency must independently evaluate the impact statement the state agency prepares.

Under the Clean Air Act, each state must prepare a State Implementation Plan (SIP) containing the control strategies it intends to use to meet the national air quality standards. States may adopt any mix of control strategies, including controls on existing sources of pollution, provided these strategies achieve compliance with the national air quality standards. Regional planning agencies and the states also select the transportation controls to be included in Transportation Control Plans, subject to review by the federal Environmental Protection Agency.

EPA can delegate the authority to administer the Clean Water Act's permit program for water polluters to the states, but the states must apply federal water pollution control standards. A number of states exercise this permit authority. State and regional agencies also have the responsibility to develop management policies in the water quality management planning process. These policies include the management of nonpoint sources of water pollution, such as agricultural and urban runoff.

States participating in the coastal zone management program adopt and must implement coastal plans through state controls. Regional agencies may participate in the coastal management planning process.

Control of state and regional performance

NEPA does not have a specific statutory compliance mechanism. The federal Council on Environmental Quality (CEQ) is authorized by presidential Executive Order to adopt regulations implementing the environmental impact statement requirement in the Act. Federal agencies are expected to adopt EIS regulations which comply with CEQ regulations, but CEQ cannot compel compliance.

Environmental impact statements are subject to challenge and review in the federal courts. Liberal judicial "standing" rules adopted by the U.S. Supreme Court allow environmental organizations and other interested parties to challenge impact statements if they do not comply with statutory requirements.[5] The federal courts have adopted a "hard look" doctrine under which they carefully scrutinize the content of environmental impact statements.[6]

State and regional authority under the Clean Air and Water Acts is delegated to state and regional agencies subject to federal supervision and review. Under the Clean Air Act, EPA reviews and must approve all state implementation plans and may prepare an implementation plan if the state plan is inadequate. EPA may enforce state implementation plans which are inadequately enforced. It may also bring direct enforcement actions against air polluters, although enforcement against polluters is also a state responsibility.

Under the Clean Water Act, EPA may withdraw its delegation of water pollution permit authority to the states if they do not comply with federal statutory requirements. It may also review state permits and may issue a permit if a state does not comply with its review decision. EPA may also review and revise state water quality standards.

Funding sanctions also are common in federal environmental programs. Withdrawal of federal assistance and termination of a state coastal program for unsatisfactory performance is the principal sanction available in the coastal management program. There is no provision for federal assumption of state program responsibilities if a state program is terminated.

Funding sanctions also are available under the Clean Air Act. Federal grants for highway projects may not be made in air quality regions which fail to achieve the national air quality standards. This restriction prevents highway construction that may increase air pollution by increasing motor vehicle use. Other funding sanctions include a statutory restriction that prohibits a regional transportation agency from approving any project which does not comply with a state air quality implementation plan.

The degree of federal supervision over state and regional participation in federal environmental protection programs clearly varies with the nature of the authorizing legislation. Although CEQ can issue regulations to implement NEPA's environmental impact statement process, the federal courts have the ultimate review authority. Judicial review is the primary method through which the environmental impact statement requirement of NEPA is enforced. The federal courts frequently must decide whether an impact statement must be prepared. They also review the adequacy of impact statements. Their review of adequacy can be more deferential, as a court may defer to the agency's judgment on what an impact statement should include.

Federal review powers are limited in federal assistance programs. Federal agencies are reluctant to incur the administrative and political costs necessary to a decision terminating a federal assistance grant for inadequate state or regional performance. Federal agency review of state and regional performance also is difficult to carry out. It requires second guessing state or regional agency actions and decisions which are often complex and discretionary. Termination of federal assistance for inadequate performance is difficult when federal legislation, such as the Coastal Zone Management Act, confers considerable autonomy on state and regional agencies.

Federal supervision is easier to accomplish under the Clean Air and Water Acts. They authorize the delegation of federal authority to the states subject to withdrawal for failure to comply with federal statutory requirements. EPA has exercised its authority to prepare state implementation plans. It prepared plans containing transportation controls when California and other states refused to adopt controls which met the Act's requirements.

This experience did not have a happy ending. EPA ultimately went to court to enforce the state plans it prepared. Some federal courts ruled that EPA did not have the statutory authority and probably did not have the constitutional power to bring this litigation.[7] The funding sanctions in the Clean Air Act now provide an alternative method of federal enforcement.

The NEPA environmental impact statement

The statutory requirements in NEPA for the preparation of environmental impact statements are straightforward. Federal agencies must prepare environmental impact statements on all of their major actions significantly affecting the human environment. This requirement applies to the projects and programs of state and regional agencies when there is a "federalizing link."

NEPA's requirement that federal agencies consider environmental impacts in their impact statements supplements the statutory authority which confers program responsibilities on these agencies. As one federal court put it, NEPA requires a balancing process which weighs the environmental costs of agency actions against their benefits.[8] This requirement does not mean that federal agencies must elevate environmental factors above others they consider. The U.S. Supreme Court held that NEPA only requires an agency to "consider" environmental impacts in its decision making process.[9] The statute does not require an environmentally preferable result.

Important statutory exemptions to NEPA limit its applicability to environmental protection programs. All actions taken under the Clean Air Act are exempt by statute from the EIS requirement. The Clean Water Act exempts most actions taken under that legislation. Important exceptions are the provision of federal assistance for a wastewater treatment plant and EPA approval of a permit for a new source of water pollution. These exemptions reflect the assumption that action taken to implement the Clean Air and Water Acts generally has positive effects on the environment. There is no NEPA exemption for the national coastal management program.

NEPA clearly requires federal agencies to consider the impact of their actions on the natural environment. Some federal courts have also required federal agencies to consider the impact of a project on regional growth and development, as well as the impact of a governmental action on problems of preservation and decay in urban areas. In one case, a California city challenged a decision not to file an impact statement on a new federally funded highway interchange intended to serve a planned industrial development.[10] The court held that an EIS was required, noting that the interchange would create secondary, growth-inducing environmental impacts which clearly fell within NEPA. These impacts included possible detrimental effects on the city's controlled growth policy. They also

The environment, legally The act of Congress that established the Council on Environmental Quality in 1969 charged that body with reporting annually on the condition of "The major natural, manmade, or altered environmental classes of the Nation, including, but not limited to, the air, the aquatic, including marine, estuarine, and fresh water, and the terrestrial environment, including, but not limited to, the forest, dryland, wetland, range, urban, suburban, and rural environment."

Source: National Environmental Policy Act of 1969 (P.L. 91-190, Title II, Sec. 201)

included a rapid increase in population, which would create a demand for residential and commercial development and the beginning of urban sprawl. Demand for city services would increase, but the industrial development creating this demand would not be taxed to provide for these services because it was not within the city's jurisdiction.

In another federal court decision, the U.S. Postal Service decided not to file an impact statement on the relocation of a major postal facility from downtown Rochester, N.Y., to a nearby suburb.[11] The court held that an EIS was required. It noted that the relocation of the facility would "contribute to an atmosphere of urban decay and blight, making environmental repair of the surrounding area difficult if not infeasible."

A state or regional plan which is federally funded may or may not be a federal action requiring an impact statement. State coastal management plans require an EIS. The Clean Water Act exempts water quality management plans from the EIS requirement. Regional transportation plans raise more difficult problems. These plans are federally funded, but federal funding of the planning process is not a federal commitment to specific transportation projects. In addition, the regional planning agency determines regional transportation planning policies. One federal court cited these characteristics of the regional transportation planning process to hold that a regional transportation plan for Atlanta, Georgia, did not require an EIS.[12]

Federally funded projects within a region may be so interrelated that they require a "program" impact statement considering their environmental impacts on a regional level. The U.S. Supreme Court considered the need for program impact statements in an important case arising out of the federal coal-leasing program in the Northern Great Plains region.[13] While the Court did not require a program impact statement in that case, it did indicate that "when several proposals . . . will have cumulative or synergistic environmental impact upon a region . . . their environmental consequences must be considered together." Federal court decisions have applied this requirement. One court required an environmental impact statement for all of the projects in a regional mass transit system.[14] Other federal courts have refused to accept impact statements limited to a small segment of regional highway and similar projects. In one case, a court required an impact statement for a regional beltway in Richmond, Virginia.[15]

A large number of states have enacted state environmental impact statement laws, most of them modeled on NEPA. The state laws apply directly to the programs and projects of state and sometimes regional and local agencies. Some of this state legislation covers state and regional plans and planning programs. A California court interpreted that state's EIS law to require an EIS on a regional transportation plan.[16] Regional facilities, such as airports, also require environmental impact statements under state NEPA legislation.

In a few states, such as California and New York, the state NEPA laws apply to private development approved in the land use control process. These state

NEPA laws add an environmental review to the planning, zoning, and similar requirements contained in state land use control legislation.

Like NEPA, the state EIS laws also add an environmental dimension to programs and actions of state and regional agencies which have an environmental impact. State and regional agencies must consider the environmental consequences of their actions under the state EIS law even though their enabling legislation does not specifically include this requirement. Another important problem under the state laws is the application of the state EIS requirement to environmental programs intended to protect the environment. Legislation in California exempts state programs from the EIS requirement if they provide an equivalent of the environmental review required by the EIS law.[17] Like NEPA, most of the state EIS laws do not require an agency to cancel or modify an action or program solely because of adverse environmental impacts disclosed by the impact statement.

The air quality program

The National Ambient Air Quality Standards (NAAQS) provide the criteria for the air quality improvement program mandated by the national Clean Air Act. EPA adopts air quality standards for air pollutants it designates, such as sulfur oxides and particulates. These standards must be achieved within Air Quality Control Regions designated by EPA throughout the country. Metropolitan areas, including bi-state metropolitan areas, usually are designated as a single Air Quality Control region.

One set of air quality standards applies to stationary sources of air pollution. An industrial plant is an example of a stationary source. Another set of air quality standards applies to mobile sources of air pollution. Automobiles are an

Figure 19–2 This coal-fired power plant is an example of a stationary source of air pollution. To improve area air quality, states must control pollution from a variety of sources, mobile as well as stationary, and balance future pollution from new sources against reductions in pollution from existing sources.

example of a mobile source. The Clean Air Act mandates specified reductions in air pollution from automobiles and other motor vehicles over a stated period of time.

State air quality agencies adopt state implementation plans subject to EPA approval. These plans are not plans of the usual type. Instead, they provide a control strategy that will achieve and maintain the NAAQS in all of the Air Quality Control Regions in the state. The major control strategy in the state plan is a schedule of air pollution reductions for existing stationary sources.

Planning and land use controls

Except for the transportation control planning process, the Clean Air Act does not authorize a planning and land use control program. The Act did originally authorize EPA to require land use controls in state implementation plans. Congress has now withdrawn this general land use control authority.

EPA utilized its land use control authority in the original Act to require controls over "indirect" sources of air pollution. An indirect source is a major development, such as a shopping center, which does not pollute the air directly. It contributes to air pollution problems by creating congested motor vehicle traffic conditions. EPA controls would have remedied this problem through a variety of techniques, including requirements for highway and public transit improvement.

Congress has prohibited EPA from requiring the states to adopt indirect source controls. States may adopt these controls voluntarily, but few are expected to do so. EPA may still require indirect source controls for federal and federally funded projects, such as highways.

A related provision in the Clean Air Act allows EPA to disapprove or modify a federally funded wastewater treatment plant if it will contribute, directly or indirectly, to a violation of the national air quality standards. This provision covers air pollution from indirect sources. An example is a treatment plant providing treatment facilities for a major shopping center which will create traffic congestion.

Nonattainment area controls and emission offsets

The Clean Air Act originally included a short deadline for compliance with the national air quality standards. The states did not meet this deadline. Practically all of the metropolitan Air Quality Control Regions are presently nonattainment areas which have yet to achieve the air quality standards for at least one pollutant. The Clean Air Act requires a program in state implementation plans to bring these areas into compliance with the national air quality standards by a designated date.

The Act requires "reasonable annual progress" toward the attainment of the standards. This phrase means that the states must achieve annual reductions in air pollution sufficient to attain the national air quality standards by the attainment date. New stationary sources of air pollution may not obtain permits in nonattainment areas unless a statutory "emission offset" requirement is met. A new source permit can be granted only if air pollution from the new source and all other sources is sufficiently less than what it was before the permit was granted to show "reasonable progress" toward attainment of the national air quality standards. In practice, this requirement means that new sources of air pollution in nonattainment areas must bargain with existing sources to reduce air pollution from these sources. The new source will usually finance the cost of the technology needed to reduce air pollution from existing sources. The offset program provides a method of allowing new economic growth without weakening the air pollution control program. When the national air quality standards are attained, the state must maintain compliance through suitable measures.

Successful implementation of the nonattainment area compliance program is critical to the success of the national air quality program. Pressure to modify this program may be substantial if nonattainment area controls limit the economic growth of metropolitan areas. Congress would then face difficult choices that may require modification of the air pollution cleanup goals of the Clean Air Act.

Transportation control planning

Many air quality nonattainment areas do not meet the national standards because of pollution from motor vehicles. The Clean Air Act attacks this problem through two strategies. One is the gradual reduction in air pollution from motor vehicles through technological controls applied to the engine. Substantial reductions have been achieved, although Congress may eventually increase the allowable levels of pollution. The reduction in pollution from motor vehicles will be substantial, but its effect on achievement of the air quality standards depends on a number of factors which are difficult to evaluate. For example, a continuing growth in the number of motor vehicles would offset the reduction in motor vehicle emissions.

The second strategy for the control of motor vehicle pollution is the Act's transportation control planning process. The objective of this process is to reduce motor vehicle air pollution by reducing vehicle miles traveled. The states must also adopt inspection and maintenance programs for the catalytic converters installed on motor vehicles to reduce air pollution.

Congress delegated the transportation control planning process to regional planning agencies and councils of government. When possible, these agencies should also be authorized to carry out the regional transportation planning required by the federal highway act. Coordination of transportation planning under the Clean Air and federal highway acts is required. The transportation control planning process produces a transportation control plan which is part of the state implementation plan.

State and regional agencies may select transportation controls for their transportation control plans from a list included in the Clean Air Act. The list includes controls such as exclusive bus lanes, control of on-street parking, and carpooling. It omits controversial controls such as gas rationing.

Nondegradation

Many rural and undeveloped areas in the nation presently enjoy an air quality which is better than that required by the national standards. The Clean Air Act requires nondegradation controls that limit the additional air pollution allowable in these areas. The Act refers to these controls as controls for the prevention of significant deterioration in air quality.

The Clean Air Act creates three classes of nondegradation areas. Additional increments in air pollution allowable in these areas are most restrictive in Class I and least restrictive in Class III areas. No increase in air pollution is allowable which will violate the national air quality standards. The Act initially classified all nondegradation areas in the Class II category, except for certain national parks and similar areas permanently restricted to Class I. States, which are expected to administer the nondegradation program, can reclassify any area except Class I restricted areas to Class III. Although the statute places virtually no limitations on state reclassifications to Class III, this authority has not been used. The nondegradation program has not yet restricted economic development, but may eventually do so as air pollution increments are used up in nondegradation areas.

The air pollution increments allowable in nondegradation areas impose an air pollution quota on new development. States allocate this quota through a permit requirement for specified major new stationary sources of air pollution. They can decide how to allocate the quota among permit applicants, but usually approve permits on a first-come, first-served basis. New stationary sources also must install the best available control technology for air pollution control.

Summary

The Clean Air Act legislates a number of interrelated control strategies intended to meet the National Air Quality Standards. Because all sources of air pollution emit all of the pollutants covered by the national standards, the effectiveness of any one of these control strategies determines how much compliance the other strategies must achieve. A weak transportation control plan, for example, requires more stringent controls on stationary sources of pollution. No mechanism in the Clean Air Act allows consideration of these trade-offs. They must be made by the state and regional agencies that administer the air quality program.

State and regional planners must also be aware of the growth management implications of air quality controls, which have a major impact on the growth and development of the states and their metropolitan regions. In the federal system, the pollution control programs have statutory priority. The Clean Air Act prohibits any less stringent state or regional controls on air pollution. This prohibition applies to the air pollution controls required for nonattainment and nondegradation areas.

The water quality program

The water quality program adopted by the Clean Water Act is intended to accomplish specific statutory water quality goals. These include the elimination of all pollution discharges into the waters of the United States, protection of fish and wildlife, and provision for recreational water use.

The Clean Water Act has two major components. One is a locally matched federal assistance program for the construction and improvement of publicly owned wastewater treatment plants. Treatment plants receiving federal funding must provide for the treatment of effluent discharged into receiving waters at treatment levels specified in the federal legislation. Industrial polluters may either send their effluent to treatment plants or discharge it directly into receiving waters.

The second component of the Act is a permit program for new and existing industrial pollution sources which discharge effluent directly into receiving waters. The permit program applies effluent limitations adopted by EPA for these new and existing sources of water pollution. EPA initially administers the permit program, but may delegate administration to states that meet qualifying statutory standards.

The states must also adopt water quality standards for waters within the state. Unlike the Clean Air Act, the Clean Water Act does not require attainment of the water quality standards but they are enforced through statutory implementation measures.

State and regional water quality management planning   The Clean Water Act also includes a combined state and regional quality management planning program. The planning program provides water quality management policies that govern federal grants for treatment plants as well as permit decisions in the permit program. A council of governments or regional planning agency usually carries out the planning program in areas, usually metropolitan areas, which have serious water quality problems. The water quality management plans have been prepared and approved by EPA.

States adopt water quality standards as part of their water quality management plan. EPA approves and may revise the state standards, which must include a policy prohibiting the nondegradation of existing water quality when this policy is necessary to protect water uses under existing water quality standards. The states must adopt more stringent effluent limitations when they are needed to achieve the water quality standards. The state must also assign maximum daily pollution loads for receiving waters whenever this measure is necessary to achieve the water quality standards. This control limits the size and location of water pollution sources by setting maximum daily limits on the amount of pollution they can discharge.

The water quality management plan must include a regulatory program, and this program must provide for the "control or treatment" of all sources of water pollution. This and other language in the Clean Water Act may require land use controls over new development but they have not usually been adopted.

Both the state and regional planning programs must also include controls over "nonpoint" sources of pollution. Nonpoint sources are sources such as agricultural, stormwater runoff, forestry, and construction activities that create water runoff which carries pollution into receiving waters. Controls over nonpoint runoff pollution sources may require "best management practices" often applied at the runoff site. Retention basins that hold polluted water until sediments and other pollutants settle are one example.

Water quality management plans must also consider and provide measures for the control of groundwater pollution. These measures can include the control of on-site septic tanks and population densities to avoid effluent overloads that may impair groundwater quality.

The water quality management plan must identify "management agencies" to implement its programs. A municipality or a special governmental district, for example, is usually responsible for the construction and operation of wastewater treatment plants. Local governments administer most regulatory controls, although the states may develop others, such as erosion controls for nonpoint sources. The effluent limitation permit program also is a state responsibility. Regional agencies could adopt land use and other regulatory controls, but they generally do not have the authority to do so.

A number of problems limited the effectiveness of water quality management planning. EPA did not initially give the program a high priority; it was delayed because of federal funding problems; and the statute provided for a short planning period. Many planning agencies also had data problems. Few plans addressed all of the required statutory elements; few considered land use control problems; and most did not deal adequately with management structures. The plans came too late to be useful in federal funding decisions for treatment plants in the early phase of the Clean Water Act program.

Many water quality management plans concentrated on nonpoint sources, which are a major source of water pollution in many areas. Effective control of nonpoint pollution sources will require innovative state and regional controls, such as erosion controls on new development and comparable controls on farming and other agricultural activities. These controls are still in a developmental stage.

The federal grant program for treatment plants and collector systems

Widespread needs for publicly owned wastewater treatment facilities led Congress to authorize a massive program of federal grants for the construction and improvement of these facilities when it adopted the Clean Water Act in 1972. The program has achieved substantial accomplishments, but it has suffered from funding delays and administrative complexities. There also have been continuing controversies on issues such as the need for advanced levels of wastewater treatment, the cost-effectiveness of publicly owned treatment systems in small communities, and the acceptability of ocean dumping as an alternative to treatment for coastal cities. Publicly owned treatment plants also have lagged behind industrial polluters in their compliance with the Clean Water Act's effluent limitation standards.

One important issue of concern to state and regional planners is the effect of the federal grant program on urban growth in the undeveloped areas of metropolitan regions. The Act originally contained a provision that authorized federal funding of "reserve capacity" in treatment plants. Studies showed that the availability of reserve capacity stimulated excessive low density growth in undeveloped areas. Congress has now eliminated federal funding for reserve capacity. The Clean Water Act also requires EPA to adopt cost-effectiveness guidelines for the federal funding of wastewater treatment plants. EPA has applied these guidelines to limit the growth-inducing effects of these plants.

Summary

The implementation of the water quality program has seen some gains in controlling water pollution. While publicly owned treatment works have lagged behind, industrial polluters have taken major steps to comply with the federal effluent limitation standards. Congress set a multi-year deadline for full compliance. Controversy still continues on issues such as the level of pollution reduction which justifiably can be mandated and the absolute "no pollution" goal the Act adopts. The Act also does not have a fully effective program for the control of groundwater pollution, which is a growing problem.

The coastal zone management program

Seventy-five percent of the nation's population will live within 50 miles of the coasts by the year 1990. This population growth will create strong pressures for development which may limit public access to the coast and destroy the natural values of coastal environments.

The National Coastal Zone Management Act of 1972 is a response to this need to protect coastal areas. The key feature of the Act is a program of federal financial assistance for state coastal management planning and the implementation of federally approved state coastal plans. The Act also authorizes a federal assistance program for the acquisition of estuarine sanctuaries and contains a financial assistance program for states whose coastal areas are affected by energy facility development.

State participation in the federal coastal program is voluntary, but practically all of the coastal states, which include the Great Lakes states, are participating. Participating states have completed the planning phase of the program and have moved into the implementation stage. Federal funding for the program is in doubt.

The national coastal legislation delegates policy making and plan implementation for coastal areas to the states but does not enact specific coastal management policies. The federal statute contains a set of congressional policies which were expanded by Congress in its 1980 amendments to the Act. These policies include the protection of significant natural systems, such as wetlands and beaches; priority consideration for coastal-dependent uses; and orderly processes for siting energy and other major facilities. These policies provide guidance for state coastal programs but give the states considerable autonomy in developing their coastal plans.

The planning program authorized by the CZMA requires the preparation of a state coastal management plan for land and water uses in the coastal zone as well as planning for coastal resource protection, energy facilities, and shoreline erosion. The federal legislation gives the coastal states considerable latitude in defining the coastal zone covered by the state coastal program. Some states include all of their coastal counties, while in others the coastal zone is a narrow strip of land adjacent to the sea.

State coastal management plans are not land use plans of the conventional type. They usually contain an elaborate set of state coastal policies that govern land and water uses within coastal areas. Some coastal states adopted coastal legislation containing the state policies. In a few states, such as California, local governments must translate statutory coastal policies into local land development plans approved by the state coastal agency.[18] State and local coastal permits may also be required for land development within the coastal area, and state coastal policies also apply to state and local government programs.

The most important implementation technique required by the CZMA is the use of one or a combination of three "means" of state control. These include direct state control, local implementation subject to state criteria and review, and state administrative review of "state, local, or private plans, projects or land-use regulations."

The CZMA also requires two selective state control measures modeled on the state-level land use controls authorized by the American Law Institute's Model Land Development Code.[19] State coastal programs must ensure "that local land and water use regulations . . . do not unreasonably restrict or exclude land or water uses of regional benefit." Other provisions in the CZMA require the preservation or restoration of coastal areas "for their conservation, recreational, ecological, or aesthetic values."

Another important 1980 amendment encourages the states to prepare "special area management plans." These plans are defined as plans for resource protection and reasonable coastal-dependent growth. They must contain standards and criteria to guide public and private land use.

These controls are intended to prevent exclusionary local land use regulations and to protect areas in coastal zones which present especially critical environmental protection problems. Valuable coastal marshlands which are vulnerable to development are one example.

Unlike the national air and water quality acts, the CZMA does not require designation of a single state agency to administer the state coastal program. States need only designate a state coastal agency to receive and administer federal coastal management grants. In practice, many states distribute coastal management authority among a number of state agencies as well as local governments in the coastal area, a technique known as "networking." Networked state coastal programs usually rely on existing laws applicable to coastal areas and do not include new coastal legislation. Wetlands legislation, which is discussed in the next section, is an example. The state relies on the networked laws to satisfy the CZMA's requirements for state coastal controls. The CZMA does not require the enactment of new state coastal legislation.

Intergovernmental relationships

The CZMA gives state coastal programs a statutory supremacy that modifes the traditional supremacy of federal legislation and programs. "Federal consistency" provisions in the CZMA require federal assistance grants to state and local governments to be consistent with state coastal programs. They also require federal agency activities "directly affecting" the coastal zone to be consistent with state coastal programs "to the maximum extent practicable." Federal agencies may not approve licenses and permits in coastal zones which are inconsistent with state coastal programs, but federal agencies need not approve a development which a coastal state has approved.

Requirements in the national Clean Air and Water Acts are an exception to the federal consistency provisions. They are binding on state coastal programs.

These sweeping state consistency provisions are modified by other provisions in the CZMA which to some extent retain and establish federal authority. A congressional finding that there is a "national interest" in the coastal zone has been interpreted to require state coastal programs to consider the national interest in a number of facilities and natural resource areas. This requirement means only that a coastal state must "consider" the national interest in a federally regulated energy facility, such as an electric power plant. If the state refuses approval of the energy facility, this decision is binding under the federal consistency provision.

The federal consistency provision has created considerable controversy, as federal agencies object to this "reverse preemption" of federal authority. One important controversy concerns the application of the federal consistency provision to offshore leasing for oil and gas exploration, which is authorized by the Department of Interior. The U. S. Supreme Court held that the federal consistency provision doesn't apply to the leasing process, but does apply to exploration and production. Congress may reverse this decision.

State coastal programs also modify intergovernmental relationships between the coastal states and their local governments. The CZMA authorizes state review of local land use decisions as a "means" of state control. The exercise of this authority by coastal state agencies would displace local authority over land use in coastal areas. Some coastal states adopted legislation authorizing the review of local land use decisions by a coastal agency, but local governments in many states successfully resisted this assertion of state authority. The national coastal agency has accepted less threatening methods of enforcing state coastal policies as an acceptable "means" of state control. The enforcement of state coastal policies through judicial action by state officials is one example.

All state agencies that exercise jurisdiction in the coastal zone must comply with state coastal policies. State agencies often resist this requirement, and compliance with state coastal policies is difficult to achieve in networked coastal programs in which there is no enforceable compliance mechanism. Governors in some states have adopted executive orders in an effort to achieve state agency compliance with state coastal policies.

State coastal programs

State coastal programs take a number of forms. In states where the coastal program is "networked" it brings together a number of existing laws applicable to coastal areas. These laws include extensive coastal development permit statutes in force in some states, such as the New Jersey Coastal Areas Facilities Review Act.[20] This Act contains a permit program for development in the coastal area, including housing, manufacturing, and electric power generation. The Act also provides for a planning program which has been used to carry out the planning process required by the CZMA.

A few states enacted comprehensive coastal legislation intended to carry out the requirements of the CZMA. Most notable among these is the California Coastal Act of 1976, the successor to the earlier interim coastal permit law adopted by voter initiative.[21] The California Coastal Act adopts basic goals for the coastal zone and amplifies them through an extensive set of coastal policies based on the California coastal plan.

Local governments in the coastal zone are to prepare local coastal programs to implement the statutory coastal policies. Local coastal programs include a land coastal plan with maps indicating land uses allowable in the coastal zone together with zoning ordinances and other implementing actions. Once the state coastal agency approves a local coastal program, the local government must approve a permit for all development in the coastal zone in addition to any other development permit authorized by law. Local permits for some development, including development within 300 feet of the sea, are appealable to the state coastal agency.

North Carolina enacted comprehensive coastal area legislation in its Coastal Area Management Act, which applies to all 20 of the state's coastal counties.[22] Local governments in the coastal zone must prepare a land development plan implementing guidelines for the coastal area adopted by the state coastal agency. The state coastal agency approves all local plans. This agency also designates Areas of Critical Environmental Concern within the coastal zone, a control technique contemplated by the CZMA.

All development within critical areas requires a permit. Major developments require a permit from the state coastal agency. Local governments issue permits for minor development, subject to an appeal to the state coastal agency. Development outside critical areas is subject to local control, consistent with local land development plans.

Summary

The National Coastal Zone Management Act was expected to create effective, federally funded state programs for the protection of coastal environments. While the national coastal program has produced many accomplishments, weaknesses in state programs and delays in their adoption and approval have brought criticisms from environmentalists and others concerned about the protection of coastal environments. Coastal-dependent developers, such as the energy facility industry, complain that coastal programs are too stringent.

State coastal programs also have been caught in a crossfire between powerful federal agencies that object to the federal consistency requirements and entrenched local governments that object to the assertion of state authority in coastal areas. The coastal program does not have enough defenders. It occupies a weak position in federal and state bureaucracies. Its successful continuation will require greater state and national commitment and public support.

State wetlands and floodplain legislation

Many states have independently addressed problems of environmental protection in "sensitive" environmental areas. Some of this legislation covers wetlands—transitional marshy areas between the land and bodies of water that have important natural and ecological functions. Another group of states has pioneered in establishing state regulatory programs for floodplains.

Wetlands legislation

Wetlands are valuable for a number of reasons. They preserve water quality by filtering pollutants and sediment, provide natural habitats for fish and wildlife, and provide recreational opportunities. State wetlands programs are intended to restrict development in order to protect the natural functions of wetland areas.

States have enacted regulatory programs for both coastal and inland wetlands. These statutes follow a common model. There usually is no formal planning program for wetlands control, but the statute usually defines wetlands and authorizes a designated state agency to map wetlands areas. The statute authorizes the state agency either to regulate wetland uses directly or to establish standards for regulation by local governments.

Owners of land in wetlands must apply for and receive a development permit. The statutes provide standards for these permits that allow the regulatory agency to review development applications on a case-by-case basis. Statutory criteria in wetlands legislation may authorize the state agency to balance a number of factors when deciding whether to issue development permits, including the effect of the development on the natural values of the wetlands area. Some statutes, such as the Connecticut statute, require an environmental balancing process similar to the one NEPA requires in environmental impact statements.[23] Applicants for permits may usually appeal permit decisions to an administrative agency and ultimately to the courts.

There have been several constitutional challenges to wetlands statutes, which can severely limit development in wetlands areas. Owners of wetlands property in these cases have argued that the statutory restriction on development in wetlands legislation is so severe that it is an unconstitutional "taking" of property without compensation.

Most state courts have upheld wetlands legislation in these cases. Some court decisions recognize a public interest in the preservation of wetlands and characterize their development as a harm to the environment which the state may constitutionally prohibit.[24]

The federal "dredge and fill" permit program

The national Clean Water Act contains a program regulating "dredge and fill" activities in the waters of the United States which the courts have extended to wetlands areas.[25] This program requires permits for the dredging and filling activities in wetlands which are necessary to development. This program is under the jurisdiction of EPA and the U.S. Army Corps of Engineers.

Federal dredge and fill permits must be consistent with state coastal zone management programs in the coastal states, and the state wetlands law often is one of the laws "networked" in a state coastal program. Delegation of federal permit authority to the states also is authorized by the Clean Water Act for inland wetland areas. States exercising this delegated authority must meet specified federal statutory requirements.

Floodplain legislation

Floodplains are another vulnerable environmental area in which governmental regulations prohibit or limit development. Most floodplain regulation is at the local level, and the National Flood Insurance Act of 1968[26] significantly increased the extent of local regulation. This Act requires local floodplain regulation before development located in the floodplain can be eligible for federal flood insurance. The Act contemplates land use controls to regulate development in floodplain areas.

While floodplain regulation is a local responsibility in most states, several states have enacted state floodplain laws. State floodplain legislation follows the pattern established by the wetlands legislation. Some states regulate development directly in floodplains designated under state law. In other states, the state law authorizes local floodplain regulation under local ordinances approved by the state floodplain agency under statutory criteria. State courts have upheld both state and local floodplain regulations challenged as an unconstitutional taking of property.

Conclusion: coordination, deregulation, and revision

Environmental protection legislation confers important program, planning, and regulatory responsibilities on state and regional agencies. This legislation differs from comprehensive planning and land use control legislation because it implements specific environmental protection objectives. The Clean Air and Water Acts, for example, contain a set of planning, development permit, and federal financial assistance programs intended to achieve federal air and water quality goals. State coastal management programs funded by the National Coastal Zone Management Act contain more conventional planning and development control elements in states which have enacted comprehensive coastal legislation. These programs serve the environmental objective of coastal protection by balancing the need for coastal development with the need to preserve coastal areas.

State and regional planners should recognize that environmental protection programs provide an important environmental overlay on state and regional planning and program responsibilities. This environmental overlay, such as NEPA's environmental impact statement requirement, may only require an environmental review process for state and regional plans and projects. Other environmental programs, such as some state coastal management programs, contain development permit requirements which provide an effective veto over development at state and regional levels.

Environmental protection legislation of this type creates what is known as a "double veto" system. New development may be vetoed both by local governments exercising traditional land use control power and by state agencies exercising environmental permit controls. Often a development project will require several permits from several different states and agencies.

Double veto systems and planning and regulatory overlaps among environmental protection programs create serious problems of coordination. Federal legislation and federal agency initiatives achieve some degree of coordination, but the responsibility for coordination rests at the state and regional level. Some states have enacted permit simplification programs and permit simplification is a program objective in the national coastal act. There also have been joint air and water quality planning programs at the regional level, and the combined regional transportation planning programs should produce a coordinated planning effort for transportation problems. Much remains to be done to integrate environmental protection programs and to coordinate these programs with related state and regional planning and control initiatives.

Coordination is not the only problem the environmental movement must consider. As environmental programs have matured, critics have argued that they overregulate the environment and place unnecessary restrictions on economic development. Critics urge Congress to reconsider the cost-effectiveness of environmental controls, and to modify controls that limit new development opportunities. Despite these pressures, opinion polls also show continuing strong public support for environmental protection programs.

The deregulation debate is likely to continue. Proposals have been made, for example, to limit nondegradation areas under the Clean Air Act to the pristine national parks and other federal land reserves. Congress may also cut back on the pollution reductions mandated by the Clean Air and Water Acts. Because the environmental protection programs have a major impact on land development patterns, the deregulation issue is especially important to planners.

1   42 U.S.C. §§ 4321–47.

2   16 U.S.C. §§ 1451–64.

3   Clean Air Act, 42 U.S.C. §§ 7401–7642; Clean Water Act, 33 U.S.C. §§ 1251–1376.

4   State and regional agencies designated as "Clearinghouses" review federally assisted projects.

5   *Sierra Club* v. *Morton,* 405 U.S. 727 (1972).

6   See Rodgers, "A Hard Look at Vermont Yankee: Environmental Law Under Close Scrutiny," 67 Geo. L.J. 699 (1979).

7   *Brown* v. *EPA,* 566 F.2d 665 (9th Cir. 1977).

8   *Calvert Cliffs Coordinating Comm.* v. *AEC,* 449 F.2d 1109 (D.C. Cir. 1971).

9   *Strycker's Bay Neighborhood Council, Inc.* v. *Karlen,* 444 U.S. 223 (1980).

10 *City of Davis* v. *Coleman,* 521 F.2d 661 (9th Cir. 1975).

11 *City of Rochester* v. *U.S. Postal Service,* 541 F.2d 967 (2d Cir. 1976).

12 *Atlanta Coalition* v. *Atlanta Regional Comm'n.,* 599 F.2d 1333 (5th Cir. 1979).

13 *Kleppe* v. *Sierra Club,* 427 U.S. 390 (1976).

14 *Inman Park Restoration, Inc.* v. *Urban Mass Transportation Admin.,* 414 F. Supp. 99 (N.D. Ga. 1975), aff'd , 576 F.2d 573 (5th Cr. 1978).

15 *Thompson* v. *Fugate,* 347 F. Supp. 120 (E.D. Va. 1972). Compare *Indian Lookout Alliance* v. *Volpe,* 484 F.2d 11 (8th Cir. 1973); *River* v. *Richmond Metropolitan Auth.,* 359 F. Supp. 611 (E.D. Va.), aff'd, 481 F.2d 1280 (4th Cir. 1973).

16 *Edina Valley Ass'n.* v. *San Luis Obispo County and Cities Area Planning Coordinating Council,* 67 Cal App. 3d 444, 136 Cal Rptr. 665 (1977).

17 Cal. Pub. Res. Code § 21100.

18 See California Coastal Act of 1976, Cal. Pub. Res. Code §§ 30000–30900.

19 American Law Institute, Model Land Development Code, Art. 7 (1975).

20 N.J. Stat. Ann §§ 13:19–1 to 13:19–21.

21 Cal. Pub. Res. Code §§ 30000–30900.

22 N.C. Gen. Stat. §§ 113A–100 to 113A–128.

23 See Conn. Gen. Stat. §§ 22a–28 to 22a–35.

24 E.g., *Just* v. *Marinette Co.*, 56 Wis. 2d 7, 201 N.W. 2d 761 (1972).

25 33 U.S.C. § 1344.

26 42 U.S.C. §§ 4001–4128.

20 Solid waste management

Ever-increasing quantities of waste, soaring costs of equipment and labor, tightening environmental standards, problems in finding sites technically suitable for landfills, and growing public opposition to the siting of any kind of waste-handling facilities are among the factors combining in recent years to make solid waste management (SWM) considerably more difficult and expensive to carry out than in the past. One result has been that planners at regional, state, and federal levels have been called upon to play an increasing role in addressing SWM-related concerns that traditionally have been considered the responsibilities of local governments (for municipal wastes) or the private sector (for industrial, agricultural, and other wastes).

Planning at the regional level was first encouraged by federal legislation in the mid-1960s, largely to promote greater efficiency in the use of available resources by participating communities. Advantages were seen to include the availability of larger geographical areas in which to find suitable disposal sites, the potential for achieving economies of scale, and the resulting possibility that fewer sites would be needed overall. On the other hand, it was recognized that transportation costs would be likely to increase (making the introduction of transfer stations worthwhile in some places); furthermore, even if they had the will, localities might not always have the authority to participate in a regional system and (perhaps most importantly) it might be difficult to find communities willing to act as "receptors" for the region's wastes.

Amendments to the federal legislation in 1970[2] shifted the primary emphasis somewhat from the safe and efficient disposal of waste to the recovery of resources. Again, regional planning was encouraged, with a particular view to promoting large-scale, centralized resource recovery and the development of regional markets for recovered products. As before, however, the initiative for undertaking planning or other activities under the federal legislative provisions had to come from the communities or groups of communities involved, and participation was decidedly patchy across the country.

Volume of solid waste

Municipal solid waste (residential, commercial, and institutional sources) amounted to about 130,000,000 metric tons in 1976, enough to fill the New Orleans Superdome from floor to ceiling, twice a day, weekends and holidays included. Per capita generation amounts to 1,300 pounds a year. By 1985, the yearly total is projected to increase to 180,000,000 tons.

With the passage of the Resource Conservation and Recovery Act of 1976 (RCRA),[3] planning was ostensibly elevated to a more significant role. Prior to this time, there had been no provision for direct regulation of SWM activities under federal legislation; rather, these activities had been regulated indirectly inasmuch as they posed threats to public health or to air or water quality. However, RCRA included provisions for the development of state programs incorporating regulatory controls on solid waste disposal, and the state planning

Definition of solid waste   The term "solid waste" means any garbage, refuse, sludge from a waste treatment plant, water supply treatment plant, or air pollution control facility and other discarded material, including solid, liquid, semisold, or contained gaseous material resulting from industrial, commercial, mining, and agricultural operations, and from community activities, but does not include solid or dissolved material in domestic sewage, or solid or dissolved materials in irrigation return flows or industrial discharges which are point sources.

Source: Solid Waste Disposal Act (P.L. 94-580), 1980.

requirements in Subtitle D of the Act were intended partly as a vehicle for the states to demonstrate their commitment to the necessary action. The Act specified that no federal funds for SWM activities would henceforth be given to states not having a duly approved plan.

With federal assistance, most (though not all) states have proceeded to prepare plans that seek to conform to the federal guidelines.[4] In some cases they have been able to draw on plans already prepared under preexisting state legislation; for example, a 1972 act in California[5] required SWM planning at the county level.

Although the federal guidelines provide for the review of a state plan (by the state) not less frequently than every 3 years, with revision and readoption where necessary, it is not clear at this time how many of the states will proceed to a formal "second round" of planning (assuming that they complete the first one) since federal assistance, except for hazardous waste management, has been essentially eliminated under the Reagan administration. It seems probable that SWM planning will continue most actively in those states which have long appreciated the benefits of planning in general. Others may be less inclined to follow up on their present efforts now that the federal pressure to do so has been drastically curtailed.

There are, however, many difficult solid waste–related problems that cannot be solved by neglect, and the advantages to states of maintaining a strong SWM planning function may become increasingly evident in the future. After a discussion on who is likely to do the planning and the importance of citizen participation, this chapter examines a selection of the major issues that planners are, or might be, called upon to address.

Responsibility for planning

Responsibility for SWM planning at the state level typically falls within a branch either of the health department (as, for example, in Virginia) or, if one exists, of a resources or environmental protection agency (as in Wisconsin). Occasionally, planning responsibility is split between two departments, although one is likely to take the lead; for example, the California State Solid Waste Management Board (in the Resources Agency) is coordinating its state's overall SWM planning effort, while the health department has special responsibility for hazardous waste management planning. Where the responsibility falls may be significant in determining the direction of policy and the setting of priorities. Thus a health department is likely to have protection of health as its primary concern and may emphasize the provision of a safe, efficient collection and disposal service, whereas a resources or environmental protection agency may be more concerned about possible impacts on natural resources and the environment and may give higher priority to reducing the rate of waste generation and to resource recovery.

Whichever is the lead agency at the state level, much of the detailed input

Some basics about solid waste In 1970, paper in its many forms—boxes, newspapers, magazines, cartons, and the like—made up 37 percent of all municipal refuse. The other large parts of solid waste by ratio were food wastes, 20 percent, and yard wastes, mostly tree branches, grass, leaves, and shrub trimmings, 14 percent. Glass made up 10 percent; metal, 8 percent; and wood, textiles, and other materials, the remaining 11 percent.

A forecast was made in 1970 that there would be a 70 percent increase in municipal solid waste by the year 2000 with the largest increases expected for paper products and plastics.

Solid waste collection, transport, and disposal is labor-intensive and very expensive. Labor makes up 70 to 80 percent of the total cost in most jurisdictions. Such costs can be offset in a few places by recycling, salvage, and generation of heat, but the economies for most local governments are to be found in three other methods: (1) educating citizens to use relatively small containers, bundle branches and yard waste, bag garbage and other waste in plastic or strong paper bags, and place waste at the easiest point (usually the curb) for collection; (2) developing collection routes that are as cost-effective as possible in relation to street patterns, location of disposal sites, traffic conditions, topography, and other transportation factors; and (3) exploiting recent advances in mechanization and automation of collection equipment, including side loaders, batch loaders, continuous loaders, oversized containers, transfer stations, pipeline transportation, compacting mechanisms, and rail loading systems

Source: Abstracted from Walter R. Niessen, "Properties of Waste Materials," in David Gordon Wilson, ed., *Handbook of Solid Waste Management* (New York: Van Nostrand Reinhold Company, 1977), pp. 17–20, and from William S. Foster, "Refuse Collection Practices," in William S. Foster, ed., *Handbook of Municipal Engineering and Administration* (New York: McGraw-Hill Book Company, 1978), pp. 13-2 to 13-7.

for planning and the primary responsibility for implementation is likely to rest at the local or possibly the regional level; indeed, it is an important function of the state plan to firmly establish which responsibilities lie at which levels (and with which particular agencies). Furthermore, it is likely to be an important component of state programs to assist the substate agencies in carrying out their responsibilities, for example, by providing needed authority, technical and financial assistance, etc.

Citizen participation

In the past, the subject of SWM did not attract a great deal of public attention. It appears that most people were content to see their waste taken "out of sight—out of mind." If a public hearing was mandated by law for the establishment of a solid waste facility, such as a landfill, the announcement was often found in the small print of the newspaper, and few people showed much interest other than those directly affected (such as those actually handling the waste or those living in the immediate neighborhood of the proposed facility). However, in recent years solid waste managers have increasingly learned, often to their considerable discomfort, that failure to ensure adequate consultation with the public prior to the making of decisions affecting solid waste facilities and services can prove most unfortunate, sometimes resulting in unexpected opposition at a late stage in the planning process and occasionally leading to costly delays, midstream changes, or cancellations.

Facility siting, especially where hazardous wastes may be involved, typically attracts the most public attention (as discussed later in this chapter), but as citizen awareness of resource and environmental issues has grown during the past 15 years, so interest has increased also in such matters as ensuring that resource conservation and recovery are given adequate weight in SWM plans. In dealing with these and other issues, if citizens are to contribute most effectively, it is important to ensure that they gain adequate knowledge about the options available, their implications, and so on. Greater efforts are needed than in the past to reach out to a broad cross section of the public, provide the necessary information, and involve them in a meaningful planning exercise.

The California Solid Waste Management Board, for example, has initiated a major effort to inform the public about SWM well ahead of the time that problems or conflicts may occur. Specifically in relation to its preparation of the state plan, the Board developed a "Contact and Coordination Program," employing techniques such as "board meetings, informal workshops, public hearings, general media, special mailings, interagency coordination and 'piggy backing' (making use of events and meetings not directly related to solid waste management)."[6] A toll-free telephone line was established to facilitate public input. One component of the Board's program consisted of a series of eight public workshops which were held in carefully selected locations around the state in late 1979, with extensive publicity. Among other things, participants were asked to respond to a draft "status report" on SWM in California[7] which was intended to provide the basis for state planning; the input provided at the workshops, together with written comments received during a formal public review period, were then summarized in a "responsiveness" document[8] prior to finalizing of the status report.

Defining objectives

States are required to work toward the federally specified objectives of achieving "environmentally sound management and disposal of solid and hazardous waste, resource conservation, and maximum utilization of recovered resources."[9] It is unlikely that any state would disagree with these objectives as broadly stated; however, if the objectives are to provide real guidance in the setting of priorities, the selection of options, and the monitoring of results, they need to be rather more carefully specified. For example, within constraints imposed by the federal legislation, each state must decide on the relative emphasis to be given to the promotion of resource conservation and recovery on the one hand, and the upgrading of more traditional services such as collection, transportation, and disposal on the other.

Phrases such as "maximum utilization of recovered resources" are unclear. Does this phrase imply that resources should be recovered and used at all costs or, more likely, does it simply call for a greater level of resource recovery than would be achieved under the influence of market forces alone? But how much greater? Unfortunately, more precise objectives may be very difficult to formulate as, for example, the Oregon Department of Environmental Quality discovered when it attempted to specify recycling levels of 25 percent and 90 percent of the waste stream within 3 and 10 years, respectively; it was soon apparent that these figures had no scientific data base for measurement, and the Department subsequently had to qualify its objectives by stating that the "25 percent figure should be regarded as a substantial move toward recovery and 90 percent as the maximum obtainable given present technology."[10]

Waste reduction and resource recovery

Increasing concern about depletion of our energy and material resources, and about the adverse environmental impacts associated with their utilization, has led to a greater interest in SWM approaches other than simply burying the waste (with or without prior reduction of its bulk by shredding, compaction, or incineration). One alternative is to reduce the rate at which this waste is generated in the first place (an approach known as "waste reduction"); another is to recover and reuse valuable resources after they have become waste ("resource recovery").

As will become evident below, there is rather little that local and regional governments can do by themselves to bring about waste reduction; for them, the waste stream is more or less a "given." Thus waste reduction is largely a state or federal option, whereas resource recovery as an option is not confined to these levels of government. Unfortunately, there are a number of economic and institutional biases currently built into our system that tend to encourage a greater use of virgin resources, a greater rate of waste generation, and a lower level of resource recovery than would be the case in an economically efficient system. It is widely felt that market forces alone are unlikely to bring about the most socially desirable levels of resource conservation and recovery for various reasons, including the following:

1. The market fails to incorporate into product prices many of the environmental costs associated with the products and the materials contained therein, as well as the costs of collecting and disposing of them (resulting in a higher rate of materials consumption than would otherwise be the case).
2. There are certain government policies (such as the favorable tax treatment given to the extractive industries and regulations governing utilities that provide a disincentive to the use of waste-derived fuels) that may in some cases excessively encourage the extraction and use of virgin resources (and the generation of waste) while discouraging conservation and recovery.
3. Relative prices often fail to reflect the fact that the extraction of virgin materials generally entails greater environmental costs than the recovery of secondary materials.
4. Many people feel that, owing to inequities in the distribution of wealth and power, the actions of private individuals and firms in the marketplace do not adequately reflect the preferences of present society as a whole, or of future generations, so that the social value of conservation may not be fully realized even in an economically efficient system.

Considerations such as these provide a strong justification for SWM planners to give special attention to waste reduction and resource recovery.

Waste reduction

Waste reduction has been defined as "prevention of waste at its source by redesigning products or changing the patterns of production and consumption."[11] It can be achieved by various means, such as the following:

1. The development and use of products requiring less material per unit of product (for example, smaller automobiles, thinner walled containers).
2. The development and use of products with longer lifetimes, to reduce discards and replacement needs (for example, longer-lived appliances, more durable tires).

3. The substitution of reusable products for single-use "disposable" products, and an increase in the number of times that items are reused (for example, reusable plates and cutlery, refillable beverage containers).
4. A reduction in the number of units of the product consumed per household per year (for example, fewer automobiles per family).

Waste reduction is the most controversial of the approaches to SWM since some people see it as implying a reduction in our standard of living. This may indeed be true if the standard of living is measured in the conventional way by the market value of the flow of goods and services through the economy (that is, by their contribution to the Gross National Product), since waste reduction measures are expressly intended to reduce at least the materials component of this flow. However, as mentioned earlier, the market fails to account for certain factors, such as the full costs of resource depletion and environmental pollution that may be important to citizen welfare; so that measuring the standard of living in this way may be very misleading.

However, it should be noted that the waste reduction options listed above cannot be assumed, under all circumstances, to bring about a decrease in the rate at which materials pass through the system and end up as waste. For example, if products that have greater durability are manufactured using more material to begin with, there may be no net saving of material over the product's lifetime (especially if the product is discarded before it is physically worn out, as sometimes seems to be the case).[12]

Various policies have been considered as potential means of promoting waste reduction, and a few have been adopted at the state level. For many people, direct regulation seems to be the obvious answer: for example, if part of the SWM problem stems from "overpackaging" (given that packaging material has been the fastest growing component of the municipal waste stream and presently constitutes about one-third of all post-consumer wastes), then why not regulate packaging? However, as the first and only state so far to adopt comprehensive packaging regulations, Minnesota is discovering that the approach is by no means straightforward to administer. Essentially it requires the regulator to decide precisely what is meant by "over packaging," which means making a myriad of tradeoffs between such factors as material usage, reusability, recyclability, and waste generation, as well as performance as a package, cost, and consumer preference. In the absence of any general agreement on how these different factors should be weighted, the regulator's task is immensely difficult. For this and other reasons, Minnesota's approach has not been adopted elsewhere, although some states are using direct regulation under limited circumstances, for example, to control potential hazards such as detachable flip-tops on cans.

The best known and most widely adopted waste reduction policy to date has been that of requiring refund values or deposits on beverage containers to promote their return and subsequent reuse or recycling. Following Oregon's lead, several states have already passed "bottle bills" (as they are somewhat misleadingly nicknamed, since they also apply to cans), while some others seem likely to follow, and there is a chance that federal legislation will come in the future. While certainly not insignificant, the impact of beverage container deposit legislation on overall resource use and the volume of waste generated is not huge in proportion to the total quantities involved; the original motivation appears to have been primarily litter control, but over the years (to the chagrin of the beverage container industry) the quest for bottle bills by those concerned about the perceived wastefulness of our economic system has taken on a symbolism whose importance should not be underestimated.

Unlike direct regulation, the use of deposits *encourages* a certain physical response (returning containers) but does not *require* it, and is an example of a financial incentive. Other financial incentives considered as possible waste reduction measures include charges levied on products to force manufacturers to take into account the ultimate costs of collection and disposal (thereby encouraging product design that minimizes waste generation), and user fees for SWM services provided to households that vary according to the amount of waste picked up (thereby encouraging minimization of this amount). However, there is presently some hesitation about adopting either of these policy options owing to uncertainties about the expected costs of administering them and the degree of waste reduction likely to be achieved.

California's draft SWM plan emphasizes voluntary approaches to waste reduction, relying largely on public education and persuasion. The state's program is attempting to "(1) raise the level of public consciousness to full recognition of all the deleterious consequences of unrestricted waste generation and environmentally irresponsible disposal methods and (2) demonstrate how a low-waste society can enable its citizens to sustain the quality of life now experienced."[13] An interesting component of the program is an examination of so-called "social marketing" techniques which might be used to "sell" the idea of engaging in socially desirable behavior (rather than selling goods and services, as marketers do in the private sector).

Resource recovery

Despite California's adoption in 1974 of the specific goal of reducing the statewide annual tons per capita of residential and commercial wastes going to landfill by 25 percent between 1972 and 1980, a review of the SWM plans prepared in the mid-1970s by the counties in that state revealed little evidence of serious effort to significantly increase the level of resource recovery.[14] One apparent reason was the technological uncertainty associated with the mechanized materials and energy recovery systems; at that time the only process to have been fully proven in full-scale continuous operation was waterwall incineration, although several variations of a process involving materials separation and the preparation of a refuse-derived fuel looked especially promising. Inexplicably, few counties seriously considered the so-called low technology recovery options, such as those involving household separation with separate collection.

Another apparent reason for the counties' hesitance in initiating resource recovery stemmed from the economic and institutional biases against recovery discussed earlier. For the state simply to set a goal of increased resource recovery was evidently not sufficient; it presumably had to do something about removing or counteracting these biases in order to make recovery an attractive local or regional option, especially in view of the ever-tightening budget constraints that most communities were facing.

As time passes and experience is gained with an increasing number of recovery plants, the problem of technological uncertainty is diminishing, although it is still too early to judge the long-term performance of some of the new processes. States can play an important role in disseminating whatever technical information is available, as well as conducting their own programs of research, development, and demonstration where appropriate. Although proponents of the "low" and "high" technology options have occasionally engaged in vociferous debates in the past about the relative advantages and disadvantages of each approach, it is probably unwise to generalize about which is the more suitable under any particular set of circumstances. Furthermore, with careful planning, the two approaches need not necessarily be mutually exclusive.

States may draw on a variety of approaches to combat the effects of economic and institutional barriers against resource recovery.[15] Programs involving grants, loans, and/or tax incentives to promote the development of recovery facilities have been popular in the past, having been tried by such states as Illinois, Maryland, New York, and Pennsylvania. Several states have assisted in the identification of markets for recovered energy and materials, and a few have attempted to influence government procurement practices in order to induce market demand. Connecticut and Rhode Island have both established special agencies to play a direct role in statewide resource recovery implementation. The Connecticut Resource Recovery Authority, for example, is charged with implementing the recovery element of the state's solid waste management plan and has the authority to issue bonds, although the design, construction, and operation of facilities is being left to the private sector.

In order to meet one of the minimum requirements for federal approval under RCRA, a state plan must provide that "no state or local government within the state shall be prohibited under state or local law from negotiating and entering into long-term contracts for the supply of solid waste to resource recovery facilities, from entering into long-term contracts for the operation of such facilities, or from securing long-term markets for material and energy recovered from such facilities."[16] Some states are also reexamining other policies currently in force that might impede the development of resource recovery facilities, such as requirements for competitive bidding and automatic acceptance of the lowest bids on all public works projects. However, abandonment of these policies should be approached with caution, since there may have been good cause for their adoption in the first place.

Land disposal

Despite efforts to promote waste reduction and resource recovery, most solid waste will continue to be deposited on land (with or without prior treatment) in the foreseeable future, as it has been in the past. However, as environmental standards have tightened, the traditional "open dump" which has been operated with little or no precautions against the potential hazards of gas migration, water pollution, rodent infestation, etc., has come to be viewed as unacceptable. RCRA requires that open dumps must be either closed or upgraded to meet prescribed standards of "sanitary landfills," and new land disposal facilities must meet stringent criteria in siting and operation. These criteria relate to the following[17]:

1. Floodplain integrity and management.
2. Endangered species preservation.
3. Surface water protection.
4. Ground water protection.
5. Application of wastes to land used for the production of food chain crops.
6. Disease prevention.
7. Air quality protection.
8. Public safety with respect to explosive gases, fires, bird hazards to aircraft, and site accessibility.

Open dump inventory

In order to obtain EPA approval of its solid waste management plan, each state is required to conduct a survey of disposal facilities and to develop an inventory of those judged to be open dumps according to the federal criteria. Recognizing that it will take a tremendous amount of time and resources to complete a survey of the 360,000 or so existing disposal facilities nationwide (e.g., the cost of groundwater monitoring where necessary has been estimated at $6,000–10,000 per site), EPA has explicitly given the states permission to prepare their inventories in stages, based on the following:

1. The potential health and environmental impact of (each) facility.
2. The availability of state regulatory powers.
3. The availability of federal and state resources for this purpose.

In Florida, for example, the Department of Environmental Regulation undertook to begin the open dump inventory under a cooperative agreement and memorandum of understanding with EPA, with 100 percent federal funding (at least, initially). The Tallahassee solid waste program staff were assigned to perform the information search and evaluation, as well as the on-site facility investigations, supported as necessary by temporary personnel and contractors. Priority levels for disposal sites were established according to the nature of the wastes accepted and the presence of monitoring wells; then priorities for the investigation of particular sites in each inventory year were set within the established priority levels, according to the following criteria (viewed in the light of local circumstances):

1. Potential health and environmental impact.
2. Type of waste known or suspected to have been accepted.
3. Location in relation to aquifers, drinking water sources, etc.
4. Location in relation to environmentally sensitive areas such as critical habitats.
5. Safety.
6. Population served by the facility.

State plans must provide for the evaluation of all existing land disposal sites and must demonstrate that the state has the powers both to eliminate open dumping and to prevent its reoccurrence. The latter is to be achieved by means of a permit program for new facilities, together with adequate surveillance and enforcement capabilities.

Some states had already adopted guidelines or regulations relating to land disposal prior to the enactment of RCRA, and one of the tasks facing state planners is to reconcile any differences between state and federal requirements. Wisconsin, for example, has had different rules pertaining to open burning at small disposal sites. In general, RCRA requires states to adopt controls that are *at least* as stringent as those specified in the federal criteria.

Potential landfill sites that meet the new technical requirements are already proving difficult to find in some places, especially in close proximity to the urban areas where the largest quantities of waste (at least, municipal waste) are generated. However, even when sites can be found that are technically suitable, their use is often vigorously opposed by local residents. This problem is the subject of further discussion in a later section.

Hazardous waste management

Subtitle C of RCRA contained provisions to regulate the storage, transportation, processing, and ultimate disposal of hazardous wastes (the so-called cradle-to-grave system). The major provisions include the following:

1. A definition of hazardous waste.
2. A manifest system to track hazardous waste from its generation to its final disposal.
3. Standards for generators and transporters of hazardous waste.

4. Permit requirements for facilities that treat, store, or dispose of hazardous waste.
5. Requirements for state hazardous waste programs.

The regulations themselves[18] (which are now essentially complete but are subject to refinement and revision in the future) have taken several years to develop, and establish both "interim" and "final" requirements; they are very complex, and each state's SWM plan should address the means by which they will be met.

An immediate issue is whether the state should develop and implement its own HWM program in lieu of the federal program; this is allowed (indeed, encouraged) under RCRA provided that the state and federal programs can be shown to be equivalent. Many states already had some form of HWM controls in place before promulgation of the federal regulations, and most are planning to take (or have already taken) the necessary steps to achieve equivalency.

Whether under a state's own program or under the federal program, action must be taken to ensure that options are available to deal with all wastes classified as hazardous. These are wastes that are "included in a list of waste sources, waste streams, and some specific wastes that are hazardous or (are) ignitable, corrosive, reactive, or toxic as determined by a specific extraction procedure."[19]

The following have been identified by the EPA as desirable HWM options, in order of priority:[20]

1. Minimize the amounts generated by modifying the industrial process.
2. Transfer the wastes to another industry that can use them.
3. Reprocess the wastes to recover energy or materials.
4. Separate hazardous from nonhazardous wastes at the source, thus reducing the costs of handling, transportation, and disposal.
5. Incinerate the wastes or subject them to treatment that makes them nonhazardous.
6. Dispose of the wastes in a secure landfill (one that is located, designed, operated, and monitored, even after it is closed, in a manner that protects life and the environment).

Among other issues that need to be addressed is that of how to handle hazardous wastes that are not covered by the federal regulations, such as those generated in "small quantities" (generally under 1000 kg per month). There is some fear that these wastes might find their way to muncipal landfills or other facilities which are not appropriate to receive them. Consequently, several states have decided *not* to exempt small generators from their HWM regulations or have made special provisions other than those specified in the federal program.

Another issue is whether to attempt to differentiate between different wastes according to some measure of their *degree of hazard* (other than simply their quantity). This approach was explicitly considered and rejected by EPA when the HWM regulations were first developed, on the grounds that (in the agency's opinion) no system had been identified which was capable of "distinguishing different degrees of hazard among the myriad hazardous wastes and also reasonably relating management standards to these degrees in a technically and legally defensible way." The agency also stated its belief that its "final regulations already achieve the objectives of a degree of hazard system; thus, such a potentially complex and challengeable system is unnecessary."[21]

However, several states (including California, Rhode Island, and Washington) have developed and implemented their own degree of hazard systems, and it appears that EPA may now be developing an approach incorporating the degree of hazard concept, based on an analytical tool known as the "waste, environment, technology (WET) matrix." In preparing an assessment on nonnuclear industrial hazardous waste, the Congressional Office of Technology Assessment[22] has indicated that it favors the use of degree of hazard in the federal HWM system. The office has criticized both EPA's existing approach and the agency's proposed use of the WET matrix (the latter for various reasons, including undue complexity), and has instead developed for the purpose of comparison a tentative proposal for an alternative regulatory framework.

Yet another issue, and one of the most troublesome at this time, relates to the siting of new HWM facilities, which are desperately needed in many parts of the country. For example, the nearest acceptable commercial disposal sites to which generators in Virginia can transport their hazardous wastes are in other states. The problem of public opposition, mentioned in the previous section, is magnified many times when hazardous wastes are involved.

Solid waste management facility siting

Solid waste facilities of all kinds, including not only landfills but also processing plants and even transfer stations, are prime examples of what Popper has termed "LULUs" or "locally unwanted land uses"; these he defines as "development projects that are needed regionally or nationally but are objectionable to people living near them."[23] Since a major responsibility of state planners is to ensure that adequate facilities are provided statewide for the handling of all solid wastes (including hazardous wastes), the siting issue is one that they cannot avoid addressing.

Despite the increasing attention given to this problem in recent years, so far no panaceas have been discovered, although various possible approaches have been proposed and/or tried. The authors of a study conducted for EPA,[24] which examined actual cases involving HWM facilities throughout the country, concluded that actions must be taken or conditions negotiated which would convince the community of the following:

1. Complete information is available about the operation of the site, proposed waste streams, and post-operation closure.
2. The risks of catastrophic or insidious dangers are slight.
3. The public and local officials will be substantively involved in the siting process.
4. The operator is a person/organization of lasting integrity.
5. There are benefits to the local area to offset the risks.
6. The site and its operation are not in conflict with other enterprises or existing activities in the area, nor are there any higher land uses for the site.
7. The government has sufficient regulations, resources, and expertise to judge independently the merits of site design and to guarantee safe operation.
8. The technical merits of the selected site and facility are unquestioned.

However, the authors pointed out that in none of the cases studied had all of the conditions been met, and that only a minority are likely to be met in the average siting attempt.

According to a survey by Becker,[25] state involvement in the siting of new HWM facilities currently encompasses the spectrum from the passive (simply reacting to and regulating private initiatives, as in Arkansas, Illinois, and Texas) to the very active (participating in the selection, acquisition, construction, and operation of facilities, as authorized in Arizona, Washington, Maryland, and Georgia). Some states, including Michigan, Indiana, Pennsylvania, and Connecticut, have established state siting boards, typically with local representation but also with the power to override local objections under certain circumstances.

Other states, such as Florida and Kentucky, also provide for preemption of local authority. However as Becker points out, "although the use of these police powers may eventually result in the successful siting of a new facility, they are definitely not the most desirable tools." They are likely to be politically unpopular, legally challengeable, and may even provoke civil disobedience by citizens opposing them. In light of past experience with state preemptive powers,[26] there is the real possibility that the infringement of traditional local rights may create more problems than it solves.

Nevertheless, states are increasingly likely to be faced with the prospect of impasse, and they must be prepared to do something if they wish new facilities to be sited within their boundaries. There are a variety of noncoercive ways whereby states can attempt to overcome local resistance, including the use of mitigation, incentive, and/or compensation measures. For example, some states, including Georgia, Indiana, and Kentucky, provide for the payment of fees or taxes by facility operators to host communities as a means of "sweetening the pot." States may encourage or require negotiation among the parties involved, and conflict resolution techniques such as arbitration or mediation may be employed under the appropriate circumstances.[27]

An example of how one state responded is the legislation enacted in Massachusetts in 1980 creating a Hazardous Waste Facilities Site Safety Council, broadly representing all those involved in and affected by the siting of hazardous waste facilities, to oversee a new siting process that incorporates innovative conflict resolution techniques—negotation, compensation, and effective community involvement in siting decisions.

The major elements of the process include the following:

1. The submission of a *notice of intent (NOI)* by the developer to the state, the host and abutting communities, and the site owner describing the proposed facility, the wastes to be processed, the siting process, the types of assistance available to communities, compensation, and other benefits which might be negotiated with the host community.

2. The holding of a widely publicized *briefing session* that gives all communities and interested individuals an opportunity to question state officials and the developer about the proposal.

3. The provision of *technical assistance grants* by the Council to host and abutting communities, giving them the resources (legal, technical, or otherwise) necessary for full participation in the siting process.

4. The creation of a *local assessment committee* by each host community to use the grants to study the proposed facility, to acquire additional expertise, and to negotiate a siting agreement with the developer.

5. The preparation of a *project impact report* by the developer that delineates the environmental and socioeconomic impacts of the proposed facility.

6. The negotiation of a legally binding *siting agreement* establishing the conditions under which the site will be built, including the services to be provided by the community to the developer as well as the compensation, services, or other benefits that the developer will provide to the community.

7. The use, when necessary, of an *arbitration board* (consisting of two members nominated by the local assessment committee and the developer, respectively, and one additional member agreeable to both) to resolve an impasse by establishing a binding settlement that conforms, as closely as possible, to the final positions of both parties.

8. The granting by communities of *local permits* of narrowly defined scope (allowing reasonable local control over facility siting), and the granting by the state of necessary permits and licenses.

9. The developer's ability to petition the state to take the site by *eminent domain,* if all requirements have been met and the community's governing board gives its approval.[28]

Abandoned disposal sites

As originally enacted, RCRA was not retroactive, which meant that it made no provision for the cleanup of abandoned disposal sites such as the one at Love Canal which attracted so much attention in 1978. Following the public revelation that there are almost certainly many thousands of largely unregulated, abandoned disposal sites across the country, many containing a variety of hazardous materials, Congress amended RCRA in 1980[29] to require states to undertake (with federal funding) a continuing program for the compilation and publication of an inventory of all sites used for the storage or disposal of hazardous wastes at any time prior to the start of the new permit program. New federal legislation, the Comprehensive Environmental Response, Compensation, and Liability Act (CERCLA)[30] was also enacted in 1980, establishing a $16,000,000,000 fund to be used for the prompt cleanup of hazardous waste spills and abandoned dump

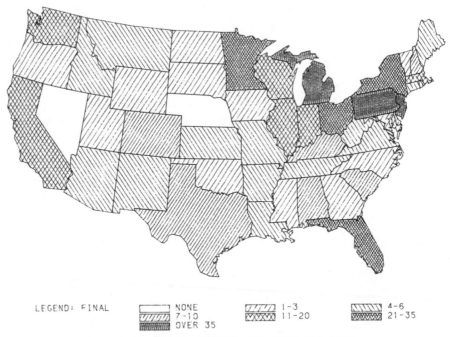

NATIONAL PRIORITIES LIST

(538 SITES)

LEGEND: FINAL   NONE   1-3   4-6
        7-10   11-20   21-35
        OVER 35

TOTAL NUMBER OF FINAL NPL SITES PER STATE

Figure 20-1   National Priorities List of hazardous waste sites, by states, 1984. The U.S. Environmental Protection Agency has identified approximately 17,000 waste disposal sites that contain potentially toxic chemicals and other hazardous wastes. This map shows the 538 sites that have been placed on the National Priorities List of hazardous waste sites. These sites will qualify first for Superfund allocations for cleanup. The majority of these abandoned sites contain wastes produced by the chemical industry. Some of them are municipal dump sites, where concentrations of pesticides and hazardous household cleaning solvents are present. Other sites are the result of dumping various kinds of industrial wastes.

sites in situations where the responsible party is either unknown or is not willing (or able) to act itself. The fund, known as "Superfund," is financed largely from a tax on oil and certain chemicals, with a small proportion (12 percent) derived from general revenues.

Although President Carter originally assigned the primary planning responsibility under CERCLA to the Council on Environmental Quality, the staff size and apparent significance of the latter have since been drastically reduced by President Reagan, and the planning responsibility has been shifted to EPA. Work has started at a number of high priority sites, and a long list of sites that are to receive Superfund allocations for cleanup has been published. Priorities will be established for future Superfund allocations based on degree of hazard, and state planners can play an important role in identifying candidate sites and documenting the need for cleanup of these sites, as well as developing contingency plans for spills. Even before CERCLA was passed, some states had already taken action by themselves in relation to the cleanup of spills and abandoned sites. For example, Arkansas in 1979 had provided for regulations "which would require the owners of abandoned disposal sites to undertake such actions as are reasonable to prevent environmental contamination." Kansas, New Jersey, and Wisconsin had established their own funds that might be used for cleanup in appropriate situations.[31]

Other wastes

In addition to muncipal wastes, and wastes classified as hazardous (and therefore subject to regulation under RCRA Subtitle C), planners need to be concerned about a variety of other kinds of solid wastes, such as nonhazardous industrial and community-generated wastes (including everything from discarded machinery to pollution control residuals to the discards from workers' lunchboxes), and wastes from agricultural and mining activities. This section briefly reviews some examples.

Pollution control residuals

With the passage of amendments to the federal Clean Air and Water Pollution Control Acts in the early 1970s, as well as of equivalent or complementary legislation in many states, emphasis was placed on cleaning up discharges to the atmosphere and to waterways. However, considerably less attention was given to the disposition of the residuals that result from these cleanup processes, such as fly ash, scrubber sludge, wastewater treatment sludge, etc. As pollution controls have tightened and continue to tighten, so these residuals have been increasing in quantity. For example, according to the application of Pacific Gas and Electric to the California Energy Commission for permission to construct a new coal fired power plant, emission controls on a single 1600 megawatt facility will produce some 3000 tons per day of residues, equivalent in magnitude to San Francisco's entire daily production of municipal solid waste.[32] More than 500 municipal treatment plants in New York State produce over 1200 dry tons of sludge per day (corresponding to as much as 117,000 wet tons, since the sludge initially contains up to 98 percent water), and this quantity is expected to increase by 50 percent by 1985.[33]

Some pollution control residuals, especially from industrial processes, do meet the criteria for classification as hazardous wastes and are therefore subject to regulation under RCRA Subtitle C. However, coal combustion wastes are explicitly excluded from RCRA hazardous waste controls at this time, and most muncipal wastewater treatment sludges are not considered hazardous. These wastes can often be put to beneficial reuse; for example, depending on its precise

Figure 20–2   Of the 1,800 wet tons of sludge produced daily by a regional sewage treatment plant in Washington, D.C., approximately one-third is composted and marketed as a soil conditioner called ComPro. Shown in this photograph is the composting operation: sewage sludge is mixed with wood chips and aerated; composting takes place at temperatures well into the pasteurization range. The compost is distributed to landscapers, farmers, and homeowners for use as a soil conditioner and fertilizer.

composition, ash can be used as a soil stabilizer, as a concrete aggregate, as a cement ingredient, and in other ways, while the sludge from utility scrubbers can be used in plastics, for mortar, and in sulfuric acid production, etc.[34] Waste-water treatment sludge can be used for the production of a gaseous fuel through anaerobic digestion (i.e., decomposition in the absence of air), or as a soil conditioner (with some nutritive qualities). However, such uses are not always possible (e.g., if sludges contain heavy metals or other contaminants that might enter food chains via uptake in crops) nor economically feasible (e.g., if they must be transported long distances to potential users), nor in many cases have markets yet been fully developed.

At this time, it appears that most of the wastes are disposed of by landfilling (solids and sludges), or by landspreading, lagooning, incinerating, or ocean dumping (sludges). Some of these options may not always be available; for example, the future of open dumping, used extensively by New York and some other states, is currently uncertain (it was to have been banned after 1981 under amendments to the federal Marine Protection, Research, and Sanctuaries Act, but the ban is now being reconsidered), and New York has also placed its own moratorium on the establishment of new landspreading facilities on certain agricultural lands.[35] Meanwhile, as discussed earlier, huge quantities of the wastes continue to be produced each day, and must be dealt with in one way or another. At the present time, however, the states lack complete data on generation rates, as well as on the potential problems and opportunities associated with these wastes.

Agricultural and mining wastes

Like the residuals just discussed, the wastes produced in agricultural and mining operations are, for the most part, either explicitly excluded from RCRA Subtitle

C controls and/or are not considered especially hazardous. Despite their production in very large quantities, their disposition has typically been left to the respective producing sectors, with little attention paid to them by public planners and other officials except when clearly identified problems have arisen. As a consequence, currently available information is poor, and there has been little or no coordination of waste-related activities on a statewide basis anywhere.

It is thought that many agricultural wastes are recycled, e.g., by incorporation into the soil (which is generally beneficial but may interfere with the application of dormant sprays, irrigation, and harvesting). Other wastes are disposed of by field burning, a procedure which causes air pollution and may be viewed as the loss of an energy resource. In California, where some 15,000,000 tons of agricultural wastes are estimated to be produced each year and where air pollution is a major concern, the state has assisted in the development of a mobile pyrolysis unit that can shred the wastes and convert them to a fuel by destructive distillation. Planners are also beginning to pay attention to the wastes from silvicultural and food processing operations in the state, together amounting to some 11,000,000 tons per year.[36]

New York provides an example of a state in which mining activities are significant, giving rise to some 30,000,000 tons of wastes annually; these include mining wastes (material removed during excavation) and processing wastes (material resulting from primary processing of mined ore at the mine site). The wastes are thought to pose a variety of water and air pollution problems, as well as causing unsightly slag piles and unproductive forms of land use, but at this time state planners have "little hard data . . . about current mining waste quantities, their disposition, or their impact on public health, environmental quality, or state economics."[37]

Coordination with other plans and programs

Although the responsibilities of planners are most clearly defined in relation to the management of municipal and hazardous wastes, it is unlikely that they can afford to continue giving little or no attention to other solid wastes such as those identified in this section; indeed, the RCRA guidelines require their consideration in state plans. It is important for planners to obtain information about the generation and disposition of these wastes, to explore the associated problems and opportunities, to assist in developing and implementing the most promising policies and programs, and to facilitate coordination among the different organizations and agencies involved.

According to the RCRA guidelines, "the State solid waste management plan shall be developed in coordination with Federal, State, and substate programs for air quality, water quality, water supply, waste water treatment, pesticides, ocean protection, toxic substances control, noise control, and radiation control.[38] The guidelines go on to list specific plans and programs with which coordination either *must* be provided (such as water quality plans prepared under Section 208 of the Clean Water Act, and state implementation plans prepared under the Clean Air Act) or *should* be provided *where practicable* (such as programs under the Toxic Substances Control Act, and solid waste management plans prepared in neighboring states).

At a minimum, planners should make every effort to ensure that there are no inconsistencies between the various related plans and programs, and that the mutual implications are explored to the greatest extent feasible. For example, if a Section 208 water quality plan calls for a significant expansion of wastewater treatment facilities, then it is important that the solid waste management plan makes provision for the associated increase in the generation of sludge.

However, planners may ultimately wish to take coordination further, so that it essentially becomes *integration*. Since pollutants often travel in pathways that cross from one medium to another, and controls typically remove pollutants from one medium by placing them (and creating potential problems) in another, some kind of *multi-media* approach to planning would seem to offer advantages over the traditional approach that considers one medium at a time. In this way it might be easier to make trade-offs according to the level of hazard posed by pollutants in different media; under appropriate circumstances, for example, it might prove desirable to modify an air quality control requirement in order to reduce a health hazard from water pollution.

At this time, the possibilities of integration have received greatest attention from those working on the control of toxic substances; for example, some studies have been made of approaches based on geographical regions, particular industries, or specific pollutants, rather than individual media. However, the research is still fairly preliminary, and the preparation of distinct solid waste management plans is unlikely to be affected significantly (if at all) for some time to come.

Conclusion

This chapter has reviewed a selection of the major issues facing SWM planners, especially at the state level. As mentioned earlier, it is apparent that federal pressure on states to undertake SWM planning has diminished under the Reagan administration; however, it is also evident that solid waste related problems can be expected to grow increasingly severe in the future, and that planners can make a useful contribution to their ultimate solution.

1   Public Law 89–272, The Solid Waste Disposal Act of 1965.
2   Public Law 91-512, Title I, The Resource Recovery Act of 1970.
3   Public Law 94-580, The Resource Conservation & Recovery Act of 1976.
4   Environmental Protection Agency, "Guidelines for Development and Implementation of Solid Waste Management Plans," *Federal Register* 44 (July 31, 1979):45066–45086 (codified as 40 CFR Part 256).
5   Nejedly-Z'Berg-Dills Solid Waste Management and Resource Recovery Act of 1972.
6   State of California, Solid Waste Management Board, *Solid Waste Management in California: A Status Report* (Sacramento: Solid Waste Management Board, 1980), p. 53.
7   Ibid.
8   State of California, Solid Waste Management Board, *Californians Look at Solid Waste Management: A Summary of Responses for State Planning* (Sacramento: Solid Waste Management Board, 1980).
9   Environmental Protection Agency, "Guidelines for Development and Implementation of Solid Waste Management Plans," p. 45080.
10 State of Oregon, Department of Environmental Quality, *Oregon Solid Waste Management Status Report 1979* (Portland: Department of Environmental Quality, 1979), p. 7.
11 Environmental Protection Agency, Office of Solid Waste, *Fourth Report to Congress: Resource Recovery and Waste Reduction* (Washington: Environmental Protection Agency, 1977), p. 21.
12 See: W. David Conn, "Consumer Product Life Extension in the Context of Materials and Energy Flows," in D.W. Pearce and I. Walter, eds., *Resource Conservation: Social and Economic Dimensions of Recycling* (New York: New York University Press,

1977), and W. David Conn, *Factors Affecting Product Lifetime: A Study in Support of Policy Development for Waste Reduction,* Final Report NSF/RA 780219 (Washington: National Science Foundation, 1978).
13 State of California, Solid Waste Management Board and Department of Health Services, *Material, Energy, Resources: Choices for California's Future,* Vol. 1: *Non-Hazardous Waste Management* (Sacramento: Solid Waste Management Board, 1981), p. 3.11.
14 W. David Conn, "Planning for Resource Recovery: Lessons from the California Experience," *Journal of the American Institute of Planners* 44 (April 1978): 200–208.
15 Environmental Protection Agency, *Waste Reduction and Recovery Activities: A Nationwide Survey* (Washington: Environmental Protection Agency, 1979).
16 Public Law 94–580, section 4003(a)(5).
17 Environmental Protection Agency, "Criteria for Classification of Solid Waste Disposal Facilities and Practices," *Federal Register* 44 (September 13, 1979): 53440–53464 (Codified as 40 CFR Part 257).
18 40 CFR Parts 260–266 and 122–124.
19 Environmental Protection Agency, Office of Water and Waste Management, *Hazardous Waste Facts,* SW-737 (Washington: Environmental Protection Agency, 1980).
20 Environmental Protection Agency, Office of Water and Waste Management, *Everybody's Problem: Hazardous Waste,* SW-826 (Washington: Environmental Protection Agency, 1980), pp. 16–17.
21 Environmental Protection Agency, "Standards for Owners and Operators of Hazardous Waste Treatment, Storage, and Disposal Facilities," *Federal Register* 45 (May 19, 1980): 33164.

22 Office of Technology Assessment, *Nonnuclear Industrial Hazardous Waste: Classifying for Hazard Management,* Technical Memorandum OTA-TM-M-9 (Washington: US Government Printing Office, 1981). See also: Statement of Joel S. Hirschhorn, Project Director, Office of Technology Assessment, before the Subcommittee on Commerce, Transportation, and Tourism Committee on Energy and Commerce, US House of Representatives (March 31, 1982), mimeo.

23 Frank J. Popper, "Siting LULUs," *Planning* (April 1981):12.

24 See: John A. Duberg, Michael L. Frankel, and Christopher M. Niemczewski, "Siting of Hazardous Waste Management Facilities and Public Opposition," *Environment Impact Assessment Review* 1 (March 1980): 84–88.

25 Jeanne F. Becker, "An Evaluation of Recent State Programs to Site Hazardous Waste Management Facilities," in *Planning 1981: Proceedings of the National Planning Conference* (Washington: Planners Press, 1981), pp. 287-294.

26 See, for example: Lawrence E. Susskind and Stephen R. Cassella, "The Dangers of Preemptive Legislation: The Case of LNG Facility Siting in California," *Environmental Impact Assessment Review* 1 (March 1980): 9–26.

27 Becker, *op. cit.*; see also: Pat M. Fox, *Siting Hazardous Waste Management Facilities,* SW-951 (Washington, DC: Environmental Protection Agency, 1981).

28 Adapted from Robert D. Wetmore, "Massachu-setts' Innovative Process for Siting Hazardous Waste Facilities," *Environmental Impact Assessment Review,* 1, (June 1980): 182–184.

29 Public Law 96–482, The Solid Waste Disposal Act Amendments of 1980. So far, EPA has not sought to have appropriated the funds authorized for the hazardous waste site inventory.

30 Public Law 96–510, The Comprehensive Environmental Response, Compensation, and Liability Act of 1980.

31 Jonathan H. Steeler, *A Legislator's Guide to Hazardous Waste Management* (Denver: National Conference of State Legislatures, 1980), pp. 38–40.

32 State of California, *Status Report,* p. 23.

33 New York State Department of Environmental Conservation, Division of Solid Waste, *Draft Solid Waste Management Plan* (Albany: Department of Environmental Conservation, July 1981), p. WT-1.

34 State of California, *Status Report,* p. 23.

35 New York State Department of Environmental Conservation, *Draft Solid Waste Management Plan,* pp. MW-1—MW-23.

36 State of California, *Status Report,* pp. 20–21.

37 New York State Department of Environmental Conservation, *Draft Solid Waste Management Plan,* pp. MW-1—MW-23.

38 Environmental Protection Agency, "Guidelines for Development and Implementation of Solid Waste Management Plans," pp. 45084–45085.

21 Health planning

We have technical specialists of all types. . . . We have far too few specialists in the composite discipline of health development. By that I mean people who are imbued with the philosophy of health development; who can generate it, plan for it, programme and budget for it, implement it, monitor it, and evaluate it; who can bring to these ends the specialized knowledge of all the other disciplines involved in the health, political, social and economic sciences, and who can marshall, master and summarize the information required for all these activities. This is the recruitment and training challenge that lies ahead of us. We must seek to create this type of person in sufficient numbers . . . to assume the responsibility of providing the new kind of support countries will require to attain the goal of health for all of their people.

Dr. Halfdan Mahler
Director-General
World Health Organization[1]

This brief statement capsulizes the philosophy and intent behind the health planning movement today. The United States is now beginning to take its place alongside many of the other nations of the world in the development and implementation of a national health policy. As may be said about much social progress, the path that has led to this juncture in our history has been long, arduous, and conflict-ridden; the proponents of health reform have fought long with mixed results—sometimes winning, sometimes losing, oftentimes compromising. But such is the way of changing in a pluralistic society.

To begin a discussion of health planning, one must clearly define the area of concern. Thus, the first task is to define "health" and present a framework for understanding the evolution of the U.S. health delivery system.

Defining health

There are many definitions of "health," but perhaps none is more widely cited than that adopted by the World Health Organization: Health is a state of complete physical, mental, and social well-being, and not merely the absence of disease and infirmity.[2] Terris expands upon this definition noting (1) that health is a relative term; there are degrees of health, and thus the word "complete" should be deleted from the definition; (2) that health and disease are not mutually exclusive states (i.e., disease may exist without illness) while health and illness are distinct; and (3) that there exists both a subjective component to health ("feeling well") and an objective component ("ability to function" adequately in one's assigned social role(s)). A revised definition would thus read: "Health is a state of physical, mental and social well-being, and ability to function and not merely the absence of illness or infirmity."[3]

Extending the earlier work of Romano, Blum's definition of health recognizes both the relative nature of "health" and its societal import: "Health consists of (1) the capacity of the organism to maintain a balance appropriate to its age and social needs in which it is reasonably free of gross dissatisfaction, discomfort, disease or disability; and (2) the ability of the organism to behave in ways which promote the survival of the species as well as the self-fulfillment or enjoyment of the individual."[4] Thus, health encompasses the concepts of homeostatic and ecological balance as well as societal productivity. The major determinants of a healthy state are heredity, environment, behavior, and health services. The latter three determinants become the major concerns of health planning in its attempt to measure the health needs of society and devise means by which they may be satisfied.

Evolution of a health services delivery system

Health services, as one of the determinants of health, has been described as "all the activities of a society which are designed to protect or restore health, whether directed to the individual, the community, or the environment."[5] Correspondingly, the health service system is "any set of arrangements in a society which assigns social roles and resources to achieve the goals of protecting or restoring health to the eligible population."[6] In reviewing this and several other definitions of the term "health delivery system," the following generalizations appear appropriate:

1. The health system is an embodiment of a society's social philosophy; its goals, organizations, and the like reflect that society's unique needs, wants, and ideology. As an institution of that society, it is not apolitical; it must vie for the allocation of scarce resources, and thus the planning, implementation, and evaluation of health policies are political issues.
2. To be a system, the inputs to health care must be functionally integrated (interdependent) and focused on a common objective—the attainment/ maintenance of optimal health status (as defined by that society).
3. A health system should have a primary emphasis on service: the application of knowledge to human problems.
4. If a health system is to meet the needs of those it is designed to serve, it must be flexible; i.e., allow for the use of socially (as well as legally) sanctioned modes of delivery. In the latter regard, Ogburn's concept of "cultural lag"[7] appears relevant in two respects: knowledge often precedes acceptable application, and legislation (a society's codified norms) often follows rather than leads acceptable social practices.
5. A health system must be comprehensive in that it touches on all aspects of human life; it is concerned with the physical, mental, and social well-being of the individual and of the larger society of which that individual is a part. This also includes a broad concern with the physical and social environmental quality of life in a society.
6. Although organizational concerns, reimbursement issues, and legal problems are not inherently "health" problems, they form part of the broad health services environment. The resolution of these issues has ramifications for the health care that is provided and are thus legitimate concerns of the health planner.

If "health" is societally defined, so is the nature and form of its health delivery system. Weinerman has discussed the evolutionary process by which a nation's unique health service delivery system develops.[8] Given the interplay among a nation's historical experience, cultural values, and societal resources, each individually and in concert affects the development of a society's unique social philosophy and, hence, its social policies. When referring to the initiation of major change within a health system, the Executive Board of the World Health Organization (WHO) notes that "there are few or no examples where a change in emphasis of the type and degree required [for major reform] has been introduced within an existing health service system without a preceding change in

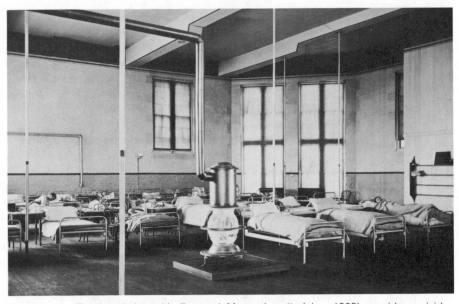

Figure 21–1   This hospital ward in Concord, Massachusetts (circa 1905), provides a vivid contrast with today's hospitals, citadels of finance, management, computerization, and technology as well as medical care.

social policies."[9] When consensus on a social policy is reached (by those who are legitimately empowered to reach that consensus which is dependent on the construct of that society), only then can national health goals and subsequently health priorities be formulated. Once formed, these statements are reflected in the organization of a system which is constrained by the state of knowledge and availability of scarce resources. Together, knowledge, organizational forms, and resources determine the nature of a society's health delivery system.

The ability of the system thus formed to serve societal needs is subject to an ongoing evaluation of its outputs and outcomes. This evaluation, together with changes in a society's experience, values, and resources (some of which are altered by the nature of the health system itself), determines whether major alterations occur in social policy. The need for social policy to reflect society's values and resources suggests that, in most cases, changes in health system delivery will be evolutionary and incremental.

Given that the dominant philosophy within the United States is one of free enterprise, what type of health system would one have expected to evolve? Roemer discusses this issue.[10] He divides the world's health care systems into five types: free enterprise, welfare state, socialist, underdeveloped, and transitional. Adoption of a free enterprise social philosophy results in a social policy of reliance on an open market to allocate goods and services with a minimum of intervention from government over demand, supply or price. In reviewing world health systems, Roemer notes that the United States is about the only country at its advanced stage of development which has retained this philosophy in relation to its health services. (Interestingly, until 1972 Australia's health system was based on the free enterprise premise; however, in that year there was a major shift in social policy away from free enterprise toward the development of a welfare state.)

The system formed under the free enterprise ethos is (in Roemer's view) characterized by sophisticated technological achievements coupled with an uneven distribution of resources and services. A mix of public and private programs exists (some complementary, others duplicative); these multiple programs reflect differences in money and power and foster wide discrepancies in access to health care; thus, the relationship of health services to health needs is often uneven. This unevenness eventually leads to political pressure to change the system. The changes that are adopted must, however, be congruent with the broader social philosophy (free enterprise); thus, when collectivization of some functions in the interest of more equitable access and more even distribution is attempted, the private sector is called upon to effect the change.

In fact, what Roemer suggests as typical of a health delivery system developed under the "free enterprise" ethos is what is occurring in the United States today. The financial support system for health services is the first aspect of our system to be "collectivized"—and attempts are being made to preserve the role of the private sector in this effort; e.g., through subsidization of private health insurance as well as reserving a major role for private fiscal intermediaries in governmentally financed health programs. As the government assumes a larger role in the financing of health care, an interest arises in regulating the costs and quality of that care. One such effort is health planning; again, in keeping with the dominant philosophy, health planning is viewed as a *partnership* of the public and private sectors. Although national guidelines have been developed, the system is to remain responsive to state, regional, and local needs. Whereas provision is made to allow health planning functions to be undertaken by public regional planning councils or single purpose units of local government, the predominant organizational form is a private one—the regional non-profit voluntary corporation.

The realm of health planning

Before discussing the specific structure and function of health planning in the United States (and its historical antecedents), it is first necessary to understand the scope of the activity and then suggest the generic planning approaches which appear most relevant to this field.

The primary focus of a health planner's activities is, by definition, the health delivery system. On first consideration, this system may appear to be a fairly self-contained one. One might simplistically define the major concerns as health and health-related manpower, facilities, and services. However, in keeping with the previously cited broad definition of "health," it seems more appropriate to view the health system as one component of the larger society. As such, it intersects with the other major sectors in a society and both supports activities provided by them and, in turn, receives support from them. This exchange may take place in many ways. For example, the health system provides services to clients of the social service system and, in turn, receives subsidization (e.g., Medicaid reimbursement) for its programs. Similarly, the health sector is a major source of employment; for example, in 1978 the health service industry accounted for nearly 7 percent of total civilian employment, and one out of every seven new jobs created between 1970 and 1978 were in the health industry.[11] Conversely, the health sector's "job" is to keep the general populace healthy and thus productive members of the employment sector.

If one accepts this broad conception of the health system and its close ties to the other major sectors, what implications exist for the planning component of health delivery? One apparent implication is that planning for health cannot be isolated from planning for the other sectors of society. Again, this relationship is a reciprocal one. Health planners must consider the impact of their health plans on, for example, education, transportation, housing, and natural resources. In turn, those with primary responsibility for planning in these sectors must consider the health implications of their own plans. Blum says this succinctly: "If health is not an intrinsic concern of the planning done in other sectors, then the health sector plan will indeed be mostly health care, without even an awareness of what other sectors are about to do to the country's health status, of the load to be placed on the health sector, or of the kinds of resources that will become or remain available to the health care sector."[12]

Fostering closer ties between health planning and other planning has many advantages. It both broadens and narrows the range of health problems defined, the possible means of intervention, and the probability of adoption and implementation of proposed strategies. If a health planner focuses only on the traditional health delivery system, he/she is tempted to define "health services" as the major determinant of health and fail to adequately recognize the roles played by environment (broadly defined) and behavior. Coordinated health planning would broaden the range of problems defined as ones of health. Alternatively, by working with planners from other sectors, the health planner can anticipate the types of health problems likely to be exacerbated or alleviated by proposals in other areas and thus focus (narrow) problem definition to those areas most deserving of immediate concern. Correspondingly, the range of useful interventions is expanded to include not only traditional health measures but health promoting interventions available through changes in educational, environmental, economic, and other policies. Finally, whereas a health plan developed in isolation must compete with other sectors' plans for a society's scarce resources, a health plan formulated in concert with other plans increases its *potential* for adoption; "it has a chance of achieving its intent for it only has to face controlled and anticipated amounts of health failures induced by the other sectors which [in turn] are alerted to the potential for good or bad health in their [own] plans."[13]

The need for the above coordination between planning in different sectors is a real one; however, one might be less optimistic about their ability to successfully carry out such coordinated planning. Demone has noted: "It is relatively easy to persuade organizations to meet together, but to persuade them to share real resources or to modify their actions is substantially more difficult."[14] The barriers to such coordination (according to Demone) are divergent ideology or beliefs, unwillingness to acknowledge the need for change, apathy, personality factors, and "reality " factors. One such "reality" factor would be the desire for discrete systems (or subsystems) to designate their own "spheres of influence" and to openly (or covertly) compete with other sectors; attempts would be made to maintain boundaries between sectors and to engage in competitive struggles over the allocation of society's scarce resources. Endorsement of this view would move us from Blum's more functional view of society to one embracing a conflict perspective.

To acknowledge the relevance of the conflict perspective for planners is not to reject the possibility of meaningful cooperation. For, although conflict may become dysfunctional, when managed correctly it has often paved the way for needed change via bargaining and compromise. The positive functions of conflict are many: it focuses attention upon critical issues and thus makes widespread indifference less likely; it may nurture intragroup integration and cohesiveness, reducing intragroup tension and leading to more effective organization and performance; and, finally, conflict is a major stimulus for innovation and change. Lewis Coser was among the first "rediscoverers" of social conflict to cite the way in which it might stimulate responsive change in human organization: "Conflict within and between groups in a society can prevent accommodations and habitual relations from progressively impoverishing creativity. The clash of values and interests, tensions between what is and what some groups feel ought to be . . . have been productive of [societal] vitality."[15]

Approaches to health planning

Others have already discussed the current state of planning theory and major planning roles and strategies (see Chapter 1); thus, it is sufficient at this point to note which generic planning approaches seem most appropriate for the health planning sector. Blum develops a typology of major planning approaches which he then evaluates as to their relevance for health planning.[16] He describes eight planning outlooks ranging from those which are the least future-oriented and most simplistic to those which emphasize future states and are more analytically complex. The typology includes the following approaches: laissez-faire; disjointed incrementalism; allocative; articulated and guided incrementalism; exploitive; normative; and total planning. With the exception of "disjointed incrementalism" and "total planning," he feels that each approach should routinely be considered as possibly relevant given the particular situation and environment with which a health planner may be faced. In his personal view, a combination of the following two approaches would provide the preferable starting point: guided and articulated incrementalism (seen as intelligent problem solving) and normative planning (seen as a form of large-goal setting).

What are the implications if Blum's preferred health planning strategies are adopted; i.e., guided and articulated incrementalism and normative planning? Normative planning is planning *from* the future; i.e., one decides upon the future desired (on the basis of current values, predicted values, or newly-created values) and then allocates resources so that trends are redirected toward the achievement of the desired state. In this type of planning, the desire for self-direction becomes paramount; one seeks what one's values indicate *should* be. Attention is focused on a composite of all systems, defining how each should be altered in order to better relate to one another. Thus, the need exists to involve all relevant system participants in the process. The desired results will, of necessity, be achieved only slowly over time.

In contrast to normative planning, guided and articulated incrementalism is planning *for* the present or near future. In this approach, one analyzes problems as systems with subsystems and unique environments, and then one designs appropriate interventions. A major departure from traditional incrementalism is that the intervenions must be chosen not only for their problem-specific efficacy, but also for their compatibility with larger sectoral goals. Thus, problem selection and solution identification must move the society *toward* a desired future state—and not merely away from an undesirable one; consequently, the process is complementary to normative planning. The goal-derived criteria "provide the 'guidance' for the guided and articulated incrementalism, of both the choice of the problem and the choice of intervention."[17] The involved participants in this planning process tend to be issue-specific. In contrast to the normative approach, guided incrementalism offers the potential for timely response to problems. When used in tandem, these two strategies encompass Blum's preferred approach to health planning.

Having suggested several planning strategies which might be particularly appropriate in the health area, it is now time to discuss the nature of the health planning program; i.e., to examine the specific structure and functions of health planning in the United States along with its historical antecedents.

Evolution of health planning

On November 3, 1966, Congress passes the "Comprehensive Health Planning and Public Health Services Amendments of 1966" and with it a renewed commitment to health planning. Whereas one might be tempted to trace the evolution of health planning to the passage of this important act, in reality the act was the culmination of nearly four decades of activity in the area.

The first stage: the CCMC report

In 1927, more than 50 persons gathered to examine the economic aspects of the care and prevention of illness. With support from eight private foundations, this committee (known as the Committee on the Costs of Medical Care, hereafter the CCMC) engaged in a five-year study of the United States' health care delivery system. They began with the identification of four pervasive problems: (1) technological advances which augured more specialization and, in turn, more fragmentation of medical care services; (2) an inadequate supply of physicians and other health care providers; (3) rising health care costs leading to greater financial barriers; and (4) the need for better organization of services and for better quality assurances regarding the care provided.

In 1932, the CCMC issued its final report entitled *Medical Care for the American People*.[18] Based on a multitude of "fact-finding studies" (26 in all) developed by the CCMC between 1927 and 1932, this report contained a comprehensive discussion of five major recommendations for planned changes in the health care delivery system. In brief, the five recommendations were concerned with the establishment of comprehensive group practices[19] linked with comprehensive prepayment, the strengthening of public health services, the need for coordination among all health services, and the broadening of health manpower education and training. For health planners, some special importance must be attached to Recommendation No. 4: "The Committee recommends that the study, evaluation, and coordination of medical service be considered important functions for every state and local community, that agencies be formed to exercise these functions, and that the coordination of rural with urban services receive special attention."[20]

In the accompanying discussion of the fourth recommendation, stress was placed on the development of temporary professional groups with lay participants, permanent local coordinating agencies, and state coordinating agencies. The need for a partnership between the professionals and an informed lay public was considered of "paramount importance." To this end, temporary professional-lay committees (appointed by professional societies) should "ascertain the facts regarding the provision of medical services, study the various possibilities for extending the service, and prepare local or state [health] plans."[21] Coordination with official and voluntary health agencies was also stressed. At the community level, permanent local agencies were to be established "to evaluate and to coordinate the existing preventive and curative medical services, to eliminate services not needed, and to stimulate the provision of additional services which are needed."[22] These agencies, utilizing representatives of the public, the medical profession, health agencies, hospitals, and social agencies would engage in continuing study of community health care needs and prepare locally-based plans to meet these needs.

In addition to the community-based local coordinating agencies, statewide counterpart agencies were advocated. These agencies would also have professional, organizational, and lay members and, like the local agencies, would be responsible for the continuing study of the state's health care system and for the preparation of a state health plan. Special attention was given to the state agency's advocacy role in the legislative process in order to implement recommended changes, maintain professional standards, and protect both the public's and the professionals' interests. The suggestion was also made that these agencies might consider regionalizing their activities by dividing the state into several "medical districts."

The recommendations of the CCMC were met with mixed reactions. While in accord with most of the suggestions, the principal (First) Minority Report registered sharp objection to the prospect of group practice and group payment. In endorsing the Minority Report, Morris Fishbein, then an acknowledged spokesman for the American Medical Association, condemned the CCMC report as being "communism, inciting to revolution."[23] Falk draws two conclusions from the CCMC experience: (1) technical studies and voluntarism in the pursuit of planned change had failed; and (2) the leadership of American organized medicine remained committed to the preservation of the status quo; i.e., fee-for-service, solo practice, and professional domination and control of the system.[24]

The foresight and care with which the CCMC undertook its work is indeed notable. The parallel between its recommendations and the current structure of health planning will become readily apparent as the subsequent history of health planning is presented.

The second stage: Social Security, grants-in-aid, and Hill-Burton

When the CCMC began its work, the United States was in a period of affluence; by the time their work was completed, the nation was in the throes of a depression. The government was responding to the need for relief by adoption of many interim emergency measures; however, the need for a sustained governmental commitment was evident. How were the CCMC's recommendations to fare in the movement toward "The New Deal"?

In 1934, the Cabinet-level Committee on Economic Security began its series of studies which were to lead in the following year to proposals for a long-term social security program. Preliminary studies and proposals addressed the need for health insurance and other health system reforms; however, "owing to widespread and intemperate objections from medical leaders and medical societies and to fears and timidities at high political levels, the recommendations which had been developed for health care benefits were not even submitted to Congress for inclusion in what became the Social Security Act[25] of 1935."[26] And so the opportunity for major health care reform was momentarily lost.

Although major reforms were not forthcoming, compromise legislation was enacted. Specifically, two important categorical grants-in-aid programs were established and added to the Social Security Act: Title V (maternal-child health program) and Title VI (the first permanent authorization for public health grants-in-aid to the states). In addition, Title VII provided authorization for the continuing national study of medical care problems and concomitant program development. The importance of these compromises was twofold: the federal government had made a major commitment to the planning and development of public health, including the medical care system; and determination of the "need" for medical care and services was no longer to be left entirely to the medical sector but would also involve the non-professional sectors of society and the active participation of the federal government.

Reeves *et al.* attribute a variety of purposes to the federal grants-in-aid programs; notably, they were to equalize availability of programs; stimulate program development and continuation; demonstrate the utility of new programs viewed as important by the federal government (a view which may or may not have been as yet shared by some states or localities); provide a means for the indirect supervision and control over local programs; enforce minimum standards; and provide a mechanism whereby federal tax proceeds could be efficiently distributed.[27] While these programs were successful in achieving many of their intended purposes, they also generated some unintended side effects; the most serious of these side effects were the fragmentation implicit in the concept of "categorization," insufficient attention to state and local priorities, and uneven and uncertain funding levels. These untoward effects were ultimately at least partially addressed by the advent of "block grants" (via the Comprehensive Health Planning and Public Health Service Amendments of 1966) and revenue sharing (via the State and Local Fiscal Assistance Act of 1974). However, many of the effects of categorization remain with us today.

Although somewhat limited in scope, the passage of the Hill-Burton legislation marked the beginning of a new era for health planning. Specifically, a grant-in-aid program entitled the Hospital Survey and Construction Act (P.L. 79-725) was passed in August, 1946 and became Title VI of the Public Health Service Act.[28] The depression and World War II had together contributed to a general shortage of hospital beds which was particularly acute in the rural areas. The Act authorized formula grants to states (based on population) to assist with facilities construction and equipment. While the primary emphasis of the program was initially on new hospital construction (and, via the 1964 amendments, on modernization of hospital facilities), subsequent amendments extended its concern to include, for example, public health centers, diagnostic and treatment facilities, chronic disease hospitals, rehabilitation centers, and nursing homes. Within this Act were the seeds for the modern health planning movement for it required (as a prerequisite for funding) that a single state agency and an advisory council be established to implement the program. The designated state agency and council would be responsible for the survey of existing hospitals and related facilities along with the development of a state medical facilities plan specifying priorities for the use of funds. Although the Hill-Burton program laid the foundation for publicly-supported health planning, it, in turn, derived its base from the early voluntary planning councils of the 1930s. Existing voluntary regional councils[29] advised the new Hill-Burton agencies and played a role in project review. In return, they received some financial support from the state.

Ironically, while Hill-Burton grew from a perceived shortage of hospital beds (particularly in the rural areas), the first hospital planning councils grew as a safeguard against overbedding. In the wake of low occupancy rates in *private* hospitals during the Depression, it was difficult for these hospitals to attract philanthropic monies; thus, "As a means of guaranteeing that the requested money was actually needed and would not be wasted on unnecessary[30] construction, regional planning agencies were established in metropolitan areas as a means of setting priorities for the collection and use of capital funds."[31] Members of these agencies/councils were generally distinguished lay community leaders who represented a community's economic and social notables.

The composition of these early councils had two major implications: (1) although formally they had little authority to implement their decisions, informally they were generally influential enough to do so; and (2) their corporate orientation focused attention on "bricks and mortar" construction and more pointedly on bed construction; "little attention was paid to matters other than beds. Non-hospital resource shortages and outpatient care were hardly addressed. Health planning became medical care planning. . . . By avoiding overexpansion, they protected the solvency of existing institutions."[32] Thus, early councils saw their task as rationalizing the hospital industry in much the same way as does other corporate planning. With this background, it is not surprising that "health planning was not an afterthought by the American Hospital Association . . . rather, the planning provision [within Hill-Burton] was from the outset an integral element of a program of federal grants for facilities construction to be administered without political favor or bureaucratic discretion. . . ."[33]

Whereas the Hill-Burton program was an important milestone for health planning, the planning which it supported had two major flaws: (1) the Act did not require coordination between hospitals or between hospitals and other health facilities—and therefore, such coordination was the rare exception rather than the rule; and (2) the planning that was done focused almost entirely on physical facilities—most notably on hospitals—and largely ignored manpower, health care financing, the environment, and other aspects of health care delivery. It was not until the 1964 amendments (via Section 318) that project grants supported the development of comprehensive regional or local area plans to encourage the coordination of existing and planned health and related facilities; planning bodies established under this amendment (i.e., state agencies or designated regional or local public or nonprofit groups) became known as "318" agencies.

By 1966, there were approximately 60 voluntary hospital/health planning agencies, including the new "318" agencies. However, "the need for a regional system with interrelationships and coordination among health facilities was apparent. . . . Thus evolved the concept of a partnership that would link government and voluntary agencies and involve the Hill-Burton program as one part of a total comprehensive health effort."[34] In that year, this concept was embodied in the passage of the Comprehensive Health Planning and Public Health Service Amendments Act of 1966 (P.L. 89-749).[35]

The third stage: comprehensive health planning (CHP)

P.L. 89-749 was the first major national commitment to health planning on a broad scale; i.e., it was the first act to address the planning function as a primary legislative intent rather than affixing a planning requirement as prerequiste to other functions; e.g., hospital construction. The Act began with a declaration "that fulfillment of our national purpose depends on promoting and assuring the highest level of health attainable for every person" and as such was viewed by many as a major societal commitment to assuring health care as a "right" of citizenship. This commitment was not, however, without reservation, for this "right" was to be assured via voluntary (noncompulsory) planning and was not to interfere "with existing patterns of private professional practice of medicine, dentistry, and related healing arts." Although some decried the "schizoid nature" of legislation designed to accomplish substantial change without such interference, such a compromise was perhaps to be expected in a pluralistic society. As Blum noted, "societies that . . . operate on a majority consensus [are] open to frequent alteration or even to the possibility of peaceful major reversals"[36] and, therefore, often employ contradictory incentives in order to preserve the predominately laissez-faire system.

True to its name, the health planning to be accomplished under P.L. 89-749 was to be "comprehensive;" i.e., it was to promote a cooperative and coordinated system of planning for all personal health services, manpower, facilities, and environmental health concerns. The partnership which it envisioned was to be multifaceted: among local, regional, state, and federal government; between the private and public health sectors; between providers and consumers of health services; and between health programs and programs in other areas such as education, welfare, and rehabilitation.

The major provisions of the Act involved revision of Section 314 (within Title III of the Public Health Service Act) and had six components. The first (314a) provided *formula* grants to states (based on population and per capita income) to establish state level offices of comprehensive health planning; these offices could reside in the Office of the Governor, in the state health department, or be an interdepartmental agency or board. The "a" agencies were to develop a state health plan and to be guided in its development by a state health planning council; the latter (an appointed body) was to include representatives of state and local agencies, nongovernmental bodies, health professionals, and others concerned with health services; a further requirement was that the majority of the membership be *consumers* of health services.

Section 314b provided *project* grants for areawide (regional) health planning. These "b" agencies (public or voluntary nonprofit) would prepare regional health plans to guide the coordination and development of new and existing health services, facilities, and manpower. Via an amendment in 1970 (P.L. 91-515), they (like their state counterparts) would be advised in their activities by a consumer-majority regional health planning council. Thus, at both the state and regional level, the major planning and policy decisions were to be placed in the hands of the private sector via voluntary consumer-majority boards. Again, this proviso should have been anticipated for (as Roemer's typology would suggest) when collectivization of some functions in the interest of more equitable access and more even distribution is attempted in a free enterprise system, the private sector will be called upon to effect the change.

Staffing of these agencies was also considered; Section 314c provided project grants for training, studies, and demonstrations to develop both the necessary manpower and the analytical knowledge base for effective health planning. As is too often the case with major legislative changes, the lead time between enactment of P.L. 89-749 and its implementation left little opportunity for the necessary education to take place. May reported that of the 60 voluntary hospital/ health planning agencies existing in 1966, only 21 made the transition to "b" agencies.[37] While some of the existing agencies were replaced by the new "b" agencies, others persisted with parallel activities until they were absorbed. A few were able to expand their boards and qualify as designated CHP areawide agencies. Nevertheless, in 1969 there were 67 wholly new agencies with an estimated 350 "health planners" on their staffs; however, relatively few of these planners had any formal education or substantial experience in the new field.

The fourth major provision of Section 318 was the availability of formula grants for public health services (Section 318d). State plans for these services (developed by state health authorities and mental health authorities) were to be compatible with the overall state health plan. The emphases of this section were threefold: (1) it was to provide monies for both public health and mental health services; (2) at least 70 percent of the grant funds were to be utilized at the *community* level; and (3) it introduced the concept of *block grants*. The block grant was to replace 15 existing categorical formula grants and, as such, was intended to address the problems associated with categorization of programs; i.e., fragmentation, insufficient attention to state and local priorities, and uneven and uncertain funding levels. In essence, these grants allowed state and local governments to focus some money on unique problem areas that might vary from state to state and from locality to locality. They would be particularly appropriate for the development of new services which did not fall under pre-existing categories or which may have fallen across such lines.

A fifth provision (Section 314e) made project grants available for health services development. Designed to promote innovative delivery modes, support was to be given to projects of limited geographic scope or of specialized regional or national significance. The "b" agencies would have "review-and-comment" authority over such grants.

The final section (Section 318f) provided for an interchange of health planning personnel between the states and the federal government for up to two years. Given the newness of the comprehensive health planning program and the relative inexperience of its staff, the opportunity for technical assistance and short-term exchange of personnel was of potential importance; unfortunately, however, this section was used sparingly.

P.L. 89-749 was in effect until 1974 when it was replaced by the passage of the National Health Planning and Resources Development Act (P.L. 93-641).[38] During its short history, the former act met with uneven success. In addition to the state level "a" agencies, by 1974 there were 218 areawide "b" agencies which covered approximately 79 percent of the nation's population.[39] Fifty-nine of these agencies were still in the developmental stages, while 159 were designated as fully operational. Thus, geographic coverage was fairly complete, and some plan development had begun. Progress had been made in the areas of health data collection and research, regionalized service programs, consolidation of hospital facilities, and reduction in unnecessary health care facilities. Public awareness of health planning was growing, and consumer input into that process was encouraged. However, there were many deficiencies which became more evident in late 1973 when the federal government undertook its first systematic assessment of the CHP program.[40]

The problems which beset many CHP agencies were not entirely of their own making. Legislatively, they began on shaky ground. In an attempt to be "comprehensive," their task became "incomprehensible." Because conceivably "everything" that affected health was potentially in the health planner's domain, many of the activities appeared (and often were) unfocused, and major accomplishments were few and far between. While the Act rang with pronouncements of a partnership, of cooperation, of coordination, in fact, "health planning was thrust into an environment which could at best be described as unfriendly and—probably more accurately—as openly hostile."[41] Not only did the Act provide little guidance as to the major intent of health planning efforts, it provided minimal direction of any kind including (e.g.) the broad goals which should be pursued and criteria for evaluating progress toward their attainment or even the processes and procedures by which health planning was to take place.

Some viewed this lack of federal guidance as intentional; i.e., an exercise in "creative federalism" whereby states and local areas could identify and remedy health problems in their own way. Others viewed it as a deficiency pointing to the immature state of health planning knowledge and techniques. Nevertheless, it was not until July, 1972 that the federal government began to identify performance expectations for health planning agencies and to assess the ability of the existing agencies to meet these criteria.[42]

In addition to the global nature of its mandate and to the lack of federal guidance, many problems were associated with the *project grant* funding mechanism. In order to generate the required 25 percent local matching monies, many "b" agencies had to spend considerable time in fund raising activities; the difficulties of attracting sufficient amounts of "untied" money also proved an insurmountable task for many agencies. Inadequate funding often meant reduced staffs, while funding contributions from local health care providers could affect the objectivity of decisions.

Consumer representation also proved to be a problem for the early CHP movement. Lacking a clear definition and any requirements for proportional representation, the assumption that consumers would function as strong advocates of the "public interest" was not justified. Many were affiliated with the provision of health care in some way. Others were intimidated by the presence of high status providers and were often content to play a passive role in the health planning process.

A final major deficiency of the 1966 legislation was its failure to provide regulatory authority commensurate with the legislation's mandate. The only real "power" was the right of CHP agencies to "review and comment" on projects which involved federal funding; e.g., hospital construction. This authority was ultimately strengthened by the passage of the 1972 amendments to the Social Security Act (P.L. 92-603). Under Section 1122 of this Act, via a state's agreement with the federal Department of Health, Education and Welfare (HEW), planning agencies were granted the right to "review and approve or disapprove" major capital expenditures (involving outlays of $100,000 or more) and/or any substantial change in services or capacity associated with any capital expenditures. Capital expenditures or service changes failing to receive approval from a state designated planning agency (who, in turn, relied heavily on advice from areawide "b" agencies) would be denied full reimbursement under Medicare, Medicaid, and the Maternal and Child Health programs. Specifically, the interest and depreciation portion of the reimbursement formula would be withheld for the disapproved service or expenditure. This program became known as "federal certificate of need" or simply "1122 review" and, together with state certificate of need legislation, was to provide a foundation for health planning's current regulatory authority. ("Certificate of need" will be discussed in more detail below in the section headed "Selected Health Planning Methods and Implementation Strategies.")

In summary, while P.L. 89-749 was a milestone for health planning, the process which it began was still far from satisfactory. While much of the criticism of this Act was warranted, "to blame comprehensive health planning agencies for not eradicating in eight years the faults which have been accumulating for decades is "to seek scapegoats rather than solutions.'"[43] Before discussing the current structure of health planning (with its associated legislation), attention must be given to several related programs which affected the development of the movement.

Other related health programs

Any discussion of the evolution of health planning would be incomplete without some mention of the following three programs: the Regional Medical Program; the Experimental Health Services Delivery Systems; and the Mental Retardation Facilities and Community Health Centers Act of 1963 (along with its amendments and extension in the Health Revenue Sharing and Health Services Act of 1975).[44]

On October 6, 1965 Congress passed the Heart Disease, Cancer, and Stroke Amendments adding Title IX to the Public Health Service Act.[45] Via this Act, authorization was provided for the establishment of *regional medical programs* (RMPs) whose mandate was to foster cooperative arrangements among medical centers, clinical research centers, and hospitals on a geographically integrated basis. In essence, the program was to strengthen the linkage among research, medical education, and health care delivery in order to assure that modern medical technology would be readily accessible to persons suffering from these three diseases; subsequently, end-stage renal disease was added to its concerns. The organization of the program was to be locally determined; each voluntary agency was to be assisted by a Regional Advisory Group composed of practicing physicians, hospital administrators, medical center officials, and representatives of other related organizations; thus, the program also forged a direct linkage between the federal government and the private practice of medicine.

Amendments to this Act in 1968 and again in 1970[46] expanded the scope of the program and, in so doing, led to some confusion as to its primary focus. In 1970, priority emphasis was shifted to primary care, prevention, and rehabilitation, ambulatory care as opposed to a preoccupation with institutional in-patient care, and innovative training and deployment of health manpower to underserved areas. Advisory group membership was to be expanded to include community-oriented public members and representatives of the designated area-wide health planning agencies. The latter agency (the "b" agency) was given "review-and-comment" authority over RMP grant proposals affecting their service area.

The RMP program improved health manpower training in a few selected areas (e.g., coronary care nurses), provided patient care demonstration projects (e.g., telemedicine and hypertensive screening programs), upgraded emergency medical services, and narrowed the gap between medical technology and its application to patient care. However, it proved to be a costly program (more than $600 million over the program's eight-year history) and one that was never able to generate sustained support from organized medicine. Similar to comprehensive health planning, an initial proviso of the RMP legislation was that should it not interfere "with the patterns, or the methods of financing, of patient care or professional practice or with the administration of hospitals." Also like CHP, it lacked any authority to carry out program recommendations; where it was successful, the success was primarily due to the ability of local programs to secure joint financing and continuation support for RMP projects from external sources. The 1970 amendments, which shifted the program's focus, "reflected the objections of private medical practitioners who expressed concern that the 'regional medical complexes' would be dominated by academic medicine and result in a redirection of patient referrals to the medical centers."[47]

The shift in focus had another adverse effect for the RMP program; its mandate became similar to that of CHP. The House evaluation of the RMP program highlighted the nature of this effect. A fundamental factor in the program's demise

was the effect of the shift made in 1970 from the original concept of RMP as a disease focused program with primary responsibilities for the dissemination of knowledge to health care providers to a concept which was similar to that of CHP (the development of primary ambulatory services, comprehensive services, emergency medical services, and generally the implementation of HEW health priorities). As long as the program had a specific responsibility to serve providers it did not need to be related closely to community health planning programs and could show a well-defined independent mission. However, as these emphases were given up and the program began to take on a responsibility to serve the needs of its communities and to respond to health planning, it became increasingly necessary to consider first its appropriate coordination and then combination with health planning programs.[48]

In January, 1973 the decision was made to phase out the RMP program and incorporate its mission within the new National Health Planning and Resources Development Act of 1974 (P.L. 93-641). Although the program had, like CHP, met with uneven success, it had reinforced two growing beliefs: a movement from categorical and institutionally-based programs toward a community-based comprehensive approach; and a reaffirmation in the principle of decentralization with its transfer of authority from the federal level to the regional and local areas.

Initiated in 1971 without legislative authority,[49] the *Experimental Health Services Delivery Systems* (EHSDS) program was designed to test whether a community management structure could improve the organization of health care delivery. Organized as autonomous non-profit corporations, their governing board membership was to consist of a coalition of the "four Ps": providers, payers (principally health insurers), politicians, and the public. Working with a staff of health analysts, health managers, and health planners, these corporations were to develop health management information systems to be used by health planning agencies and other organizations in order to improve decision making regarding the accessibility, cost-effectiveness, and quality of health care delivery.

The EHSDS program, however, was felt by some to have been misnamed. It was never a true experiment for, although 19 programs were funded, none were matched with "control" communities; further, community baseline data in the project areas proved inadequate as a basis for evaluation of the program's effectiveness. In addition, the programs were not "health delivery systems" in the sense that they neither owned nor operated any facilities or services and generally lacked authority to implement suggested changes. Finally, without its own legislative authority (and, therefore, its own appropriations), Congressional interest and support for the program was absent. In fact, there was some antagonism toward a program which was potentially competitive with comprehensive health planning; i.e., many felt that it was inappropriate for HEW to fund EHSDS at a time when CHP was known to be suffering from inadequate financial support.

The ill-fated EHSDS program was not without some merit, however. The stress which it had placed on management skills and on the need for strong health data systems was later incorporated into the 1974 health planning legislation (P.L. 93-641).

The 1963 Mental Retardation Facilities and Community Health Centers Act[50] was an important milestone not only for the mental health movement but also for its contribution to the evolution of health planning. It delegated mental health planning and administration to the states, provided constrution and staffing monies, stressed the need for service coordination, and required statewide program planning for mental health services. Specifically, each state was required to identify a responsible state agency which, with the direction of an advisory council (with consumer representatives), would develop a state mental health plan. Planning requirements were further strengthened in Title III of P.L. 94-63, the Health Revenue Sharing and Health Services Act of 1975.[51] Via Section 237, requirements for state mental health plans were specified, including the provision that such plans parallel and be consistent with the state health plans and state medical facilities plans required under P.L. 93-641.

In the ensuing years, mental health planning was to become more integrally linked with that of general health planning. However, several important concepts which were later to be reaffirmed in health planning legislation had their beginnings in the 1963 mental health act. The movement away from a preoccupation with institutionalization toward community-based care was stressed, as was the need for the coordination and systematizing of health services; e.g., in this instance, linking state hospitals, community mental health centers, and other community support services. The "catchment area" concept regionalized planning for mental health services in much the same manner as the subsequent 1966 CHP legislation mandated for all health services. Consumer involvement in both state advisory councils and catchment area boards was encouraged; again, such citizen participation became a hallmark of the CHP movement.

The preceding discussion examines the foundation upon which modern day health planning is based. The program built upon the insights of the CCMC, the reformism of Social Security, the pragmatism of Hill-Burton and other grants-in-aid programs, the idealism of comprehensive health planning, the innovativeness of RMP, and the technical expertise of EHSDS. Many of the pieces needed for effective health planning were tested. It remained to reassemble the best points of these previous efforts and refocus them into a strong and effective health planning program. It was time to realize that reform meant change and thereby could not be carried out without some degree of "interference" with the status quo. It was time to realize that responsibility without commensurate authority was an exercise in futility and authority without accountability was fraught with danger. These lessons (and others) were at least partially learned, and, thus with the passage of the National Health Planning and Resources Development Act of 1974, a new era began for U.S. health planning.

The fourth stage: national health planning

On January 4, 1975 the National Health Planning and Resources Development Act[52] became law, marking the beginning of present-day health planning. As previously noted, the new law replaced four existing programs—Hill-Burton, the Regional Medical Program, the Experimental Health Services Delivery Systems, and Comprehensive Health Planning. These multiple planning efforts were combined into a single planning program, one which incorporated the following principles in its structure:

1. Active participation by providers, consumers, private and public organizations in the health planning process.
2. Adequate and sustained levels of financial support.

3. Emphasis on plan implementation with commensurate regulatory authority to effect needed changes.
4. Authority to guide *new* health resource allocation decisions as well as the fiscal capability to seed innovative demonstrations.
5. On-going support for staff development, technical assistance, and evaluation of planning effectiveness.
6. A federal commitment not only to guide the state and regional health planning process, but to engage in a parallel effort at the national level.
7. A growing recognition that health services are only one of the determinants of health status and thus adequate planning must also address health-related behavioral and environmental concerns.

Briefly summarized, P.L. 93-641 added two new titles to the Public Health Service Act: Title XV, which revised the three existing health planning programs (i.e., RMP, EHSDS, and CHP); and Title XVI, which revised the existing health resource development program (i.e., Hill-Burton). Specifically, the Act was to foster the development of a national health planning policy, augment state and regional health planning efforts, and assist in the orderly development of needed health resources. In so doing, the problems of access, quality, and cost of health care could be more adequately addressed.

Title XV contained four major sections. Part A mandated the enactment of a national health planning policy based upon a set of national health priorities. This policy would take the form of national guidelines and contain both a statement of quantifiable national health goals and the establishment of resource development standards. The former would provide a framework for state and regional goals, while the latter would provide some criteria for state and local resource development decisions. Section 1502 enumerated the ten national health priorities which were to be considered by state and regional agencies in the conduct of their programs; the subsequent 1979 amendment to the Act added seven additional priorities (see the section below headed "The National Health Priorities").

Section 1503 established a National Council on Health Planning and Development within HEW (now the Department of Health and Human Services (HHS))[53]. The Council (composed of 12 voting members, at least five of whom were to be consumers) was to advise, consult with, and make recommendations to the Secretary concerning activities conducted under the two titles.

Part B (the second major section of Title XV) specified criteria for health service area designations, described the organization and functions of health systems agencies (HSAs) and established procedures for HSA designations and formula grants. Annual grants to designated HSAs would be based on the area's population (i.e., $0.50 per capita) with a maximum and minimum grant of $3,750,000 and $175,000, respectively. Additional federal funds were made available for up to $0.25 per capita to match local monies.

Part C provided similar authorization for the designation of state level health planning agencies. Known as state health planning and development agencies (SHPDAs), these entities would be eligible for federal grants of up to 75 percent of their operating costs provided an average maintenance of state effort was assured. The organization, composition and functions of statewide health coordinating councils (SHCCs) were also specified. Since much attention had been focused on the sharply rising costs of health care, a limited number of demonstration grants (six) were authorized to assess the potential effectiveness of hospital rate review and regulation.

The final section, Part D of Title XV, addressed several important issues. Section 1532 specified the procedural and substantive criteria for SHPDA and HSA review of proposed changes in institutional health services; i.e., the broad criteria upon which certificate of need and other regulatory decisions should be based (As previously stated, certificate of need and other regulatory mechanisms will be discussed in more detail below in the section headed "Selected Health Planning Methods and Implementation Strategies").

The issue of federal technical assistance was the focus of Section 1533. A national health planning information center was established. In addition, via direct and/or contractual assistance, HEW was to prepare materials related to health plan development, identify components of a necessary health data set, and devise health planning methodologies and standards including uniform systems for cost accounting, rate setting, institutional classification, and institutional reporting. To accomplish this technical assistance, the Bureau of Health Planning and Resources Development (BHPRD) was established in March, 1975 within the Health Resources Administration; the latter was part of the U.S. Public Health Service within HEW. Finally, due to the decentralized nature of the health planning function, grants and/or contracts were to be let for the establishment of several multidisciplinary centers for health planning; serving one or more of the HEW regions, these centers would conduct research, develop health planning methods, policies, and standards, and, in general, provide technical assistance to SHPDAs and HSAs in their regions. By February, 1979 there were ten such centers in existence; at that time, a decision was made to reduce the number of centers to four and emphasize their role in staff development (e.g., continuing education workshops).

The new Title XVI (which replaced Hill-Burton) had six major sections. Financial assistance would be available to states on the basis of population, financial need, and need for medical facilities. Via allotments and low interest loans and loan guarantees, impetus would be provided for the construction of new outpatient facilities and for the modernization and/or conversion of existing inpatient facilities. Eligibility for these monies would be contingent on the existence of a separate state medical facilities plan which had been approved by the SHCC as consistent with the overall state health plan.

An important addition to health planning's authority was contained in Section 1640 of Title XVI: the area health services development fund (AHSDF). Under this Section, designated health systems agencies, with approved health systems plans, could establish a fund from which monies could be drawn to contract for projects and programs which the HSA deemed necessary for plan implementation. While these monies could not be used for construction or delivery, they could provide "seed" money for encouraging and planning important projects. (This section was (and is) a potentially useful tool for implementation; to date, it has never been adequately funded.)

The current health planning program

P.L. 93-641 ushered in a new era for health planning. As Fiori noted, it brought with it a new reality for American economics—one that focused on less rather than more, and on conservation and planning rather than expansion.[54] It was a law which stressed local health planning, provided unprecedented regulatory authority over health resource development (particularly institutional services), recognized the need for substantial technical assistance (the responsibility for which should rest with the federal government), and reaffirmed a belief in strong consumer-provider participation in the process.

Health service area designation

The first step toward implementation of the new act was to designate the "health service areas" upon which areawide planning was to be based. The designation process (to be completed by the governor of each state) was designed to be self-executing; i.e., no federal implementing regulations were to be issued. Section 1511 of Title XV contained seven requirements for the designation process, essentially based on population (i.e., from a minimum of 500,000 to a maximum of three million, with some exceptions allowed) and compatibility with existing planning areas. In achieving this compatibility, specific reference was made, for example, to state planning and development districts (clearinghouses) as constituted under the Intergovernmental Cooperation Act of 1968 and revised in the Office of Management and Budget's Circular A-95. Under this circular, a state was to establish planning districts which could provide a consistent geographic basis for coordinating federal, state, and local programs. Thus, when a new federal act called for the designation of planning districts (as called for in P.L. 93-641), the new areas were to be congruent insofar as possible with existing designations.

On September 2, 1975 the Federal Register announced the completion of the health service area designation process.[55] A total of 202 areas in 46 states (and in the Commonwealth of Puerto Rico) had been defined. Delaware, Hawaii, Rhode Island, Vermont, and the District of Columbia were granted exemption from designating service areas under Section 1536 of the Act; such exemptions were allowed if a state had no county or municipal public health institution or department and had, prior to enactment of P.L. 93-641, maintained a health planning system which essentially complied with the specifications of the Act. In such cases, the SHPDA assumed both state and regional health planning functions.

The 202 areas differed in population, geographic size, number designated per state, urban-rural composition, and congruity with existing planning districts. The different composition of the health service areas around the nation, should, on the whole, be viewed as a strength of the program; i.e., although health planning under P.L. 93-641 was more regulatory in nature than previous efforts, it attempted to keep the major decisions at the state and local level. The designation process—the first major step in implementing the Act—reflected this attempt. "Some states . . . by designating a greater number of smaller health service areas, sought to maximize the potential for community and grassroot inputs to the HSAs and local health planning efforts. . . . Other states gave greater weight to the desirability of including a more comprehensive range of health resources and services within their areas and thus designated fewer but larger areas."[56]

The national health priorities

P.L. 93-641 began with a declaration that "the achievement of equal access to quality health care at a reasonable cost is a priority of the federal government." As previously noted, a set of 17 priorities was explicitly stated within the Act and its subsequent 1979 amendments. These priorities reflected the three overall purposes of the law: equal access, quality care, and reasonable cost. For example, equal access was addressed by at least seven of the priorities; i.e., priorities number one (primary care for the underserved), four (utilization of physician extenders), seven (appropriate levels of care), eight (disease prevention), ten (health education), fifteen (community mental health centers), and sixteen (concomitant concern for both mental and physical health). Cost considerations were reflected in at least twelve of the priorities; i.e., priorities number two (coordination of health services), three (medical group practices), five (sharing of support services), seven (appropriate levels of care), eight (disease prevention), nine (uniform reporting systems), ten (health education), eleven (energy conservation), twelve (elimination of duplicative services), thirteen (cost containment, appropriate utilization and production efficiency), fourteen (deinstitutionalization), and seventeen (strengthening competitive forces). Inclusion of explicit priorities within the Act "was to identify policies which Congress believes are especially important for improving the health system, but to do this in such a way as to give health planners the widest possible latitude in adapting them to the particular needs and situations of their areas."[57]

The seventeen national health priorities were to be used by the Secretary of HEW in the development of national health planning goals. The process by which national health goals and standards were developed is worthy of discussion.

The national health guidelines: goals and standards

Section 1501 of the 1974 Act mandated that the Secretary of HEW issue national health guidelines including a statement of national health planning *goals* based on the national health priorities and establish *standards* for resource allocation decisions. In turn, these goals and standards would be used by SHPDAs and HSAs in the development of their own plans.

A task force was established within HEW and, together with the National Council on Health Planning and Development, it began working on the Guildines in mid-1975. Although primary responsibility lay with the federal government, recommendations and comments were solicited from the state and regional health planning agencies throughout the process. As a result of this process, the first set of standards was issued on March 28, 1978; proposed national health planning goals were issued on April 17, 1980.

Initially, the task force chose six areas within which specific goals and standards would be established: health status; health promotion and production; health care services; health data systems; health innovation; and health financing. Goal statements were then evaluated as to their compatibility with the national health priorities, potential for improving the health of the population, relevance to health planning's statutory mandate, consistency with other national health policy statements, achievement potential, and severity and importance of the health problem which they addressed.

The proposed set of national health goals released in April, 1980 contained three broad goal categories.[58] The first category, "health status outcomes," included 11 goal statements addressing health status improvements, infant and child health, substance abuse, oral health, and the three major diseases—heart disease, cancer, and stroke. The second category, "disease prevention and health promotion," included ten goals reflecting concerns with prenatal care, consumer education, immunization, nutrition, smoking, fluoridation, accidents, and environmental and occupational health. The last category, "institutional and personnel resources and systems of care," contained 19 goals related to concerns of service delivery, systems of care, and coordination of community resources. At least one goal addressed each of the national health priorities, and, in most cases, the priorities were reflected in several goal statements.

The relationship between national goals and state and regional goals is intended to be a direct one; inconsistencies between these goals and state and local goals must be explained. However, SHPDAs and HSAs are encouraged to develop additional goals which reflect unique state and local needs and the current level of specificity in the national goals leaves much latitude for state and local initiative. The intent is not to set goals which create a uniform standard for every state and area in the country; rather, they are to provide a link (and thus compatibility) between national health policy and state and local health planning. The information flow is designed to be two-way; i.e., the national government develops the goals with substantial input from the states and the regions; these goals should be reflected in regional health systems plans (HSPs) and, in turn, since state health plans (SHPs) are "made up of" HSPs, each SHP should reflect a combination of national, state and local goals.

The process used to develop "national standards respecting the appropriate supply, distribution and organization of health resources" (as stated in Section 1501(b)(1) of the 1974 Act) is similar to that employed in the development of the national goals; i.e., a federal initiative with input from health planning (and other health-related) state and regional organizations. The report issued on March 28, 1978 consisted of 11 resource standards addressing the following nine areas: hospital bed:population ratios and occupancy rates; obstetrical, neonatal and pediatric services; open heart surgery and cardiac catheterization; radiation therapy; computerized tomographic scanners; and end-stage renal disease services.[59] For example, in relation to general hospital-bed supply, the standard states that "there should be less than four non-federal, short-term hospital beds for each 1000 persons in a health service area except under extraordinary circumstances." With regard to general hospital occupancy rates, it specifies that "there should be an average occupancy rate for medically necessary hospital care of at least 80 percent for all non-federal, short-stay hospital beds considered together in a health service area except under extraordinary circumstances."

The focus of the initial set of standards (more are to follow) is upon the short-term opportunities for cost containment and quality promotion in the *institutional* sector. This is to be achieved by promoting efficient and appropriate utilization of services and (in some cases) limiting their availability. In reference to the standards (and with illustration to the two mentioned above), there are several generalizations which might be made:

Cost containment is a major intent of all the standards; e.g., the intent is to reduce supply to that which is "medically necessary" and, in turn, monitor the appropriateness of its use.

Most of the standards contain the phrase "except under unusual circumstances;" this is a reflection of the emphases placed on the role and responsibility of SHPDAs and HSAs to adjust the guidelines to meet unique state and local needs. For example, age, seasonal population fluctuations, the rurality of a service area, and existence of referral hospitals in an area may justify alterations in the desired bed-supply.

Although adjustments are possible, they must be explained; i.e., an HSA must explain the unusual circumstances which preclude adherence to the standards; in turn, the SHPDA and the SHCC must review such requests and, if approved, incorporate these adjustments into the state health plan. Thus, both HSPs and SHPs must reflect national standards and/or justify inconsistencies between regional/state and national guidelines.

In many cases (not all), the emphasis is on regional rather than institution-specific adherence to standards; with regard to occupancy rate, for example, the standard need not be realized by all institutions but should be achieved on a collective ("considered together") basis.

The concept of regionalization (a complementary network of differentiated resources ranging from those which provide routine services up to those which provide highly specialized care) is reflected in many of the standards; e.g., required occupancy rates may vary with the size of a unit and the complexity of the care it provides.

In setting minimum caseloads per service and maximum resources per capita, the standards acknowledge the deleterious relationship between quality of care and under-utilization/over-utilization of resources; e.g., to maintain skill levels, minimum case loads are essential; conversely, unnecessary or inappropriate care can lead to iatrogenic illnesses.

In essence, the guidelines (goals and standards) attempt to *balance* state and local agencies' need to be responsive to local health conditions with the federal government's statutory mandate to provide national health planning guidance and leadership. (As previously noted, the lack of federal guidance had been cited as a major shortcoming of the earlier CHP movement.) To achieve the necessary balance, the guidance provided must be accepted as legitimate (not as "backdoor regulation") and as such must be a true reconciliation of local, state, and federal concerns. Such reconciliation is a time-consuming and arduous process; e.g., Navarro[60] discusses the inherently rigid and issue-specific concerns of a local constituency vis-à-vis a state or national one; as one moves from the local to state to national level, concerns broaden and the number of constituencies with a stake in an issue increases and the opportunity (and perhaps the necessity) for bargaining and compromise becomes greater. However, as a consequence of such bargaining, contradictory messages are transmitted, goals support two or more sides of an issue simultaneously, and, thus, ultimately they support neither side effectively.

Failure to resolve the dissonance implicit in reconciliation of local with state and national priorities leads to problems in the implementation of the national guidelines. For example, in some states, forces are split into two camps—the cost control advocates versus the access/quality control advocates; the 1974 law provides substantial support for both groups, while the guidelines (by their own admission) stress cost containment. Formally, no prioritization of the three major goals—access, quality, and cost—has taken place; however, federal directives have emphasized cost considerations. This instance of administrative policy making may be at odds with state and regional priorities. Until incompatibilities among the three goals are reconciled and until the prioritization of these three goals can be agreed upon at all levels (federal, state, and regional), the health planning program will be caught in a dilemma:

The resulting product has become a curious mixture of grassroots planning by HSAs and SHPDAs constrained by a federal framework of strict "top-down" [often contradictory] planning standards and directives. . . . the guidelines, as they are written, do not represent national health policy per se but are, in fact, a statement of the potential regulatory criteria that would facilitate the implementation of a broader statement of national [health] policy.[61]

Whether that broader statement of national health policy will be forthcoming is largely dependent on the commitment health planning is given at the state and regional levels. According to Diamond, evidence of this commitment would be the incorporation of the guidelines into the states' own policy structures, strategic placement of SHPDAs and SHCCs in government bureaucracies, and the use of HSAs as publicly-recognized forums wherein local issues and concerns are translated into state-level health policies.[62] Diamond's suggestions lead logically to the next subject of inquiry: the functions of state and regional health planning agencies.

State and regional health planning functions

The new law establishes a three-tiered network of health planning agencies. At the federal level is the National Council on Health Planning and Development. Initially a 12-member body, its size was expanded in 1979 to include 20 voting members, of whom eight are required to be consumers. This council advises the Secretary of HEW, makes recommendations about the development of a national health planning policy (via the establishment of the national health guidelines), evaluates the implications of new technology on health care delivery, and provides an appeal body for disputed Section 1122 project review decisions. A nongovernmental body, the council serves as a contact point and forum for both private and public participants in the health planning process. Staff assistance for the council comes from a newly established Bureau of Health Planning and Resources Development (BHPRD); the latter is divided into four offices responsible for policy coordination, evaluation and legislation, operations monitoring, and program support, respectively.

At the state level, two entities—the state health planning and resources development agency (SHPDA) and statewide health coordinating council (SHCC)—are established. The consumer-majority SHCC is appointed by the Governor from a list of eligible candidates submitted by a state's health systems agencies (HSAs); the SHCC might also contain other gubernatorial appointees including state agency representatives and public elected officials. A major responsibility of the SHCC is to annually review and coordinate the health systems plans (HSPs) and annual implementation plans (AIPs) of the regional HSAs; in 1979, the frequency of HSP review was reduced to every three years. A state health plan (SHP), based on the *preliminary* state health plan prepared by the SHPDA which (in turn) is to "be made up of" HSPs, is a second major responsibility of the SHCC. In 1979, the SHCC was given the added task of developing a uniform plan format which each HSA is required to follow. Other review responsibilities of the SHCC include the annual review of HSA budgets, HSA applications for health planning grants and use of area health services development funds (AHSDF), review and approval/disapproval of state plans involving funds under three federal acts, and, in general, overseeing all SHPDA activities. The intent of the SHCC, like the national council, is to keep the private sector—with an emphasis on consumers as well as direct providers—actively involved in the health planning program.

The SHPDA is essentially the staff arm of the SHCC. As such, its responsibilities include the general conduct of state health planning activities, the preparation of the preliminary state health plan (which would be subject to final approval by the SHCC), and the implementation of those parts of the SHP and the HSPs which relate to state government. Initially, the agency was to review a *separate* state medical facilities plan to ensure its compatibility with the general SHP; however, in 1979, both SHPs and HSPs were required to include a plan for health facility development *within* their general plans; such integrated plans are prerequisite to receipt of federal allotments for facility construction, conversion, and modernization under Title XVI. The end result is a firmer basis for project review decisions under Section 1122 and state certificate of need laws.

The "teeth" in the new health planning movement are contained in the remaining major responsibilities of the SHPDA. Specifically, the SHPDA is to serve as a state's Section 1122 agency and administer a state-enacted certificate of need (CON) program. The CON review process is one in which planners must approve all new health facility construction, major capital development projects, and major service changes proposed in their health services areas (and thus within the state); as previously discussed, Section 1122 involves a similar review but is specifically aimed at construction and capital projects involving facilities which receive Medicare and Medicaid reimbursement. Based on Section 1122 and CON reviews and recommendations from the HSAs, the state agency is given decisional authority over new institutional health services to be offered in the state. Finally, the SHPDA is given authority to review existing institutional health services to determine their "appropriateness" and to make its findings public; in this task, the SHPDA again relies upon reviews and recommendations by the HSAs. (CON, Section 1122 review, appropriateness review, and "proposed use of federal funds" review (PUFF) will be discussed below in the section headed "Selected Health Planning Methods and Implementation Strategies.")

In reviewing the functions of both national and state level health planning bodies, one is struck by the repeated opportunities for input from the regional/local HSA level. For example, the national council seeks substantial input from the HSAs in the development (and revision) of the national guidelines; the SHCC is composed largely of members nominated by the HSAs; CON and appropriateness decisions are to rely heavily upon HSA recommendations. Thus, although one might initially perceive the health planning structure as being hierarchial, it (in fact) is felt by many to be a last attempt at grassroots health planning. As one commentator notes, "the law [P.L. 93-641] strongly emphasizes local health planning and unprecedented control over health service development is vested in the local and state health planning agencies. . . . The Department [HEW] will help in developing the framework, but the major impetus must come from the local level if we are to succeed.[63] Since regional HSAs are considered so important to the success of health planning, what major functions are they required to perform?

The HSA is responsible for assembling and analyzing data (perferably extant data) on the health of area residents and the status of the health care delivery system, including an inventory of health resources (manpower, facilities, and services), patterns of utilization, and an assessment of environmental and occupational factors affecting health. Initially, environmental concern was broadly defined; in 1979, responsibility was focused on environmental hazards associated with health care equipment and with health services provided by health institutions and providers. Utilizing this data along with consideration of the national guidelines and priorities, each HSA is to develop a regional health systems plan (HSP). The HSP contains long-range goals (a five-year planning horizon) and as such provides a statement of the region's health goals and objectives. In a reaction to "paper plans," the emphasis in areawide health planning is placed on plan implementation. To facilitate this process, an HSA is also responsible for preparing an annual implementation plan (AIP) detailing, on a yearly basis, how parts of the HSP are being pursued and reporting progress in implementing the previous year's plan.

Again, focusing on implementation, the HSP is to be the basis for project review decisions. For example, in reviewing applications for new institutional services (under CON or Section 1122), consistency of the proposal with the HSP is expected. The plan also provides support for other HSA review functions: reviewing and approving/disapproving proposed uses of federal funds to be expended in the health service area (PUFF review); annual recommendations to the state for the modernization, construction, and conversion of health facilities in the region along with priorities for their funding; and periodically (at least every five years) reviewing the "appropriateness" of the existing institutional health services (AR). Another implementation authority is also placed in the hands of the HSA; the HSA is to extend technical assistance to individuals and organizations wishing to develop health resources and services in the area and, if such projects would further the HSP, area health services development funds (AHSDF) can be provided for the *planning and development* costs associated with approved proposals.

Regional coordination between an HSA and other planning bodies is also addressed in the statute. The HSA is required to coordinate its activities with the area's designated Professional Standards Review Organization (PSRO),[64] other general or special purpose regional planning or administrative agencies, agencies which are part of the A-95 project notice and review system, and other regional health-related organizations. As previously noted, in designating the health service area covered by an HSA, an attempt was made to accommodate existing planning boundaries wherever possible.

The structure of HSAs

Further comment on the background leading to the predominantly private nature of most HSAs should be made. The 1974 Act (via Section 1512(b)(1)) specified that HSAs could be nonprofit private corporations, public regional planning bodies, or single units of general purpose local government. As of November, 1979, the vast majority of the 202 HSAs were private nonprofit agencies; 20 were public regional planning bodies; and five were units of local government.[65] The governing body or executive committee (if any) of the HSA was required to have a majority of consumer members (but not more than 60 percent) with at least one-third providers. Via the 1979 amendments, at least one-half of the provider members were to be *direct* providers. By mid-1980, more than 9000 persons were serving on their local HSA governing bodies as consumers (on average, 53 percent) or providers (on average, 47 percent).[66] The question remains, however, why were so few regional planning bodies and units of local government designated as HSAs? A corollary question might be how have public health planning bodies performed vis-à-vis private ones?

Early drafts of P.L. 93-641 limited HSAs to private nonprofit corporations. Further, as specified in H.R. 16204, Part B, Section 1412(b), an HSA was not a subsidiary of or controlled by any other private corporation or other legal entity. Exclusion of regional planning councils and other public bodies from designation as HSAs evoked strong criticism from several groups including the National Governors' Conference, the National Association of Counties (NACo), the National Conference of State Legislators, the U.S. Conference of Mayors, the National League of Cities, and the U.S. Conference of City Health Officials. In the House debates, the following issues were presented for limiting HSA eligibility to the private sector:[67] (1) the House bill already required participation by publicly-elected officials in the health planning process; to allow public HSAs was tantamount to encouraging public control of the process; (2) CHP agencies (under P.L. 89-749) that had been controlled by councils of government had often been "development" oriented and thus inclined to promote industry, approve unnecessary facilities, and, in general, contribute to the cost escalation in the health area; (3) constrained by public sector personnel policies, public CHPs had been unable to offer competitive salaries and thus often lost qualified planners to private CHPs; and (4) since the vast majority (85 percent) of health services in the U.S. are offered through the private sector, planning and development in that area should involve private sector providers at the highest level. (It was argued that control of health planning by the governing bodies of public agencies (e.g., COGs) might preclude such high level involvement by the provider sector.)

The arguments presented in the House against the establishment of public HSAs were not without merit. In a series of several articles written between 1971 and 1974, Ardell[68] documented his experinces in a public CHP agency— in his case, a multifunctional regional planning council which assumed responsibility for CHP functions in 1970. Initially, Ardell began with an impressive list of reasons for placing CHP within a regional planning council structure:

(1) the need to reduce program fragmentation at the areawide level by improving coordination and effecting linkages between related programs; (2) the compatibility of areawide CHP review functions and the broad review mandate of the regional council "clearinghouse"; (3) the trend toward vesting of governmental powers in CHP agencies, which seemed inappropriate for private, non-profit health organizations but consistent with the role of quasi-public regional councils; (4) the alleged failings of the

single purpose [CHP] voluntary councils and the absence of persuasive alternatives to a strong form of new regional leadership; (5) the prospects for better accountability and lessened dominance by provider interests obtained by separating final policy making jurisidiction from the health types; and (6) the judgment that health system change and program effectiveness would be served by the act of marshalling all planning resources under a single group of decision makers who could best glimpse the big picture and thus set regional policies more likely of implementation.[69]

By late 1974, Ardell reluctantly concluded that the promise of multifunctional council leadership in health planning had not been realized; "the concept remains valid, the case is still persuasive, but unfortunately, it does not seem to work."[70] The relationship between the governing board of the regional council and the advisory Health Board had, in Ardell's experience, deteriorated over time. Among the problems he noted were intra-program rivalries, clash of constituencies, regional council time constraints that prevented adequate study of health issues, personnel policies that interfered with recruitment and retention of qualified personnel, financial strain on the regional council's budget caused by the need to match local CHP monies, lack of workable mechanisms for effective coordination between the work plans of the council and that of its advisory Health Board, and political interference with the health decision-making process. In sum, in place of a structural integration of CHP with regional planning councils, Ardell concluded that interorganizational collaborative mechanisms (e.g., joint work programs) were called for.

Lobbying by NACo and the other associations was effective; i.e., public regional planning councils and units of local government became eligible for designation as HSAs. Having "won" that battle, these organizations turned their attention to involvement in the drafting of regulations necessary to implement the 1974 law.

Altman[71] discussed several of the controversies surrounding the drafting of the regulations. The Governors' Conference and NACo had lobbied extensively to "open up" the regulatory drafting process; specifically, they worked for the repeal of the "Weinberger Rule" which prohibited the circulation of draft regulations and also advocated the creation of an Office of Regulations Development within HEW. Initially, in keeping with the 1974 statute, the Secretary (HEW) was given discretion in the designation of HSAs; subsequent regulations stressed the major role which state governors should play in the process. The 1974 law required that the SHCC select its chairperson from its membership; concern was expressed that, since HSA nominees make up 60 percent of the SHCC's membership, states would lack adequate control over the state health planning process. Thus, partly in response to a Governors' Conference proposal, the 1979 amendments provided state governors with an option: they could select the SHCC chairperson (with the advice and consent of the state legislature), or, alternatively, they could allow the SHCC to select its own chair.

By and large, two of the most controversial issues in the implementation of P.L. 93-641 involved the relationship between local governments and regional HSAs. In particular, controversy surrounded the percentage of HSA governing body membership allocated to governmental representatives and the relationship between the health planning governing body of a public HSA and its parent organization's governing board. The 1974 legislation stated that no more than one-third of the total membership of the governing body of a private HSA or the health planning governing body of a public HSA could be public officials. The intent was "to insure that a private agency is not so dominated by public members that it becomes, in effect, a public agency."[72] Similarly, in the case of a public HSA, the intent was to insure that the private sector would be adequately represented in the public agency's deliberations. The law, however, was felt by some to potentially weaken the input of publicly-elected officials into the health planning process. For example, although all HSA governing bodies were to include publicly-elected officials and other representatives of local government, no minimum percentage of local officials on the body was specified. In response, NACO proposed a requirement that elected officials comprise one-third of public HSA and subarea council governing bodies. Although this was not adopted, as of 1980, nearly all HSA governing bodies included public elected officials who, overall, represented approximately 20 percent of the consumer membership and about 8 percent of the total membership.[73]

The relationship between the consumer-majority governing body of a public HSA and its parent organization's (e.g., council of governments (COG) or regional planning council) governing board requires further discussion. Under the Act (Section 1512(b)), a public regional planning body could be designated as HSA if it had a governing board composed of a majority of elected officials and if its area of concern was identical to the designated health service area boundary; a single unit of general purpose local government could become the HSA if its boundaries conformed with the health service area. In the early House debates, it was suggested that the governing body for health planning of a public HSA would be identical with the public agency's governing board. However, via a legislative compromise, the final statute provided for the establishment (within public HSAs) of a separate consumer-majority health planning governing body; this latter governing body was to have "exclusive authority" to perform all health planning functions. Prompted by lobbying efforts of NACo and other groups, floor debates ensued in the House and the Senate in an attempt to clarify *legislative intent.*[74] Reportedly, the intent was to give the governing body of the parent organization (e.g., a COG) final authority over certain functions of a public HSA including the development of the health systems plan and annual implementation plan. However, as noted, the language of the law was in direct conflict with this intent. NACo and the National Association of Regional Councils were concerned that a literal interpretation of the statute would give a public agency health planning responsibilities but without concomitant final authority over the major functions. They argued that public bodies (if they choose) should control the process and not merely participate in it.

On the advice of the General Counsel, the Department (HEW) decided to follow the language of the statute and preclude the general governing board of the public agency from exercising final authority over the health systems plan and other major health planning functions. Via guidelines and policy statements, however, public HSAs were encouraged to give their parent agency, for example, the right to be involved in the selection of the separate health planning governing body's members, to be adequately represented on said body and to review and comment on major HSA decisions.

Regardless, the extent of the public agency's authority over the health planning body remained unclear. Subsequently, Montgomery County's public HSA brought a suit against then-Secretary Joseph A. Califano charging that P.L. 93-641 was unconstitutional; i.e., both the Act and the regulations promulgated under the Act offended the guarantee clause of the Tenth Amendment.[75] In essence, the plaintiff charged that the Act allowed the decision-making process to take place outside of state government. The District Court held that: (1) the HEW regulations pertaining to public HSAs were invalid to the extent that they did deprive the regional planning body and general local government of its authority to control the separate health planning governing body (within a public HSA) which exercised "exclusive authority" in the conduct of its health planning functions; (2) Montgomery County was not entitled to prevail upon Califano the contention that the Act violated the guarantee; and (3) the "exclusive authority" clause did *not* violate the Tenth Amendment. Further, the Court interpreted the "exclusive authority" clause to mean that the health planning governing body did have the sole undivided authority to act for the agency in the performance of such functions (as specified in the Act) provided that: (1) it does not preclude the public regional planning body or unit of general local government from establishing procedures related to the function of the agency including an opportunity to comment on any action proposed by the health planning body pursuant to fulfillment of its functions; and (2) the public regional planning body or single unit of general local government must be given the opportunity to comment on the health systems plan and its implementation prior to its establishment.

It was not until the 1979 amendments that the relationship between the two governing bodies in a public HSA was statutorily clarified. The public council or unit of local government is responsible for personnel policies and the budget of its health planning unit; however, the separate health planning consumer-majority governing body is responsible for all its other internal affairs. Although the regional planning body or unit of local government must be given the opportunity to *"review and comment"* on the health systems plan and annual implementation plan (and append suggested changes), the separate governing body for health planning has "exclusive authority" to perform all major health planning functions.[76]

The states, the SHPDAs, and the HSAs[77]

With the enactment of P.L. 93-641 came a new network of planning and regulatory structures. Acting under federal guidelines, the states and regions are to *share* major responsibility for the implementation of the program. Over time, it has become clear that health planning is a highly political activity rather than a purely technical or analytical one. Altman analyzes its political nature and, in so doing, notes the implications the Act has for federal/state/local relationships.[78]

There are four broad political issues addressed by P.L. 93-641: federalism; bureaucratic competition; citizen participation; and interest group representation. In a federal form of government, power is distributed between a central authority and a number of constituent territorial units; in this case, among the federal, state, and local governments. The question arises as to which level will achieve preeminence in the new health planning activity. Initially, the 1974 law was heralded as a return to grassroots planning—strengthening federal-local ties between HEW and the regional HSAs. Due to the predominantly private nature of many HSAs, concern has been expressed by governmental officials at both the state and local levels that the new HSAs might become "para-governments" similar to the OEO days and thus bypass traditional governmental channels. Thus, the states (and counties) are beginning to reassert their authority under P.L. 93-641. Have they been successful in doing so?

The law does, in fact, mandate a considerable sharing of authority between the states and the regions. For example, the regulatory responsibilities—CON, Section 1122 review, PUFF review, and appropriateness review—are all shared at least to some degree by both states and regions. Whereas Section 1122 and certificate of need involve initial reviews by the regional HSAs, the state retains final decision authority; however, if the state rejects the HSA recommendations, they must forward a reason for the rejection to the applicable HSA. A similar situation exists with regard to appropriateness review; the states are to make the decision as to which types of existing institutional services are to be reviewed every five years; while the actual review takes place at the regional level, the states are to have final authority in this area as well. The SHCCs are to review federal funds affecting statewide health activities (PUFF review); the regions exercise review and approval/disapproval of such funds affecting their own health service areas.

Another important area in which the states have retained considerable authority is the area of rate regulation. Via rate review experiments, eventually the states may be able to effectively link health financing with planning. As Kennedy notes at the federal level, "it makes no sense to separate planning, quality control, and the delivery of health services from the financing and review of them."[79] In approximately 20 states, separate institutional rate review commissions have been established; although separate from the SHPDA and HSAs, these commissions work closely with both of these agencies. Approximately one-half of the existing rate review commissions function as budget *approval* rate setting bodies, while the remaining one-half still confine their activities to budget *reviews* of rates. This latter type of rate review body was established in Florida under the state's Hospital Care Cost Containment Act of 1979 (P.L. 79-106).[80] Florida's Hospital Cost Containment Board is placed for administration purposes within the state's Department of Insurance; however, it retains its independent board status. Its financial support is self-generating; i.e., it is funded by a state-imposed assessment of all hospitals in the state; to date, the assesement amounts to 0.04 of 1 percent of a hospital's gross operating costs. Other states that have established institutional rate review boards include e.g., Maryland, New York, New Jersey, Connecticut, Massachusetts, and Washington. Several of these states were recipients of rate regulation demonstration monies authorized under P.L. 93-641.

In contrast to certificate of need which is reactive, "rate setting, on the other hand, is proactive; it includes control over present hospital budgets. Thus, in theory linking the two activities provides the biggest stick yet in health planning."[81] Retaining this authority at the state level could significantly alter the balance of power in health planning toward the state.

As previously noted, the states have allied themselves with other governmental units and associations (e.g. NACO) to lobby for further control in the health planning program. The question Altman poses is "why do the states care?" His answer centers on the financial, political, and regulatory impact which many health planning decisions entail.

Health planning affects (and could potentially affect) the financial obligations of the states in several ways. The states are concerned that regional HSAs— accountable not to the states but to HEW—might become administratively central in national health insurance program; if so, "HSAs would control the public sector in health, from data to dollars."[82] State and local governments are fearful that HSAs might set priorities in their HSPs that impinge upon state and local dollars; e.g., HSAs may approve services (via certificate of need) that channel funds into one area and ultimately force cutbacks in others; via PUFF review, HSAs may approve federal funds that require state matching monies and thus affect state budgets.

Many of the finance-related health planning decisions have political ramifications as well. As Altman notes, the new style of government emphasizes fiscal management. Governors and county and city officials want maximum control over federal dollars coming into their states and into their localities—and they want to place them in areas which meet *existing* political priorities; in other words, they want to use them (where possible) to pay for existing services so that demands placed on state and local revenues will be minimized (and thus contain the need for additional unpopular state and local taxation). Similarly, health planning agencies are concerned with economy; however, they are also committed to playing the change agent role, exploring innovative ways to provide health services and perhaps in the process curtailing existing service arrangements. Certificate of need and other regulatory responsibilities of the HSAs and SHPDAs, by their nature, involve "winners and losers" and thus are politically volatile.

The regulatory authority that has been placed in the hands of a privately-dominated organization (the HSA) also worries state and local officals. "Should

HSA . . . develop into autonomous and powerful quasi-governments, elected officials will come to act even more as umpires, mediating disputes between agencies and industries over which they have little direct control, but which may have a significant impact on state economies."[83] This has led some to argue that HSAs are usurping police powers that have been guaranteed to the states under the Tenth Amendment; as previously discussed, this argument was the basis of the *Montgomery County v. Califano* suit which held that P.L. 93-641 did not violate the guarantee clause. Nevertheless, in the exercise of their authority, HSAs and SHCCs will infringe upon what has heretofore been considered the prerogative of state and local government. In so doing, it is worthwhile to consider the accountability issue upon which the justification for such authority may ultimately rest.

Altman suggests that P.L. 93-641 tests the compatibility of two policy trends: public accountability and control, and technocratic accountability and control. With regard to the former, health planning stresses citizen participation in all stages of the decision-making process; it provides a forum wherein consumers, providers, elected officials, and planners meet in an attempt to resolve common problems. Further, both the 1974 Act and its 1979 amendments include requirements for public hearings, public access to its data and records, widespread dissemination of its plans and annual reports, and an appeals process. Although one cannot equate "consumer majority" with "consumer control," the possibility of the latter is at least enhanced by the statutory mandate. Involvement of elected officials also does not ensure the public interest; while it undoubtedly enhances the legitimacy of the planning process, it also increases its political vulnerability. As West notes (and Ardell's experiences confirm), "public officials are more closely attuned to political pressure than to planning considerations;" while they "may not have a vested interest in existing patterns of health care, they usually favor incremental approaches to decision making" which will not radically alter the status quo; consequently, it is unlikely that they "will face up to serious health problems when it means assuming political risks or taking a stand on issues that divide their constituents . . ."[84]

Whereas participation by consumers and public officials in the health planning process increases the potential for public accountability, due to the emotionally charged (and thereby political) nature of many health planning problems, a second form of accountability is necessary: technocratic accountability. Planning is the primary means by which such accountability is to be achieved. Planning (at least in theory) connotes rationality, objectivity, empirical evidence, evaluation, and the like. Combined with the voluntarism and consensus building nature of the public accountability component of health planning, professional planning is viewed by many as an appropriate vehicle for focusing debate and thus ultimately rationalizing the health system.

To understand further the relationship between state level health planning and its regional counterpart, Altman points to the differences that exist with regard to constituencies, modes of operation, and professional orientation:

1. With respect to constituencies, HSAs live on a day-to-day basis with local providers and consumers; SHPDAs must answer to cost-sensitive state governments.
2. With regard to operating modes, state agencies can act directly through CON, rate setting, or licensing. HSAs must bargain and cajole, always attempting to accommodate their various component groups. When they emerge from this process, HSAs still cannot act authoritatively but rather act through recommendations to the state.
3. With regard to professional orientation, SHPDAs view themselves as agents of state government; they are governmental decision makers

operating within the bounds of departmental and gubernatorial policy. In contrast, HSA staff members view themselves as professional planners and advocates for a set of beliefs and skills obliged to bargain for their positions within a highly pluralistic and participatory structure.[85]

Given these differences, it is no wonder that tensions exist between state and regional health planners. However, recalling Coser's comments on the positive functions of conflict, recognition (and ultimately reconciliation) of these differing perspectives may provide a firmer basis for productive change which either alone could not provide.

Selected health planning methods and implementation strategies

Health planning has been given the mandate to ensure accessibility to high quality health care at a reasonable cost. It remains to discuss the various methods and strategies which have evolved to accomplish this mandate. Health planners (like all planners) apply many existing analytical tools developed by other disciplines, e.g., population projections, economic base and gravity models, cost/benefit and cost/effectiveness analysis, systems analysis, and computer simulation techniques. In addition, health planning has devised several techniques and strategies unique to the field. Although it is not possible to discuss all of these techniques within the context of this chapter, several deserve attention: a health system taxonomy for plan development; the health plan development process; resource-based planning versus population-based planning models; health data sources; and project review functions and criteria.[86]

A health system taxonomy

As previously discussed, the SHPDAs and HSAs are responsible for the development of a health plan. To assist the states and regions, the Division of Planning Methods and Technology within the Bureau of Health Planning and Resources Development (HEW) developed a two-dimensional analytical framework of the health system.[87] The intent of the taxonomy was threefold: to provide a *system-wide perspective* for the development of long-range plan documents; to allow for a *service-specific classification* schema upon which reviews of proposed and existing services might be based; and to provide a *common frame of reference* between health service areas to promote uniformity in planning efforts across regions and states.

In developing the taxonomy, a number of classification schema were considered: medical specialties; settings; resources; intervention modes; disease categories; level of specialization; consumer age groupings; and geographic subdivisions. For the final taxonomy, two parameters were selected: personal health care services grouped by modes of intervention (e.g., health promotion, diagnosis and treatment, rehabilitation); and health care settings (e.g., home, hospital) subdivided into organizational types (e.g., ambulatory care provided by hospital and ambulatory care provided in non-hospital settings). The selection of these two parameters was based on the assertion that one must *first* determine the appropriate health care services to be delivered along with the appropriate setting for its provision *before* resource requirements (e.g., manpower and facilities) can be adequately assessed.

As depicted in Figure 21-2, the services are first grouped according to their intended effects (e.g., prevention); similarly, the settings are first grouped according to the expected locational relationship between provider and consumer. Figure 21-3—the complete taxonomy—adds a second refinement to each of the broad groupings. In the case of the service dimension, the services are further classified

Figure 21–2   A simplified taxonomic classification of health system services and settings.

Health systems services	Health system settings						
	Home	Mobile	Ambulatory	Short-stay inpatient	Long-stay inpatient	Free standing support	Community
Community health promotion and protection							
Prevention and detection							
Diagnosis and treatment							
Habilitation and rehabilitation							
Maintenance							
Personal health care support							
Health system enabling							

to reflect differences in areas of concern or in technique. In the case of the setting dimension, the settings are classified into organizational type.

The health plan development process

Utilizing the above health system taxonomy, Reeves suggests the key steps to be considered in both the development of the health systems plan (the long-range plan) and the annual implementation plan.[88] Figures 21-4 and 21-5 depict each of these processes, respectively.

As noted in Figure 21-4, policies and assumptions, community description, health status, health services, and health resources encompass the major components of the health systems plan development process. As shown, it includes all three levels of planning: policy, strategic, and operational. Throughout the process there are many decision points; e.g., observed disparities between what exists, what is likely to exist without intervention and what one's goals/objectives suggest should exist must, in turn, be prioritized relative to one another; again, one must choose the preferred means of remedying each priority disparity and identify it as a "long range recommended action (LRRA)." Although the process of plan development, as presented, may appear to be sequential, Reeves emphasizes that many of the tasks are undertaken concurrently; e.g., the process of forecasting can occur at the same time that goals and objectives are being formulated.

The process, as depicted in Figure 21-4, is fairly self-explanatory. In essence, it begins with the governing board (with community input) developing a statement of overall health goals which provide guidance for all subsequent health planning activities. Such community-based statements provide the basis for the determination of the "public interest" as well as increase the likelihood that decisions made are consistent over time. In this first step, the governing body is also responsible for specification of assumptions about the health care system and its future along with expectations about the level of investment and operating costs that will meet with community acceptance.

Health systems services		Health system settings									
		Home	Mobile	Ambulatory		Short-stay inpatient		Long-stay inpatient		Free standing support	Community
				Hospital	Other	Hospital	Other	Hospital	Other		
Community health promotion and protection	Health education services										
	Mental health promotion										
	Environmental quality management										
	Food protection										
	Occupational health and safety										
	Radiation safety										
	Biomedical and consumer product safety										
Prevention and detection	Individual health protection services										
	Detection services										
Diagnosis and treatment	Obstetric services										
	Surgical services										
	Diagnostic radiology services										
	Therapeutic radiology services										
	Clinical laboratory services										
	Emergency medical services										

Figure 21–3 An analytical framework of health system services and settings.

The community description which follows the development of policies and assumptions must be population-based; as Reeves explains, it must be "based on the needs of area residents as a whole, rather than a process that deals with the proposals of individual institutions or providers as a basis for making planning decisions."[89] Since it is assumed that many determinants of community health lie outside of the traditional health services system (recall Blum's four determinants of health—heredity, environment, health services, and behavior—as discussed in a preceding section headed "Defining Health"), a community profile must include an assessment of the social, political and economic conditions in the community. The description must include an explicit recognition of the relationship between the community characteristics described and the health status of the populace to be served.

Health systems services		Health system settings									
		Home	Mobile	Ambulatory		Short-stay inpatient		Long-stay inpatient		Free standing support	Community
				Hospital	Other	Hospital	Other	Hospital	Other		
Diagnosis and treatment	Dental health services										
	Mental health services										
	General medical services										
Medical habilitation and rehabilitation	Medical habilitation and rehabilitation services										
	Therapy services										
Maintenance											
Personal health care support	Direct patient care support services										
	Administrative services										
Health system enabling	Health planning										
	Resources development										
	Financing										
	Regulation										
	Research										

Figure 21-3   (continued)

Again, based on the initial set of policies and assumptions, *health status* goal levels are determined, checked for internal consistency, and then prioritized. From this set of optimized goals, time-related objectives are formulated. These objectives are then compared with a forecast (projection) of future health status. Via this comparison, discrepancies can be noted, estimates can be made as to their determinants (health system related or non-health system related) and appropriate LRRAs can be suggested.

Similarly, optimized *health system* goals and then objectives are derived based on the initial set of policies and assumptions and the community description. A check is then made as to the compatibility of the health system objectives with those which have been developed for health status. The health system objectives must then be compared to an inventory of the health system projected to the planning horizon (i.e., the health system forecast). Discrepancies are noted between the health system objectives and forecast, and LRRAs are formulated to remedy these discrepancies.

Finally, *resource needs* are assessed relative to the overall policies and assumptions, the health system goals, and the health system LRRAs. In essence, consideration of resource requirements at this point in the process reflects the assertion underlying the health system taxonomy that one must first determine

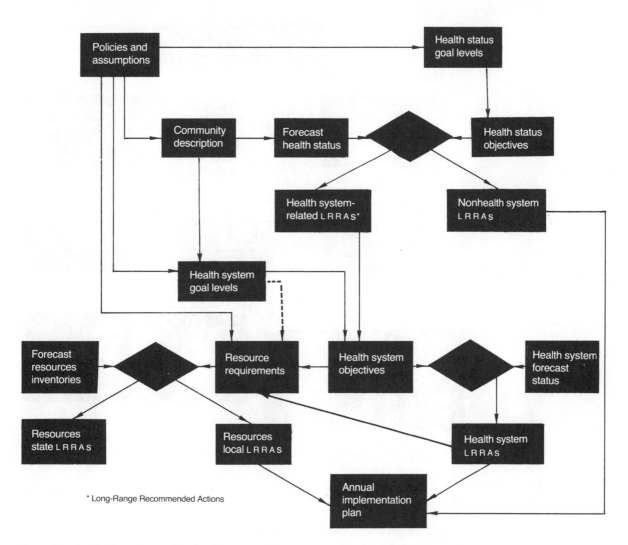

Figure 21—4   Health systems plan development process.

the appropriate health care services to be delivered along with the appropriate setting for its provision before resource requirements can be adequately assessed. Again, an inventory of existing resources is made, discrepancies between what resources are projected to exist and what resources are needed to achieve health status and health system goals are noted, and suggested LRRAS are made. As depicted in Figure 21-4, the LRRAs may be directed to actions which should be taken at the local level or, alternatively, identify those which need be taken at the state (or federal) level.

Figure 21-5 depicts the process of developing an annual implementation plan (AIP). The AIP, on a yearly basis, details how parts of the HSP are being pursued and reports progress toward the completion of the previous year's plan. As Reeves describes, a decision is made as to which of the LRRAs are to be chosen for implementation the following year; this decision is based on a knowledge of priority needs and constraints such as financial and political feasibility and HSA and community resource availability. Once the decision is made, annual objectives are formulated for the health system, related non–health system, and health resource development. Ultimately, "short range recommended actions (SRRAs)" are devised and become the focus for *community initiated* actions.

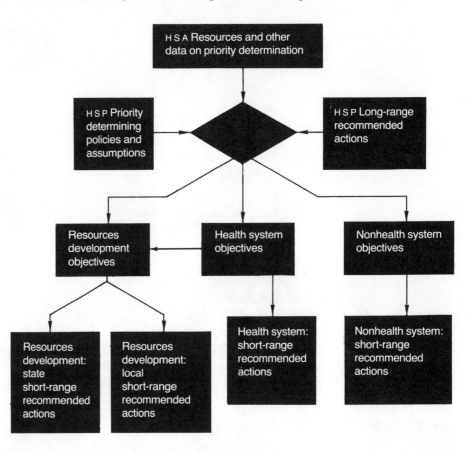

Figure 21—5   Annual implementation plan development process.

Alternative planning models

Reeves' approach to plan development assumes the use of a population-based planning model. As in Blum's approach, agreement must first be reached on broad health goals and objectives, followed by an assessment of health status. Once priority health problems are identified, the search for strategic actions to be taken to resolve these problems can begin.

In a population-based planning model, one first "determines health needs and establishes resource requirements based upon an assessment of risk levels and health status of a given population. The determination of need is derived solely from attributes of the population, *initially* [emphasis added] ignoring all existing resources."[90]

By focusing on health status problems, one is free to identify *all factors* (e.g., medical, economic, and social) which might contribute to the problems. In turn, these factors can be evaluated as to their distribution within the target population. Since both health service related and non–health service related contributing factors are assessed, one is not confined to alterations in the traditional health system in order to remedy the problem(s). Once programs and standards are identified to manage the risks, these programs can be compared to existing programs; discrepancies can be noted; and strategies for resource adjustment can be determined. The process is cyclical, since periodic re-evaluation of problems and interventions must be made.

In contrast to the population-based planning model, one might employ a resource-based approach. As Tannen notes, resource-based planning attempts

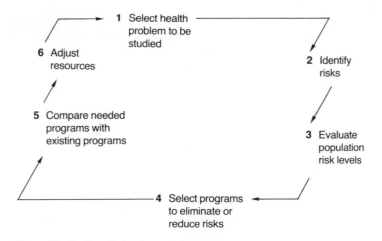

Figure 21–6   Population-based planning model.

to match resource supply with the demand for health services. It begins with the identification of services to be studied based on problems of under- or over-utilization of resources, need for modernization, replacement, or the like. Based on an assessment of past utilization and current demand, the size and nature of future demand is projected. A comparision is then made between this future demand and the capacity of the existing system to accommodate it. Changing standards of use (e.g., occupancy rate) are taken into account. Finally, discrepancies between projected demand and expected supply are noted, and interventions are devised.

Tannen makes an interesting comparision between the two models with regard to both their underlying assumptions and their potential impact on change in the health care system. When one adopts a resource-based planning model, the focus tends to be on the development of institutionally oriented modes of health care delivery—and thus on a perpetuation of the status quo. In his view, there are two basic problems associated with this planning approach: (1) because the model implicitly sees the treatment of illness as the sole purpose of the health system, the linkage between health status and the existence and use of health resources is seldom made clear; it is simply *assumed* to exist; and (2) in its concern to balance supply with demand, it perceives the health systems as a health care "marketplace" where change is equated with "fine tuning" of the market and limited to incremental adjustments within the existing system. Thus,

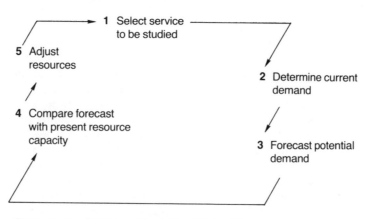

Figure 21–7   Resource-based planning model.

not only is change limited to an extension of the status quo, but it oftens fails to take into account the many factors (both health and non-health) which intercede between a direct translation of need into effective demand; e.g., differential reimbursement policies, racial and ethnic barriers, geographic inaccessibility, dietary, and other lifestyle behaviors.

In contrast, population-based planning is premised on a "social view of health."[91] By focusing on health problems and the many factors which exacerbate them, attention is directed to the population at risk and thus suggested interventions are not confined to the status quo. Health promotion, prevention, and primary care activities are more likely to be stressed as appropriate change stategies. However, Tannen does feel that there are two obstacles to the use of such models: (1) since attention is directed to causes of ill health which may fall outside of the realm of the traditional health system (e.g., environmental pollution and social conditions), suggested stategies might not prove to be politically feasible; and (2) the type of data required to support the models may not be available; i.e., while institutional data (need for resource-based models) are generally available, planners do not often have access to reliable sources of detailed demographic, attitudinal, medical, and environmental data (on a sufficiently small geographic basis) to effectively drive population-based models.

A national health data policy

Partially in recognition of the need for population-based health data, the Cooperative Health Statistics System (CHSS)[92] was established within the National Center for Health Statistics (NCHS) in 1970. In order to ensure access to baseline health statistics, NCHS let contracts to states to establish CHSS minimum data sets in seven areas designed to address the three major concerns of health planners: accessibility, quality, and cost of health care. The seven components of CHSS include selected data on vital statistics, health manpower, health facilities, hospital care, household interview data, ambulatory care, and long-term care. While the data collected is important for effective health planning, even more important is the "shared network" concept which it epitomizes.

P.L. 93-641 (section 1513(b)) mandates that HSAs assemble and analyze data on health status, inventory health resources and services, assess utilization behavior, and determine the nature and extent of environmental and occupational exposure factors affecting health. To the maximum extent practicable, they are to obtain these data from extant sources rather than collect their own primary data. In addition to coordination with the CHSS, health planning agencies obtain data from a myriad of sources: state and local health departments, state mental health planning agencies, hospital associations, third-party payers, state and local planning organizations, colleges and universities, and professional standards review organizations (PSROs).

To assist SHPDAs and HSAs in their data responsibilities, the Bureau of Health Planning and Resources Development (now the Office of Health Planning) published several sets of guidelines for the acquisition and use of health information.[93] In addition, the Bureau developed several techniques which allow state and substate health planning agencies to utilize national health data at a lower geographic level. One example is the "synthetic estimate" whereby individual state or regional "improvised estimates" can be obtained by applying national rates to corresponding population groups at the respective lower level, holding constant a number of demographic and socioeconomic factors.[94] Several excellent sources of national health data should be mentioned: these are the population-based national survey data systems of the NCHS. Included in these sets are the Health Interview Survey, the Health and Nutrition Examination Survey, the National Ambulatory Medical Care Survey, the Vital Statistics Data

Systems, the Vital Statistics Follow-Back Surveys, the National Survey of Family Growth, the Hospital Discharge Survey, and the National Nursing Home Survey System.[95]

Project review functions and criteria

The major review responsibilities of health planning agencies include certificate of need (CON), Section 1122 review, appropriateness review (AR), and proposed use of federal funds review (PUFF). They provide the primary means which SHPDAs, SHCCs, and HSAs have at their disposal in order to encourage compliance with the goals, objectives, LRRAs, and SRRAs of their plan documents. Other implementation stategies include the use of discretionary "seed" monies (via Title XVI's Area Health Services Development Fund), cooperation with rate-setting and other regulatory bodies, promotion of joint planning ventures between separate institutions to consolidate underutilized services and facilities, and informal agreements with third-party payers. While these stategies are all potentially important in the context of this chapter, there is only opportunity to explore the four major review functions.

Certificate of need and Section 1122 review functions

In response to the sharp rise in national expenditures for health care (e.g., from 5.2 percent of the GNP in 1960 to 8 percent in 1973 and later to 9.1 percent in 1978) and to the belief that this increase stemmed largely from an excess of hospital beds and duplicate facilities and equipment, several states initiated certificate of need (CON) statutes; among the early adopters were New York (1964), Maryland and Rhode Island (1968), and Connecticut and California (1969). Relying on input from the then-existing CHP agencies, the states withheld licensure and/or imposed court injunctions or fines on health facilities and services which did not recieve a prior certification of need from the state and applicable regional health planning body.

The American Hospital Association (AHA) officially endorsed the certificate of need concept in 1968, and defined the process as one in which "the state grants permission to health care providers to change their scope of services, or, in the case of a prospective provider, to introduce new services."[96] In 1972, the federal government became formally involved in certificate of need through the passage of the Social Security Amendments of 1972 (P.L. 92-603); Section 1122 of that Act specified that designated state agencies should determine the consistency or inconsistency of proposed "major" capital expenditures by health care facilities with areawide and state health plans.

Under Section 1122, disapproved health facility and service changes do not receive total reimbursement under the Medicare, Medicaid, and Maternal and Child Health programs; specifically, allowance for depreciation, interest, and return on equity capital is withheld on costs attributable to the capital expenditure for the unneeded construction. Whereas the portion disallowed might not be large, the impact of Section 1122 review has been substantial; for example, many commercial lenders and governmental loan programs require Section 1122 approval before agreeing to finance a health facility construction project.

By late 1975, 30 states had enacted CON laws and 38 had signed agreements with the Secretary of HEW to implement Section 1122 review; 20 of these states had both CON and Section 1122 programs. By 1982, all states except Louisiana had CON programs; whereas at one time 40 states had Section 1122 programs, by mid-1982 all but 15 of the states had allowed their Section 1122 agreements to expire (apparently assuming their state CON programs were sufficient). Although section 1122 and CON are similar, there are two major differences between the programs. As previously noted, the sanctions differ; Section 1122 employs a financial sanction, while CON is tied to state licensure, court injunctions, and fines. The coverage of the two programs also differs; Section 1122 covers only capital expenditures while CON, in many states, covers major capital expenditures, any major change in service (even when little or no capital expenditure is involved), as well as acquisition of high cost medical equipment.

P.L. 93-641 gave added impetus to the CON concept. Via Section 1523(a)(4), the SHPDA is to serve as a state's designated Section 1122 agency (should an agreement be signed with the Secretary) and is required to adopt and

administer a state certificate of need program which applies to new institutional health services proposed to be offered or developed within the state and which is satisfactory to the Secretary. Such program shall provide for review and determination of need prior to the time such services, facilities, and organizations are offered or developed or substantial expenditures are undertaken in preparation for such offering or development, and provide that only those services, facilities and organizations found to be needed shall be offered or developed in the state.[97]

A two-level review system is established in that SHPDAs are required to consider recommendations as to the disposition of CON applicants made by the appropriate HSA. All state CON programs are to meet minimum national standards relating to coverage, procedures, and review criteria. CON, Section 1122, and Appropriateness Review (AR) are all subject to a similar set of review criteria. As shown, the criteria are very broad, allowing for latitude in their interpretation and operationalization at the state and regional level.

The CON program was expanded in the 1979 amendment to P.L. 93-641. Major equipment serving in-patients *regardless of its location* is are subject to review. While not required to cover equipment in independent clinical labs or in doctors' offices, state CON laws *may* require such coverage if the state wishes to do so. The state can now withdraw certificates of approval if applicants do not adhere to a prearranged time schedule or if they greatly exceed their approved expenditure level. Some states had, in the past, placed "informal requirements" on applicants; in essence, informal trade-offs and agreements were often attached to approvals; e.g., if a hospital received approval for "X" service, it would informally agree to expand "Y" service and/or allow another hospital in the area to expand "Y" service. The 1979 amendments disallowed this practice; states are not allowed to attach any condition which is not directly related to criteria in the Act, in federal regulations, or in state law. Finally, the concept of "batching" CON proposals was introduced in 1979; i.e., CON applications at both the state and regional level are now batched so that similar proposals can be evaluated relative to one another; batched reviews must take place at least twice a year at both levels.

CON and Section 1122, by their nature, involve winners and losers. Thus both processes are often fraught with controversy. An interesting example of the controversial nature of CON is the Bon Secours case which is discussed at length by West.[98] Use of CON sanctions has led to charges that HSAs and SHPDAs are in violation of national antitrust legislation. This charge and its current status will be discussed in the final section of this chapter.

Appropriateness review (AR)   The law requires that SHPDAs and HSAs undertake a periodic review (at least every five years) of all *existing* institutional health services in its state or health service area, respectively. The legislative history of this requirement suggests the ambiguity which has surrounded the implementation of this authority. As reported in the *Federal Register*, "the function of periodically reviewing existing institutional health services developed from a review combined with recertification authority, to a periodic determination as to the continuing need for a service (with sanctions not required), to the present requirements for periodic reviews of services as to their 'appropriateness.'"[99] While the publication of the outcomes of the review remains the only "sanction" attached to the AR, the imposition of other types of sanctions are not prohibited.

The purpose of AR is to identify existing problems, inefficiencies, and service gaps, and to correct these problems through suggestions for change. The intent is, thus, not to simply label some services as "inappropriate"and seek through punitive measures to eliminate the offenders; rather the HSA and SHPDA are required to work with the affected institutions to alleviate the problems and, through cooperative efforts, attain the goal of improved service delivery. Other strategies—such as the medical facility component of HSP, AIP, and SHP, the use of area health services development funds, and the use of CON review— are all activities complementary to the AR process. Any reduction of capacity that may result through the use of any of these strategies must be justified by the net benefit it produces within the health system rather than assuming that a reduction in capacity is in itself a useful pursuit.

As previously noted, the criteria which are used for AR are similar to those developed for CON and Section 1122 reviews. Apart from the differences in sanctions, AR is initiated by the planning agencies rather that being a reaction to outside proposals. Finally, AR is concerned with existing facilities and services rather than addressing the need for proposed or new services.

MacStravic outlines the roles assumed by the HSAs, SHPDA, and SHCC in AR.[100] First, the SHPDA develops (with SHCC review and approval) the guidelines for the AR; i.e., what institutions and services are to be reviewed along with the relevant criteria and standards. These guidelines are then forwarded to the HSAs who, in turn, carry out the actual review process. The HSAs make judgments as to the "appropriateness" of the services and pass these findings on to the SHPDA and the SHCC. The findings are reviewed at the state level and, if approved, are published. Stategies for accomplishing suggested changes are developed through cooperation between the affected institutions, the HSAs, the SHPDAs, and the SHCC.

Proposed use of federal funds review (PUFF)   To promote coordination of federal health monies with general health planning activities in a health service area (and in a state), the HSAs (and the SHCC) are required to review and approve/disapprove applications for grants, loans, or loan guarantees authorized under the following three Acts: the Public Health Service Act, the Community Mental Health Centers Act, and the Comprehensive Alcohol Abuse and Alcoholism Prevention, Treatment, and Rehabilitation Act of 1970. Certain research monies are exempt from the PUFF review unless they would directly affect the development of resources or the delivery of services in the health service area. The SHCC's responsibilities under PUFF are to review and approve/disapprove any state plans and applications for allotment funds made to a state under the above three acts. Although the Secretary of HEW may approve funding over the HSAs or SHCC's disapproval, each of the latter agencies must be given written reasons for HEW's disregard of their decision.

The HSAs (or SHCC) must work closely with the grant applicats to assure that early in the application process proposed projects are cognizant of community (or state) health needs. In turn, the applicants must demonstrate that their projects are consistent with the health plans and review criteria of the HSAs and the SHCC. The overall intent of PUFF, like all of the other regulatory activities of the health planning agencies, is to encourage the development of timely innovative approaches addressing documented health problems in the state and regions.

Health planning: a controversial future

More than a decade ago, Ranney queried whether mixing planning with politics was an unholy alliance.[101] He concluded that it was not; in fact, the admixture was a fact of life, for there are no planning-related policy decisions which do not involve value judgments; with this clash of values comes conflict and, hopefully, out of the conflict comes thoughtful change. Falk has aptly summarized the need for and value of such a process:

It is not enough toward the achievement of constructive action to be critical of the status quo, to be articulate by voice or pen about what is wrong or bad or not good enough, or for the disaffected to talk only to one another or even only to the general public. This would be an accustomed ignoring of the lessons of history. We are free enough to reject the past, but it is not wise to ignore its lessons.[102]

Ranney addressed the planners' role in the politics of planning. In essence, planners have three choices: (1) they can alter their decisions so as to avoid further conflict; (2) they can make decisions in line with their own personal and/or professional values and ignore the political implications; or alternatively, (3) they can actively generate support for their proposals and plans. To be sure, the health planner of today faces such a decision for health care delivery and health planning have been and continue to be fraught with political controversy.

There are many controversial issues in the health planning arena. Should the health planner's role be one of facilitator, arbitrator, antagonist, or protagonist? What is the consumer's role in the process? Should one seek to "educate" them as to health planning's philosophy and methods or is this a form of "cooptation" as offensive as cooptation of consumers by the provider sector; does it not just as effectively disenfranchise consumers and negate their most valuable contribution to the health planning effort—representation and advancement of the public interest?[103] Should the federal government, the state, or the regions dominate in health planning? Should the governmental sector assume major responsibility for health care in the interest of efficiency and equity? Or should the private sector retain supremacy in the interest of free choice, individual freedom, and free enterprise? These are difficult issues; while much has been written on each, they have not been resolved—which does not, however, mean that they are "irresolvable."

Regulation versus competition   While all of the above issues (and many more) are of major importance to the future of health planning, one of particular importance at this juncture in the evolution of health planning is that of regulation versus competition. For some, the passage of P.L. 93-641 signalled an acceptance of the necessity for regulation in the health field:

The planning law is significant because it signals a choice of direction in health. It follows a series of laws that toyed with the issue of regulation, and embodies regulatory powers appropriate to the present balance of interest and political groups active in the health area. The law reflects the view that the imposition of external controls will be necessary to check soaring costs and to make any form of national health insurance a practical alternative. This posture is one that the health sector has been moving toward for some time.[104]

While Altman feels that the regulatory authority delegated to health planning is "appropriate" and (to date) sufficient, others might disagree. Some feel that health planning could easily become overburdened with regulatory obligations; not only is it time-consuming, but it could become self-defeating; i.e., rather than viewing health planning as a collaborative element in the health sector, those who are regulated might become antagonistic and resistant to suggestions emanating from a regulatory body. As Havighurst has cautioned, "regulation is a negative process, occasionally preventing bad behavior, but rarely bringing about good."[105] In this view, pehaps P.L. 93-641 has given health planning "too much" regulatory responsibility.

Conversely, others might feel that health planning has "too little" regulatory power. For example, Beauchamp views the expansion of regulatory authority over a medical care system which has been dominated by self-interest, "market justice," and "radical individualism" as both socially and ethically justifiable.[106] Advocates of the "right to health" must provide a countervailing force to the established vested interests if the public interest is to be served; if health planners choose to play this role, they must have substantial regulatory authority to influence the necessary changes.

A fourth view of health planning's regulatory "teeth" is that such authority is easily coopted and therefore unworkable. As Krause[107] notes, the risk of cooptation of the regulators by the regulated is always present; this is especially likely when the regulated possess a high level of technical expertise. The latter is certainly true in the health area. Thus, if one depends on peer review (e.g., PSROs), one might legitimately wonder who is supervising the peer expert? Correspondingly, if health planners are to be the guardians of the public interest in the health field, one might ask who is guarding the guardians? Consumer participation helps, as do the many requirements for public disclosure, an appeals process, and the like; however; are these safeguards sufficient?

If one questions the wisdom of regulation, one might be equally wary of its alleged alternative—competition. In keeping with our society's free enterprise ideology, it is not suprising that there are those who resist regulation in the health field. Health planning has attempted to be responsive to the advocates of competition; to wit, the 1979 amendments specifically addressed the need "to strengthen competitive forces in the health services industry wherever competition and consumer choice can constructively serve . . . to advance the purposes of quality assurance, cost effectiveness, and access" (National Health Priority No. 17). Reviews performed under Section 1122, CON, or AR must consider the positive or negative impact of proposed or existing services on competition. Some of the impetus behind federal support of health maintenance organizations (HMOs) can be interpreted as an attempt to provide consumers with a competitive alternative to traditional fee-for-service practice.

Although cognizant of the advantages of competition, Congress was aware of its limited utility in the health care sector. In passing P.L. 93-641, Congress acknowledged the failure of the medical marketplace to adequately deal with the problems of equitable access, maldistribution of resources, and soaring costs. Significantly, it did not choose to dismantle the medical marketplace but rather to enter into a public-private partnership and rely on voluntary planning (albeit with a modicum of regulatory authority) to provide the vehicle wherein "rational" alternatives and solutions might be explored.

Klarman addresses the role of competition in the health market as does a recent report of the Institute of Medicine (National Academy of Sciences). "The conditions under which the free market is said to promote the benefits of all parties are well known; namely, the presence of large numbers of knowlegeable consumers and producers, all of whose interests are captured in the transactions in which they participate, with each party acting as if none exerted any influence on price."[108] The health sector, however, meets few (if any) of these conditions. For example, there are many "market imperfections" in the health system: the lack of medically knowledgeable consumers, the existence of provider-generated demand as well as the more traditional consumer-generated demand, the non-profit nature of most health care institutions, the availabilty effect (i.e., Roemer's Law[109]), the impact of insurance on price and income, and the existence of externalities which leads to "false signals" in the marketplace.

Figure 21–8 National health care revenues and expenditures, 1983.

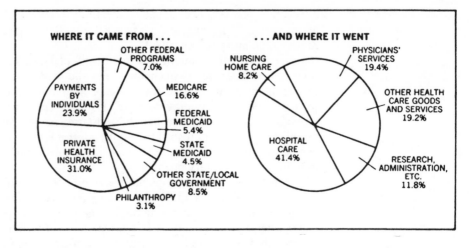

Acknowledging these market imperfections, the Institute of Medicine believes that it is neither "sensible nor safe to return health care to laissez-faire philosophy, although regulation should be used as sparingly as possible so that market forces can operate when appropriate." Both the Institute and Klarman conclude that the case for health planning rests largely on the divergence that has been shown to exist between the interests of autonomous health providers and those of the broader public interest—interests which cannot adequately be resolved in an unrestrained free market.

The antitrust implications of the health planning law provide an appropriate vehicle in which the relationship between regulation and competition in the health care sector can be further explored. While much has been written in the area,[111] it is sufficient in this context to briefly review a recent controversial court case.[112]

In 1978, the National Gerimedical Hospital and Geronotology Center filed a suit against Blue Cross of Kansas City (and the Blue Cross Association). In dispute was a denial by Blue Cross to enter into a member contract with the new hospital allegedly because the hospital had not been reviewed and approved by the Mid-America Health Systems Agency; in essence, National Gerimedical argued that Blue Cross had violated the antitrust laws by requiring the hospital to obtain a capital expenditures review from the HSA before it applied for a Blue Cross contract. The inital decision (by the U.S. District Court for the Western District of Missouri) held in favor of Blue Cross, ruling that the intent of Congress was to immunize this type of voluntary activity from the antitrust laws. On July 22, 1980, the 8th Circuit Court of Appeals reheard the case and in essence reaffirmed that voluntary cooperation of a provider with a health planning agency is anticipated by the health planning act and covered by an implied immunity from antitrust laws.

Several months prior to the Court of Appeals' ruling in the Kansas City case, the Department of Justice (DOJ) had been asked its opinion regarding possible antitrust activities by the Central Virginia HSA. In a May 6, 1980, review letter, the DOJ opined that the health planning law did not create complete antitrust exemption for all efforts by HSAs and providers working with them to implement their plans. In January, 1981, the DOJ submitted an amicus brief to the U.S. Supreme Court requesting that the Court hear the antitrust case involving National Gerimedical and Blue Cross. According to the brief, the "Court of Appeals' decision has a substantial adverse impact on competition and antitrust enforcement" in the health sector, and further, that there "exists no plain repugnancy between the National Health Planning and Resources Development Act and the Sherman Act."[113]

The medical marketplace The dynamics of the system in everyday life are simple to follow. Patients want the best medical services available. Providers know that the more services they give and the more complex the services are, the more they earn and the more they are likely to please their clients. Besides, physicians are trained to practice medicine at the highest level of technical quality without regard to cost. Hospitals want to retain their patients, physicians, and community support by offering the maximum range of services and the most modern technology, often regardless of whether they are duplicating services offered by other institutions nearby. Though insurance companies would prefer to avoid the uncertainty that rising prices create, they have generally been able to pass along the costs to their subscribers, and their profits increase with the total volume of expenditures. No one in the system stands to lose from its expansion. Only the population over whom the insurance costs and taxes are spread has to pay, and it is too poorly organized to offer resistance.

The obvious defect is the absence of any effective restraint. . . . No limits were placed on the number or variety of medical specialties, while specialists received higher insurance reimbursements than general practitioners. Almost every conceivable encouragement was given to hospitals to grow. Most insurance covered hospital care; doctors' services, if given in hospitals, were more likely to be covered and paid at a higher rate.

So just as the financing system promoted overexpansion in some areas, it produced an undersupply of services in others. The incentives that favored hospital care promoted the neglect of ambulatory and preventive health services; the incentives that favored specialization also caused primary care to be neglected. Paying doctors according to the fees prevailing in their areas encourage doctors to settle in wealthy suburbs rather than in the rural or inner-city areas.

Source: Paul Starr, *The Social Transformation of American Medicine* (New York: Basic Books, 1982), pp. 386–87.

On June 15, 1981, the Supreme Court overturned the holdings of the lower courts and ruled in favor of National Gerimedical; in essence, the court determined that voluntary cooperative activities of providers to implement the plans of an HSA are subject to the antitrust laws. As Justice Lewis Powell wrote,

Nothing in the [planning act] requires Blue Cross to take action that, in essence, sought to enforce the advisory decision of [a local HSA]. . . . There is no reason to believe that Congress specifically contemplated such 'enforcement' by private insurance providers . . . to put 'teeth' into the noncompulsory planning process. Congress expected HSA planning to be implemented mainly through persuasion and cooperation.[114]

Although the decision will undoubtedly discourage cooperative efforts by private entities in implementing health systems' plans, a footnote in the decision leaves the door open for further litigation: "the holding does not foreclose future claims of antitrust immunity in other factual contexts. . . [and further] there are some activities that must, by implication, be immune from antitrust attack if HSAs and state agencies are to exercise their authorized powers.[115] Thus, the competition versus regulation controversy is far from being definitively resolved.

Recalling the previous discussion of regulation and competition, however, it becomes apparent that the issue is somewhat of a "false dilemma." It is just as possible for the establishment to capture a regulatory process as it is to manipulate a competitive one. The center of power in the health field has been (and remains with) the provider sector. Unless the center of power shifts (which in the short

Horizontal vs. vertical integration of health care financing   There is no evidence for significant savings from for-profit over nonprofit organizations and little evidence for savings from multihospital systems over freestanding institutions. Horizontal integration has more advantages for the organizations than for the society. Similarly, corporate restructuring—the emergence of the polycorporate enterprise—has as its main motive the maximization of reimbursement. These are primarily adaptations to an incentive system that continues to be skewed; there is no reason to expect that they will meet the demands of the government or employers for containment of medical costs.

On the other hand, vertical integration—comprehensive prepayment—has the potential to yield significant savings of money and improvements in effectiveness. There is clear and convincing evidence for substantial savings from HMOs; the main reason is the reduction in expensive hospital care—hardly surprising in view of the effects on the rest of the health care system of the long-standing tilt toward hospitals in government policy, private insurance, and relative prices paid physicians for hospital and office services.

Source: Paul Starr, *The Social Transformation of American Medicine* (New York: Basic Books, 1982), pp. 440–41.

run is doubtful), the most change advocates can hope for is to achieve some semblance of balance within the system—both in the sense of a balance between regulation and competition as well as maintaining broad public and private participation in the process.

Transition

We would be remiss in light of the changing political and economic climate of the early 1980s not to comment on the future changes that health planning is likely to undergo. While it is still too soon to depict definitively how the structure and function of health planning might change as we proceed into the decade, one must be prepared for changes in emphases.

One such change of emphasis will be a concentration of health planning's regulatory authority and responsibility at the state level. With the shift of initiative from the federal to the state level will come a corresponding diminution of regional/local responsibilities. State responsibilities will focus on capital expenditure control and on rate review/regulation—each guided by a state health plan. While the SHCC (or its counterpart) will remain at the state level to provide consumer/provider input, its authority vis-á-vis the state health planning office will be reduced. Data collection and analysis will also reside at the state level. Federal support for health planning will be reduced to be replaced by reliance on both state support and self-generating sources of revenue; e.g., certificate of need application and processing fees; assessments on hospital revenues. Alterations in reimbursement formulae may provide additional support for health planning functions; e.g., allowance for "planning" as part of reimbursed costs under Medicare and Medicaid.

At the regional/local level, health planning will continue to stress community involvement, public information and education, advocacy, and implementation. The latter will be accomplished through a state-local partnership; the state will provide regulatory authority and financial incentives to implement proposals coupled with a reliance on local level negotiations, bargaining, and compromise to facilitate community input and approval. The regional agencies will continue to be organized as nonprofit private agencies with consumer-majority advisory councils; however, consumers will be broadly defined and include major representation from the purchasers of health care; i.e., business, labor unions, third-party payers, and public officials. Financial support for local health planning will of necessity rely on private sector contributions; such reliance will bring changes of vested interest and undue influence—some of which will require judicial resolution.

Health care coalitions will become increasingly important; coalitions—representing the labor and business communities—will work with providers and regulators to identify and implement needed changes. In a few cases, the coalitions themselves might assume major health planning responsibilities at the regional/local level; in many cases, the coalitions will provide valuable input into the process, providing a forum for education and the exchange of ideas on needed health care reforms, and becoming active in planning activities on task forces, subarea advisory councils, and agency governing boards. These coalitions will represent a second change of emphasis in the health planning program—encouragement of private sector activity in health planning.

Overall, the problems health planners will face in the 1980s will be familiar ones—cost, access, and quality. However, the system itself will change; thus, the way these problems need be addressed will be altered. Health planners will need to become more familiar with pro-competitive options such as health maintenance organizations and private health insurance reform strategies. Since they will increasingly work within the private health sector (e.g., with individual hospitals; hospital chains; coalitions; third-party payers), health planners must become more proficient in the areas of health care administration, health care micro-economics, and institutional long-range planning. To implement effectively, they must have greater knowledge of health care marketing principles and strategies. Health planners will become involved in conflict resolution; for example, conflict is likely to arise between large hospital chains and small independent health care institutions, between business/labor coalitions and hospitals (over cost shifting issues), and between group practice physicians and independent physicians. With greater private sector involvement and cooperation will also come antitrust concerns.

Health planning remains a potentially strong countervailing force to unrestrained free enterprise, on the one hand, and national centralized authority, on the other. Many view the program as a last attempt at grassroots health planning. It has had a long history. It has had its successes and its failures. It has often been asked to respond to "mixed signals"—and, in its attempts to do so, has not always been able to accomplish all it aspired to do. It grew out of the CCMC concept and the voluntary hospital planning councils of the 1920s and 1930s, to the Hill-Burton agencies of the 1940s and the "318" agencies of the early 1960s, to the CHP partnership of the mid-1960s and the national health planning movement of the 1970s and 1980s. Throughout nearly seven decades, it has kept its community orientation and commitment to public participation and voluntary action. Although over time, the scope of its activities has broadened and the tools to accomplish its mandate have changed, the intent has remained constant: to improve the health status of the American people.

1 Dr. Halfdan Mahler, Director-General of WHO, in an address to the twenty-ninth session of the Regional Committee for Africa, Maputo, September 1979, quoted in *World Health Forum: An International Journal of Health Development* 1 (1980):7.

2 United Nations, World Health Organization, "Constitution of the World Health Organizations," *Handbook of Basic Documents—World Health Organization* (Geneva: Palais des Nations, 1951):3.

3 Milton Terris, "Approaches to an Epidemiology of Health," *American Journal of Public Health* 65 (October 1975): 1038.

4 Henrik L. Blum, *Planning for Health : Development and Application of Social Change Theory* (New York: Human Sciences Press, 1974), p. 93.

5 E. Richard Weinerman "Research on Comparative Health Service Systems," *Medical Care* 9 (May–June 1971): 272.

6 Ibid., p. 273.

7   Don Martindale, *The Nature and Types of Socio-logical Theory* (Cambridge, MA: The Riverside Press, 1960), pp. 324–327.

8   Weinerman, "Research on Comparative Health Service Systems," pp. 274–275.

9   United Nations, Executive Board of the World Health Organization, *Organizational Study on Methods of Promoting the Development of Basic Health Services* (Annex 11 to *Official Records of the World Health Organization*, no.206), 1973, p. 110, quoted in Ray H. Elling and Henry Kerr, "Selection of Contrasting National Health Systems for In-depth Study," *Inquiry* 12 Supplement (June 1975): 25.

10 Milton I. Roemer, *Comparative National Policies on Health Care* (New York: Marcel Dekker Inc., 1977), pp. 1–24.

11 US Department of Health, Education and Welfare, *Health United States 1979*, DHEW Pub. No. (PHS) 80-1232 (1980): 205.

12 Henrik L. Blum, review of *Approaches to National Health Planning* by H.E. Hilleboe, A. Barkhuus, and W.C. Thomas, in *International Journal of Health Services* 4 (1974): 367.

13 Ibid., p. 368.

14 Harold Demone, "Simulating Human Service Reform," *Human Services* 8 (June 1978): 29.

15 Lewis A. Coser, *The Functions of Social Conflict* (New York: The Free Press, 1956), p. 153.

16 Blum, review of *Approaches to National Health Planning*, pp. 370–380.

17 Ibid., p. 377.

18 Committee on the Costs of Medical Care. *Medical Care for the American People* (Chicago: University of Chicago Press, 1932; reprint ed., New York: Arno Press and the New York Times, 1972).

19 The term "group practice" was defined by the Committee as " . . . a group which is so organized that each professional person in it is responsible to the group for the quality of his work rather than solely to himself." Ibid., p. 109.

20 Ibid., pp. 134–135.

21 Ibid., p. 135.

22 Ibid.

23 Morris Fishbein, cited by James E. Bryan, "View from the Hill," *American Family Physician* 20 (November 1979): 216.

24 I.S. Falk, "Medical Care in the USA—1932–1972: Problems, Proposals, and Programs from the Committee on the Cost of Medical Care to the Committee for National Health Insurance." *Milbank Memorial Fund Quarterly/Health and Society* 51 (Winter 1973): 4.

25 US Congress, House, *Social Security Act*, sec. 1, 49 *Stat.* 620 (1935), 39 *U.S.C.*, sec. 498(d), 1970.

26 Falk, "Medical Care in the USA," p. 5.

27 Philip N. Reeves, David E. Bergwall, and Nina B. Woodside, *Introduction to Health Planning*, 2d ed. (Washington, D.C.: Information Resources Press 1979), pp. 13–15.

28 US Congress, House, *Hospital Survey and Construction Act*, sec. 1131 (64), 60 *Stat.* 1041 (1946), 5 *U.S.C.*, sec. 73(c) (1966).

29 The Hospital Council of Greater New York was the first (1937) voluntary hospital planning council to be established. By 1964, there were 33 such bodies in the major metropolitan areas.

30 As Tannen notes, the early hospital planning councils defined an "unneccessary facility" " . . . as one

that does not have adequate demand to support it; the appropriateness of its utilization or its relationship to health status was only indirectly addressed." Source: Louis Tannen, "Health Planning as a Regulatory Strategy: A Discussion of its History and Current Uses," *International Journal of Health Services* 10 (1980): 122

31 P. Thompson, "Voluntary Regional Planning," in *Regionalization and Health Policy*, ed. E. Ginzberg (Washington, D.C.: Health Resources Administration, 1977), as cited by Tannen, "Health Planning as a Regulatory Strategy," 121.

32 Tannen, "Health Planning as a Regulatory Strategy," p. 122.

33 Herbert E. Klarman, "Health Planning: Progress, Prospects and Issues," *Milbank Memorial Fund Quarterly/Health and Society* 56 (Winter 1978): 91.

34 Reeves, *Introduction to Health Planning*, p. 18.

35 US Congress, House, *Comprehensive Health Planning and Public Health Service Act*, sec. 1-2. 80 *Stat.* 1180 (1966), 42 *U.S.C.*, sec. 201 (nt) (1977).

36 Blum, review of *Approaches to National Health Planning*, p. 380.

37 J. Joel May, "Will Third Generation Planning Succeed?" *Hospital Progress* (March 1976): 61.

38 US Congress, House, *National Health Planning and Resources Development Act*, sec. 1, 88 *Stat.* 2225 (1975), 42 *U.S.C.*, sec.201 (nt) (1977).

39 In 1974, the organizational structure of the 218 areawide comprehensive health planning agencies varied: 161 were nonprofit private organizations, 16 were economic development districts, 18 were planning commissions, 8 were councils of governments, 3 were local governments, and 12 were state-assisted local councils. Source: US Congress, House Committee on Interstate and Foreign Commerce, *Report on National Health Policy, Planning and Resources Development Act of 1974*. 93rd Cong., 2d sess., No. 93-1382, 26 September 1974, p. 11.

40 US Department of Health, Education and Welfare, *Interim Analysis of Results of Comprehensive Health Planning Agency Assessments* (Washington, D.C.: Division of Comprehensive Health Planning, March 1974), pp. 1–3.

41 John T. O'Connor, "Comprehensive Health Planning: Dreams and Realities," *Milbank Memorial Fund Quarterly/Health and Society* 52 (Fall 1974): 401.

42 US Department of Health, Education, and Welfare, *Interim Analysis*, p. 1; also see US Department of Health, Education, and Welfare, Health Resources Administration, *Areawide Health Planning Agency Performance Standards* (Washington, DC: The Comprehensive Health Planning Service, October 1973); and US Department of Health, Education, and Welfare, *State Health Planning Agency Performance Standards* (Washington, DC: The Comprehensive Health Planning Service, November 1973).

43 O'Connor, "Comprehensive Health Planning," p. 405.

44 The acts being considered in this chapter are not inclusive of all federal health legislation and programs which may affect health planning. Other acts which might have been discussed (e.g.) include: The Appalachian Regional Development Act of 1965 (P.L. 89-4), the Demonstration Cities and Metropolitan Development Act (P.L. 89-754), the Office of Management and Budget's Circular No. A-95,

the Health Professions Education Assistance Act of 1963 (P.L. 88-129 along with its numerous amendments), and the Social Security Amendments of 1965 (P.L. 89-97) which authorized the Medicare and Medicaid programs—Titles XVIII and XIX of the Social Security Act, respectively. For a discussion to these acts (and others), see Reeves, Bergwall, and Woodside, *Introduction to Health Planning*, pp. 6–34; and/or Florence A. Wilson and Duncan Neuhauser, *Health Services in the United States* (Cambridge, MA: Ballinger Publishing Company, rev. 1st ed., 1976), pp. 117–201.

45 US Congress, House, *Heart Disease, Cancer and Stroke Amendments*, sec. 1, 79 *Stat.* 926 (1965), 42 *U.S.C.*, sec. 201 (nt) (1977).

46 US Congress, House, *Heart Disease, Cancer, Stroke and Kidney Amendments of 1970*, sec. 102, 84 *Stat.* 1297 (1970), 42 *U.S.C.*, sec. 299 (1977).

47 US Congress, House, Committee on Interstate and Foreign Commerce, *Report on National Health Policy, Planning and Resources Development Act of 1974*. 93rd Cong., 2d sess., no. 93-1382, 26 September 1974, p. 14.

48 Ibid., p. 20.

49 The Experimental Health Services Delivery Systems program was initiated in 1971 by the Health Services and Mental Health Administration within its National Center for Health Services Research and Development. It never received legislative authority.

50 US Congress, House, *Mental Retardation Facilities and Community Health Centers Act*, sec. 1,1000, 77 *Stat.* 282 (1963), 42 *U.S.C.*, sec. 2661 (nts) (1977).

51 US Congress, House, *Special Health Revenue Sharing Act*, sec. 101, 89 *Stat.* 304 (1975), 42 *U.S.C.*, sec. 201 (nt) (1977).

52 US Congress, House, *National Health Planning and Resources Development Act*, sec. 1, 88 *Stat.* 2225 (1975), 42 *U.S.C.*, sec. 201 (nt) (1977).

53 In 1980, the Department of Health, Education, and Welfare (DHEW) was reorganized and became the Department of Health and Human Services (DHHS) and the Department of Education (DOE). DHHS now assumes responsibility for health planning. Since the early planning activity was the responsibility of DHEW, the author chose to refer to the major federal-level health agency as DHEW rather than DHHS throughout the chapter.

54 Florence B. Fiori, "Bureau of Health Facilities' Increasing Responsibilities in Assuring Medical Care for the Needy and Services Without Discrimination," *Public Health Reports* 95 (March–April 1980): 164.

55 The discussion of the health service area designation process closely follows that presented in Roland L. Peterson, "The Designation of Health Services Areas," *Public Health Reports* 91 (January–February 1976): 9–16.

56 Ibid., p. 16.

57 US Department of Health, Education, and Welfare, Health Resources Administration, *Papers on the National Health Guidelines: The Priorities of Section 1502*, DHEW Pub. No. (HRA) 77-641 (January 1977): iii.

58 US Department of Health and Human Resources Administration, *National Health Planning Goals: The National Guidelines for Health Planning*, draft copy (17 April 1980): 4, 21–134.

59 US Department of Health, Education, and Welfare, Health Resources Administration, *Papers on the National Health Guidelines: National Guidelines for Health Planning*, DHEW Pub. No. (HRA) 78-643 (28 March 1978): 1–75.

60 Vicente Navarro, "Methodology on Regional Planning of Personal Health Services: A Case Study: Sweden," *Medical Care* 8 (September–October 1970) as cited by Kenneth J. Diamond, "Trying to Take the National Guidelines for Health Planning Seriously: Issues for Thought," *American Journal of Health Planning* 3 (April 1978): 30.

61 Diamond, "Trying to Take the National Guidelines for Health Planning Seriously," p. 30.

62 Ibid., pp. 30–33.

63 Eugene J. Rubel, "Implementing the National Health Planning and Resources Development Act of 1974," *Public Health Reports* 91 (January–February 1976): 4,8.

64 The PSRO program (established under the Social Security Amendments of 1973, P.L. 92-603) is a utilization review and quality assurance program required as a condition of participation for hospitals under Medicare.

65 The reader is referred to footnote 39, which describes the varied organizational structure of areawide "b" agencies existing in 1974.

66 Colin C. Rorrie and Frances V. Dearman, "Health Planning—A New Phase," *Public Health Reports* 95 (March–April 1980): 178.

67 US Congress, House, "Discussion on National Health Policy Planning and Resources Development Act of 1974 (H.R. 16204)," *Congressional Record* (13 December 1974): H11845–11846.

68 Donald B. Ardell, "Public Regional Councils and Comprehensive Health Planning: A Partnership?" *Journal of the American Institute of Planners (November 1970): 339–404;* Idem, "CHP, Regional Councils and the Public Interest: A Case for New Leadership," *Inquiry* 8 (December 1971): 27–35; Idem, "The Metropolitan Council CHP Experience—A Search for Balance Between Control and Delegation," *American Journal of Public Health* April 1972: 516-521; Idem, "Health Planning: Some Alternatives for Change," *Planning* (July 1972): 114–116; and Idem, "CHP and Multifunctional Regional Councils: A Reappraisal," *Inquiry 11 (December 1974): 263–268.*

69 Ardell, "CHP and Multifunctional Regional Councils," p. 264.

70 Ibid.

71 Drew Altman, "The Politics of Health Care Regulation: The Case of the National Health Planning and Resources Development Act, *Journal of Health Politics, Policy and Law* 2 (Winter 1978): 566–568.

72 Rubel, "Implementing the National Health Planning and Resources Development Act of 1974," p.7.

73 Colin C. Rorrie and Frances V. Dearman, "Health Planning—A New Phase," *Public Health Reports* 95 (March–April 1980): 178.

74 US Congress, House, *Public Protection Activities of HEW, Hearings before a Subcommittee on Oversight and Investigation of the Committee on Interstate and Foreign Commerce*. 94th Cong., 2d sess., 8 April 1976, pp. 10–11.

75 *Montgomery County, Md. v. Califano*, 449 F. Supp. 1230-1250 (United States District Court, D. of Maryland, 30 March 1978).

76 In implementing the holding of the *Montgomery*

County Md. v. Califano decision, provision is made to allow the four existing HSAs which are units of local government (Montgomery County; City of Chicago; Santa Clara County; Navajo Nation) to retain their right to review and *approve* the health systems plan and annual implementation plan. See US Congress House, *Health Planning and Resources Development Amendments of 1979: Conference Report to Accompany S. 544.* 96th Cong., 1st sess., August 1979, pp. 67–68.

77 The discussion in this section follows closely the information presented in Altman, "The Politics of Health Care Regulations," pp. 560–580.

78 Ibid., pp. 566–572.

79 Edward M. Kennedy, "The Congress and National Health Policy," *American Journal of Public Health* 68 (March 1978): 241.

80 Florida, *Hospital Care Cost Containment Act, Florida Statutes* (1979): Chap. 395.501-514, *Florida Statutes* (1980 Supplement): Chap. 395.512, 395.5125.

81 Altman, "The Politics of Health Care Regulations," p. 568.

82 Ibid., p. 569.

83 Ibid., p. 570.

84 Jonathan P. West, "Health Planning in Multifunctional Regional Councils: Baltimore and Houston Experience," *Inquiry* 12 (September 1975): 189.

85 Altman, "The Politics of Health Care Regulations," p. 571.

86 The following references are devoted in whole or part to a discussion of health planning methods: Allen D. Spiegel and Herbert Harvey Hyman, *Basic Health Planning Methods* (Rockville, MD: Aspen Systems Corporation, 1978); Blum, *Planning for Health: Development and Application of Social Change Theory*; Reeves, Bergwall, and Woodside, *Introduction to Health Planning*; Health Planning/Development Center, Inc., *Selected Methodological Approaches to Address the National Guidelines for Health Planning in Local and State Health Plan Development* (Atlanta: The Center, 1979); G.E. Alan Dever, *Community Health Analysis* (Rockville, MD: Aspen Systems Corporation, 1980); US Department of Health, Education and Welfare, *A Data Acquisition and Analysis Handbook for Health Planners*, Vol. I (HRA 77-14506) and Vol. II (Hra 77-14507), 1976: Idem, *Health Planning Information Series: Guidelines for the Acquisition and Use of Data Under Public Law 93-641*, HRA 78-14013 (June 1978).

87 US Department of Health, Education, and Welfare, *Health Planning Methods and Technology Series: A Taxonomy of the Health System Appropriate for Plan Development*, HRA 77-14534 (May 1979).

88 Reeves, Bergwall, and Woodside, *Introduction to Health Planning*, pp. 51–61.

89 Ibid., p. 54.

90 Tannen, "Health Planning as a Regulatory Strategy," p. 128.

91 Ibid., p. 126.

92 US Department of Health, Education, and Welfare, *Health Planning Information Series: Guide to Data for Health Systems Planners*, HRA 76-14502 (April 1976): 17–19, 199–274.

93 For example, see reference no. 92; also see US, Department of Health, Education, and Welfare, *Health Planning Information Series: A Guide to the Development of Health Resource Inventories*, HRA 76-14504 (August 1976); Idem, *Health Planning*

Information Series: Guidelines for the Acquisition and Use of Data Under Public Law 93-641, HRA 78-14013 (June 1978); Idem, *Health Planning Methods and Technology Series: Organizing and Maintaining a Document Collection in a Health Systems Agency: Suggested Resources*, HRA 79-14011 (December 1978).

94 US Department of Health, Education, and Welfare, *Health Planning Methods and Technology Series: A Data Acquisition and Analysis Handbook for Health Planners*, Vol. I (HRA 77-14506), October 1976, pp. 160–164.

95 For a brief description of these surveys, see Dorothy P. Rice, "The National Center for Health Statistics and the Data Needed for National Health Insurance," *Bulletin of the New York Academy of Medicine* 53 (December 1977): 893–900.

96 Steven Sieverts, *Health Planning Issues and Public Law 93-641* (Chicago: American Hospital Association, 1977): p. 81.

97 US Congress, House, *National Health Planning and Resources Development Act, sec. 1523(a)(4)*.

98 West, "Health Planning in Multifunctional Regional Councils," pp. 180–192.

99 US Department of Health, Education and Welfare, "Health Systems Agency and State Agency Reviews of the Appropriateness of Existing Institutional Health Services," *Federal Register* 44, no. 239, (11 December 1979); p. 71754.

100 Robin E. MacStravic, "Appropriateness Review." Report to TAC/X, Center for Planning, Boise, ID, January 1979, p. 3 (mimeographed)

101 David C. Ranney, *Planning and Politics in the Metropolis* (Columbus, OH: Charles E. Merrill, 1969), pp. 109–137.

102 Falk, "Medical Care in the USA," p. 30.

103 For a thorough discussion of the issues raised by consumer participation in health planning, see Theodore R. Marmor and James A. Morone, "Representing Consumer Interests: Imbalanced Markets, Health Planning, and the HSAs," *Milbank Memorial Fund Quarterly/Health and Society* 58 (Winter 1980): 125–165.

104 Altman, "The Politics of Health Care Regulation," p. 563.

105 Clark Havighurst, as cited by Jere A. Wysong, "Health Planning and Health Systems Agencies," *Health Services Research* (Winter 1975): 402.

106 Daniel Beauchamp, as cited by Wysong (see note 105), p. 401.

107 Elliott A. Krause, "The Political Context of Health Service Regulation," *International Journal of Health Services* 5 (1975): 593.

108 Klarman, "Health Planning: Progress, Prospect and Issues," p. 89.

109 Milton I. Roemer, "Bed Supply and Hospital Utilization: A Natural Experiment," *Hospitals* 35 (1 November 1961): 36–42, as cited by Klarman, "Health Planning: Progress, Prospects, and Issues," 1978, pp. 89,93.

110 Institute of Medicine, *Health Planning in the United States: Issues in Guideline Development* (Washington, DC: National Academy of Sciences, 1980): 12.

111 For example, see J.C. Avellone and F.D. Moore, "The Federal Trade Commission Enters a New Arena," *The New England Journal of Medicine* 299 (July–September 1978): 478–483; P.C. Kissam, "Antitrust Law, the First Amendment, and Professional Self-Regulation of Technical Quality," in *Regulating the Professions: A Public Symposium,*

ed. R.D. Blair (Lexington, MA.: Lexington Books, 1980): 143–183; Clark C. Havighurst, "Antitrust Enforcement in the Medical Services Industry: What Does It All Mean?" *Milbank Memorial Fund Quarterly/Health and Society* 58 (Winter 1980): 89–124; Idem, "The Antitrust Laws, the Federal Trade Commission and Cost Containment," *Bulletin of the New York Academy of Medicine* 56 (January–February 1980): 169–179.

112 American Health Planning Association, *Today in Health Planning*, 2 (9 May, 23 May–6 June, 1 August, 19 September 1980); 3 (9 January 1981).

113 Ibid., 9 January 1981.

114 Justice Lewis Powell as cited in *Today in Health Planning*, 3 (19 June 1981).

115 Ibid.

22 Social services and education

This chapter focuses attention on the evolution of a variety of services which have become an accepted part of everyday life in the United States. An initial discussion presents a framework for discussing services and the states' practices in planning for them. Included in the framework discussion are several compatible classification schemes. The history and structure of state patterns for carrying out the variety of social service functions is viewed both from the states' acceptance of their responsibilities and federal involvements and initiatives. State practices are given heavier emphasis than regional practices, primarily because of the temporary and amorphous nature of the regional planning bodies. There is some discussion of the needs assessment phase in the planning process, especially within the context of Title XX social services planning. The section on social services ends with some emerging principles for social services planning.

Education and educational planning are treated separately, but as a part of the total human services system. Since the function of education has always been a responsibility of the states, it is from this perspective that both the practices and the principles for educational planning are presented. Examples covering elementary through higher education are given. Regional aspects are presented within the context of vocational education.

The framework of social services planning

The boundaries of a field or a system of service are the product of historical accident, vested interest, professional assessment, conceptualization of problems at a given moment—and a host of other factors. In The United States, the historical events following the "Great Depression" and World War II and the rediscovery of "poverty" in the 1960s gave rise to reviewing and rethinking the field of social services.

Human services (with or without planning) has been seen in the past as the exclusive turf of the social work profession; human resources planning has been staked out, more or less, by economists and the education professionals with sociologists having a little piece of the action; social policy development, for the most part, has been seen as the prerogative of political scientists, public administrators, and the legal professionals with an assist from economists and sociologists.

It was not until the 1960s when federal legislation focused on so many different social concerns and called for comprehensive, program, and project planning that the skills and knowledge of planners were seen as necessary and useful outside the boundaries of the physical and economic development domains; even planners themselves had not previously stepped far outside these limits. Efforts at all levels of government and in the private sectors (business and human service organizations) have begun moving toward more cooperative and/or collaborative arrangements in planning for the future. Unfortunately, these efforts are currently being made within the limits of previously defined, or newly expanding definitions of, certain fields and only tentatively or tenuously crossing those boundaries.

Human needs and human services

It has been generally agreed that there are four categories of basic need shared by all human beings:[1]

Physical survival

The need to grow and develop—and ultimately reach one's potential

The need to overcome specific pathologies (any illness, disease, or defect whether by reason of birth, accident, or contagion)

The need for support in times of crisis or trauma.

The knowledge areas which have been developed in these categories of need comprise what has come to be referred to as the "human services."[2] Some are provided selectively either through public financing or individual purchasing, depending upon one's economic means. It is when an individual or family does not have adequate economic means that services in many of these categories are necessarily provided through public resources—governmental or voluntary.

Development of classification systems: a theoretical base

Although there is yet no single uniform classification system, there has been steady movement in this direction, especially since 1968. The various schema which have been developed and are being used at present are derived from studies conducted in several fields of endeavor. Alfred J. Kahn's work is particularly important to an overall framework of categories.

In his studies of social services as they relate to the theory and practice of social planning and social policy, Kahn makes a strong case for the addition of a "personal social services" category to the five traditionally accepted social welfare categories of health, education, income maintenance, employment, and housing. The philosophy underlying the personal social service system holds that a complex technological society is a difficult environment for many of us, and that *good* government works actively to make life easier for its citizens. The traditionalist viewpoint limits the thrust of social welfare to those in temporary trouble and thus would withdraw or redirect services once people are restored to some predetermined level of adequacy.[3]

The distinction that Kahn makes between "social utilities" and "social services"[4] is of particular importance for planners and decision makers at the state and regional levels of government. A *social utility* is defined as a social invention, a resource or facility designed to meet a *generally experienced need* in social living. It is considered so vital that the broader community suffers from the results of the deprivation faced by an individual. The provision of a social utility is not left to the market economy even though some people, especially those who are affluent, may continue to resort to the marketplace. Public education, public health, social insurance, income maintenance, employment service, public and subsidized housing, senior service, and children's day care centers are all forms of social utilities. They are not considered as temporary or transitional.[5]

A *social service,* on the other hand, may be interpreted in an institutional context as consisting of programs made available by other than market criteria *to assure a basic level* of health-education-welfare provision. Objectives of such programs are set forth to enhance communal (within family; within community) living and individual functioning, to assist those in difficulty and need, and to facilitate access to services and institutions, generally.[6]

The emphasis on the notion that some services are social utilities and others are social (case) services represents, first, a conviction that community well-being and the success of the economy depend on the existence of social utilities and, second, a belief that we must organize such utilities *so as to make them as accessible and nonstigmatic* as the water supply and postal service.[7]

Three types of social services are suggested by Kahn as useful in sorting out issues of access, financing, and service delivery. The first two services are directly related to general resources and facilities (or social utilities); the third encompasses "case" services (what traditionalists generally understand as social services).

1. Services or resources to be used by the individual as he chooses to do so (the park, for example). Symbolically, at least, such facilities have no locked door.
2. Services or resources available to users by status (age—school, senior center; or income level—public housing and income maintenance are examples). One's status provides the key for opening the door.
3. Services or resources, which become available on the basis of professional judgment or evaluation or some assessment of need (e.g., a residential treatment center, compensatory education, therapeutic counseling). An appropriate diagnostic judgment or social assessment (e.g., handicapping condition, nonconformity, inappropriate responses to stress, etc.) provides the key to the doorway of service.[8]

It is the third service type which seems to present the most problems to planners, administrators, and elected public officials at all governmental levels. Some of the services in this category have been and still are provided through the voluntary sector; others have been provided through the public sector, especially in institutional settings.

State attempts at classification: target groups, goals, services

In a study conducted by the Council of State Governments (1975), a classification of 13 client or "target groups" was set forth, reflecting state governments' views as to those most frequently in need of human services. As can be noted in the identification of the target groups, all presume some handicapping condition or impairment, and thus fall into Kahn's third service type of social (case) services. The services to be provided as well as the types of facilities are grouped into four levels of care, indicating the client's degree of dependency on the system of human services.[9]

One of the underlying assumptions of the level of care arrangement is that institutional care is the most expensive to the public (i.e., the government-in-charge). There is, however, the recognition that there are and will continue to be clients or target groups in need of human services; general purpose state and local governments will have continuing responsibilities for providing some human services to those in need; and other specialized categorical approaches to the provision of public social services has become too cumbersome for the general purpose government officials to deal with, both financially and administratively.

The level of care categories, as presented in the Council of State Governments' study, are almost parallel with the Title XX goals of self-sufficiency, protection, reduced or appropriate institutionalization, and self-support as presented below.

Levels of Service Goals—Title XX

The five broad national goals to which all services must be directed and under which all other goals and objectives are to be subordinated are:

1. Achieving or maintaining economic self-support to prevent, reduce or eliminate dependency;
2. Achieving or maintaining self-sufficiency, including the reduction or prevention of dependency;
3. Preventing or remedying neglect, abuse or exploitation of children and adults unable to protect their own interests, or preserving, rehabilitating or reuniting families;

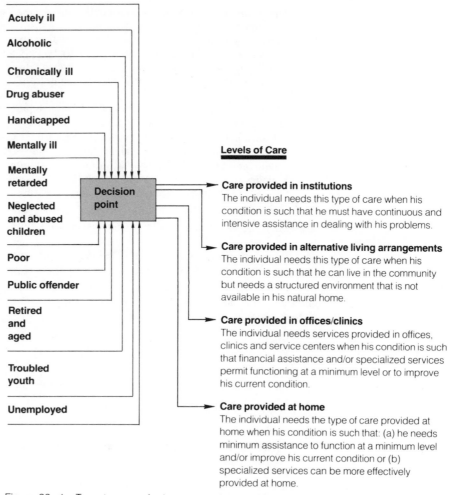

Figure 22–1 Target groups for human services and levels of care required.

4. Preventing or reducing inappropriate institutional care by providing for community-based care, home-based care or other forms of less intensive care;
5. Securing referral or admission for institutional care when other forms of care are not appropriate, or providing services to individuals in institutions.[10]

In their study of state, regional and local government organizations involved in human services planning, Horton and Armentrout found among the three state case studies (Arizona, Florida, Georgia) that Arizona's Department of Economic Security had outlined five levels of self-sufficiency intended to be achieved toward the economic security of the individual.[11] These levels and their descriptions seem to take into account the full range of possibilities and realities of a community and the human condition. They are similar in nature to the "levels of service goals" set forth in Title XX of the Social Security Act, 1974 and the "levels of care" described in the Council of State Governments document. They are presented as an example of state initiatives which reflect genuine concern about service fragmentation, costs, efficiency, and the need for planning and policy control over state provision of social services.[12]

Levels of Self-Sufficiency; *Arizona Department of Economic Security*

1. *Fully Self-Sufficient*—An individual economically and socially self-sufficient and therefore, independent of DES services.
2. *Partial Self-Support*—An individual who has some earnings but is partly

dependent upon DES programs for subsidized services and/or income supplementation.

3. *Family Self-Care*—An individual who has attained physical and/or emotional independence within his own home and may be dependent upon income maintenance. This level has an important prevention focus attached to it. Services are provided to prevent an individual or family from deteriorating and thereby requiring out-of-home care.

4. *Alternative Care*—An individual who does not require full-time supervision of daily activities (has not attained physical and/or emotional independence and does not have in-home family care available) but requires care in a community-based facility for continued growth and development *and* normalization.

5. *Institutional Care*—An individual who requires full-time supervision of his daily activities or who requires special settings to assist in the development of his ability to function at another level.

UWASIS: a comprehensive human services taxonomy

Another significant contribution to the classification process has been the development of a services identification system by the voluntary sector.[13] United Way of America Services Identification System (UWASIS) consists of seven substantive goal categories and one which is supportive in nature but also listed as a functional category.

1. Income security and economic opportunity
2. Health
3. Provision of basic material resources
4. Opportunity for the acquisition of knowledge and skills
5. Environmental quality
6. Individual and collective safety
7. Social functioning
8. Assurance of the support and effectiveness of services, through organized action

Almost every local and areawide United Way of America agency and many state and county as well as municipal government human services or social services departments are using some adaptation or variation of UWASIS' program categories.[14]

The structure of social services and planning efforts

The structure of social services was built largely without benefit of planning. Different parts were developed at different times to meet different needs. In its most rudimentary form, the conditions for public provision of social services began when "helping" was taken over from the extended family and its informal community by a host of private (charity) and public (welfare) organizations and institutions.

The evolution of social services: from the beginning

From the earliest days in the United States, rights of the individual to "Life, Liberty, and the pursuit of Happiness" have been linked inextricably with a common bond to "promote the general welfare." During the several hundred years of our history we have been constructing a vast network of community-supported services whose intent *is* to promote the *general* welfare.

Many of these services, orginally founded for the benefit of the disadvantaged, now have become indispensible to the general welfare of everyone. The early pauper lists and poor farms have grown into a system of income maintenance and social insurance. From the first institutions for the sick poor has come the modern community hospital. The gaols, the stocks, and the whipping post have been supplanted by different notions of criminal justice and corrections institutions. For the mentally abnormal of an earlier day there were few institutions established—mostly to protect the community against the so-called "criminally" insane. Today, we have a variety of mental health, casework, and other agencies which strive to aid those whose circumstances and behavior handicap their adjustment to society or society's adjustment to them. Where, in the past, we had abundant nature surrounding every doorstep, now we have parks and playgrounds for hundreds of thousands—at varying distances from those doorsteps.

The pressures and complexities which have accompanied changes from the relative social independence found in a rural agricultural society to the necessary interdependence of an urban industrial society, impelled a rapid expansion of many different types and targets of services, approaches to delivery, means of financing, and separate professions. Public policy, for many decades, has supported a categorial approach to meeting human needs. At best, the governmental sectors have been reactive to the conditions which accelerated the phenomena of uncoordinated, nonintegrated, and fragmented approaches to both planning *and* delivery of social services. And in the private sector as well, conflicting traditions, fears, misconceptions, matters of sponsorship, financing, and administration, have contributed to the continuation of a categorial treatment of individuals.

Federal involvement and the establishment of administrative structures

To gain a perspective on how social services came to be in this seemingly incoherent predicament, and to continue planning for change, it is necessary to look at some of the history of federal social legislation and the administrative structures which evolved. The provisions made in each piece of legislation have either directed, guided, or influenced the practice of social services planning at all levels of government as well as in the private (profit and nonprofit) sector. The legislative specifications and requirements laid out for the state have impacted the planning at substate governmental levels as well as the organizational structures for administration and service delivery. Each different legislative enactment outlined the target populations to be served, the problems on which to focus, which organizations may or may not provide services, how those services may be delivered, and what kinds of research shall be conducted.

Although not the first piece of federal social legislation, the Social Security Act of 1935, and all of its succeeding amendments, has had the most profound effect on what states, and thence local jurisdictions, can do and have done with regard to social services. In effect, it laid the foundation of the present public welfare system. It also served to establish the social acceptability of a national attack on need, suggesting that at least to some extent poverty was coming to be seen as a societal rather than an individual problem. Over the years, the programs and procedures established in 1935 have been expanded and/or modified. However, the basic structure has changed little in the categories of persons to be served and administrative units to oversee those services. The original purpose as stated was:

To provide for the general welfare by establishing a system of federal old age benefits, and by enabling the several states to make more adequate provisions for aged persons, blind persons, dependent and crippled children, maternal and child welfare, public health, and the administration of their unemployment compensation laws; to establish a Social Security Board; to raise revenue; and for other purposes.

Separate titles were oriented to categories of persons (aged, children, mothers, blind, potential delinquents) or fields of endeavor (public health, vocational rehabilitation). Within each of the categories, states were required to submit, and have approved by the specified federal agency, "state plans" for programs and/or services to be delivered and to establish or designate the state agency for administration of the plan, the method of administration, financial participation and reporting.

Subsequent amendments to the Social Security Act have done the following: encouraged the separation of income maintenance from social services (1962); initiated Medicare and Medicaid (1965), Work Incentive Programs, and emphasis on day care (1967); created Supplemental Security Income for disabled adults and indigent elderly (1972); provided for consolidation of federal financial assistance for social services and promoted planning for coordinated and comprehensive delivery of services through Title XX (1974).

In addition to the Social Security Act, other federal legislation affected the states and their local governments as they organized and planned for human services.

Federal legislation oriented to *the handicapped* was initiated under the Vocational Rehabilitation Act (VRA) of 1920, providing grants to states to develop programs of vocational rehabilitation for the physically disabled. In 1965, this act was amended to assist in the expansion and involvement of services and facilities and *for planning comprehensive vocational rehabilitation programs* in each state. The amendment of 1967 created a National Commission on Architectural Barriers and a National Center for Deaf-Blind Youth and Adults. In 1973, the Rehabilitation Act replaced the VRA of 1920, created the Rehabilitation Services Administration within the Department of Health, Education, and Welfare, established an administration for program evaluation, and required that for states to receive funds there had to be a *written plan for each handicapped individual*. Section 504 of the 1973 legislation established the bases for antidiscrimination toward the handicapped.

The National Mental Health Act of 1946 was the first federal legislative enactment directed toward psychiatric disorders. It provided funding for research in the development of methods of prevention, diagnosis and treatment of such disorders and created the National Advisory Mental Health Council. It also encouraged states, through grants, to get involved with mental health. In 1963, the Mental Retardation Facilities and Community Mental Health Centers Construction Act was passed. This act focused on facility construction and the training of teachers for the mentally retarded. It was through this legislation that a number of research and demonstration projects were initiated to bring about coordination of services for the mentally retarded.[15] The amendment in 1970, "Developmental Disabilities Services and Facilities Construction Act," was designed to assist states in *developing plans for the provision of comprehensive services* to persons affected by mental retardation or their developmental disabilities originating in childhood, assist states in the provision of such services, assist states in the construction of facilities to provide the services needed to carry out the plans, and outlined what is expected to be included in the state plans. The emphasis was focused primarily on education of the mentally retarded.

The Developmentally Disabled Assistance and Bill of Rights Act of 1975 amended the 1970 legislation to provide funds for the resocialization of inappropriately institutionalized persons. Among the programs eligible for assistance under this act are: parent counseling and training, early screening and intervention, infant or preschool care, legal advocacy, community-based planning, coordination of resources, and facilities for the deinstitutionalization of persons inappropriately placed.

A closely allied piece of legislation, the Education for All Handicapped Children Act of 1975, assured that all handicapped children have a free, appropriate education which emphasizes special education and related services designed for meeting their unique needs. It also provided for grants for the removal of architectural barriers and built in evaluation requirements for assessing the effectiveness of the efforts to educate handicapped children, including both physical and mental disabilities.

This stream of legislation directed at the handicapped has its roots in Title V, Part II of the Social Security Act of 1935, representing the concepts of locating such individuals; diagnosing and providing a wide range of services for treatment and follow-up; and *cooperation and coordination with other departments at the federal and state levels of government.*

The Older Americans Act in 1965 gave cognizance to the plight of the elderly by providing *assistance to the states* for the development of new or improved programs, for planning, for training, and for services found lacking. Again, a National Advisory Committee was established, this time for the aging. Research and development projects abounded; state and regional councils on the aging were created; new approaches to working with older people were developed; and senior centers were constructed. The amendments which followed added to or modified the original legislation as well as amending other acts (Higher Education, Library and Construction, Adult Education, Employment, etc.) for the benefit of senior citizens. It was not until the 1973 amendments, however, that grants for state and local planning began *requiring that needs assessments be conducted and that services be coordinated.* The roots of this legislation for older Americans can be traced back through the amendments to the Social Security Acts through the years. The foci, until 1965, had been on income transfers for basic survival and health benefits, without due consideration to normal growth and development and patterns of living and contributing to the community.

During the Great Depression, surplus commodities were provided to those suffering economic hardships and willing to stand in line for those staples which were doled out. The National School Lunch Act of 1946 was a policy declaration on nutrition and education for low-income children. Assistance was provided to state by the federal government to establish and operate school lunch programs wherein meals were to be free or at reduced costs for low-income children. This legislation did not go through any major revisions until 1966, when the National School Lunch and Child Nutrition Act was passed. This act was designed to strengthen and improve food service programs for children. Funds were provided through state education agencies for school breakfast programs, nursery schools, day care centers, and settlement houses through subsequent amendments from 1968 to 1975. The administration at the federal level was transferred from Agriculture to the Department of Health, Education, and Welfare in 1975.

In addition to these acts directed specifically to child nutrition programs, there is another stream of federal legislation directed toward provision of basic foodstuffs for needy individuals and families receiving income assistance through public welfare departments. The Wheatflour and Cornmeal Act of 1954 established precedents for the acts which followed, namely the Food Stamp Act of 1964 and its amendments. The purpose of this legislation was twofold: to strengthen the agricultural economy, and to help achieve a fuller and more effective use of food abundances. Thus, provisions were made to improve levels of nutrition among low-income households through a cooperative federal-state program of food assistance to be operated through normal channels of trade. Administration was carried by the Department of Agriculture and required participation of state welfare agencies.

Declaring a national policy on employment, production, and purchasing power, this legislation called for an annual economic report by the President of the United States, established a Council of Economic Advisors to the President, and created a Joint Committee of the Congress to review the Economic Report.

Most of the employment legislation which followed has focused on ways and means of dealing with unemployment problems, manpower development, training and education for the low-skilled unemployed and underemployed, and the youth who chronologically are ready to enter the labor market but for many reasons are being excluded. Major legislation designed to address these problems included the Manpower Development and Training Act of 1962; the Economic Opportunity Act of 1964; the Emergency Employment Act of 1971; the Comprehensive Employment and Training Act of 1973; and the Youth Employment and Demonstration Projects Act of 1977, and their amendments to date.

All of the foregoing federal social legislation and much more has set in motion the many programs and services which now require a more rational framework for organizational structures, planning, financing, coordinating, and the delivery of services to those in need. A close review of these federal enactments indicates the degree of organizational and intergovernmental complexity which was built into the state social services and why, after 45 years, there is still a great deal of institutional resistance to change.

The Federal Security Agency (FSA) created by Congress in 1939 brought together four human service functions: the Public Health Service, the Social Security Board, the Office of Education, and the Civilian Conservation Corps. Prior to this time, the Public Health Service was located in the Treasury Department (since 1912); the Office of Education was located in the Department of the Interior (since 1867). The Children's Bureau, which was established within the Department of Labor in 1912, remained outside of the FSA. It was not until 1953, when President Eisenhower submitted a reorganization plan calling for the dissolution of the Federal Security Agency and the creation of a cabinet-level department (U.S. Department of Health, Education, and Welfare) that most of the health, education, and welfare programs and offices were brought together "under one roof." By 1975, DHEW had five major units large enough to be designated as cabinet-level departments in some countries: the Social Security Administration; the Public Health Service; the Social and Rehabilitation Service; the Education Division; and the Office of Human Development.

The passage of the Department of Education Organization Act (PL 96-88) in 1979 established cabinet-level status for education and redesignated DHEW as the *Department of Health and Human Services* (Title V, Section 509). It is the Office of Human Development Services which is charged with a broad range of responsibilities related to personal and general social services for specific populations. These responsibilities include leadership for planning and coordinating efforts and the administration of human services and human development programs. The specific populations or special constituencies are children, youth, and families; persons with mental or physical handicaps; the elderly; and native Americans. The major components are designated as "Administrations For. . . ." Each administration works through the ten principal HDS regional offices in direct, official dealings with state and local government organizations.

The pattern of state structures for social services

For the most part, the state's structures for social services followed an evolutionary pattern as the administrative need was determined within each state or as conditional grants-in-aid were enacted by the Congress. Thus, there are both similarities and differences among the states, depending upon the purpose and function of the unit and political form for structuring organizational units within each state.

Units for *education* and *public welfare* were established early in each state's history, since these were *considered as responsibilities of the states and their local governments*. As populations and costs increased, and the capacity of units of care (almshouses, county poorhouses) went beyond the abilities of local communities to maintain, the state institutions care agencies were created.

States first enacted measures for *building facilities* to house all public assistance recipients *within the counties* (New York, County Poorhouse Act, 1924). These sheltering facilities were undifferentiated, i.e., the old, the young, the sick, the poor, the emotionally ill, the blind, the addicted, and the criminal were all housed together. The financing of care and maintenace was left to the counties (from tax funds); county superintendents of welfare were authorized as administrators. As the number of cases in each category increased, the need for differentiation became apparent. Differentiation occurred gradually, and not all within one state. For example, Virginia established a state hospital for the insane in 1773; Ohio and Kentucky, homes for the deaf in 1819 and 1823, respectively; Ohio, a home for the blind in 1837; and Massachusetts, a home for juvenile delinquents and the retarded in 1848. Persons in these need categories were accepted from other states through negotiation. Some of these institutions were initially designed as experimental in order to encourage other states to establish similar operations as well as to encourage federal participation in the care and/or the education of the handicapped. Thus as the state established these service functions, organizational and administrative units were also created. As federal conditional grants-in-aid legislation was passed by Congress, additional units (agencies, departments, divisions, commissions, etc.) were put in place to accommodate the various conditions and requirements of the legislation.

These organizational arrangements remained fairly stable from the mid-1930s until the 1960s when federal legislation began focusing on planning, coordination, citizen participation, and demonstration programs for specific "needy" populations or target programs. These foci plus the plethora of grants for developing improvements in systems for treatment and rehabilitation of "societal deviants," improvements in the administration of social services, and for the training of both professional and nonprofessional service providers, led to the creation of new and/or expanded organizational units, both at the state and federal levels of government.

The development of programs to provide services to solve specific problems of specific groups took precedence over assessing the impacts of these programs on other groups, on individuals or communities as a whole. Little thought was given to the logic of the organizational arrangements for operating and maintaining the new kinds and levels of service, or to determining whether or not there would be a continuing, expanding, or diminishing need for these programs and their associated structures.

The proliferation of state and federal administrative units, resulting from requirements associated with federal enactments during the 1960s, may have been seen as cause for concern by some, but the general attitude precipitated by "The Great Society" movement drew attention away from the logic of structure and form. It was soon discovered, however, that the pressure for immediate solutions was bringing to light, or creating, more problems for the future.

For example, the Social Security Amendments of 1962 encouraged states to separate social services from income maintenance and devise programs to reduce dependency on welfare. However, the separation did not occur at federal level until 1964, when the Department of Health, Education, and Welfare underwent administrative reorganization and created the Social and Rehabilitation Services (SRS) unit. SRS brought together vocational rehabilitation and other categorical social service programs, including Aid to Families of Dependent Children and Medicaid. Although the states did separate social services from income maintenance, they did so with a great deal of reluctance, generally by creating two divisions in the department. For the most part, they did not incorporate rehabilitation services within those divisions.

At the state level, attention to the dilemmas of administration and the constantly expanding organizational structures peaked in the late 1960s. New programs, new responsibilities, new arrangements, and new rules represented encroachment on old turfs, agencies, and structures which had been established since the 1930s. Fiscal problems and management issues, as well as intergovernmental conflicts motivated reorganization efforts.

By 1969 approximately 20 states had already combined several services and many other states were seriously considering reorganizations. In Massachusetts, for example, the Executive Office of Human Services was created to coordinate the traditionally separate public health, mental health, rehabilitation, and social welfare programs of the state. A survey in 1972-73 by the Council of State Governments indicated that 26 states had by then reorganized their own agencies to create comprehensive human resource departments that administer both public assistance and social service programs, and at least three other major types of human services programs.[16]

Initiatives for social and human services planning

The planning system designed by Arizona's Department of Economic Security identifies human services as those services provided by the state which maximize "the self-sufficiency — both economic and social — of which Arizona residents are capable, thereby reducing the cost of publicly financed assistance programs to a level consistent with the public good."[17]

The overall goal and sub-goal found in Arizona's Department of Economic Security first five-year plan document are indicative of many of the trends emanating from theoretical studies, demonstration projects, research, and experimentation with processes and procedures in planning for human services. The goals are directed toward a redefinition of the purpose, attitudinal frameworks, and the means for the end-product of effective service delivery or breaking down the barriers to individual self-sufficiency. The goals and objectives are *not* specific services to be delivered. Instead they are oriented to many of the problems which impede or inhibit those services from being delivered to the appropriate individuals and in the appropriate places. For example, the plan established the goal of providing economic security programs in a manner reasonably accessible to all eligible residents. To achive this goal, several objectives were identified:

1. Services not currently available on a statewide basis will be so distributed.
2. Generalists will be trained to provide a broad spectrum of services to those communities too small to provide adequate workloads for individual program specialists.
3. Means of service delivery other than permanent stationing of staff will be examined for service to smaller communities such as mobile service, contracted service delivery, contracted information and referral, or telephone scheduling.
4. Services to those with multiple service needs shall be made available at a single location[18].

The plan document completed in March 1974, through the efforts of the Bureau of Planning of the Resources Planning Division within the DES, represented the first formal attempt at "specifying a set of comprehensive goals and objectives to guide the Agency." Its uses were to provide: (a) a common direction for planning by organizational elements of the Department; (b) a means to prioritize service programs and activities; (c) a vehicle for public comment; and (d) a vehicle for interagency coordination and planning. The approach taken was that of planning within the parameters of a statewide multiagency service delivery system.[19]

Title XX: The carrot and the stick

The passage of the 1974 Social Security Act amendments, which created Title XX and instituted social services planning requirements, provided a significant impetus to states' human services reorganization and planning efforts. It was through some of the new planning requirements that new opportunities were to be realized. Services could now be provided not only to "welfare recipients" but also to those who were struggling just above the designated poverty line.[20] State and local human service agencies, community groups, and the general public were encouraged to participate in assessing needs, setting priorities, and reviewing recommendations for the Comprehensive Annual Social Services Program Plan (CASSP). Although many states had previously prepared plans for categorical grant programs, few had prepared a comprehensive plan requiring the establishment of a detailed planning process, incorporating the views of the state's citizens. It was only to the extent that traditional state and substate public welfare units were flexible and open to participation and that a given state had built-in human services planning capabilities or a readiness for comprehensive social service planning that the first-year CASSP reflected the full intent of the legislation and incorporated the full range of the planning requirements.[21]

The plan requirement which refers to the assurance that needs of all residents be considered in social services planning under Title XX has received a great deal of attention since 1974, both in the public and the voluntary sectors. The section which follows discusses some facets of this seemingly new term "needs assessment."

Needs assessment: a basis for planning social services

Tasks and activities now associated with the term "needs assessment" have been a part of the planning and or research processes encompassed by gathering data and information for decision-makers for as many years as planning and social research have been around. However, only within the recent past (since the early 1970s) has it come to have a specific meaning and application for planning. Its now common usage is found primarily in the subparts of social planning: human services planning and human resources planning.[22]

Much of the systemization of needs assessment approaches, methods and techniques grew out of the study project entitled "Analysis and Synthesis of Needs Assessment Research in the Field of Human Services," conducted by Gretchen A. Heller and Edward C. Baumheier and financed by the U.S. Department of Health, Education, and Welfare.[23] Gerald Horton and Edmund Armentrout, in working with the Human Services Institute for Children and Families, Inc., and studying state and regional as well as local human services planning organizations, have developed, and continue to refine, useful manuals for conducting needs assessments.[24] The requirements in federal legislation and regulations that the needs of the citizens in all geographic areas be described and that the methods for determining those needs be documented[25] have had a significant and positive effect in the further development and use of more systematic needs assessment, especially in social services and broader human services planning.

Information about community, individual and/or group needs is a vital component of human services and human resources planning and program development. Need assessment information provides the contextual framework for evaluating the relevance and adequacy of the available services and resources, the general quality of life, and the magnitude of problems or undesirable social processes in a community (state, region, or local).

It is important to understand that the principle of needs assessment and the practice can vary. For example, one survey showed that needs assessment is the base of a good planning process. Planners should decide what types of services to provide based on the basis of need. However, when there is widespread agreement that everyone can see the need for any given service, that it serves no useful purpose to measure it. In fact, in numerous states, there was no needs assessment system before the planning process began.[26]

Early practice in Title XX social services planning

The needs assessment efforts of the eight states studied by The Research Group, Inc. are indicative of the trends which have been established in the use of needs assessment methods and techniques in social and human services planning.[27]

After states established their planning cycles they made various initial steps in developing alternative techniques. For example, most state agencies obtained information from other state human service agencies, key state or local advisory councils, and reviewed previous surveys or plans. A smaller number of states surveyed private service providers, regional service providers or studied secondary data relating to social indicators. Only a few analyzed budget systems or surveyed clients or the general population.

As needs assessment practice has evolved the assessments are becoming increasingly structured and require a competant staff with specialized skills. Assessments are increasingly being conducted jointly with other human services surveyed, and needs assessments increasingly involve district and local service providers, agencies and planners, and local staff conducting surveys.

The type of data that are being collected include general and specific population characteristics, age, employment status, health, income, education, and specific surveys of various categories of aid recipients.

In New Jersey, for example, the needs assessment had several goals. First, to measure the types of need for social services. Types of need include, for example, family planning, day care, counseling, transportation, and job-related needs. Some needs may receive no attention by existing agencies and others may be met, but inadequately, by other agencies. The second goal is to measure the severity of need. This assumes the goal of providing a limited amount of funds for programs to those in greatest need. Third, to measure the distribution and need throughout the state. And, fourth, to measure public support for funding and conducting social service programs.[28]

Probably the most important consideration when conducting any kind of needs assessment is that of purpose. Far too many surveys have been made and data collected without goals for their use. The primary purpose should be to gather and present valid information to be used as a bases for planning — services to people and resources to be allocated for the delivery of such services. Any other purpose is secondary.

Regional planning for human services?

Human services planning in regional organizations has been largely federally financed and in response to federal legislation. Intended primarily as planning and coordinating bodies, the many single-purpose regional planning organizations (e.g., Comprehensive Health Planning Agencies, Health Systems Agencies, Regional Criminal Justice Planning Boards, Area Agencies on Aging, and Mental Health and Mental Retardation Boards) have been continuously hampered by limited funding and statutory mandate as well as often disputed political jurisdiction. Most have been able to effect coordination in planning; some have been successful in coordinating service delivery; all have been able to bring

Figure 22–2   Example of the use of social indicators to develop a regional statistical profile.

Population	734,140 (13.9% of state population) (ranks fourth out of seven)
Age	0–4 years: 7.8% of regional population (ranks seventh out of seven)
	65+ years: 11.2% of regional population (ranks fourth out of seven)
Employment	47,920 are unemployed (ranks third out of seven)
	11.9% unemployment rate in the region
	15.2% of the state's unemployed persons live in region
Health	133 infant deaths recorded in 1974 (ranks fifth out of seven)
	Infant mortality rate of 16.9%
Income	64,946 live below the poverty level (ranks fourth out of seven)
	8.8% of population live below the poverty level
	14.2% of the state's below-poverty-level population live in the region
Education	Median school years completed—12.1 (ranks fourth out of seven)
Categorical aid	52,474 people receive AFDC (15% of total AFDC recipients) (ranks fourth out of seven)
	15,769 people receive SSI (13% of total SSI recipients) (ranks fourth out of seven)
	7,685 people receive General Relief (16% of total GR recipients) (ranks second out of seven)
	19,272 people receive Medical Assistance (14% of total MA recipients) (ranks fourth out of seven)
	77,174 people receive food stamps (13% of total food stamp recipients) (ranks fourth out of seven)

together other agencies of like interests and service needs. As block grant legislation came into being, the regional organizations saw changes in their functions and structure, jurisdictional boundaries, and most of all reduced funding. Many have been reorganized as county-wide units for planning, services management and delivery under state auspices. Relationships among the governmental hierarchies within the state may benefit as a result of some of these changes. At the same time as the public sector is decreasing the size of its "regions" the voluntary sector (health and welfare councils, social planning councils, United Ways) seems to be expanding its geographic areas of purview, for both planning and fund raising.[29]

Principles and prospects for social (services) planning

A need, a crisis, or a dissatisfaction too often propels individuals and groups into action without giving attention to any notion of planning or least of all to a recognition of important preplanning considerations and activities. The limits and parameters of what is to be planned, possible questions to be asked, political power positions to be considered and negotiated, resources and capabilities available, and community organization and participation elements to be woven together are preplanning actions which must be settled before planning can take place. These are the items frequently overlooked or not given sufficient attention even when an authorization to plan has been given. Thus, problems which cry out for solution have caused and most likely will continue to cause the creation of many fragmented programs which later appear to be in desperate need of planning or coordination.

In the United States, there must be sanctions created at state and local levels of government in order for public planning to occur. State enabling legislation for physical planning and economic development has been around for many years; local governmental jurisdictions have created mechanisms and structures for physical and economic planning; but legislation for any kind of social planning, including social services or, for that matter, any of the human services, has not yet come into favor as a public function for state and local governments. Until the states recognize not only the legitimacy of, but their obligation to carry out, a planning role related to the social aspects of their territories, that level of government will continue to find itself beleaguered from above (federal) and below (local governments).

Principles for social planning have come from many sources: from the theories and experiences of all kinds of planning professionals, from problems encountered in program implemetation by other professionals (social service, public administration, *et al.*), from experiences of public officials and political processes, and from the studies of academicians about the many facets of living. Alfred J. Kahn presented in 1969 what he called "a very tentative summarization of emerging principles," in the light of municipal and state experiences, general dissatisfactions, and trends in both the public and private sectors.[30] More than 10 years later, these principles seem to be still emerging and have not been rendered invalid.

The emerging principles

As an underpinning and confirmation for the principles which Kahn has outlined, he also made firm statements about some lessons learned from urban planning and social welfare experts. Accordingly, he states that the lesson of all available experience argues against monopoly by one discipline: there should be no economic planning with only economists on the staff, no physical planning completely in the hands of architects, no social welfare planning reserved completely to social workers and sociologists. Further lessons:

There is no economic planning without serious social consequences to be taken into account, social programming to support economic measures, and socially relevant options to be assessed.

Bricks, mortar, and zoning maps do not make real communities.

Social welfare programs that list requirements without assessing costs, resources, manpower, and benefits are truncated, at the very least. Economic plans require capital construction planning.

Social welfare efforts need to be staged with reference to the phase of economic development.

The eleven principles suggested by Kahn focus primarily on the organizing, staffing, and process functions of social planning. These principles, when used by the states and their regional subunits, can further a more rational approach in the provision of social services to the general population and especially to those in dire need.

Principle I *Planning (should) remain a coalitional activity, requiring a variety of roles and the perspectives of several disciplines.* Practitioners from human services as well as from behavioral and social science are needed.

Principle II   *The supporting organizational framework (i.e., structures) should avoid imagery, conditions, or requirements which would preclude the above principle.* Preoccupation with one particular planning aspect over another (e.g., coordination, developing resource allocation formulae, management information systems, case management systems, etc.) tends to project images and set conditions.

Principle III   *Planning should be so organized as to support a process and not the mere production of a plan.* Those who must implement, support, finance, and take advantage of output should be included in the process of thinking, choosing, and evolving in various relationships.

Principle IV   *Whatever the governmental level, statutory planning should be a staff function in the office of the executive*—with only occasional exceptions. If impartial boards and committees produce plans, they will lack adequate support. If specialized offices are expected to coordinate and plan with other specialized offices, the process lacks adequate sanction and support. If finance divisions take on planning roles, the output is unduly affected in terms of budgetary considerations. If governmental planning responsibilities are assigned to non-governmental or semi-independent bodies, winning adequate political support within the government must be added on.

Principle V   *Planning offices (and planning personnel) should not operate programs or projects.* While this principle may be implied in the foregoing discussion, it is in need of repetition. The majority of experts hold that operation confuses the role and undermines the status of a planning office.

Principle VI   *Less-developed countries, cities and states with very limited resources, and voluntary agencies with rudimentary organizational structures should not attempt to develop a complete structure for planning all at once.*

Principle VII   *There should be organizational provision for a diversity of planning, official and unofficial, central and local.* Democratic societies may seek rationality and coherence, while protecting preferences, by avoiding monolithic planning. *The state can provide an overall framework, enunciate basic objectives and targets as well as instruments of policy by which they are implemented.* It can guide and coordinate local activities with national objectives and goals *without unduly undermining the essential autonomy and diversity of local planning and service-providing organizations.*

Principle VIII   *Task force, commission, and other short-term ad hoc and interim planning mechanisms (should) continue to have their place, supplementing departmental, legislative, and overall governmental planning machinery.*

Principle IX   *The decision as to whether to create separate official machinery for social planning or to assume that one planning staff will undertake economic, social and physical planning, must depend on the total context and the view of planning in the culture.* While the interplay among these elements should be obvious and the ultimate validity of socially oriented criteria for all aspects of public policy may be recognized, there are many mitigating circumstances which causes separateness to prevail. There are differing degrees of readiness to plan; there are different legislative mandates and sanctions to plan—for different sectors and at different levels; and there are different prerogatives among governmental departments and among voluntary organizations. All of these differences are a matter of historical fact, timing, precedent, and practice—they may represent barriers or they could represent opportunities.

Principle X *Whatever the organizational structure, staffing by interdisciplinary teams or conditions is essential.* The diversity of planning substance and context is such that no one disciplinary field can accommodate all of the knowledge or skills *or* roles necessary to carry out a total and comprehensive planning process.

Principle XI *Devices to coordinate statutory and voluntary planning are (and will continue to be) needed at all governmental levels.* Both state and local governments across the United States define their roles and responsibilities as well as their service categories differently. The private nonprofit (voluntary) sector, although not limited by public statutes, displays many of the same kinds of variances. Although it has been given no legal authority per se, the voluntary sector has been involved in social and human services planning throughout our country's history. Its sanctions have been derived through participation of powerful and influential community leaders in local and areawide community chests and councils (United Way of America). These agencies carry on a social planning function either in addition to or in coordination with governmental organizations.

Education and educational planning

Education is most often omitted from discussions of social or human services. Historically, the function of education has been delegated to the states and not seen as a responsibility of the federal government. Within each state, education departments and their separate governing boards have been established by state statute as separate entities apart from other public service functions. This separation, of course, has effectively separated education from other public services at local governmental levels. The recent (1979) creation of the federal Department of Education may even reinforce this separation. However, the effects of cabinet level status for education remain to be seen. Under Public Law 96-88 (the Department of Education Organization Act), all of the education activities and functions are "under one roof."

Like the health sector, schools to train teachers were established long before training institutions for welfare and human service workers were created. This historic separation has discouraged the inclusion of education in efforts to consolidate human service organizations and been problematic for theoretical definitions of what constitutes the human service field. Yet the planning principles which have developed coincide with health, social services, and human resources planning principles. All are based on human needs.

Public education is included here as a human service system. It is a vast, multilevel system. The scope of this subsection on educational planning only begins to describe this complex system, some of its history, and legislative origins.

In this complex context, educational planning practices and mandates are carried out to varying degrees. The purpose of this section is to set forth the planning principles and techniques at several programatic levels and to highlight the major planning issues which are facing our education administrators and legislators.

Context and scope

The educational system in the United States is not a simple one. The laws, organization of administrative and governing functions, and the planning and delivery of educational services vary from state to state. Typically, a state will have all or most of the educational program components, such as universities and colleges, community colleges, high school or post–high school vocational programs which are contained in a regular high school, at special area vocational schools or in community colleges, and elementary and secondary school districts.

All of these educational enterprises may be linked administratively through the state education agency, or they may function under independent boards. Usually, the institutions of higher education are governed by a board of regents, while vocational, elementary, secondary, and special education services (blind, deaf, or handicapped) function under a local school district served, and regulated, by a state board of education and state department of education. For example, in New York and Rhode Island, all education is under the aegis of one governing body and agency. In Idaho, there is a single governing board with dual staffs. Montana's state governing board is made up of two boards, a board for higher education and a public school board.

Public elementary and secondary education is universally a state constitutional responsibility. In all states, except Hawaii, tradition and political culture have dictated that this responsibility be delegated to local school districts; that each district elect its own governing body and raise taxes. The state legislature and its administrative arm, the department of education, have specified the organization of local public school districts, governing structures, methods of financing, and various regulatory standards.

Postsecondary education is a direct state-delivered and financed service through its universities and colleges. State involvement in higher education was given its initial boost with the land grant colleges established by the federal government over 100 years ago. Since then, the original state universities have expanded to large systems, with branch campuses, two-year colleges, extension and continuing education programs and special institutes, as well as research programs. The federal government was instrumental, also, in the institution of state vocational education beginning with the Smith-Hughes Act of 1917.

In the last 15 years, federal education initiatives have been largely responsible for enhancing the role of state education agencies and education planning. The primary impact of these mandates have resulted in greatly expanded staffs of state departments of education, and a broadening of their responsibility to coordinate and plan for public education. The provisions of the Elementary and Secondary Education Act (ESEA) of 1965, Title V, were intended to improve the planning, research, and personal resources of state departments of education. Title III of this act, which provided funds for innovative educational projects, required a comprehensive educational needs assessment as part of the justification for funds. In 1969, state education agencies were given the responsibility to administer these funds directly and to conduct statewide needs assessments. State education agency responsibilities were even further expanded with the passage in 1973 of the Education for All Handicapped Children Act. This act mandated a "free appropriate public education for all handicapped children" and a requirement that each handicapped child have an individualized plan for instruction. The state education agency was given the responsibility to supervise the implementation of these provisions.

Under the Vocational Education Act of 1963, states were required to submit comprehensive five-year plans for the allocation of vocation education funds. Critical evaluation of vocational planning efforts in the 1970s resulted in the Education Amendments of 1976 (Title II, PL 94-482) which set forth elements of a planning process rather that plan content. Two major elements of the process were the inclusion of a number of educational system actors into a state planning committee, and the use of a manpower planning data base.

At the higher education level, too, planning for the allocation of funds has been fostered by federal actions. The Education Amendments of 1972 authorized states to designate or create state postsecondary commissions for planning (Section 1202) and provided some funding for five-year master plans.

The concept of regional planning in education is more of a concept than any widespread, common administrative or governmental reality. Historically, there have been some actions to establish area-wide education entities. When rural school systems were predominant, states often established an intermediate administrative unit, a multidistrict service which provided a trained educator to oversee and guide the one-room schoolhouse system. Similarly, special education services have often been provided on a multidistrict basis so that a district with few handicapped students would not have to bear the entire burden of hiring a special teacher. Title III of the Elementary and Secondary Education Act (1965) provided that states establish sub-state area centers to perform certain education functions or carry out regional needs assessments. The California PACE centers and the Regional Education Research Laboratories are two examples. Due to lack of federal support or a real administrative need for these regional units, many are dormant or no longer serve an integral educational function. Some have substantial accomplishments to their credit, such as the Regional Education Service Agency of Appalachian Maryland. One such accomplishment is the planning and use of educational television to serve remote areas. Currently, some experts in education see the objective of desegregation and problems of managing large urban school systems as a reason to institute an areawide or multidistrict metropolitan system which would perform certain educational service functions, while devolving other functions to the school building or neighborhood level.[31]

Regional planning principles and considerations are more a reality in vocational and higher education. The service area, enrollment sources, and employment opportunities of vocational institutions, community colleges, universities, and other postsecondary educational enterprises are regional in nature. Because of this, planning involves regional, demographic analyses and, in the instance of vocational education, state and regional labor market supply and demand analyses.

Principles and purpose of educational planning

Educational planning is based on human resources principles and cultural values about the quality of life and equality of opportunity. From the societal point of view, the purpose of education is the development of our human resources— training individuals in skills and knowledge needed to sustain a productive society, and developing their capacity to realize their greatest potential as members of society. Educational planning principles, then, are based on self-development and matching individual human needs and societal needs.

Legislative enactments for educational planning have established a rudimentary technical foundation for such planning in the United States. The effectiveness of these practices are determined by the complexity and structure of our educational decision making and financing system. The limited authority of state departments of education have constrained the use of statewide needs assessments' goals and objectives to direct and improve the quality of the classroom experience of the local school district except in an advisory capacity. Comprehensive master plans for the allocation of funds for vocational education have achieved this purpose but do not effectively enable planners and administrators to redirect vocational programs as is desired. The politics of state legislatures which decide the allocation of higher education funds are shaping the production of static, comprehensive master plans on the role and scope of each institution in the higher education system into the practice of policy analysis. Planning practitioners are tackling one policy issue at a time, for example, the implication of demographic trends on future enrollments. Planning practices are becoming a greater part of the budget decisions, in the form of highly specific program objectives.

In the future, the role and practice of educational planning will concern the refinement and dissemination of human resources planning techniques. Also, planning practices will continue to broaden their scope to include the goals of equality and equal access to education. The demands of increased productivity and new technologies engendered by the changing role of the United States in the world economy are expected to encourage the inclusion of educational planning principles in decision making structures of the education system. Planning will focus on three goals: productivity of our human resources, equality, and quality of the educational experience.

Educational planning techniques

Planning touches on all aspects of the education system. Since education concerns teaching people, planning must address how best to teach and what is the best thing to learn. Since there needs to be a physical location in which this teaching and learning occur, planning for the financial and human resources to provide these things must consider all potential students who need to learn and what teaching should prepare them for. Planners must use demographic analysis to determine who has needs; they must assess those needs in social, economic, and instructional terms and decide upon desired objectives. What is desired will depend upon the cultural values and productive needs in the community and society. These objectives will concern what are the best opportunities available (economic and social), how many and who will learn (equality), and how and what they will learn (quality).

Needs assessments: from individual to community A needs assessment is a systematic method and process for determining:

1. What ought to be—a desired goal or objective.
2. What present condition exists.
3. The discrepancy between the desired objective and the present condition.
4. The reason for the discrepancy.
5. Which discrepancy (need) areas should be given the highest priority?[32]

The scope of educational needs assessments and objectives for the reduction of need extends from individual pupil instructional objectives, to grade levels or groups of students, to entire social groups, potential student populations, and the community. The expansion of the scope of needs assessments broadens as higher levels of education are reached because the role of these higher education institutions is a broader one.

Needs assessments and objectives at the elementary and secondary school level are pupil centered, geared to the objectives of basic public education in the community, i.e., certain knowledge and social and physical skill levels and socialization into the community. A given student population is assessed. At the postsecondary education level, needs encompass not only existing postsecondary student population, but the educational needs of a potential population. Even broader than that, vocational and higher education assesses the education needs spanning a complete demographic profile of young adults, older adults, minorities, women, working people, unemployed, and so on. Accordingly, the method of assessing needs will differ. It is relatively straightforward to assess the needs of an entire existing elementary and secondary student population by testing them in their classroom. It is more difficult to assess the needs of a potential enrollment group. Methods at these higher education levels include analyses of market demand for different types of education.

At some point, the educational goals and the "what is" must be compared, to identify need and to use to make decisions about redirecting and improving the quality of education. New Jersey carried out a testing program to measure educational progress simultaneously with its needs assessment program. The state education agency chose to present these test results in such a manner that each district could compare its achievements with other districts. Each district, however, had to decide if its test results were "good," "bad," or "needed improvements."

A needs assessment can begin with the assessment of education progress and analysis of data and then proceed to develop education goals, or it can develop goals before assessing needs in the goal areas. The program can consist of ongoing evaluations of education programs which are fed continually into the curriculum development and policy making process of school administration. Much more than specific skills and traditional knowledge subjects can be included in an assessment of needs. Pennsylvania's State Department of Education greatly expanded the concept of need by including such things as student self-concept, understanding others, citizenship, health habits, creativity, preparation for a changing world, and many others. Also, in Pennsylvania the local school rather than the district grade level is the unit of performance assessed on a broad range of indicators.

Effective needs assessment planning is problematic at the state level. State departments of education do not directly govern elementary and secondary local school curriculum and education activities. While state legislatures may require local districts and the state to conduct assessments of educational progress, there is no means to assure that effective processes exist to insure that needed and desired changes in education can be instituted. State legislatures, which provide about 50 percent of local school funds, are increasing their demands for school district accountability. As local schools have had to rely more on state funding, questions of performance and accountability have naturally arisen. Presently, four states (Maryland, North Carolina, Tennessee, and Virginia) have minimum performance standards for high school graduation.

Needs assessment and human resources   Region-wide needs assessments use methods similar to those used by states and local districts for elementary and secondary school pupils. Public meetings, public opinion surveys, and question-naires are all part of the task of finding out what are considered the most important goals for education. The Regional Education Service Agency of Appalachian Maryland conducted a needs assessment before setting up a rural educational television network by interviewing a stratified sample of more than 1,300 families in several isolated communities. Many innovative region-wide needs assessment techniques were developed and pioneered by the 21 regional centers in California (PACE Centers) set up under Title III of the Elementary and Secondary Education Act.

At the vocational and community college level, needs assessments are expanded from pupil-centered learning skills, knowledge and self-development skills to include the needs of the community such as business needs and employment opportunities. Educational goals are translated into curriculum objectives and programs at specific vocational institutions or colleges and related to the job market and needs of the *potential* student population, e.g., adults, high school graduates, minorities, and women.

Manpower planning techniques have been formally required for states since the Vocational Education Act of 1963. State Vocational Education Plans for the allocation of funds are completed for five years, annually updated and monitored.

The plans must specify objectives for vocation programs, the number and types of courses and vocational degrees offered, high school or two-year post–high school; these objectives must be based upon a detailed analysis of employment supply and demand in the area which is served by the vocational institutions. Provisions must be made in each plan to improve the participation of minorities and women.

One detailed needs assessment program was developed by the Central Florida Community Colleges Consortium. The basic component of the program is an assessment of the occupation needs of business which collects data on present and future occupational training requirements and determines priority job skills. Monthly status reports from the Florida State Employment Service for the service area of each community college are analyzed by computer. The jobs are coded by occupation and weighted by the number of net job openings each month. The occupational codes are prioritized for needs and fed into curriculum planning activities.

Manpower data bases are difficult to construct because of several problems: (1) Are the jobs with the most vacancies now, going to be the same jobs in two years which could absorb newly trained workers? (2) What are the new, emerging kinds of jobs which may require trained personnel in the future but which do not show up as high demand in the present? It is equally difficult to make an accurate count of the present number of trained and available people in each region. Special skills can be obtained in a variety of ways—high schools, community colleges, private technical institutions, and the military. Even dropouts from special programs have some skills which enable them to meet the employment demands in their area of training.

Despite improvements in data and the ability to analyze the demands of the labor market, it is an individual decision to take a job or hire someone. The periodic waves of feast and famine of engineers or teachers can be mitigated but never eliminated.

Conclusion

Responsibility for the planning and delivery of social services has been floating back and forth between state and local governments since the earliest days in the United States. The federal government has nudged, offered incentives in the way of appropriations for demonstration projects, established requirements for planning attached to funding, and more. These efforts were designed to bring some order to the evolving patchwork quilts in the social services, to determine where and how planning for each state's citizens and their social well-being should occur. Breaking down the entrenched categories which have been established through past funding patterns continues to be the most difficult task. However, many states are finding that reorganization of the bureaucratic structures, determining needs at substate levels, and establishing overall goals with attendant priorities is going a long way toward smoothing out some of the intergovernmental hassles between state and local governments in the social service arena.

Since the function of education has always been the responsibility of the states, jurisdictional disputes between the state and its local school districts have not been the predominant problem, historically. The quality, type, and degree of financial support and setting of standards, however, has been in the forefront of planning for education. Much attention, most recently, has been (and probably will continue to be) given to needs, numbers, and the employment scenario. Skirmishes between urban, suburban, and rural educational appropriations will continue until state formulas and/or legal battles are settled.

1   Richard S. Bolan discusses both the concept of human need and related divisions derived from Maslow's "hierarchy of needs" and Erikson's developmental concepts of personality growth in Chapter 4 "Social planning and policy development in local government" of *Managing Human Services* (Washington, DC: International City Management Association, 1977), pp. 100-102. Also Robert M. Moroney offers more on the concept of need as he introduces factors influencing the definition of need in Chapter 5 "Needs assessment for human services" in the same book. The four categories of need suggested by Lotspeich draws on these concepts; however, there is no hierarchy implied.

2   Income security and economic opportunity, housing assistance, education, recreation, justice and safety, health (physical and mental) and social support services (for families, individuals and groups) are considered as parts of the current human service system. For a brief but thorough presentation of human services definitions and perceptions, read "The human services function and local government" by Robert Morris in *Managing Human Services* (Washington, DC: International City Management Association, 1977), pp. 5-8 and 17-28.

3   Sheila B. Kamerman and Alfred J. Kahn, *Social Services in the United States: Policies and Programs* (Philadelphia: Temple University Press, 1976), pp. 3-5.

4   Alfred J. Kahn provides generally accepted definitions for both, in addition to presenting arguments by economists, social planners, and social philosophers in the United States and other countries. For a detailed discussion and other references, refer to Chapter VI in *Theory and Practice of Social Planning* (New York: Russell Sage Foundation, 1969).

5   Ibid., p. 178.

6   Ibid., p. 179.

7   Ibid., p. 179.

8   Ibid., p. 180.

9   The Council of State Governments. *Human Services: A Framework for Decision-Making* (Lexington, KY, December 1975), p. 13.

10 Public Law 93-647, Social Services Amendments of 1974. 42 USC 1397.

11 Human Services Institute for Children and Families, Inc., *Alternative Approaches to Human Services Planning* (Arlington, VA: Human Services Institute for Children and Families, Inc. 1974), p. 39.

12 The levels of self-sufficiency can be found in the section on Mission of the five-year plan document completed by the Department of Economic Security (State of Arizona) in March, 1974. It should be noted that this document preceded the passage of Title XX of the Social Security Act of 1974. The overall goal is the maximization of self-sufficiency, both economic and social. The underlying assumptions for these descriptions or definitions do not seem to presume exiting the system.

13 United Way of America, UWASIS II: A Taxonomy of Social Goals and Human Service Programs (Alexandria, VA: United Way of America, November 1976), p. 3.

14 In March 1974, United Way of America conducted a survey to determine the nature and extent of the use of the first UWASIS publication. This survey revealed that there were over 5,000 users, including voluntary human service organizations, governmental agencies, commercial organizations, and academic institutions. Since that time, it is esti-mated that the number of users has more than doubled. See Ibid., p. iii.

15 For an excellent analysis of coordination of services, see Michael Aiken *et al.*, *Coordinating Human Services* (San Francisco: Jossey-Bass Publishers, 1975).

16 The Council of State Governments. *Human Services: A Framework for Decision-Making* (Lexington, KY: The Council of State Governments, December 1975), p. 5.

17 Human Services Institute for Children and Families, Inc., *Alternative Approaches to Human Services Planning* (Arlington, VA: Human Services Institute for Children and Families, Inc., 1974), p.37.

18 Ibid., pp. 39-41.

19 Ibid., p. 37.

20 The basic Title XX eligibility criteria allows each state to receive federal support for the provision of services to all those in need whose income is not greater than 115 percent of the state's median income adjusted for size of family. This income-related criterion is a sharp philosophical break from the traditional welfare-related categories in Title IV-A and VI. It was to help alleviate the "taint" of welfare programs as it encouraged services planning and delivery on a needs-oriented basis. It should be noted, however, that the state is not obligated to serve people up to the 115 percent limit.

21 For a detailed analysis of some of the first and second year efforts in social services planning under Title XX, see *State Experiences in Social Service Planning*, case studies of eight states, conducted by The Research Group, Inc. under contract with U.S. Department of Health, Education and Welfare, July 1976. Gerald T. Horton and Edmund H. Arment were principal researchers and authors.

22 Refer to the section on "Educational Planning" for a more detailed discussion of needs assessment, especially related to education and human resources planning.

23 An essay, "Needs Assessment Research and Human Services Planning," which comprises Chapters 2, 3, 5 and 7 of this study can be found in *Readings on Human Services Planning* (Arlington, VA: Human Services Institute for Children and Families, Inc., September 1975), pp. 109-126. See also *Assessing Social Service Needs and Resources*, the final report of a project to "develop alternate methodologies for assessing social services needs and resources as related to Titles I, IV, X, XIV and XVI of the Social Security Act as amended from 1962 through 1972. This study was one of a special group of contracts awarded to promote and facilitate the National Service Reform Effort initiated and developed by the Community Services Administration of the Social and Rehabilitation Service. This document can be secured through "Project Share."

24 See, for example, *Needs Assessment in a Title XX State Social Services Planning System* (1975), *Techniques for Needs Assessment in Social Services Planning* (1976), and *Approaches and Techniques for State and Local Human Service Needs Assessment* (1977), (Atlanta: The Research Group, Inc.).

25 Title XX of the Social Security Act, 1974 may have had the strongest impact toward the development of needs assessment methods and techniques. Other major pieces of federal legislation also contain requirements or incentives for assessing and documenting needs, e.g., The Older Americans Act, the Developmental Disabilities Services and Facil-

ities Construction Act, the Health Planning and Resources Development Act, Vocational Rehabilitation Acts, the Drug Abuse and Alcohol Abuse Acts, the Vocational Education Acts, and the Elementary and Secondary Education Act of 1965 and its amendments.

26 Gerald T. Horton and Edmund H. Armentrout. *State Experiences in Social Service Planning* (Atlanta: The Research Group, 1976), p. 18.

27 Ibid., pp.18–29.

28 Ibid., p. 262.

29 Alvin Taylor discusses some of the history of regional planning for human services in Chapter 2, "Relations with other agencies delivering human services," in *Managing Human Services* (Washington, D.C.: International City Management Association, 1977),

pp.46-48. Ironically, he states that the present regional planning efforts has as ancestors the health and welfare (or social planning) councils of earlier decades.

30 For a more detailed discussion of the eleven principles which follow, see Alfred J. Kahn, *Theory and Practice of Social Planning* (New York: Russell Sage Foundation, 1969), pp. 308-323.

31 Raold F. Campbell *et al.*, *The Organization and Control of American Schools, 4th ed. (Columbus, OH: Merrill Publishing Co., 1980), p. 133.*

32 Belle Ruth Witkin, *An Analysis of Needs Assessment Techniques for Educational Planning at State, Intermediate and District Levels* (Alameda, CA: Office of Alameda County Superintendent of Schools, May 1975), p. 15.

23 Criminal justice planning

In July, 1965, the Commission on Law Enforcement and Administration of Criminal Justice was established through Executive Order 11236. This Commission, established by President Lyndon B. Johnson, was charged with inquiring into the causes of crime and delinquency and reporting to him, in early 1967, with recommendations for preventing crime and delinquency and improving law enforcement and the administration of criminal justice. Through the work of the 19 commissioners, a staff of 60, and over 150 consultants, the Commission called three national conferences, conducted five national surveys, and interviewed tens of thousands of persons.

As a result of this Commission's work, more than 200 recommendations were made. In characterizing these recommendations the Commission stated: "The recommendations are more than just a list of new procedures, new tactics, and new techniques. They are a call for a revolution in the way America thinks about crime."[1]

In its seventh and final recommendation to the President, the Commission report discussed the "responsibility for change" if this revolution were to become a reality. In that regard the Commission stated:

The Commission recommends that in every state and city there should be an agency, of one or more officials, with specific responsibility for planning improvements in criminal administration and encouraging their implementation.

Planning agencies, among other functions, play a key role in helping state legislatures and city councils decide where additional funds and manpower are most needed, what new programs should be adopted, and where and how existing agencies might pool their resources on either a metropolitan or regional basis.

The planning agencies should include both officials from the system of criminal justice and citizens from other professions. Plans to improve criminal administration will be impossible to put into effect unless those responsible for criminal administration help make them.[2]

In a related recommendation the Commission noted that criminal justice agencies would require substantially more money if they are to control crime better. Noting that the federal government was already financing a broad range of programs to address the social problems associated with crime, it recommended a federally financed program to strengthen law enforcement, crime prevention, and the administration of justice.

The Safe Streets Act and planning

As a result of these recommendations Congress, in 1968, passed legislation entitled The Omnibus Crime and Safe Streets Act. This was the first national effort to attack the American crime problem comprehensively. The legislation focused on the need for comprehensive, coordinated planning. Millions of dollars were earmarked for the establishment and operation of planning agencies in every state for the sole purpose of developing a nation-wide strategy for the prevention and control of criminal behavior.

The beginning of professional police work Modern police work usually is dated from the Metropolitan Police Act of 1829, which authorized Sir Robert Peel, home secretary for Great Britain, to organize and centralize the London police force. In this country the comparable date would be 1844 when New York City consolidated separate day and night watches into a single law enforcement organization. New York's action was followed in the next few years by Chicago, New Orleans, Cincinnati, Boston, and several other large cities. The following excerpts summarize the arduous task police chiefs faced at that time and the continuing task of adjusting to societal change.

What those first chiefs of police found in their newly consolidated forces was a motley, undisciplined crew composed, as one commentator on the era described it, principally of "the shiftless, the incompetent, and the ignorant." Tales abounded of police officers in the 1850s who assaulted their superior officers, who released prisoners from the custody of other officers, who were found sleeping or drunk on duty, or who could be bribed

for almost anything. The nation's first top police administrators, therefore, faced the task not only of imposing organizational order on what had previously been two separate and independent operations, but of doing so with a personnel force that, by anyone's estimation, left a great deal to be desired.

Ever since that time, the American police service has faced a dual role— that of constantly refashioning the machinery of policing to meet the problems of public safety and social order in a rapidly changing society, and that of reshaping the attitudes, perceptions, and skills of the men and women who must carry out this vital social responsibility. This remains as important a challenge for police administrators today as it was almost a hundred and fifty years ago.

Source: Hubert G. Locke, "The evolution of contemporary police service," in Bernard L. Garmire, ed., *Local Government Police Management* (Washington, D.C.: International City Management Association, 2nd ed., 1982), pp. 15–17.

Several aspects of this national effort should be of vital interest to the planning profession. First, the challenge of crime to American society is a contemporary issue of immense sociopolitical importance. National, state, and local elections have been, and will continue to be, decided largely on the issue of crime. Regardless of one's attitude toward the problem and its solution, its political significance is a fact of life.

Second, planning was thrust into the forefront in the "war on crime." Since the program's inception in 1968, the Congress has appropriated in excess of 10 *billion* dollars to be expended in state, local, and national efforts to prevent and reduce crime. Many continue to question the efficacy of this tremendous expenditure of public funds to attack a problem that has its basis deep within the foundation of our society. Thus, the promise to reduce crime was, and is not, one that could be realistically attained through the expenditure of vast amounts of money. This has important implications for the planner and the manner in which the planning profession becomes involved in criminal justice planning. The first of these implications is that one can no longer simply look at crime as a single social force and attempt to address it through a single-faceted approach. Rather, the planner must, as with any other social problem, determine the underlying and contributive social problems. If the "war on crime," as we know it today through hindsight, has had a significant weakness it was this attempt to reduce crime as if it were a single entity to be dealt with. The vicissitudes of American society almost dictate that there shall always be criminal acts which

Figure 23–1   Crime has many descriptions and takes many forms.

will gain the attention of the public and lead to demands for new and more stringent laws and sentencing practices. Thus, the planner's role in the criminal justice field will be one of working in a coordinated fashion with planners in other fields and those working within the criminal justice system and identifying and developing methods to improve the effectiveness of police, courts, and corrections agencies in dealing with crime.

This multidisciplinary approach must include urban planning specialists to address the housing and transportation needs of the jobless and working poor, recreational facilities and opportunities, as well as social service specialists to provide the counseling services often needed by individuals who have entered the system. Architectural planners have developed the concept of crime prevention through architectural design by incorporating structural as well as visual barriers in their plans. They also must be included in this multidisciplinary, multifaceted approach to crime control.

Financial support for criminal justice planning

In the past, financial support for state and local criminal justice planning efforts had been provided primarily through the Safe Streets Act and the various amendments that were enacted. The Justice System Improvement Act of 1979,[3] in setting forth the purpose of the legislation, states: "Congress further finds that although crime is essentially a local problem that must be dealt with by state and local governments, the financial and technical resources of the federal government should be made available to support such state and local efforts." The financial assistance that has been made available to state and local governments was through formula grants, national priority grants, and discretionary grants.

Formula grants were intended to provide assistance "in carrying out specific innovative programs which are of proven effectiveness, have a record of proven success, or which offer a high probability of improving the functioning of the criminal justice system."[4] Twenty-three general areas were eligible for federal funding under this part of the Act and included the following:

1. Neighborhood programs that enable citizens to develop programs to deal with crime and delinquency.
2. Improving and strengthening police operations and administration.
3. Developing investigations and prosecution of white-collar crime, organized crime, public corruption-related offenses, and fraud against the government.
4. Reducing trial court delay.
5. Improving the prosecutorial process against habitual offenders.
6. Providing assistance to crime victims and witnesses.
7. Improving conditions in adult and juvenile correctional institutions.
8. Coordinating the various components of the criminal justice system, establishing criminal justice information systems, and supporting the training of criminal justice personnel.
9. Developing statistical and evaluative systems in state and local governments to assist in the determination of the effectiveness of the program areas previously mentioned.

Thus, the intent of the formula grant funds was to improve each of the system components as well as coordinate their activities and measure component and system improvements through the use of this financial support.

National priority grants were made for those programs that the Law Enforcement Assistance Administration (LEAA) had determined were effective or innovative and thus likely to have a beneficial impact on criminal justice. These programs were identified through suggestions requested by the administration of the various offices, bureaus, and boards within the LEAA as well as other appropriate public and private agencies.

The discretionary grant program was originally intended to provide additional federal financial assistance for those programs that might not otherwise be undertaken through the states' criminal justice plans. Programs that were included in this allocation were:

1. The modernization of state court operations by means of financial assistance to national nonprofit organizations operating in conjunction with and serving the judicial branches of state governments.
2. National education and training programs for judges and those in positions directly related to the operation and administration of the courts.
3. Community and neighborhood anticrime programs.
4. Victim-witness assistance programs.
5. Those efforts to improve the administration of justice through the development, dissemination, implementation, evaluation, and revision of criminal justice standards and guidelines.

These programs were identified through the same process as the national priority grants and were intended, in part, to offset any identified inequities resulting from disproportionate funding allocations among the various components of the states' criminal justice systems.

In the early 1980s, however, federal budget cuts reduced significantly the level of funding available for various crime prevention/suppression, research, and

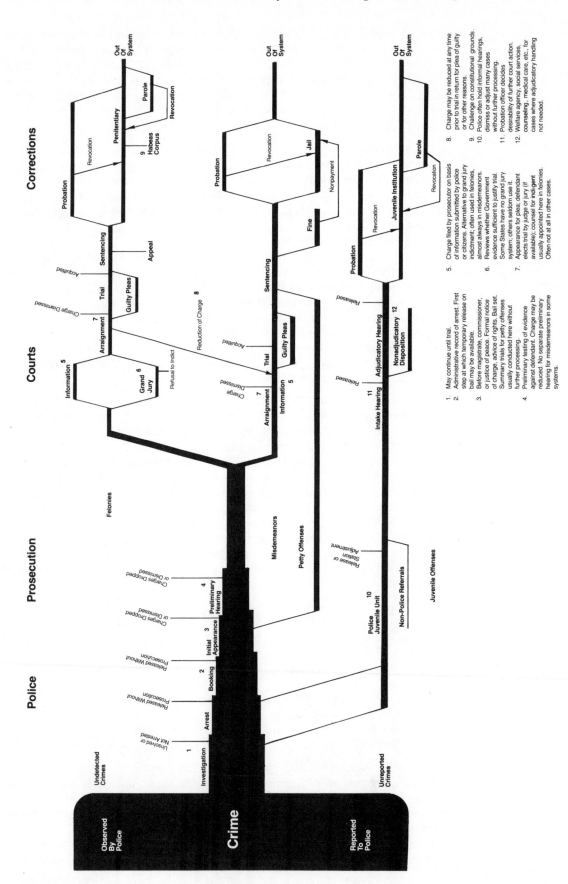

Figure 23–2   A general view of the criminal justice system.

juvenile delinquency prevention programs. While federal appropriations for state and local criminal justice planning declined precipitously during the late 1970s, the early 1980s produced even more drastic budget cuts and the elimination of several programs basic to the crime control program. Those eliminated included the Law Enforcement Assistance Administration—the original agency that disbursed program and planning funds to state and local governments. A restructuring of program priorities resulted in increased funding for the Bureau of Justice Statistics to support various statistical programs and a maintenance level of funding for the research and demonstration activities carried out by the National Institute of Justice.

Despite the vast amounts of federal monies appropriated for criminal justice planning and programming, these funds represented a very small portion of the total funds expended annually by the various criminal justice agencies throughout the United States. From 1969 to 1972, when the LEAA appropriations were at their peak, the resources available to the states under the Safe Streets Act amounted to only 3.1 percent of the total state and local government criminal justice expenditures.

The Safe Streets Act played a major role in the development of criminal justice planning. Through this federal legislation, its mandate for statewide planning, interorganizational coordination, and the grant funds made available for planning and programs, the criminal justice planner evolved. A body of knowledge of planning practices and procedures was formalized and attempts were made, with varying degrees of success, to improve a system that had long gone without a coordinated approach to the problem of crime and the handling of criminal offenders.

With the elimination of most of the federal appropriations for crime control programs, criminal justice planning should not simply cease to exist. It has become clearly evident that the planner's concern must go beyond that associated with the development of federally funded programs. In order to have any major influence upon the future of the criminal justice system, planning efforts must now be directed toward the 96 percent of criminal justice expenditures that are appropriated at the state and local levels of government.

Organizing for criminal justice planning

During the early stages of regional planning primary concern was the development of regional or substate groups (regions) comprised of clusters of adjacent counties. These were to serve as the local source for program development and review before requests for funding reached the state planning agency (SPA). The Illinois SPA, like many others, began with an inordinate number of substate planning agencies. In 1969 there were 80 such regional planning agencies in the state. The next year this was reduced to 36 and finally, in 1978, there was a total of 19 planning regions. Some states chose not to establish regional units, while others organized anywhere from two to 25 such groups. The state of Ohio established originally 15 substate units and later reduced this to four. This approach was somewhat unique in that the four planning units served the four largest cities in the state, while the SPA provided planning services to the remaining governmental jurisdictions within the state.

Many states developed regional criminal justice planning bodies which conformed to the boundaries of preexisting regional planning commissions. Councils of government, regional planning agencies responsible for 701 reviews, and general land-use and physical planning agencies were asked to expand their jurisdiction to include the criminal justice planning function.

While some of these efforts proved profitable, many failed simply due to the inability of traditional planning agencies to effectively address a social planning problem.

Criminal justice planning was to be a new area for planning and one which called for analysis and solutions other than land-use, zoning, and wastewater planning. In criminal justice planning the demand was for short-term planning for specified amounts of money with considerable risks involved. Action-oriented groups such as police, prosecutors, and jail wardens were the key actors. While many sought to improve police operations, increase criminal prosecutions, and expand correctional facilities, the social reformists sought to implement programs to address these problems through treatment and diversionary programs. Many traditional and tranquil regional planning regions wanted no part in these highly controversial planning efforts.

One of the few areas where the criminal justice planning effort encountered an existing framework compatible with its demands was in urban areas where model cities programs had begun to take hold and where crime and the criminal justice system were considered priority issues.

Most of the 1970s was devoted to the organization of substate planning regions and later the development of a planning process which encouraged local needs and priorities to be systematically channeled to the SPA for inclusion in the annual state plan. Regardless of the findings at the local level, however, federal funding to the states depended almost exclusively on population, and state spending was dictated by the state plan. Local input did not necessarily find its way into the plan.

Today we have witnessed a dissolution of regional planning regions and an almost complete elimination of SPA staff as a result of the large reductions in federal appropriations and the elimination of LEAA by Congress. A role that was born in controversy—the criminal justice planner—and an analytical system that had only begun to mature now faced one of the greatest of problems: the institutionalization of criminal justice planning within local and state government.

About the time that the federal appropriations for local criminal justice planning were reduced and then eliminated entirely, state and local governments experienced increasing financial pressures as a result of a wavering economy. The issue of crime had lost some of its political luster, and, more importantly, many local governments found themselves facing large shortfalls in revenues with which to fund basic services. Spurned by inflation and the multitude of social programs enacted in earlier years, local governments had to find new ways of financing the costs of programs and services considered essential. With their priorities stated, many local governments found they could not afford to provide financial support to a planning effort that promised little hope of additional federal funds to implement planned programs. Since criminal justice planning had become so inextricably associated with federal grant support, the luster of criminal justice planning began to tarnish. In addition to these financial problems, the concept of state and regional criminal justice planning was just beginning to mature and had only begun to be generally accepted as a viable approach to the problem of an uncoordinated and often fragmented system.

Several larger metropolitan areas institutionalized criminal justice planning into the general purpose planning agencies. However, the majority of regional planning units existed for the sole purpose of providing program planning assistance to suburban and rural jurisdictions. The ability of these jurisdictions to provide continued financial support to the regions is the factor that most influenced the future of these planning regions. In those areas where the value of regional criminal justice planning was readily recognized—despite the nonavailability of grant funds—planning regions were merged, staffs reduced, and the costs distributed among more governmental units. In some cases, individual criminal justice agencies saw the value of hiring trained and experienced planners

Distinction between urban and rural police The historic distinctions between urban and rural police services *are rapidly disappearing*. In discussions of municipal police administration the sheriff's office is frequently overlooked, not out of disregard for its importance but because, historically, the tasks and roles of sheriffs and police chiefs have been fundamentally different. Much of the difference, of course, remains. Sheriffs are generally responsible for jurisdictions that include large, sparsely populated areas. Sheriffs are elected rather than appointed; as elected officials, they normally have a significant political as well as policing role in their jurisdictions, and custody of criminal offenders or of persons awaiting trial is still a much larger part of their responsibilities than is the case with police administrators in municipal police agencies.

These differences, while important, tend to become secondary in light of the challenges that both sheriffs and urban police administrators share. The nature of these challenges is such that the tasks that sheriffs and police chiefs have in common are rapidly becoming far more significant than the historic differences. Certainly, from the standpoint of professional police administration, there is little that divides the two offices.

Source: Hubert G. Locke, "The evolution of contemporary police service," in Bernard L. Garmire, ed., *Local Government Police Management* (Washington, D.C.: International City Management Association, 2nd ed., 1982), p. 21.

---

to conduct internal planning, while others hired these planners in various non-planning administrative capacities.

The criminal justice planner's role

While the criminal justice planning field was born through the appropriation and dissemination of federal crime control funds, this planning effort must not continue to be dependent entirely upon the availability of these funds. Given the nature of crime, the need for continuing improvement and upgrading of the criminal justice system, as well as the need to continue the coordinative efforts within the system, it is essential that criminal justice planning be continued at the local and regional levels of government. In furthering this continuation of criminal justice planning the planner must not only make himself aware of the general nature of criminal justice planning, but should also attempt to maintain a broad perspective of the planning field. The interrelationship between criminal justice planning and other social and physical planning processes holds the promise of offering a wide range of interdisciplinary solutions to the problem of crime and social disorder. Crime prevention through the physical design of buildings and their immediate environment has been shown to be effective. The planning and development of social programs to meet many noncrime related needs will, and should, have an impact upon the incidence of crime in a community.

Program planning and crime specific planning techniques must be maintained and refined as a means of improving the operations of the system. Program planning to address the rational use of scarce resources within the system agencies is necessary to improve the ability of these agencies to prevent, deter, prosecute, adjudicate, and incarcerate or treat those who come to the attention of the system.

Because the criminal justice planner is dealing with a system, if in name only, it is essential that the impact of a particular program be analyzed with respect to the effect it may have on other system components. A program to increase arrests of felony offenders, for example, must be analyzed to determine the impact it would have upon the prosecutor's office, whose staff must review the formal charges and evidence for legal sufficiency and prosecute the case in court. An increase in prosecutions may require additional assistant prosecutors, create additional demands for courtrooms, require more judges, and, ultimately, may lead to an increase in the prison population. In locales where these resources are already overtaxed, means must be identified to improve the efficiency and productivity of the justice system agencies.

Crime-specific planning, a technique widely adopted in the late 1970s, meets crime head-on by analyzing conditions under which crime occurs. This technique involves the identification of the types of offenders and victims involved, and then the development of preventive measures that the police can utilize in patrol and citizen crime prevention programs. Alternative correctional programs for various types of offenders—nonviolent misdemeanants, habitual felons, or first-time offenders—can be developed based upon the crime-specific planning process. Since crime-specific planning examines a crime from its commission to the incarceration of the offender, it enables planners to detect inadequacies and to design countermeasures ranging from prevention to rehabilitation.

An example of crime-specific planning for an armed robbery problem might involve the following elements: prevention, deterrence, apprehension, and prosecution. In this example a formal program would be established with the following quantified objectives:

1. Reduce the rate (or rate of increase) of armed robberies by x percent through crime prevention methods including:
    a. Development of an awareness program for businessmen to inform them of the methods used by offenders to commit robberies.
    b. Development of a business owner education program that will provide them with methods and procedures for reducing cash on hand, increasing visibility into store interiors, and reporting suspicious persons in and about their place of business.
2. Reduce the commission of robberies in a specific area by x percent by:
    a. Increasing patrol strength in the affected area by five officers.
    b. Implementing a program of aggressive patrol, stopping and interviewing all known offenders and suspicious persons.
    c. Increasing plain clothes tactical strength in the area by two officers.
3. Increase the apprehension rate of robbery offenders by x percent by:
    a. Implementing a portable radio controlled robbery alarm system in high risk commercial establishments.
    b. Developing robbery offenders profiles, trends and patterns through crime analysis techniques, and provide stakeouts of most probable businesses to be victimized.
4. Increase the conviction rate and sentencing of robbery suspects x percent by:
    a. Assigning a special prosecutor to handle all case reviews, prosecutions, and post-trial hearings involving robbery cases.
    b. Refusing to negotiate (plea bargain) robbery cases.
    c. Seeking the establishment of career criminal legislation to impose additional sentencing on those convicted of armed robbery on two previous occasions.

Additional strategies may involve the determination of why these offenses are being committed, i.e.: to support a drug habit, serious unemployment, fund raising for gang activities, etc. Appropriate measures can then be taken to address these problems, which are of a more basic social nature, and develop strategies and programs to deal with causes of criminal behavior.

Without the continued attention to the criminal justice system and the ever-evolving problems of coordination and development, meaningful comprehensive criminal justice planning will not be attainable. Since the criminal justice system in the United States is largely a function of local government, there are a great many autonomous police agencies, prosecutor's offices, courts, and correctional institutions with independent jurisdiction. This structure poses many problems for the planner and requires that some coordinative planning be conducted. Using the planning techniques mentioned above, a systems perspective can be maintained, even if it were to be restricted to an overview of system operation.

An early monograph on criminal justice planning identified and discussed a number of basic challenges that professional planners to confront. Those which have current applicability to the criminal justice effort are presented below:

1. Planners in the criminal justice arena find themselves in an action-oriented environment. For political and professional reasons the national program must perform and perform quickly. The millions of dollars being invested cannot wait for the normal time lapse which planners prefer before completing their blueprints for action. In fact, planning and funding began simultaneously with the onset of the program in 1969. Whether two such strange bedfellows as planning and funding can productively coexist under one roof (the state planning agency) remains to be seen.

   Certainly the need for such a pairing exists where impact programs focus on institutional and social change. If planning is going to be relevant in this arena, a strategy for effective short-term planning is going to have to be developed soon. Planners in the criminal justice field are not merely giving advice; they are being asked to call the shots, to spell out priorities, to choose among functional areas, and to develop a strategy for the expenditure of hundreds of millions of dollars annually.

   The situation calls for the involvement of skilled planners at every level of government. In such a context planners will be highly visible and, even worse, most of the criminal justice planners will have to live with their decisions. Such a situation is enough to frighten many a planner.

2. Few programs present a more urgent need for a coordinated and systematic approach to problem solving, and few professions place a greater emphasis on just such an approach than does planning. The criminal justice system is fragmented and suffers from a lack of coordination. Planning has always prided itself on its systematic approach to multifaceted problems. As demonstrated earlier, the criminal justice system drastically needs such an approach.

3. In addition to being interdisciplinary the criminal justice system is intergovernmental. Federal, state, and local governments all have key roles in the administration and execution of the system. Any meaningful and comprehensive plan must take into account the critical relationship between governmental units if an effective and efficient system is to be formed. Planners have historically advocated regionalization where governmental cooperation enhanced the delivery of public services. This intergovernmental aspect is sufficient cause for planning to make a significant commitment to the effort.

4. The issue of representation on planning boards has always been one of historic importance in the development of the planning process, both here and abroad. Planners have always been on guard for "vested interests" in the planning process and this very issue is a key one for the current criminal justice reform effort. The quality of planning in the overall program will be directly related to the quality and the representativeness of those numerous commissions who are responsible for policy formulation and planning effort.

5. Very little rational planning is going to take place in the criminal justice field until basic data needs are satisfied. The challenge of attaining consistent and reliable data is a sizable one, but one which planners are familiar with. The overall profile of the national crime problem is suspect in spite of the emphasis police place on data. Much of the information they receive from the public is simply inaccurate, a considerable amount of crime is never reported, and a significant percentage is interpreted in ways that relieve the reporting agencies of any blame.

   A detailed account of the effectiveness of the criminal justice system in treating the crime problem at every point along the system's continuum and in every geographic location throughout the country is vitally needed. Because the planning profession has always placed a top priority on data collection, and because planners are normally trained in data collection techniques, the skilled planner is needed in the criminal justice field. . . .

6. The ultimate challenge to planners is the very aspect which provides the greatest risk. The whole criminal justice program is fraught with obstacles and booby traps which only the most sensitive and skilled can survive. If planners do, in fact, respond to the need for their services, they are being thrust into the center of the age-old battle between city and state, between black and white, and between repressionist and reformist.[5]

The planner's responsibilities

In addition to the challenges facing the criminal justice planner, he is faced also with a set of professional responsibilities which only he is fully suited to address. Since the criminal justice system is comprised of a large number of autonomous agencies with independent jurisdictions, it involves a wide array of participants whose motives are often divergent and whose perspectives are often in conflict. The continuing existence of these vested interests and often subjective appraisals require the planner's priority be afforded to fact finding, standard setting, and the systems approach to problem solving. While there are many techniques that can be used and services that the planner can provide in the effort to upgrade the criminal justice system, there are several fundamental responsibilities that the planner must fulfill.

A comprehensive framework

The development of a planning framework, a comprehensive strategy or game-plan that encompasses not only the problems or needs of the particular agency being addressed, but also the related elements of the other components of the system, is the first responsibility of the planner. Since the criminal justice system operates, at least in theory, as a system, the component parts of the system must be addressed in a coordinated manner recognizing the interactive nature of the criminal justice process.

It is the planner who must ensure that findings are systematically validated and that the strategy moves from its conceptual beginnings through planning and eventually to the implementation stage. Numerous isolated activities must be related to one another and arranged logically during the planning cycle. The vested interests to be encountered will naturally tend to frustrate the interdisciplinary solutions that the planner identifies. The feasibility, and at times the desirability, of these solutions will often be questioned by those whose interests and involvement in the system are restricted to their own agency or element within the system. The police planner, the court administrator, the fiscal officer, and the city executive must all serve and satisfy constituents with differing needs and desires.

The criminal justice planner relies on the substantive experts to identify problems, select those factors that are critical, and decide on the course of action that will ultimately be followed. The planner, however, is personally responsible for identifying the actual *cause* of problems, for developing alternative courses of action and for comparing achievements, costs, and developing various time schedules for the alternatives.

A flow of relevant information

The planner must continually work toward providing relevant information. He must seek out sources of such information among the tons of irrelevant and

The police and the courts Police and the courts in the United States are not systemic, but there is a pattern that generally follows the federal, state, and local levels of government.

The local government agencies include city and county police departments, sheriffs' departments, and police agencies for special purposes such as harbors, tunnels, and parks. State police agencies include general-purpose police departments, as well as agencies for public health, insurance, parks, liquor control, and other special purposes. The federal government does not have a national, general-purpose police force, but there are specialized police agencies for narcotics control, tax collections, prison management, immigration, border control, customs, and other purposes.

Courts of general jurisdiction in the federal government include three levels: district courts, courts of appeals, and the U.S. Supreme Court. The federal government also has special courts for taxes, claims, patents, international trade, and other purposes.

State courts are generally divided into three levels. The initial level includes the trial courts of general jurisdiction and a wide variety of courts of limited jurisdiction, including justice courts, municipal courts, probate courts, juvenile courts, traffic courts, and others. In about half of the states the only appellate level is the state supreme court. The remaining states have an intervening appellate level.

---

misleading information which serve only to complicate an already difficult task. A number of reliable information collection and analytical techniques are available to the criminal justice planner. Each planner must seek out those techniques that have applicability to the situation and apply them in an objective manner. Several of these analytical techniques are addressed later in this chapter.

Facilitation of the establishment of basic priorities

The planner must facilitate consensus on fundamental priorities and the direction in which to channel planning activities. By allocating financial and personnel resources to appropriate program areas basic philosophies are implicitly stated. Therefore, in terms of total justice system planning the planner must recommend which of the system components must receive priority attention and, in general, what the overall priority relationships will be among the system components. Providing assistance in the setting of basic priorities and the allocation of resources to meet these priorities can be a difficult task for the planner. As mentioned earlier, the divergent and often conflicting interests of those in the criminal justice system serve to increase the complexity and difficulty of the priority setting task.

Application of standards

Criminal justice planners must continually work for the establishment of new standards, the refinement of existing standards, and their dissemination.

The establishment of such standards has received considerable attention in recent years. The National Advisory Commission on Criminal Justice Standards and Goals has issued a multivolume set of standards that address all of the elements of the criminal justice system as well as related private sector interfaces with the system.

The National Advisory Commission recognized that these national standards were not enough. In the various volumes they repeated often the statement that local and state criminal justice agencies should adopt certain standards depending upon their size and complexity. To date most states have developed and enacted laws governing the minimum training an individual must have before he or she can be certified as a permanent police officer. Similar standards exist for other positions within the criminal justice system yet these are only a beginning. Much more must be done by the criminal justice planner to bring these standards to the attention of criminal justice administrators and, of ultimate importance, to push for the adoption of these standards and their application in the day-to-day operations of these agencies.

Evaluation

Evaluation is more than the last task to be completed before the conclusion of a program. In order to realize the full benefits of program evaluation the evaluation process must commence with the first efforts at planning the program. The criminal justice planner's role in the program planning process is one of assisting the program manager in developing program goals and objectives that lend themselves to the evaluation process. Goals and objectives that are quantitative, as well as qualitative, are essential to an efficient and reliable evaluation. These goals and objectives are established upon the assumptions of the program, i.e., certain givens that are taken at face value based upon a theoretical construct or past experience. Based upon available information, standards adopted for the program or the organization, relative priorities, and the planner's skills and knowledge, the criminal justice administrator can learn of the merits of the program and make informed decisions.

The LEAA requirement for program evaluation of funded projects has led to not only an increase in the number of programs evaluated, but also an interest in evaluation as a management tool. Yet, despite all this information and interest, many still retain their suspicions and negative feelings toward program evaluation.

In far too many cases program sponsors know little more of a program's value and cost effectiveness after a year or two than they did at the outset. Perhaps a new or expanded program put a few more people to work, but whether the program's original objectives were met or whether the experience is worth replicating elsewhere is unknown. Qualified evaluators are not found as readily as are those who portend to be evaluators. Some programs would cost half again as much to evaluate properly, and yet few agencies are willing to develop such a capacity when allocating funds and other resources to a program.

One key to the overall criminal justice effort rests with our learning from past experiences. The planner should be continually stressing the need for sufficient, first-rate evaluation. There is every likelihood that if the planner does not supply this sensitivity, it will not be supplied.

One method of ensuring that some degree of program evaluation occurs is to build an evaluation component into the program during the initial planning phase. Programs are intended to address an observed set of problems. It follows, therefore, that the problem statement should serve as the basis for the development of the goals and objectives, and tasks and responsibilities, to be fulfilled by the program effort. Stating these problems, goals, and objectives in quantitative terms is an initial step not only in program planning, but also program evaluation. A clear statement of the results and benefits to be realized through program operation supports the evaluation phase of the program.

In an era of reduced revenues, economic inflation, and cut-back management, program evaluation becomes more meaningful. Decisions to expand, reduce, or eliminate programs should be based upon objective data which establish program worth. A sound program evaluation design, originated during the initial planning process, is the most reliable, and often the least expensive, means of developing and collecting these data.

Ongoing program monitoring provides opportunities to check on program status and further develop and refine the data collection process. As a result of these initial and ongoing efforts for evaluation and monitoring data are collected, analyzed, and refined while the program is in effect. Thus, cost-saving steps can be taken immediately, and time-consuming, post-program data collection avoided.

Sources of information for the criminal justice planner

One of the earliest efforts to collect criminal justice system information was that of the U.S. Bureau of the Census which began to count criminal offenders in 1850. From that early effort, annual censuses of prisoners in federal and state prisons were started in 1926 and, in 1924, the Uniform Crime Reporting system (UCR) was initiated.

Uniform Crime Reports

The UCR system, now under the aegis of the Federal Bureau of Investigation, regularly collects information from numerous municipal, county, state, and special district police forces throughout the country. In many states, statewide reporting systems, with mandatory reporting requirements, have been established to meet the needs of law enforcement officials for crime-related data.

While the UCR statistics provide data on crime and criminality, they have been scrutinized by innumerable researchers and law enforcement officials and have been found to be lacking in many respects. Because these statistics are collected through a voluntary program, there are numerous cases in which law enforcement agencies under-report the number or nature of offenses reported to them by victims of crime, or do not report at all. The information provided by the UCR system is primarily a count of offenses that have been reported to the police and the police response to these offenses in terms of arrests.

The UCR information is by in large useful for reactive decision making. To the extent that the data collected are reliable and valid indicators of crime, the use of the information is restricted almost entirely to the comparison of one jurisdiction's reported crime and arrests over a period of several years. To a certain extent this information can be used to compare the crime clearance rate of one jurisdiction with other comparable jurisdictions. The user of UCR information is cautioned to read and consider carefully the caveat contained in the introductory section of the annual UCR reports. This addresses the fact that a number of social, economic, cultural, and geographic factors play major roles in influencing the type and extent of crime in a community. Therefore, it is difficult, even under optimal circumstances, to accurately compare the crime rate of one jurisdiction with another that appears, on the surface, to have similar characteristics.

In addressing the shortcomings of the UCR system the National Advisory Commission on Criminal Justice Standards and Goals stated:

The UCR system was designed to provide measurement of changes in the pattern of criminal activity. It was not designed to provide detailed data for planning and program evaluation or to meet other current needs for crime data.

For these reasons, it is suggested that UCR be used as a basic standard and upgraded to satisfy additional needs for information. Additional needs for information should be met by collecting data beyond that prescribed by UCR.[6]

As a result of the studies and recommendations of various commissions and legislative committees, a renewed interest in criminal justice statistical and data reporting systems has been created. This interest resulted in the funding by LEAA of several efforts to improve the collection of criminal justice information.

Computerized criminal justice information system (CJIS)

As a means of overcoming one of the most serious inadequacies of the UCR system, LEAA funded Project SEARCH (System for Electronic Analysis and Retrieval of Criminal Histories). The goal of this project was to design and develop a computerized criminal justice statistics system that would store information on individual offenders proceeding through the criminal justice system.

Prior to the inception of this system it was difficult, if not impossible, to reconcile the arrest process of the police with the prosecution and adjudication processes and the eventual incarceration of the offender. Because each one of the system's components was using a count that met its own internal needs for reporting purposes, the same individual might be processed through the system yet be counted as an arrest by the police, a case by the prosecutors and the courts, and as a person (inmate) by correctional agencies. Thus, the available data did not show the proportion of arrestees released at various stages of the criminal justice process nor the type and frequency of initial and amended charges. Also, the efficiency of the system in processing offenders, in terms of time and dispositions, could not be determined since no system processing times were collected and stored for future reference and analysis.

The SEARCH project resulted in the development of the Offender Based Transaction System (OBTS). Through the OBTS individuals, multiple charges against an individual, time expended in processing an individual through the system, and criminal justice agency inputs/outputs can be recorded, tracked, and analyzed. Through the analysis of these data more rational decisions can be made regarding the allocation of resources to various programs and interagency performance standards can be developed and agency performance comparatively assessed. In addition, the impact of the incidence of crime on the system elements can be determined and more reliable predictions made of criminal justice agency workloads.

Computerized criminal histories (CCH)

The CCH system, like the OBTS, is an offender-based system. The offender is the common element of count and allows interfacing between the two systems. The CCH is directed primarily at the interchange of information between criminal justice agencies. While the FBI presently operates the National Crime Information Center (NCIC) and collects such offender-based information, there is a need to have such information collected at the state level to support the OBTS.

Figure 23-3 depicts the unique and common data elements of the OBTS and CCH systems. A review of this table will give the reader some insights into the types of data necessary to conduct criminal justice systems planning.

Opportunities in criminal justice planning

Since the passage of the Safe Streets Act in 1968 the role, and in fact the existence, of criminal justice planners has evolved into a professional pursuit. Where criminal justice planners were once unknown to the criminal justice community and at the various levels of government, they eventually evolved into a highly visible group. Through the activities engaged in by criminal justice planners, the planning regions, and the state planning agencies created under the Safe Streets Act, a common knowledge has evolved. Through accredited college and university courses and programs there are thousands of qualified practitioners in the field of criminal justice planning.

In assessing the evolution of criminal justice planning, the Task Force on Criminal Justice Research and Development stated:

Researchers in criminal justice prior to the passage of the . . . Safe Streets Act . . . consisted largely of behavioral and social scientists, including sociologists associated with criminology. By and large, the criminal justice research community was small, generally tangential to the mainstream of social and behavioral science, widely scattered at different academic institutions, and of uneven quality. The stress imposed on the community of criminal justice researchers by the rapid infusion of R&D [research and development] dollars has resulted in a sharp increase in the number and types of researchers who do criminal justice R&D. Today, the research community includes individuals from law, operations research, economics, political science, and engineering; the scope of the performer community has been considerably broadened.[7]

Thus, from its seminal beginnings in the late 1960s criminal justice planning has grown from a few whose interests were directed toward sociological inquiry into the nature and causes of crime to an ongoing force to study not only the causes of crime but also the changes necessary to bring about more effective operation of the criminal justice system. There exists today an opportunity for the criminal justice planner to interact with a variety of individuals engaged in the total spectrum of issues, concerns, and programs associated with the criminal justice system.

The opportunities available today and in the near future have been influenced negatively by the decision of the federal government to reduce substantially its support to the criminal justice planning structure and programs initiated under the Safe Streets Act. However, programs to educate and familiarize local and state officials as well as community leaders with the process and benefits of criminal justice planning have been an integral part of many criminal justice planning programs.

State and local Chambers of Commerce, Leagues of Women Voters, Conferences of Mayors and Managers, as well as various other associations have been involved in the criminal justice planning process to one extent or another. It is because of this knowledge and the recognized need for criminal justice planning on the part of many of these officials that the criminal justice planner will not become obsolete after the federal government has ceased to support a national crime reduction effort.

As mentioned earlier in the introduction to this chapter, federal crime control funds accounted for less than 4 percent of the total criminal justice expenditures in the United States. It is the remaining 96 percent of expenditures that must be planned for and allocated if the planning process is to have any major impact upon crime prevention and reduction, and increase the efficiency of the criminal justice system.

Considering these facts, it becomes evident that any reduction or elimination of federal crime control funds, while it may impede the continuing progress that has been made through the availability and use of the funds, will not portend the end of an era in the criminal justice system in this country. Instead, it may point out the need for more concentrated efforts to analyze the crime and operational problems that the system agencies are and will be facing in the future. Without the availability of federal crime control funds to initiate new or innovative programs, administrators will have to rely more upon existing resources and identify ways and means of reallocating priorities and dollars in order to fund these new programs. This emphasis on internal program planning and resource allocation may create the need for qualified planners: planners with a

OBTS	CCH
IDENTIFICATION ELEMENTS	**IDENTIFICATION SEGMENT**

OBTS	CCH
	Message key
State identification no.*	Originating agency
FBI no.* →	FBI identification no.
State record no.	Name
Sex ←	Sex
Race ←	Race
	Place of birth
Date of birth →	Date of birth
	Height
	Weight
	Color of eyes
	Color of hair
	Skin tone
	Scars, marks, tattoos, etc.
	Social security no.
	Miscellaneous identification no.
	Fingerprint classification
	Identification comments
	State establishing record
	Date record established
	Date of latest update

OBTS	CCH
POLICE/PROSECUTOR ELEMENTS	**ARREST SEGMENT**

OBTS	CCH
Arresting agency no.*	Message key
	Arrest agency identifier
	Date of birth
	State identification no.
	FBI identification no.
	Name arrestee used
Sequence letter ←	Sequence letter
Date of arrest ←	Date of arrest
	Arrest charge no.
	Date of offense
	Statute citation
	General offense character
Charged offense—most serious ←	Arrest offense—numeric
	Arrest offense—literal
Police disposition ←	Arrest disposition—numeric
Prosecutor disposition	Additional arrest disposition data
Police/prosecutor disposition date	

OBTS	CCH
LOWER CRIMINAL COURT ELEMENTS	**JUDICIAL SEGMENT**

OBTS	CCH
Court identification no.*	Message key
	Agency identifier
	State identification no.
Initial appearance date	FBI identification no.
	Sequence letter
	Date of arrest
	Court count no.
Disposition date	Court disposition date
	Statute citation
	General offense character
Charged offense (most serious) →	Court offense classification— numeric
	Court offense classification— literal
Lower court disposition ←	Court disposition—numeric
Release action	Sentence suspended

Figure 23–3 Comparisons of OBTS and CCH data elements (arrows indicate corresponding data elements).

OBTS	CCH
Release action date	Confinement
Final charge (most serious)	Probation
Type of charge	Fine
Plea (at trial)	Other court sentence provisions—literal
Type of trial	Other court sentence provisions—numeric
Date of sentence	Date case appealed
Type of sentence	On bail pending results of appeal
Confinement term (days)	
Probation term (months)	
Type of counsel	

COUNTY PROSECUTOR GRAND JURY ELEMENTS	**SUPPLEMENTAL SEGMENT**
	Message key
Prosecutor identification no.*	Agency identifier
Date of filing	State identification no.
Type of filing	FBI identification no.
Filing procedure	Sequence letter
Date of arraignment	Date of arrest
Charged offense (most serious)	Court count no.
Initial plea	Court (chief executive) disposition date
Release action	Court (chief executive) disposition
Release action date	Sentence suspended
	Confinement
	Probation
	Fine
	Other court sentence provisions—literal
	Other court sentence provisions—numeric

FELONY TRIAL ELEMENTS	**CUSTODY—SUPERVISION SEGMENT**
Court identification no.*	Message key
Trial date	Agency identifier
Trial type	State identification no.
Final plea	FBI identification no.
Trial ending/disposition date	Sequence letter
Final charge (most serious)	Date of arrest
Type of charge	Status change character
Court disposition	Custody or supervision status starting date
Sentence date	Custody or supervision status—numeric
Sentence type	Custody or supervision status—literal extended
Confinement—prison (years)	
Confinement—jail (days)	
Probation (months)	
Type of counsel	

CORRECTIONS ELEMENTS

Agency identifier*
Receiving agency
Status
Date of exit
Exit

* Data element should be in data base at state level but is
 not required to be reported to LEAA in Comprehensive Data
 Systems Program.

Figure 23–3   (continued)

knowledge of the intricacies of the interrelationships among the components of the criminal justice system. This will create additional needs for planners with specialties in training and organizational development, program monitoring and evaluation, as well as agency-specific planning (police, courts, corrections, etc.). Other opportunities of a general nature will include multipurpose planning agencies, research organizations, and county and state budget offices.

In early 1981, shortly after it was learned that the Reagan administration was severely curtailing federal appropriations for criminal justice planning and programs, the Ford Foundation announced that it intended to focus on the problem of crime in the 1980s. This foundation, the wealthiest philanthropic organization in the country, often sets the pace for other foundations. Their stated intentions to examine the impact of crime on neighborhood life, location of businesses, job opportunities, and the availability of goods and services may prove to be the continued support criminal justice planning requires. While the Foundation's total annual grant awards are significantly less than the federal appropriations to LEAA for criminal justice purposes, their decision will direct some ongoing attention to the problem of crime.

Training and organizational development

The concept of organizational development is a "whole systems" approach to the change process in an organization. That is to say that organizational development (OD) deals with the totality of an organization: individuals, technologies, and the structures and processes employed in the organization. For the planner interested in the process and implementation of organizational change within the criminal justice system, this planning role can be rewarding.

The operationalization of this concept has been described in practical terms by one practitioner of OD as follows:

At the first level, OD focuses on change in the person: skills, knowledge, values; work style, management style, interpersonal style; personal growth and development. Second, OD practitioners are concerned with modifying the technology of the organization—the flow, pace, and arrangement of its technical procedures and resources—the application of its art, craft, and skill toward some productive end. Third, OD practitioners are concerned with improving organizational structure and process—the sense of relationships among people, work roles, and the interaction dynamics within work teams, between various groups or departments, and within the total organization. Since no organization exists in an environmental vacuum, the fourth concern of OD practitioners is to analyze and deal with the various pressures and needs of the organization's external environment.[8]

In this role the planner would be analyzing the needs of the organization and the individuals in it and developing strategies that would meet the needs of both the organization and the individual. This role is that of the planner as a management analyst: employing his analytical skills, knowledge, and interests to bring about change in criminal justice agencies.

Program monitoring and evaluation

Program monitoring can be best described as the "quality control" component of the program evaluation effort. The evaluation effort itself encompasses a series of related tasks or steps. These include: the quantification of goals and objectives, establishing goal/objective relationships, identifying evaluation measures, and determining data needs.

The need for criminal justice evaluators has become one of increasing importance in recent years. With the growing sophistication of the criminal justice planning and programming processes has come an attendant need to involve the criminal justice planner in all phases of the program planning process. In asking the question of where the criminal justice planner fits into the program evaluation picture, one author states:

The response to this query is assertedly in the foreground of all planning, program implementation, and evaluation. We would predict, in fact, that the CJS planner will become more immersed in decisions that deal with productivity, measurement of the impact of various services, and the evaluation of both. As a mix, productivity, measurement, and evaluation form an invaluable planning tool. Conversely, without them the CJS planner is missing a fundamental capability for *controlling* his or her assigned *responsibilities* (italics in original).[9]

Program monitoring and evaluation have become increasingly more important as the emphasis on productivity, cut-back management, and cost-avoidance has increased. Establishing quantified goals and objectives are essential first steps in the program planning process, yet are meaningless unless serious, continuing effort is made to assess the progress of the program and program results. In this respect, the planner becomes involved in identifying, developing, and applying reliable performance measures. Continuing on with the data gathering, collation, and analysis phases of evaluation the planner will be required to modify and improve upon these performance measures based upon actual program experiences. In the final stage, analysis and documentation of program results, the planner may again find him or herself in the role of the management analyst. Interpreting the results of a program in terms of dollars expended, services provided, and results obtained from the perspective of productivity and the use of relatively decreasing resources will present a major challenge.

In essence, the criminal justice planner's role will be primarily one of evaluating alternative courses of action to provide existing services as opposed to evaluating the process and impact of new and additional services. At the same time, the planner, as an evaluator, may be analyzing existing programs and services to identify those that can be reduced or eliminated to meet available resources.

Integration with social and physical planning

Recognizing that the criminal justice system is one whose components must be interrelated with one another, so must the criminal justice system be interrelated with the various social and physical systems that comprise our society. Systems such as education, welfare, housing, highways, and parks each have an impact, individually and collectively, upon the manner in which the police, courts, and correctional components will operate and the resources that they will require. The nature and quality of housing will determine in part the way in which the police will patrol an area. The availability of jobs, and the manner in which the welfare and unemployment systems are administered, will also play a role in the incidence of crime and the manner in which the courts and correctional agencies will respond and provide services. The criminal justice planner in interaction with the physical and social planner has an opportunity to assess the planning process and its products from the perspective of the eventual impact upon the crime and the criminal justice system.

Continuing federal interest

The LEAA ceased operation April 15, 1982. Despite the absence of LEAA funds, federal interest in the chronic problems of state and local corrections has not disappeared. For instance, in what undoubtedly amounts to the most significant and sustained federal involvement in prisons and jails, district and appellate judges have gone to great lengths and minute detail to assure at least minimal constitutional conditions in a large number of overcrowded and deteriorating state and local facilities—often at considerable expense to state and local coffers.

The trend toward federal "mandates" of this sort was intensified in 1980 by passage of the Civil Rights of Institutionalized Persons Act[10] which directs the Attorney General to initiate suits against states, their political subdivisions, and agents believed to be violating the rights of inmates. Moreover, in December of 1980, the Justice Department released a set of *Federal Standards for Prisons and Jails.*[11] While strictly voluntary, these extensive standards are expected to heavily influence the remedial decisions of federal judges.

A different sort of mandate—grant-related—was attached to the Juvenile Justice Amendments of 1980.[12] In relevant part, that Act requires participating states to remove all juveniles from local adult lockups and jails by 1985—an admirable goal indeed. Yet, while the costs of removal vary greatly from jurisdiction to jurisdiction—from nothing for the many "footdraggers" to as much as $69,740 for jurisdictions holding 100 children in secure facilities for ten days—the overall estimated $118.8 million pricetag of the order is viewed with some hostility by many hardpressed participants.[13]

Thus, in spite of continued, if not heightened, federal involvement in state and local institutional arrangements, one observer has noted that:

[t]he federal approach of providing financial resources, technical assistance and useful research is on the wane. In its place the federal government is showing signs of shaping a new role for itself—that of regulator.[14]

Continuing state and local interest

Fewer federal criminal justice dollars have not meant an end to creative state-local correctional arrangements.[15] Though initiated in 1973, the leading example is Minnesota's Community Corrections Act. The much-acclaimed law—popular with both county and state officials despite a somewhat negative official evaluation[16]—authorizes the state to provide subsidies to counties that plan, develop,[17] and operate community-based correctional programs for adults and juveniles. The formula grant is conditioned upon counties spending their own funds at the same level as the previous year. Thus, the subsidy is used for expanded services. Counties with small populations may elect to join contiguous counties in developing regional plans. In the past several years, Kansas, Oregon, and Iowa have all passed community corrections acts using the Minnesota legislation as a model.

1　President's Commission on Law Enforcement and Administration of Justice, *The Challenge of Crime in a Free Society.* (Washington, DC: US Government Printing Office, 1967), p. v.
　Ibid., p. xi.
　Public Law 96-157, December 27, 1979.
　Ibid., Section 401(a).
　Mark Hoffman. *Criminal Justice Planning* (Chicago: American Society of Planning Officials, 1972), pp. 22–23.
　National Advisory Commission on Criminal Justice Standards and Goals, *Report of the Task Force on Criminal Justice Research and Development* (Washington, DC: US Government Printing Office, 1976), p. 31.
　Ibid.
　Frank Friedlander, *OD: Purpose and Values in OD* (Madison, WI: American Society for Training and Development, 1976), p. 9.
　Donald Shanahan and Paul Whisenand, *The Dimensions of Criminal Justice Planning* (Boston: Allyn and Bacon, 1980), p. 403.
10　P. L. 96-247 (1980).
11　U.S. Department of Justice, *Federal Standards for Prisons and Jails* (Washington, DC: US Department of Justice, December 16, 1980).

12　P.L. 96-509 (1980).
13　University of Illinois, Community Research Center, "Jail Removal Cost Study," Summary Report of the Office of Juvenile Justice and Delinquency Prevention, May 1982.
14　Mark A. Cunniff, "Unannounced Shift in Federal Programs," *Nation's Cities Weekly* September 1, 1980: p. 5.
15　A useful report on the institutionalization of criminal justice planning both with and without reference to federal funding is *Criminal Justice Planning in the Governing Process: A Review of Nine States* (National Academy of Public Administration, February 1979).
16　Both the assumptions underlying and the methodology of the evaluation have been subject to widespread criticism.
17　Initial plans and annual comprehensive plans are to be developed by a representative board composed of members from law enforcement, the judiciary, prosecutorial services, the education community, the county welfare board, the public defender's office, probation and parole boards, corrections, social and health care service agencies, private citizens, and the sentenced, convicted population itself.

24 Comprehensive emergency planning and management

The word disaster is overused and much abused in our daily conversations. An extreme geologic or weather event, such as an earthquake or a flood, is not a natural disaster *per se*. A natural event is termed a catastrophe or disaster when "damage to property, human health, social structure, or processes are of such severity that recovery and rehabilitation is a long, trying process."[1]

Many trying natural events have occurred periodically, such as droughts in the West or blizzards in New England. Such events were not perceived as disasters until recently, when they began to cause serious hardships for people and damage to the manmade environment. In the United States, nine kinds of hazards have been responsible historically for most building damage: earthquake, landslide, expansive soil, river flood, hurricane wind/storm surge, tornado, local flood, local wind, and tsunami (seismic sea wave). As the population and the density of residents in disaster-prone areas increase, the United States is becoming more vulnerable to catastrophes caused by natural events. Although the main focus of this chapter will be on natural disasters, the preparedness and recovery planning processes are similar for many manmade disasters, such as explosions, fires, dam breaks, and subsidence. Nuclear disasters, however, would have significantly different characteristics and requirements for response and recovery.

While natural disasters may be "acts of God," settlement patterns and building practices in the United States contribute directly to the losses of lives and property and indirectly to the social and economic disruption resulting from such events. Presently, floods are the most numerous and costliest natural disasters experienced in this country. Recent studies, however, have highlighted the growing potential damage that can be caused by hurricanes, which may soon surpass floods as the costliest hazard in the United States:

Destruction of buildings by hurricanes is expected to grow from today's almost $2 billion to about $5 billion (constant dollars) annually by the year 2000. This is largely due to population growth and movement, coastal development, and higher construction values.[2]

The so-called manmade hazards, which include chemical and toxic spills, explosions, nuclear accidents, crashes, and conflagrations, are increasing at an alarming rate in the United States. Currently, manmade disasters occur at least twice as often as natural disasters and the rate climbs steadily.

A community that experiences any type of disaster usually goes through several identifiable stages. The key stages are named and defined here to reduce confusion about the various terms used. The four terms most commonly used are the following:

Mitigation, which covers activities that could prevent or alleviate the impact of a catastrophic event before the event occurs; this includes stringent building codes, flood insurance, and public education.

Preparedness, which includes installing warning systems; stockpiling supplies;

maintaining resource inventories; devising special hazard plans; making structural adjustments, such as dams and levees; and implementing nonstructural measures such as relocation; in other words, planning and implementation to guide development away from disaster-prone areas.

Response, which includes search and rescue operations; debris removal; and provision of resources, such as food, shelter, and medicine.

Recovery, which refers to the activities that contribute to the restoration and reconstruction of the community to at least predisaster conditions. After the emergency repairs have been made, the restoration of repairable and restorable structures begins. Next, the emphasis is on the replacement of capital stock to return to predisaster levels or greater. Finally, major construction that will contribute to the improvement of the community often is undertaken.

These four phases are interrelated and should be thought of as an unbroken chain. Many recovery activities, such as rebuilding and land use decisions, may contribute to mitigation of future severe geophysical events. To be successful, mitigation activities must be linked to appropriate preparedness and recovery activities and carried out as part of a comprehensive emergency preparedness program.

While the preparedness and response phases have received the most attention to date, emergency services officials at all levels of government are becoming increasingly concerned with the need for longer term mitigation measures and with the often lengthy, and not well-understood, recovery period. Planners probably would have the greatest involvement in mitigation and recovery activities, both of which are covered in more detail in the subsequent sections of this chapter.

The states and comprehensive emergency planning and management

Since the advent of the Federal Emergency Management Agency in April of 1979, the concept and term "comprehensive emergency management" has come to the fore. The centralization of the national level disaster relief and emergency services agencies—formerly dealing separately with civil defense, fire, and natural disaster relief—has contributed to both the consolidating of agencies and the broadening of thinking at the state, regional, and local levels. Consequently, the concepts of comprehensive emergency planning and management have gained far more currency recently. Further, many organizational arrangements at the state and substate levels are being changed to reflect the full spectrum of disaster activities in which those governments may be involved.

In a recent survey of states (and commonwealths and territories), the National Governors' Association noted that most states have a single agency which takes the lead responsibility for emergency preparedness and response activities. While the nature of the lead organization as well as its functions varies, nevertheless, state organizations generally fall into five types. Those five types are as follows:

1. Authority legislated to the governor and operated in the executive office.
2. Authority legislated to the governor and delegated to a civilian department.
3. Authority legislated to the governor and delegated to the adjutant general.
4. Authority legislated to the governor and delegated to the state police.
5. Authority legislated to the governor and delegated to a council which oversees departmental activities.[3]

The budgets of the lead state organizations as well as their functions vary con-

Preparedness assessed in California   In June 1980, the California Legislature (via one of the three oversight subcommittees of the Assembly) evaluated the emergency planning and disaster relief activities in California. The resulting report was candid and highly critical of the state of emergency preparedness in California. After reviewing California's past experiences with disasters and hearing testimony about the high probability of such disasters occurring in the future in California, the subcommittee became convinced of the need for a high level of emergency preparedness in the state.

"In fact, the basic principle behind all the recommendations contained in this report is the belief that improved emergency preparedness can result in a significant reduction of the amount of casualties and damage occurring due to a disaster."

The general findings of this evaluation were that the state of California is poorly prepared to respond to a major disaster affecting a metropolitan area and, consequently, could incur unac-

ceptably high levels of casualties and damage from such a disaster. While noting that a real test of emergency preparedness could come only from experiencing a major disaster, nevertheless the evaluation was based on reviewing three major aspects of preparedness in the state. Those three were: (1) administrative priority, (2) local government preparedness, and (3) state agency preparedness. Each of these three aspects was analyzed, and specific findings and recommendations put forward.

This example is important because it shows state legislative interest; an effort to evaluate the state of preparedness for a large and hazard-vulnerable state; and an effort to improve public awareness and, hopefully, action regarding the noted deficiencies.

Source: "Preparing for Disasters, An Evaluation of California's Emergency Preparedness," by Joe Lang, Assembly Committee on Energy Planning and Disaster Relief, January 1980.

siderably. In 1978, the state budgets ranged from $50,000 to more than $1.2 million.

All states have an emergency services office, although the titles vary; and all have designated one organization with the lead responsibility for disaster *preparedness* and *response* activities. Nevertheless, the state structures and responsibilities for other phases of emergency planning and management—most notably for mitigation and long-term recovery (and also for attack and manmade emergencies as well as natural disasters)—appear to vary widely.[4]

Characteristics of comprehensive emergency planning and management

Prior to a disaster, the plans and activities appropriate for preparedness for an emergency or disaster are essentially the traditional ones. Traditional land use and economic planning will contribute importantly to the well-being of a community both in normal times and after a disaster.

In fact, researchers have noted that a community usually recovers from a disaster far more easily if it has done some predisaster planning and has thought through the necessary organizational arrangements as well as the emergency response and recovery functions before the disaster event occurs.[5] Not only having a plan, but exercising it, produces the best results. Researchers have also documented that a community (or state) should plan to use existing organizations for disaster response and recovery activities, to the extent possible. Such agencies work best because the organizational arrangements and functions performed are familiar and comfortable. Finally, although the value of planning before a disaster has been well documented, few localities do so. Communities rarely plan ahead for a possible disaster just as individuals rarely do so—each thinks it will not happen to me. Consequently, desirable mitigative measures usually are taken after the fact, during the recovery period.

The aftermath of a disaster may range from extreme devastation, such as 85 percent destruction of an entire community on the Gulf coast after Hurricane Frederick (1979) to the loss of a roof off a school in a Texas city after a tornado briefly touched down in one spot. Not only is the physical impact significant after a major disaster, but also the disruptions to the economic and personal system usually are serious. Using the descriptions of some recent disasters as background, one can imagine the extent of the disruptions to both community and human systems and networks.

The tornado that struck Xenia, Ohio, in April, 1974, caused 34 deaths and 500 injuries, destroyed 1,300 buildings, and damaged thousands more in only three minutes, resulting in an estimated $100 million damage. The tornado (in reality, three tornadoes that merged) left a swath of destruction almost three-quarters of a mile wide and four miles long through suburban as well as downtown properties.[6]

Although a tornado can demolish in seconds what might take a hurricane hours to destroy, the tornado's swath is usually less than one-tenth of a mile, while a hurricane can cover a distance 50 to 1,000 miles wide and last for weeks.[7] During four days in June, 1972, Tropical Storm Agnes and its accompanying flash floods killed 118 people and caused about $3.5 billion in property damage. The damage Agnes caused stands as a record for losses of private and public property and facilities.[8]

Between 1960 and 1970, 13 significant disasters occurred in the United States, each responsible for at least $100 million damage and 10 lives lost. Six of the 13 were hurricanes and were responsible for more than 60 percent of the total damage. The single most destructive natural event in the 1960s was Hurricane Camille, which struck in August, 1969, and caused $1.4 billion in damage and 256 deaths.[9] During 1978, 25 major disasters and 14 states of emergency were declared by the President, costing $635 million and $79 million, respectively.

Perhaps the most dramatic natural hazard is an earthquake, which is neither as rare nor as limited in locale as most persons think. In the United States, California and Alaska are thought of as most earthquake prone, yet 39 states have areas of potential seismic hazard. Persons living in an earthquake-prone area are at risk from not only the shaking of the earth, but also from one or more of its secondary effects, such as ground failure, ground displacement along a fault, waves, flood from dams and levee failures, and fires.

Many hazards may have indirect effects that can cause at least as much damage as the triggering incident. As serious as the 1906 San Francisco earthquake was (it measured 8.2 on the Richter scale), the conflagration that followed caused approximately 80 percent of the estimated property damage ($400 million). The known deaths totaled 700.[10]

In the United States, floods are the most widespread hazard and also the most destructive to buildings. Because people like to settle near rivers, river flooding takes an enormous toll of life and property. "Overflowing waterways destroy or damage approximately 410,000 buildings across the nation each year . . . with an aggregate cost of over $3 billion (1978 dollars).[11]

River floods also cause more damage in a greater number of states than any other type of natural hazard. "Although nine widely separate states suffer from over 50 percent of the building damage from such floods, 35 experience more than $20 million in building losses during an average year."[12]

Figure 24–1   The tornado that hit Xenia, Ohio, in 1974 cut a path through the city that was three-quarters of a mile wide. These photos show the damage to a church and houses on West Market Street and the recovery in that area with the development of a shopping mall, Xenia Towne Square. Note the contemporary feeling of the mall that arose from the devastated area.

Planning and developing procedures to cope with disasters, both natural and manmade, are fundamental to the protection of life and property and should be performed by appropriate public practitioners at all levels of government. A wide variety of public practitioners becomes involved after a major disaster. At the city and county levels, an emergency services (or civil defense) coordinator usually does the planning prior to a disastrous event. After the event, top elected and administrative officials usually take charge. At the state level, the governor (or his/her designated representative) takes charge and provides central leadership and policy guidance. The governor's office usually works closely with the state emergency services office. Later, planners and budget directors are involved in the recovery process.

In actual fact, after a major disaster strikes, few local governments, by themselves, are able to effectively respond and then deal with disaster recovery. After a major disaster, local governments usually find themselves in circumstances that exceed their resources; thus, they appeal to state government to help. If additional assistance is required after all state and local resources have been committed, the Governor may appeal to the President for either a "major disaster" or "emergency" declaration. After receiving a Presidential Declaration, a state will face a very complex set of intergovernmental relationships as at least three levels of government bring their resources to bear to aid in disaster relief and recovery.

Federal disaster assistance Few local governments can handle a major disaster or emergency without help from the state government, usually through the office of the governor. When the disaster is of a magnitude that exceeds the state's capacity, the governor can ask for federal help to meet either a "major disaster" or an "emergency," and a presidential declaration can be issued.

According to the Disaster Relief Act of 1974, the president's declaration of an emergency or a major disaster is made only upon the request of the governor of the affected state, based on the governor's finding that the disaster "is of such severity and magnitude that effective response is beyond the capabilities of the State and the affected local governments and that Federal assistance is necessary." The governor informs the president of the extent and nature of state resources available to meet the disaster and guarantees that state and local expenditures "will constitute . . . a reasonable amount of the funds of such State and local governments for alleviating the damage, loss, hardship, or suffering resulting from such disaster."

Disaster aftermath

After a disaster has occurred, the public planning and management decision making often require different techniques and processes than are needed in normal times. New organizations and leaders tend to emerge, and many volunteers usually offer their services. The postdisaster community undoubtedly will pose some significant challenges and differences to decision makers, both public and private, at all levels.

Depending on the magnitude of the disaster event relative to the size and population of the community or communities affected, virtually all aspects of community life may experience disruption.

Since a disaster may affect virtually all segments of a community—housing stock, transportation system, public service buildings and equipment, for example—all types of state and regional plans may be affected. Some of the indicators of the extent of local disruption include: the number (and percentage) of the local population without homes; the rate of unemployment; estimated dollar loss of structures (public and private); and the number (and percent) of deaths and injuries.

The disruption might also affect the home and/or workplace and living or working conditions of the locally based public planners and managers. In short, public officials may have experienced disruptions in home and family life as well as other difficulties arising from destruction of community systems. Another different characteristic, therefore, is that decision making regarding response and recovery may be done under extreme stress.

Many important, long-lasting decisions affecting future land use patterns and major buildings have to be made quickly and in a context of conflicting demands and interests in the aftermath of a disaster. Local decision makers will find that these pressures compound their difficulties:

Most policy issues involving reconstruction arise because some element of the community wants to avoid a similar future disaster. This usually happens shortly after the disaster and may cause conflict with the widely held desire to return to normal as quickly as possible. The strongest pressure of all for prompt return to normalcy comes from the existence of displaced families and businesses. Such pressures do not necessarily make for orderly, well-planned reconstruction processes.[13]

The confusion and lack of coordination during disaster recovery periods result in part from the lack of systematic procedures for maintaining a strategic overview of the disaster:

Lack of coordination also stems from the natural human tendency to feel a great sense of urgency to get something done to help the victims, which makes taking time to communicate and coordinate decisions seem a luxury. Under stress it is also difficult to exercise the more complex intellectual process such as looking ahead and thinking about the indirect consequences of a decision.[14]

Another major difference in postdisaster planning is that usually the locality or localities impacted become heavily dependent upon external resources, both public and private, to return to normal. As was noted earlier, local and even state capabilities and resources are quickly overwhelmed after an extensive disaster. Consequently, requests for aid quickly escalate from local to state to federal government. The high cost of disaster response and recovery lead officials to request state and federal assistance for all kinds of catastrophies, manmade and natural.

Furthermore, public officials should not assume that decision makers in the private sector will hold off their decisions until the most important public policy decisions have been made.[15] Just as publicly employed planners at the local, regional, state, and federal levels will be making a host of decisions regarding the reconstruction of buildings, so too will local plant managers, together with their regional and national corporate executives, be making decisions about possible rebuilding, relocation, or termination of their facilities.

Finally, postdisaster planning for reconstruction and recovery must take into consideration the fact that depending on the nature of the disaster from which the community is recovering, the community may continue to be vulnerable to the same or similar hazards (e.g., riverine flooding, deficient dams) and thus subject to more such disasters in the future. Many hazardous situations that may become disasters can be identified (such as a floodplain or fault zone); and in some cases, destruction may be preventable. Public planners and managers should be alert to opportunities to identify threats to public safety and to advocate preparedness or mitigation measures. In an area that is known to be at risk from seismic hazards, or from flooding, or from unstable soils, strong land use management controls could prevent the erection of new structures that can be anticipated to experience serious damage from such hazards. In such known risk areas, the only question is *when* an incident will occur.

In other cases, such as a tornado that struck in Connecticut, far from the usual tornado belt in the United States, or a hurricane (which is a water-based storm) hitting Pennsylvania as Hurricane Agnes did, the vulnerability of an area to a *specific* hazard is far less predictable.

Nevertheless, far more knowledge about natural hazards, such as floods and earthquakes, is available than is acted upon by public officials in the United States. Planners can help to close the gap in many ways, such as by integrating earth science information with public policy analysis. More planning time and

Love Canal, a man-made disaster In August 1978 the New York Health state health commissioner officially acknowledged the existence of a "great and imminent peril to the health of the general public" in the Love Canal area of Niagara Falls. He recommended that "families with pregnant women" and the "approximately 20 families" living on the streets bordering the southern end of Love Canal "with children under 2 years of age, temporarily move from the site as soon as possible." In contrast to this rather modest set of recommendations, by the summer of 1981, more than 500 families had moved out—with their homes purchased by the state; hundreds more purchase applications were pending; and the large public-housing project was more than half empty. The neighborhood, once full of sound and life, was empty and silent, with grass growing tall among the boarded-up homes and apartment buildings and over the huge, gently sloping clay cover that makes the old Love Canal look like a great grave, with the abandoned school as the tombstone.

After the U.S. Congress approved an emergency appropriation in the summer of 1980, allowing the president to spend up to $20 million to relocate Love Canal families . . ., there were weeks of negotiations between the Federal Emergency Management Agency (FEMA) and the state task force representatives. They finally agreed that the federal government would lend the state of New York $7.5 million at 8.25 percent interest and

would grant them another $7.5 million, while the state provided $5 million in revitalization funds—earmarked by the New York legislature and governor nine months earlier for Love Canal. . . .

Home purchases and neighborhood revitalization were then administered through the Love Canal Revitalization Agency, an entity established June 4, 1980.

[That agency] worked to satisfy conflicting mandates. The $20 million was to fund not only home purchases for hundreds of families and relocation expenses for the renters, but also revitalization of an area ten blocks wide. They performed these tasks in the limelight, working with residents who were angry, worried, confused, and "totally sick of the whole thing," and who did not trust the revitalization agency.

By the terms of the complex federal-state loan-grant agreement, only $2.5 million of the $20 million in combined funds were available for all purposes other than purchasing homes whose owners were living in them. The $2.5 million had to be stretched to cover, among other items, temporary housing costs, the needs of the renters, neighborhood revitalization, and payments for commercial properties.

Source: Abstracted and excerpted from Adeline Gordon Levine, *Love Canal: Science, Politics, and People* (Lexington, Mass.: Lexington Books, D. C. Heath and Company, 1982), pp. 213–14.

---

investment in predisaster planning would result in significant reductions in life and property loss in this country.

The recovery process

Historically, cities usually survive the destruction and disruption of disasters and stay in the same location. Although disaster recovery may take a city from two to ten years, in the United States the public disaster-related programs tend to focus on a relatively short-term (two-years) recovery period.

A capsule summary of the findings of many disaster researchers is contained in the book *Reconstruction Following Disaster:*

Disaster recovery is ordered, knowable, and predictable. The central issues and decisions are value choices that give varying emphasis to the early return to opportunities for improved efficiency, equity, and amenity. Overambitious plans to accomplish these goals tend to be counterproductive. Major opportunities to improve the reconstruction process lie in early recognition of overlooked problems, people, functions, and areas; the reduction of uncertainty about the future for those who live and work in the city; and the preparation for reconstruction before the disaster comes.

Invariably it is found that much more is left than destroyed. What's more, the time needed for reconstruction reflects not only the amount of damage and the available recovery resources, but also predisaster trends. Predisaster growth or decline trends tend to continue after a disaster, although postdisaster reconstruction policies may accelerate the pace for a time.[16]

The long-term recovery phase is a critical part of the process of recovering from a disaster, yet little research about this phase has been conducted or shared to date. In describing the characteristics of this phase and in describing the process, special attention will be given to public planning and management concerns. From the standpoint of public planners and administrators with responsibility during and after a disaster, very little existing research is relevant.[17]

Figure 24-2 shows the observed phases of recovery from a variety of disasters (both domestic and foreign) in recent decades.

The recovery process is comprised of four overlapping activities:

1. Emergency period. For the first few days to a few weeks, attention is focused on the dead, injured, homeless, and missing. The primary activities are search and rescue, emergency mass feeding and housing, and debris removal. During this time, normal social and economic activities are disrupted.
2. Restoration period. The main activity during this period is restoration of repairable public utilities, housing, and commercial and industrial structures. This phase usually lasts for several months, the end of which is marked by the return to relatively normal social and economic activities.

Figure 24–2 Phases of recovery from disaster.

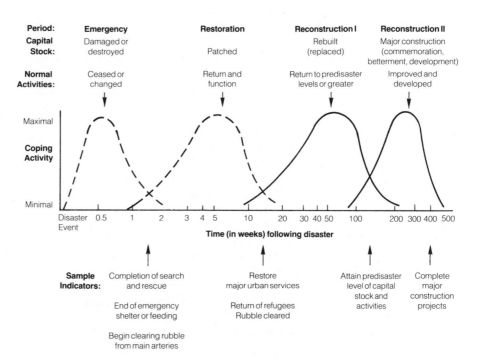

3. Reconstruction I. During this period the emphasis is on replacement of buildings, with capital stock rebuilt to at least predisaster levels. During this time, social and economic activities usually return to predisaster levels or higher.

4. Reconstruction II. During the long-range phase, the activities focus on commemorative, betterment, and developmental reconstruction. The three different but often interrelated functions of this final phase of restoration are to memorialize or commemorate the disaster, mark the city's betterment or improvement, and serve future development.

As indicated in Figure 24-2, each of the last three periods is approximately 10 times longer than the previous one, although specific reconstruction decisions may affect the time period.

The authors of *The Environment as Hazard* have observed that the rate of recovery is directly related to the extent of damage, the available resources, the prevailing disaster trends, and qualities such as leadership, planning, and organization for reconstruction. The existence of some sort of a plan (for downtown renewal, for example) is also of considerable importance.

The same authors have documented seven basic issues that public decision makers usually encounter during the long-term recovery planning process. At the heart of these seven basic, interrelated policy issues is the subject of money—since funds allocated for one purpose are not available for another. The seven basic reconstruction issues are:

1. Should normal or extraordinary decision making mechanisms be used in deciding how, when, and where to rebuild the city? For example, should a special task force be created?

2. Should there be change in land use? This question is most likely to arise after a flood or earthquake.

3. Should the building code be changed? Timing is the critical factor in changing building codes. Such changes usually take months if not years to achieve.

4. Should a concerted effort be made to make the city more efficient and more attractive? Normally, changes in the attractiveness or efficiency of a community come in small increments, "but on the heels of a major disaster, giant steps are possible—forward or backward!"

5. Should there be compensation or special financial assistance for private property losses? "Policy decisions involving governmental programs make a great difference to the speed and level of individual family recovery. If federal help is contingent upon the enactment and enforcement of local hazard mitigation policies—land use regulations, building codes—these can be long delays, and the victims of the disaster become pawns in the political struggle.

6. How should disaster-produced personal and family problems be handled? The availability and cost of housing, employment opportunities, and health and emotional problems raise larger questions about communication and decision making in the community. "Many community policy decisions must be made before large-scale construction begins; some community leaders wonder if the victims' needs and desires are being taken into account. They may organize and demand to be heard. Politicians may try to use these issues for their own purposes."

7. How should the increased local expenditures be financed? At the same time tax revenues are decreased, there is an increased demand for government service, repair of facilities, and acquisition of land and condemned properties.[18]

During local recovery operations, officials often will find themselves making decisions about repair, restoration, or removal of buildings or neighborhoods that invariably become intertwined with nondisaster planning and development. While recovery planning sometimes is dealt with separately, integrating recovery planning into the locality's master plan should be done, if at all possible.

Only a few weeks after the disaster, the local public and private sectors begin restoration and reconstruction activities. Figure 24-3 depicts the many categories of functions that contribute to the recovery planning process. While the time span for the recovery segments can readily be shown, it is not easy to depict the web of relationships and interaction among government officials (local, regional, state, and federal); citizens; business owners and mangers; and consultants, such as architects, engineers, economists, and planners—all of whom are engaged in recovery activities. It is expected that a large number of participants depends upon the organization and its planning processes.

Figure 24-3 shows the first steps that are typically performed at the local level during long-term disaster recovery. While these functions usually go on in each community impacted by a major disaster, they may be carried out by local, county, regional, and state officials, in varying combinations depending on the extent of the damage and local public planning and management capability.

The functions and time frame shown are generally representative rather than definitive or prescriptive. The duration of Phases I and II may vary considerably, depending on the type and magnitude of the disaster and also on the capability and sophistication of the local and state governments affected. The figure emphasizes the many simultaneous activities that usually occur during early stages of recovery.

Mitigation

Mitigation measures are the hardest type of actions to plan for because (1) it is hard to convince persons to take action now for future payoff, and (2) mitigative effects can be seen only in a long-range time frame. The differing perceptions of local, state, and federal officials about what constitutes a "disaster" and what constitutes "mitigation" increase the complexity of the problem of determining responsibility for disaster assistance. Definitions may be critical in that they determine what locally incurred costs are eligible for state and federal assistance.

Another aspect of the dilemma involves disaster frequency. A community may experience a major disaster, such as a flood, once in the lifetime of most of its residents, while national disaster relief officials may receive requests for major disaster aid monthly or even weekly. If local officials think a disaster will never happen in their lifetime—or think only one will occur in their lifetimes—unfortunately, they do not tend to take mitigative measures against future disasters.

Mitigation measures may be taken both before and after a disaster event. Sample mitigation measures for some major types of disasters are listed in Figure 24-4. In many instances, mitigation measures taken by one locality may not be adequate because the hazard affects the region, such as a watershed area or an area in a seismic fault zone. Such geophysical hazards may require both a multijurisdictional and intergovernmental approach. For example, to become well prepared, a locality may need technical assistance from the state geologist in assessing its risk from a seismic hazard. Services of a federal agency, such as the U.S. Geological Survey, may also be required. Disaster planning is also complicated by the fact that many natural hazards do not fall in the bailiwick of only one government. At times, regional, state, and national agencies must cooperate for efforts to be effective.

Figure 24–3   Major steps for long-term disaster recovery

Function	Phase 1: First two weeks	Phase 2: Third through twelfth weeks

Information gathering and assessment	Assess damage:
	● To environment ● Social impact
	● Relative to prior ● Economic impact
	  plans
	● Physical impact
	Clarify disaster assistance needed and available:
	● Clarify objectives ● Assign expediters
	  and policies
		Continue assessment of damage, identification of needs, and sources of assistance
		Continue determination of assistance needed

Organizational arrangements	Create ad hoc recover task force	Establish reconstruction agency: ● Combine planning and operational functions ● Hire or acquire needed staff Implement recovery component of local and/or state plans
Resource mobilization	Expedite disaster relief Restore vital community facilities Organize local contractors	Clarify resources available Identify outside investment and aid for: ● Public facilities ● Private investment Integrate local and outside resources
Planning, administration, and budgeting	Construct temporary community plan: ● Housing facilities ● Transportation ● Commercial ●Acquire vacant land ● Community ● Secure hazardous facilities property, facilities ● Utilities Assess hazards Assess existing plans for implementation potential	Formulate master plan for community development, including consideration of local hazards and recovery plan for affected areas Refine plan; obtain approvals Obtain state and local appropriations
Regulation and approval	Assess need for special laws, permits, construction moratoria	Obtain approvals for special laws, permits, moratoria
Coordination and intergovernmental relations	Establish contract with key community agencies Establish intercommunity, regional, state, and federal liasons	Apply for state and federal aid Coordinate key community service agencies
Monitoring and evaluation	Establish monitoring and feedback sources	Determine data needs React to planning studies Review availability of resources Assess needs for organizational changes Implement auditing system

Recently, the National Governors' Association (NGA) assessed the roles of all levels of government and the private sector in emergency mitigation. They used the term mitigation to include "all long-term activities which either prevent a hazard from striking or reduce the overall damages to people and property from a strike." Other activities reduce damages but are more suitably classified as preparedness or response measures (typically short-term actions like warnings, emergency medical assistance, or temporary housing). Mitigation activities focus on the hazard (like hail suppression), human systems (like relocation of com-

Figure 24—4 Sample mitigation measures for natural disasters.

Categories of functions	Flood	Hurricane	Landslide	Earthquake
Vulnerability analysis	Flood plain mapping	Pattern of past hurricanes	Soil tests Geological analysis	Delineation of seismic risk
Land use regulation	Flood plain management	Coastal zoning Land use controls	Land use restrictions Strip mine regulations	Zoning Land use controls
Public information	Information, maps of flood plains Disclosure for realty sales	Information, maps of storm surge areas Disclosure for realty sales	Information, maps of land movement Disclosure for realty sales	Information, maps of fault zone Disclosure for realty sales
Warnings and predictions	Warning systems Prepare evacuation routes and facilities	Prepare evacuation routes and facilities		Improved prediction and warning
Insurance	Federal flood insurance	Federal flood insurance		Earthquake insurance
Building codes and standards	Building codes	Building codes	Building codes	Building codes
Structural solutions	Construct dams and levees	Anchor mobile homes; use shutters Flood and windproofing techniques	Special construction techniques Drainage, vegetation	Earthquake resistant construction Retrofit buildings Reduction of secondary and lifeline hazards

munities out of a floodplain), or their interaction (like adding scent to liquid propane gas).[19]

After studying 82 sites and meeting with public officials responsible for mitigation at all levels of government, the NGA staff discerned ten areas of activities that cut across all mitigation sites. Those areas are:

1. Rules—codes, statutes, and ordinances; private covenants and agreements; legislation; and litigation.
2. Economics—financial incentives and disincentives; funding; fund raising.
3. Influence—lobbying; politics; and referenda.
4. Monitoring—enforcement and compliance; and, monitoring and inspection.
5. Management—administration; coordination and liaison; and planning.
6. Planning—anticipating future needs; and programming resource expenditures.
7. Public participation—community and public relations; public information; public hearings; surveys and polls; and public education.
8. Professional training—technical instruction in professional skills.
9. Research—scientific investigations; applied research; demonstration projects; feasibility studies; evaluation studies; and utilization research.
10. Assessment—risk mapping; structure assessment vulnerability analysis; and cost-benefit analysis.[20]

This NGA study provides an in-depth analysis and identification of mitigation measures; further, it demonstrates just how broadly and wide-ranging state and local efforts must be to accomplish mitigation of hazards.

In summary, achieving successful recovery from a disaster usually requires a full array of planning and management talents and tools. Among the most important functions are:

1. Obtaining and coordinating public and private participation in the planning process.
2. Facilitating complex intergovernmental relations.
3. Applying for outside grants (state and federal), not only to take advantage of special disaster assistance programs, but also to capitalize on existing programs to replace or improve capital stock and to provide programs and services for local residents.

1   Gilbert F. White and J. Eugene Haas, *Assessment of Research on Natural Hazards* (Cambridge: M.I.T. Press, 1975), p. 71.
2   J. H. Wiggins Company, *Building Losses from Natural Hazards: Yesterday, Today, and Tomorrow* (Redondo Beach, CA.: J. H. Wiggins Company, 1978), p. 4.
3   "The 1978 Emergency Preparedness Project, Final Report"; the National Governors' Association, 400 North Capital Street, N.W., Washington, D.C. 20001, p. 8.
4   Ibid., p. 13.
5   See Russell R. Dyner and E. L. Quarantelli, *A Perspective on Disaster Planning* Wash., D.C.: Defense Civil Preparedness Agency, 1972; and National Governors' Assoc., *op. cit.*
6   Richard V. Francaviglia, "Xenia Rebuilds: Effects of Predisaster Conditioning on Postdisaster Redevelopment," *American Institute of Planners Journal* 44 (January 1978): pp. 14-15.
7   Woody Gelman and Barbara Jackson, *Disaster Illustrated* (New York: Harmony Books, 1976), pp. 117–118.
8   National Academy of Sciences, *Geophysical Predictions* (Washington, D.C.: National Academy of Sciences, 1978), p. 1.
9   Executive Office of the President, Office of Emergency Preparedness, *Report to the Congress on Disaster Preparedness* (Washington, DC: Government Printing Office, 1972), p. 184.
10 Bruce A. Bolt, *Earthquakes, A Primer* (San Francisco: W. H. Freeman and Company, 1978), p. 198.
11 J. H. Wiggins Company, *Building Losses from Natural Hazards*, p. 13.
12 Ibid.
13 J. Eugene Haas, Robert W. Kates, and Martyn J. Bowden, *Reconstruction Following Disaster* (Cambridge: M.I.T. Press, 1977), p. xxix.
14 *International Encyclopedia of the Social Sciences*, 1968 ed., "Disasters," by Charles Fritz, p. 205.
15 Haas et al., *Reconstruction Following Disaster*, pp. xxxii–iii.
16 Ibid., p. xxvi.
17 The book *Reconstruction Following Disaster*, by Haas et al. does highlight some public policy issues. A synthesis of the existing practical literature on recovery is contained in the monograph "Natural Disaster Recovery Planning for Local Public Officials," by Claire B. Rubin, available from the Academy for Contemporary Problems or the Federal Emergency Management Agency, both in Washington, D.C.
18 Haas et al., *Reconstruction Following Disaster*, p. xxxi.
19 Preliminary Research Summary prepared by the National Governors' Association, July 1980.
20 Ibid.

Bibliography

1 Approaches to Planning

General planning theory

American Institute of Planners. *The Comprehensive Planning Process: Several Views*, Readings for the AIP Examination. Washington, DC: 1975.

Bolan, Richard S. "Emerging Views of Planning," *Journal of the American Institute of Planners* (July 1967): 233–245.

Friedmann, John. *Retracking America: A Theory of Transactive Planning*. Garden City, NY: Anchor Press/Doubleday, 1973.

Kent, T.J., Jr. *The Urban General Plan*. San Francisco: Chandler Publishing Company, 1964.

LeBreton, Preston P., and Henning, Dale A. *Planning Theory*. Englewood Cliffs, NJ: Prentice-Hall, Inc., 1961.

Meyerson, Martin. "Building the Middle Range Bridge for Comprehensive Planning," *Journal of the American Institute of Planners,* 22 (Spring 1956): 58–64.

Perloff, Harvey S. *Planning the Post-Industrial City*. Chicago: Planners Press, 1980.

Wilson, David E. *The National Planning Idea in U.S. Public Policy: Five Alternative Approaches*. Boulder, CO: Westview Press, 1980.

State planning theory

Choate, Pat, and Walter, Susan. *America In Ruins*. Washington, DC: CSPA, 1981.

Council of State Planning Agencies. *State Planning Series*, 16 volumes. Washington, DC: 1977. 1. *History of State Planning—An Interpretive Commentary*, Harold F. Wise. 2. *Concepts of State Planning*, Lynn Muchmore. 3. *Evaluation of State Planning*, Lynn Muchmore. 4. *The Legal Basis for State Policy Planning*, The Research Group, Inc., Atlanta, GA. 5. *State Urban Development Strategies*, Harold A. Hovey. 6. *State Development Strategies for Rural Communities*, William E. Bivens, III. 7. *State Intergovernmental Planning Strategies*, Robert I. Remen, Robert N. Wise, and John Montgomery. 8. *State Strategies for Multistate Organizations*, Leonard U. Wilson. 9. *State Strategies for National Economic Policy*, David K. Hartley. 10. *Statewide Policy Instruments*, Cogan and Associates, Portland, OR. 11. *Techniques of Public Involvement*, Cogan and Associates, Portland, OR. 12. *Financial Planning for State Government*, John Petersen. 13. *State Economic Modeling*, Robert W. Rafuse, Jr. 14. *Intergovernmental Data Issues*, Jay O. Tepper. 15. *State Economic Resource Planning: Four State Examples*, David K. Hartley. 16. *State Planning in Action: Proceedings of CSPA Regional Meetings*, Fall 1976, David K. Hartley, editor.

Council of State Planning Agencies, *Studies in Development Policy*, 12 volumes. Washington, DC: 1979–1981. 1. *State Taxation and Economic Development*, Roger J. Vaughan. 2. *Economic Development: Challenge of the 1980s*, Neal Peirce, Jerry Hagstrom, and Carol Steinbach. 3. *Innovations in Development Finance*, Lawrence Litvak and Belden Daniels. 4. *The Working Poor: Toward a State Agenda*, David M. Gordon. 5. *Inflation and Unemployment: Surviving the 1980s*, Roger J. Vaughan. 6. *Democratizing the Development Process*, Neal Peirce, Jerry Hagstrom, and Carol Steinbach. 7. *Venture Capital and Urban Development*, Michael Kieschnick. 8. *Development Politics: Private Development and the Public Interest,* Robert Hollister and Tunney Lee. 9. *The Capital Budget*, Robert DeVoy and Harold Wise. 10. *Banking and Small Business*, Derek Hansen. 11. *Taxes and Growth: Business Incentives and Economic Development*, Michael Kieschnick. 12. *Pension Funds and Economic Renewal*, Lawrence Litvak.

Regional planning theory

Advisory Commission on Intergovernmental Relations. *Factors Affecting the Voter Reactions to Governmental Reorganization in Metropolitan Areas*, Report M–15. Washington, DC: U.S. Government Printing Office, May 1962.

——. *Governmental Functions and Processes: Local and Areawide*. Washington, DC: U.S. Government Printing Office, 1974.

————. *Regional Decision Making: New Strategies for Substate Districts,* Report A–43. Washington, DC: U.S. Government Printing Office, October 1973.

Friedmann, John, and William, Alonso, editors. *Regional Policy: Readings in Theory and Applications,* rev. ed. Cambridge, MA; The MIT Press, 1975. See especially the bibliographical essay by John Friedmann at the end of this book.

Rondinelli, Dennis A. *Urban and Regional Development Planning: Policy and Administration.* Ithaca, NY: Cornell University Press, 1975.

Regional planning cases

Advisory Commission on Intergovernmental Relations. *Regional Governance: Promise and Performance,* Report A–41. Washington, DC: U.S. Government Printing Office, May 1973.

Costikyan, Edward N., and Maxwell, Lehman. *New Strategies for Regional Cooperation: A Model for the Tri-State New York-New Jersey-Connecticut Area* New York: Praeger Publishers, 1973.

Gerther, L. O. *Regional Planning in Canada: A Planner's Testament.* Montreal, Canada: Harvest House, 1972.

Rothblatt, Donald N. *Regional Planning: The Appalachian Experience.* Lexington, MA: Heath Lexington Books, 1971.

2 The Evolution of American Planning

Advisory Commission on Intergovernmental Relations, *A Catalog of Federal Grant-In-Aid Programs to State and Local Governments: Grants Funded in FY 1981.* Washington, DC: U.S. Government Printing Office, February 1982.

————. *A Crisis of Confidence and Competence,* Vol. 1, The Federal Role in the Federal System. Washington, DC: U.S. Government Printing Office, 1980.

————. *Categorical Grants: Their Role and Design.* Washington, DC: U.S. Government Printing Office, 1978.

————. (Citizen Participation in the American Federal System. Washington, DC: U.S. Government Printing Office, 1980.

————. *Multistate Regionalism.* Washington, DC: U.S. Government Printing Office, 1972.

————. *Regional Decision Making: New Strategies for Substate Districts.* Washing-

ton, DC: U.S. Government Printing Office, 1973.

————. *Regionalism Revisited: Recent Areawide and Local Responses.* Washington, DC: U.S. Government Printing Office, 1977.

————. *State and Local Roles in the Federal System,* chap. 5, "Areawide Organizations." Washington, DC: U.S. Government Printing Office, 1982.

Bosselman, Fred, and Callies, David. *The Quiet Revolution in Land Use Control,* prepared for the Council on Environmental Quality. Washington, DC: U.S. Government Printing Office, 1972.

Clawson, Marion. *New Deal Planning: The National Resources Planning Board,* published for Resources for the Future. Baltimore, MD: The Johns Hopkins University Press, 1981.

Council of State Governments, Task Force on Natural Resources and Land Use Information and Technology. *Land: State Alternatives for Planning and Management.* Lexington, KY: 1975.

Gerkens, Laurence Conway. "Historical Development of American City Planning," in Frank So *et al.* editors, *The Practice of Local Government Planning.* Washington, DC: The International City Management Association, 1979.

Graham, Otis L., Jr. *Toward a Planned Society: From Roosevelt to Nixon.* New York: Oxford University Press, 1976.

Hagman, Donald, and Misczynski, Dean. *Windfalls for Wipeouts: Land Value Capture and Compensation.* Chicago: American Planning Association, 1978.

Muchmore, Lynn. *Concepts of State Planning,* State Planning Series 2. Washington, DC: Council of State Planning Agencies, 1977.

President's Commission on National Goals, *Goals for Americans.* Englewood Cliffs, NJ: Prentice Hall, 1960.

Scott, Mel. *American City Planning Since 1890.* Berkeley, CA: University of California Press, 1969.

Steiner, George A. *Strategic Planning.* New York: The Free Press, 1979.

Sundquist, James L. *Dispersing Population: What America Can Learn from Europe.* Washington, DC: The Brookings Institution, 1975.

The President's Commission for a National Agenda for the Eighties. *A National Agenda for the Eighties,* Report of the Commission. Washington, DC: U.S. Government Printing Office, 1980.

U.S. Bureau of the Census. *Governmental Organization,* Vol. 1, No. 1, 1977 Census of Governments. Washington, DC: U.S. Government Printing Office, July 1978.

————. *Regional Organizations,* Vol. 6, No. 6, 1977 Census of Governments. Washington, DC: U.S. Government Printing Office, August 1978.

Walter, Susan M., editor. *Proceedings of the White House Conference on Strategic Planning.* Washington, DC: Council of State Planning Agencies, 1980.

Wilson, David E. *The National Planning Idea in U.S. Public Policy: Five Alternative Approaches.* Boulder, CO: Westview Press, 1980.

Wise, Harold F. *History of State Planning: An Interpretive Commentary,* State Planning Series 1. Washington, DC: Council of State Planning Agencies, 1977.

---

3 State Planning Today

Clawson, Marion. *New Deal Planning: The National Resources Planning Board;* published for Resources for the Future. Baltimore, MD: Johns Hopkins University Press, 1981.

Coordinating State Functional Planning Programs: Strategies for Balancing Conflicting Objectives; a report prepared by the American Institute of Planners for the U.S. Department of Housing and Urban Development, August 1977.

Geiss, Alan Walter. *A Framework for Planning State Government.* Council of State Governments, September 1968.

Governing the American States: A Handbook for New Governor, published by the National Governors' Association, November 1978; chap. 6, "Policy Development."

Graham, Otis, L., Jr. *Toward a Planned Society.* New York: Oxford University Press, 1976.

Healy, Robert G., and Rosenberg, John S. *Land Use and the States;* published for Resources for the Future. 2nd ed. Baltimore, MD: Johns Hopkins University Press, 1979.

Levin, Melvin R., Rose, Jerome G., and Slavet, Joseph S. *New Approaches to State Land-Use Policies.* Lexington, MA: Lexington Books, 1974.

Model State and Regional Planning Law. New York: National Municipal League, 1955.

Planning the Fourth Migration: The Neglected Vision of the Regional Planning Association of America, ed. Carl Sussman. Cambridge, MA: MIT Press, 1976.

Preliminary Report of the Pennsylvania State Planning Board to the Honorable Gifford Ginchot, Governor of the Commonwealth, and to the National Resources Board. Harrisburg, PA: December 1934.

Relevance, Reliance, and Realism; 1968 Report of the Committee on State Planning, the National Governors' Conference.

Rosebaugh, David L. "State Planning as a Policy-Coordinative Process." *Journal of the American Institute of Planners,* 42 (January 1976): 52–63.

Sanford, Terry, *Storm Over the States.* New York: McGraw-Hill, 1967.

State Legislative Program of the Advisory Commission on Intergovernmental Relations; vol. 10: *Environment, Land Use, and Growth Policy,* Report No. M–96, November 1975. State Planning and Growth Management Act and Joint Legislative Committee on State Planning.

State Planning and Federal Grants; a report of the Public Administration Service to the Council of State Governments, 1969.

State Planning: Intergovernmental Policy Coordination; a report by the Council of State Governments for the U.S. Department of Housing and Urban Development, August 1976.

"State Planning: Its Function and Organization; Report of the Committee on State Planning, American Institute of Planners." *Journal of the American Institute of Planners* 21 (November 1959).

The State Planning Series; published by the Council of State Planning Agencies, 1977.

State Responsibility in Urban Regional Development, a report by the Council of State Governments to the National Governor's Conference, 1962.

"Survey of State Planning Agencies, 1960"; conducted by the National Committee on State Planning, American Institute of Planners; review prepared by Aelred J. Gray, Chairman of the Committee. *Journal of the American Institute of Planners,* 27 (November 1961).

White House Conference on Strategic Planning; Proceedings; a report of the Council of State Planning Agencies, 1980.

4 Techniques for Implementing State Plans

Barker, Michael, editor. *Studies in State Development Policy.* Washington, DC: Council of State Planning Agencies, 1979.

Council of State Governments. *Book of the States.* Lexington, KY: Council of State Governments, semiannual edition.

―――. *State Planning: Intergovernmental Policy Coordination.* Washington, DC: U.S. Department of Housing and Urban Development, 1976.

Hartley, David, and Jensen, Dwight, editors. *The State Planning Series.* Washington, DC: Council of State Planning Agencies, 1977.

Howard, S. Kenneth. *Changing State Budgeting.* Lexington, KY: Council of State Governments, 1973.

National Governors' Association, *The Critical Hundred Days—A Handbook for New Governors.* Washington, DC: National Governors' Association, 1982.

Patton, Milton H.; Stubbs, Anne D.; and Wilson, Leonard U.; editors. *State Environmental Resources Management Series.* Lexington, KY: Council of State Governments, 1975–1982.

State Government, quarterly editions. Lexington, KY: Council of State Governments.

Walter, Susan, editor. *Studies in Governance.* Washington, DC: Council of State Planning Agencies, 1982.

Wise, Harold F. *History of State Planning; State Planning Series No. 1.* Washington, DC: Council of State Planning Agencies 1977.

5 State Planning Administration

Hand, Irving. "The States and Urban Strategies: A Comparative Analysis and Ten Case Study Reports (California, Connecticut, Florida, Massachusetts, Michigan, New Jersey, North Carolina, Ohio, Oregon, Pennsylvania)." (book review) *Journal of the American Planning Association* 48 (April 1982).

Muchmore, Lynn. *Concepts of State Planning.* State Planning Series 2. Washington, D.C.: Council of State Planning Agencies, 1977.

Warren, Charles R. *The States and Urban Strategies: A Comparative Analysis.* Washington, D.C.: National Academy of Public Administration for the Office of Policy Development and Research, U.S. Department of Housing and Urban Development, September 1980.

6 Regional Planning Today

Advisory Commission on Intergovernmental Relations. *Governmental Functions and Processes: Local and Areawide,* Report A–45. Washington, DC: U.S. Government Printing Office, February 1974.

―――. *Multistate Regionalism,* Report A–39. Washington, DC: U.S. Government Printing Office, April 1972. The second printing, in 1978, contains a new introduction with updated information.

―――. *Regional Decision Making: New Strategies for Substate Districts,* Report A–43. Washington, DC: U.S. Government Printing Office, October 1973.

―――. *State and Local Roles in the Federal System,* Chapter 5: "Areawide Organizations," Report A–88. Washington, DC: U.S. Government Printing Office, 1982.

Derthick, Martha. *Between State and Nation: Regional Organizations of the United States.* Washington, DC: The Brookings Institution, 1972.

National Association of Regional Councils. *Regional Council Representation and Voting.* Washington, DC: March 1979.

Perloff, Harvey S. "Key Features of Regional Planning," *Journal of the American Institute of Planners,* 34 (May 1968): 153–159.

Stam, Jerome M. and Reid, J. Norman. *An Overview of Federal Programs Supporting Multicounty Substate Regional Activities,* ESCS Staff Report. Washington, DC: U.S. Department of Agriculture, May 1980.

U.S. Bureau of the Census. *Regional Organizations,* Vol. 6, No. 6, 1977 Census of Governments. Washington, DC: U.S. Government Printing Office, August 1978.

Wheaton, William L. C. "Metro-Allocation Planning," *Journal of the American Institute of Planners,* 33 (March 1967): 103–107.

7 Techniques for Implementing Regional Plans

Advisory Commission on Intergovernmental Relations. *Regional Decision Making: New Strategies for Substate Districts.* Washington, DC: U.S. Government Printing Office, October 1973.

―――. *Regional Governance: Promise and Performance.* Washington, DC: U.S. Government Printing Office, May 1973.

Haar, Charles M. "Budgeting for Metropolitan Development: A Step Toward Creative

Federalism," *Journal of the American Institute of Planners* 34 (March 1968): 102–104.

Henton, Douglas C., *et al. Rethinking Urban Government: An Assessment of the Negotiated Investment Strategy.* Menlo Park, CA: SRI International, July 1981.

McDowell, Bruce D. "White House Casts a Cold Eye on A–95," *Planning* 48 (January 1982): 6–7.

Mediation and New Federalism: Proceedings of a Roundtable on the Negotiated Investment Strategy. Dayton, OH: Charles F. Kettering, Foundation, July 8, 1981.

Mogulof, Melvin B. *Governing Metropolitan Areas: A Critical Review of Councils of Governments and the Federal Role.* Washington, DC: Urban Institute, 1971.

Naftalin, Arthur, and Brandl, John. *The Twin Cities Regional Strategy.* St. Paul, MN: Metropolitan Council of the Twin Cities Area, November 1980.

National Association of Regional Councils. *Regional Capital Improvement Programming: An Evaluation and Analysis.* Washington, DC: February 1976.

"Negotiating the City's Future: A Report on an Experimental Plan for Pooling Urban Investments and Bargaining to Coordinate Policy Goals," a special supplement to *Nation's Cities Weekly,* November 26, 1979.

Pressman, Jeffrey L., and Wildavsky, Aaron B. *Implementation.* Berkeley, CA: University of California Press, 1973.

Rosenthal, Donald B. "Bargaining Analysis in Intergovernmental Relations," *Publius* (Summer 1980): 5–44.

So, Frank S. *Metropolitan Planning Policy Implementation, Planning Advisory Service Information Report No. 262.* Chicago: American Society of Planning Officials, October 1970.

Sundquist, James L., with the collaboration of David W. Davis. *Making Federalism Work: A Study of Program Coordination at the Community Level.* Washington, DC: Brookings Institution, 1969.

U.S. Office of Management and Budget. *Conceptual Outline of Proposed Revisions to OMB Circular A–95.* Washington, DC: August 1980.

———. *Office of Management and Budget Circular No. A–95: An Assessment.* Washington, DC: May 15, 1978.

Warren, Charles R. *National Implications of a Negotiated Approach to Federalism.* Dayton, OH: Charles F. Kettering Foundation, July 8, 1981.

Wheaton, William L. C. "Metro-Allocation Planning," *Journal of the American Institute of Planners* 33 (May 1967): 103–107.

———. "Operations Research for Metropolitan Planning," *Journal of the American Institute of Planners* 29 (November 1963): 250–259.

8 Managing Regional Planning Organizations

Advisory Commission on Intergovernmental Relations. *Citizen Participation in the American Federal System.* Washington, DC: U.S. Government Printing Office, 1980.

Drucker, Peter F. *Management: Tasks, Responsibilities, Practices.* New York: Harper and Row, 1974.

Emerson, Lynden V. *Evaluating Your Staff— A Guide for Regional Council Directors.* Washington, DC: National Association of Regional Councils, 1978.

Friedmann, John. *Retracking America: A Theory of Transactive Planning.* Garden City, NY: Anchor Press/Doubleday, 1973.

Knudson, Ed. *Regional Politics in the Twin Cities: A Report on the Politics and Planning of Urban Growth Policy.* St. Paul, MN: Metropolitan Council of the Twin Cities Area, September 1976.

McDowell, Bruce D. *ABCs of a Metropolitan OPD: The WashCog Experience, Technical Report Number 1,* Metropolitan and Regional Planning Department, AIP. Washington, DC: American Institute of Planners, 1972.

McGregor, Douglas. *The Human Side of Enterprise.* New York: McGraw-Hill, 1960.

Metropolitan Council of the Twin Cities Area. *The Politics and Planning of a Metropolitan Growth Policy for the Twin Cities: An Executive Summary.* St. Paul, MN: September 1976.

Miller, Robert W. *Schedule, Cost, and Profit Control with PERT: A Comprehensive Guide for Program Management.* New York: McGraw-Hill, 1963.

National Association of Regional Councils. *Managing Your Regional Council: Techniques for the Director.* Washington, DC: 1978.

———. *Regional Council Communications: A Guide to Issues and Techniques.* Washington, DC: 1973.

———. *Working With Your State: A Guide for Regional Councils.* Washington, DC: 1978.

————. *Your Regional Council—A Guide for the New Policy Maker*. Washington, DC: 1978.

Novick, David, editor. *Program Budgeting: Analysis and the Federal Budget*. Cambridge, MA: Harvard University Press, 1965.

Odiorne, George S. *Management by Objectives: A System of Managerial Leadership*. New York: Pitman Publishing, 1965.

Ouchi, William. *Theory Z: How American Business Can Meet the Japanese Challenge*. Reading, MA: Addison-Wesley, 1981.

Pyhrr, Peter. *Zero Based Budgeting: A Practical Management Tool for Evaluating Expenses*. New York: Wiley, 1973.

Reichert, Peggy A. *Growth Management in the Twin Cities Metropolitan Area: The Development Framework Planning Process*. St. Paul, MN: Metropolitan Council of the Twin Cities Area, September 1976.

Sellers, Robert E., and Spaier, Burton. *Evaluating Your Regional Council*. Washington, DC: National Association of Regional Councils, 1978.

Steiner, George A. *Strategic Planning: What Every Manager Must Know*. New York: Free Press, 1979.

Van Dersal, William R. *The Successful Supervisor: In Government and Business*. New York: Harper and Row, 1962.

Walter, Susan M., editor. *Proceedings of the White House Conference on Strategic Planning*. Washington, DC: Council of State Planning Agencies, 1980.

9 Policy Analysis

Bardach, Eugene. "Gathering Data for Policy Research." *Urban Analysis* 2 (April 1974):117–144.

Dunn, William. *Public Policy Analysis: An Introduction*. Englewood Cliffs, NJ: Prentice Hall, 1981.

Hatry, Harry; Blair, Louis; Fisk, Donald; and Kimmel, Wayne. *Program Analysis for State and Local Governments*. Washington, DC: The Urban Institute, 1976.

Lynn, Laurence E., Jr. *Designing Public Policy: A Casebook on the Role of Policy Analysis*. Santa Monica, CA: Goodyear, 1980.

MacRae, Duncan, Jr., and James A. Wilde. *Policy Analysis for Public Decisions*. North Scituate, MA: Duxbury, 1979.

Majone, Giandomenico, and Quade, Edward S. *Pitfalls of Analysis*. International Series on Applied Analysis, Vol. 8. Chichester, Great Britain: John Wiley & Sons, 1980.

Meltsner, Arnold J. *Policy Analysts in the Bureaucracy*. Berkeley: University of California Press, 1976.

Quade, Edward S. *Analysis for Public Decisions*. New York: American Elsevier, 1975.

Stokey, Edith, and Zeckhauser, Richard. *A Primer for Policy Analysis*. New York: W. W. Norton, 1978.

Wildavsky, Aaron. *Speaking Truth to Power: The Art and Craft of Policy Analysis*. Boston: Little, Brown and Co., 1979.

10 Environmental Impact Analysis

ABT Associates, Inc. *Integration of Environmental Considerations in the Comprehensive Planning and Management Process*. Washington, DC: U.S. Department of Housing and Urban Development, Office of Policy Development and Research, August 1977.

Advisory Commission on Intergovernmental Relations. *Regional Decision Making: New Strategies for Substate Districts*. Volume 1. A–43. Washington, DC: U.S. Government Printing Office, October 1973.

Categorical Grants: Their Role and Design. A–52. Washington, DC: U.S. Government Printing Office, 1978.

Andrews, Richard N.L. "Elements and Methods of Impact Assessment," Chapter 9.3 in *Environmental Analysis: for Land Use and Site Planning*. William M. Marsh, editor. New York: McGraw-Hill Book Company, 1978.

Council on Environmental Quality. *Environmental Quality*. Washington, DC: U.S. Government Printing Office, annual.

Dee, Norbert; Baker, Janet K.; Drobny, Neil L.; Duke, Kenneth M.; and Fahringer, David C. *Final Report on Environmental Evaluation System for Water Resource Planning*. Prepared by Battelle-Columbus Laboratories, Contract No. 14–06–D–7182 from Bureau of Land Reclamation, U.S. Department of the Interior, 1972.

Dickert, Thomas G., and Domeny, Katherine R., editors. *Environmental Impact Assessment: Guidelines and Commentary*. Berkeley: University Extension, University of California, 1974.

Finsterbusch, Kurt, and Wolf, C. P. *Methodology of Social Impact Assessment*. Stroudsburg, PA.: Dowden, Hutchinson, and Ross, Inc., 1977.

Glickman, Norman J., editor. *The Urban Impacts of Federal Policies.* Prepared for the U.S. Department of Housing and Urban Development. Baltimore, MD: The Johns Hopkins University Press, 1979.

Kane, Julius; Vertinsky, Ilan; and Thompson, William. "A Methodology for Interactive Resource Policy Simulation," *Water Resources Research* 9 (1973 No. 1.).

Keyes, Dale, *Land Development and the National Environment: Estimating Impacts.* Washington, DC: The Urban Land Institute, 1976.

Kitto, William, and Burns, Ann Forest. "The ABCs of NEPA Regs." *Planning* 46 (June 1980): 17–18.

Leopold, Luna B.; Clarke, Frank E.; Hanshaw, Bruce B.; and Balsley, James R. *A Procedure for Evaluating Environmental Impact.* Circular 645. Washington, DC: U.S. Geological Survey, 1971.

Liroff, Richard A. "NEPA—Where Have We Been and Where Are We Going?" *Journal of the American Planning Association* 46 (April 1980):154–161.

McEvoy, James, III, and Dietz, Thomas, editors, *Handbook for Environmental Planning.* New York: Wiley-Interscience, 1977.

McHarg, Ian L. *Design With Nature.* Garden City, NY: Natural History Press, 1969.

Ortolano, Leonard, editor. *Analyzing the Environmental Impacts of Water Projects.* Alexandria, VA: U.S. Army Engineer Institute for Water Resources, 1973.

Pearlman, Kenneth. "State Environmental Policy Acts: Local Decision Making and Land Use Planning," *Journal of the American Institute of Planners* 43 (January 1977):42–53.

Rau, John G., and Wooten, David C. *Environmental Impact Analysis Handbook.* New York: McGraw-Hill, Inc., 1980.

Sorenson, Jens C. *A Framework for Identification and Control of Resource Degradation and Conflict in the Multiple Use of the Coastal Zone.* Berkeley, CA: Department of Landscape Architecture, University of California, 1971.

11 Basic Studies for State and Regional Planning

Andrews, R. B. "Economic Studies" in *Principles and Practice of Urban Planning;* edited by William I. Goodman and Eric C. Freund. Washington, DC: International City Managers Association, 1968, pp. 76–105.

Brown, H. J. "Shift and Share Projections of Regional Economic Growth: An Empirical Test." *Journal of Regional Science* 9 (1969): 1–18.

Division of Planning and Research, New Jersey Department of Labor and Industry. *Statistical Source Directory for New Jersey State Government.* Trenton: The Department, February 1980.

Executive Office of the President, Office of Management and Budget. *Standard Industrial Classification Manual.* Washington, DC: U.S. Government Printing Office, 1972.

Gass, Saul I. and Sisson, Roger L., editors. *A Guide to Models in Governmental Planning and Operations.* Potomac, MD: Sauger Books, 1975.

Greenberg, M. R., Krueckeberg, D. A., and Michaelson, C. O. *Local Population and Employment Projection Techniques.* New Brunswick, NJ: Rutgers University, Center for Urban Policy Research, 1978.

Hewings, G. "On the Accuracy of Alternative Models for Stepping-Down Multi-County Employment Projections to Counties." *Economic Geography* 52 (July 1976): 206–217.

Isserman, A. "The Location Quotient Approach to Estimating Regional Economic Impacts." *Journal of the American Institute of Planners* 43 (January 1977): 33–41.

James, F. J., and Hughes, J. W. "A Test of Shift and Share Analysis as a Predictive Device." *Journal of Regional Science* 13 (1973): 223–231.

Koebel, C. Theodore. *1979 Housing Report for Kentucky.* Louisville: University of Louisville, Urban Studies Center, 1979.

Krueckeberg, D. A., and Silvers, A. L. *Urban Planning Analysis: Methods and Models.* New York: John Wiley and Sons, 1974.

Kutscher, R. E. "Revised BLS Projections to 1980 and 1985: An Overview." *Monthly Labor Review.* Washington, DC: U.S. Government Printing Office, March 1976.

Miernyk, W. *The Elements of Input-Output Analysis.* New York: Random House, 1965.

Sternlieb, George, and Hughes, James W. "Housing in the United States: An Overview," in *America's Housing: Prospects and Problems;* edited by George Sternlieb and James W. Hughes. New Brunswick: Center for Urban Policy Research, 1980, pp. 1–92.

Thompson, W. *A Preface to Urban Economics.* Baltimore, MD: The Johns Hopkins University Press, 1965.

Tri-State Regional Planning Commission. *Tri-*

State Data Resources. New York: The Commission, October, 1981.

U.S. Bureau of the Census. *Census of Business*. Washington, DC: U.S. Government Printing Office.

———. *Census of Manufactures*. Washington, DC: U.S. Government Printing Office.

———. *Census of Mineral Industries*. Washington, DC: U.S. Government Printing Office.

———. *Census of Population 1970 and 1980*. Washington, DC: U.S. Government Printing Office.

———. *County Business Patterns*. Washington, DC: U.S. Government Printing Office.

———. *Data User News*. Washington, DC: U.S. Government Printing Office, monthly.

———. *Federal State Cooperative Program for Population Estimates*. Series P–26. Washington DC: U.S. Government Printing Office.

———. *Population Characteristics*. P–20. Washington, DC: U.S. Government Printing Office.

———. *Population Estimates & Projections*. Series P–25. Washington, DC: U.S. Government Printing Office.

———. *Special Studies*. Series P–23. Washington, DC: U.S. Government Printing Office.

———. *Statistical Abstract of the United States*. Washington, DC: U.S. Government Printing Office.

———. *Consumer Income*. Series P–60. Washington, DC: U.S. Government Printing Office.

U.S. Bureau of Economic Analysis. *1972 OBERS Projections*. Washington, DC: U.S. Government Printing Office.

———. *Survey of Current Business*. Washington, DC: U.S. Government Printing Office.

U.S. Bureau of Labor Statistics. *Employment and Earnings*. Washington, DC: U.S. Government Printing Office.

———. *Employment and Wages*. Washington, DC: U.S. Government Printing Office.

———. *Monthly Labor Review*. Washington, DC: U.S. Government Printing Office.

———. *Patterns of the U.S. Economy,* Bulletin 1672. Washington, DC: U.S. Government Printing Office.

U.S. Department of the Interior, National Cartographic Information Center. *Map Data Catalog*. Washington, DC: U.S. Government Printing Office, 1980.

12 Citizen Participation

Advisory Commission on Intergovernmental Relations. *Citizen Participation in the American Federal System*. Washington, DC: U.S. Government Printing Office, 1980.

American Institute of Planners. *Survey of State Land Use Planning Activity*. Washington, DC: U.S. Department of Housing and Urban Development, 1976.

Arnstein, Sherry. "A Ladder of Citizen Participation." *Journal of the American Institute of Planners* 35 (July 1969): 216–244.

Cogan & Associates. *Techniques of Public Involvement*. Washington, DC: Council of State Planning Agencies, 1977.

Federal Interagency Council on Citizen Participation. *At Square One: Proceedings of the Conference on Citizen Participation in Government Decision Making*. Washington, DC: U.S. Government Printing Office, 1977.

Friedmann, John. *Retracking America: A Theory of Transactive Planning*. Garden City, NY: Anchor Press/Doubleday, 1973.

Rosenbaum, Nelson. *Citizen Involvement in Land Use Governance: Issues and Methods*. Washington, DC: The Urban Institute, 1976.

U.S. Community Services Administration. *Citizen Participation*. Washington, DC, 1978.

U.S. Department of Transportation, Federal Highway Administration. *Effective Citizen Participation in Transportation Planning: Vol. 1, Community Involvement Processes; Vol. 2, A Catalogue of Techniques*. Washington, DC: U.S. Government Printing Office, 1976.

13 Urban Development

Advisory Council on Intergovernmental Relations. *Improving Urban America: A Challenge to Federalism*. Washington, DC: Government Printing Office, 1976.

Bosselman, Fred, and Callies, David. *The Quiet Revolution in Land Use Control*. Washington, DC: Government Printing Office, 1971.

Choate, Pat, and Walter, Susan. *America in Ruins: Beyond the Public Works Pork Barrel*. Washington, DC: Council of State Planning Agencies, 1981.

Godschalk, David R., *et al. Constitutional Issues of Growth Management*. Revised edition. Chicago: Planners Press, 1979.

Healey, Robert G., and Rosenberg, John S. *Land Use and the States*. 2nd ed. Baltimore: Johns Hopkins University Press, 1979.

Hovey, Harold A. *State Urban Development Strategies*. Washington, DC: Council of State Planning Agencies, 1977.

Naftalin, Arthur, and Brandl, John. *The Twin Cities Regional Strategy*. St. Paul, MN: Metropolitan Council of the Twin Cities Area, 1980.

Popper, Frank J. *The Politics of Land Use Reform*. Madison: University of Wisconsin Press, 1981.

Warren, Charles R. *The States and Urban Strategies: A Comparative Analysis*. Washington, DC: U.S. Department of Housing and Urban Development, 1980. See also the 10 separate volumes on the strategies of California, Connecticut, Florida, Massachusetts, Michigan, New Jersey, North Carolina, Ohio, Oregon, and Pennsylvania.

14 Rural Development

Bonner, William S., and Middleton, Robert K. *Regional Communities: A Planning and Development Concept for Nonmetropolitan Areas*. Washington, DC: American Institute of Planners, 1972.

Browne, William P., and Hadwiger, Don F. *Rural Policy Problems: Changing Dimensions*. Lexington, MA: Lexington Books, 1982.

Carlson, John E; Lassey, Marie L.; and Lassey, William R. *Rural Society and Environment in America*. New York: McGraw-Hill Book Co., 1981.

Christenson, James A., and Robinson, Jerry W., Jr. *Community Development in America*, Ames, IA: Iowa State University Press, 1980.

Corbett, Michael N. *A Better Place to Live: New Designs for Tomorrow's Communities*. Emmaus, PA: Rodale Press, 1981.

Fitzsimmons, Stephen J., and Freedman, Abby J. *Rural Community Development: A Program, Policy, and Research Model*. Cambridge, MA: Abt Books, 1981.

Ford, Thomas R., editor. *Rural U.S.A.: Persistence and Change*. Ames, IA: Iowa State University Press, 1978.

Getzels, Judith, and Thurow, Charles, editors. *Rural and Small Town Planning*. Chicago: American Planning Association, 1980.

Hawley, Amos H., and Mazie, Sara Mills, editors. *Nonmetropolitan America in Transition*. Chapel Hill, NC: University of North Carolina Press, 1981.

Lassey, William R. *Planning in Rural Environments*. New York: McGraw-Hill, 1977.

Northeast-Midwest Institute. *The 1983 Guide to Government Resources for Economic Development*. Washington, DC: Northeast-Midwest Institute, 1983.

Rogers, David L., and Whiting, Larry R. *Aspects of Planning for Public Services in Rural Areas*. Ames, IA: North Central Regional Center for Rural Development, Iowa State University, 1976.

Rural Development Perspectives. Washington, DC: U.S. Government Printing Office, 1980.

Sargent, Frederic O. *Rural Environmental Planning*. Burlington, VT: University of Vermont, 1976.

Small Community and Rural Development Policy. Washington, DC: U.S. Government Printing Office, 1980.

Weber, Bruce A., and Howell, Robert E., editors. *Coping With Rapid Growth in Rural Communities*. Boulder, CO: Westview Press, 1982.

U.S. Congressional Research Service, Library of Congress, *Rural Development: An Overview*. Washington, DC: GPO, 1979.

U.S. President. Task Force on Rural Development. *A New Life for the Country*. Washington, DC: U.S. Government Printing Office, 1980.

15 Economic Development

Aldrich, Mark. *A History of Public Works in the United States 1790–1970*. Report prepared for the U.S. Department of Commerce, Economic Development Administration, December 1979.

Appalachian Regional Commission. *A Report to Congress on the Continuation of the Appalachian Regional Commission*. Washington, DC: March 1979.

———. *Areawide Action Program, A Guide to Its Preparation and Use*. Washington, DC: 1978.

Arronson, Leanne, and Shapiro, Carol. *The State's Role in Urban Economic Development: An Urban Government Perspective*. Urban Consortium Information Bulletin: September 1980.

Bivens, W. E., III, and Marinich, Joseph S. *State Departments of Community and Economic Development*. Washington, DC: Council of State Community Affairs Agencies, 1978.

Choate, Pat, and Walter, Susan. *America in Ruins*. Washington, DC: Council of State Planning Agencies, 1981.

Clawson, Marion, *New Deal Planning*. Baltimore, MD: The Johns Hopkins University Press, 1981.

Council of State Community Affairs Agencies. *Economic Development—the State's Perspectives*. Washington, DC: January 1981.

Council of State Planning Agencies. "State Development Strategies, A Policy Maker's Guide to Their Design," Washington, DC: 1981 (unpublished).

Council of State Planning Agencies. "Public Pension Funds and the Housing Problem." Washington, DC: July 1980.

———. "State and Local Investment Strategies." Washington, DC: September 1980.

———. *State Regulation and Economic Development*. Washington, DC: March 1981.

Darwent, David F. *An Analysis of Recent Survey Data on the Economic Development Administration's Growth Center Policy*. Unpublished, undated.

Eichner, Alfred S. *State Development Agencies and Employment Expansion*. Ann Arbor, MI: Institute of Labor and Industrial Relations, The University of Michigan—Wayne State University, 1970.

Graham, Otis L., Jr. *Toward A Planned Society*. London: Oxford University Press, 1976.

Heilbroner, Robert L. *The Making of Economic Society*. 4th ed. Englewood Cliffs, NJ: Prentice-Hall, Inc., 1972.

Kerr, William O. *Exports and Export Development Program in the CONEG States*. CONEG Policy Research Center, Inc.: May 2, 1979.

Keynes, John Maynard. *The General Theory of Employment, Interest and Money*. New York: Harcourt, Brace and World, 1936.

Legis 50/The Center for Legislative Improvement. *The Economic Development Project Final Report to the United States Department of Commerce, Economic Development Administration, Office of Economic Research*. Englewood, CO: December 1977.

———. *Legislative Policymaking in Economic Development: Four Case Studies*. Englewood, CO: 1977.

Levitan, Sar. A. *Federal Aid to Depressed Areas*. Baltimore, MD: The Johns Hopkins Press, 1964.

National Council for Urban Economic Development. *State Development Programs: A Catalogue*. Washington, DC: National Council for Urban Economic Development, 1981.

National Resources Board. *A Review of Activities and Progress*. Washington, DC: U.S Government Printing Office, June 1935.

National Resources Committee. *The Future of State Planning*. Washington, DC: U.S. Government Printing Office, March 1938.

National Resources Planning Board. *State Planning*. Washington, DC: U.S. Government Printing Office, June 1942.

National Resources Planning Board. *Circular XI—Current Programs of State Planning Boards*. Washington, DC: U.S. Government Printing Office, April 22, 1943.

Public/Private Ventures. *Critical Issues in Development Finance*. Report prepared for the U.S. Department of Commerce, Economic Development Administration, February 1981.

"State and Local Government in Trouble." *Business Week,* October 26, 1981, pp. 135–155.

TERA, Inc. "Evaluation of and Recommendations for Improvement in the State OMBE Program." Report prepared for the U.S. Department of Commerce, Office of Minority Business Enterprise, Washington, DC, April 1978.

U.S. Department of Commerce, Bureau of the Census. *The Metropolitan Statistical Area Classification*. Prepared by the Federal Committee on Standard Metropolitan Statistical Areas. August 1980.

U.S. Department of Commerce, Economic Development Administration. *The EDA Experience in the Evolution of Policy: A Brief History September 1965–June 1973*.

U.S. Department of Commerce, Economic Development Administration. Growth Evaluation Task Force. *Program Evaluation: The Economic Development Administration Growth Center Strategy*. February 1972.

U.S. Department of Commerce, Economic Development Administration. *Local Public Works Programs, Final Report*. Washington, DC: 1980.

U.S. Small Business Administration, Office of Advocacy. *Planning a State Small Business Conference*. Washington, DC: November 1980.

U.S. Small Business Administration, Office of the Chief Counsel for Advocacy. *Directory of State Small Business Conference*. Washington, DC: July 1980.

———. *The States and Small Businesses*. A Report on the First National Conference on State Small Business Programs. Denver, CO: 1979.

Vaughan, Roger J., and Bearse, Peter. *Federal Economic Development Programs: A Framework for Design and Evaluation*. Prepared for the Commission on Employment Policy, October 1980.

Vaughan, Roger J., and Verney, George. "Countercyclical Public Works Programs." A paper prepared for a conference on "The Fiscal Crisis and The American City: The Federal Response," Economic Development Administration, U.S. Department of Commerce, Washington, DC: June 1978.

West, Robert Craig. "The Depository Institutions Deregulation Act of 1980: A Historical Perspective." *Economic Review*, Federal Reserve Bank of Kansas City (February 1982), pp. 3–13.

16 Housing Planning

Advisory Commission on Intergovernmental Relations. *The States and Distressed Communities: The 1981 Report*. Washington, DC: U.S. Department of Housing and Urban Development, May 1982.

Council on Development Choices for the '80s. *Interim Report: Development Choices for the '80s*. Washington, DC: Urban Land Institute, 1980.

Nenno, Mary K., and Brophy, Paul C., et al. *Housing and Local Government*. Washington, DC: International City Management Association, 1982.

Peterson, George E., with Brian Cooper. *Tax-Exempt Financing of Housing Investment*. Washington, DC: The Urban Institute, 1979.

President's Commission for a National Agenda for the Eighties. *Urban America in the Eighties*. Washington, DC: U.S. Government Printing Office, 1980.

U.S. Department of Housing and Urban Development. *The President's National Urban Policy Report: 1980*. Washington, DC: U.S. Government Printing Office, 1980.

U.S. Senate. *Impact of Building Codes on Housing Rehabilitation*. Washington, DC.: U.S. Government Printing Office, March 24, 1978.

17 Transportation Planning

Adams, Brock. "New Directions for Transportation Policy in Last Half of 1970s," address to Transportation Association of America, October 7, 1976.

Advisory Commission on Intergovernmental Relations. *Toward More Balanced Transportation: New Intergovernmental Proposals*. Washington, DC: Advisory Commission on Intergovernmental Relations, 1975.

Altshuler, Alan. *The Urban Transportation System: Politics and Policy Innovation*. Cambridge, MA: MIT Press, 1979.

Barton-Aschman Associates, Inc. *Evaluation Manual: Energy Saving Traffic Operations Project*. Illinois Department of Transportation, August 1980 [draft].

———. *Guidelines for New Systems of Urban Transportation, Volume One: Urban Needs and Potentials*. 1968.

———. *Petroleum Shortage Response Program for the State of Illinois, Phase One: Thirty Day Actions*. Prepared for the Illinois Institute of Natural Resources, June 1979.

———. *San Diego/Los Angeles Corridor Study*. California DOT, Southern California Council of Governments, Comprehensive Planning Organization of the San Diego Region, 1975.

———. *State-Wide Transportation Plan. Phase One: Interim Report February 1975; Phase One: Summary Report August 1976; Phase One: Technical Report January 1976*. Prepared for the North Carolina Department of Transportation.

———. *Urban Transportation and Land Use Coordination*. Prepared for the Erie and Niagara Counties New York Regional Planning Board, July 1969.

Barton-Aschman Associates, Inc., and Creighton Hamburg, Inc. *Development of a Transportation Planning Work Program for the Delaware Valley Regional Planning Commission; Work Papers Numbers 1–10 and Summary Report, 1972–1973*.

Barton-Aschman Associates, Inc., and Ernst & Ernst. *Alternative Solutions to Railroad Impacts on Communities in Minnesota and North Dakota*. MnDOT and North Dakota State Highway Department, 1979.

Bellomo, Salvatore J. *Issues and New Directions in State-Wide Transportation Planning and Programming*. Prepared for the TRB 56th Annual Meeting, January 1977.

Castel, Gilbert, and Engelen, Rodney E. "Joint Transportation and Development Planning at the State Level: A Case Study." Presented to the Committee on Transportation and Land Development Policy at the 55th Annual Meeting of TRB, January 1976.

Dickey, John W., and others. *Metropolitan Transportation Planning*. New York: McGraw-Hill Company, 1975.

Engelen, Rodney E., and Stuart, Darwin G.

New Directions in Transportation Planning. Chicago: American Society of Planning Officials, 1975.

Federal Highway Administration. *Planning Process Memorandum 50–9*, 1965.

———. *Planning Process Memorandum 90–3*, 1974.

Gray, George E., and Hoel, Lester A. *Public Transportation: Planning Operations and Management.* New York: Prentice-Hall, Inc. 1979.

Harris, Roy J., Jr. "Regional Airlines, Using Efficient Planes over Short Hops, Outpace Trunk Carriers," *The Wall Street Journal*, July 22, 1980.

Manheim, Marvin L.; Suhrbier, John H.; and others. *Transportation Decision-Making: A Guide to Social and Environmental Considerations.* Cambridge, MA: MIT Press, July 1974.

Miller, David R. *Equity of Transit Service Study.* Vol 2. W. V. Rouse and Company, June 1977.

Minnesota Department of Transportation. *Minnesota Looks at Transportation: A Report on Phase One of the MN/DOT Plan.* St. Paul: Minnesota Department of Transportation, July 1977.

———. *Minnesota Moves Toward a State Transportation Plan: A Report on Phase Two of the MN/DOT Plan.* St. Paul: Minnesota Department of Transportation, January 1978.

———. *A Transportation Plan for the State of Minnesota.* St. Paul, Minnesota Department of Transportation, July 1978.

National Academy of Sciences, Transportation Research Board. *NCHRP Report 208: Market Opportunity Analysis for Short-Range Public Transportation Planning, Procedures for Evaluating Alternative Service Concepts.* Washington, DC: National Research Council, 1979.

———. *NCHRP Report 209: Market Opportunity Analysis for Short-Range Public Transportation Planning, Transportation Services for the Transportation Disadvantaged.* Washington, DC: National Research Council, October 1979.

———. *NCHRP Report 210: Market Opportunity Analysis for Short-Range Public Transportation Planning, Economic, Energy, and Environmental Impacts.* Washington, DC: National Research Council, October 1979.

———. *NCHRP Report 211: Market Opportunity Analysis for Short-Range Public*

Transportation Planning, Goals, and Policy Development, Institutional Constraints, and Alternative Organizational Arrangement. Washington, DC: National Research Council, October 1979.

———. *NCHRP Report 217: The No-Action Alternative, Impact Assessment Guidelines.* Washington, DC: National Research Council, December 1979.

———. *Research Record 686: Effects of Transportation on the Community.* Washington, DC: National Academy of Sciences, 1978.

———. *Research Record 701: Applications and Use of Transportation Data.* Washington, DC: National Academy of Sciences, 1979.

———. *Research Record 707: Urban Transportation Planning, Evaluation, and Analysis.* Washington, DC: National Academy of Sciences, 1979.

———. *Research Record 714, Impact of Air Quality Control Measures.* Washington, DC: National Academy of Sciences, 1979.

———. *Research Record 723: Travel Behavior Methodology.* Washington, DC: National Academy of Sciences, 1979.

———. *Special Report 187: Transportation Planning for Small and Medium Size Communities.* Washington, DC: National Academy of Sciences, 1980.

———. *Special Report 190, Transportation System Management in 1980, State-of-the-Art and Future Directions.* Washington, DC: National Academy of Sciences, 1980.

———. *Urban Transportation Policy Research: Workshop Report.* Prepared for the US Department of Transportation, December 1979.

National Transportation Policy Study Commission. *National Transportation Policies Through the Year 2000.* Washington, DC: National Transportation Policy Study Commission, June 1979.

Petzinger, Thomas, Jr. "Inadequate U.S. Port Facilities Threaten Potentially Huge Export Market for Coal." *The Wall Street Journal*, July 29, 1980.

Railroad Revitalization and Regulatory Reform Act of 1976.

Schnepf, Max *Farmland, Food and the Future.* The Soil Conservation Society of America, 1979.

Stobaugh, Robert, and Yergin, Daniel, editors. *Energy Future: The Report of the Project at the Harvard Business School*

Energy Project. New York: Random House, 1979.

U.S. Department of Transportation. *A Prospectus for Change in the Freight Railroad Industry.* October 1978.

U.S. Department of Transportation, Federal Highway Administration.*1981 Federal Highway Legislation: Program and Revenue Options. Discussion Paper Number 1,* June 26, 1980.

U.S. Department of Transportation, Office of the Secretary. *Transportation and the Future.* Washington, DC: U.S. Department of Transportation, 1979.

Voorhees, Alan M. and Associates, Inc. *Colorado State Wide Transportation Planning Project: Final Report.* Prepared for the Colorado Department of Highways, AMV and Associates, September 1977.

Weiner, Edward. *Evolution of Urban Transportation Planning.* Washington, DC: U.S. Department of Transportation, April 1976.

Wisconsin Department of Transportation. *State Transportation Policy Plan.* January 1980.

18 Energy Planning

Energy: The Next Twenty Years, Report by Study Group sponsored by the Ford Foundation, administered by Resources for the Future. Cambridge, MA: Ballinger Publishing Company, 1979.

Energy Tomorrow: Challenges and Opportunities for California, 1981 Biennial Report to the Governor and the Legislature, California Energy Commission, Sacramento, CA, 1981.

Garreau, Joel. *Nine Nations of North America.* Boston: Houghton Mifflin Company, 1981.

Mid-America Economics Institute. *Consumer's Guide to the Economics of Electric Utility Ratemaking.* Springfield, IL: Illinois Office of Consumer Services, 1979.

New York State Energy Master Plan and Long-Range Electric and Gas Report. Albany, NY, New York State Energy Office, 1980.

1980 Energy Policy and Conservation Biennial Report, Report from Minnesota Energy Agency to the Minnesota Legislature, St. Paul, MN, 1980.

Rodberg, Leonard, and Schachter, Meg. *State Conservation and Solar Energy Tax Programs: Incentives or Windfalls.* Washington, DC: Council of State Planning Agencies, 1980.

Ross, Mark H. *Our Energy: Regaining Control.* New York: McGraw-Hill, 1981.

Sant, Roger, and Carhart, Steven C. *Eight Great Energy Myths, The Least-Cost Strategy 1978–2000.* Arlington, VA: Energy Productivity Center, 1981.

Schelling, Thomas C. *Thinking Through the Energy Problem.* New York: Committee for Economic Development, 1979.

Schurr, Sam H. *Energy in America's Future: The Choices Before Us.* Baltimore, MD: Johns Hopkins University Press, 1980.

Stobaugh, Robert, and Yergin, Daniel, editors. *Energy Future: Report of the Energy Project at the Harvard Business School.* New York: Random House, 1979.

19 Environmental Protection

"Areawide Planning Under the Federal Water Pollution Control Act Amendments of 1972: Intergovernmental and Land Use Implications." *Texas Law Review* 54 (June 1976): 1047–80 [comment].

Chasis, Sarah. "The Coastal Zone Management Act." *Journal of the American Planning Association* 46 (April 1980): 145–153.

Council of State Governments. *Diffuse Source Pollution: Policy Considerations for the States.* Lexington, KY: The Council, 1977.

Environmental Law Institute. *Federal Environmental Law.* St. Paul, MN: West Publishing Company, 1974.

Finnell, Gilbert L. Jr. "The Federal Regulatory Role in Coastal Land Management." *American Bar Foundation Research Journal* 1978, No. 2 (Spring 1978): 173–288.

Hagevick, G.; Mandelker, D.; and Brail, R. *Air Quality Management and Land Use Planning.* New York: Praeger, 1974.

Healy, R., and Rosenberg, J. *Land Use and the States.* 2nd ed.; Baltimore, MD: Johns Hopkins University Press, 1979.

"The Implementation of Transportation Controls Under the 1977 Clean Air Act Amendments." *University of Colorado Law Review* 50 (Winter 1979): 247–275 [comment].

Kusler, J. *Regulating Sensitive Lands.* Cambridge, MA: Ballinger Publishing Company, 1980.

Liroff, Richard A. "NEPA, Where Have We Been and Where Are We Going? *Journal of the American Planning Association* 46 (April 1980): 154–161.

Mandelker, D. *Environment and Equity.* New York: McGraw-Hill, 1981.

————. *Environmental and Land Controls Legislation.* Indianapolis: Bobbs Merrill, 1976; and *Supplement,* 1982.

Mandelker, D., and Cunningham, R. *Planning and Control of Land Development.* Indianapolis: Bobbs-Merrill, 1979; and *Supplement,* 1981.

Martin, Kenneth R. "The Wetlands Controversy: A Coastal Concern Washes Inland." *Notre Dame Lawyer* 52 (June 1977): 1015–34 [note].

Natural Resources Defense Council, Inc. *Land Use Controls in the United States.* New York: Dial Press, 1977.

Pearlman, Kenneth. "State Environmental Policy Acts: Local Decision Making and Land Use Planning." *Journal of the American Institute of Planners* 43 (January 1977): 42–53.

Pelham, T. *State Land-Use Planning and Regulation.* Lexington, MA: Lexington Books, 1979.

Phillips, Michael B. "Developments in Water Quality and Land Use Planning: Problems in the Application of the Federal Water Pollution Control Act Amendments of 1972." *Urban Law Annual* 10 (1975): 43–143.

Rodgers, W. *Environmental Law.* St. Paul, MN: West Publishing Company, 1977.

"Sewers, Clean Water, and Planned Growth: Restructuring the Federal Pollution Abatement Effort." *Yale Law Journal* 86 (March 1977): 733–81 [note].

Thurow, C.; Toner, W.; and Erley, D. *Performance Controls for Sensitive Lands.* Chicago: American Planning Association, 1975. (Planning Advisory Report Nos. 307–08).

To Breathe Clean Air. Report of the National Commission on Air Quality. Washington, DC: 1981.

"Who Owns the Air? The Emission Offset Concept and its Implications." *Environmental Law* 9 (Spring 1979): 575–600 [comment].

20 Solid Waste Management

Cole, Leslie. *Waste Management in the States, RM–706.* Lexington, KY: Council of State Governments, 1982.

Conn, W. David. "Regulatory Control over Solid Wastes in the United States," in *Progress in Resource Management and Environmental Planning,* Vol. 4, ed. Timothy O'Riordan and Kerry Turner. Chichester, England, John Wiley, forthcoming.

Environmental Protection Agency, Office of Solid Waste Management Programs. *Decision-Makers' Guide in Solid Waste Planning, SW–500.* Washington, DC: Environmental Protection Agency and US Government Printing Office, 1976.

Gavrich, David A. *Developing a State Resource Conservation and Recovery Program, SW–791.* Washington, DC: Environmental Protection Agency, 1979.

Goddard, Haynes C. *Managing Solid Wastes—Economics, Technology, and Institutions.* New York: Praeger, 1975.

Kovalick, Walter W., ed. *State Decision-Makers Guide for Hazardous Waste Management, SW–612.* Washington, DC: Environmental Protection Agency and US Government Printing Office, 1977.

Steeler, Jonathan H. *A Legislator's Guide to Hazardous Waste Management.* Denver: National Conference of State Legislatures, 1980.

Tchobanoglous, George; Theisen, Hilary; and Eliassen, Rolf, eds. *Solid Waste—Engineering Principles and Management Issues.* New York: McGraw-Hill, 1977.

U.S. Congress, Office of Technology Assessment. *Materials and Energy from Municipal Waste, OTA-M–3.* Washington, DC: Office of Technology Assessment, 1979.

Watson, Tom; Hall, Ridgeway M., Jr.; Davidson, Jeffrey J.; and Case, David R. *The Hazardous Waste Handbook.* 3rd ed. Rockville, MD: Government Institutes, 1981; with update, 1982.

Worobec, Mary. "An Analysis of the Resource Conservation and Recovery Act, with a Summary of EPA Hazardous Waste Regulations." *Environment Reporter* 11 (August 1980): 634–646.

21 Health Planning

Berry, David E. "The Transfer of Planning Theories to Health Planning." *Policy Sciences* 5 (1974): 343–361.

Blum, Henrik, L. *Planning for Health: Generics for the Eighties.* New York: Human Sciences Press, 1981.

Committee on the Costs of Medical Care. *Medical Care for the American People.* Chicago: University of Chicago Press, 1932, reprint ed., New York: Arno Press and the New York Times, 1972.

Cooper, Philip D., ed. *Health Care Marketing: Issues and Trends.* Rockville, MD: Aspen Systems Corporation, 1979.

Dever, G. E. Alan. *Community Health Analysis.* Rockville, MD: Aspen Systems Corporation, 1980.

Ford, Ann S. "The Health Planning Professional: A New Opportunity for Planning Education." *Journal of Planning Education and Research* 1 (Summer 1981): 18–28.

Hyman, Herbert Harvey. *Health Planning: A Systematic Approach.* 2nd. ed. Rockville, MD: Aspen Systems Corporation, 1982.

———. *Health Regulation: Certificate of Need and 1122.* Rockville, MD: Aspen Systems Corporation, 1977.

Institute of Medicine. *Health Planning in the United States: Selected Policy Issues.* 2 vols. Washington, DC: National Academy of Sciences, 1981.

Joskow, Paul L. *Controlling Hospital Costs: The Role of Government Regulation.* Cambridge, MA: The MIT Press, 1981.

Reeves, Philip N.; Bergwall, David E.; and Woodside, Nina B. *Introduction to Health Planning.* 2nd ed. Washington, DC: Information Resources Press, 1979.

Roemer, Milton I. *Comparative National Policies on Health Care.* New York: Marcel Dekker, Inc., 1977.

Spiegel, Allen D., and Hyman, Herbert Harvey. *Basic Health Planning Methods.* Rockville, MD: Aspen Systems Corporation, 1978.

Starkweather, David B. *Hospital Mergers in the Making.* Ann Arbor, MI: Health Administration Press, 1981.

22 Social Services and Education

Social services

Anderson, Wayne F., *et al.*, editors. *Managing Human Services.* Washington, D.C.: The International City Management Association. 1977.

Demone, Harold W. Jr., and Harshbarger, Dwight. *A Handbook of Human Services Organizations.* New York: Behaviorial Publications. 1974.

Hasenfeld, Yeheskel, and English, Richard A. *Human Service Organizations.* Ann Arbor, MI: The University of Michigan Press, 1977.

Horton, Gerald T., and Armentract, Edmund H. *State Experiences in Social Services Planning.* Atlanta: The Research Group, Inc. 1976.

Kahn, Alfred J. *Theory and Practice of Social Planning.* New York: Russell Sage Foundation, 1969.

Kamerman, Sheila B., and Kahn, Alfred J. *Social Services in the United States: Policies and Programs.* Philadelphia: Temple University Press, 1976.

Magill, Robert S. *Community Decision-Making for Social Welfare.* New York: Human Sciences Press, 1979.

So, Frank S., *et al.*, editors. *The Practice of Local Government Planning.* Washington, DC: The International City Management Association, 1979.

The Council of State Governments. *Human Services: A Framework for Decision-Making.* Lexington, KY, December 1975.

United Way of America. *UWASIS II: A Taxonomy of Social Goals and Human Service Programs.* Alexandria, VA: November 1976.

Education

Campbell, Roald F.; Cunningham, Luvern L.; Nystrand, Raphael O.; and Usdan, Michael D. *The Organization and Control of American Schools,* 4th ed. Columbus: Charles E. Merrill, 1980.

Colorado State Board for Community Colleges and Occupational Education, "Annual State Plan for Vocational Education, 1980." Denver, June 1979.

Education Commission of the States, *Challenge: Coordination and Governance in the '80s.* Report No. 134, Denver, July 1980.

Hershkowitz, Martin. *Statewide Educational Needs Assessment.* Silver Spring, MD: Consortium of State Education Agencies, 1974.

National Project and Task Force on Desegregation Strategies. *Progress: A Report on Desegregation Trends in the States.* Education Commission of the States. Denver, Winter 1980.

Ohio Department of Education, Division of Vocational Education. "Ohio 1981 State Plan Accountability Report. Vocational Education." Abridged, Columbus: 15 April 1980.

The National Institute of Education. *The Vocational Education Study: The Interim Report, Publication No. 3.* Washington, DC: September 1980.

The University of the State of New York. *The Simulation of College Enrollments, New York State, 1978–1994.* The State Education Department, Office of Post-Secondary

Research, Information Systems and Institutional Aid. Albany, February 1980.

Witkin, Belle Ruth. *An Analysis of Needs Assessment Techniques for Educational Planning at State, Intermediate and District Levels.* Office of Alameda County Superintendent of Schools, California, 19 May 1975.

23 Criminal Justice Planning

Agopian, Michael. "A Selected Bibliography in Criminal Justice Planning, Analysis and Evaluation," *Vance Bibliographies Public Administration Series: P–420,* February 1980. Monticello, IL: Vance Bibliographies, 1980.

Arthur D. Little, Inc. *Local Criminal Justice Planning and Analysis: Activities and Capabilities.* Washington, DC: Law Enforcement Assistance Administration, 1976.

Council of State Governments. *The Future of Criminal Justice Planning.* Lexington, KY: CSG, 1976.

Cushman, Robert C. *Criminal Justice Planning for Local Governments.* Washington, DC: U.S. Department of Justice, National Institute of Law Enforcement and Criminal Justice, January 1980.

Friedlander, Frank. *OD: Purpose and Values in OD.* Madison, WI: American Society for Training and Development, 1976.

Gibbons, Don, *et al. Criminal Justice Planning: An Introduction.* Englewood Cliffs, NJ: Prentice-Hall, 1977.

Hoffman, Mark. *Criminal Justice Planning.* American Society of Planning Officials, Planning Advisory Service Report No. 276, January 1972. Chicago: American Society of Planning Officials, 1972.

Loving, Nancy, and McKay, John W. *Criminal Justice Planning: Five Alternative Structures for Cities.* Washington, DC: National League of Cities and U.S. Conference of Mayors, 1976.

National Advisory Commission on Criminal Justice Standards and Goals. *Report of the Task Force on Criminal Justice Research and Development.* Washington, DC: U.S. Government Printing Office, 1976.

National Criminal Justice Reference Service. *Directory of Criminal Justice Information Sources.* Washington, DC: NCJRS, May 1979.

O'Block, Robert L. *Criminal Justice Research Sources,* Cincinnati, OH: Anderson Publishing Company, 1983.

Shanahan, Donald T., and Whisenand, Paul M. *The Dimensions of Criminal Justice Planning.* Boston, MA: Allyn and Bacon, 1980.

U.S. President's Commission on Law Enforcement and Administration of Justice. *The Challenge of Crime in a Free Society.* Washington, DC: U.S. Government Printing Office, 1967.

24 Comprehensive Emergency Planning and Management

Overview

Barton, Allen H. *Communities in Disaster: A Sociological Analysis of Collective Stress Situations.* New York: Anchor, Doubleday and Company, Inc., 1970.

Council of State Governments, *The States and Natural Hazards,* Lexington, KY: The Council of State Governments, 1979.

Dynes, Russell R., and Quarantelli, E. L. *A Perspective on Disaster Planning.* Washington, DC: Defense Civil Preparedness Agency, 1972.

Executive Office of the President, Office of Emergency Preparedness. *Report to the Congress on Disaster Preparedness,* January 1972.

Federal Disaster Assistance Administration, US Department of Housing and Urban Development. *Directory of Disaster-Related Technology,* HUD Report No. 401. Washington, DC: Federal Disaster Assistance Administration, 1975.

Haas, J. Eugene; Kates, Robert W.; and Bowden, Martyn J. *Reconstruction Following Disaster.* Cambridge: M.I.T. Press, 1977.

The disaster aftermath: physical impact on the community

American Institute of Architects Research Corporation. *Architects and Earthquakes.* Washington, DC: American Institute of Architects, 1975.

Baker, Earl J., and McPhee, Joe Gordon. *Land Use Management and Regulation in Hazardous Areas.* Boulder, CO: University of Colorado, 1975.

Brinkman, Waltrand. *Hurricane Hazard in the United States: A Research Assessment.* Boulder, CO: University of Colorado, 1975.

Cochrane, Harold C. *Natural Hazards and Their Distributive Effects.* Boulder, CO: University of Colorado, 1975.

Committee on the Alaska Earthquake, National Academy of Sciences. *The Great Alaska Earthquake of 1964, Vols. 1–8.*

Washington, DC: National Academy of Sciences, 1973.

Mileti, Dennis S. *Natural Hazard Warning Systems in the United States: A Research Assessment*. Boulder, CO: University of Colorado, 1975.

Mileti, Dennis S.; Drabek, Thomas E.; and Haas, J. Eugene. *Human Systems in Extreme Environments: A Sociological Perspective*. Boulder, CO: University of Colorado, 1975.

National Academy of Sciences. *Geophysical Predictions*. Washington, DC: National Academy of Sciences, 1978.

U.S. Water Resources Council. *A Unified National Program for Flood Plain Management*. Washington, DC: Water Resources Council, 1976.

White, Gilbert F. *Flood Hazard in the United States: A Research Assessment*. Boulder, CO: University of Colorado, 1975.

The recovery process

Dynes, Russell R. *Organized Behavior in Disaster*. Lexington, MA: D.C. Heath and Company, 1970.

Laffoon, Polk, IV. *Tornado: The Killer Tornado that Blasted Xenia, Ohio in April 1974*. New York: Harper and Row, 1975.

Rubin, Claire B. "Long-Term Recovery from Natural Disasters: A Comparative Analysis of Six Local Experiences." Final Report to the National Science Foundation, September 1981.

Decision making under extreme pressure

Haas, J. Eugene. "Lesson Learned for Coping with Disaster," *Human Ecology*, The Great Alaska Earthquake of 1964, Committee on the Alaska Earthquake, National Academy of Sciences. Washington, DC: National Academy of Sciences, 1973.

William Spangle and Associates, Inc. "Post-Earthquake Land Use Planning," final report to the National Science Foundation, 1980.

Recovery planning and comprehensive community planning

Haas, J. Eugene; Kates, Robert W.; and Bowden, Martyn J. *Reconstruction Following Disaster*. Cambridge: M.I.T. Press, 1974.

Petak, William J.; Atkisson, Arthur A.; and Gleye, Paul H. *Natural Hazards: A Public Policy Assessment*. Redondo Beach, CA: J. H. Wiggins Company, December 1978.

Rubin, Claire B. *Natural Disaster Recovery Planning for Local Public Officials*. Washington, DC: Federal Emergency Management Agency, November 1979.

Intergovernmental relations

Federal Emergency Management Agency. "Digest of Federal Disaster Assistance," 2nd ed. Washington, DC: October 1979.

National Governors' Association. *1978 Emergency Preparedness Project Final Report*. Washington, DC: U.S. Government Printing Office, 1978.

———. *Comprehensive Emergency Management, A Governor's Guide*. Washington, DC: U.S. Government Printing Office, 1979.

Community examples

Adler, Steven P., and Jansen, Edmund F. *Hill Reestablishment: Retrospective Community Study of a Relocated New England Town*. Durham, NH: University of New Hampshire, 1978.

Francaviglia, Richard V. "Xenia Rebuilds: Effects of Predisaster Conditioning on Postdisaster Redevelopment." *American Institute of Planners Journal* 44 (January 1978).

Laffoon, Polk, IV. *Tornado: The Killer Tornado that Blasted Xenia, Ohio in April 1974*. New York: Harper and Row, 1975.

Mayor's Disaster Review Task Force. *Disaster Response: The 1975 Omaha Tornado*. Omaha, NB: City of Omaha, 1977.

Peirce, Neal R., and Hagstrom, Jerry. "One Community's Answer to Flood Relief." *National Journal* 10 (October 14, 1978): 1648–51.

About the authors

Persons who have contributed to this book are listed below with the editors first and the chapter authors following in alphabetical order.

Frank S. So, AICP (Editor, Introduction) is Deputy Executive Director of the American Planning Association. He has worked previously in local and area-wide planning agencies. He is the senior editor of the companion volume to this book, *The Practice of Local Government Planning*. He holds a bachelor's degree in sociology from Youngstown State University and a master of city planning degree from Ohio State University.

Irving Hand, AICP (Editor, Introduction, Chapters 3 and 5) is Director of the Institute of State and Regional Affairs and Chairman of the Graduate Degree Program in Urban and Regional Planning at Pennsylvania State University, Capitol Campus. He was Executive Director of the Pennsylvania State Planning Board, 1964–1972, and prior to that held executive positions in local and regional planning in Nashville, Tennessee; Tulsa, Oklahoma; and Westchester County, New York. He is a past president of the American Planning Association and held national office with its predecessor organizations, the American Society of Planning Officials and the American Institute of Planners. He is a graduate of the City College of New York and holds a master's degree in city planning from the Massachusetts Institute of Technology.

Bruce D. McDowell, AICP (Editor, and Chapters 1, 2, 6, and 8) is Senior Analyst, U.S. Advisory Commission on Intergovernmental Relations. His former positions include those of Senior Planner with the Maryland-National Capital Park and Planning Commission, Assistant Director of Regional Planning and Director of Program Coordination with the Metropolitan Washington Council of Governments, and consultant to the Housing and Home Finance Agency

(predecessor of the U.S. Department of Housing and Urban Development). He teaches community planning at Montgomery College, Rockville, Maryland. He holds bachelor and doctoral degrees from American University and a master of city planning degree from the Georgia Institute of Technology.

Frank Beal, AICP (Chapter 18) is Manager of Marketing and Coal Development for the Inland Steel Company. He was previously Director of the Illinois Department of Energy and Natural Resources, the state's energy policy office and environmental research agency. He also served as Deputy Director of the American Society of Planning Officials before it was merged with the American Institute of Planners to form the American Planning Association. He holds a bachelor's degree in engineering from Antioch College, and a masters is urban planning from the University of Illinois.

Robert G. Benko (Chapters 3 and 5) is Director of Governor Thornburgh's Office of Policy and Planning in Pennsylvania. He was formerly the Director of Pennsylvania's land policy program and was the recipient of the 1980 Soil Conservation Society of America National Honor Award for outstanding contributions and dedication in the field of soil and water conservation. He has been associated with state planning in the Commonwealth since 1964. He is lecturer in the Graduate Degree Program in Urban and Regional Planning in The Pennsylvania State University, Capitol Campus. He holds a bachelor's degree from Franklin and Marshall College and a master's degree in Regional Planning from Pennsylvania State University.

William S. Bonner, AICP (Chapter 14), is Chairman of the Department of Community and Governmental Affairs at the University of Arkansas–Fayetteville. He has been involved in rural planning and research and has served on several task forces and networks addressing rural problems and issues. He holds a master's degree in regional planning from the University of North Carolina, and a bachelor's degree in sociology from Michigan State University.

Stephen E. Brown (Chapter 18) is public information officer for the Illinois Department of Energy and Natural Resources. He formerly was energy/environment writer.for the *Chicago Daily News*. Mr. Brown, educated at the University of Illinois–Urbana and Northwestern University, writes on environmental and energy topics.

E. Drannon Buskirk, Jr. (Chapter 10) teaches environmental planning, project development, and quantitative methods at Pennsylvania State University. At other colleges and universities he has taught biology, chemistry, and environmental science. He has conducted numerous impact assessments in Southeast Asia and the northeastern United States. In recent years he has co-directed projects on water quality management planning for the U.S. Environmental Protection Agency, and water conservation under a Ford Foundation grant. He holds a bachelor's degree from St. Andrews Presbyterian College, and master's and doctoral degrees from the University of Michigan.

Arnold Cogan, AICP (Chapter 12) is managing partner of Cogan & Associates, a planning and public affairs consulting firm in Portland, Oregon. He was Oregon's first state planning director, first Executive Director of the Oregon Land Conservation and Development commission, and the first planning director of the Port of Portland. He graduated with honors in civil engineering from Oregon State University and has undertaken graduate study in planning and political science at Portland State University.

W. David Conn (Chapter 20) is Associate Professor and Chair of the Ph.D Program in the College of Architecture and Urban Studies at Virginia Polytechnic Institute and State University. He was previously Associate Professor of Urban Planning at UCLA. He has served as an independent consultant at federal, state, and substate levels, and is an associate of the London-based consulting firm, Environmental Resources Ltd. He holds a bachelor's degree in chemistry, a master's degree, and a doctorate in economics from Oxford University.

Linda Donnelly, AICP (Chapter 22) is Planning Coordinator for the Community Planning and Development Division of the Mid-Ohio Regional Planning Commission in Columbus, Ohio. She has studied school finance policy extensively and has served as guest lecturer for policy analysis and planning strategies in the Department of Educational Administration at Ohio State University.

Robert A. Doran (Chapter 23) is President of R.A. Doran and Associates, Public Management Consultants. He served as Deputy Chief of Police of Mount Prospect, Illinois. Previous positions include Senior Consultant with Public Administration Service, executive director of a multicounty criminal justice planning council in the metropolitan Chicago area, and Criminal Justice Specialist with the Illinois Law Enforcement Commission. He has a bachelor's degree in administration of criminal justice from the University of Illinois and a master's degree in public administration from Roosevelt University.

Rodney E. Engelen, AICP (Chapter 17) is Director of Planning for Clark/Van Voorhis Architects, Inc., and was a Senior Vice President of Barton–Aschman Associates, Inc. He has held key public positions in planning in Minneapolis and St. Paul, Minnesota. His work covers a wide range of areas including land and community planning, transportation, and urban design. He has participated in numerous regional and state planning projects involving transportation and land development in areas throughout North America. Mr. Engelen holds a degree in architecture from the University of Minnesota and a master of city planning degree from Harvard University. He has written more than a score of articles and papers dealing with a range of planning and development questions.

Ann Suter Ford (Chapter 21) is on the faculty of the Department of Urban and Regional Planning, Florida State University, where she directs the health planning degree program. She has conducted research and written in the following health areas: planning, consumer education, and manpower. Her past publications include a book, *The Physician's Assistant: A National and Local Analysis* (New York: Praeger Special Studies, 1975). She is currently working on a graduate level health planning text entitled *Health Services Planning*. Dr. Ford received her RN after education at White Plains Hospital School of Nursing, her bachelor's degree in nursing from the University of Kentucky, and her master's and doctoral degrees in urban and regional planning (health planning and policy analysis) from Florida State University.

David R. Godschalk, AICP (Chapter 13) is Professor in the Department of City and Regional Planning at the University of North Carolina at Chapel Hill. He has been vice president of a planning consulting firm in Tampa, planning director for Gainesville, a faculty member at Florida State University, and editor of the *Journal of the American Institute of Planners*. He has served on the boards of the American Society of Planning Officials and the American Planning Association. He holds a bachelor's degree from Dartmouth College, an architectural degree from the University of Florida, and master's and doctoral degrees in planning from the University of North Carolina.

Joe Hertzberg (Chapter 12) manages public affairs projects for Cogan & Associates, a planning and public affairs consulting firm in Portland, Oregon. He formerly was an instructor at Yale University. He holds a bachelor's degree from Oakland University and advanced degrees from the University of Pennsylvania and Yale University. He is involved in citizen participation activities as a consultant, researcher, and activist.

Connie O. Hughes (Chapter 11) is Staff Director of the New Jersey State Data Center, a federal–state cooperative program with the U.S. Bureau of the Census. Prior to her present position, she developed the first demographic–economic population projection model for New Jersey and its counties, and assisted in the development of the Federal–State Cooperative Program for Population Projections. Ms. Hughes received a

master's degree in city and regional planning from Rutgers University and conducted research on the modeling of employment growth at the University's Center for Urban Policy Research.

Donald A. Krueckeberg, AICP (Chapter 11) is Professor of Urban Planning and Policy Development at Rutgers University in New Brunswick, New Jersey. He is also a consultant in demographic analysis, the author of several books in the field, and a former editor of the *Journal of the American Planning Association*. He holds a bachelor's degree from Michigan State University and masters's and doctoral degrees from the University of Pennsylvania.

Margaret L. Lotspeich (Chapter 22) is Associate Professor of Community Planning at the University of Cincinnati. She teaches human services planning and evaluation at the School of Planning. She has provided extensive volunteer planning consultation to human service agencies in the Cincinnati metropolitan area. Her professional practice is carried out through her partnership in Planning ～～ ～ces Associates.

Daniel R. Mandelker (Chapter 19) is Stamper Professor of Law at Washington University in St. Louis, where he teaches courses in land use and environmental law. His books include *Environment and Equity* (1981) and *Environmental and Land Controls Legislation* (1976). He served on the American Bar Association's Advisory Committee on Housing and Urban Growth and the U.S. Department of Transportation's National Advisory Committee on Outdoor Advertising. He also has consulted with state and local governments on environmental and land use questions.

Feather O'Connor (Chapter 16) is Executive Director of the New Jersey Housing Finance Agency. She was Acting Deputy Assistant Secretary for Policy Development of the U.S. Department of Housing and Urban Development during 1980–1982, and Director of HUD's Division of Policy Development 1977–1980. She holds a bachelor's degree from the University of Arizona and a master's from the University of Texas.

Carl V. Patton, AICP (Chapter 9) is Dean of the School of Architecture and Urban Planning, University of Wisconsin–Milwaukee. Previously he was Professor and head of the Department of Urban and Regional Planning at the University of Illinois at Urbana–Champaign, director of the Department's Bureau of Urban and Regional Planning Research, an associate in the architecture and planning firm of Richardson, Severns, Scheeler, Green, and a planner with Ladislas Segoe and Associates, city planners and consulting engineers. He holds a bachelor of science degree in community planning from the University of Cincinnati, a master's in urban planning from the University of Illinois at Urbana–Champaign, and a Ph.D. in public policy from the University of California at Berkeley.

H. Milton Patton, AICP (Chapter 4) is a principal partner of State Research Associates, Lexington, Kentucky, specialists in state policy and program development. He has served as executive secretary of the Council of State Planning Agencies and associate director of research at the Council of State Governments. He has been a state planner in New York, West Virginia, and Washington and worked on the community renewal program for San Francisco. He holds a master of city planning degree from the University of Pennsylvania.

Janet W. Patton (Chapter 4) is Associate Professor of Political Science at Eastern Kentucky University, Richmond, Kentucky. Her major areas of teaching and research are intergovernmental relations and state and local government. She has served on state and local commissions, boards, and task forces dealing with juvenile justice, welfare, transportation, and solar energy. She is a graduate of Mount Holyoke College and received master's and doctoral degrees from the University of California at Berkeley.

Thomas H. Roberts, AICP (Chapter 7) is an Atlanta-based planning consultant specializing in local and regional planning, zoning, and land develoment regulations. He is the former Planning Director of the Atlanta Regional Commission and of the Metropolitan Washington (D.C.) Council of Governments. He has also served as the

Executive Director of the American Institute of Planners, President of the American Society of Planning Officials, and Founder of the American Planning Association. He received a bachelor of science degree in civil engineering from Case Western Reserve University and a master of regional planning degree from the University of North Carolina at Chapel Hill.

Claire B. Rubin (Chapter 24) is a consultant in public management and emergency management. She previously was Director of the Natural Disaster Research Center at the Academy for State and Local Government in Washington, D.C. She also served as Director of Contract Research at the International City Management Association. She is the author of numerous publications and training programs in the field of natural hazards and disasters, with emphasis on public planning and management decision making at the local and state levels.

Sumner Sharpe, AICP (Chapter 12) is a Senior Associate with Cogan & Associates, a planning and public affiars consulting firm in Portland, Oregon, and an Associate Professor of Urban Studies at Portland State University. He graduated with honors in geography from Dartmouth College, earned a master's degree in regional planning from Cornell University, attended the London School of Economics as a postgraduate student in government and public administration, and received his doctorate in urban planning from the University of Washington.

Michael A. Stegman (Chapter 16) is a Professor of City and Regional Planning at the University of North Carolina at Chapel Hill where he has taught courses in housing policy and programs since 1966. He was appointed Chairman of the Department in July, 1983. From July 1979 to January 1981, he served as Deputy Assistant Secretary for Research in the U.S. Department of Housing and Urban Development. He holds a bachelor's degree from Brooklyn College and master's and doctoral degrees in city planning from the University of Pennsylvania.

Pamela H. Wev (Chapter 15) is an economic develoment consultant in Washington, D.C. At the Economic

Development Administration during the late 1970s she worked on program development and administration for the 302(a) State and Metropolitan Planning Programs. Prior to that she was with the Institute for State and Regional Affairs at Pennsylvania State University doing applied research in state and regional economic development. She holds a bachelor's degree in political science from Mary Baldwin College and a master of urban and regional planning degree from Pennsylvania State University.

Illustration credits

Chapter 1   Figure 1–4: National Association of Home Builders; Figure 1–5: U.S. Air Force photo.

Chapter 2   Sidebar (Landscape, cityscape and planning, a portfolio): Text by David S. Arnold. Photo and line cut research by Christine Ulrich. Page number references to John R. Stilgoe are from his book, *Common Landscape in America: 1580 to 1845* (New Haven: Yale University Press, 1982). Other credits as follows: Fort Caroline, Florida: Reproduced from the collections of the Library of Congress; Williamsburg, Virginia: Christopher Tunnard and Henry Hope Reed, *American Skyline: The Growth and Form of our Cities and Towns* (New York: New American Library, 1953), p. 47; George Washington, surveyor: Library of Congress; Columbus, Georgia: Library of Congress; Aberdeen, Dakota Territory: Library of Congress; Johnstown, Pennsylvania: Library of Congress; Immigrants debarking in New York: Library of Congress; East Side market, New York: Library of Congress; Skyscrapers, New York: Library of Congress; Telephone, 1910: Library of Congress; Radio, 1926: Library of Congress; Auto on rural road: Federal Highway Administration; Housing in Queens, New York: Louis B. Schlivek; NO MEN WANTED: Library of Congress; Farm for sale: Library of Congress; WPA: Library of Congress; TVA: Library of Congress; Ford plant at Willow Run: Library of Congress; Housing development, Woodbridge, New Jersey: Louis B. Schlivek; Baby carriages, Waldwick, New Jersey: Louis B. Schlivek; Housing development, Bergen County, New Jersey: Louis B. Schlivek; Boarded-up store fronts: Baltimore, Md., Department of Housing and Community Development; Office in 1984: Courtesy of NBI, Inc; Metrorail station: WMATA photo by Phil Portlock.

Chapter 4   Figure 4–1: Drawn by Herbert Slobin; Figure 4–2: Drawn by Herbert Slobin.

Chapter 5   Figure 5–2: Drawn by Herbert Slobin; Figure 5–3: Drawn by Herbert Slobin.

Chapter 6   Figure 6–1: Advisory Commission on Intergovernmental Relations, *State and Local Roles in the Federal System* (Washington, D.C.: U.S. Government Printing Office, 1982), Chapter 5, Figure 5–4; Figure 6–2: Compiled by ACIR staff, based upon: Reid, Stam, Kestner, and Godsey, *Federal Programs Supporting Multi-county Substate Regional Activities: An Analysis*; ESCS Staff Report (Washington, D.C.: U.S. Department of Agriculture, May 1980); Reid, J. Norman, and Stam, Jerome M., "Funding cuts hit substate regions," *Public Administration Times*, January 15, 1982, p. 3; Figure 6–6: Adapted from a preliminary analysis developed by Patricia S. Atkins, doctoral candidate at the University of Maryland, as reported by her in *Intergovernmental News*, Vol. 5, Number 2 (Washington, D.C.: American Society for Public Administration, Section on Intergovernmental Administration and Management, September 1981), p. 5; Figure 6–7: Adapted from Howard Hallman, *Government by Neighborhoods* (Washington, D.C.: Center for Governmental Studies, 1973), p. 24.

Chapter 7   Figure 7–1: Drawn by Herbert Slobin; Figure 7–2: Drawn by Herbert Slobin; Figure 7–3: Drawn by Herbert Slobin.

Chapter 8   Figure 8–2: Office of the Chief of Public Affairs, U.S. Department of the Army; Figure 8–3: National Capital Transportation Planning Board, *Program Design for Comprehensive Transportation Planning in the National Capital Region* (Washington, D.C.: Metropolitan Washington Council of Governments, July 1967), Figure II-1.

Chapter 9   Figure 9–1: Drawn by Herbert Slobin; Figure 9–3: Drawn by Herbert Slobin.

Chapter 10   Figure 10–1: All three photos, Library of Congress; Figure 10–2: Photo by B. L. Lambeth; Figure 10–3: U.S. Department of Transportation; Figure 10–4: Drawn by Herbert Slobin; Figure 10–5: Housing development (top), U.S. Department of Agriculture, Soil Conservation Service; farm land restoration (center), U.S. Office of Surface

Mining; hazardous waste site (bottom), U.S. Environmental Protection Agency.

Chapter 11   Figure 11–1: Drawn by Herbert Slobin; Figure 11–7: U.S. Executive Office of the President, Office of Management and Budget, *Standard Industrial Classification Manual—1972* (Washington, D.C.: U.S. Government Printing Office, 1972).

Chapter 12   Figure 12–3: Adapted from Sherry R. Arnstein, "A Ladder of Citizen Participation," *Journal of the American Institute of Planners*, Volume 35, Number 4 (July 1969), p. 217; Figure 12–6: U.S. Government auto (top) David Hulse, *The River Reporter*, Narrowsburg, New York; public hearing (Washington Public Power System), Gray's Harbor County, Washington, photo courtesy of the *Seattle Times*; Ride Match Fair (bottom), Southeast Michigan Council of Governments.

Chapter 13   Figure 13–1: Drawn by Herbert Slobin; Figure 13–2: Regional Planning Federation of the Philadelphia Tri-State District, *The Regional Plan of the Philadelphia Tri-State District* (Philadelphia: 1932), inset between pp. 10–11; Figure 13–3: State of New York, Office for Regional Development, *Change/Challenge/Response: A Development Policy for New York State* (Albany: State Office of Planning Coordination, reprint, n.d.), p. 15; Figure 13–4: *The President's Urban Policy Report, 1980*, Executive Summary, p. 25; Figure 13–5: State of California, Office of Planning and Research, *An Urban Strategy for California* (Sacramento: Office of Planning and Research, 1979), p. 13; Figure 13–6: Oliver Byrum and Robert Hoffman, "Development Framework Guides Regional Land Use, Public Facilities," *Practicing Planner*, Vol. 7, No. 1, (March 1977), pp. 20–21.

Chapter 14   Figure 14–1: Breakatron (top), Department of Community Affairs, Arlington County, Virginia; sack race (bottom), photo by Duane Dailey, U.S. Department of Agriculture; Figure 14–2: Top photo from the Library of Congress; bottom photo by Michelle Bogre, U.S. Department of Agriculture.

Chapter 15   Figure 15–1: Library of Congress; Figure 15–2: Council of State Planning Agencies, "State Development Strategies, A Policy Maker's Guide to Their Design" (Washington, D.C.: Council of State Planning Agencies, July, 1981), draft paper, unpaged.

Chapter 16   Figure 16–1: Data from 1980 Census of Housing; data do not include group quarters (hospitals, military barracks, college dormitories, etc.). Photos: single-family house, National Association of Housing and Redevelopment Officials; row houses, National Association of Home Builders; apartment house, National Association of Housing and Redevelopment Officials; manufactured home, Manufactured Housing Institute.

Chapter 17   Figure 17–2: Drawn by Richard Hedman.

Chapter 18   Figures 18–1 through 18–4: U.S. Department of Energy; Figure 18–5: R. L. Heminger, *Across the Years in Findlay and Hancock County* (Findlay, Ohio: R. L. Heminger, 1965), plate following p. 32 taken from drawing that originally appeared in 1886 in the *New York Illustrated*.

Chapter 19   Figure 19–1: Drawn by Herbert Slobin; Figure 19–2: Photograph by Daniel S. Brody, provided by the Environmental Action Foundation.

Chapter 20   Figure 20–1: Map furnished by U.S. Environmental Protection Agency, Hazardous Site Control Division, Discovery and Investigations Branch. Quote from U.S. Council on Environmental Quality, *Environmental Quality, 1983*, 14th Annual Report of the Council on Environmental Quality, p. 61; Figure 20–2: Photo courtesy of Metropolitan Washington Council of Governments.

Chapter 21   Figure 21–1: Library of Congress; Figure 21–2: Government Studies and Systems, *A Taxonomy of the Health System Appropriate for Plan Development*, prepared for Bureau of Health Planning and Resources Development, HRA, PHS, HEW, Publication No. (HRP) 0100401, May 1977, p. 18; Figure 21–3: Government Studies and Systems, *A Taxonomy of the Health System Appropriate for Plan Development*, prepared for Bureau of Health Planning and Resources Development, HRA, PHS, HEW, Publication No. (HRP) 0100401, May 1977, p. 19; Figure 21–4: Philip N. Reeves, David F. Bergwall, and Nina B. Woodside, *Introduction to Health Planning*, 2nd ed. (Washington, D.C.: Information Resources Press, 1979), p. 53; Figure 21–5: Philip N. Reeves, David F. Bergwall, and Nina B. Woodside, *Introduction to Health Planning*, 2nd ed. (Washington, D.C.: Information Resources Press, 1979), p. 58; Figure 21–6: Louis Tannen, "Health Planning as a Regulatory Strategy: A Discussion of Its History and Current Uses," *International Journal of*

Health Services, Vol. 10, No. 1, 1980, p. 128; Figure 21–7: Louis Tannen, "Health Planning as a Regulatory Strategy: A Discussion of Its History and Current Uses," *International Journal of Health Services*, Vol. 10, No. 1, 1980, p. 127; Figure 21–8: Health Care Financing Administration.

Chapter 22   Figure 22–1: Council of State Governments, *Human Services: A Framework for Decision-Making* (Lexington, Kentucky: December 1975), p. 13.

Chapter 23   Figure 23–1: Drawn by Herbert Slobin; Figure 23–2: President's Commission on Law Enforcement and Administration of Justice, "The Challenge of Crime in a Free Society," 1967; Figure 23–3: National Advisory Commission on Criminal Justice Standards and Goals, *Criminal Justice Systems* (Washington, D.C.: U.S. Government Printing Office, 1973), pp. 100–101.

Chapter 24   Figure 24–1: Photos furnished by the city of Xenia, Ohio; Figure 24–4: Adapted from Council of State Governments, "States and Natural Hazards—Responsibility and Fulfillment," report to the National Science Foundation, May 1979; supplemented with information from disaster workers, planners, and researchers.

Municipal Management Series

**The Practice of
State and Regional
Planning**

Text type
Times Roman, Helvetica

Composition
EPS Group, Inc.
Baltimore, Maryland

Printing and binding
Kingsport Press
Kingsport, Tennessee

Design
Herbert Slobin